"Hell, I Was There"

"Hell, I Was There!"

By Elmer Keith

Petersen Publishing Company
Los Angeles, California

ACKNOWLEDGEMENT
The publisher wishes to acknowledge
the able assistance of the editorial
staffs of *Guns & Ammo* and *Hunting*
magazines, with special thanks to
Slim Randles who prepared the original
manuscript for publication,
and Dr. Ralph C. Glaze, editor of
Guns & Ammo's Specialty Books.

Contents

Foreword

The acknowledged dean of American gun writers, Elmer Keith tells his own life story in this new, revised and expanded edition. One of the last of a vanishing breed of men who were there when the American frontier was laid to rest, Keith writes vividly of his experiences in a West that is no more.

Throughout his days as a cowboy, broncbuster, hunting guide and rancher, Elmer Keith maintained an abiding and active interest in firearms that led to his writing hundreds of articles and several books on the subject over a period of more than 50 years.

Although firearms are a part of this book, as they have been a part of Elmer Keith's life, "HELL, I WAS THERE!" is not a gun book. It is a book about fascinating people of a bygone era; about animals, both wild, and tame; and about a rugged life in the great outdoors—as seen through the eyes of a man who was really there!

The recipient of the first Outstanding Handgunner of the Year Award, Keith is presently Executive Editor of GUNS & AMMO Magazine.

Let Elmer Keith take you along as he rides wild broncs, hunts big game from Alaska to Africa, or follows a frozen trail in the dead of a Montana winter.

Read Keith's own story of his role in developing the .41 and .44 Magnum revolvers, his work for the Army during World War II, his shooting days at old Camp Perry, and much, much more!

"HELL, I WAS THERE!"—the life story of ELMER KEITH is a truly remarkable book by an even more remarkable man.

The Editors

Introduction

ELMER KEITH: Here are two brief stories about the hunter, naturalist and outdoorsman—and an analysis of him as a writer.

Keith and a guide were scouting game ahead of a hunting party. They were not carrying rifles but both had a heavy pistol. In the middle of the afternoon they saw a grizzly bear below them, near the creek. Keith studied the situation briefly and then whispered to the guide, "I have always wanted to get a grizzly with a pistol." (I have no such ambition, myself.) "This looks like my chance. Give me your gun and climb a tree." He made a successful stalk and was about to open fire when a sound behind the animal drew his attention. A cub came tumbling out of the brush, and then another and still another. Keith reversed his stalk and returned to the guide. The grizzly family went on their way blissfully unaware of how near they had been to disaster. Keith's laconic comment: "I never wanted a bear bad enough to make orphans of three cubs."

Keith's writings are based on three aspects of his personality. The first is his remarkable gift for accurate, detailed observation. The second, his prodigious and exact memory. The third is his uncompromising honesty.

It is impossible for Keith to build up a story for a better effect or to tone one down to make it sound more plausible. He must tell it as he saw it, regardless of where or how it impacts. If a phrase seems provocative or a sentence challenging, it is not argumentative. It is his conception of the truth—defiant.

The reader who settles himself in an easy chair with one of Keith's books can let down the drawbridge of his mind and dismiss his mental sentries. Keith parades his thought openly. His sentences contain no double-entendre. His paragraphs offer ambush to no bravos of propaganda.

Keith is not a philosopher. Concrete facts interest him, abstractions do not. Psychologically he is inclined toward the decision-action type. He is never found sitting on an ideological fence.

When Keith writes there is some conflict between the technician and the artist. So far the disburser of facts has won most of the points but there are indications that the sensitive, imaginative Keith is gaining in strength. If so, it is all to the good. His occasional descriptive paragraphs of nature in action are the best of his work—etchings in prose. He should give us more canyons, mist-filled after a night of rain, more mountain peaks, copper-washed by the last rays of evening.

Keith is best known as an arms expert, a term he dislikes. At least 40 years have elapsed since his first gun article was published. There have been many since. Like General Hatcher (handguns), Colonel Whelen (rifles) and Major Askins (shotguns), Keith writes from personal experience and observation. He keeps his fingers on the pulse of world thought through an extensive correspondence that is nearly world wide. Hunters in Alaska and Canada, European sportsmen, a scientist in Africa, all write him long letters. He is careful about his statements of fact. They can be accepted at face value. His conclusions are open to question as is all personal opinion. But be warned. He has a penchant for getting ahead of current thought. Time frequently corroborates him.

Keith's knowledge of wildlife is categorical and intimate. It flickers in and out of his hunting stories but he has never quite given it a free rein. He could, if he were so minded, write a cradle-to-grave biography of any game animal, game bird, fur bearer or predator in the Rocky Mountains. He knows what they eat, how they live, the type of country they like, their romances, their natural enemies, and their geographical dispersion. He does not make "guesstimates." His comments, however casual, are authoritative.

Keith and I were hunting. We could have found deer but we were looking for something else. It was a rugged day. Half-melted snow and wet brush on the north hillsides—slippery rocks—mazes of crisscrossed down timber—tough going all the way.

Just after sundown we came out on a hill a quarter of a mile above camp and sat down to rest. There was a sound in the brush.

Two grand mule deer bucks, their noses up and their antlers thrown back, sneaked craftily along the edge of the timber 40 yards below us. When they had passed out of sight I looked at him. His rifle lay across his knees forgotten. His pipe hung loosely from his mouth. The big hat was pushed carelessly up on the side of his head; his face was a picture of absorbed interest. He caught my glance. A twinkle came into his gray eyes.

"Beauties, weren't they?" he said softly.

To know Elmer Keith, an authentic brother of the backlands needs no more introduction.

DON MARTIN
Salmon, Idaho
1972

Chapter 1

GROWING UP IN THE OLD WEST

MISSOURI BEGINNINGS...

I was born at Hardin, Ray County, Missouri, March the 8th, 1899, the son of Forrest Everett and Linnie Neal Keith. Mother was a Merrifield and her mother was a descendant from Benjamin Merrill, who started the first revolution against the British four years before the American Revolution. His small army was crushed by the British. He was captured, hung, and drawn-and-quartered on the scaffold. My Grandmother Keith was Druzilla Ann Cummins before her marriage to Silas Keith in Cynthiana, Kentucky in 1850. She was a descendant from Captain William Clark of the Lewis and Clark Expedition. Captain Clark had a daughter named Hannah who married an Irishman named Elliot. They in turn had a daughter who married a Cummins.

The Cummins family had a daughter that they named Druzilla, a name that Captain Clark wanted carried down in the family. Druzilla Ann Cummins became my Grandmother Keith. Many years later we named our girl Druzilla.

On both sides my ancestors were Kentuckians who moved in with Daniel Boone or shortly afterwards. When the game became scarce there, they moved on to Missouri and during the Civil War they fought on the southern side. My uncle, Oleander J. Berry,

who married my father's oldest sister, was wounded in the Battle of Lexington across the river from Hardin. They was rolling cotton bales up against the northern fort, which they later took. When he reached up over a bale to ram another ball down his old squirrel rifle, a minieball took him through the right arm, breaking his arm. Uncle Oleander was out of the fight for the rest of the war.

Mother had three uncles in the war also. Two of them died in the prison camp at Rock Island Arsenal after being taken prisoner. Granddad Merrifield had a big family so he didn't go to war. He was too busy trying to keep his family fed, with first the Confederates coming by hungry, and then a bunch of Northern troops coming by hungry.

After the Civil War my grandfather, Anson Merrifield, was the first marshal of Hardin that lived for any length of time. He finally straightened the town of Hardin out. It was well named at that time. He used an old double-barreled ten gauge for the purpose.

Two of Granddad Merrifield's brothers went west to Texas after the war, and settled near Amarillo. I remember them coming back for a visit when I was a little boy and telling about the big rattlesnakes they found out there, and how they'd take a shotgun and get on a horse in dispatching them. Two of their sons, A. W.

Merrifield and Enoch Merrifield, moved north. A. W. Merrifield became Teddy Roosevelt's ranch foreman in Medora, North Dakota, and Enoch became foreman of the Drum Lomond mine cyanide plant at Marysville, Montana.

Granddad Merrifield told of many hard times he had while marshal of Hardin, after the Civil War. One one-legged man owned a farm out of Hardin and had rented it to a man for several years. Each year the river would flood the land and after that possibly he would get a crop and possibly not. For two years he'd been flooded so long that the corn crop had drowned out. He went to this one-legged man in town and told him he would pay him the rent as soon as he could get a crop. The one-legged gentry pulled out a sheath knife and stabbed him through the heart. He fell on the sidewalk and a friend of his came along, stooped over to pick him up, and the one-legged man stabbed him through the heart also and he fell across him. Then he got on a horse and high-tailed it to a ferry going over to Lexington, Missouri, across the Missouri River.

Granddad Merrifield took a deputy and went after him. They trailed him up over the south side of the river and corraled him beneath a big bridge across a gulch. Granddad had his deputy shoot into the culvert from one end and attract his attention, while he sneaked around behind and got the drop on him and took him alive. They got him back across the Missouri River via the ferry, and they tied his peg leg and good foot together under the mule's belly and handcuffed him to the saddle horn. They got back in about the neighborhood of Father's farm, three miles west of Hardin, and a hard thunder shower came up.

They stopped under some water oaks, and took the man off the horse and tied him to a tree. They left the saddle horses and mule that he was riding under another tree and Grandfather and the deputy got under a third tree. Lightning was coming down in heavy bolts all around. The prisoner started cussing "God Almighty". Finally he says, "Damn You, if you're so smart, hit this tree."

A bolt came down the tree, killed him instantly, blew his wooden leg off, and took a strip of hair off the top of his head. Granddad said they tied him across the mule and took him on to Hardin for burial.

Granddad Merrifield used a double-barrel shotgun and buckshot most of the time in cleaning up the town of Hardin after the Civil War. During the thirties I had a good many letters from people saying that there was an article in the *Saturday Evening Post* about border marshals and sheriffs that included quite a write-up on Granddad Anson Merrifield. However, I did not take the magazine at the time and never got to see a copy.

My uncle, Oleander Berry, served under General Price during the Civil War. I remember many tales he told us of the service before he was wounded at Lexington and put out of the fight. Once he was stationed out in a big old hollow tree in a swamp, sniping. They forgot all about him and left him there three days and nights with no way of getting ashore with his old rifle. Water extended for several miles between him and his outfit. He said he got so hungry that his mouth would water when he thought of his mother's old soap grease barrel at home.

We lived on the prairie some twelve miles north of Hardin on a little farm along with Granddad Keith. Father bought, sold and traded mules in addition to farming. He was also a fancier of trotting horses, and usually had some Hambletonians around. When I was three years old he took me to Carrollton, Missouri, to watch the trotting horses. Frank James was starting the races at that time after the Governor had pardoned him, (he was Jesse James's brother.) We drove up and Frank came over and says, "Hello, Farry." (They called my dad "Farry.") Frank says, "That's an awful pretty girl you have there, Farry."

Dad says, "Girl hell, Frank. I'll have you understand that's a boy."

Well, they had me dressed in a polka-dot dress, long black socks, button patent leather shoes, a Windsor tie, and long yellow curls down to my shoulders. There was no ready made clothing for little boys at that time, and we had to wear what the women put on us. Until I was four years old it was dresses, which I hated. Father told me that he wore homespuns until he was twenty-one. I still remember Grandma Keith's old loom in the attic of the first house that Granddad Keith built, and her old spinning wheel. Each year a bootmaker would come around and spend a week or two with each family making boots and shoes for the whole family, then he'd move on the next farm. Things was different in those days.

I still retain some other memories of my toddling days, which is now over seventy years past. Father and Ed Hale kept a pack of hounds and ran foxes just for their own amusement, just to hear the dogs. When they would never bring in a fox, Mother was provoked and wanted to know why they didn't

Elmer in one of the dresses he wore as a tiny lad. This photograph was taken in 1902, when Elmer was three.

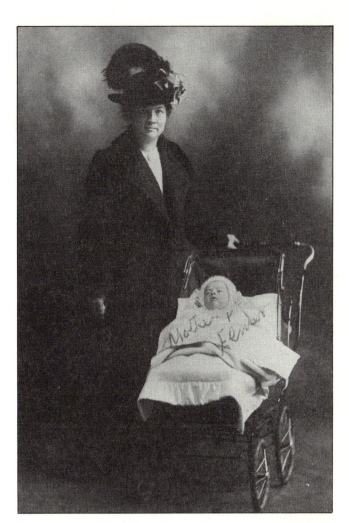

Elmer's first baby picture was taken in the spring of 1899. The young lady in the plumed hat is his mother.

catch the fox. Dad told her they didn't want to kill the fox, they wanted to hear the music.

Granddad Keith and old Tommy Hale would sit on the front porch of Granddad's and talk over the Civil War for hours. Grandmother Keith died before I was born, and was buried in the little family graveyard.

From my earliest years I was more interested in guns and ammunition than other things. My Aunt Molly gave me a pretty doll. I promptly rapped its head off on the foot of the bed and went to playing with some of Dad's empty shotgun shells.

My brother Silas was born two years after I was, and I can still remember rocking him to keep him from crying.

Granddad Keith would come to see us and he always rode a big mule. He would stop at a little store on the way and buy some stick candy. His coming was always welcome.

Dad had a pet coon named Jim. I still remember when Mother would scrub the board floor scrupulously clean, Jim would sit down on one side of it, hook one of his claws in the crack and back up clear across the floor, stir-

ring up any dirt that he could. Then he would look up at Mother to show her that she hadn't done her job right. Mother usually gave him a dusting with the broom.

Mother also had a black house cat named Dinah, the best behaved cat that I ever saw. When Dad was away, Mother would milk the cow, and she'd set a pail of milk down out in the yard. Dinah would keep the chickens and pigs away from it while Mother milked another cow. One day a mule came up and tried to get a drink of the milk. Dinah scratched him on the nose, he reversed ends, and kicked poor Dinah to Kingdom Come.

The deer and turkeys were gone from Missouri at my earliest remembrance. There were still prairie chickens, sandhill cranes, geese, ducks, rabbits, and a lot of small game. My dad hunted quite a lot. In fact all the families there that I knew of hunted a great deal to keep up the family larder. As Missouri was quickly getting settled up, my folks decided to move to Montana, and in 19 and 5 they made plans for the trip west.

Getting ready for a trip west was quite a

3

Elmer's parents, Linnie Neal and Forrest Everett Keith.

problem in those days. Mother packed up the things she had to have in a couple of big trunks. She converted the family exchequer into gold pieces, and sewed them into my brother's and my underwear along the back, with a little patch over each gold piece. In that way, if we got stuck up we wouldn't lose all the family resources.

When everything was ready, Dad loaded the trunks into the spring wagon. Mother had a big basket of fried chicken and other lunch goods and we set out through deep mud for Hardin. The gumbo was so thick it would cake the wheels until they would hardly turn around the sides of the wagon. I remember Dad getting out and taking a limb off a tree and prying the mud off occasionally.

We reached Hardin a few minutes too late to get the Kansas City train that evening. Dad was very perturbed about missing the train as we had to stay all night and take another train the next morning. However, before morning word came back that the train wrecked short of Kansas City and there were 48 killed and a lot more injured, so Father

was not quite so unhappy about missing the train.

EARLY MONTANA YEARS . . .

We rode the Santa Fe to Kansas City and then the U.P. to Salt Lake City. We finally took some branch line from Salt Lake over to Helena, Montana. I remember seeing antelope running alongside the train after we reached the prairie country. It was a great experience for us little boys. I was six and Silas was four years old.

When we arrived in Helena, we took a little branch railroad up to the mining town of Marysville where Mother's cousin, Enoch Merrifield, was foreman of the cyanide plant. He gave Father a job, and we rented a house. The track ended in town, and a great turntable was used to reverse the engine. It took every man, woman, and kid joining on the long beam to help turn the engine around for its trip back to Helena. We lined the engine up on a side track and then switched it back to head the three-car train back to Helena.

Si and I played in the gulch above the

cyanide plant where Enoch Merrifield and his big crew were putting all the tailings from the Drum Lomond rich quartz mine through a recovering system, and they recovered a great amount of gold at the cyanide plant. One day we found some huge cat tracks going into an old prospect drift. We told Dad about it, and he and some others got flashlights, dogs, and a rifle and went in and killed a big cougar.

We spent some two years at Marysville, as I remember it. One day Si and I decided to cross the canyon on the railroad trestle. The track came around the shoulder of a mountain and then square across the canyon. It must have been at least two hundred feet from the trestle down to the floor of the canyon and the trestle was open between the ties. Why we decided to do it I'll never know. We were half-way across, carefully stepping from one tie to another, and staying close to the rail so we could grab it if we missed a tie. Just then the train came around the corner. The engineer blew the whistle, put on all his brakes, and with nothing else he could do, we were in bad shape. There was a barrel of water hung on the side of the trestle about the middle and level with the top of the tracks. So I chucked Si in the barrel of water, and grabbed ahold of the rim with both hands, and let myself down on the side as the train thundered past. It stopped with the caboose just barely across the trestle. The conductor came a-running down the steps and hopping the ties as fast as he could, yelling encouragement to me to hang on. I hung on all right, but between the jar of the train and the shake of the trestle, I thought I was gone several times. As soon as the trainman reached us, he grabbed me by the belt, put me under one arm, then he fished Si out of the water barrel, chucked him under the other arm, and carefully stepped the ties back to the caboose. There he sat down, turned us over his knee, and gave us the hiding of our lives. That was one licking I enjoyed getting. The conductor then instructed us not to say anything to our folks or the next time he saw us he would give us a real paddling.

Like most western mining towns around and after the turn of the century, Marysville had plenty of tough kids. My brother's ears set out from his head about like an old buck deer, very noticeable. One day the boys caught Si by the ears and lifted him up off his feet, and he was screaming bloody murder. I found about a third of a brickbat so I picked that up and I hit the big kid in the ribs under his right arm as hard as I could throw it. He gasped and dropped Si. Si lit a

At age nine, Elmer was already an experienced hunter. With his trusty .22, his hunting dogs, and a belt of ammunition, he was ready for almost anything!

runnin' and I wasn't slow to take off behind him because the bunch of them was going to have some fun with us. They started throwing rocks and I got one in the back of the head. I hit the dirt on my face. I got up and took off again and we made it home, but the back of my vest and shirt and underwear was soaked with blood from the cut on my head.

One Fourth of July the bigger boys pooled all their pennies and bought the biggest giant firecracker they could find. Then they took it and spliced it underneath the belly of a big black tom cat, started him on down the main street after touching off the fuse. He exploded about the middle of the street. As several ladies were out dressed in white, they were pretty well splattered.

An old German lived in a little cabin on a sidehill. A trail ran around the hill about thirty yards to his private privy. One Halloween the boys decided to play a trick on the old German. They didn't like him and he didn't like any of them. As a rule he would go out to the backhouse about nine o'clock, then go to bed and blow out his lantern. This night the boys all hid and waited. When the old man went to the privy, a couple of them rushed up, slammed the door and turned the button. Then all of them rushed up and started to give it the old heave ho. It was set on stilts on the lower part and not too substantially built. With the combined efforts of the boys, finally over it went. The steep hill, about thirty yards to the bottom, tapered out into a little meadow. The old backhouse toilet disintegrated as it went down the hill, with the old man rolling around in the melee. He came up at the bottom in the moonlight with the seat board around his neck, cussing all the boys in German.

One day a kid picked a fight with me at school by punching me in the back of the neck with a sharp pencil when the teacher's back was turned. At recess I proceeded to give him a good licking. Word later got home to my folks via the teacher, and some of the boy's friends put me to blame. So they made me go over across town and apologize to his mother. I went across town all right, knocked on the door, and apologized to his mother. The kid stuck his head around her shoulder and thumbed his nose at me, so I reached up and glommed him and I proceeded to give him another good licking until his mother beat me off with her broom.

During that summer, Granddad Merrifield, my Aunt Molly, and Aunt Dean came out for a visit, and Enoch Merrifield took us all out on a picnic back in the hills. He had a 95 Model Winchester caliber .35 WCF, and I remember him and Granddad shooting at a piece of paper on a big yellow pine at one hundred yards with solid or full patch bullets. I remember the slugs went through and kicked dust up on the hill in the back. I wanted to shoot it too, but they said it was too big for a little kid. Later on Enoch took us down to the assay office of the cyanide plant and he ran a big gold brick from the cleanings that they had there. We watched the whole process. He'd pour the amalgam in and a white powder of some kind, and when the crucible of gold was red hot he poured it into a big mold. As I remember the mold was about 8-10 inches long and 3 or 4 inches wide at the top and narrower at the bottom. Anyway when he had the ingot, he took a cold chisel and cut out a chunk of one corner for assaying to get the fineness of the gold, and then he shouldered the piece. He had to lift to get it up on his shoulder and a shotgun guard went in front of him and another one behind him while they went out to the express car, and locked it up in the car to go to Helena. It makes me laugh today to see the movie stars handle big bricks of gold with one hand. That one was a pretty good load for a strong man.

During the summer, a girl named Sally Autin took my brother and I in tow. She was considerably older than we were. She showed us how to find bumblebee nests, kill the old bees, and dig out the batch of honey. Each globule of honey was sealed in a round ball of wax. It looked about, oh, a half-inch in diameter. We'd break these open and eat the honey. She also showed us where there was a good huckleberry patch. My brother and I filled our hats, took them home and asked Mother to bake us some pies. As soon as we got in the house she could smell the strong odor of huckleberries and she didn't like it, but in deference to our work picking them all, she made up some pies out of them. Si and I sat down and we ate one right now. Mother became curious after awhile and she came over and cut a little piece and nibbled on it. Then she cut a larger piece, and then another. She said, "Boys, go back, take the buckets, and get all you can find."

HARDIN WAS A TOUGH TOWN . . .

Father still had considerable property in Missouri; a house and lot in town and a fifty-acre farm in the Missouri riverbottom, plus a bit of livestock. So the family decided to move back to Missouri for a year and get things in shape and sell this property, and then come back to Montana. With that thought in mind we moved back to Missouri. We spent the next year and a half there.

By this time I was old enough to understand and really appreciate the primitive life in Missouri at that time. Father had 250 early Richmond cherry trees on the farm, and he would hire twenty Negro women to pick them, giving them five cents a gallon. And then he would peddle the cherries and sell them at twenty cents a gallon all over the community to different farms. This was quite a project while the cherry crop lasted. One little Negro lady would pick twenty gallons a day, which was big money those days. There was an abundance of small game—cottontails, squirrels, quail, and ducks. Father bought me a .22 Hopkins & Allen rifle. I had been previously shooting some game with a muzzle-loading squirrel rifle that belonged to a neighbor, but the little .22 was much handier, and it soon became my job to furnish the family with table meat the year around.

UMC .22 shorts and black powder cost ten cents a box in those days, and hollow points and Lesmoke, fifteen cents. I had to account

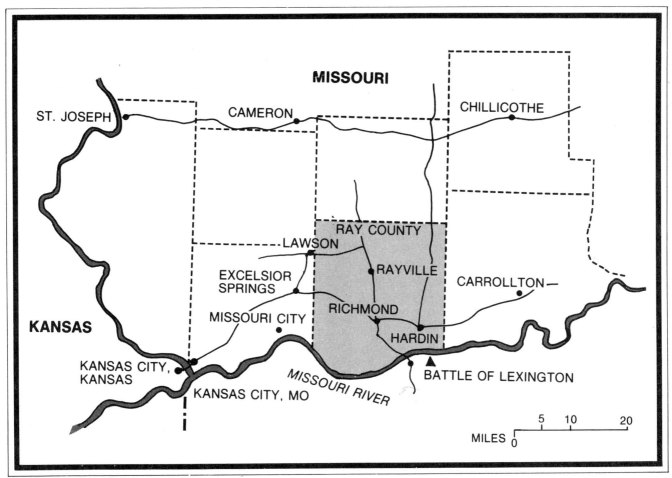

MISSOURI

ST. JOSEPH

CAMERON

CHILLICOTHE

RAY COUNTY

LAWSON

RAYVILLE

EXCELSIOR SPRINGS

CARROLLTON—

MISSOURI CITY

RICHMOND

KANSAS

HARDIN

KANSAS CITY, KANSAS

BATTLE OF LEXINGTON

KANSAS CITY, MO

MISSOURI RIVER

MILES 0 5 10 20

for all of the ammunition I used. Father didn't believe in promiscuously shooting up ammunition at any time, and being as I started with a muzzle loader, I learned to make every shot count.

One day I decided to try a neighbor boy's shotgun for squirrel hunting. Dad tried to persuade me to leave it alone. But I took it and went into the heavy oak timber beyond Dad's farm on Crooked River. I finally spotted a big old fox squirrel that had seen me, in the top of a water oak. The wind was blowing hard and the limb was swaying back and forth. I thought you had to aim a shotgun the same as you would a rifle, so I found a drooping limb on another water oak with a knot on it. I rested the barrel on that, took careful aim on the squirrel as he swayed back and forth, and timed it so as to intercept him when the top of the tree brought him back in line. When the gun went off, the knot on the limb that I had the barrel rested over broke and the muzzle turned down and plowed into another water oak ten feet in front of me. What part of the gun hit me, I don't know, it cut my upper lip clear through to my teeth until the upper lip hung down over the lower lip. I woke up about three hours later in a

pool of blood. That was my first experience with a shotgun on game. I got up, reloaded the gun, scrubbed the blood and leaves off my face the best I could, and limped sadly home.

I had two little rat terriers—hunting dogs. They were good squirrel dogs and they loved to hunt possums. They'd chase a possum into his hole or trail him into it, then they'd go in. A fight would ensue and then finally they had a peculiar howl they'd let loose when they had the possum by the nose. I'd brace my feet on each side of the hole, reach in and get the dog by the tail, and pull the whole works out. I've seen Dad hold a possum by the tail with one of those rat terriers clamped on his nose until his arm would get tired. He'd change hands and still that little dog would just shut his eyes, and grin and hang on.

One spring Bernie Bowman and I caught eleven female possums. We penned them up in a screen crate we made for them in the yard. The Negroes claimed that possums didn't breed like any other animal at all, but fertilized the female's nose and she in turn fertilized the little tits inside of her pouch and the possums grew on it. I still believe the colored people were right in spite of what science says. At any rate, we were watching

7

those possums and the first little young possums would appear on the tits in the pouch and they were less than a half-inch long. Each one was clamped firmly to his tit and we'd take a match and carefully pry one off. It seemed like he was glued to it, though, but when they would finally separate, none of them ever went back and got on the tit. Every one we pried off died. We watched them until they were up over an inch long and the same procedure. If they lost that little tit they were apparently glued to or grown to, they died. So I still believe that the Darkies have the right picture on the possums.

This was a very religious community. Every Sunday we had to go to Sunday School. Hunting was prohibited on Sundays, but I would put my little .22 in a flour sack, sneak out of town after Sunday School, and hunt squirrels. One day I got farther into the timber than I had been before. At that time Missouri was largely heavy timber. Since then it has been cleared and turned into farm land. I got overheated. I'd killed four or five squirrels and was packing them. It was a hot day in late June. I came to a clearing and I was just about all in from heat prostration. There was an old Darky there that had a little clearing, a milk cow, a spring, his little log cabin, and a spring house. He came out and he says, "Son, you look a mite tuckered. You'd better come in." So I went in the cabin with him, sat down, and I felt better then. He got me a glass of cold milk from his spring house. He had a bunch of meat, it looked to me like dried eels, hanging above the fireplace. Anyway they were curled around and smoked and salted, and he got one of these strips down, got his knife and board, and sliced me off several slices of that. Then he opened a Dutch oven and got a big slice of cornbread and butter and fixed me a lunch. I ate it. The meat was white inside and smoked and salted to a turn and it tasted very good. I felt better after that. Then the old colored gentleman wanted to know if I knew what kind of meat it was. I told him I supposed it was eel. "No," he says, "It's rattlesnake." He took me out in back of the cabin and showed me a big canvas sack with a burlap sack inside of it, and shoulder strap, and a long forked stick and an axe. He said he hunted the rattlesnakes and, when he found one, he pinned its head down with the forked stick and chopped it off and put the snake in the sack. Then he'd go home and skin them, take out the stomach contents, then he'd soak them overnight in salt and pepper. Then he'd hang them above the fire-

place and smoke them. So I ate rattlesnake once in my life.

During the summer my folks would take either Si or I out to Granddad Keith's and let one of us spend a week at a time there. We always had a great time. My Aunt Emma was a good cook. There was lots of squirrels and young cottontails around, and Granddad would take me down by the pond and along the hedge with his old Colt .32-20 rifle in which he shot some .32 Smith & Wesson shorts. He'd pack the gun, but when I'd find a cottontail he'd let me sit down and shoot him through the head with this old .32-20 Colt. At that time that was a big gun for me.

Snakes were in abundance—rattlers, some copperheads, blue racers, and along the creeks and swamps the old cottonmouth moccasins, and a lot of black snakes. One day my little rat terriers located a big black snake. When I got through the brush to them, he had a coil around one of them and the little dog's tongue was out. He was about to be crushed. The other dog had him by the neck a chewing on him, so I shot him through the head just clear of the dog. I put a string on him and drug him up to the house. He was six feet nine inches long and it was about all I could do to drag him.

Granddad Merrifield had a sawmill and a batch of timber just west of Hardin, Missouri, along the Santa Fe railroad track. There was a patch of timber there he wanted to log and it was literally alive with rattlesnakes. So he had my dad and other men build a fence around it, a good tight woven wire fence, and he filled it with hogs, put a whole bunch of them in there. Bob and Rollie Foster and I were chums and we used to go up the track, sit down on the rail and watch the hogs hunting snakes. Every once in awhile they'd find a snake and you could hear the woofing. They'd all congregate. I've seen an old sow grab a rattler, he'd be a-striking her, and she'd put a foot on him, tear him in two, eat him right down while he was striking, his rattles a-going and his head striking at her. Hogs loved those rattlesnakes and they seemed to be impervious to their poison.

In the spring and summer we had good fishing for catfish, perch, crappie and some bass. There was a wide variety of fish. An old gentleman named Shackleford used to take me down to Crooked River and we'd bait the hooks with corn for some of the fish and with little balls of dough for others. We caught about everything in the book. We really had a great time.

SKUNKS AND BUSTLES . . .

Mother taught both oil and china painting and she had a huge china kiln that stood in the living room in which she would fire the china after each painting. It took three coats and three firings before that china came out with the paint burnt under the glaze so it was permanent. I'd do my lessons in the flickering light from that china kiln.

I well remember the first suit of clothes I had, Mother found them in a store. She dressed me up in it while she had a china painting class on. There were fifteen or twenty women in the room. I went out in back of town and was prowling around with my two rat terriers and they ran a civet cat in a hole. The dogs dug after him until the little skunk perfumed them good and they beat it and started rubbing their noses in the ground. I plugged the hole with a rock and then found another hole up on the sod and plugged that with a rock. All I could think of was the thirty cents that civet cat hide would bring, so I took my jackknife and dug down halfway between the holes. The first thing that came up was that little skunk's tail. So I picked him up by the left hand, whacked him in the back of the head with a club and killed him. By that time I couldn't smell anything, I was so skunked up that I was absolutely perfumed. So I skinned the little spotted skunk, and turned his skin with the fur side out, and put it in the pocket of my new coat and headed for home. I was pretty happy, since I'd made thirty cents.

When I went in the front door, all those ladies rushed to the window, it was a warm afternoon in the fall, swung their legs out, and stepped out until only Mom and I were left in the room. She ordered me to take a tub, pack it up in the barn, pack water to it, and go up and shuck all those clothes, have a bath and change, which I did. It took a long time to get the skunk scent out of my little suit.

During the summer months the whole community would have picnic gatherings at some prearranged site. The women would fry huge baskets of chicken, bake cakes and all the other good food they could possibly gather. We'd all have a good time. I can still remember the women and their long dresses with several petticoats dragging through the dust, and it's a sharp contrast to the miniskirts the girls wear today.

In those days the women wore tight laced corsets and big puffed sleeves. I can still remember Mother helping neighbor women with their dresses, putting her knee in their backs while she cinched their corsets as tight as she could. Then after they got them cinched up almost to a wasp waist, they'd hang a big bustle on their backside before they put on the dress. It was quite amusing to a young lad.

Our summer clothing consisted of three items: a straw hat, a blue shirt, and a pair of bib overalls. Shoes and stockings were reserved for fall when we started to school. After a rain, especially in spring, our barnyard would be a loblolly of mud a foot deep. Father decided to put concrete walks in and a concrete feeder in the center there for the milk cows. While this was in progress he had us take the milk cows from Uncle Will's pasture, through town and down to the Santa Fe stockyards and put them there, lock them up, and come home and get the buckets and go milk the cows. One evening Si and I had herded the cattle through town, put them in the stockyard, and we had just shut the gate when a big Negro came running towards us. He scared us. My brother could run like the wind, and I never could run good, so Si soon left me. Well, the big black man kept right after me. I seen that I couldn't outrun him, and I had a slingshot in my hip pocket with some good dime rubbers I'd bought at the drugstore. In another pocket I had a bunch of .36 caliber Colt round balls. To get them, we had dug the babbitt metal out of the boxes on the axles of the Santa Fe freight cars and run it in this old .36 Colt mold.

Those .36 Colt round ball molds made very good ammunition for the slingshot. One day I killed three cottontails and a quail with this outfit. Seeing that the man was going to catch me, I jerked the slingshot out of my pocket, unwound it and put a bunch of .36 balls in my mouth, put one in the bed and just as I figured he was going to get me, I whirled around, pulled it to my ear and let him have it, right in the face.

I saw his two front upper teeth go. They clicked quite loud. He grabbed his face with both hands hollering, "Oh, lawdy" and staggered around behind a spring wagon. I got another ball in the bed of the old slingshot and I let that go and heard it hit the seat of the wagon. The next two though I heard go "plunk", and they go nearly through a cottontail and through a quail, so I figured he took them pretty good. Then I lit out and headed for home.

Just as I got around a ten-foot fence around this mule yard, I met Si and my dad coming back. Dad had the old shotgun over his shoulder and both hammers back and he says, "Where is that man?"

Well, we went back and all around the stockyard, and about that time a freight train pulled out. We never did see the man. Dad sent Si and I home and he prowled the town the rest of the night and the next day until he was satisfied whoever he was was long gone. That .36 round ball that I hit him in the mouth with took those upper teeth. I saw that clearly, and must have gone on back and done him considerable damage. Where the other two hit him I don't know, but from the plunk of them I know that they hit.

During the winter school months, most of us boys ran trap lines and practically every day some of us would catch a skunk. Teacher had a place reserved over in one corner for every kid that came in with skunk scent on him. We were very unpopular.

Several of us made some muzzle-loading pistols. We'd take a piece of copper pipe, bend one end over and hammer it tight, whittle out a pistol stock, bed the pipe in it, wrap it with copper wire, and file a touch hole. We'd load it with a charge of black powder, some newspaper, then a charge of shot and some more newspaper. When the pigeons were thick around the barn, one of us used to hold the gun and aim it at the pigeons and another one would strike a match and touch it off. Then we'd take the pigeons, a bunch of corn, and an old five-gallon can and boil the works down along the Santa Fe tracks out of sight. Us kids had some wild times and good feeds that way.

After school started, a lad named Charley Alcorn was making fun of our muzzle-loading pistols. His dad ran a clothing store and had given him a fine heavy overcoat. He told Pat Tracy that gun wouldn't even shoot through his coat. Pat told him it would, so at recess we decided to try it out. Charley humped up in his big coat, turned his rump to us, and Pat loaded the gun too heavy. I was elected to aim it while Pat touched it off. It went off all right—it blew up.

Just the same, enough of the shot got to Charley. It went through his coat and he took off in the opposite direction and he was bent the other way as he ran. He had to go to the doctor and have the shot dug out.

My face was splattered all over with powder, and I was a sorry-looking mess. The gun ruptured the copper tube, I don't know how much powder Pat had in it, but it certainly blew up. The principal decided we didn't have any more recesses coming for the next two months, so it worked a hardship on Pat and me.

At school that first winter, we had a professor named Holland. He was very severe with everybody. None of the boys liked him. I don't believe even the teachers liked him. One day Bob Foster and I were sitting on a bench talking and planning our next trapping expedition. Another lad came along about that time and poked a live snake around my neck. Well nothing would scare me more than a snake. When Mother was carrying me, she stepped on a snake and it coiled around her ankle, and I was born with a birthmark around my right ankle of a snake. I was whittling on a stick at the time and it made me so furiously mad that I whirled around and cut the snake in two. On the next slash I cut through his coat lapel and nicked his ribs, and after that he was going so fast all I could do was nick his coattails. He could run faster than I could.

Professor Holland soon had me up on the carpet. He had a huge hickory paddle with holes bored through it. He took me by the scruff of the neck and every time he'd hit me he'd lift me off the floor. Unluckily, I had a bottle of indelible ink. In those days we'd break up an indelible pencil, put the lead part in an ink bottle, fill it with water, and make our own ink. Well, his old hickory paddle smashed the bottle and he proceeded to drive segments of the broken bottle into my right hip. Finally he shook me and threw me across the room and let it go at that. But he had a big square ink well on his desk, and that time my dander was up too. I picked up the ink well and I let him have it. I hit him aside of the head and knocked him colder than a wedge. Down the stairs I went.

I told the teacher we'd had a good fight and that she could go take care of him, and I went home. The next day Father came down and told him that if he ever hit me with that paddle again, he'd have to account to him.

There was another boy named Henley, who he beat so badly with the paddle that he went home, got pneumonia and died. George Henley, his bigger brother, wanted to square accounts. He got out a knife, sharpened it up and took the stairs three steps at a time. But before George got to the top, Professor Holland had piled the desk and everything against the door.

The whole school was irate, and most of the community was against him, so we decided we'd rotten-egg him when school was over. I saved up a basket of eggs and hid them in the

10

hay mow. All the other kids did the same thing. I can remember when Mom's china painting class would be talking, they'd wonder what had become of their nest eggs. They said there must be snakes getting our nest eggs. They'd marked them because they knew they were rotten but they wanted them to nest for the old hens to deposit fresh eggs. But when school was out in the spring, we had a grand collection of rotten eggs, all reserved for Professor Holland.

The night that they was to leave town, (there was an evening train to Kansas City), I passed my basket of eggs out the back window of the barn. Bernie Bowman took them, and just as I was going to crawl out after him, Dad nailed me by the seat of the pants and hauled me in, so I didn't get to see the party.

They caught Mr. Holland and his wife on a high board-walk up above the mud at Cunningham-Beckenmeier's hardware and feed store. They surrounded them, using a few rocks and all the rotten eggs in town. After that, they couldn't go to the train or anywhere else, and finally an old colored lady on the south side of town let them in and gave them some other clothes to get out of town. Several of the parents told Mr. Holland before that if he ever came back they would kill him. He never came back.

One day Bob and Rollie Foster and I were hunting squirrels down along Crooked River, and met a Negro there who was hunting geese. He had a big single-barrel 8-bore muzzleloader. I don't know how much powder he put in it, but he said he used heavy charges. Each charge of shot was soaked in tallow, and saturated until it was a ball. Wrapped in tow, and with about a two-ounce load of BBs, he'd ram them down after the powder and newspaper. He dared us kids to shoot it, and I was always willing to take a dare. Finally we spotted a yellow hammer about thirty yards away beating on an old snag and I managed to get the big gun up in line with him. It was so heavy I could hardly hold it up, let alone aim it properly, but I finally got on the yellow hammer and pressed the trigger.

That knocked me cold as a wedge.

I didn't know exactly what happened, but Rollie and Bob told me later. Part of the hammer came back and cut my cheek, the gun got out of my hands and landed muzzle down in the mud of the slough along the edge of Crooked River, and I was turned a back summerset into the slough. All we found of the yellow hammer was his bill and tail feathers. Our Darky friend was very put out. He had to go home and boil out his gun, get all the mud out and dry it before he could even reload it, let alone finish the day's hunting.

During spring high water and the resultant floods, it used to flood all of Father's ground, a good part of it, anyway, and many more of the Missouri riverbottom farms were often under water. The men would take nets with several lengths to them and rope off with wire screen each little outlet from a big puddle of water. As the water sank, the fish would head back for the river and these hoop nets they put in there would catch a conglomeration of everything during the night.

I've seen as many as three muskrats in one, four or five mud turtles, a lot of gars with their heads stuck through and hanging by their gills, as well as perch, crappie, buffalo, and catfish.

They'd stick a stick through and catch the muskrats and pry them up against the netting and whack them on the head to kill them. In the meantime, the rats would run around and bite the gars open on the tummy.

An old Darky lived about half way between Hardin and Granddad Merrifield's place and he wanted turtles, all the turtles we could get. He'd put them in the slop barrel and fatten them up. These were the big old snappers, big old mud turtles. So whenever us boys could catch one we'd get him by the hind legs and drag him down there, being careful to keep clear of that awful bill. The old gentleman would give us fifty cents apiece for big turtles and two bits for small ones. That was big money in those days. He said there was seven kinds of meat in them and when he butchered them he had a steady demand for them.

In the fall when we were trapping, the Negroes would offer us six bits for a big possum if we didn't skin him. If we did skin him, they'd give us fifty cents for him. The hide would bring fifty-sixty cents so we'd skin all the possum and the boys would have to take the possum skinned instead of with the fur on. When they did buy one from some kid with the fur on, they scalded him like a hog and scraped him before they cooked him. They were very much in favor of scalding and scraping, but we couldn't see selling a possum for four bits when he'd bring double that if we skinned him.

Each spring the Negroes who lived on the south side of the Santa Fe tracks would have a big celebration lasting several days. They had a platform built up and in one corner of it was a still higher platform for the music. They would hold meetings there and dance half the night. The Foster boys and I cut a trail down through some six-foot horse weeds into the middle and had a little bivouac of our own there and a peephole cut out so we could watch them dance. One night there was a big fat black man, very dark colored, and a tall mulatto, quite fair skinned, got into a fight over a tall mulatto girl. Both of them pulled razors out. They gripped the handle and let the blade fold back over their knuckles. Well, the big fat Darky, he was a whale of a man, he made a pass at the yellow-colored Negro and he cut one ear right off, just flopped it down on his collar, scraping the side of his head. I remember the long, slim Darky says, "You will, will you?" And he reached up around the fat man's belly just above the belt and went half way around him. Instantly all of his intestines popped out all over the floor. The big Negro says, "Oh, lawdy" and he tried to catch the intestines as he sank down on the floor. Soon they brought in a stretcher, some sheets, and some water. They finally got him and all his intestines on this sheet, wrapped them up and took them away to the doctor. I don't believe it was over two months later I saw this big Negro walking down the street, smoking a cigar, apparently as well as ever. I also saw the mulatto, or light-colored Negro, and on that side of his head was no ear, but kind of a pink patch with a little hole in it. Us boys were very careful not to tell our parents about that incident. If we had, we'd have got a good hiding and that would have been the end of our watching the celebration.

"NEVER EATEN ANY BETTER . . . "

In those days we had no refrigeration, and during the winter the farmers would all gather at one farm and kill their year's supply of pork. Then they'd move on to another farm and do the same thing. I got in on a lot of it on Saturday and Sundays. My job was to shoot the hogs. By that time I was pretty proficient with a rifle, and each farmer would turn the job over to me to shoot the hogs with my .22. My other job was turning the sausage stuffer. In those days they lost no part of the hog. They made head cheese and souse meat of the head, the jowls were taken off and cured, as well as the bacons and the hams and the shoulders. For some unknown reason the good back straps were put in the sausage. I never could understand that. Then we'd boil the back bones and pick the meat from them. Later on, my job was to cut second growth hickory and keep the fire going in the smoke-house and keep some green hickory on it.

They would take all the hams, bacons, and jowls and soak them quite awhile in a salt-and-pepper solution and some sugar. Then they would hang them up in the smokehouse and smoke them for two or three weeks. When they were finished, they were really fine. The ladies would take the small intestines, and dip them in lye water that they made by running rain water through a big trough. It was V-shaped and full of wood ashes. They'd pour water through them and get the lye from it. They used that for making homemade soap, and they would also use it for cleaning the pig intestines. They'd dip them through that, then they'd scrape off the outer layer. There's three layers to the intestine. They'd turn them wrong-side out and scrape the inner layer off. The center layer was what they used to stuff the sausage. It looked about the same as high-class frankfurters we get today—very thin and transparent. They had a sausage stuffer that would hold three or four gallons, with a spout on it about an inch and a quarter in diameter. We'd slip this pig intestine over it and tie it, and I'd turn the crank to feed the sausage into this. When we had a coil of it that would fill a big skillet, it was put on the stove and fried until the sausage was thoroughly done. As soon as one skillet was full, they'd bring another one. I was too weak then and too small to turn the sausage grinder, but I could turn the stuffer. When the sausage was thoroughly cooked, they put it down in the bottom of a big stone crock and poured melted lard on it. This continued until they got near the top, then they'd pour another batch of hot lard over it, which sealed it. They covered the top of the crock with cheese cloth, and tied it down. That was the way the sausage was put away for the summer. I wish we could still get hams cured with that old hickory smoke the way we did when I was a little boy.

Beef was always killed during the cold weather, and then whatever farmer killed a beef, he would go around to all the neighbors and divide it up so it could be eaten before it spoiled. Then another neighbor would kill a cow and spread it around. But the hogs seemed to be the mainstay; the cured meat, the sausage, the fresh pork while it was in season.

The women would also make hominy. I can remember Aunt Emma taking the lye water from their big old ash hopper and boiling the corn until it would take the outside hull off. It was quite a process, but when she got through the hominy was excellent.

Each farm had a barrel for soap grease and all the fat from frying or cooking was thrown in the soap grease barrel. Then with lye from the hopper, they would make sort of a soft soap and sometimes they would harden it into bars and cut it with a knife. I remember having to stir soap with a big paddle many times. It was strong and known simply as lye soap. It would not only take off the dirt, but the hide as well if you was too generous with it.

In those days in Missouri we had only dirt roads, which were often either four inches of dust, or six inches to a foot of mud and very narrow. All transportation was by saddle horse or mule, buggy, surrey, spring wagon, or old dead-axle wagon with a spring seat. My uncle, Will Merrifield, was one of the first to get an automobile. I remember it as having brass furniture, a big old rubber bulb to squeeze for a horn, and a lot of gear shift levers. It would scare the devil out of all the horses and mules. Uncle Will became very unpopular with his "skunk buggy" among the residents. The narrow roads permitted only limited passing. About the only way horses or mules could be gotten past the car was to stop and kill the motor.

I spent some time with Uncle Oleander J. Berry and Aunt Mary. She was Father's oldest sister, and a little tiny woman. She did most of her cooking in the fireplace. She had Dutch ovens, with a crane at each end of the thing for kettles and long-handled skillets and spiders. I've never eaten better cooking. Although Uncle Oleander gave her a cooking range, she seldom used it. She preferred using the old fireplace.

At that time one side of the road was covered with heavy virgin forest. It was excellent squirrel hunting and I had a good time there. There was a great oak tree grew in one corner of the yard and Uncle Oleander told me he'd fired both barrels of his muzzle-loading ten gauge into it when it was loaded with passenger pigeons, and he and Aunt Mary picked and dressed pigeons for two days.

To my knowledge there were no game laws in Missouri at that time, but everyone frowned on any waste of game. They believed in utilizing everything possible from any game animal. The deer and the turkey were gone, but the small game was plentiful. I've never seen them shoot more than they could use, and at that time I never saw anybody kill a lot of ducks and leave them lying around for several days to spoil. They always took care of their game as a matter of course and appreciated having it to use.

Although there was a great deal more timber land there in Ray County, Missouri, when I was a little boy than there is now, a lot of the game was gone. Today the deer, at least, have come back in worthwhile numbers in a considerable part of the country due to good management.

One of the gala times for us boys was when they cleaned up a corn crib. Farmers stored their corn in great cribs. The rats lived in there by the thousands. They would undermine the whole thing with a series of dens and holes and they destroyed an awful lot of corn. Whenever a farmer got down to the last stages, he would bring in some wagons, and all the kids in the country, black and white and all the dogs they could find. With clubs they would converge on the old corn crib, pull out the last few bushels of corn, and then get busy on the rats. I've seen as many as a barrel-and-a-half of the rats come from under one huge corn crib.

Our little rat terriers were the prime dog used, but for two weeks after a corn crib was cleaned up, their little heads would be swelled all out of shape from the rat bites they received. We had one little dog that would put her feet over a rat hole and let just one rat out. She'd slap her forefeet back over the hole while she killed him, then let another one out. It was really interesting to watch how that little dog worked. But she suffered because invariably they would curl up and bite her while she was crushing them through the shoulders.

Most of the farmers raised their own sorghum. I can remember helping Dad fork a load of sorghum cane on the wagon and haul it to the mill. There they would grind it. A horse went around and around a big hopper with a grinder. The sorghum cane was all forked into that and after it was ground, all the juice was compressed out of it and put into big vats and boiled. The men would stand around and swap yarns, sometimes have a keg of moonshine, and share a drink or two. By evening we had our wagon load of sorghum cane contained in a small keg of sorghum molasses. Then we'd hitch up and go home.

The local mills also ground the corn for human consumption. My folks would never use anything but white corn for bread. The yellow corn, they said, was only good for the mules. We'd take the corn to the mill and have them grind it all to the desired granulation and bring it home. Each family in those days was self-sufficient. They practically raised everything they ate and they knew how to take care of it. Food was plentiful and very good. At least it stayed with you. Cooking, of course, presented long laborious hours at times. There were no stores to go to and pick up a TV dinner, or any of the canned material, vegetables, and things we enjoy today. 'Twas primitive in the extreme. Those old Kentucky hill people that moved into Missouri knew how to make practically everything they needed, and knew how to take care of it.

In the fall, we gathered hazelnuts, hickory nuts and black walnuts. In the winter when the ice was all over the ponds, we kept the yonkie pins as we called the little nuts that were in the lillies that dried up above the ice that we could get at. Cider was made by the barrel, and usually when it became sharp they would put a quart of pure grain alcohol in each barrel and four ounces of salicylic acid. This was supposed to hold the cider at a sharp, biting stage when it was good. My father, along with the rest of them, always barreled several barrels of cider for winter consumption. What wasn't used would usually get flat and then turn to vinegar.

I never saw any of the Keiths or Merrifields in the least degree drunk, but they usually had some liquor in case of need, and used it more as a medicine than for social purposes. Father usually had a gallon jug set behind the kitchen door. If I came in soaked and wet from trapping and hunting, he'd say, "Well, Elmer, you'd better take a pull on the jug before you go and change clothes—get warmed up."

I can remember him hitching up the mules, taking the empty jug, and we drove into the deep woods. Finally a fellow says, "Is that you, Farry?" Dad says, "Yes". He says, "Come on in." We went on into the moonshiner's, where Dad and he had a drink out of tin cups and he filled Dad's jug. He gave him a dollar, I believe, and we went back home.

We boys tanned a lot of skins. Coon hides were especially tough, and old fox squirrel hides also were tough. We'd put them in wood ashes and water for several days until the hair slipped and clean them off. Then if the folks didn't watch us and catch us at it, we'd put them in a barrel of soft soap and leave them there awhile, then take them out, wash them, and work them thoroughly over a beam to break up the grain. In that way we made excellent string leather, bullet pouches, and one thing and another.

I hunted possum with my little dogs more than coon. The coon business I didn't get in on very much. However, the Darkies, and many of the whites as well, ate coon and claimed they were even better than possum.

In the fall when the persimmons got ripe, they had to freeze first. If you tried them before that, they'd pucker your mouth up until you couldn't get a BB shot in it. But after they freeze they are delicious. You would always find out where the possums were by looking at the trees. They'd have their muddy tracks up and down the trunks where they climbed up to eat the persimmons.

All kinds of fruit were canned and dried, as well as corn and peas. Practically all the various lentils and blackeyed peas that were so famous in the South grew there too. My Aunt Emma raised salsify. It was a root that looked considerably like parsnip, but when made up into a soup with butter and milk, it very closely resembled oyster soup. It was excellent.

During the summer and fall, fruits and berries were either dried or canned. Then after the cold weather, came the hog killings at each ranch, or farm as they called them there. We really, I believe, lived better then than we do today in many cases. It was good and wholesome food, no antibiotics and no preservatives in it except drying and smoking and salt. Everybody worked. When a kid was seven or eight years old, he had to work. By the time he was twelve or thirteen, why he was supposed to take a man's place in most jobs that his strength would allow. I remember riding a bucking mule pulling a Jackson fork and stacking hay all day for two bits a day. I thought I was making big money. Wages in many places were simply a place to sleep and board. Others paid four bits a day, and a dollar a day was considered very good wages at that time, along in 19 and 8, 9 and 10. However, the small amount of money a family received in a year would in turn buy something in those days. Today you need a hat full of money to buy anything.

We lived in a nice bungalow off Main Street in Hardin. I remember one time my brother had been out to Granddad Keith's for a week, and Aunt Emma had given him an old Plymouth Rock hen and a bunch of little chickens. He tethered the old hen in our front yard with the little chickens feeding around, but what he didn't figure on was a colored girl that was hired for a maid next door at the doctor's.

My brother and I had been out fishing, and when we came home the girl had a broom and was on the other side of the fence. When Si's little yellow chickens would get through the fence, she'd squash them with the broom. We had only two little chickens left. Si was so mad he went berserk. He jumped over the fence, clouted the colored gal on the jaw, and knocked her out. Next he opened the front gate, and grabbed her by the heels. The mud was about knee deep in front of the place. He drug that colored gal up and down the street in the mud until you couldn't tell one end of her from the other before he deposited her back on the walk in front of the doctor's house. We never heard any trouble over it, but the next time Si was out to Granddad's and Aunt Emma gave him an old hen and chickens and brought them home, she was still a maid there but she never squashed any more of Si's little chickens when they crawled through the fence.

At that time the colored people and the whites got along very well in Hardin, Missouri. No trouble at all that I can remember. Many of the colored people we thought the world of, and many of them had been slaves during the war. I still remember hearing a lot of them talk about the good old days "Befo de wa when Master took care of us and we didn't have any worry about money or clothes or food."

There were, of course, mean black folks the same as there were mean white folks. I have found in all colors, creeds and races there's good people and there's bad people, but no one can differentiate and say that a certain race is all bad, because it certainly is not true. That wasn't so awful long after the Civil War, and a great many of the blacks and the whites got along together fine. Most of the people there would fight for the good black people just as quick as the black people would fight for the good white people. They were friends. They were neighbors. They worked together.

Father had varied interests in Ray County and drove about quite a bit with his mules and spring wagon. I remember one mule wanted to run away every time he'd hitch him up. We were going up to Granddad Keith's north of Hardin. There was a steep hill from the mill pond up, and this team of mules decided to run away uphill. So Father got the whip and went into action with them and he ran them up the hill. When he stopped at the top, one of the mules dropped dead.

When not in school, I rode around with him, taking care of the farm as much as possible, shooting small game along the road with my little rifle. Both of my granddads were fine rifle shots. During the war the northern soldiers had confiscated Granddad Merrifield's rifles and pistol so he went out in the deep woods, built a forge and a little shop, and proceeded to make him another rifle and pistol. They were single-shot muzzle loaders, but they kept the family in game during the war.

I remember being out at Granddad Keith's old white house on the hill before we left for Montana. Granddad was then over eighty. He quit riding his mule and used to spend a great deal of his time with a chair cocked up against the house in the shade. Both Granddads chewed tobacco and he'd tell me what a nasty habit it was and to be sure and never start it. He had a big barn he built and painted red in back of the house and the woodpeckers were usually busy at one time or another drilling holes in it. That Granddad didn't like. One day one was playing a tat-tattoo on the south side of the barn and Granddad said, "Get your rifle, Elmer. I want to kill that woodpecker." He sat down about thirty yards from the barn, maybe thirty-five. The woodpecker would peck a tat-too, then he'd turn around and parup-parup at us. Granddad says, "Next time he swings his head, I'm going to put one right down his neck." He was as good as his word. The little .22 bullet took off the mandible of his bill.

My Aunt Emma never married. Neither did Uncle Joe. They and Granddad lived together in the old house. Grandmother Merrifield was still alive then, and I remember her as a tiny little woman, who always wore lace cuffs and a lace collar, was very neat and prim and a wonderful cook. Grandmother Keith I never knew because she passed away before I was born. My Aunt Emma, Uncle Joe, and Granddad lived there. My Aunt Martha married Doug Jacobs and they lived near Richmond in a big brick house. I used to go up there for a week at a time. Uncle Doug Jacobs' mother was still alive. She was a prim little southern lady, also usually wore a lace collar and lace cuffs. She had a buckskin bag hung on the mantle of the fireplace. Every evening she'd get it down. She had a long clay pipe there, would tamp it full of home-grown tobacco, get a coal of fire from the fireplace to put on it until the tobacco was burning good, and then get her knitting needles and go to knitting socks.

Several of my cousins are still living in Richmond and Hardin, Missouri. Victor Jacobs now owns the old Ford place, and has modernized the house where Jesse James and his gang hung out, and where they killed one of their members. I never knew the particulars of the fight but my folks knew all of them.

Father raised corn on the farm west of Hardin in addition to his 250 cherry trees, and one part of the farm still carried a lot of heavy timber. I can remember holding up one end of the crosscut saw while he cut down black walnut trees. I wasn't strong enough to do much pulling, but I could hold it level so he could do the work. I wish now that we had

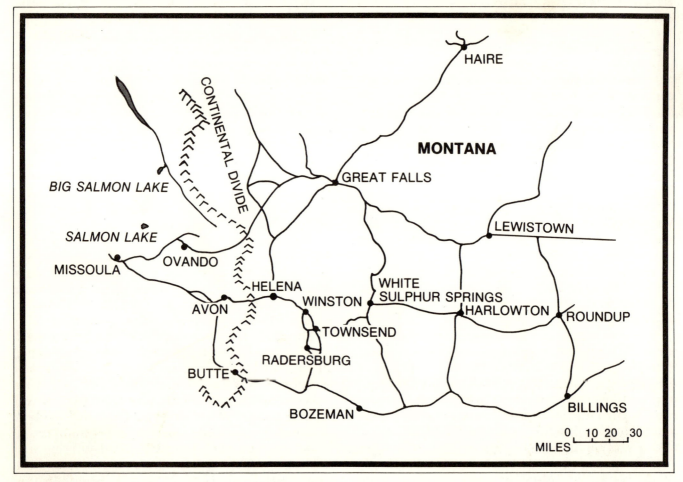

the black walnut timber that we felled there and burned up. It would be worth a fortune. He augered holes in the stumps and blew them out with heavy charges of black powder. They would make some beautiful burl walnut gunstocks if we had them today.

My Aunt Martha's family, the Jacobs, was very large, Mary, Anna, Lucy and Druzilla were the girls, and Vic and Monroe, the boys. Lucy taught elocution and toured the country with groups of girls for some time and put on plays. Druzilla was the youngest of the girls and she was older than I and a tomboy. She took me in tow and we hunted squirrels together. Also cleaned up on a lot of wild housecats. Where all the wild housecats came from, I'll never know, but so many people let them raise prolifically and then turned them loose to live on the game. They were a pest at that time in Missouri.

I can still remember the red-checkered tablecloths at Aunt Martha's and Aunt Mat's and Aunt Emma's tables and the huge piles of fried chicken, squirrel, bullfrog legs or whatever we had, including heaps of corn bread, butter, and milk. It was plain fare, but we really lived in those days. There were plenty of big green bullfrogs all around the lower country near Crooked River. I used to hunt them quite a bit, chop off their legs, skin them, and soak them in salt water. They were wonderful eating.

Grandfather Keith would take me in the woods back of the house squirrel hunting at times. He wouldn't carry a gun or shoot, but would go along just to watch me. We'd always stop at Grandmother's grave on our way back to the house. The squirrels were practically all fox squirrels, although I did get a very few grays. The big fox squirrels would mature about the first of June, and Father wouldn't let me shoot them or cottontails until they were big enough to harvest. Grandfather Keith taught me to tan squirrel hides, coon hides, and one thing and another for string leather. In fact I found a good old-time tom housecat skin made excellent shoe strings.

BACK TO MONTANA . . .

After living a couple of years in Montana, the folks were never again satisfied in the State of Missouri. Father was busy settling up affairs, finally sold our residence in Missouri, and we were soon ready to go back to the wilds of Montana.

After the hot, humid summer in Missouri,

we arrived in Helena in the fall and we nearly froze for the first month we were there. The high mountain air was entirely different from the damp, humid climate of the Missouri riverbottoms.

Father bought a home on Ninth Avenue with a German family for neighbors. He immediately went back to Missouri and brought out an immigrant car with livestock in one end of the car, boarded up, cows, horses, even a pair of pet coons. In the other end was our furniture. We lived on Ninth Avenue for some time.

My brother and I were put in Central School. Si's ears still stuck out like those of a big mule buck, and everybody made fun of him on account of his ears. There was a bully at the school that ran the boys. He was a big husky lad about twice as big as either of us. He had to pick on us and pick on us until finally he made us mad and we had a fight. Well he left us in a sorry state. We went home with broken lips and bloody noses, much the worse for the fight.

Dad looked us over and said, "Well, boys, I'm not going to lick you for fighting," he said. "From what you told me it was justified, but I'll give you one week to lick that guy." Then he said "I don't know how you'll do it, but get clubs or whatever you want. If you don't lick him, I'm going to give you a good hiding."

Knowing that Dad always kept his word, we went to the blacksmith shop and managed to get a couple of old spokes, made for the front wheel of a stagecoach. The blacksmith kindly drove holes in the small end of them, and we put buckskin strings through them and ran our belts through them and dropped them down inside our pants.

For several days Si and I studied this bully's behavior. We finally figured the way he went home every evening after school, and we hid in a big lilac bush he had to pass about two blocks from the school house. When he came along that evening, we jumped out and confronted him.

I hit him over the head with my wagon spoke and he just laughed at it and proceeded to clobber me. In the meantime, my brother got him in back of the ear and down he went. We proceeded to stomp his teeth out and we broke his nose, cut his lips, and blacked both eyes—in fact I think we would have killed him if a preacher hadn't come along and pulled us off of him.

The next day the truant officer was down to see Father and tell him what he was going to do. I remember Dad hopping over the fence and offering to take him on. The bully didn't come back to school for two weeks, and he was pretty badly patched up then and had to get front teeth all put in false with braces to hold them.

After that we never had any more trouble with him or anyone else at the school. When a new boy would arrive there, the bully would tell him, "Well, you can fight with anybody you want here, any of the boys in school except those two little Missourians. Don't ever start a fight with them.

"They won't fight," he said. "They'll just kill you."

LIFE IN OLD HELENA. . . .

Dad had brought out some trotting horses, and each Saturday and Sunday we would take off across the sagebrush flats on hunting trips one way or another. I still remember the smell of the high mountain air permeated with the scent of sagebrush, and the sweet acrid smell of fresh horse manure as the team would trot us along.

We hunted jack rabbits and sage hens mostly. Father liked the wing shooting, and I liked to shoot at the big bouncing jackrabbits. I finally got so I could pick them off on the run, first with a 19 and 6 Winchester .22 with long rifle cartridges, and then I traded for an 1890 Model Winchester, in .22 Winchester Special, with ivory bead front sight and a Lyman peep. With that rifle I got pretty good. The big jacks would jump, and usually by the third shot I'd roll them. Sometimes I'd get lucky and get them on the first shot, but they'd bounce high and long and they'd jump out right under our feet. Other times they'd break when they were thirty yards away.

I remember one day when Dick Tinker went along with us. His father had given him a new 1897 12-gauge pump gun. Dick shot at rabbits all day without hitting them, shooting behind them. He couldn't seem to figure out that they needed to be led. Finally Dick came to a big sagebrush, spread his legs wide apart, shoved the long pump gun down into the brush and pulled the trigger. Out boiled a lot of dust and out kicked a big jack rabbit sans any trace of a head. Dick says, "I finally got one, anyway."

Father worked at various jobs around Helena, and during the school months and evenings I sold papers to make some extra money. I found out that the saloons were good places to sell them. Helena was a lively town in those days. There were no automobiles; only horses, carriages, surreys, buggys, spring wagons, and old dead-axle wagons. Cowpunchers dropped their reins in the hay market, which is all built up now. The ranchers would drive in, unhitch, and turn their team around to the back end of the wagon, and feed 'em while they shopped over Helena for groceries, clothing and what-have-you. I sold papers up and down the street, and in the saloons.

Charley Russell was painting some of his most famous paintings then, including the meeting of Lewis and Clark with the Indians at Ross's hole. A great mural, it's one of his greatest works.

There was a Chinese laundry in Helena back of the meat market, terraced into the side of the hill. At times we would gather there and watch the Chinamen when they would stop work and serve their lunch. They would spread a big mat in the middle of the floor and set a huge kettle on that with a ladle in it. Then each would gather around the kettle with their small bowls and chopsticks. They would ladle out a bowl of soup all around and then they would start chattering and hold the bowl up close to their chin and twiddle their chopsticks and a stream of soup would go down their necks. We got quite a kick out of watching them shovel soup with chopsticks. They were certainly adept at it.

One noon we came down there, just to watch them again, and they had a big row going on. After considerable palaver, one of them picked up one of the heavy irons they have for pressing clothes and crowned another one, crushing his skull in and popping his eyes out. Almost instantly another Chinaman got a knife and nearly beheaded that one. Then he was stabbed from behind by another Chinaman. Us kids ran down the slope there. We ducked into the Helena Meat Market and had them call the police station and clean up the mess. Helena had a very large population of Chinamen in those days that had moved in to clean up the placer diggins after the whites had quit and given up.

The Dixon family was from Missouri, and Dad knew all of them. Coon Dixon lived at Wolf Creek. He and Charley Russell would come in and get drunk at the California Winehouse. Father would bring Coon home and Mother would sober him up on black coffee. He was a brother of Billy Dixon who was in the Adobe Walls fight and also in the Buffalo Wallow fight. Several years later I had considerable correspondence with Olive Dixon, his widow, when she was on a newspaper at Amarillo, Texas.

I continued to sell papers after school, and the ladies of ill repute that lived in the rear of some of the saloons would often send me to run errands for them; to get a dress, a hat, or a box of candy because they didn't want to be seen on the streets. They would nearly always tip me a dollar and quite often make me a sandwich from the salver at the end of the bar.

I remember one evening an old cowpuncher bought a paper. It was dark and I thought he gave me a nickel, but when I got up under a light to make change for another man, I found out he'd given me a five-dollar gold piece. I started hunting up and down trying to find that cowpuncher to give him back his gold. Finally I located him in the back of the California Winehouse in a poker game. The sheriff was there too, so I went up behind him, waited until he'd made his play and tapped him on this shoulder. I told him, "Mister, you gave me five dollars instead of a nickel for this paper," and I laid it down on the table. Everybody stopped playing and he says, "Son, you're honest. You may keep the five dollars."

The sheriff reached over in his pile of gold pieces there and picked another five dollars off it and laid it on top of it. He says, "Take this also, son. You're an honest kid." So I made more money in one night than I usually made in a week selling papers, just by being honest.

A German family named Hildebrand lived next door to us on Ninth Avenue. We all became good friends. He worked on a newspaper and Father became his good friend and he'd go hunting with us. I remember one morning at three o'clock, Mother woke up and started crying. Dad couldn't understand it and she said, "My Mother is dead." Father went over and got Mrs. Hildebrand to try to console her, but it was no use. Mother started packing up to go back to Missouri to her mother's funeral. Mrs. Hildebrand told her she was silly to have such a dream. Mother said, "No, it was not a dream."

At nine o'clock the telegram came. "Mother is dead. Come at once."

Mother had the uncanny ability to forsee things that were going to happen. How, nobody knew. In later years when I would be gone months punching cows or running a government pack string, and possibly hadn't written her for a month or two, I'd go home and find Mother sitting up waiting for me at two o'clock in the morning when I got off the train. She'd usually have a big chocolate cake baked and a lamp burning while she crocheted. I asked her how she knew I was coming home. She said, "I just knew, that was all." She had that gift.

Father later sold the Ninth Avenue property and bought a bungalow and a big barn with a Bull Durham sign painted on the back of it out at 1012 Billings Avenue. At that time it was out on the flat, and only one house next to it, with others scattered around 200 yards to a quarter-mile away. It was just across an old placer diggings and us boys liked that much better because we could play in the placer diggings. There was a spring about 200 yards from the house with wonderful water. We'd pack our drinking water from there, as it was better than the piped water from the city. The ditch from this spring ran down to what we called the China Gardens back of the NP depot where some Chinamen raised vegetables to peddle all over Helena. There were some cottontails in the diggings and we had some fun getting a mess of them now and then. Also some wild house cats. My little rat terriers would trail them in a hole and fight them until they finally killed them and dragged them out.

We had chickens, cows, and horses at this place, and it was much better than living up in the thickly settled Ninth Avenue district. While living here my second brother was born and Father named him Francis. He was a grand playmate as soon as he was old enough, and we thought the world of him.

About this time, about nineteen and nine as near as I can remember, the first automobile came to Helena. A doctor bought it. It was very similar to the one that my Uncle Will had had in Missouri. He stopped in front of the California Winehouse and a great crowd gathered to see it. I remember an old Chinaman with his long black smock, his hands in his big sleeves across his chest, and he eyed the thing for some time. When the doctor put it in gear and started off, the old Chinaman says "All pushee, no pullee, go like hellee all samee."

In those days, three four-horse stages went out of Helena. They would stop at the old Beatty House across the street from where the old Placer Hotel now stands. One of them went to Radersburg, one of them went across Canyon Ferry to a mining camp, and another went over to Seven-Up Pete's towards the Blackfoot Country. I often watched the stage drivers pull on their silk gloves, then a pair of buckskin gloves if the weather was nippy, gather up their strings after all the passengers and the freight was loaded, kick off the brake

and away they went down Main Street just as hard as the ponies could run. When they hit the turn into Helena Avenue that went on to the depot, the hind wheels would usually slide clear up and over the curb as they bounced around.

The coming of that first automobile, however, raised hob with the peaceful life of Helena. Horses had never seen such a thing and they stampeded in every direction. He drove past the Hay Market and half the horses tied to the wagons broke their halter ropes and took off across the flat. The cowpunchers' ponies took off. There were broken bridle reins all over the streets, and cowpunchers walking around hunting horses. The merchant's delivery company that delivered all the groceries in spring wagons all over town, had one runaway after another. It was a sight.

It wasn't long before more automobiles came to town, and then the problem worsened. Ranchers coming to town would usually stop, take their rifles and shoot on each side of the car, kick up dust until the automobile stopped. Then they'd drive wide around it out on the prairie and come on to town. They called them "skunk buggies." The ranchers certainly hated every man that owned an automobile. Quite a few people were killed, and others were hurt in runaways. It was simply a case of a bunch of wild Montana broncs wanting nothing to do with automobiles.

OF FIRE AND PAIN . . .

In the fall of nineteen and eleven, the folks decided to move from Helena to Missoula and see how they liked the western Montana country. Arriving at Missoula, they found most of the hotel rooms taken. They finally found a rooming house across a vacant lot from the courthouse and rented two rooms. They couldn't get the two rooms together, so they got one on the third floor for my brother and I, and theirs was on the second floor. Father found a house on the south side he wanted to rent, but the owner lived up the Bitterroot and wouldn't be in until the end of the week, so we took our meals downtown and spent the nights in this rooming house.

My brother and I had a premonition the place was going to burn. We begged the folks to take the bedding from the room on the third floor and spread it out on the floor of their room and let us sleep with them. But Father insisted we had a good room and a good bed up there and to go ahead upstairs and stay there. I have always been a light sleeper, while Si was very hard to wake up.

19

At about three o'clock in the morning, I woke up and the building was on fire. The hallways were a roaring mass of flame. I shook my brother until I finally got him awake and raised the window overlooking the front of the rooming house. I told him to jump and try to hit the porch. It would break his fall somewhat before he landed on the ground. Si jumped and he landed on the porch and then on his side on the ground. He was pretty well knocked out for several months.

Just then the transom over the door caved in and a wall of flame shot from there out through the window where my brother had jumped. It was a roaring furnace. I managed to put my left hand over my eyes and save them and staggered around the bed to another window. A brick building was fairly close to this side window. Between it and the rooming house was an ornamental iron fence with spearheads scattered along the top. I could feel my flesh curling up on me and I heard Father yell, calling my name twice. I remember answering him once and drawing my arm back to knock the window out, as I intended to jump. Then everything turned black on me.

The roar of the fire awakened Dad and Mother and Dad opened the door to be met by a wall of flame. He slammed it and went to the window and raised it. Mother proceeded to throw her clothes, suitcases, belongings out the window and even an old family clock she wrapped in some bedding and threw that out, too.

The fire department was soon there, but before they arrived Dad hung with his hands from the window sill and had mother crawl down the length of his body and then drop. Some men ran under her and caught her so she was uninjured. Dad then went around to the front of the building to the fire truck and told them that his boy was in the northwest corner of the bedroom on the third story. So they turned the hose in there.

Dad wanted the ladder put up but they said it was too hot and they couldn't do anything. While the hose was pouring water into the bedroom and scalding me further, Dad got a ladder off the truck and put it up to the porch, climbed to the top of the porch, pulled the ladder up and jammed it into the roof of the porch, and climbed to the top of the ladder. Then he jumped to the right and tried to catch the window. He fell back to the ground the first try. Then the firemen put a ladder up to the porch and he tried it a second time. On his third try he grasped the window sill with one hand, and, being very active, he crawled in.

He hung on to the bed, the floor was all a mass of coals, in case it caved through, the bed, he thought, might catch on the rafters. He felt around for me until he got to the foot of the bed and found me near the window. He picked me up and passed me out to the firemen who by this time had put ladders up to the window. Father remembered the fireman say, "He's still alive," when they passed me out.

They took me to the brick house next door and tried to put me to bed. They called a doctor named Flynn, who said he gave me enough chloroform to kill three men before I stopped screaming. I would jump from the bed to the ceiling, they said, and was screaming in agony. The old gentleman that owned the house, seeing me in the condition I was in, died of a heart attack.

They finally piled blankets over me and roped me in bed and put me to sleep with an enormous dose of chloroform. When they removed my underwear, a great deal of flesh came off my right shoulder, along the top of my right leg, my face, and my left hand. Evidently I'd laid on my left hand on the burning floor. I spent the next ten days in the hospital soaking in olive oil with a fan some six inches from my face. I was blind, couldn't hardly tell the difference from daylight 'til darkness, and my tongue was swelled out of my mouth. I remember wanting water, and they'd take a medicine dropper and drop a little out on the end of my tongue where it did me mighty little good.

In the meantime, Father rented the little house out on the south side and they finally got me out of the hospital and took me to this new home. They got a sanitary cot with folding wings. Instead of leaving them horizontal, they'd pull the wings up to a 45-degree angle and wired them across that way, then put a sheet under me and another one over me, and that's the way I spent the next three months. The flesh was rotting, falling off me, and the doctor was coming and cutting it off and doctoring me the best they could in those days. They knew nothing of present procedures of treating burns then, and would put dry powder on the burns and then cheese cloth. It would adhere to the burn and pus and blood would form, so they'd tear them off and chunks of cooked flesh would come with it.

I was burned in October and Christmas Day the folks thought possibly I could sit up and have Christmas dinner with them. However, when they propped me up in a chair, blood vessels burst along my leg and arm and sprayed the house and they had to put me back in the old sanitary cot.

My chin was welded down to my right shoulder. My left hand was a claw turned upside down on the back of my left wrist. I would hook this under my chin and grasp it with my other hand and push until I'd tear the scar tissue and scabs loose between my jaw and my right shoulder. Then blood vessels would burst and spray the room. The doctor would give me the devil, saying I was going to bust my jugular vein. I told him, "Well enough. Either I'm going to have a neck so that I can straighten my head and turn it once in awhile, or I'll get it over with."

In time skin grew from my back and my chest allowing me to turn my head and to straighten it up. This was a great help.

Father took a job as shipping clerk with the Missoula Mercantile Company while my little red-headed mother put in most of her time caring for me. After some three months on my back in this sanitary cot, practically all of my back was a solid bed sore. I was a total wreck. However, my eyes cleared up so I could see and I developed an enormous appetite which Mother tried to satisfy, as I had a lot of tissue to rebuild. I was so sick much of the time that my memory is very faulty during those months.

Finally spring came and I'd managed to pry my chin loose from my shoulder, grow a little skin there and started learning to walk again by pushing a chair in front of me. However, it didn't take very much exercise until I had to lie down again. As spring progressed, I managed to get dressed and walk, and I would head towards Mount Sentinel and the University of Montana. I'd walk as far as I could, then sit down on the curb. Father would get off work and come looking for me. When he found me, he'd put me on his shoulders and pack me back home. I remember the day that I finally got to the foot of Mount Sentinel. Dad had a long haul packing me back home that evening. I had a lot of first-degree burns; my face, hands, practically everything except my chest and back, and the back of my left leg and buttocks, were covered with first-degree burns. But my right leg, the whole top of it below the knee, and completely around below the knee on the left leg, and a big patch on the inside of the left leg, my right arm, my right shoulder, the right side of my face and my left hand were third-degree burns where the flesh came off down to the bone in

places. It was two years before the deep burns on the top of my right leg finally healed over with scar tissue. They had to be dressed every day. I was a wreck, hardly worth saving, but Mother persevered and pulled me through it. I ate enormous quantities of beefsteak that Mother would cut up in bites for me, as my left hand was not of much use, being doubled back on my wrist.

Dad bought a pair of Remington .22 pump guns for Si and I and as soon as I was able to carry it in one hand, I would hike out towards Mount Sentinel. Ground squirrels were in profusion and a few woodchucks lived along the base of the hill, so I spent my time hunting. Along towards fall I could travel pretty good both ways. I got a job setting traps at the trap club which only required one hand anyway, and I put in some time at that. The next fall, I remember Si and my Dad hunted deer together, but I was unable to go, being too much of a cripple to cover much ground at that time.

A man named Chevigny, a French Canadian, owned the rooming house and an investigator soon turned up the fact he had it insured with three companies. They contacted everyone they could find. Finally they contacted Bert Conner. Chevigny had tried to hire him to fire the place and Bert had asked about the people in it. Chevigny said, "Oh let them get out the best way they can." Bert Conner turned state's evidence and helped convict Mr. Chevigny. Mother identified him as the man she'd seen crossing the vacant lot during the fire.

One lady had jumped out of the third story window and had curvature of the spine and was a wheel-chair patient the rest of her life. I was the worst burn case of all, but my father's hands were terribly burned and required quite awhile for them to heal up.

The court finally sentenced Mr. Chevigny to nine years in the state pen at Deer Lodge. He had poured thirty gallons of coal oil on the three hallways, all three stories of them, and touched it off. No wonder it was such a furnace. The sheriff, deputy sheriff, and a lot of people begged Dad to shoot Chevigny, but Dad preferred to let the court take its course.

A year after I was burned I was able to get around pretty well and attend school. I also again sold newspapers, the Missoula Sentinel as I remember. The top of my right leg was still proud flesh from my knee to my hip and had to be dressed every day. By that time they used olive oil to soak the dressings, so that they could peel off clean and not tear out pieces of flesh at the same time. My left hand wasn't much use, but I still managed to shoot squirrels that second summer, resting the rifle over my wrist.

Missoula was a small town then as compared to today. The whole flat south of the river was practically empty, except Spruce Street and a couple of streets that led into the bridge. The rest of it was just open prairie out to the University. Two brothers named Mapes had a shoe store. They had a big pointer dog that was well-known all over town. One day he disappeared. Us news boys knew that the new dog catcher was grabbing every dog he could find. If they had a tag on them, he'd pry it off and throw them in the city dog pounds. It was located on the south side between the ball park and the lower bridge, in a big open meadow.

One day the Mapes brothers contacted us urchins, and asked us if we could find their dog. We had a good idea where the dog was, all right, so we went to the blacksmith shop and borrowed an old cold chisel, and an old wagon spoke with a hunk of iron shrunk on one end of it for a hammer.

I put DeBarge on top of the bridge across the Missoula river and Pearson climbed up on the ball park fence to watch, in case of interference. I proceeded to cut the padlock and open the door into the hallway. Pens of dogs were on each side, some 500 dogs in all, and each was in a muddy pen. As soon as I cut the padlock and opened the door they all started barking. I was determined to find the Mapes' dog and take him back. They'd promised us all the ice cream we could eat plus fifty cents apiece if we could find the dog.

Each time I opened a pen, out came a rush of dogs and they'd knock me down in the mud. I finally got to a big pen in the back. Then I spotted him. When I opened that and the rush of dogs carried me part way down the hallway, I managed to grab the old pointer's collar and slip my belt through it.

He dragged me out in the open, and the other boys joined me. We sneaked back into town and to the back door of Mapes' shoe store. The Mapes brothers took us in and cleaned me up the best they could. They they took us to the drug store next door and ordered them to give us all the ice cream we could eat. The Mapeses gave us each four bits, to boot.

When I got home that night, Mother asked me how I got so muddy. I told her that I'd fallen down in the mud. The next morning, Mrs. Elman came over with the morning paper and showed it to Mother. Across the front page ran a big advertisement: "$500 reward offered for the miscreants who tore down the City Dog Pound and turned five hundred dogs loose." I was a very quiet lad, knew nothing about it, and had nothing to say! But I still remember about five hundred of the happiest dogs I've ever seen, going in all directions across that green meadow, their tails up, barking, with each headed for his own home.

After Chevigny's trial was over, and I was on my feet again, Dad and Mother were ready to forget Missoula and move back to Helena—and I was, too.

When we moved from Missoula back to Helena I was considerable of a wreck. My left hand was turned upside down and back on my wrist, just a claw extending from the top of my wrist. I used to wrap a towel around it when Father sent me to school so the girls wouldn't cringe at the sight of it. The right side of my face was all drawn down towards my shoulder also. I was a horrible-looking sight. The girls didn't like to look at me.

I told Father I had to have a left hand so I could hold a rifle and do normal things. Father contacted every doctor in Helena, as he had in Missoula, to try to get them to operate on that hand and break it over and straighten it out. None of them would tackle the job. They all said I would never live to be 21 anyway and they were not going to torture me any further.

Finally, I had had enough of going with only one hand, so I asked Dad if he would break it. Mother says, "Can you stand it?" I says, "I don't know, but you can go ahead and do it anyway."

So Mother got a bunch of cotton bats and gauze, soaked them in melted deer tallow, and had a lot of bandages ready. Father went down to Goodkind's wholesale liquor store and bought a gallon of Old Granddad, 100 proof, and came home with it.

He said, "Son, do you still want to go through it?" I said, "I do." I said, "Regardless of how much I howl or pass out or whatever, get the job done. I want this hand straight whether I'll ever be able to use it or not."

It was just a bunch of drawn cords, bones, and fingers and you could see daylight between the bones if you looked close. It was just thin membrane. Father poured me a water glass of 100 proof Old Granddad.

"Son, get drunk. Get damn good and drunk." I drank it. Dad said, "Are you drunk, Elmer?"

I said, "No." He says, "Can you whistle?" I

tried. I said, "I can't even pucker, Dad. I feel pretty good so go ahead."

Dad put my arm on a heavy table and sat down on it with my hand between his legs. When he picked up those fingers that were doubled back of my wrist and broke them, the pain was terrific and I passed out. Father took a board he used for stretching mink and sanded it until it was as smooth and slick as glass and would reach from my elbow out past my fingers. When I came to, my hand was straight. It was all laced down solid to the mink board. An old black silk scarf was bound around it and tied around my neck for a sling. It hurt. I never had anything hurt any worse I don't believe, but it was straight and I was proud of it.

I walked the floor for three days and three nights. I couldn't eat anything as I couldn't sit still long enough, but I did drink a gallon of Old Granddad. The pain seemed to hit me more up in my shoulder and the back of my neck and the left side of my head. Finally after the third day, the pain subsided.

Mother said when Dad broke the fingers over, the scar tissue broke across the back of my hand, and she said she could see the joint water in every one of the joints in my hand.

It bled, and in a few days that taped hand was a dirty-looking mess. Mother wanted me to let her unwrap it and re-bandage it. I wouldn't do it. I wore it for two weeks. I wouldn't let anybody touch it. I says, "It's straight now, and I'm proud of it."

Finally it began to stink. Mother says, "Elmer, you're going to mortify if we don't take that bandage off and clean it up." After two weeks, I figured that it surely wouldn't spring back. I was afraid if they opened the bandages too soon that my hand would pop back on my wrist and I'd be out of luck.

She got a foot tub, filled it with warm water, soap, sheath knife, and scissors and cut the bandage away. Lo and Behold! My fingers were all straight and a thin membrane had grown over the top of my knuckles and hand where she had looked at the joint water when Dad broke them over. She re-bandaged it, and put it back on the board for a time.

Father had a squaw make about a dozen buckskin gloves to fit my left hand. Mother would drip melted deer tallow in these and I put them on, and started riding. I'd go out to Bear Tooth and ride broncs with Bill and Fannie Steele. I'd wrap the rope around my left hand and in the excitement of riding the bucking horse, I'd grip it. Of course the old scar tissue would break clear across my knuck-les, and when one glove got caked with dried blood and filthy, I'd throw it away, wash my hand, and put on a new clean buckskin glove filled with the deer tallow.

In this way I finally made a new left hand but it was a long struggle. At first I could hold it up to the light and see daylight between the bones right down the palm of my hand. After a couple of years working with it every time I could and also riding broncs and pulling on the rope with that hand, I finally wound up with a pretty good hand. Even today it's a sorry-looking hand but it's useful, and for a time I even did two-gun demonstrations with six-guns.

EARLY GUNS . . .

While living at 1012 Billings avenue, we had several very happy years. My little brother Francis was born there. On Sundays we would drive to some of the streams like Prickly Pear or Beaver Creek for fishing. In the summer and in the fall we put in every Sunday hunting, either down to Helena Lake for ducks, or else go deer hunting up by Priest Pass or over on Nevada Creek.

I traded for an old Remington 1854 .58 caliber brass mounted smooth-bore musket, which was my first shotgun. It was only effective at very close range due to the extreme spread of the pattern. I did wreck a covey of green wing teal that came up the river past us one time, and was death on muskrats swimming down the river if I aimed about a foot in front of them. The concussion would kill them and they'd come up kicking and I'd have another muskrat skin to handle.

As I was not expected to live anyway, the folks let me put in part of a summer with Waldo P. Abbott. He had been a school teacher in Kansas after the Civil War, and a buffalo-hide hunter, then was a scout for General Crook at the Battle of the Rosebud. When General Crook asked for volunteers after his defeat to carry the news to Fort Laramie and ask for reinforcements, Abbott volunteered. Crook offered him the best horse in the outfit, including his own, but Abbott told him he didn't want any horses, but said to go out and pull the moccasins off of six dead Sioux they thought would fit him, as he was going to travel on foot by the stars and shack up in thickets during the daytime. He wanted to leave only Sioux tracks in Sioux territory. Abbott taught me a lot about hunting and he was a very fine rifle shot.

Another summer I put in a good part of the time with Samuel H. Fletcher, an old Civil

War veteran that fought through the Civil War with the 2nd Illinois Cavalry, being one of the few of that outfit who came home alive. He was a fine pistol shot and also taught me a great deal.

I put in a good part of one summer during school vacation working for the National Biscuit factory. My salary was $10.80 per week. I was paid at the end of each week with a ten dollar gold piece and some small change in a little brown envelope. In the morning I had to shovel three tons of slack coal in a wheel-barrow, wheel it onto an elevator, up a couple of stories, and up a steel incline, and dump it in the bake furnace. That occupied the whole morning. Then I would wash up and in the afternoon I had to take the small cartons of half a dozen or a dozen boxes of cookies or crackers and pack them in huge cartons, put them on a truck to the elevator, and stack them as high as I could throw them. It helped develop my crippled left hand. From age 12 to age 16 I didn't grow in stature at all, being too busy rebuilding what the fire had taken away from me.

I began to realize that if I was going to get my share of the ducks that were so plentiful, I had to have a real shotgun. So I wrote the Ithaca Gun Company when I'd saved enough money for a No. 2 Ithaca double hammerless shotgun. I wanted Damascus barrels, but Lou Smith, the president then, wrote that during the war which had started then in nineteen and fourteen in Europe, he could no longer get Damascus barrels, and for that reason was sending me the higher grade No. 3 at the same price. It was my first fine shotgun and I did very good work with it. I shot that gun for seventeen years.

Father gave me a new model 1894 .25-35 Winchester long-barrel rifle. I killed my first deer with it on Nevada Creek. The first shot was three hundred yards up a steep mountain. The deer had seen me and I couldn't get any closer, so I raised the rear sight two notches, got a rest, and hit her square in the shoulder. It broke the shoulder, but the little 117-grain bullet never even went on into the chest. The deer pitched off down the hill in a run and I trailed her around the mountain for a half a mile, getting three more running shots before I got enough of those tiny bullets in the deer to put her down to stay. That was enough .25-35 for me for big game. Then I went to a .45-70 trapdoor Springfield carbine that had been given to me by an old stage driver. That and a case of 500-grain infantry loads of 70 grains of black powder and 500 of lead was a power-

ful rifle for a tiny kid then, but it did the job.

I asked to join the Helena Rifle Club, which was composed almost totally of much older men. The club members didn't want a kid in the outfit, but my friend, Bill Strong, sided with me and told them that I would qualify, and asked if they would let me in if I qualified expert over at the Fort Harrison military range.

They agreed, thinking it impossible that a skinny kid could handle a .30-06 and qualify expert. I bought a dollar-and-a-half Krag rifle through the N.R.A., practiced with it, and went over the course from two hundred to a thousand yards three times. Then I borrowed Bill Strong's Springfield and shot the full course with that. When the day came for the annual match, I managed to qualify expert with three points over, so they allowed me to join the Club.

That winter, the club shot in the National Indoor matches. They were mail order matches. Each club shot its own and mailed in the results. It was quite a lengthy match and we shot for weeks. At any rate, I wound up as high man for the Helena Rifle Club using an old .22 Winchester musket I'd bought from Holder Hardware Company for $10, and Mother loaned me another $10 to buy a Stevens scope, which Johnny Linder put on for me free of charge.

Bill Strong became my good friend and mentor. I would cast bullets, reload all his pistol ammunition and we shot together and hunted together whenever we had a chance. He was the state accountant at the Capitol building. His brother, George V. Strong, became a General in charge of G-2 during World War II.

About this time the right side of my neck started to abscess just below my lower jaw. Evidently the scar tissue had formed and healed over some burned tissue. Father took me back to Beaudeau and Johnson in St. Paul, Minnesota, where I spent two weeks in the hospital. The doctors operated on my neck and removed all the burned tissue there. It healed up and never gave me any further trouble. Each day they would have me up in the office, strip me, and exhibit me to doctors who came from New York, New Orleans, Frisco, and all over the country. They couldn't believe their eyes that I had lived after such terrible burns.

Father's next project in Helena was to buy the little store of an old Civil War veteran named Grosbugge at the corner of the Hawthorne School. We worked like troopers and ran this store for about two years, ending up with a bare living and some five thousand on the books that we could never collect.

SALOON ROBBERY...

While carrying the horse paper route for the Helena Independent, my route led down Helena Avenue to the NP depot where my friend, Bill O'Connell, was a night cop.

At that time, Helena was quite a tough town. Most of the beams that held up the porches were studded with six-gun slugs or bullet holes or gouges from different gun fights. The depot area was the toughest part of the town, and O'Connell was one of their best men. On the corner was a wedge-shaped saloon. There was one door in the apex of it and a counter ran down the east side with a break in it and then a counter was to the left. There was a side door that opened into the street that led down to the fur buyers. I gave Bill his paper one morning and he says, "Elmer, things are too quiet over at that saloon. Ride your horse by at a trot and see what's going on in there, swing around the block and come back and let me know."

On my saddle horse I could see over the curtained windows, from which everything was perfectly visible to me but not to anyone walking along the street. Two men had everybody lined up against the bar, one man holding two guns on them while the other was taking all their belongings and putting them in a hat. I rode around the corner, doubled back and told Bill what was going on.

Bill says, "I'm going in, Kid. If I don't make it, you ride down to the saloon across from the NP depot and tell the bartender to give you my ten-gauge and a box of buckshot. You come back where you can cover both doors and keep everybody in there until help arrives. Have the bartender phone the police department for help."

Bill went in the front door and as he went in I rode alongside to see what was going on. A man whirled around and shot at Bill, but hit the transom over the door. Both of them then jumped over the counter of the bar. Everybody else fell flat on the floor.

One man raised up over the bar and aimed at Bill, but before he could shoot Bill hit him between the eyes with the old forty-five and he collapsed. The other ran down the back bar and I yelled at Bill to watch the opening. I don't know whether he heard me or not through the windows, but anyway he swung and leveled his gun on that opening. The other man was crouched down low, running be-

hind the bar. When he crossed the opening, Bill took him through both shoulders with the old .45 Colt. He fell on his face, while one leg came up in the air and stayed there.

As soon as I saw the thing was over, I rode around to the front. Bill came out and he says, "Elmer, go down to the depot and have the bartender phone for the coroner, the sheriff, and the undertaker, and bring the dead wagon." I did as directed. Bill said, "Do you want to go hunting next Sunday?" I told him I did. So we went duck hunting down at the lake the next Sunday.

Bill's work gun was a .45 Colt single-action with a 5½-inch barrel and Remington black-powder loads, 40 grains of black, and 250 of lead. He carried it in a shoulder holster on the left side and was a very good man with it.

SCHOOL DAYS...

I finished the 8th grade at the Hawthorne School by the time Dad sold the store and the place on 1012 Billings Avenue and bought a ranch six miles from Helena in the Helena Valley.

I walked six miles from the ranch to Helena to get in my one year of high school. For a time I was the head of the class in algebra and most other studies except talking German. I never could twist my tongue around to doing a good job with that language.

I got caught in a blizzard hunting jackrabbits one Sunday and froze both feet harder than rocks. Dad thawed them out when I got home with coal oil and snow. Some of my toenails came off, and all the skin came off, and I had to hobble around in house slippers for two weeks.

When I did get back to school, Mrs. Richmond, the algebra teacher, and I had a good row. She tried to make fun of me before the whole class for being silly and fool enough to go hunting in the winter time.

We had the one-arm chairs in the algebra room. Leighton Burley sat on the corner in the front row and I was next to him. Leighton would always pick on me whenever he got a chance and, as he was the teacher's pet, he got away with it. He would write on my collar and she would look out over the class, paying no attention to him. I even got a rubber collar, and he would write on that with ink and I'd have to wash it off. I was in bad with Mrs. Richmond on account of the frozen feet and being out two weeks, and I asked her to let me make up the work, but she wouldn't do it. She said she was going to flunk me, and she did.

Elmer took this doe near Helena, Montana in the fall of 1916 with a 220-grain bullet from a .30-06 Springfield.

About that time Leighton Burley decided to write on my collar and I told him to quit it, I hauled off and hit him with everything I had, right on the edge of his jaw. I knocked him out of the chair and over by the door and he went to sleep. Mrs. Richmond jumped up and down in her high-heeled laced shoes, told me off in good shape, and rushed around to Professor Roberts' office. Professor Roberts came back to look the situation over. He looked at me, he looked at my collar, and he said, "What did you do, Elmer?" "I couldn't get him to stop, so I figured I'd better stop him," I said.

He said, "I think you did a good job." However, Mrs. Richmond flunked me in Algebra anyway, so I told the folks that was enough of that.

I decided to go to Business College. Professor J. Lee Rice ran the Helena Business College at that time and I put in six months there. I learned a great deal more in that six months in Business College than I had in my year in high school. After Business College I put in six months in the U. S. Weather Bureau and then had to stay another three months after I resigned before they got another boy to take my place.

I hired out to the survey crew with the U.S. Government Land Office. While on that job, I incurred the enmity of a man named Adrian, who they called Canuck. We all packed six-guns on the line every day, and I would run into a bunch of fool hens or young blue grouse and get a mess of chickens every few days. Canuck carried a 4½-inch New Service .38-40 in a holster, and he was always bragging about how fast he was with it. He would stick his finger in the trigger guard, lift up and spin the gun with the muzzle forward and shoot it. One day on the line he pulled that gun and threw it on me. I didn't like it, so I clobbered him, and the fight started.

Finally he got me by the throat with his right hand and was choking me. I couldn't get him loose any other way, my left hand still wasn't very strong, so I reached up and got hold of his long finger on the right hand and bent it back and broke it off short with his hand. That ended his choking me right quick. Canuck went a long time with that hand in a sling, so the rest of us had to do more work because he was useless except for carrying the flagpole and giving Rigby a shot across gulches while we were running the township line. However, this ended his quick-draw practice and throwing a gun on us. Finally, when his hand healed up, one Sunday the boys told

him he couldn't hit anything anyway. They set up a quart beer bottle and a little half-pint whiskey bottle at the foot of a tree at 110 yards and told him to hit it. He couldn't even hit the tree. I sat down with my back to a stump, pulled my knees up, took an old 7½-inch .32-20, and asked them to spot the first shot for me. It was a little low, so I raised a little more front sight up and I broke my two bottles with the next two shots. That didn't endear me to Canuck in the least.

Several of the boys on the crew had been school mates in the same class at school. Before fall Canuck wrote a letter to Pat Scherer's girl. I guess it must have been a very nasty letter although I never saw it, but he signed my name to it. That fall when I got home off the survey and went to town, Pat Scherer wanted to lick me as soon as he saw me. I told him I couldn't fight him. He was a bigger man that I was, and I only had one good hand, but he insisted. So I told him to get his gun and I'd meet him in the alley in back of Bronson's Pool Hall and we'd have it out. I went, but he didn't show. Then my friend, Dick Tinker, talked to him. He says, "I know Elmer never wrote that letter or had anything to do with it."

Finally Canuck bragged to some of the boys about what he'd done and the truth came out. Pat Scherer came to me and apologized. But after that tale I didn't have much use for Canuck.

In nineteen and eighteen, there were twenty of us already inspected and ready to go to Camp Lewis the next morning, on the 10th of November. The war ended on the 11th. So, instead of shipping up to Camp Lewis, they turned us all loose. Helena went wild that night. Everybody was on the streets and celebrating. My brother, Barty Lightworth and I were coming down Main Street on the right side just above where Broadway runs down the hill and into Main Street. There was a saloon there in the first block above Broadway. As we came along, Canuck came out of the saloon. He leered at me as he started to go by. Without even thinking I jerked my right hand out of my mackinaw jacket and clobbered him. I hit him an awful blow on the jaw and he curled up alongside the Copenhagen snuff sign by the left side of the door. We watched him a few minutes and he didn't show any signs of coming out of it.

A couple of hours later, I saw Canuck coming down the middle of the street with a pug with him, who boxed around Helena, and two other men. He was looking right and left, and

I knew he was looking for me, but I made no attempt to move. I thought we might as well get it over with. I had a good six-gun in a shoulder holster, but didn't have any idea of using it in a crowded street with people in every direction. Canuck marched up to me as soon as he spotted me and he jerked that old New Service .38-40, jammed it in my belly and he started to say, "I'm going to kill you." But I hit him under the chin so hard he sailed out between the car tracks. His gun clattered off to one side of him. He sat up and was holding his head. I was standing there low and balanced, and I thought if he made a move for the gun I'd just jump out and see if I couldn't kick his head off with my steel-capped boot heel.

All the while I was watching him I wasn't paying any attention to the others. The big pug came in from the side, hit me in the mouth and knocked me clear back into the plate glass window of Sandean and Ferguson's store. He cut my upper lip so it hung down over the lower one. I managed to get my hands up and he backed me along the sidewalk across the street from Bronson's Pool Hall. By that time a cop came a-runnin' after him. He made a pass at the guy's head with his billy. The pug dodged and he missed him, but he turned and ran.

By that time I could look around and see what was happening. My brother Si had the other two knocked colder than a wedge and he was watching them to see if they wanted to get up and have any more of it. The pug grabbed Canuck's gun, jerked him to his feet and took off up an alley. I never saw any more of him, but for some time he told all and sundry he was going to kill me on sight.

About that time, after I started going to business college, I went to the sheriff, the chief of police, and my friend Bill O'Connell, and they told me to wear my gun because if I didn't Canuck would likely shoot me in the back. And they said, "Call him whenever you see him and kill the rat because he's paid for. He's been threatening you all over the town."

My first day at business college, I went in and Mr. J. Lee Rice, the professor, had given me a seat about halfway back. I unbuckled my six-gun, rolled the belt around the holster and shoved it in my desk. Some girls behind me saw the gun, and rushed up to Professor Rice to tell him. Professor Rice came back, sat down with me, put an arm around my shoulders, and he says, "Elmer, that your gun?" I says, "Yes." He says, "Is it loaded?" I says, "Yes." "What is it?" I says, "a .45." He says, "Why are you packing it?" I told him. Professor Rice went back, called the class to order and he says, "It's necessary for Elmer to carry his gun because his life's threatened and he may have to use it any time when he's out of this classroom. So," he says, "I don't want to hear anything about it. I don't want any of you kids to touch that gun. It's loaded and Elmer knows what he's doing," he says. "Leave it alone."

Finally I saw Canuck coming down the street below the Marlow theatre. He saw me coming and I wanted to get close enough to be sure he had a gun on him before I shot him. I could easily have killed him at 100 yards with the old .45, but I wanted to get close enough so that he could go for it and make it a fair fight. That's what the sheriff had advised me to do; be sure he had his gun.

As soon as I crossed the street to brace him, he turned around the corner, ducked down an alley and I never saw the man again. I'm glad of it now because I surely would have killed him or tried to if it had come to that.

Chapter 2

BRONC
BUSTING DAYS

LEARNING A TRADE...

My brother Si, and my little brother, Francis enjoyed life on our new ranch much more than living in town, and so did I. This was more like it! I started riding broncs—determined to learn to be a professional bronc rider.

I had gotten acquainted with Bill and Fannie Steele, who lived out at Bear Tooth. Fannie was at that time the lady world champion bronc rider, and I rode out to spend a few days with the Steeles every chance I had. They would put me on one bucking horse after another.

The first one I tried they called "Sagehen." That was about as crooked a bronc as I ever rode. She would sunfish until your stirrups on the near side would hit the ground, swap ends, come down, turn the other way, in fact she knew all the tricks. The first time I tried her, she threw me higher than a kite. My feet were clear up above the saddle and I yelled at Bill to catch her. I says, "I'm bucked off." Bill says, "Hell, no! You're riding good. Keep a-kickin'." The horse jumped under me and I came down in the saddle, managed to get a-hold with both spurs, and I did set her. This riding of broncs greatly strengthened and improved my left hand.

I lost no opportunity to try out anything that would buck. Bill Steele loaned me a bucking horse and had me put a halter on it and a hobble on one foot, run the halter rope down through the hobble, and then picket it. I tried that out. The horse ran to the end of the rope, turned a summerset, got up, ran the other direction until he hit the end of the rope, and turned another summerset. After that he was picket broke, but that horse could still buck pretty good. Finally I decided to take it back to Steele's ranch. I'd played with that one as long as I wanted to, so I saddled it up in the corral. On one side of the corral was a machine shed and it was just high enough to allow a horse with a saddle to walk under it. I gave Charley Stout a neckyoke, and told him to stay in the machine shed and keep the horse from going under there with me. I crawled on a gentle horse, slid over on the bronc and we had it out. He could buck all right, but finally headed for the machine shed. Stout dropped the neckyoke and ran. I turned all holds loose, kicked my feet out of the stirrups and fell off. But I lit on my left side pretty hard. I was a sick boy for the rest of the day.

The next day Jim Galen came down from Helena and wanted to go out to Bear Tooth and ride broncs with me, so we saddled the bronc again and he said, "I'll snub it up until we get out in the road." So he put a rope on

Fannie Steele of the Bear Tooth Ranch, showing the riding style in 1914 that carried her to the world's championship among lady bronc riders.

Early-day rodeos in Montana were often impromptu events, lacking the fine seating and arena facilities available today. Here Mike Reed rides a horse named Bill Steele.

the bronc, and snubbed it up, in addition to my hackamore that I always rode with. When I climbed the bronc, he went to pitching and swapped ends. He bucked around Jim until the rope wound Jim down against his big pinto's neck. The pinto started bucking. Well, with the two horses pitching, first one way and another, with the rope around them, my Dad was yelling, "They'll both get killed! They'll both get killed!" However, Jim and I got them sorted out after awhile and went on to Bear Tooth with them.

I made a little money then by buying a couple of green colts, getting on one and riding him until I could steer him with my hat and spurs. Then I'd get the other one in a round corral, and wool him around for half a day, pulling him sideways until I had him halfway broke to lead. Then I'd tie this one to the other's tail, get my saddle on it, and head for the ranch. The bucking horse couldn't do much bucking with the other one tied to his tail. This way I'd take two broncs home, break them out and sell them, and then go get two more.

Next I bought an old bucking horse that had been traded from one ranch to another and rode him while I put in six months in the Helena business college. I'd ride him in and stable him at Charley Stout's. I'd hauled in a load of hay for him to eat and that worked pretty good. At least I had a way to get to town and back. I ran a coyote trap line from the ranch to town, so I could run my traps and attend business college and had a means of transportation. The old pony bucked every time I saddled him up mornings, but I enjoyed the job of riding him.

I traded an old six-gun, a .41 Colt rod ejector with a Derringer butt, known as the Lightning Model, for a bucking mare to practice

on. I found out after I got her that she was loco. She would snap at you as you went by, and if you bucked her out about three times, the third time she'd get pretty rough.

The Al G. Barnes Circus came to Helena, and Jim Galen told me to come in and see the show. Barnes said he'd give twenty dollars in gold to anybody that would bring in a bucking horse, any kind of a nag that would make his clowns ride. He said "Bring her in." George Lamb and I led the old mare to town. On the outskirts of town I saddled her up and I bucked her out twice until she was getting pretty rough, and was well heated-up. We led her on in. Mr. Barnes put his two clowns on her to double-deck her. We called her "Maggie Murphy" and old Maggie was in good fettle by the time the clowns got on her. She turned a summerset over them, broke one's leg and broke the other one's shoulder. Mr. Barnes said to get that animal out of here.

I said, "Mr. Barnes, you promised me twenty dollars in gold if she made your clowns ride. I don't see your clowns riding her any." He paid off and took the mare.

Jim Galen went on with the show to Great Falls and he said old Maggie crippled another clown up there, so Barnes had her shot and fed her to the lions. I wound up with a nice shiny twenty-dollar gold piece out of the deal at any rate.

While riding for a cow outfit one summer, I was riding broncs. We were riding in pairs, roping, throwing, building a sagebrush fire and putting the running iron on a bunch of cattle that the rancher had bought, right out on the range. I had three broncs gored that summer by those wild longhorn cows. They were descendants of the old Texas stuff that had come North in the early days. On two of them, the cows killed the horses, and I then killed the cows with a .45. The third one we managed to get home, as he was hit farther back. The horn had rammed into his intestines, so we poked them all back, sterilized them, sewed him up with fish line and he got well. But he had a big knot on his tummy thereafter.

Aside from a few fenced-in ranches around the lake, Beaver Creek, and Ten Mile, much of the country was open. You could ride all over the country. Today it's all fenced up, squared away now to where you have to go down the highway in an automobile.

In the winter they would hold dances and box socials, either at the school house or at various ranches. In the summer, when time permitted, they would run in all the broncs we could find and us young bucks would ride them for entertainment. The ladies would bring lunches and we'd have a big feed after the bronc riding, usually winding up with a dance, then we'd have breakfast, saddle up our horses, and head for home. Times were hard, money was very scarce, and lots of Jim Hill's homesteaders had to wait for the old hen to cackle of a morning to have breakfast. But we seemed to have more good times then than I remember having since. Every neighbor would help each other in case of sickness or any trouble, and we had a lot of fun in spite of all the hard work.

One morning I saddled up my horse down at the ranch intending to go out to Bear Tooth and ride broncs for a couple of days. I'd just pulled on a brand new pair of handmade Hyer boots, buckled on my spurs, and started out past the cellar to the barn to get my horse.

Dad had an old Rhode Island Red rooster, quite old, with spurs over an inch long. He was a belligerent old chicken, always wanting to fight something. He bristled up in front of me and I stuck my toe out to push him aside. Instantly he jumped in the air and spurred me with both feet. Those long spurs went through my new boots just at the bottom of my right ankle and drove into the bone. Man, they hurt! I just jerked the .45 and plugged him right down through the center. Mother came out of the house when she heard the old six-gun and wanted to know what was the matter. I backed over to the cellar door, sat down and worked my boot off. It was already filling with blood in the bottom. He'd cut an artery on the inside of my right ankle and the blood fairly squirted after we pulled my sock off. The ankle swelled up until it was impossible to get a boot on and I didn't go to Steele's for two weeks or do any bronc riding. Mother

Fannie (left) and Bill Steele on their ranch at Bear Tooth in 1928, when Fannie was the World Champion Lady Bronc Rider. Elmer learned his bronc-riding skills from this pair of experts on some of their rankest horses.

put on the kettle and it was chicken and dumplings for supper.

PUSHING A PACK STRING...

I put in nine months in the U. S. Weather Bureau in Helena as messenger boy. My job being to print the weekly weather bulletins and daily forecast cards, then break up and distribute the type. Many times the forecast would read fair and warmer when a good blizzard was on, and the postal officials would laugh at me when I took all the cards and bulletins up there for distribution. After nine months of it, I had had enough of indoor work, so in spring I hired out on a U. S. Geological Survey for the summer.

We started at Clemons on the Dearborn, and for a time I worked as axman on the line. Later I packed from Augusta, freighting in food and supplies for the double survey crew. We ran that township line up over Scapegoat Mountain, the Divide, down to the East Fork of the North Fork of the Blackfoot, and finally over to the head of the South Fork of the Flathead. Much of it was township line that we were surveying, and half a dozen of us would take a blanket or stag shirt and fold up our share of grub in it, put that on our back, work all day and cook our own meal that evening, and sleep in the stag shirt or blanket around what wood we could gather for a big camp fire.

Being good with horses, and with our head packer having to go home on account of sickness, I inherited the pack string. I had to pack twenty miles from Ovando up to the bridge at the dry fork of the North Fork.

It was wonderful fishing there those days, big trout were in profusion, and I remember when we pulled out from the bridge to go up

The Gilman Stampede in 1920 saw Joe Daly ride "Midnight," a famous bucking horse of that period.

on Scapegoat Mountain, our engineer asked me to catch all the trout I could. We'd been on frowzy bacon and ham that had been on a pack horse for two months, and the fish were a welcome change. He asked me how many men I needed to pack the fish and I told him four. I had the only fly rod in the outfit. That day I caught a wash tub full of trout. I'd hook a two to three pound cutthroat and then a big bull trout would grab him by the tail and I'd finally get him away from the bull trout, and land the cutthroat. Then I'd put on a big hook with a little piece of fin, throw it in again, and hook the bull trout. I'd play him around until I'd get him close enough to the surface to kill him with a six-gun and drag him out.

There was an old trail camp that had piled about 30 prune boxes under a spruce tree, so we packed the dressed trout in moose grass, tight, and loaded them into the boxes. We packed them on the horses up the hill the next day. When we got up to Scapegoat Mountain, we selected a big snow drift near the camp on the north side of the mountain, tunneled back in it about twenty feet, made shelves, and placed the prune boxes of trout on them. In a week's time that crew of 16 men ate every fish.

The next year I took a job as smokechaser for the U. S. Forest Service out of Montour Station outside of Ovando. It was a three-day ride from the ranch over to the Montour Station, so I took my saddle horse and pack horse and made it through okay. We had some awful fires that summer, one of them covering twenty square miles in Anaconda Copper Company saw timber. Another one went twenty-five square miles up the Montour and there was a huge one over on Babcock Creek that covered thirty-six square miles before it was through.

Again I inherited a packing job. I had seven head that I packed up to the fire camp on McCabe Creek. One day I packed up there and unloaded all the packs. I tied up all the horses except an old white horse that I always turned loose. He was a grand old pack horse. I went in and had lunch, and while I was about it, the cook had set about 15 lemon meringue pies out on the top of a lodgepole that was flattened off, to cool. I went out to gather up my horses to go back to Montour and, bless Moses, old Whitey had stuck his big face in every one of those pies. He was smeared with meringue all around his lips. He ruined every one of them. The cook came out about the time I forked my horse and got the

After breaking camp in the morning, the survey crew packed and guided by Elmer Keith is ready to head deeper into the forest. This picture was taken in 1920.

lead rope of the horses that were tailed together. He ran back in the tent and grabbed a cleaver, came out and threw it at Old Whitey's head. Whitey dodged and the cleaver stuck in a tree. I knew my welcome was all through at that fire camp, and I told the ranger that he would have to send someone else up there with the next load of food.

A few days later the ranger called me in and asked me how much lemon and vanilla extract I'd taken to that camp. We got out the papers and found out that this cook had been ordering a considerable amount of it. Finally the ranger asked me if they were serving any undue amount of pastry. All I'd seen was the pies that Old Whitey had ruined. He figured it all up, and there were too many cases of lemon extract and vanilla extract, so he rode up there. He found a big cache of empty bottles behind the cook's tent. Next thing I knew he fired the cook and ordered me to pack him up and take him to Ovando. He had been drinking the extract for the alcohol that was in it.

One day I was making the rounds over onto the Dry Fork, up the North Fork, across Dry Fork then drop down Falls Creek—my regular smoke route. I went through the fire camp, had lunch there, and when I got almost to the top of the divide a high wind came up and the fire crowned behind me. It was a roaring inferno, and going as fast as the horse. I spurred and dragged my pack horse over the top of the divide, and I'd just got down on the other side when I met an old grizzly in the trail. The horses were afraid, whirled, and wanted to go back into the fire. I got my hand pretty badly rope burned before I got dallies on the lead rope to my pack horse. It took me back to the top of the hill, where the fire drove us back. Needless to say, when we came back the old grizzly had gone on about his business.

I remember packing into the South Fork of the Flathead, which meant three days and nights without sleep. We needed many supplies in there, and had to keep the strings going. Coming back with an empty string, I stopped at Falls Creek. I'd been asleep in the saddle, I don't know how long, but I remember I was awake when I left the Montour cabin. The horse must have stepped over my hackamore rope when he was getting a drink out of Falls Creek, because I woke up with my spurs about under the fork of the saddle and the old pony a buckin' for all he was worth. He rammed my left shoulder into a big pine tree and it was numb, but I had the rope in

In a storm but still spurring well over the shoulders of "Glass Eye" at a rodeo in Montana in 1921 was Smoky Branch, illustrating some of the spectacular moves made by broncs.

Winters were cold at Winston, where Elmer (left) and Si Keith bagged these two mule deer for winter meat. The rifle at left is a .44-105-520 Sharps, the other is a 94 Winchester.

my right hand and managed to set him. That night I decided I'd had enough of going without sleep, as riding broncs asleep was poor business, so I rolled into bed for a good 24-hour rest.

When I started breaking broncs and punchin' cattle, I soon found out my little .32-20 six-gun, while a fine grouse and rabbit gun, was too small to stop a mean cow or a bronc. I acquired a good 5½-inch .45 single-action Colt. When I went any distance I usually rolled one in the bed and wore the other one. In the Ovando country there were lots of fool hens and quite a few blue grouse. I like the .32-20 for them. They furnished us many a good meal.

One day we got into deer and I killed one. I wrote Dad a note and sent it out with the packer to come over and get it. In the meantime while the letter was in transit and before he got there, I killed two more with the old .32-20 for the camp. We enjoyed the fresh fat

venison but found out that the .32-20 was a bit small for deer shooting. One deer I hit five times in the shoulder and those little bullets that would dig into a dry lodgepole or green lodgepole and merely smear the lead off the soft point jacket, when they hit a deer they flattened out to the size of a penny. Finally the deer went up the hill after I'd put them in him. I hit a limb with the sixth shot and missed, the seventh broke his neck and killed that one. The third one was running down the hill. The boys above had jumped it, a big old dry doe. I led it quite a ways and broke its neck with one shot. That convinced me that whenever there was big game on the menu, I'd better put the .32-20 in the bedroll and pack the old .45. However, I did kill three mule deer and a coyote that summer with the .32-20, and the next year I killed a cow elk with it.

Before moving to the valley ranch, a coyote came by the house one morning and I grabbed the .25-35 and followed it over to where the Wesleyan University is now. In three shots, I made it so hot that it turned back into the gulch out of sight and headed towards the State Capitol. I followed along behind and I got to where the cordwood was piled to heat the Capitol. The coyote appeared on the mountain south of there a good six hundred to seven hundred yards away and about thirty people getting ready for their day's work in the Capitol watched. I rested my left shoulder against the cordwood, aimed at the coyote, raised the rifle fairly high above him, knowing that the little bullet would drop a long way, and fired. I'd reloaded the rifle and was aiming again when the first bullet got there and hit the coyote and he rolled down the hill for quite a distance. I emptied the gun, but could never hit him again, so I went home and got a belt of shells and told

Dad what had happened. He said he'd go with me and help get him. We trailed the coyote up over the hill, down into Dry Gulch into deep snow, finally coming on him in the snow. I started to shoot him but Dad says, "Just get a club. That's all you need." So I finished him with a club. That hard point solid 117-grain .25-35 had broken the right shoulder and went about an inch into the right lung and lodged there. But the hemorrhage from the broken shoulder had simply bled the coyote out. Dad stepped the distance from the cordwood rick in back of the Capitol to where the coyote had rolled, and said it was between six and seven hundred yards. It shows the futility of trying to kill anything with a little rifle at that distance when a hard-point bullet merely got into the right lung after breaking the shoulder.

SPUDS AND TRAINS...

At this time the Great Northern railroad was known as the Big Potato route. They brought in all the homesteaders they could find from all over the country and homesteaded much of the old buffalo range of Montana. A railroad man named Jim Hill seemed to be responsible for much of the homesteading and the advertisement of free land that went with it. The settlers plowed the land and put it in wheat, and up until World War I they did very well, many building fine homes. But after we were in World War I, it stopped raining. Before that it would rain twenty to thirty days in June, and they had wonderful crops. After the war started, the rain stopped, and most of the dry farmers went broke and left their farms. Tumbleweeds took over, and you could see any number of ranch houses with windows out, the fences piled high with tumbleweeds, and the machine sheds full of them.

There were people in the Helena valley who grew potatoes to sell to the Great Northern railroad. One spring they dumped an awful lot of cull potatoes out that they didn't sell. My brother and I hauled several loads of them home with the wagon and decided to try raising spuds ourselves. We put in ten acres of spuds. That year Ten Mile Creek had plenty of water, we had plenty to irrigate with, so we raised a big crop of spuds. In the fall we dug them and filled the cellar. Having no place for the rest, we dug great pits in the field and pitted them. One pit froze and we lost it all. Spuds went to $16 a hundred that winter and we really capitalized on it. We paid off the little ranch, and bought Dad a new Ford. The predecessor of the Model Ts, it

was brass mounted. We also gave him a good bank account from our crop of spuds.

The next year I decided to get rich and put in five acres of spuds myself, but that was the summer of nineteen and nineteen, and it was a dry year. No water ever raised in Ten Mile Creek and none in our ditch, and never a spud came up. So my second venture at farming was a complete flop.

Pete Hilger had been raising great quantities of spuds and selling them to the Great Northern railway for a living. One fall after a successful crop, he went to Helena, tied up at the Hay Market, and went over to the store and decided to buy himself a new outfit of clothes. He bought new socks, shoes, underwear, shirts, suit, hat, topcoat and all, packed them all up, raised the lid on the back of his buggy, and put them under the seat. Then he went up the street across from the Helena Meat Market and had a couple of drinks at the saloon, came back, got in the buggy, and drove down to Helena Valley.

When he came to the bridge over the creek, he stopped the horse in the middle of the bridge, and looked up and down the road both ways for a couple of miles. No one was in sight, so he sailed his hat in the creek, pulled off his coat and shirt, threw them in the creek, took off shoes, socks, underwear and everything, stripped down and threw them all in the stream. Then he reached around, turned up the lid in the back of the buggy to get his new clothes—and discovered someone had stolen the whole works!

He says, "Giddup, Dobbin. We'll fool the old lady anyway," and he drove into the ranch yard naked as the day he was born.

One day Dad, Mother and little Francis, who was still a baby, had driven to Helena, and as they were crossing the NP railroad tracks below the depot, high board fences obscured the view on each side, and Dad drove out on the track and his Ford stalled.

A freight train was coming along at the same time. Dad couldn't get it started, you had to crank those brutes, so he grabbed little Frank and just reached to grab Mother and pull her out of the Ford, when the train hit. It carried the Ford and Mother 67 feet, and she was pretty badly bruised up, not able to do much for about a year. I remember during that time I did the family washing on an old washboard. Many times I rubbed the skin off my knuckles trying to get the clothes clean.

A lawyer named Mills had a ranch in the Helena Valley, and Dad farmed me out to him for a week's work. Old man Haines, an old ex-wolfer, and I and Lawyer Mills had to

One of the more popular events in early-day rodeo was the single steer roping contest, where the roper "wild wests" the steer (as shown) then dismounts and ties both hind feet.

load a four-horse alfalfa frame on another wagon to haul it to Helena. There was a log chain around some of the beams underneath this four-horse frame. It was made out of two-inch stuff for hauling enormous loads. The three of us lifted it up. I was at one corner, Mills at another and old man Haines volunteered to go underneath and undo the log chain and get it out. He hadn't much more than got under when Mills said, "Hold it, Keith, while I get a prop." He turned the whole works loose on me. I had to either hold it or kill old man Haines, so I held it.

Something popped in my hip. Finally Lawyer Mills came back and put a prop under it to hold it up. It made me sick and I almost passed out it hurt so. I didn't think too much of it at the time after the pain quit, but I was in for trouble. For seven years after that I would have terrific pains in my back there and my hip. Father took me to Helena and the doctor pronounced it kidney stones, so he had me take four ounces of glycerin every other day, then a wad of crackers on top of it.

It didn't do a bit of good. Sometimes my back and hip would hurt until I'd lay down on the floor and cold sweat would run off me. Dad would get me by the hands, get me on his back, pull my arms over his shoulders and shake me and that would relieve me for a time. I had ordered a fine and fancy saddle

from Al Furstnow of Miles City, Montana. It was a beautiful saddle, basket-stamped and with matching 22-inch tapaderos. When it came I put it on a horse. I cinched it up good and tight and it would still pull to the left side of the horse when I hit the saddle. Finally I sent it back to Furstnow at Miles City. He wrote me that he had every old cowpoke in town ride it and nothing was wrong with the saddle. I still didn't tumble. Of course, I was so bowlegged at that time it was hard to tell which leg was the longest. Finally in desperation Dad took me to Helena to a chiropractor, and he X-rayed me. My right hip was two inches above the ball socket. It had come out of the socket, it had started a new socket of its own and my right leg was two inches shorter than the left one. No wonder the saddle set on one side of the horse when I had all the holes laced at exactly the same on each stirrup leather.

The chiropractor put me on a table and strapped me down, took a block and tackle and pulled my right heel up by my right ear, twisted sideways and jerked down. The hip popped back in the socket, and it's been there ever since, thank God.

BACK TO THE PACK...

In nineteen and eighteen we had a double survey crew on the North Fork of the Black-

Ready to leave the Lamb Ranch in Helena Valley, in 1920 and all "duded up" for a wedding, were (left) George Lamb, Elmer Keith, and Joe Spurzan.

foot, finishing up a lot of work around the Dry Fork and over around the Little Lake. After that work was done, we pulled out for Ovando and a day's celebrating, and then the government sent us down on Gold Creek above Missoula a few miles. Before we broke up our Lake Creek camp, a man named Hanrahan said he had to go out and see his mother who was sick. Smokey Hess was the head packer then and he took Hanrahan to Missoula. However, some of the boys wanted to send down for some things in town and the boss, George F. Rigby, had everybody's money in his strong box. This man Hanrahan had been sick, or pretended to be sick, for two days and had been around camp.

When they looked in the strong box everybody's money was gone except mine. I had it in my gunbelt. No one knew who had done it, but a bunch of us boys figured it was Mr. Hanrahan because when he came back from Ovando he brought a lot of candy, cigars, and everything for everybody. He'd done pretty well. Both Rigby and Jim Flynn thought that Smokey Hess, the head packer, had stolen the money. I didn't believe it for a minute, and neither did the rest of the crew.

When we got to Ovando they fired Smokey, so I inherited the pack string. I had to take them down to Gold Creek alone, and went past a good many ranches that night. I had saddles on all of them, cinched up as tight as I could, but after they'd trot for a few miles, they'd come loose and I'd have saddle blankets to pick up, then I'd have to rope that horse, re-saddle him, and turn him loose again.

I finally reached what they called the Clearwater. There was a settlement of people there, some religious sect or other, and they wouldn't take me in. They wouldn't pasture the horses, they wouldn't feed me, and they wouldn't honor the government vouchers that I had to pay for it. I kept on into the night and finally reached Gold Creek.

At that time it was a logging camp. There were corrals there, and a barn. I pulled the saddles off and fed the horses, but there was no place I could eat that night at all. The saloon was open, however, and the bartender let me roost on a stool there and eat all the pretzels I wanted, along with a couple glasses of beer. I slept in the saloon that night.

The next morning the boss of the logging camp told me to come over there to the camp and have breakfast with them, then I had to move about seven miles up over the divide. At the end of the road there was a deserted ranch. At one time there had been a town there in this little meadow and all the furniture, pianos, silverware, everything was still in the houses. The packrats were having a grand old time. They trucked the material in there as far as the logging road went, then I had to pack it back about fifteen miles. We worked at that until fall. Two horses quit the bunch and I spent a week and over trying to cut their tracks, until I finally found them.

When I did get them it was pouring down rain and we packed up just as it was getting dark. I moved one load down to this old deserted mining town in the meadow. During the day the cook had made a washtub of doughnuts, so we put an oilcloth over the tub and I loaded it on top of the pack. When we got down to the meadow about midnight we put this tub of doughnuts underneath a table that the boys brought out from one of the houses.

Finally it quit raining, cleared off, and we all bedded down around the table. The packrats, however, wouldn't let us sleep. They'd come out of the cabin, go over to this tub, get a doughnut, go back over to Jim Flynn's bed and set up on that.

When they went between the bed and the cabin, I got my six-gun out and started killing rats in the moonlight. Every time I'd shoot a rat, however, I'd get a barrage of boots from the other boys that wanted to sleep. A good time was had by all. I was very unpopular and had most of the boots off the whole crew piled on my bed by morning.

Rigby came back up from Missoula and gave us orders for Justin Postel and I to move the pack string to Wolf Creek. It was a long trip but we lit out. We made it to Ovando, the next day we went up to Lincoln. We changed off horses, riding everything in the outfit.

I finally rode a mule that Shenkle had rid-

Keith on a bronc at a rodeo in Claysoil, Montana in 1922.

den. She was a grand saddle mule but once somebody had knocked a pipe out on the saddle horn and burned her. When we got up just out of Lincoln we stopped to let the horses all drink. An old horse shed a pack saddle and got it under his belly and the blanket went down the river. Postel got the blanket and I got the saddle and piled it on in front of the fork of my saddle. I guess she thought I was knocking another pipe of fire out on her neck because she started pitching. I had to quit hanging on to the saddle, and let it go. I rode the mule until she quit bucking. When she got tired, there was nothing left to ride that hadn't been rode hard but this one old outlaw, so I told Postel to get a string on him and saddle him. I got on him and he could really buck. He wiped it up for quite awhile with me but I set him.

We headed out and over the divide and down the old trail to Wolf Creek. It started raining and then turned to snow as we climbed higher until we were soaked wet, even our chaps soaking through. I rode this old outlaw around the stock yard in Wolf Creek and was going to jump off and open the gate while Justin Postel ran the pack string in. I got my feet clear of the stirrups and threw myself just as far from him as I could. He

kicked with both heels and they went under my right arm, but didn't quite touch me. However, when I hit the ground my legs just collapsed. They were numb. I sat there like a fool. Postel laughed at me and he says, "I'll have to open the gate." And he jumped off. His legs collapsed under him too, and he set down. An old cowpuncher sitting on the porch at the hotel across the street got up laughing. He says, "Boys, when you can straighten out your legs, go over to the hotel." He says, "I'll take care of your pack string."

MULE BUSTING . . .

I remember the last time Buffalo Bill and his wild west show came through Helena. Bill was riding a big white horse, had on a white shirt, white pants, white Hyer boots, a white Stetson hat, and his long white hair. The next year the show came back to Helena again but Bill wasn't with them. They were simply making the circuit to pick up what money they could before they disbanded. They offered $50 to anybody that would rope, throw, saddle and ride a jenny mule they had in the outfit until she quit bucking.

Jake Jackson and I asked them if us two kids would be allowed to try. They thought it

What goes up must come down, as Montana bronc rider (and later famous movie director) Yakima Canutt illustrates, being unseated by "Monkey Wrench" in a 1918 bronc-ride.

would be great sport so they told us we could. We got the mule in a small round corral and I told Jake to beat her over the tail with a saddle blanket and get her running just as hard as he could, then I thought I could throw her. When she was going around the corral in high gear, I flipped out my loop, got both forefeet, threw the rope around my hips and set back for all I was worth, and I threw her. Jake sailed out, lit over those flying heels, grabbed her nose and turned it up. She kicked his hat off, but he kept her nose turned up until I could get around, grab one foot then another, and finally had her hog-tied. We used Jake's double-rig saddle, poked the cinches under with a scantling, and then we cinched both cinches as tight as we could get them. Jake took his piggin' string, went around from the front cinch ring for a breast collar, and I took another around under her tail for a crupper from the rear cinch rings. We took a buckskin string and tied it on top of her tail so we'd have the saddle in place where it couldn't move. We fished out the stirrups and I told Jake I would ride the flank and wrap the cantle strings around my hands, hook my spurs in her flank, and Jake was to ride the stirrups and the saddle. I told him to be sure and holler "right" or "left" if she fell, because I figured she'd probably throw herself.

We went out on her. Sure enough, after about three jumps Jake hollered "left," I kicked up my left foot and down we came on that side. She threw herself twice more, both times on the right side, but Jake would holler "right" and I'd kick up my foot. Finally we got her to running instead of bucking. We rode her around the arena and asked the old boy with the cauliflower ears that we'd propositioned if she was ridden enough. He said, "No, you used a crupper and a breast collar.

That wasn't fair." So I told him we'd just keep the mule for $50. She was a good animal to practice on. I yelled at Jim Galen and Ed Weber to get our horses and open the gate, and we'd take off. About that time a lot of ranchers and cowboys fell out of the grandstand and bleachers and surrounded this gentleman with the cauliflower ears. One of them said, "I think it would be an awful nice gesture if you paid those little boys off right now." He paid off and when they hollered they had our money, Jim Galen rode up by the mule and picked me off, then Ed Weber rode up and Jake Jackson grabbed him and we got clear. We got our saddle off.

MY FIRST SIX-GUN . . .

I took my $25 and went to Talley's gun store and bought the first real six-gun I ever owned. Before that I'd been using a .36 Navy. I'd killed a lot of rabbits and grouse with it. This .32-20 had checkered walnut stocks and 7½-inch barrel. As I remember, it cost me $18.75, new. I went down to Nye's saddle shop and had them make me a chap-leather belt with loops for fifty rounds of ammunition, a double belt, a money belt that I could put my wages inside, and a holster. I carried that long six-gun wherever I went. I had enough money left out of the $25 to buy three boxes of ammunition. As I remember they were 60 cents a box, black powder and lead bullets. Father was very perturbed when I first came out of the house with that gun and gun belt. He was going down to Charley Marteen's to trade his Jersey bull for a Jersey bull that Marteen had so they wouldn't inbreed the stock. He told me to get my .22, which he called a target, and get some rabbits. I came out with the six-gun instead of the rifle. Dad was very mad. He wanted to know where I got it. I told him I bought it. He wanted to know where I got the money. I wouldn't tell him. Finally he said, "Did you get it honestly?" I told him I did.

We drove down Prickly Pear Creek. Just before crossing it, I spotted a cottontail about twenty yards from the road. I told him to stop and I'd get out and get the rabbit. I'd been practicing up at the city dump and knew where the old six-gun shot all right. Dad just whipped up the old trotting mare and didn't stop. So I just rolled out of the back of the spring wagon, over to the fence and rested both elbows on a fence post, and I killed the cottontail. He stopped across the bridge, I retrieved the rabbit and threw it in the back end of the spring wagon, and climbed in again. A short distance farther, I saw another cottontail. I said, "Stop, Dad, and I will get that one." He said, "Giddup, Truce" to the old trotting mare, so I rolled over the seat and out the back again, and repeated the performance. He stopped when he saw I was going to shoot anyway, so I put that rabbit in the spring wagon. Then we drove to Charley Marteen's ranch. While he and Dad were looking over the cattle and trading bulls, I spotted a rabbit run into a patch of rosebushes, just got a glimpse of him, so I circled the bush. Finally I could see his eye. I took both hands and I took the eye out all right at close range, then I had to get down on my belly and under the brush to retrieve the rabbit. Imagine the shock when instead of a cottontail, I found I had a big old ten or twelve-pound buck Belgian hare. I dragged him sadly out, told Mr. Marteen I was sorry, and that I would pay him for the rabbit. Mr. Marteen said, "Think nothing of it, Son. The man that owned this ranch before I bought it raised them and turned them loose." He says, "You've got yourself a fine eatin' rabbit. Take him home."

He was very fine eating and after that when Dad and I went anywhere, he didn't say any more about the .22 rifle. He'd say, "Get your old pop, Elmer," and I'd get the six-gun and take it along.

MOVING CATTLE...

Charley Marteen had a ranch up Beaver Creek across Canyon Ferry where he summered his cattle. He wintered them there at the ranch in the Helena valley, then would have them trailed across the flat and down to Canyon Ferry and up Beaver Creek to the ranch, a three day trip. He gave me the job of moving his cattle. I had a blanket, a loaf of rye bread, and a stick of salami for the three-day trip. I camped with the cattle, rolled up in the blanket of a night, started them again before daylight, and tried to move them as far as I could before the sun got hot. There was a lot of little calves with the cows and I had a good job to keep them all a movin', but I found one old steer that strung out for a leader, and fed the others in until I had them strung out for a quarter of a mile and they went pretty well.

The last day, the third day, we were going up Beaver Creek and I saw two eagles diving at something on the high cliffs on the right side of the creek. The creek was all covered with cottonwoods and willows and the cattle were very tired, and the little calves were get-

In from a day's range work in 1918 were (from left) Ed Lamb, Joe Spurzan, Elmer Keith, and George Lamb.

ting footsore, so I let them shade up while I rode on up to see what the eagles were after. When I got about a quarter of a mile away, I left my horse and sneaked up through the bottom in the cottonwoods and willows on foot. It was an old ewe mountain sheep with a lamb. The lamb was quite sizable, and the little lamb would get between her hind legs. One eagle would dive and hit the old ewe. She'd hook at him with her horns, paw at him with her feet, and then another would dive. Finally one of them got his long lunch hooks in her withers and while she was fighting him off, the other one grabbed her lamb. The lamb was probably heavier than the eagle and he couldn't lift him. But he dived off the cliff with him, soared downhill until he was out two hundred yards from the cliff and dropped the lamb, which fell over one hundred fifty feet and burst open on the rocks. Then both eagles went down and went to eating on the lamb. I crawled up through the brush until I could get within 60 yards. A tree had fallen and lodged in another one, making an ideal rest for both arms. I aimed at one and squeezed the trigger. It didn't kill him but it broke the wings and he couldn't fly. The other bird took off and came sailing right over me, not very high, possibly 15-20 yards. I aimed at the front end of him and hit him in the belly. One hind leg came down and he went on down Beaver Creek with that leg a swinging, and I emptied the gun but couldn't hit him again. I reloaded and went up and shot the other eagle through three times before I finally got him killed. In the meantime, the old ewe was standing up on the ledge blatting and stomping her feet. That was the first of a great many eagle kills I witnessed

Elmer demonstrates his steer riding ability in this photo taken at Bozeman, Montana in 1922.

over the years. Those were golden eagles, the largest of the species.

HUNTING THE BIG MOUNTAINS...

We were allowed three deer then in Montana, and the mountain sheep season was still open, during the last hunt Dad and I made over on Beaver Creek. I remember we were working along the top of a plateau that had burned over and black stumps stuck up out of a foot of new snow when I spotted a big buck coming about half a mile away across this table land. We sat down beside some stumps. The deer kept coming. As it got closer, I could see it wasn't a deer at all, but a big ram. He came to three or four hundred yards from us, right towards us. We sat motionless against the blackened stumps and he probably never saw us. Dad says, "Elmer, you'll have a lot of time to hunt sheep and I won't. Let me have him this time."

The big ram trotted by within thirty yards of us and Dad raised that long, octagon-barreled .25-35 that he used and shot the sheep in the heart. He set the rifle back between his knees. That old ram, never flinched, never broke his stride, but just trotted on past. I couldn't understand it. I told Dad to shoot

again. He says, "It's no use, I put that one in his heart and there's no use shooting anymore." I says, "Well, Dad, I'm not going to let him get away." When he was a hundred yards away I turned the safety over on the Springfield. I had a Sheard gold bead on the front of it for hunting. I used that with a battle sight which shot about right at two hundred yards with the 220-grain bullets I was using. So I held on his rump, took up the slack, and just as I was going to squeeze the trigger, the ram stopped, whirled around and faced us. He shook his head up and down three times, then seemed to stiffen, and rolled over like a wooden sheep down the mountain. Dad's little bullet had gone through the heart and lodged under the skin on the other side. It was a beautiful full-curl head which Dad had mounted.

Wood was very scarce in the Helena valley, and coal was $20 a ton. My brother and I used to hitch up the team to the old dead-axle wagon and drive out to the hills north of there towards Bear Tooth where there were millions of stumps that the miners had left in the earlier days of Helena. We'd take a log chain, put it on the stump after grubbing around and cutting the roots, hook the team on it, jerk it over, and load the wagon with

41

stumps. It was a hard day's work to get a wagon load of them, but they were full of pitch. We'd haul them home, then chop them up, which was quite a chore, but they made wonderful heating wood, and sometimes were a bit too hot for the family range. Mother complained about burning it until we got some cottonwood to go with it.

One fall Dad farmed me out to a man over near Bear Tooth where the power line had gone through and they had cut down a lot of big yellow pines. He was sawing them up into blocks for stove wood, and for a month I was on the short end of a crosscut saw working ten hours a day.

By this time I'd bought a .256 Newton rifle, serial No. 129, and I had this along. Jackrabbits would bed down of a night on the south sidehill across a forty acre field. There was a big log there by the house, and I rigged up a stool and a good sheepskin on top of the log for a bench rest. It was 440 yards across the field to this steep rise in the hill, and old white jacks would get out there and bed of a night. The next day the sun would melt the snow off and we could spot them across there under the sagebrush, and I got so I would get two out of four, sometimes three out of four shots. I would dress them, hang them on the north side of the cabin, and, when we quit the wood sawing, I had a nice load of jackrabbits to take in and sell to the Helena Meat Market for forty cents apiece.

The rifle had a double-set trigger and a good peep sight. It was wonderfully accurate. All the ammunition I ever did get for it, however, was 129-grain paper insulated bullets. I killed several deer, a number of coyotes, and one cow elk with that rifle before I decided it was too small and went back to the old '06. I also used several Sharps rifles that I'd bought off Chauncey Thomas of Denver, Colorado.

We had chickens, ducks, a couple of pair of geese, some pigs, and a whole group of milk cows, as well as horses on the ranch, and managed to live pretty well with that and a big garden. The sheep were always through the fence in Ot Aggins' second-crop alfalfa. One day we had a rain storm and the lambs went over and filled up on the second-growth alfalfa. When they came back home, several of them were badly bloated. I remember two of them crawling up on the old cellar which was dug into the ground. They laid on the cellar, poor little things, and Si and I didn't know enough to stick them until finally they went "poonk" and their little side blew out right over the paunch, and they died. Later we had a cow bloat and Dad showed us how to take a

butcher knife and stick her in front of the left hip and into the paunch and relieve the gas and they'd get well.

One day we saw a cyclone coming from the direction of Helena. Mother got us kids in the cellar, as Dad was gone to town on business. This twister came right down the valley towards us. We had an old cavalry barn that had been moved from Fort Harrison after the horse cavalry had left there, and it was quite long and open on one side. We all got in the cellar until the storm was over. Our house was brick and it withstood it all right, as did the chicken house, but we finally found the barn a half-mile away in Ot Aggins' second crop alfalfa and scattered all over the place.

Little Francis was a sleep walker. He'd get up and prowl around of nights in his sleep. One morning we missed him, and we hunted all over the place for him and happened to look up on the roof, and there on top of the ridge pole sat little Frank sucking his thumb. How he got up that brick wall and on that steep roof no one will ever know. We put up a ladder and got the little fellow down, but that has always remained a mystery to me how that little fellow could get up on top of that high roof.

After I got home from one summer's work, Father, Si and I drove back to Ovando and had a packer take us up on the left side of the Montour where we hunted elk and got our winter's meat. It was tough going. The snow got very deep, right up to our hips. We had to quarter an elk, then cut the quarters in two, take them down into a box canyon and up a gutter on the other side. Si and Father accomplished this while I went back to town and got the pack string and came back to pack them out to the car.

In the fall of nineteen and seventeen, Charlie Stout, my dad, and Si and I drove down on the West Gallatin to hunt elk. We hunted hard for ten days and didn't get a shot. I trailed seven big grizzlies into Yellowstone Park and never caught up with any of them. I desperately wanted one of the big bear, but they were feeding on the pine cones and the nuts the squirrels had cached, and all I found was their big droppings and tracks leading into the park. Father, Mr. Stout, and my brother finally pulled out. They went down to Ennis, bought me a supply of grub, and left me in a camp with a man named Riley. I stayed there for the next ten days and finally got my elk.

There were about two hundred people camped there and each morning about three or four o'clock they'd light up their gas lanterns and walk up the trail towards Lightning Mountain. Bud Storey had a lodge at the foot of the mountain, just to the right of the trail. They'd go up to see if any elk came out of the park, or rather out of the three-mile preserve adjacent to the park, and across the West Gallatin above camp. If they picked up a track, they'd take it and trail it. It was twenty below zero and the timber wolves would howl out on the flat every night. One morning I got up at two o'clock, pulled on my three pairs of socks, moccasins, two pairs of pants, wool shirt, sweater and buckskin shirt, muskrat cap and mittens, took my old Springfield, and decided to go out ahead of them. It was a nice moonlit night, and the wolves were howling over below Storey's camp. I'd only gone about a mile when I saw two tracks coming out of the river. I couldn't make them out, but I was sure they had to be elk. I trailed them over into the timber. About three o'clock, along came the lantern brigade and they started following the tracks. One fellow says, "Oh, there's some foxy hunter ahead of us."

As soon as daylight arrived and I could see my sights, I picked up the trail, went downwind on it, and started circling. Finally I got a glimpse of the two of them. Just as I raised my rifle, one turned and ran around a tree. I caught him in the left flank with a 220-grain, .30-06 and down he went, but he was up instantly and gone. I picked up their tracks and began trailing them.

As the day progressed, five fellows cut in ahead of me on the tracks. I made a big circle and got ahead of them, then they circled and got ahead of me. Finally I got to the park line, where the soldiers were patrolling every hour with their rifles and snowshoes. I was ahead of the party of five, and I stood behind a big old spruce tree until a soldier went by. Then I knew I had an hour. So I tightened up my belt and took the trail into the park. Illegal, but I wanted my elk, and I knew I had a 220-grain slug in one.

I circled to the wind side of them in a big basin to give them my wind, making about a two-and-a-half, three-mile circle in the deep snow, and I came back out on the park line just as another soldier came along. He went down to where he saw my tracks going in and stopped. Just then the other five fellows had collected there and waited for him. So he strapped on his snowshoes and loaded his rifle and took off after my tracks in the park. I wished him luck because I had the two bull tracks just below me, out of the park and going around the side of Lightning Mountain.

I trailed them around about a quarter of a mile. The snow got so deep that they would go underneath the overhanging bows of the spruce trees rather than out in the open. Finally I came to an open park where they had crossed. I ran out from under the trees and I could see them both running away, one seven-point bull and the six pointer that I had hit. I gave him another slug in the flank, and down he went, but he was up instantly and turned down the mountain. I floundered a little higher in the snow. It was deep enough, and the crust hard enough, that it made a good elbow rest. He was running straight down the hill, about two hundred yards away, when I aimed on his tail and gave him another one. That stopped him. It must have gone into the paunch. He turned around broadside, so I worked down the hill until I was about thirty yards from him. Not knowing how tough an old elk is, I put in a 150-grain service load and thought it wouldn't tear up as much meat as a 220-grain. Just as I raised my rifle he whirled and came for me. I plugged him square in the bulge of the neck. He had his head thrown back and his hair all turned the wrong way. The little bullet broke his neck all right, but it turned. I later found the slug lodged against the left jawbone where it had turned and come back toward me.

I had the bull about dressed when the five men who had been following me all day, trying to cut me out, came over on the other side of the clearing. They yelled at me and wanted to see my elk. I laid the Springfield in the crotch of a big old pinon pine and told them I'd shoot the first guy that came out in the open. They argued for awhile, and I told them to just show their nose and I'd let them have it, so they pulled out. I waited until they were long gone, then took the heart and liver and made my way to camp, getting into Riley's tent at two o'clock in the morning. The packer loaned me a horse the next day and Bill Riley and I went back up and tied the elk's lower jaw to the horse's tail, after we had worked him down the steep mountain. We'd dally one on a lodgepole, let him slide until he hit the end of that, then dally the other one and let him go again. But when we got to the bottom, we just tied his lower jaw to the horse's tail and the old packhorse dragged him into camp in nice style. I mailed a note to my father and he came back with my brother in the old Ford to haul me and our winter's meat home.

In the meantime, a lady came into camp one day wringing her hands, saying she'd killed a big bull and two men had taken it away from her. There was a man named

Elmer Keith brings up the rear of a pack string used on the South Fork of the Flathead River in 1919.

Bradley there playing cards with Riley, and he says, "Elmer, get your rifle and go with me. Let's go see about it." So we went back with the lady. Sure enough, the fellows were just finishing dressing him. Bradley told me, he says, "You sit down with your rifle here a hundred yards away and watch things." Which I did. Bradley went up to them and I had my rifle on them. The lady got their guns and Bradley proceeded to beat both of them unmercifully. He really gave them a working over. We took their guns and marched them back to camp and sent word down to Ennis to phone the sheriff at Bozeman. He came out and took them both in tow. The little lady had her elk, a nice bull. When I dressed my six-point bull, I found that all three of my 220-grain slugs that entered from the rear had all stopped in the paunch. That convinced me that a .30-06 was hardly an elk gun. I wanted something that would penetrate the length of them, or at least go through broadside, so I decided to get something heavier for my next elk hunt.

WINSTON WAS A ROUGH PLACE...

The summer of 19 and 19 was a dry one. No water in Ten Mile Creek and no water in our irrigation ditch. Likewise no crop. Father decided we had to have a bigger and better ranch and be where we'd have water the year round. So he sold the place in the valley and bought a cow ranch on Antelope Creek, some seven miles from Winston (around twenty miles east of Helena.) It was a beautiful place. The rear end of it sloped right back into a big heavy-timbered mountain. There was lots of fir timber, and Antelope Creek ran through the middle of it, and was piped into the old log house. We had an abundance of buildings; barns, cowsheds, hog pens, sheep shed. It was a first-class ranch for its size.

That fall Tex Clark and I took a contract with the state fair to clown at the fair. Tex let his hair grow long until it was down to his shoulders and had it marcelled, got a pink silk shirt waist and a buckskin divided skirt, and paraded as a woman. We were supposed to be a man-and-wife team. When he got all his powder on, and his kid gloves, he really looked like a woman. He had a 7½-inch .45 single-action, and a belt and a holster, and we would pull the bullets out of Remington black powder loads with pliers, and rub soap in the end of the case to hold the powder in place. Our job was to double-deck steers out of the chute to entertain the crowd between the

44

Taking a short rest while packing on the South Fork of the Flathead River in 1919.

bronc rides. Tex would ride the neck backwards with a surcingle around back of the steer's shoulder, hold it with one hand, and shoot his six-shooter until it was empty with the right hand. Then putting the gun in the holster, he'd hop off and grab me around the waist and take me off. I rode the rear deck, also backwards, and as tight as you could cinch a surcingle on the flank of the steer. Every jump he'd make he'd have six inches to a foot of slack. The only way I could stay on was to lie flat on my back on the steer, spur him in the rear end, and keep the handholds up tight against my leg. We got by with a good many rides that week, to the amusement of the crowds.

One day there was a big Holstein steer in the pen. He'd weigh about 1500. He was fat and round, and my rear end was getting pretty sore from those razor backs that we'd been riding, so I proposed to Tex that we take that big fat Holstein out. We got the surcingles on, and wired a bell on the tail. But instead of putting on a cowbell, there was a big Swiss bell there made of cast material with figures all over it. I thought a big steer ought to have a big bell, and wired this Swiss bell to his tail. We got nearly to the grandstand and I heard Tex shoot three times and then I saw him

lying on the ground with his gun by one side of him. Then I was left alone on that bucking old Holstein. He jumped the fence and went out into the middle of the half-mile circular track. He bucked around until I could stand no more, so I turned all holds loose and hoped he'd throw me clear. My hand with the glove on it caught in the handhold and he dragged me for considerable distance kicking me. The latigo handholds were flat and doubled, should have been round. That pinched in against my glove and my hand. He finally kicked me loose, and I went over to the front of the grandstand. Tex was still lying there. I picked up his gun, got an arm around him, and dragged him over in front of the grandstand. Just then a boy came along yelling, "Ice cold pop!" I bought a bottle, and poured it in Tex's face. Pretty soon he commenced spluttering. I put a little in his mouth. Finally he was able to straighten up. He had a big knot on his jaw. I didn't know what had done that unless the steer had kicked him. So I says, "Tex, what happened?" He says, "That d-d-d-d-damn bell hit me in the jaw."

Another time Father bought a big Clydesdale stallion at Wolf Creek. He sent me to get him from the ranch. It was a long two-day ride each way. I stopped at the Lamb ranch,

45

and Ed and George decided to go with me for the ride. We stayed all night with Harry Berry at Bear Tooth, on to Wolf Creek the next day, got the old stallion and headed back, again stopping overnight at Bear Tooth.

I was riding a bay saddle mare that I'd bought at Ovando. She had a mean habit of pitching downhill when she could find a good place that was real steep, and as she had low withers, twice she'd thrown me, saddle and all. When I quit rolling I had a stirrup on each foot, and a saddle between my knees, but no nag. We were going up the road from Berry's, up quite a grade with a deep arroyo on the left side. About half way up, the road went close to the edge, a nice steep slope there of about thirty degrees. The mare decided to get rid of me, made about two jumps, and sailed out into the air over the canyon. Then she came right back where she started from. She tried it again with the same results. I wondered how she'd learned to jump backwards. That was the first time she'd ever done that, and looking around I saw the reason. When I dropped the throw rope, she was a "wring tail," always switching her tail, and she'd switched it over the rope as I'd dropped it and it had half-hitched on her tail. The big Clydesdale stud was braced and settin' back with all four feet braced. Each time she'd jump ahead, he'd yank her back.

I had a barber friend in Helena, an old gunfighter who'd been lookout on faro tables and poker games throughout the southwest in his earlier years. He was a small man, but one of the fastest men I've ever seen with a single-action Colt. I used to go in and get a haircut, and Sam would pull the curtains down, get out his guns and give me lessons in quick-draw work. He used a holster in his hip pocket and carried six rounds to one side of the muzzle of the gun, exactly fitting the pocket of his pants, and the butt of the gun was to the right. He would slip his hand in under that gun and come out with it as fast as any man I've ever seen, and he was very accurate.

At that time Remington brought out their first smokeless powder loads in a short case, really about the length of the .44 Russian or the .45 Smith & Wesson cartridge. They were just squib loads, with only four or five grains of Bullseye. Sam would practice at jerking the gun and shooting at each of the linoleum patterns. The loads were so light they would just bury the bullet level with the linoleum.

While I was packing for the government over at Ovando, Sam got into trouble. He was in the saloon, in a poker game in the back. A big man came in and ordered everybody up to the bar for a drink. Sam was hard of hearing and didn't hear him. The other people got up, but Sam's back was to the bar and when he looked around mildly to see what the disturbance was. The big man says, "Come on, you little s.o.b. I mean you too."

Sam says, "Say it with a smile, Mister, and I'll be with you." The fellow says, "Nah, I'm not saying it with a smile. That's what I say you are."

Sam told him, "Mister, I never took that off no man. I won't take it off you. I'm unarmed, but I'll be back."

Sam left by the front door, and cornered up the street to his barber shop. He took the .45, cocked it, draped a silk handkerchief over the short 4¾-inch barrel, and stuck the handkerchief, ends up, in his cuff. He went up the street and crossed over and came down the back alley.

In the meantime, the bartender had told this big man he was in trouble. "Oh", he says, "I'm not worried about that little guy." So he pulled a gun and watched the front door. However, Sam did not come in the front door. He came in the back door. The big man heard the door creak behind him, he whirled around to shoot but Sam shot first, through his right arm, and through his body. Down he went for keeps. They gave Sam three years in the pen on account of it, and the judge took his gun. Afterwards Sam had a friend steal the gun off the judge. I later traded Sam out of it and wore it for many years and still have the old gun.

Our ranch at Winston was a beautiful place, high mountains covered with fir timber directly behind it, extending around in an arm, ending up in bunch grass hills to the north. I put up 200 tons of hay regularly, and also put in forty acres of oats. The oats did wonderfully well that year. The neighbors said they would go a hundred bushels to the acre, but before I could cut them, we had a big hail storm that left them all flat as a hotcake. I never harvested an oat.

Father had taken a job as manager of the Singer Sewing Machine Company in Helena, and was gone a good part of the time. Mother and I ran the ranch, as my brother had also taken a management job for another Singer Sewing Machine office at Harlowton, Montana. In August I cut the hay and raked it, then took a buckrake and swept it all up into huge piles around the stack yard.

My little brother, Francis, would go with me a lot of the time when I'd irrigate. I'd take an old muzzleloading rifle, along with my six-gun, and shoot ground squirrels. We had a lot of fine days together. We had a big garden, our own chickens and hogs, and raised about everything we needed. There was good deer hunting behind the ranch in the fall, and plenty of ruffed grouse and big blue grouse. Down on the flats in the grain fields between our ranch and Winston were plenty of sharp-tailed grouse, so I did well with the old 16-gauge Ithaca each fall on them. There were quite a few small trout in the stream, and Mother would catch us a mess of them occasionally for a change of fare. The neighbors usually kept me supplied with broncs to break at ten dollars a head for saddle stock. In the evenings I would work on them in the corral, then take them for a ride. About once a week I would go to Winston, some seven miles away, and get the mail.

I bought a buckskin bronc out of George Hammond's bucking string at Ovando, the meanest outlaw I ever broke in my life. He wouldn't kick but he was wicked with those front feet. I never had to open gates with him, however. I'd ride him up to a four-strand barbed wire fence, whirl him around and back off fifty yards, then he'd sail right over it.

One day I was headed for Winston to get the mail, and had just crossed Beaver Creek when I heard an awful lot of shooting. Soon I came on Jim Meyers and old Sut Ellis, the old buffalo hunter, in a little cut at the side of the road where the highway department had dug out gravel. They were shooting at the northwest corner of the hotel building. I stopped my horse and asked them what was going on.

"Oh," he says, "some silly guy tried to hold up Winston. He's up in the northwest corner bedroom now." I got the dope from them. Evidently he'd held up a Frenchman's store and went over to hold up George Meyers at the post office. George had phoned Taplan the depot agent, as the man ran for the depot. Taplan came out of the depot and gave him both barrels of his old sawed-off shotgun, one pellet catching him through the leg. He hobbled back up the street while Taplan was hunting for more ammunition, went into the hotel, climbed the stairs and got in this upper bedroom.

The whole town turned out, got their deer rifles, and decided to settle accounts with this robber. They knew where he was holed up, and the old hotel was an old ramshackle two story affair anyway, so they were shooting through it from two sides. I asked Jim and Sut how best to get into town. They said it was safe enough if I rode up the road, and parked behind Valentine's saloon. I did and went in the saloon. A bunch of the boys was

talking it over there and the shooting was still going on. Finally Bert Lanning said, "If you'll stop all the shooting, I'll take somebody and go up and see what shape that guy's in." I volunteered to go with him, so we sent a kid around the perimeter on a bareback horse to tell everybody to quit shooting, that we were going up into the room. We pulled off our boots and spurs, and slipped up the stairway. Getting up there, both of us had our six-guns, Bert took a run, smashed the door open and rolled across the room while I went in behind him. There was no use in our precautions. The man was on the bed. The bed itself was shot to pieces, and so was he. He was still alive, but he'd been hit several times. They made a stretcher out of a couple of poles and a blanket, and packed him down to the depot. Taplan flagged the next train and put him on it. He died, they said, before they got to East Helena. We later found out he was from Chicago, which was probably the reason he was fool enough to try to hold up a little Montana cow town.

I NEVER LEARNED TO LOVE SHEEP...

In addition to the cattle we had on the ranch, a bunch of Jersey milk cows and some stock cattle, Dad decided to get rich quick and bought a small band of sheep. That was a sad mistake. We were surrounded by cow ranches and they didn't like sheep. As he was gone most of the time, and my brother as well, I inherited the job of herding sheep. Little Francis and I would reload .45 Colt ammunition of an evening to heave lead in front of those old black-faced ewes the next day. I didn't have a cow dog. I ran a lot of broncs to death trying to keep them on our property, but if I turned my back on them for a minute, they were gone somewhere. I never learned to love sheep, but I did learn long-range six-gun shooting. I could sit across on one hill and drop a big slug in front of them and they'd turn and go back.

That winter I was alone most of the time, as Mother had moved to town with Dad. My brother was still gone, so I inherited the job of lambing out that bunch of sheep. I never worked any harder in my life, and for two months I never had my clothes off. I had a Big Ben alarm clock that I would set for an hour later, sit down in a big rocker in front of the stove to go to sleep, and when the alarm went off I'd get up and make my rounds again. Some of my ewes would have twins and some would lose their lamb, so I'd skin the dead lamb, put the skin on one of the others, and put that lamb on the ewe that had lost her lamb. Some of them wouldn't own their own lambs, and I had to drive spikes and bend them up in the shed and rope the old ewe up there and make her take her lamb. After a few days, she would accept him as a rule. I worked like a dog for two months and finally wound up with a pretty good lamb crop. One of the happiest days of my life, however, was when Dad sold the sheep, and we trailed them down to Townsend and turned them over to their new owner. Then we went across the river and bought forty head of fine Hereford heifers and two big registered bulls from the A. B. Cook ranch. It was a joy to get on old Satan and trail that bunch of stock home.

Dad always had a bunch of Jersey cows. It seemed like it fell to me to do most of the milking. We sold the cream, and the skimmed milk was turned over to the hogs and chickens. Milking all those Jerseys developed a good pair of hands. Even my crippled hand came out of it from the incessant work.

The season after the hail got my forty acres of oats, that forty acres came up volunteer in sweet clover. Where the seed came from, I'll never know, unless it was in the oat seed. That stuff grew up higher than a horse's hames. Some of it was six feet high and as big around as your thumb at the base. I'd mowed, then I tried to rake the stuff. I couldn't do anything with it. So I'd take the buckrake and take a swath at a time, piled it all up in huge piles. Then I phoned Dad to bring a crew and come out and stack it. We had a great long rick of this sweet clover, as we'd move the overshot stacker as soon as one stack was finished. The neighbors all laughed about Keith and his sweet clover. I told them we might have a winter that year and need it. I put up 200 tons of good wild hay, and God knows how much of this sweet clover I had on the forty acres, but it was an enormous long rick.

That fall the winter started during the fair week in September. It went completely through to June, and we had another foot of snow on the 6th of June. It was one of the worst winters Montana had experienced since the bad one in the eighties. It wiped out Stadler and Kaufman's herd in the Judith Basin.

On the first of September I saw a coyote down in the field. Mother was home then and said, "You'd better kill him, Elmer, even though his hide is no good, because he'll be catching the chickens." I stuck the old .45-100 Sharps through the netting fence in front, set the sight for 300 yards, got on Mr. Coyote, and touched the set trigger. After the cloud of smoke dissipated, we saw him lying in the meadow. I went down and got him. I was amazed. Where I expected to see a rattailed summer skin, that coyote was prime. His tail was a good four or five inches through, and beautifully furred, so I dragged him up to the house and skinned him. When I put him on the board there was no black streak down the back whatever. He was perfectly prime, a good sign that we were in for a tough winter.

There was always friction between East Helena and Winston, although I never learned the cause. Jim Meyers had a dance hall and the East Helena boys would come out with the intention of breaking up the dance. The first time they did it, they fairly broke up the dance all right. They started several fights within the hall, and when they got outside it became a free-for-all. I remember Harry Berry and my brother Si and I got in the corner where the steps came out from the dance hall and it was about six feet to the ground. We got in that corner with a beer bottle apiece and abated all comers. I saw seven guys picked up and packed out. We never heard of anybody dying from it, but it was sure a grand old free-for-all. After that when Jim Meyers held a dance there he'd have me come and sit on a stool back of the piano with my six-gun to back him up in case he had trouble. No trouble resulted, though a time or two I stood up and let them know I was there and the argument stopped very quickly.

George Meyers, Jim's uncle, had a patch of grassland between Winston and Townsend about three or four miles down the flat from Winston. I came down one day and George says, "That mean cow I've got just gored my other horse and killed him this morning, and I wish you boys would dehorn her. I'll give you five dollars in gold and all the lunch you can eat out of the store if you'll go down and dehorn that cow."

That was big money to us so I told Jim to get his nag and we'd go rope her and stretch her and saw her horns off. Jim said his horse was sore-footed and he didn't have any new shoes to put on. He had an old bug Ford and he says, "Let's take the Ford." So away we went in the Ford with ropes and a dehorning saw, and drove to the gate. We got out in the pasture, sorted out this old longhorn cow and we took after her. I tried standing up in the back end of the Ford in a little jockey box he had, but the cow would turn and he would follow and nearly throw me out several times. That didn't work, so I got up and straddled the hood of the car while he drove. He was supposed to dally the rope on a brace he had at the side of the door, or where the door would have been had it been there. I roped the old cow all right, but Jim didn't get his dallies, and she got away with my rope.

The field extended up the hill a quarter of a mile above the flat. It was a big pasture and the cow went up on the hill. We left the Ford, and took the other rope. I told Jim, "I believe if we get up there she'll come for us and maybe we can grab the rope and dally it on a fence post."

Sure enough when we got up the hill opposite her, here she came. Through the fence she went, so we dodged back, and I grabbed the rope and got a dally on the base of a fence post. When she took after George on the other side she hit the end of the rope and turned a summerset. George ran back and got her tail, pulling it up between her hind legs, and he held her until I got there. I came over and hog-tied her. Then we looked down on the flat a quarter of a mile to the car and I says, "Jim, I'll watch her and hang onto her tail here, while you go get the saw."

Jim says, "I've got a better idea." He picked up a big rock and started beating on her horn until he knocked it off. Then he hit the end of the bone shell inside the horn after the shell came off, and patted it on the end with a rock until he flattened it. So we rolled her over and he performed the same operation on the other side. Then we took the piggin' string off and turned her loose. That old cow didn't want anything to do with us, and just took off across the flat. We drove back to Winston and George was as good as his word. He gave us five dollars apiece, sardines, crackers, cookies, and everything we could eat, and asked if we did a good job. We told him we were sure she'd never hurt anything anymore.

That was in the spring.

Along towards fall I came down to get the mail and George Meyers collared me. "Elmer," he says, "I want you to tell me how you dehorned that cow. Jim won't tell me."

I says, "Mr. Meyers, the job was satisfactory wasn't it?" "Very," he says. "She hasn't hurt anything since."

Then, he says, "I'll give you and Jim each five dollars apiece and all the lunch you can eat out of the store if you'll tell me what you did. But first you've got to go down and look at that cow."

So we saddled up our horses and rode down to take a look at her. On each side of her head the horns came out about three inches, ending in a flat hotcake of horn at least four inches in diameter; just a round disc on both sides. She was the oddest looking cow I'd ever

seen. We went back and told George what we'd done, and he was as good as his word once again.

One time Father and Si and I got caught in a blizzard a few miles out of Winston. We got to the N.P. railroad and walked on that, as we could follow the tracks even though you couldn't see ten feet in front of you. Suddenly out of the snow came a train. We hadn't heard it, and didn't see it until it was on us. I dived to the left side of the track and rolled clear of the rail, and the train thundered past. I yelled, wondering if Dad and Si had gotten off. They were on the other side of the track, and they were wondering if the train got me.

A CROOKED LAYOUT . . .

I also remember the fall of 19 and 18 when the survey crew disbanded at Finn, north of Avon. It left us all on our own to get out the best way we could so they hauled our baggage down to the depot. I set out walking, and a blizzard caught me about half way between Finn and Avon. At the crossroads were some old deserted houses with the windows out and doors off. I got in one and tried to set it afire, but I couldn't do it. The wind blew out any match as fast as I lit it, even inside the house.

I finally took off down the road as darkness was coming on. My cheeks were frozen, and my right hand froze around the forestock of my rifle. Finally I was getting sleepy and had just about had it when I saw a light ahead. I finally found a cabin off to the right of the road. I went in and bumped the muzzle of my rifle against the door. An old stage driver who knew Father came to the door. He held a gas lantern up, took one look at me and took me out to the woodshed. Then he got a can of coal oil and a tub of snow and he proceeded to rub my cheeks, nose, ears, and feet in this coal oil and snow. It was miserable. The hand was frozen to my rifle, and he cut the palm of my right hand quite a bit, even through the glove, with the gold bead front sight when he finally twisted the rifle out of my grasp. After he got some semblance of life in my hands and feet, he took me back in the cabin and put me up in the attic, and plied me with hot tea and whiskey. I walked the floor all night.

After it came out of my hands and feet, the frost acted just like a burn. I was sure in misery. The next day I decided to hobble on down to Avon anyway and get a train home. I arrived there too late. By that time some of the survey crew that stayed at Finn were getting in. One man owned the restaurant, saloon and the hotel. It was all a big combination building at that time. Several of the boys that thought they were poker players got in a game, and the usual old crowd played against them and they were soon shy of their summer's wages. I had my summer's checks in my gun belt, but it was devoid of cash, and we had to eat to get a room. So I asked the bartender to cash a check for me. As I remember I was getting $55 a month. I endorsed the check, handed it to him, and he turned around and says, "Everybody up to the bar. It's customary to buy a drink for the house when you cash a check."

I didn't know anyone in the place except some of the crew that I'd been with all summer, and I told him I wasn't buying a drink for anybody I didn't know. He hollered, "Everybody up to the bar. He's going to buy 'em a drink."

I jumped up on the bar, boot heels and all, and I told him to give me my check back. He started to reach under the bar, and I told him if he did, I would shoot him. Just then Jim Flynn, the assistant cadastral engineer, came through the door out of the restaurant. He yelled at him. He says, "Mister, you better do what the kid says or he'll sure plug you." So I got my check back. Justin Postel and I went into the restaurant and we ordered a big steak. My hands were so sore and swollen from being frozen the day before that I had a hard time handling a knife and fork. I tried to cut that steak but I couldn't. I think it was carved off a bull that Noah had on the Ark because it resisted my best efforts. Just as I thought I was going to whittle a piece off the end of it, the fork slipped, the steak took off in the air, and the pretty little waitress came through the swinging doors at the same time. That big greasy steak hit her right in the breast. I lost all respect for that little hasher then and there. I found out she could cuss better than any old mule skinner I'd ever seen. Justin got mad too, so he laid the money under our plates and we got up and left. We went over to the blacksmith shop and started up an acquaintance with the blacksmith, asked him if there was any place in town where we could get a decent meal. He says, "Boys," he says, "I know what you're up against." He says, "That outfit runs the whole town, and it's a crooked layout."

He says, "You go up to the last house on the left side of the street and knock there and tell my wife that I sent you up, and to feed you. You'll find a cow elk a hangin' in the woodshed and you get a saw and knife and go out and cut you some steaks and let her thaw them out and cook them for you."

The lady cooked us a fine meal. When we left we thanked her and we also slipped a dollar apiece underneath the plates without her knowing it. We had to sleep in this hotel, and the room they assigned us, had just a hole in the door instead of a lock. As the crew in the bar had fleeced several of the boys of their whole summer's wages, the proposition didn't look good to Justin and I. He looked at me. I looked at him. Not a word was spoken, but we just went to the bed, picked up the mattress and everything, packed it over to the door, and jammed the foot of the mattress against the door. I always slept with my old .45 six-gun in bed with me.

About two o'clock in the morning I felt the mattress trying to curl up on my feet. Justin put a hand over my mouth, and poked me in the ribs as he'd felt the same thing. Somebody was trying to get in. So Justin picked up one of his boots, slammed it hard against the door. "Now," he says, "that's a warning. We'll put .45s through it next." They left us alone after that. The next morning we were glad to get out of Avon and head for Helena.

MOONSHINE AND SOUR MASH . . .

One fall Con Sweeny and I were riding for cattle back on the big mountains back of the ranch at Winston. We'd gathered up about twenty head, some belonging to us, some belonging to Sweenys, and some to the Miles Brothers. We were trailing them down a little wet meadow high on the mountain when we ran into a moonshine still. The first I knew I saw a guy step around behind the tree and put a rifle on me. I jumped off my horse on the other side and Con rode up. Con knew the moonshiners and he yelled at them that everything was all right. So the feller took his rifle down and invited us in. We went into the log cabin he had there adjacent to his still, and he poured us each a pint tin cup half full of his raw whiskey. We drank it and set there and talked awhile. Finally we gathered up the cows and thanked him for his treat and started on down the gulch towards the ranches. By the time we got down to the foot hills, Con was so drunk he could hardly stay in the saddle. We decided to go to Sweeny's ranch, as that was the closest, and corral the cattle there. I rode up to the corral, opened the gate and went back to help Con drive the cattle in. Con fell out of the saddle. Mrs. Sweeny came out of the house wanting to know what was the matter with Con. I told her we had just had a big forced drink.

An old gambler named Ross Degan always

wore a black coat, with diamond studs in his shirt, and a little dude plug hat. He had a cabin several miles back of our ranch on the mountain in a little clearing. I'd never been right at the place, though I'd been by it several times hunting grouse or hunting deer. One day a big black car went by the ranch, drove past the cow barn, and took this road to Ross Degan's. There were four men in it. After a while they came back and they had Ross Degan with them and handcuffs on him. They stopped and I went over to see what the trouble was. Ross says, "Elmer, these men just raided my still."

That was the first knowledge I had that Ross was running a still up the gulch. He says, "There's a whole wagon load of fresh mash up there that was ready to run, and they chopped up all the barrels and poured it out. You're welcome to it if you want to feed it to your hogs."

Dad had a good tight wagon box, so I screwed up the endgate, hitched up the team and drove up there. I loaded it with the fermented corn mash clear to the brim.

We had about twenty hogs in the pen down below the house on the creek, and Father had a pet Poland China sow that won first prize at the fair. She was a beautiful white hog. He also had a speckled rooster. I never did remember the breed of chicken he was, but he was the only one in Montana, so Dad always got first prize at the fair on him. When I was unhitching the team, George Lamb came in to spend a few days with me. We shoveled some of the corn mash into the trough, fed this Poland China sow a feed, and also Dad's speckled rooster. We had a show. The sow got drunk. Finally she sat down, as she couldn't eat any more. Finally her little short legs folded up, and as the corral sloped, she rolled clear over into the fence. We hopped down and turned her over on her belly so she wouldn't have her heart stop on her. At the same time the rooster was filling up. He got to feeling real good. He crowed a couple of times, then he ate some more. Then he put a wing out on each side of him, cocked his tail down on the ground for further balance, and tried to crow. All he could do was "Ur-ur-ur" a few times. He couldn't finish the job at all.

Next we loaded up the trough down where the big batch of hogs were, and they all proceeded to get to various stages of drunkeness. We had more fun watching those drunken pigs. George stayed a week with me. Every day we'd have a session. The rooster would get drunk, try to crow and brace his wings, the Poland China sow's little legs would fold up and she'd roll over to the fence, and we'd straighten her out, then we'd get the big batch drunk. We were setting on the corral one morning there just after feeding them, watching the show, when Dad sneaked up in his Ford. He peered through the fence, and saw the sow fold up her legs and, the rooster stick out his wings, and was he mad! He says, "You poisoned my sow . . . you poisoned my rooster!" We told him what had happened, that they'd been drunk for a week with no ill effects, but were getting fat on it, so that was the end of the trouble.

BRONCS AND RODEOS . . .

The neighbors usually kept some broncs on hand for me to break at $10 a head. George and Ed Lamb and I all liked to ride. George and I always rode saddle broncs and Ed practiced for bareback bronc riding for the show. He was a good bareback rider with his old two-handed surcingle. One day we were down at Winston and some of the Tomchek boys had brought in a bunch of broncs they were going to ship. So we decided to ride them in the stock pens there before they shipped them. We had bucked several of them out, and I saddled up another good looking bronc. The boys kept kidding me about him. Finally I told them I could ride him without a hackamore. So they held a hackamore on him until I got in the saddle and got my stirrups, then jerked everything off his head. I managed to set him, but I was all over the saddle and was nearly out of it three or four times, and when they finally picked me off of him I was very glad to quit that bronc. I swore never again would I ever try to ride one without a rope to pull on his nose.

One day a bunch of us were at Valentine's saloon across the street from George Meyers' store. The saloon adjoined a two story hotel. Somebody brought in a big rough looking bronc on the end of a halter rope, and they wanted to see if any of us would ride him. I elected to take a setting at him, so we got my bronc saddle on him, cinched up good and tight, got the hackamore on him, and they turned me loose. That bronc could really wipe it up. He sunfished until my stirrup hit the ground on one side, then the other and then he'd swap ends. He came up out of a long sunfishing jump and landed on the porch of the hotel, which is about two feet above the road. All four feet went through the planking on the porch. On the next jump he landed back in the road, then headed for Mother Meyers' clothesline. It was a double line of clothes, a yardarm at each end, with a little break in the middle. She had it festooned with the week's family washing. The bronc came up between the two clotheslines and I was soon engulfed with clothes until I couldn't see anything of the horse or know where I was going. I had an arm over each clothesline, and both arms full of clothes. I kicked my feet free of the stirrups, and when I hit the yardarm at the other end, I let the bronc go. Mrs. Meyers was very put out about her washing. However, I hadn't seemed to hurt it much, it was nearly dry, so I got by with that deal. I then went over to the hotel manager and asked him what I owed him for lumber to put some new planks in his porch. "Oh, hell," he says, "the show was worth the planks. I'll take care of it."

Bill and Fannie Steele had a bucking string, and George and I would go out to Bear Tooth, take a setting at various broncs in that string now and then, and when they decided to take the broncs to the Bozeman Roundup, George and I helped Fannie drive them down. We also took along a couple of broncs we'd caught out of the Spokane hills. They were the meanest pair of broncs I believe I've ever seen. One of them won third place as the best bucking horse at Bozeman. When we came back up to Three Forks to the next show, Al Brassfield drew him in the finals. He threw old Al higher than a kite. I traded one of those horses to George for a rawhide rope. George kept him in a barn, fed him oats and hay in a box stall that winter. When spring came he took him out and tried to ride him. He couldn't make it. He called in all the boys he knew; Johnny Sandez, Slim Ring, Jim Galen, and Ed Weber. They all took a setting at him and he threw them all. I happened to ride into the Lamb ranch at Helena so they insisted I take a setting at him. Hearing how he bucked all of them off, I put two buck ropes on my hackamore so that I could get a hold with each hand down pretty short, screwed my old bronc saddle down on him tight, and I managed to set him. But I had cow manure from the corral in both stirrups and on my spurs when he quit bucking.

The larger of the two broncs I kept, and he was still a harder bucking horse than the other one. I remember one fall when John Lawther and I were going to the south fork of the Flathead on an elk hunt, we put 'em all in the corral, and was intending to pack this bronc until we got to Ovando and see if we could tame him down and then I'd try and break him. When I went out to saddle up in the morning, there were tracks where this bronc had taken a run across the corral, jumped the seven-foot fence and was gone. He went back to the Spokane hills and I never saw him again.

The forest ranger had a big gray outlaw, all of twelve years old. He was a beautiful horse, weighed about 1500, and stood about seventeen hands high. He'd go to the end of the field, stick his tail out, and whistle at you. He was all horse. The ranger offered me a Model 1895, .30-03 Winchester if I'd break him. The rifle was practically new and took the forerunner of the .30-06 case. It had a longer neck and used a 220-grain bullet. I accepted. I rode the old boy. He could really buck.

I remember I was alone at the ranch with Mother one time. I got him in the corral, crowded him over against the side with my saddle horse, worked my saddle on him, got a hackamore on him, and was all set to go. Then I crawled from a gentle saddle horse over and fished out the stirrups gingerly until I got both of them on my feet, and turned him loose. The corral had a big gate for driving under with four horse loads of alfalfa, and a pole went up at each side of the gate and a crossbar at the top. When you load a four horse load of alfalfa, it's a pretty high load, but it would still go under that gate. I remember when he bucked around by there, I reached down and slapped the top of the pole with my hat with one hand as he ducked past it, so you know he could get in the air. When I had the initial spasm over with, Mother opened the gate and I took off for Winston. The ranger said I did a good job, but he said anytime that horse wanted to get rid of him, he'd just come apart and throw him higher than a kite. Then he'd wait for him to get on him again. He was a one-man horse, and I tried to trade him out of him. I could have made a real rope horse out of him, but he wouldn't part with him, even though the big horse threw him anytime he decided it was time for him to get off.

Another man at Winston, whose name I now forget, offered me $20 to break a big outlaw, seventeen-hands high and about 1350 pounds. I took the job. After two weeks riding him whenever I had a chance, I had him coming along fine. This bronc had a strip of long hair down the center of his long hook nose, and little snake eyes. He was a mean horse by every angle. He would kill you if he had half a chance. He'd kick, strike, and bite, but I finally got so I could manage him pretty well, and was getting along with him. After riding him for a couple of weeks, I decided to take him home.

I was going across a meadow when the horse, traveling at a good easy lope, stuck both feet in a badger hole and turned a summerset. Over and over we went. I lost the hackamore rope. When I came up, my left spur had somehow got around in front of the stirrup leather and my foot was still in the stirrup I was hung tight. He took off across the flat, running and kicking. I was so close to him he was hitting me with his hocks, and I knew I was a goner unless I stopped him. My old six-gun had got up under my right arm, but I managed to get it and poured .45s into his rear end. At the third shot I broke his back. Then we really turned summersets. I wound up in front of him with that stirrup stretched towards him, and he was trying to strike at me with one foot though his back was broken. I shot him in the forehead with the fourth round in the old six-gun and that settled him.

I managed to crawl over to the horse, get up on the saddle and get my spur out from behind that stirrup leather and then I passed out. It must have been two or three hours later that I came to. I unbuckled my spurs and chaps and ran the belt through the spurs and hung them on the saddle horn, kept my six-gun, and headed for the ranch. I got in long after dark and for two weeks I was only able to get out of bed and go to the bathroom and eat a little. I was sure black and blue from one end to the other. I was really bunged up. I told the owner what had happened and he was a very generous man. He says, "You damned well earned your money, I'm paying you." And he did.

A bunch of gentle horses ranged in the Spokane hills, and one day a little wild stallion took up with them. The Lamb boys and I got behind the whole bunch, and by yelling, and shooting our six-shooters on each side of them to throw up dust, we ran the whole bunch into the corral. As soon as they were in the corral, the old gentle horses stood still, but this little wild stallion would run to one side of the corral, climb as high as he could, fall over on his back, jump up, run to the other side and climb up until he fell over. I put a rope on the little guy. I don't think he'd weigh over 800. He was an awful pretty little stallion. So I took him home on a rope and proceeded to break him out. He was too light for me to ride steady. I didn't want to injure him or stove him up, so I handled him careful, and broke him out.

John Moody lived about halfway between our ranch and Winston. He had a girl about fifteen years old named Maxine, and she needed a horse to ride to school. John seen me riding this little wild stallion and wanted to know if I wouldn't trade him to him for Maxine. I told him I would if the girl could handle him. He was gentle as a dog. Like most wild horses, they're the easiest horses in the world to break. An old outlaw that's been fooled with is one thing, but a wild horse that's never had a rope on him tames down quicker than any other animal, in my experience. John offered me a 4-inch Smith & Wesson Military and Police .38 Special, brand new, and a box of shells, so I traded. Maxine liked the little horse and he liked her. She'd go out in the pasture of a morning with her hackamore, and pan of oats, and she'd whistle at him. That little horse would run to the other end of the field, stick his tail out and snort. He'd do that several times, from one side of the field to the other, finally he'd come up and stick his head in the hackamore and eat his oats. She'd ride him to Winston. When I left there in '24, her and the little stallion was still getting along swell.

We had a five-year-old Jersey steer at the ranch that we used as a decoy duck. In other words if we was going to trail the cattle anywhere, we'd take him as he'd take the lead and then we could feed in the other stuff behind him until we had them strung out and they'd travel good. Also, when we was branding, the old Jersey steer would go through the branding chute just as often as we wanted him. That way the other cattle would follow, and we'd squeeze them and put the iron on them. George Lamb and I taught the old steer to buck. We'd put on one spur, the right one, leave the other one off, and put a surcingle on him. We'd spur him on the right side until we taught him to spin. He'd take three or four jumps in the middle of the corral, and then he'd swap ends like a merry-go-round. When we had him well-trained, we went to Helena to the Lamb ranch. We told Ed Lamb we had a steer he couldn't ride with both hands on his surcingle. Ed had to take it up. He had a bunch of friends in Helena, and they came out in three cars to watch him try the steer. He took three settings at the steer, but the steer threw him every time.

One winter George Lamb and I decided to play a trick on Ed. Ed was a rather bashful sort anyway, so we gathered up all the magazines we could find and we answered every marriage agency ad we could find . . . and signed Ed's name to it.

We stayed at the ranch about a month, and was wondering how Ed had come out, so we saddled up and rode into the Helena valley.

Fannie Steele shows the double buckrein used in early-day bronc riding, and the lack of the flank strap ruled mandatory in rodeos since the 1940's.

We talked with Ed a little while and he said, "You'd better come up in my room, boys." So we went up to the room. All around the room were pictures of women and girls; elderly women and young ones, he had a real collection. We pretended to be ignorant as the dickens, and asked him how come. "Oh," he says, "them's some of my friends I'm writing to all around, corresponding." We didn't let on. The thing went on for some time before George told his sister what we'd done. Then the fat was in the fire. Ed didn't want anything to do with us for a long time.

At the Bozeman Roundup in '22, Clyde Finch and I teamed up to ride wild horses. They had to run them out of the chute on the end of a thirty-foot rope, then dally it on to one wing of the chute. When they started the procedure, they broke three horses' necks in short order, so they stopped it. From then on we put the halter on them and thirty feet of rope—two men to each rope—and they'd turn them loose. We had to stop them, then crawl up the rope. One man would ear him down while the other one saddled him, then gather up the hackamore rope and try to win. The wild horse race was a complete circle of the

arena at Bozeman.

Clyde was a little man, short-legged and a wonderful bareback rider. He could get a mane hold and ride most horses, so he elected to ride. I was taller and could get a hold of the horse's ears. We got a good forked pony and I managed to get up and get a hold of his ears, ear him down, Clyde saddled him and got on, gathered up a hackamore rope, we cut the long rope loose and he took off. The horse bucked straight ahead. Each jump Clyde would get a little higher. Finally he was six feet in the air over the horse. He came down on his feet, reversed from the way the horse was going, and walked off. Everybody said Clyde should have had a prize for being throwed the prettiest of anybody at the show.

The next day I helped Clyde ear the horse down, and I elected to ride. I got my saddle on him and bucked him out, and he bucked straight ahead for quite a ways. I got clear around the arena and was doing fine. Just before I got to the finish line, however, he swapped ends and went to pitching the other way. Three horses went by me and won all the day money.

The wild cow milking at that show was a

scene. They turned 30 head of Angus cows in the arena at once. They'd taken the calves away from them the night before, and Angus are notorious mean cows anyway. They had to be milked on the end of a thirty-foot rope. You couldn't dally them up close. I searched around for a roper, and finally found an old cowman from up the West Gallatin who said he'd rope for me. We had a little pint bottle to milk in and we'd tie them to our wrists with buckskin.

That wild cow milking about broke up the Bozeman roundup that year. Johnny Sandage, the arena director, after six days of it, said, "One more day of wild cow milking and I won't have any more boys to ride in the bronc contest."

The ambulances would make three trips to the hospital every day after the cow milking. One day there were cows going every direction on the ends of thirty-foot ropes. They'd run around the saddle horse and throw him, run around another cow and throw her, it was a mad melee. My old roper roped the last cow that was caught. I had my head buried in her flank, had her tail between my legs, and I was doing pretty good when another cow came along from behind, hit me in the rear and rooted me over the top of this cow. When she did so she turned a summerset, so while she was still on her back I managed to get up there and get some more milk. I had my bottle about filled, and headed for the grandstand. However, when I got there three guys were ahead of me. I found out afterwards a clown and two others had brought bottles of milk, stirred 'em up, warmed them up in a little fire under the grandstand, and won first, second and third.

We made our eating money and hotel money, when we could find a hotel room, riding Brahma bulls. One year they shipped up a bunch of longhorns from Texas. Those things were impossible. We had to put a rope on the horn, and keep one horn pointed ahead and one behind in order to get them through the chutes. Then when we got them up there, and one horn outside the chute, with just a rope holding the gate shut, we'd get on them. I had to go across a thirty-foot deadline in order to get my $5. Those steers made about three jumps and they'd just swing one horn around underneath your arm and throw you off. There was nothing we could do about it. On the old Brahmas, however, we had some terrible rough rides. I would still rather take out a very rough saddle bronc than a Brahma bull. Their hide will slip from

their hips to their ears, and it is about the toughest animal there is to ride.

One day I was setting on a chute when it was just ready to open and let a boy out. The man that was taking down our names so we could get our money, he says, "Five dollars, Keith, if you double-deck him." I just jumped, landed behind the fellow, and hooked my spurs in the bull's flanks. Out we went. I crossed the deadline, but I don't know whether I bucked off over the top of that fellow or from behind. I remember hitting the ground hard and seeing the bull's belly as he jumped over me. I got the five bucks anyway.

Red Sublette, a clown, and a darned good one, decided to put on a show, so we got a breaking cart and put it up in front of a chute and to the side. We finally worked a steer up between the shafts and ran the shafts through loops on the surcingle. Red got a-hold of his tail and got in the breaking cart with his six-shooter. We pulled the bullets out of .45 Colts and rubbed soap in the cases to hold the black powder in. So Red went out in this breaking cart on this wild steer, shooting him in the rear end with the blanks which would burn plenty. He got about to the middle of the arena and the steer got clear of the shafts, backed off, whirled around, and the shafts turned straight up in the air. The steer hit it about the center, turned it upside down on old Red. Then the steer was going around trying to get one horn under the cart to get at Red, when some cowpuncher came along and roped him.

We had some wild shows in Montana in those days and at that time there were plenty of real honest-to-God cowboys and plenty of real bucking horses, something that is long gone from the scene today. Today all they have left is a bunch of horses that will kick up. I remember at Cody, Wyoming, of all the bucking horses they had there, I saw one real bucking horse. Today you can see a lot of shows. The horses will go out with their heads in the air, kicking up at a flank rope, just running and kicking up. That, to my notion, is not a bucking horse at all. A bucking horse needs no flank rope. He does not kick up. He drags his hind end and those front feet hit hard as rocks, his nose usually down between his forelegs. Only old Charley Russell could paint or draw a bucking horse as they really were in those days.

COW HORNS AND COYOTES...
Coming back from the Bozeman Roundup one time, a man stopped Clyde Finch and I

at Townsend, and asked us if we'd take a bull over to Radersburg for him. That was some twenty miles across the hills on the old stage road out of Helena. It was a big old Shorthorn bull. He had short, stubby horns, but they were sharp on the end and about a foot long. He offered us five bucks apiece to take him over there, so we decided to do it. We got across the river all right and headed across the sagebrush flat and scattered junipers. We started up a hill to intersect the old stage route road to Radersburg. The bull got on the fight and wanted to go back. We turned him time and again. Finally he gored Clyde's horse about the middle and threw him. I got my rope down, roped him, wild-wested him, and Clyde ran over and hog-tied him. His poor horse had a lot of his intestines sticking out through a big hole in his side, so we worked the bull around until his feet were downhill and he couldn't do any harm.

There had been an old homestead cabin there and it had burned down. There were sections of steel pipe about two inches in diameter and 5 to 6 feet long lying around. Clyde walked over and picked one up and he proceeded to hit one of the horns, the one that was upward, as hard as he could. He pounded it until the shell came off.

I got my horse, rolled the bull over on the other side, and he beat the other horn off. We let him lie there while Clyde took my horse and went across the flat about one-half mile to another homestead. There he borrowed a horse and the rancher came back out with a can of water and creosote and some fish line and a buckskin needle. We proceeded to disinfect the intestines out of Clyde's horse as good as we could. He was a fine old gentle cow pony. We poked them all back in and sewed him up. The rancher led him back home and we took off to Radersburg after turning the bull loose. From then on all we could do was ride like the devil to stay in his dust. He had no intention of going back to Townsend. He headed for Radersburg as though he knew where he was going.

Chapter 3

RANCH LIFE

"THERE WAS ALWAYS GUNS AROUND..."

During these years I experimented with every type of gun I could get, six-guns and rifles as well. My first good six-gun was .36 Navy; the second, .32-20 single-action Colt. I kept a record for three years and killed 41, 43, and 42 blue grouse with that six-gun alone in the three seasons. After killing three deer and an elk with the .32-20, I found out it was much too small for my purpose. Before I started punching cows in earnest and fighting broncs, I got hold of a good .45 caliber 5½-inch single-action Colt. That gun with 40 grains of black Remington loads and 250 grains of lead, did the business. It would go into an old cow's skull and back into her neck and would stop anything.

I corresponded a lot at that time with Chauncey Thomas of Denver who was then a writer for *Outdoor Life. Outdoor Life* was published at that time in Denver under John McGuire. Harry, McGuire's boy, was associate editor. Later the magazine went to Minneapolis and Harry McGuire ran it there, and still later was bought by New York interests and moved to its present location in New York.

I bought several Sharps rifles off of Chauncey Thomas and he taught me a great deal about loading and sizing shells. He was an old westerner and a very fine friend. Between him and Waldo P. Abbott, and Samuel Fletcher,

as well as Sam Russell, I had most excellent instructors in all phases of rifle and pistol shooting.

I bought an 18-pound Sharps off J.D. O'Meara, who was then chief of police, and also head of the guards at the Homestake Mine at Lead, South Dakota. O'Meara told me it was Hank Water's old buffalo rifle that he'd used throughout the hide-hunting days in the Dakotas, Montana and Wyoming. It had killed a pile of buffalo. The bore was bad and O'Meara had bought a blank that would make up into an 18-pound rifle from Bannerman. Bannerman at that time had a bunch of these old heavy .45 caliber Sharps blanks on hand. He did a good job on it. He said there was one tight place in the barrel and he lapped that out. He sent me a target with five shots in one hole at 40 yards. I gave him $18 for the big rifle. It was too heavy to pack on the side of the saddle, so I lugged it home from Winston across the fork of my saddle on a bronc. First I bucked him out, and then had the rifle handed up to me.

Mother and Little Frank were at the ranch at the time, Dad and my brother being away selling sewing machines. I loaded up a batch of ammunition and sighted it for 100 yards, using 100 grains of soft coal and a heavy card wad and a quarter-inch of deer tallow and

Even the popular jackknife position can't eliminate the sharp recoil of the .45-100-566 Sharps buffalo rifle.

Keith dropped this fine bull buffalo with a single shot from his 16-pound .45-120-566 Sharps Model 1874.

then the paper patch bullet. It shot exceptionally well. It would stay under an inch and sometimes I'd get five shots in one ragged hole at 100 yards.

That weekend Father came out from town in his old Ford and said Andy Tomchek was having a big turkey shoot at Montana City. Montana City at that time was barely a railway station along with Tomchek's big dance hall. Dad proposed we go over there, so Mother and Dad and I and Frank drove over to Montana City in his old brass-mounted Ford. We arrived just before lunch and I got into three matches.

The match was a six-inch bullseye at 200 yards, ten shooters at four bits apiece, and nearest-the-center takes the turkey. They were shooting off a car fender, having parked it across the road. A buffalo robe was piled between the fender and the hood. They'd lay down partly on the running board and shoot that away. There were several Springfields from the Helena Rifle Club, along with Krags, Winchesters, Remingtons, and about everything you could name, about 50 shooters on deck.

Not liking their makeshift rest, I shot prone with my Springfield, lying down in the muddy road, as it had just had a hard rain. I was in the black with three shots, but somebody beat me each time. Then we had lunch. In the afternoon Mother says, "Why don't you try the old Sharps?"

I said, "I don't know where to shoot at 200 yards. I'm sighted at 100." So I asked the officials if they'd allow me three shots to sight the old Sharps. They were all interested in the big gun and wanting to see how it would perform, so they told me to go ahead. I got a beer case from Andy Tomchek and a saddle blanket out of the back of Dad's Ford and laid on the case and laid down in the middle of the road. I jacked up the front sight to about what I thought would be right, set the set triggers, put the pinhead at the bottom of the black, and touched her off. Ross Degan was lying, half reclining, on the hood of this car on the buffalo robe where he'd been shooting. He was just about on a line with the muzzle of the big Sharps. When the gun went off, Ross's plug hat fell in the mud, he dropped his cigar, and staggered back holding both ears from the concussion. The boy at the target marked my shot just above the black.

I proceeded to lower the vernier sight, held exactly the same again, and shot again and I was just the same distance below the bullseye. Having made notes as to where I had the sight set each time, I split the difference. The next shot was a pinwheel. They shot off seven turkeys that afternoon. I took them all with the old .45-100-550 Sharps and my home-grown loads.

My brother Si was quite a ladies' man. Father bought him a Ford to take the girls to dances and socials. Ed and George Lamb and I weren't interested in girls in the least. All we were interested in were guns and broncs. If we'd hear of a horse that couldn't be rode, we'd ride fifty miles to take a setting at him.

Likewise we were always experimenting with guns. One election day at Winston there was quite a crowd there. Ranchers had all come in for the election. Con Sweeny had a new Stetson hat he'd just bought. Out in the middle of the street there was quite a crowd and he started kidding George and I. He said, "What are you two kids always wearing them old .45s for? You can't hit anything with them. You can't even hit my new hat."

He sailed it straight up and George and I drew at the same time and shot when it was just about at the height of its throw. Down came the hat. One .45 had hit the edge of the brim, split it clear to the sweat band, and cut through both sweat bands. The other one had punctured the brim and put two holes through the crown of the hat. Con took one look at it, and threw it aside. I took another look at it and had another thought. I says, "George, that will make awful good wads for our cap-and-ball six-guns."

I wadded it up and stuffed it in the saddle bags, later to be soaked in tallow and have wads cut out of it to put on top of powder before we seated the round ball in our cap-and-ball guns. Con never kidded us anymore about being able to shoot with those old six-guns.

TRAPPING, PACKING, AND THE LAW . . .

I ran a trap line from our ranch around over past Billy Geiger's, down Beaver Creek to the bridge, and then on to Winston. Another man ran down Beaver Creek with his trap line, clear down to Stadler & Kaufman's old home ranch on the Missouri River. He was always kidding me about packing a gun to shoot bobcats in the traps. I found it was easier to shoot the cats in the chest, so it come out the rear end, than it was to club them. Coyotes I'd tap on the nose, stun them, and stomp them behind the foreleg with my boot heels and not have any holes in the hides. But bobcats were a different thing. Sometimes you'd catch them by a hind foot on a long chain and they'd fight a buzz saw.

One day this trapper that worked down Beaver Creek came staggering into Winston. On the left side of his face the cheek was cut and was lying down on his throat and you could see all his teeth on that side. His left ribs were all bare and his intestines showing in one place and one arm was badly chewed. We asked him what had happened. He had caught a big bobcat in a #3 Victor trap, an old trap. He picked up an old black birch to kill it with, and black birch are notorious for

rotting in a year or so after they lay on the ground. He batted the cat over the head with it, and the stick broke and the cat jumped and nailed him, got him down, and he really chewed him up. The trap came all apart at the first jump the bobcat made. So we put him on the first train that Catlin flagged to go to Helena and he spent a month in the hospital. He came back pretty badly scarred on the left side of his face, and a much wiser man. That fall I noticed he was packing a six-shooter when he started trapping. I used to kid him, asking him why he packed a six-gun to shoot bobcats.

The first bobcat I ever trapped was in the Spokane hills north of Helena when we were still living at 1012 Billings Avenue. I was a little shaver, and learned a valuable lesson about that breed of kitties. I had a trap pen built against a fir tree right on the edge of a ledge. Behind the tree it dropped off down to another ledge and successive ledges down into the canyon. I'd rocked up side walls, covered it all with fir boughs and I'd stapled the chain, a rather long chain about six feet long, to a root of the tree, and then covered it all with fir needles. I had a snowshoe rabbit in the back of the pen for bait and the trap covered lightly with fir needles in the mouth of the pen.

I'd run it every weekend and as often as I could get away from school. It was quite a hike. So when I ran the trap, the pen was all torn to pieces. I didn't see any sign of a chain or a thing, and no sign of the cat. I kneeled down and started digging at the root of the tree where I'd stapled the chain to see if it was still there. When I uncovered it, bless Moses, the chain was still there, and it extended over the ledge! Like a fool I peeked my head over the ledge.

There sat the cat three feet below me. With one snarl he was in the air. I threw myself backwards, jerked the .45, and shot at the same time. The old cat landed on my chest. My bullet had gone up through his neck and through his spine and he was all done. But it taught me a lesson about bobcats . . . they will fight. He was a big bobcat and, being my first, I had Steve Camp make a rug of him with an open mouth.

Later at the ranch at Winston we had lots of bobcats, and I trapped a lot of them. I had one set on the hill back of the cow barn. One night my brother and I were milking cows and we heard the doggonedest cat yowl I've ever heard in my life. It apparently came from a little point of rocks about a quarter of a mile from the barn. My brother said it was

59

a lion. I'd never heard a lion holler and I didn't know. It was no scream or shriek like a woman. It sounded like an old tom cat on the back fence magnified several times.

The next morning I took my rifle, as I wanted to run my traps on the hill anyway, and went up there. There had been a foot of wet snow and the only tracks I could find on the hill were those of a pine squirrel, a snowshoe rabbit, a few grouse, and one enormous cougar following my trail from one trap to another. I had caught a bobcat in one, not a very big cat, and the pen was torn to pieces and the cat was dead. The lion had killed him. Evidently the cougar didn't like bobcats. He hadn't eaten him, though, and I saved the hide and sewed up the fang holes.

In the summer of 19 and 20 I signed up with the U.S. G.L.O. to run a government pack string from Ovando as far down as Big Salmon Lake; six days one way on the South Fork of the Flat Head. They had hired this big string from a man named Stanley Arkwright at Miles City in addition to two more small strings, so we had 23 head of packs and our two saddle horses. Arkwright had never packed but he was a good cowpuncher and a big powerful man. I let him do the lifting while I lashed stuff on.

We had only sawbuck saddles, had to pack the sides and the top pack, then throw a diamond hitch on top of it all. I used the old government three-quarter diamond most of the time. It always worked well for me with sawbuck saddles. A man named Harris was the U. S. cadastral engineer. I told him that one pack string wasn't enough to handle a double survey crew of 16 men, plus the cook, his wife, and little five-year-old daughter that far from Ovando unless he let us buy the grub. I says, "If you'll let me buy the grub and let me take in only dry food, dried fruit, dried beans, and stuff of that sort, I believe I can supply you with these 23 head of horses. But if you are going to order canned goods to any extent at all, why it's impossible."

He decided I could handle it, and he would buy the grub. So he bought canned peaches, apricots, pears, pineapple, canned pork and beans. He bought all the canned goods he could, and I had to freight all that water in over the divide. We had no manties, so we had to get good wooden boxes as much as possible, or sack up stuff for top packs in order to move it. We moved the whole outfit into Sullivan's cabin over the Montour Divide and arrived at Babcock Creek to find it in flood stage. I told him it was impossible for a string to get through without drowning. He

wanted me to tackle it. I wouldn't do it. So I says, "The only thing to do is to set here a week until this water comes down."

Another man came along with a seven-mule string and decided to try it. He got out with his saddle horse and one of the six mules and the others all drowned. Then Mr. Harris agreed to let me go back to Ovando and freight in another load of grub and pile it up there. When Babcock Creek started dropping he changed his mind, and decided we ought to go on. He says, "Why don't you go out and kill an elk for us and then we can make it until you get us over to Big Salmon Lake and come back for another load of grub?" I told him I was at loggerheads already with the game department and the forest service on account of a fire I had had on McCabe Creek the year before when I was working for the forest service. A man named Tatro and I fought the fire a week and it was getting away from us all the time and I asked the ranger for a crew and a cook and bedding so we could stay with it and get it out. Finally he said us punks didn't know what we were doing anyway. He pulled twenty men off of the trail crew and went over and took charge of the fire. It got away from him and burned up twenty square miles of Anaconda Copper Company's private saw timber.

There was hell to pay.

The supervisor came up from Missoula and he questioned everybody. Finally he questioned Clarence Herring. Clarence says, "I been the cook here all this time." He says, "Keith has come in and asked for men for a week." He said, "Him and Tatro stayed out there three days on one lunch fighting that fire, trying to hold it, and" he says, "Beard, the ranger, wouldn't give them any men. Finally when he did go, it was too late and the fire got away from them." I knew Beard held that against me and there was nothing I could do about it.

When Harris wanted me to kill an elk I told him, I says, "He's got two smokechasers here and if they hear a rifle shot they will investigate."

"Well," Harris says, "you get me an elk." I says, "Will you be responsible, Mr. Harris?" He says, "I will." He says, "It's customary for survey crews to kill meat in the hills and live on it when they can't get any fresh meat and the camp is far into the wilderness." I knew that because I'd already acted as meat getter on a couple of surveys. I had my six-gun and a little .250-3000 Savage for a saddle gun, so I went over to a lick I knew about and sconched myself behind a log 50 yards from

The finale to an elk hunt on the Lochsa in 1933 saw these fine trophy bulls taken by (from left) Elmer Keith, Forrest Keith (Elmer's father), Everett Pruit, and Dru Keith.

the lick. I laid there and after a while I saw an old cow elk coming with several more behind her. She came up to some timber about fifty yards from the lick on the other side. She poked one eye and one ear around the bole of the tree, and watched for several minutes. Then she slowly pulled her head back and those elk all disappeared without a sound. I laid there until nearly night. Finally a five-point bull came in. I took a bead on his heart, and was going to pull the trigger, when I had a feeling somebody was watching me. I put the safety on, made a circle, and found tracks of a man, but I never found him. So I went a couple of miles farther over where I knew there was another elk lick and I waited there. Just before dark a big dry cow came in. I shot her right in the front of the neck, and down she went in a pile. She jumped up and whirled to go around. I shot her again in the side of the neck. I didn't know it at the time but I cut the jugular vein that time, too low for the spine. She went down in a pile again and jumped up and ran again. I chucked the darn Savage, pulled the six-shooter and taking both hands, I hit her in the back of the head and that did it.

I took the feet, hide, head and all the guts, dug a hole, piled them in it, covered them up neat, sacked the four quarters and with ropes I had along, pulled them up in fir trees and tied them. I took the heart and liver and went to camp. The next morning Harris says, "We'll break camp today and head on up Babcock Creek, over the ridge and down to Big Salmon Lake from the back side."

We had most of the camp down and when we pulled down the cook tent, bless Moses, there was the heart and liver laying in a dish-pan. At the same time along came Bud Beard and two of his smokechasers and sat down in the camp. They knew darn well I'd killed an elk. They had a pow-wow with Harris and wanted to take me to Ovando, Harris told me. They had quite a pow-wow. Finally they said if I would turn over my guns to them they'd let me go on and pack. I had no intention of going anywhere with them. If they wanted a gun fight they could have it because I knew them too well. I didn't know if I would get to Ovando if I did go with them after turning my guns over to them. So finally I agreed to turn my rifle over to them.

When they first came to camp they walked over by my saddle. My rifle and six-gun were on it so I walked over, buckled the six-gun on and ran the strap around my leg, threw a saddle on a horse and led him over to the other side of camp. After the pow-wow and they decided I'd turn a rifle over, they let me go on the pack. So I pulled the little Savage out of the scabbard, walked over and turned it on the three of them. I slowly worked the shells out of the magazine while I looked them in the eyes. Their faces got as white as chalk. I reversed the gun and handed it to Beard. He says, "Let me have your six-gun."

I said, "Never. I'm not going to be in the hills with you birds without a gun." They let me go on and pack.

We finally made it up Babcock Creek and over Holbrook Ridge, down into the head of the creek that fed Big Salmon Lake and established camp. There Arkwright and I pulled out for Ovando. We left the elk with them, but even so I knew they were going to run out of grub. It was six days one way back to Ovando, then a day to go over the packs, cargo up the grub, and start the next six-day trek back. We did our part of it, but the survey crew at Big Salmon Lake ate all the food they had, ate all the elk, boiled the bones, and they were counting the number of beans each man got with his soup the day before we got back. They said they intended to try to hike out to Ovando the next day, but without grub they never would have made it.

We packed out of Ovando for about half the summer, then went down past Holland Lake to the head of Swan River to a ranch there. From there we took a Dodge truck and went to Missoula, and freighted the food up to the ranch in this Dodge truck. It would twist an axle off about every trip so we carried a couple of spares. Then we'd pack up around the old goat trail above Holland Lake, over the divide, and down Holbrook Ridge into the camp.

Horses had never been taken around the mountain on the right side of the lake to intercept the old South Fork of the Flathead trail. I asked a ranger that came in one day if it was possible. He said he didn't think so, but we could try it. So Arkwright and I elected to go out that way and save the long climb up over Holbrook Ridge, down into Babcock Creek, and down to Sullivan's cabin. We had a rough time of it getting off that mountain. We skinned some of the horses up but we didn't break any legs, and we made it. Up past Big Prairie Ranger Station we intercepted the trail over the Montour at Sullivan's cabin.

After the survey was over and I was home, Dad wrote Bud Beard for the return of my rifle. It didn't come. Dad said, "Send it, Bud, or I'll come over after you and it too." Then the rifle came. In the meantime they killed an elk, for evidence, probably one of Bud Beard's,

took the front quarters, shipped them to Helena and put them in cold storage. They were determined to get us some way.

George Lamb and I were trapping muskrats at the head of Helena Lake. I remember we got 88 rats, 3 mink, and a skunk in the ten days. We'd broken camp at the lake there in a little cabin, and packed up all our fur on a packhorse, and were heading for Lamb's ranch. A big car came along, stopped, and two men got out. One each side, both were in full-length beaver overcoats. At that time all the game department men and their wives had full-length beaver coats. There was a lot of politics in the beaver industry in Montana in those days.

One of them named Bosler came over and he says, "You Elmer Keith?" I says, "Yes." He says, "You're under arrest." I says, "What's that all about?" "Oh," he says, "I've got a warrant for you. We're going to take you up to the state game warden." I says, "O.K."

I unbuckled my six-gun and handed it over to George. He looped it around the fork of his saddle. Bosler rushed over and said, "Give me that gun." George drew it and cocked it. He says, "Where do you want it, Mr. Bosler? This gun was left in my care, and all you'll get out of it is the contents." They desisted, so I got in the car with them. I asked them if I could stop and shave, so they stopped at Lamb's ranch, let me shave, change clothes, and then took me up to the state capital. Immediately they said that I'd killed an elk and they had half of it in cold storage.

I says, "Mister, I never done anything that I'm ashamed of in my life. I did kill one elk for a double survey crew and the cook's wife and little girl, and they ate it, they cracked the bones for marrow, they boiled it, and every sprig of it was eaten."

I says, "If you're going to prove that this half elk you got here is mine, you can just go ahead and hop to it."

I phoned Dad at Winston. He was on the warpath instantly. He got hold of the state game warden, told him to go right ahead. He says, "I watched Harry Morgan killing grouse out of season last year when it wasn't necessary." He says, "My kid killed an elk when it was necessary to feed people, and we'll fight it to the last ditch if you want it."

So Dad came to town and we went up to the survey office and asked Mr. Harris what he wanted to do about it.

"I can't be mixed up in it in any way. You'll have to take the rap, Elmer."

"Well," I says, "I've no intention of taking any rap. I've done nothing I'm ashamed of in my whole damn life, and I'm not about to start in now."

So they turned me loose, and went after Mr. Harris. They got him to 'fess up and pay a $200 fine. Next time I came to town, Harris wanted me to ante $20 to help him with the fine. I told him to go plumb straight to.

That was the first and only time I've ever been arrested.

Next summer at the ranch several people came in from Ovando. They said to tell Elmer to never go back to Ovando, that Morgan and Beard are going to get him if he ever shows up. Dad heard it all. Finally one morning he says, "Elmer, I guess you and John Lawther want to go to Ovando elk hunting this fall, don't you?"

I says, "Yes, dad, I think we'll go up there." Dad never said any more but when he came back from Helena he had 200 pounds of pig lead, 25 pounds of black powder and 5000 caps for my old .45 Colt. I asked him what this was all about now that the sheep were gone. "Oh", he says, "I thought you might want to do a little practicing 'fore you went to Ovando this fall."

Practice we did, both John and I. I was very good with a single-action then, and could draw and hit a gallon can at ten yards in about a quarter of a second or a shade over. I had two .44-77 Sharps, and plenty of hand-loads for both rifles. We elected to use them for the elk, as they had proved adequate and far better than any .30 caliber for me. We saddled up, loaded our beds and grub on packs, took extra pack horses, and lit out for the long trek to Ovando.

When we came in sight of the town, I just ran the strap of my old six-gun around my leg and buckled it down. I told John, "The first thing we've got to do is call those crooks." Ovando at that time was in the form of a little square. Scoop Moore ran a billiard parlor and a restaurant, and to the right of it was Kit Young's saloon and across the street the other way was the post office. We rode up where we could look into the billiard parlor. There was curtains around the lower part of the window. Harry Morgan and another man were playing pool. John laid his old Sharps across the saddle, cocked it, and I fell off my horse and went in the door. Morgan whirled around when he saw me. He looked like he'd seen a ghost. I called him everything I could think of that would make a chipmunk fight. He wouldn't. I knew he had a .41 Colt in a shoulder holster and another one on his hip. I begged him to take one hand off the billiard cue so I could kill him, but he wouldn't do it.

I says, "Mister, you sent word you was going to get me if I ever came over here. I'm here now and I'm calling you publicly. Fight or get out." He wouldn't fight so I backed out while John watched him, went over to the store and found the ranger and I called him. He wouldn't fight either.

We went to see some friends named Holler and stayed overnight with them. I remember we got six inches of snow that night. They had a cow that had bloated and died, and the coyotes had been working on her. At daylight one of the Holler boys, John and I sneaked down to the last timber overlooking the little meadow where the cow lay and, sure enough, a big coyote was on it. As soon as he spotted us, he took off on a run. It was early in the morning and I held a little too much front sight, and went over his back on the first shot. He lit out in a hard run around the sidehill. My next slug threw up mud and snow right under his tail. I increased the lead for the third shot. At that shot he jumped high in the air, made a twisting turn, and headed up over the hill.

We went over and picked up his tracks. There was not a drop of blood anywhere, but right where he made the twisting jump was a bunch of food, hair, and cow meat that could only have come out of his intestines. So we trailed him up over the hill and there he lay in a pool of blood. My 470-grain paper-patch slug hit in front of the right hip and came out back of the left shoulder.

We stayed a day at the Holler ranch resting our horses, and the next day we packed up and headed for the South Fork of the Flathead, over the old Montour trail.

We had ridden up the Montour River several miles past the ranger station when here came Harry Morgan and a deputy down the trail. Evidently they'd been looking for us and didn't know we'd stayed. I cocked the old Sharps, set the set trigger, let it lay over my left arm, and pointed it at his chest.

He says, "Where's your license?"

I says, "It's in the barrel of this old Sharps, Harry. Where do you want it?"

The deputy's face got white and he rode way up in a wide circle around the trail. Harry looked at me a minute or two, and I says, "That's it, Harry. You can go for it or you can take the slug out of this Sharps, just as you want."

He too then rode up the hill and went around. Then John Lawther hollered from the back of the pack string, he says, "Shall I show him my license?"

I says, "Only in case you want to. You just

as well show him the Sharps." That's what John Lawther did. They went on into Ovando and we went on into the South Fork on our elk hunt.

Those were rough times in Montana in those days, and a man carried his law with him. If he didn't, he might not last too long. Suffice it to say we never had any more people coming from Ovando and telling us that anybody was going to get us if we came back over there.

Many years later, after being married and living various places, I was over to Missoula and stayed all night with friends there and they had a big sportsman's meeting. They asked me to attend. Oddly enough, when we set down to the table, there was Harry Morgan on the other side. The game department was just going to give him a medal and one thing and another, for all his years of service as game warden. When he looked across the table and saw me, he looked like he'd swallowed a green persimmon. I made no mention of the fact, had nothing to do with him, and the party went on as scheduled.

The summer of 19 and 20 I put in packing out of Ovando. While we were trucking food from Missoula to the Holland ranch, I decided to hunt up this fellow Chevigny that had burnt me up. If I could find him, I intended to kill him.

I crossed the slugs with a knife clear down to the brass on the .45s for my old six-gun, and I traveled all over Missoula trying to find him. I found the man that was deputy sheriff at the time. He says, "Elmer, I think he left and went to Canada. If you can find him, kill the rat. I'll take my car and take you anywhere you want to go and give you some money to start on."

However, I never found him. In later years I'm glad now that I didn't, because I surely would have killed him. He had caused me untold suffering for years, as well as a lady that jumped out and was an invalid for the rest of her life.

I didn't think he had any right to live, but I never saw the man again. I am glad though, after all these years, that I let the good Lord handle the case, but I was very bitter about it at that time.

A FEW GOOD WRECKS . . .

All the doctors claimed I would never live to be 21, but they don't know it all. I believe thoroughly that a man won't die until his time comes. When that time comes, he's a goner even if he has to fall off a step and break his neck. But until that time comes he may go through hell and then some, but he'll still live some way or other. I've been in so many scrapes where, by all rules and regulations, I should have got bumped off and didn't. I'm a fatalist. I never was afraid of anything on two legs or four, and I intend to continue that way.

During the next to last year we put in at the ranch at Winston, my brother Si and I gathered up some of our cattle that had strayed over on Beaver Creek. We were bringing them over to dump them in the lower end of our ranch, down at the east end of it. There was a deep arroyo that ran down just outside our land.

Some of the cattle broke and started to go back. I rode old Satan up to the arroyo. He could jump it easy, but it had rained before that, and just as he took off to jump the arroyo, the bank peeled away with him.

Down we went, and over he came on top of me with his head uphill. The arroyo was quite steep, and I was underneath him. The saddle horn punched my shirt through right near my ribs, skinned me a little, but didn't hurt me, but I couldn't get out and old Satan was on top of me. My brother finally missed me, and started riding around looking for me. He saw us down in the bottom of the arroyo, the horse on top. Si was a very powerful boy. He jumped down, grabbed the horse by the ears and hackamore and rolled him off. Outside of being skinned up a little bit and one side of my shirt gone, I was all right. We proceeded to take the cattle on and poke them in the lower end of the ranch.

In those days I was very active. I didn't figure a horse could fall fast enough to catch me. I've had many of them go down on icy slopes, but I was always able to kick my foot up and let them hit on the side.

One day I was riding a big Hambletonian I was breaking, 17-hands high, through East Helena. The wind was blowing hard. Just as I came along, a lady was standing out in the street waiting for a streetcar. The wind blew her dress up in the air and the old Hambletonian snorted and went to bucking. He bucked up the street a ways, and then turned into a cross street.

I was setting him pretty until he came down on the far side on a slant. His shoes slipped on the concrete and down he came. I jerked my left foot as fast as I could, but the fork of the saddle caught it against the concrete and bent my spur shank right down so that the rowel was right down under my boot heel. Man, that spur strap was so tight it was killing me when I got off the horse and got him up. I had to take a knife and rip the spur strap off my foot. It was choking my instep, but there was no further damage. But I did have to get another pair of spurs.

I had learned to ride on a balance and on my spurs, and I used them. Every time a horse hit the ground I dug those old gut hooks in good and deep, got my balance, and looked to see which way he was going on the next jump. A good rider, with his spurs, can tell which way the horse is going to turn for the next jump by the feel of his spurs. Later, when they came out with good bronc saddles, it was much easier. With the high fork and undercut swells, you had a good leg grip.

One night John Lawther and I were sleeping in the back bedroom of the old log cabin at the Winston ranch. The window had little panes about four inches square, a whole block of them, and one of them was out. Along about two or three in the morning I woke up. It was like I was in a nightmare. I was paralyzed. I couldn't move. An old brindle house cat that we'd had around for a couple of years was on my chest with her nose jammed on my nose. It was one of the most awful nightmares I ever had. Only it was no nightmare, it was real. Finally I got my right toes a wiggling and tickled John Lawther on the ankle. John woke up. He looked over, he says, "What the hell?" The moonlight was coming through the window, and he could see the cat on my chest. He drew back his arm and hit that cat so hard she flew clear across the room and banged into the wall. Then I got a gulp of air and I was all right. I jumped up, pulling the six-gun out of the holster where I'd hung it on the bed, told John to get the flashlight, and we'd get the cat. John got out and I said, "Get in front of the window so she can't get out the hole." He did, and shined the light all around. Finally he spotted her under the bed, but before I could shoot she ran between his legs, and out the hole. I got up, put on all my clothes, it was 20 below, and spent the rest of the night and the morning going through cow sheds, hay barn, everything, looking for that cat. We never did see her again.

She may have been picked up by a coyote or an owl after she went out the window. Or possibly John hit her so hard that she crawled under the house or some place and died.

At any rate, I've since wondered about so many baby deaths in the crib with a cat in the house. I'm sure if I'd been alone that cat would have killed me, so what would happen with a little baby when I was a grown man right in my prime? Since then I've had no use for house cats of any description, let alone having one in the bedroom with me.

By this time I had acquired quite a collection of Kentucky rifles and Sharps rifles, having 25 or 30 of each. I was experimenting all the time, wanting to learn more. Each time I had one rifle working good, a problem would come up with another one and it's still the same today. I'm still learning.

One summer Mother sent away for a bunch of Plymouth Rock chicks. Those chickens progressed rapidly and grew like weeds, but they failed to develop any feathers. They had feathers on their tail and on the wing tips, but the rest of them was bare. They sunburned brown as biscuits. Towards fall, they were hard put to keep warm. At that time us kids, before we'd grown up, had worn long black stockings, and there was a lot of them laying around in a box on the ranch. Mother took these old black sock legs, cut holes for their wings, legs, and gathered the rear end a little bit, leaving them room for a vent.

A big goshawk found it out while I was gone. He'd swoop, reach one leg down, grab a sock, and take a chicken off. Two hundred yards from the house was an old dead snag up on the mountain, and there he'd eat the chicken. I came home and Mother told me about it. About the time we sat down for dinner here came the hawk. He nailed another one of Mom's chickens with his sock overcoat, and away he went. I went to the door and saw him land in the old snag, so I took the old .45-100 Sharps, set the sight for two hundred yards, poked it through the netting fence, set down beside it, put the pin head on the old hawk's breast and touched off the set trigger. The old gun kicked back out of the fence, but the hawk came down in a heap. I went up and got the hawk. The old 566 paper patched slug took him square in the breast. He'd only eaten the head and neck off the chicken so I brought it to the house, Mother dressed it, and we had fried chicken for supper that night.

In the spring of 19 and 20 I petitioned the Masonic Lodge at Helena and was elected. By spring of 19 and 21 I became a Master Mason. In 19 and 71, they gave me my fifty-year pin and told me I no longer had to pay dues.

All the Keiths were Masons as far back as we could trace them. I remember Granddad Keith telling that Bill Keith served General Washington and his staff at a dinner, toasting in Madeira the night before they forded the Delaware. Father went through the Shrine, Algeria I believe the name of it was, in Helena. There he became acquainted with a man

65

who raised wheat on a large scale in eastern Montana and up in Canada. Our government had sent him to Russia once to show the Russians how to raise wheat on a large scale. When the press of business got too hard on him, Dad would send him out to the ranch and he'd spend a few days with me shooting gophers. I remember one time he followed me around while I shot gophers with an old .36 caliber half-stock rifle, a muzzle-loader. I killed 33 ground squirrels without a miss from 20 to 60 yards with the old rifle that day, all offhand work, but it had set triggers and shot perfect.

There was a funny thing about that rifle, however. About in the middle of the barrel was a place that must have been rusted out, because when I rammed the round ball down with its tight patch it would jump for about six inches in the middle of the barrel until the rifling would catch it again. It didn't seem to affect the accuracy in the least.

Dad and Mother were living in a series of rooms in Helena while Dad ran the Singer Sewing Machine office. Along towards spring I told John Lawther I'd like to go in for a few days and see the folks if he'd take care of things at the ranch, which he agreed to do. I rode into Lamb's ranch and stayed the night. There was a dance down at Canyon Ferry, on the lake at a ranch house. So George and Ed and I saddled up and rode the twenty miles down there, danced all night, had breakfast, and came home. We hadn't much more than got to sleep when Mrs. Lamb came down and woke us up. It was pretty cold weather, around twenty below, and Mrs. Lamb says, "Boys, you've got to get up. The East Helena butcher is over at Middlemass's and he's shot a bull and wounded him. The bull's got him up a tree and he's freezing to death."

George got a couple of broom straws, and we pulled straws to see who had to go. I lost.

I saddled old Satan up, rode over, and sure enough, the East Helena butcher was up a tree over there and the bull was going around after him. His .41 rod ejector Colt had shorts in it. I never heard of such a light load being used for the purpose, as an old bull has two inches of cartilage over the frontal skull plate, and his bullets were stopped by the skull. As soon as the bull saw me he came for me. I shot him square in the forehead, killing him instantly, and he turned a summerset towards me. The old .45 Colt slug went clear through his skull. My horse, jumped over the top of him and watched him, but the bull was dead.

The East Helena butcher slid down out of the tree. I got his knife, cut the bull's throat so he could bleed out and took the butcher to the Middlemass ranch were he could thaw out. Then I rode back to Lamb's, stabled my horse, went in my bedroom, shucked my clothes and went back to sleep. I slept the clock around.

One day when George Lamb was at the ranch we decided to ride down to Winston. During the night we got about 18 inches of snow. I had on a pair of bat-wing angora chaps. The leather-lined wings were quite heavy and cumbersome, but wonderful for keeping warm on a horse.

I elected to ride a grey bronc that belonged to my brother. As I was attempting to get one stirrup, he whirled and struck me in the face with a left forefoot. He smashed my nose flat as a hotcake. I just didn't have any nose. Some of the bones were out under my left eye, and some out under my right eye. Of course he knocked me senseless in the snow. George Lamb beat him off, got on him, and rode him to a finish.

George got me in the house. There was a big blood clot under my right eye the size of a bantam or pigeon egg. I opened that with a knife. George found a mirror and a lead pencil with a rubber eraser on it. I worked the eraser up in where my nose had been, and with him holding the mirror, started pushing the bones back from my cheekbone and re-building my nose. It was a very painful operation. Then I put the pencil in the left side of my nose and worked the bones in from that side. Finally George said it looked pretty good to him. I did the best I could to shape it up and put the bridge back in place with the end of the pencil. Then I shoved the pencil up the right side and left it so I could be sure and get air. For three days I had to breathe through my mouth while the nose bone knitted together again. We were 20 miles from Helena and it was 20 below zero so we had to do our own surgery in those days. My nose is still a little crooked, but not much the worse for wear and tear.

One day when the folks were going to be at the ranch for a couple of weeks, I decided to ride out to Bear Tooth and ride broncs and chase wild horses with Bill and Fannie Steele for a week. I took off on old Satan, got east of Helena, and cut across the flat to Bear Tooth. There were no fences there then. I came to the last ranch near Scratch Gravel, owned by an old Swede who had a nice bunch of cattle. Just as I came along, the cattle had gotten into his second-crop alfalfa and he put the dogs on them with the end result that the whole herd stampeded to the fence and turned

66

Lorraine Keith displays a golden eagle that Elmer rendered inoperative in 1927 on their ranch in Durkee, Oregon, with a single shot at 500 yards with a .300 H&H Magnum.

Horse bridges across the Salmon River were used often on Keith's goat hunts in Idaho in the 1940s, and Art Kirkpatrick pauses to rest on one after a successful hunt.

over nearly a quarter of a mile of it. He was very irate and asked me to corral the cattle for him. Then he asked me to help him set up the fence as it was a two-man job. I pitched in and helped him and we finally got the fence straightened up. Then he told me, "I'm going to Helena and sell every darn one of them cattle right now." I looked the cattle over. They were fat, a nice little bunch. I asked him how much he wanted for them, and he told me. By doing a little bit of figuring, I decided there was good money in that bunch of cattle so I told him I'd buy them.

He said, "Have you got any money?" I said, "No, but my dad has. The bank will honor his check with my name under it."

So I bought them by the head. In the bunch was one purebred heifer, a beauty. I decided I was going to keep her. I gave him a check signed "F. E. Keith by Elmer", and started the cattle back to East Helena. I put in the night with them, driving along the irrigation ditch, letting them feed and water all

they wanted, and eased them into the stockyard at the slaughter house the next morning. I got hold of the East Helena butcher, asked him what he'd give for them, and we ran them on the scales. I told him I wanted to keep that one white-faced heifer, and asked if he had any place he could keep her.

"Yeah," he says, "you can put her in my little horse pasture here." I told him I'd be gone a week. So we put her in the horse pasture, weighed the others up, and I came out with a check a couple of hundred dollars heavier than the one I gave the Swede. I buttoned the check in my shirt pocket and went on to Bear Tooth, rode broncs and chased wild stuff with Bill and Fannie for a week.

Finally I came back to East Helena, got my heifer, and started her down the road to Winston. She wanted to go into first one gate, then another, so I put a rope on her and let her run ahead of me. I pulled her out whenever she wanted to go the wrong way, and finally got her to the ranch. As I rode up the field, I saw dad come out from the house. I pulled the rope off the heifer and dad was irate. I didn't know what was wrong. He says, "Elmer, what have you been doing? Here I'm overdrawn at the bank, and I thought I was in good shape. Bill Dixon phoned me and wanted me to cover an overdraft."

"Well," I says, "take a look at this." And I pulled the check out of my shirt and gave it to him. His anger turned to a smile in short order. I told him, "The heifer is my part of the deal. I'm going to keep her myself." He agreed.

Father bought the ranch at Winston from a farmer named Baum. They had a sawmill, and they cut an enormous amount of fir timber around on the back part of the ranch. All the limbs were still lying there, and the country was studded with knife-edged granite seams that came up through the ground. I used to get my wood supply very easy; just drive the wagon up to where one of these big firs had been limbed and pick up the limbs, and rap them over the edge of one of these sharp boulders. When it was 20 below, they'd snap off short. I could get a wagon load of wood in short order. I used to haul it 20 miles to Helena, get $10 a load for it, put my team up in the stable, and come home the next day. It was certainly a hard way of making money, however.

TO SHOOT A GROUSE...

I had an old tanned sheepskin in the back of the wagon seat, and carried my .44-77 Sharps lying across it. On the way to Helena I'd usually spot several jackrabbits, and now and then a bunch of short tailed grouse. One day near a little spring I saw a bunch of grouse, so I wrapped the reins on the brake, got the old Sharps, and started killing short-tailed grouse. I had three or four of them killed when the primer pierced and the gas came back. It was an old '69 action, without the dovetail plate in back of the firing pin, and it drove a piece of the primer right into the center of my right eye. It hurt like fury.

One look through the Sharps and I could see it was pretty badly corroded. I was shooting some old factory ammunition that I'd got from Chauncey Thomas, and God knows how old it was. The paper patch had evidently rolled up on the bullet when I forced it into the chamber. I remember the last one had gone in hard. So I got a stick and spit on it and swabbed the throat good until it was all loosened up, wet the next patch, shoved in another shell, and killed two more grouse

shooting lefthanded at about 75 yards off the wagon seat.

I gathered up my birds, drew 'em, and threw them in the corner of the load of wood so they would keep and freeze, and drove on to Helena. I unloaded my wood, put my team in the stable, and then I hunted up Doc Copenhamer, the eye doctor. One look at me, and he called in a nurse, put me in a chair and doped up my eye until it was numb. Then he took some kind of a little sharp knife and started digging. He said there was a piece of metal, evidently a piece of primer, driven right through the cornea, half inside my eye and half out. Finally we heard a tiny "zing" as it left. He was very perturbed that it might have gone in my eye, but evidently it did not. Then he had to cauterize my eye with an electric needle. For years after that I had a black spot right in the center of anything I looked at with that right eye, but it finally disappeared and left me in perfect condition again. After that I was careful to get '74 model Sharps rather than '69, using a dovetail plate across in back of the firing pin. Also, if shooting old loads, I'd swab the throat out with a wet patch after every two or three shots so it wouldn't cake up and strip the patch back on the bullet when the cartridge was inserted in the chamber.

I had a dozen dark Brahma hens and a rooster at the ranch and they laid, not as prolific as leghorns, but great big eggs when they did. I enjoyed those eggs for breakfast every day. One morning I saw a little spotted dog come out of the henhouse with an egg. He headed for the mountain, and took off over it. The next morning he repeated the performance.

I found he was getting about as many eggs as I was. I had an old muzzle-loading Austrian elephant rifle, an eight-bore single-shot, so I loaded it up with about 120 grains of black powder and a grease patch around the big two-ounce ball, capped it, and stood it in the corner. The next morning here came the little dog out of the hen house with another one of my eggs. I picked up the old rifle, cocked it, stepped out the door, leveled it on him and just the cap went. The charge failed to fire. The dog ran, heading back up the mountain the way he came in. I went back in the house, got a needle, picked the tube open, rubbed a little real fine powder in it, put on another cap and came back out the door.

By this time the dog was 200 yards away in the snow up on the sidehill. I aimed at him, holding up a lot of front sight, and then I raised it still higher because I knew it had an awful trajectory, and touched it off. It kicked me back into the door and when I ducked down under the cloud of smoke I got a glimpse of the big heavy ball hitting the snow about six feet short of the dog.

It ricocheted, however, and down he went. It caught him in the right ham, near as I could tell. He howled like a good fellow while I was reloading the old gun. But before I got it reloaded, he got up and into the timber, but he never came back for any more eggs.

About a week or maybe ten days, later, Mother and Dad came out from town and Mother wanted me to take an elk roast over to Mrs. Gatey. The Gateys lived over that mountain but only about two or three miles in a air line.

I took the elk roast and rode around to the Gatey ranch. Mrs. Gatey was a very particular old German lady. She made everybody pull off their boots or shoes before they came in her kitchen. She kept it scrupulously clean. After getting my boots and spurs off, I tiptoed in to warm up before heading for home, gave her the elk roast, and, bless Moses, there was this spotted dog lying on a pallet in the corner behind the cook stove and with his right hind leg all done up in bandages. I didn't say anything but pretty soon Papa Gatey came in with a big round ball.

"Elmer," he says, "do you know anybody with a gun that would throw such a thing as this?" I told him I had no idea. He said it went halfway through the little dog's leg and lodged there and he'd dug it out. Anyway it didn't hit the bone and the little dog recovered. But I sure cured him of sucking eggs on our place.

LIFE IN THE HIGH COUNTRY . . .

I well remember the first mountain goat I killed. That was back in 19 and 17 on the Dry Fork. George Rigby, U. S. cadastral engineer, was in the lead with a solar compass, and had set it up to take another shot. It was a steep mountain. We'd been on moldy bacon and ham for nearly two months with no fresh meat except a few bunches of fool hens and blue grouse I'd killed with a six-shooter. We came around a mountain and spotted this old billy goat. I asked George if he wanted him. He said, "No." He grabbed two legs of the transit, folded it, put it over his shoulder and stepped around behind me and then he says, "Yes, get him if you can."

By that time, the goat had started off in that shambling trot of theirs. I shot him in the seat of the pants with a 5½-inch .45

single-action. The slug ranged forward and broke the left shoulder, although we didn't know it at that time. The goat went out of sight over a hillock. We were on the edge of a long ridge.

I ran to the top, and followed him around that ridge for nearly two miles, shooting at him whenever I could get a chance. Some of the shots were a good 200 yards as he was below me, traveling on three legs as that first shot had broken his left shoulder after penetrating the length of him. I managed to hit him with ten out of 18 shots I fired. All were body hits except one that went through the right forefoot and crippled him further. By that time I was down to six shells and as it was grizzly country, I didn't want to be unarmed. The goat lay down behind an old snag and I worked down there and knocked him in the head with my Marbles belt axe.

The old .45 slugs had made tiny holes through him, and no meat damage. The goat was too tough to be damaged anyway. I packed the hams and the loins back that night to where the crew was, and the next day Rigby told me to go ahead and get the rest of the goat and they'd work my part of the survey some other way. So I went back and packed in the rest. Then we loaded the horses and went down to the main camp at the mouth of the Dry Fork.

We had a Russian cook named Charley. We worked up from that camp to another high camp running the township line and Charley would put on a pot of goat meat and boil it three days before it softened up. Water boils at very low temperatures up high anyway and that old billy needed strenuous cooking. He put on another pot of goat meat every day, and by the third day we would eat it. It was delicious. We certainly made good use of that wild billy goat, from his hocks to his ears.

One fall day I rode down to Winston to get the mail and was over at Valentine's saloon talking to some of the neighbors when Bert Lanning's mule came in to town, kicking and bucking for all he was worth. Con Sweeney and Tom Miles jumped their saddle horses and roped the mule. They threw the mule and stretched her out.

The saddle was under her belly, but part of the sack went back up to the top of her back. There was something moving in the sack. I couldn't figure what it was so I pulled the .45 out and put two slugs through the sack just so it could clear the mule's belly. They hit the hard ground and howled away. That limbered up whatever was in the sack. So I undid the cinches, got the saddle off, and bless Moses, there was a bunch of long black claws hooked right around the mule's back. I took my knife, cut the sack open, and there was a big old golden eagle he had in there. I cut the eagle's leg off at the joint, but I still couldn't get the claws out. One of the boys came out of Valentine's saloon with a pair of pliers and we got hold of the heads of the cords and retracted the claws and got the foot clear of the mule's back. Ross Degan came out then with a bottle of moonshine, poured that on the mule's back and she sure did bray. We tied the mule up and went back in the saloon.

About an hour later Bert Lanning came limping in. His whole backside was frosted with prickly pear. He had a tale of woe. He'd caught this eagle in a trap and he had it sold for $25 to the zoo, so he put it in a sack and tied it on behind the saddle. Then the eagle worked one foot around, got a-hold of the mule's back, and all hell broke loose. She bucked Bert off in a pile of prickly pear, and took off. We laid Bert on the pool table, got his pants down, and the boys picked the prickly pear spines out with pliers. They barb like a porcupine quill, and are very painful. When we got Bert's backside pretty well cleaned out, Ross Degan came around with a bottle of moonshine and doused him with that. Poor old Bert just about went through the roof. He was certainly mad. He says, "Keith goes and shoots my eagle, I get bucked off in the prickly pear, and then, Degan, you damn fool, you pour whiskey on it."

I had a friend named Martin on the police force, and one day I was riding up Main Street when Martin saw me. He signalled me to come over, so I rode over to him. He said, "I want you to look at my new six-shooter." He pulled out a new Smith & Wesson .38 Special, a beautiful little gun. He handed it to me, and I checked it over. He says, "What do you think of it?" "Well," I says, "It's an awful nice little grouse and target gun, but it's too small for your job."

Just as I handed it back to him a boy came running down Sixth Avenue from up towards the Grandon Hotel. "Police! Police!" he says. "There's a holdup in the Chink parlor." Martin says, "Well, here we go." He holstered his gun and walked up the street. I rode alongside, and we got to the Chink parlor. The right side of it was booths, curtained off, then the main part was tables, and at the back end of the tables was a cross bar and the cash register. When Martin went in the front door, a man was holding up the Chink at the cash register with a little nickle-plated .32 revolver. Hearing the door open he whirled around and

shot. The bullet hit Martin right over the heart, but he had a notebook in his pocket there. It went through the notebook and lodged in the bottom of his pocket as we later found. He continued firing.

Martin pulled his .38 and put all six shots in the man's chest. Then the man threw the revolver at Martin. It came through the window and bounced across the street. I rode over and picked up the gun and came back. Martin got on the phone and called for an ambulance and took the guy, for what reason I'll never know, to the Catholic hospital. The Protestant hospital was much closer. At any rate, they hauled the man to the Catholic hospital, and when they were climbing the hill he died. Martin was very upset about it all.

I told him he had no other choice. One of the man's .32 bullets went so wide that it went through one of the curtains and a booth where a boy and his girl was peacefully eating noodles, and it went through the calf of the lad's leg. While he was crippled up for a few days, he recovered all right. The others went through the window, so we accounted for all five shots from the little nickel-plated gun.

I told Martin, "Now if you'd used a heavy gun, you could have shot him in the shoulder and put him out with one shot and then probably not had to kill him." He agreed with me and later came up with a new .45.

Years later, when I was living on the North Fork, my friend Dick Tinker came over from Helena for a visit, and told me that another lad we'd gone to school with had killed Martin in a gunfight. I never learned any of the particulars or the reason.

THE SHOOTING OF BILL STRONG...
In the fall of 19 and 19 Captain W. R. Strong, Father and I had planned an elk hunt on the South Fork of the Flathead. However, before we made final arrangements, men we'll call H. and D., both big officials in Montana, insisted that Bill had to go with them. Bill said he had planned the trip with Dad and I while he was in France, but they insisted, and Bill finally said he would go if they would take me along.

My horses were still at Ovando, so they agreed that I would pack them in and pack the meat out, and we'd hire extra horses if we needed them. They would put up the grub and take care of any other expenses. So the four of us took the train over to Avon, and then the stage from there over to Helmville and Ovando.

As we were going over some of the low hills

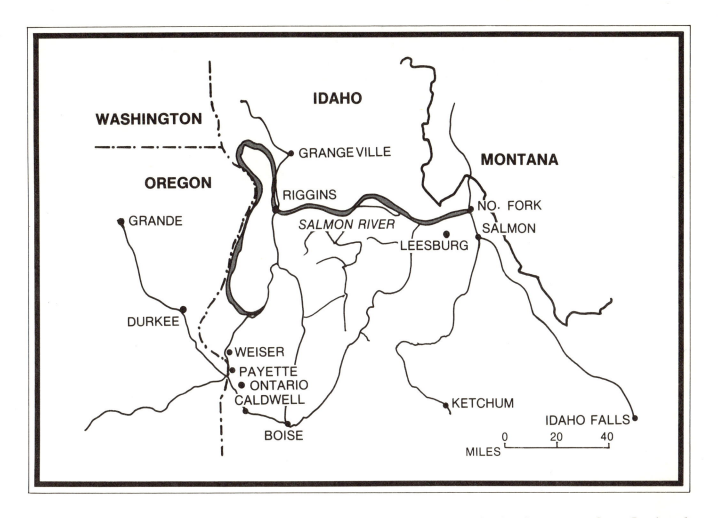

there, a lake off to our left was literally covered with white geese. We didn't know what they were at the time, but thought they were big white geese. The stage driver stopped. Bill Strong and D. each had Model 95 Winchester .30-06 carbines. A Springfield that I was going to use was rolled up in my bedroll. H. didn't have a gun handy either. I had a .38-40 I was trying out with a 5½-inch barrel.

The flock of geese practically covered the whole lake. It didn't look like it was possible to put a bullet between them without hitting something. D. and Bill both fired and I fired with the old single-action. Their bullets got there almost instantly and there was an awful uproar as the geese took off. My slug landed what seemed like quite an interval after the two '06 bullets hit. Bill broke one's wing and it swam ashore. That great flock of geese headed north, so I started holding up the front sight, as I had to drop a bullet in the middle of them. I emptied the gun, reloaded it, and my eleventh shot killed a goose a good quarter of a mile away. Bill says, "I'll go get yours, Elmer, if you'll run my crip down and kill him." So I went down to the lake and took after the goose. I shot at its head twice, but he was a waggin' it back and forth as he

ran. I missed both times, so then I aimed right where his neck joined his body and that did the business. Instead of an ordinary goose, though they were swans. I found out when I picked this bird up a I had nearly a yard of neck besides the bird. They were enormous, fat, heavy birds, well over 20 pounds. Bill came in with mine. I'd hit it square through the center of the body with the old .38-40 and it went clear through. We took them on to Ovando and gave them to a packer's wife to serve us a meal when we came out.

We packed in over the Montour, down to Sullivan's cabin, and up Babcock Creek. Going up the creek we ran into a five-point bull elk. D. and H. both shot at him with their '06s, and finally got him down after they had pounded one shoulder five times. We dressed him, hung him up, went on up Babcock Creek within about three miles of the head of it and made a nice camp.

The next morning H. says, "I will hunt the left fork, and Bill, you and D. and Elmer take the right fork. It's the biggest drainage. Then, if you get in any trouble, have any accidents or anything—shoot three times."

This sounded funny to me at the time, and I had an uneasy feeling that something was

Loaded down with elk, Elmer's pack string heads over the Montour toward Ovando in the snow at the close of the hunt.

wrong. Anyway, the three of us lit out up the trail. I remember a squirrel jumping from one branch to another. Instantly D. had his rifle cocked and on the squirrel. I didn't like being around anybody as jumpy as that. Finally Bill peeled off, and I was to go a ways farther and leave. However, when I left D. I turned and went back down the trail until I caught up with Bill. We sat down and talked for awhile. He says, "Elmer, I feel something is wrong on this trip. I know one thing I forgot. I forgot to pay my army insurance and it is past due." We gave D. plenty of time to get on up towards the head of the creek, then Bill peeled off up the right slope. I hunted hard. The snow was up to my hip, but by going underneath the spruce trees I could get around pretty well. Finally I ran onto an enormous old bull, great record head, six points, but very heavy, very long tines. He was about 70 yards away and broadside, so I aimed on his neck with the old Springfield. I had a gold bead on the front and its height made the battle sight about right for 200 yards. I was loaded with 45 grains of Pyro DG and a 220-grain softnose bullet. I heard the slug whack him, and down he went in a pile in the deep snow. I

went up like a fool in front of him. I was looking at the enormous horns and thinking what a fine bull I had. I decided to see if he was dead. His head and eyes were under the snow, so I poked him in the top of the withers with the muzzle of the Springfield. He just exploded out of the snow, caught me on the brow points, and threw me down the hill. My left elbow hit a log under the snow and the whole left arm went numb. When I quit rolling, my feet were up the hill and the bull was jumping up and down with his feet bunched where he'd been like he thought I was in the snow underneath him. I lost the rifle in the melee. The six-gun was up under my arm, but I got it out. It was the same .38-40. I had it loaded alternately in the cylinder with the first Remington nickel primer soft-nosed bullets, smokeless, and then my own handloads with the 260-grain .40-82 bullet sized down with about 40 grains of black behind it.

When I cocked the gun, the bull stopped jumping up and down and looked down at me. I centered his forehead and shot. He just shook his head and came for me. Cocking the gun instantly on the recoil, I shot him again in the forehead just as he was almost on me.

Elmer (center) with two hunters on Babcock Creek elk hunt that ended tragically with the death of Bill Strong.

That bullet hit him too low, between the eyes. The first one, the Remington soft-nose, penetrated his hide and just splattered out on the skull. But the second one that I had alternated in the cylinder with one of my good old black powder loads, drove clean through under the brain pan, too low to hit the brain, but it put him down. He slid up against me. The only sensible thing I did, I was just a 20-year-old kid then, was to reload my six-gun, run the strap around my leg to hold it in place, and I got my rifle and finally found a long slim snow brush and got the snow out of the barrel and reloaded it. Then I thought, "I'll go around behind you this time and see if you are dead," because his head was again under the snow. His feet were up hill, and his back downhill. I worked in behind him, poked him in the rump with the Springfield. He lashed out with both hind legs and knocked me a rollin', jumped up and took off. As I went over backwards, I lost the rifle again, and I jerked the old six-gun and started thumbing the hammer and throwing them into him. The first one hit the sword point on the left side, went in halfway and turned wrong side out. Another one of those darn

Remington light loads. The second, however, was black powder and the third as well. In the reloading I put in more of my own loads. The third shot broke his back. Down he went behind. Then he turned around with his forefeet and his hair all turned the wrong way and he came pulling himself back to me. I waited until he was ten feet away and shot him in the bulge of the neck, breaking his neck and killing him. I dressed the old boy out, took his heart and liver and spitted them on a forked willow and lit out for camp.

I got in way late that night after the others were in. The next morning H. again said he would hunt the left fork and D. and Bill and I would go back together. And Bill says, "Elmer, I'll go up with you and help you quarter the elk, and skin him out, and then we can go on and get me a shot." But D. was to hunt the head of the creek. Again, H. admonished us, if we had any trouble, or anything happened, to be sure and shoot three shots quick. Bill and I went back to my kill and we skinned and quartered the old bull, took off the cape for a fine mount, and hung it all up in good shape. It was getting late by then and I told Bill we'd go ahead around the mountain and see if we could get him a shot.

"No," he says, "It's late, Elmer. Let's figure out where a horse can get through this bog, and blaze a trail out because it's starting to spit now and it's going to snow tonight." So we worked down the mountain and out onto the flat. The trail up Babcock Creek had ended a mile or more below there.

Picking our way around fallen logs and brush, we figured out where a horse could go. I'd bend over little fir trees and whack them so that they would pop open as markers and also blaze trees. We came to a big heavy spruce tree and Bill broke a bar of Hershey chocolate in half and he says, "Elmer, I can help more if I get ahead and pick out where a horse can go while you're doing the blazing." He'd just stepped ahead of me when I heard the ping of a bullet go between me and the big spruce. It caught Bill in the back. He just gasped, doubled up, and fell backwards. I nose dived behind the spruce tree. Having been on the target range marking targets for years, I well knew what that sharp ping was. I yelled until I was hoarse. I pulled the six-shooter and shot three times in the air. No answer. Then I got mad. I reloaded the six-gun and started on hands and knees and I made a wide circle and came in behind where I knew that shot had come from. Finally I worked down and I saw some alders a-moving. So I sat down and turned the safety over on the Springfield and waited.

Out came D. I was surprised.

I had a bead on the center of his chest, the slack taken up and only an ounce or two left on the trigger pull. Had I known what I did later, I think I would have given him that 220-grain slug right then. I hollered at him, "You shot Bill."

"No," he says.

I says, "You sure have," and he turned his gun up like he was going to shoot himself so I got up and walked towards him, watching him all the way, and kept my gun on him. When I got close enough to him, I kicked the rifle out of his hands.

"Now," I says, "Come on. Let's go see what we can do for Bill." We ran over there and Bill was just gasping. The bullet had caught him just inside the right shoulder blade and came out near the center of his chest, just to the right of the breast bone. It was a 150-grain Winchester umbrella-point that I had loaded myself for him. Some of his lung was outside the bullet hole. I happened to have a clean white handkerchief and I plugged both holes and got him in a sitting position, but he just gasped and his eyes were turned back. I

told D. to run to camp and get H. and a bottle of whiskey, a medicine kit, blankets and come back and see if we could do anything for Bill. It was getting dusk then. D. says, "I can't go. I can't do it."

"Well," I says, "Stay here and hold Bill's head up so he won't drown in his own blood and I'll go." So he took hold of Bill, very reluctantly, and I lit out for camp.

It got dark and started snowing heavy. I'd get on a log, run the length of it, fall off in the bog, wallow through it until I came to another log and get on it. Finally in the dark I found the head of the trail up the Babcock. Then I ran for all I was worth. I'd stop every few minutes and shoot the six-gun three times. When I got to camp H. was cooking supper. I says, "H, did you hear me shoot?"

"Sure," he says, "What did you do, kill all your elk and shoot up your ammunition?"

I says, "Damn fool! You never knew me wasting ammunition. It costs too much. D. shot Bill. Grab some blankets, Bill's medicine kit, and that quart of whiskey we got, and let's go back."

He says, "We can't do anything now. It's dark and snowing. We just as well wait until morning." I says, "Wait, hell. I'm going." I grabbed the blanket, medicine kit, bottle of whiskey and I took off. I ran to the end of the trail, then floundered through the mud and water in the swamp there, climbed on logs, fell off them, until finally I knew I was getting close. I shot the six-gun and D. answered me, then I headed his direction and I soon found where he was. He'd built up a big fire off to one side of Bill. Bill was still sprawled in the logs. I got there and I said, "Help me get Bill out of them logs," and I asked him how he was doing. He said, "He died just a few minutes after you left." I wanted to get him out of that awful log jam that he was piled up in, but D. wouldn't help me. Then we heard a shot. D. answered it. It was H. and he came on in.

I tried to get them both to help me. All they would do was hold the flashlight, and I finally drug Bill's heavy body out of the logs, spread out the blanket and wrapped him up in it. I took off his glasses, took everything out of his pockets, rings and everything, and put them in my silk scarf, tied it in a knot and put it inside my shirt. Then H. says, "Well, he's in better hands than ours. Let's go to camp. We can't help him any now."

That made me see red. I jumped across the fire from them and I says, "I'll kill the first man that leaves. The very least we can do is stay with our friend until morning." Stay we did, whether they liked it or not. When daylight came we lit out, finally got to the head of the trail, and arrived back in camp. D. started cooking something to eat. H. says, "You get me a good horse and I'll ride to Sullivan's cabin and the McKinnon party should be out by then. I'll get help and come back." So I set out after the horses. It was a long time before I even cut a fresh track. They'd headed on the back trail. Finally I caught up with them at ten miles. I bare-backed one and got them all back in camp. I saddled up the best saddle horse I had and turned him over to H. Meantime they'd cooked and eaten and I set down to get a much-needed meal. H. promised me faithfully as soon as he got to Sullivan's cabin he'd get help and come back. We never saw him again. The next day D. worked faithfully, I'll say that for him. We went back up and packed my elk into camp and hung him up. Then we went back and stayed all night with Bill's body. D. had killed a spike bull before he shot Bill, so the last day we went back and packed that elk down to camp and went back and stayed with Bill's body. The next morning I told him I was going to start packing Bill's body out some way if we had to cut half the timber down to get out of that log jam. Soon Earl Watts came along with a little doctor from Great Falls, Montana. It was getting dusk when they arrived. We cooked up another feed. The little doctor was fooling with a pen knife, and when he went to wipe it shut on his leg, he turned the blade the wrong way and ripped his leg open for six inches. We had an awful time stopping the blood. I finally got some pitch out of a balsam fir, smeared it with that and then some flour, then bandaged it and got the bleeding stopped. D., Earl Watts and I took the tallest mule he had, and we went back up to Bill's body. By that time it was frozen hard, and it was still snowing. The snow was pretty well up to our knees at camp, and clear up to our hips where Bill's body was.

When you have to bend the body of your best friend over a pack horse and throw a diamond hitch on him, it takes a lot out of you.

Earl says, "I'll take Bill's body right straight through to Ovando. I'll travel night and day."

It was a day down to Sullivan's cabin and either two to three days, depending on how hard he pushed it and how deep the snow was over Montour Pass. We still had seen no sign of H. and when I asked about it they said he had gone out with the McKinnon party, and the cook and the two packers were still at

Sullivan's cabin waiting for us to come down.

D. and I loaded up everything, took a load down, came back and got the three elk and the rest of the camp. Then that night the McKinnon party's cook stepped backwards into a Dutch oven of boiling water and burned his foot and leg bad and we had another crip on our hands.

All the next day, and for two days thereafter, I broke trail in front of all those horses right up to to Ovando, we learned H. had gone right out to Helena.

H. had put a piece in the paper saying that Bill's rifle stuck up over his shoulder and D. thought he was an elk. In reality the muzzle of that carbine hung level with the top of Bill's shoulder. They had held one inquest, and they held another to get the testimony of D. and myself. The packer's wife cooked up one of the swans that we had killed and I never ate a better goose dinner in my life than we had that night. Results of the inquest was that Bill met death as an accident, that D. had mistaken him for an elk. It's true Bill and I wore buckskin shirts, just the color of an elk, but I never saw any man in a buckskin shirt that looked like an elk in the hills, and I've hunted all my life.

After getting my stock home, I saddled up and rode back to Helena and went up to see Mrs. Strong I gave her my silk handkerchief with all of Bill's belongings in it and she showed me a bill that H. and D. had sent her for seventy-odd dollars. I couldn't understand it. I says, "What's this for?" It was itemized, including $40 that Earl Watts charged for bringing Bill's body out, and the rest was for grub. I says, "They was to pay for all expenses so long as I furnished the horses." It made me mad, so I took it up to the State Capitol, up to H.'s office, and asked him about it.

"Oh," he says, "she's got insurance. She just as well pay for part of the thing."

"Well," I says, "this isn't part of it. It's all of it. I'll pay half of it if you will pay the other half."

"I won't do it." he says, "that's her share."

"Hell," I says. "it's all of it."

So from there I went to D.'s office and I told him, "Will you pay half of it, and I'll pay the other half?" He agreed to do it. So I wrote a check for half of it, signed it, "F. E. Keith by Elmer," and gave it to Mrs. Strong. Erma tore the check up in front of me. The next time I came to Helena I went up to see Erma. She showed me her cancelled check and the bill marked "paid". She'd paid it all; all the expenses of the hunting trip.

It was then I began to piece things together.

H. was state treasurer of Montana. D. was chief clerk in the treasury office. Bill was state accountant, and Bill had been gone to France and to California to training camp for a couple of years. I am sure in my own mind now that they had something they had to cover up and they had to take Bill on their hunting trip and get rid of him.

Had I known when I was in Babcock Creek what I learned later, I am quite sure I would have brought Bill's body out and the elk and that would have been all. I took it up with the Masonic Lodge as all of us were Masons, told the Lodge the whole story just as it happened. The next year when H. ran for office I understand he got soundly beaten.

A BAD MONTANA WINTER . . .

Harry Lamb, George and Ed's father, and J. L. Stewart and Father came over when they heard about the tale. They wanted me to pack them back in up Falls Creek and over to Dry Fork to try to get an elk before winter set in earnest. We got to Falls Creek, a beautiful place with all the big trees and the stream pouring down over the falls, and set up camp. This was an ancestral campground of the Flathead Indians. Their tepee poles stood up under the spruce trees all around. Lamb started to get a pole to cut it for firewood, and I stopped him.

That evening an enormous band of Flatheads came out of the South Fork of the Flathead, with over 100 pack horses, most of them loaded with boned elk meat and hides, their winter's meat.

It started snowing in earnest, but the squaws soon had places brushed clear and the tepees all up and a little fire going in the center of each of them. We had a big 12'x14' tent with four-foot walls set up. It snowed hard all night. By morning, there was two feet or over, and before morning came our ridgepole broke and the whole works came down on us. We had a hard time even crawling out from under the mass of snow. We got outside and an old buck Indian and his squaw who was camped nearest to us came out. Stewart managed to salvage a flashlight and we took a look around. The horses were about snowed under too. It was clear up to their bellies where I'd tied them and fed them oats. The old Indian took one look at our camp. He said, "White man tepee no damn good."

We agreed. He said, "You gottum flour, sugar, coffee?"

"Sure," I said. "We've got everything." He said, "Mo' better you come my tepee. My squaw good cook." So while one of us held the flashlight, we managed to dig grub and beds out from under the mess, and pack them over to his big 18-foot tepee. We did right well there. We had plenty of elk meat and his squaw *was* a good cook.

The storm lasted a couple of days. We finally got all our belongings dug out from under the tent, and the snow beaten off it. We folded it up and put it on a packhorse, and made it back to Ovando. It was hopeless to try to go any farther.

Dad, Stewart, and Lamb took the Ford and lit out and was one of the last cars over Priest Pass. I had my horses to move, so I set out. I made it to Helmville the first night. I remember I gave my Springfield to Lamb to take home and took his little .30-30 Model 94 carbine for a saddle gun going home as it would be lighter on my horse. I ran onto four big timber wolves about 300 yards away, emptied the carbine at them and, holding as careful as I could, I couldn't even throw snow on them. In disgust I pulled the six-shooter and I soon ran them over the hill, hitting just under and just over. I was awful close with the six-gun, but that carbine had a worn muzzle and it wouldn't stay in a washtub at 50 yards I found out later.

The next day I made it up to just below the pass, and stayed all night at a ranch. By that time Priest Pass had blowed full, and was closed. I started up the foot of the hill in the evening. The horses were breaking through up to their bellies. When one would play out, I would get on another one and ride him because I only had my bedding with me for a pack. My old horse that I later named Satan was a bronc then that I'd bought off George Hammond, so finally I saddled him up, bucked him as far as he would go and left him standing there in the snow panting while I led the rest of the string up to him. In this way I finally got over Priest Pass at two in the morning. From there I rode on down to the Lamb ranch in the Helena Valley, getting in there about 10 o'clock in the morning.

I was more dead than alive.

George and Ed came out of the house and pulled me out of the saddle. Ed took the pack string on to the corral to feed them and unsaddle them. I told him to be careful of the bronc because he was a man eater. They put him in a box stall, but he tore half of it up before they were through. Harry Lamb took me in the house, poured me a big slug of

This spike elk was downed by Elmer with a single shot from his 450/400 double rifle.

whiskey. After Mrs. Lamb served me a fine dinner, I pulled off my clothes and went to bed for 24 hours.

Back at the ranch, the winter of 19 and 19 hit us at the tail end of Fair week in September. It had been blowing and snowing for sometime when we were over elk hunting, but about the first of November it set in in earnest. It was the hardest winter Montana had seen since a real bad one in the '80s when the cattle pool in the Judith Basin, owned by George Stadler, Louie Kaufman and Jesse Phelps, had been wiped out by a blizzard. Louie Kaufman told me that he had stayed with the boys at the line camp. The cattle were all dying. Towards spring a cow puncher came in and had a note from Phelps and Stadler wanting to know how the cattle were doing. Louie said he wrote a long letter of lament and told them they were wiped out. Only a few horses had survived, and they were feeding them cottonwood and willow bark, and they would have to start in the cow business all over again.

Stadler and Kaufman recorded the first cow iron in Montana territory, the old Bar R on the right stifle. Louie said Charley Russell was at the camp. He got out a set of water colors and painted that old Bar R cow that they use on so many calendars and renamed it "The Last of 10,000." Charley's caption on it was "Waiting For a Chinook."

Louie said, "I just tore up my letter and sent the picture back to them." Later they gave it to the Montana Historical Society and I guess it's now in the State Capitol at Helena. At any rate Louie said this cowpuncher loused up the whole outfit, as the boys had doubled up with him and he was lousier than a pet coon.

The fall before I left Montana in 19 and 24, I had ridden into Helena on old Satan and Louie Kaufman was going up the street in his old full length mink coat. He waved at me and motioned me over.

He says, "Elmer, put your horse in the stable and come up and stay all night with me. I've got a man I want you to meet." So I did as directed. His housekeeper served us a nice dinner.

Old Nelson Storey was his guest. He must have been in his 80s and was living in California, but would come back to Helena to see old friends each summer or fall. He was tall, straight, white haired, white mustached and was a grand old gentleman. After dinner we repaired to the bedroom. It was a big room with two alcoves on one side with a double bed in each of them. The other side was paneled in different kinds of hardwood and was a solid liquor cabinet from one end to the other.

Louie had all kinds of whiskey, brandies, and wines, some of them dating back to before the Civil War. He plied us with them and Nelson Storey told his tale of the first cow drive from Texas to Abilene and then to Wyoming where the Fort Fetterman massacre occurred a short time later, and then over the Bozeman Trail to where Bozeman now stands, with the first Texas cow herd. When they got to Dodge City, he said, the cow market was off and he decided to drive on into Montana on account of the mines had opened up there and he heard there was a big demand for beef. He said they had 50 Remington rolling-block .50-70 caliber rifles for sale, and a wagon load of ammunition for them. It was the old copper-case inside-primed centerfire .50-70, with 70 grains of black and 470-grain lead slug. He bought the whole works. He said he had around 32 men in the outfit. They had cap-and-ball six-shooters and some muzzle-loading rifles, but weren't well armed until he bought these fifty Remington rolling blocks. In due time they arrived at the Fort in Wyoming and Colonel Carrington, in charge of the Fort, forbade them to go over the Sioux trail or the Bozeman Trail. It was covered with Sioux, and they had been fighting them for some time then. Storey, however, told his ramrod as soon as it got dark to move the cattle into Sioux territory just as far as they could, and bed them in a good place that could be defended. In the meantime he and his best-looking cowpokes went to the fort and they held a big dance where they swung the officer's wives and the non-com's wives around until about three o'clock in the morning. Then they excused themselves and lit out on the trail of the cattle.

They fought Sioux all the way from there to the Musselshell River. Each night they'd travel, and each day they'd corral just before daylight in some basin where they had good cover all around. He'd post a string of sharpshooters out all around, and keep a half-a-dozen men at the wagon, with the horses saddled and a couple of rifles and a nose bag of ammunition on them. Whenever the Sioux hit them hard in any one place, these men would ride over and fall off and join the fracas. He said those old .50-70s would go right through an Indian pony and the Indian on the other side. The Indians had nothing but muzzle loaders (it was in '66 as I remember him telling us), and bows and arrows, and he said they were no match whatever for those old .50-70 Remingtons.

In spite of all the fights they had, they just decimated the Sioux and I believe he said they only lost two men. We talked and drank Louie's good liquor until three o'clock in the morning before we went to bed. It was one of the most interesting evenings I ever put in.

When hunting elk on the West Gallatin in 19 and 17, I became acquainted with Nelson's boy, Bud Storey, who had a hunting lodge there just outside the park boundary on the West Gallatin.

An old buffalo hunter named Sut Ellis told me he and three other fellows were across the river one time prospecting when the Indians ran off some of their horses. They managed to catch a few the Indians didn't get and took after them. He said the chase lasted up the river for some 20 miles. He said they managed to shoot a horse out from under one Indian, who jumped into a pile of granite boulders. Sut said as they rode up he raised up and aimed a rifle at him and Sut said, "I shot him in the face with a .45 I knew he was good, and we just went on after the others."

They finally caught up with them and killed the other Indians and got their horses back. He said, "We never came back past the place where I'd shot this Indian." I asked him if he still knew where it was. He was an old man in his 80s then.

"Yes," he said. "I'm going over there this summer prospecting again. I'll take a look around and see if there is any evidence of that Indian left. I know I killed him."

That fall he came in from the trip, bringing an Indian skull with a .45 Colt slug hole through it, and an old cap-and-ball Colt revolving rifle in .36 caliber. There was two chambers fired out of it, and the others were still loaded. The stock was broken and it was just a mass of rust. I took it up to the ranch and hung it up. Mother didn't like that grinning skull around at all, and told me I had to get rid of it. It was quite a keepsake I figured.

About that time I had a friend named Bill Emerson who lived at Bozeman. He was a gun crank and collector. He gave me quite a few of Russell's pictures and traded guns with me several times. Knowing that old Bill would dearly love such stuff, I gave him the skull and the old Colt rifle.

That winter of 19 and 19 broke about every cowman in Montana. Dad had bought two

carloads of hay. I hauled one with a four-horse team from Placer siding and put it in the barn, and the forty acres I'd had in oats the year before came up in sweet clover, and I put that all up. That winter we had one little alcove, or cove you might call it, extended with high fir timber all around on three sides, studded with big granite boulders around the perimeter. I worked our cattle in there and fed them. The wind blew so hard you couldn't load anything on a hay rack and sled, so I'd take a throw rope, pile hay on that and get on a bronc and drag it over there, a jag at a time, probably 500 pounds, all I could get a rope around, and fed them in that way. The neighbors drug all the straw off the straw sheds, cut down willows and cottonwoods, and wintered a lot of stock that away. One man across the river from Townsend dug pits for his cattle and put sheepskin in between. He'd roll them in the pits, the forelegs in one pit, the hind legs in the other, and on this sheepskin of a night, he'd roll them out of a daytime and let them stretch and kick around. He had a lot of cottonseed cake shipped in and he managed to pull a lot of them through.

One day I was going to Winston after the mail and George McCartney, who ran the big Kriskenk Ranch then, says, "Elmer, come over here. I want to show you something." So I went over to his straw shed. It was a whale of a shed, covering half an acre I presume, and at each end of it was an opening about seven or eight feet across, pointing to the south. In each corner next to the wall was a big Hereford bull frozen hard as a rock, some blubbers on his nose, his eyes glassy. George says, "I'm going to have the boys drag them out."

I says, "Hell, no. You better leave them right there or you'll have two more to take their place." So there they stood until May when the boys finally drug them out and I skinned them. I skinned stock that spring until my fingers and hands were so cracked Dad would have to help dress me mornings.

I had some more broncs, and they were poor too, not much strength to them. It was easy to break them out when they were in that shape. I'd skin the legs and head and neck on the cattle, get a rope on it and get on a bronc. Every buck jump he made I got another foot of hide. When the whole hide came off, I'd drag it up to the ranch and throw it in the little jockey box on the back of Dad's old brass-mounted Ford. He'd haul them to Helena and get $12 a skin. That was big money in those days, so I worked at it with a vim. I saw horses standing in fence corners drifted over with snow, head to tail, frozen hard as rocks. Cattle the same way. Some bunches of sheep were piled up in just a big frozen mass.

For two months it never got above 30 below. For three months it never quit blowing, the sun never came out and it stayed around 20 below. It got down to 55 below one clear morning towards the middle of the winter.

Dad let the neighbors have all the hay that I had piled in the barns to help them out, and that great rick of sweet clover that we put up that came in volunteer on my old oat field was a godsend and a lifesaver. The old cows would go around there chewing on one of those sticks. But they did well at it. I had to chop holes in the creek and set by there on a sharp shod saddle horse and let them drink. Every once in a while one would slide into it and I'd have to rope them and drag them out to keep them from drowning. We had quite a time that winter. I never want to see another one like it. I swore then if I ever got out of Montana I was never coming back to live. I kept my word.

Towards spring a cowman between Wolf Creek and Great Falls phoned Dad and wanted to know if he had any hay. Dad still had this carload in Helena. He wanted it and Dad says he can have it for just what he's got in it. I believe he paid $30 for it, and then there were the storage charges and handling. Anyway Father says, "I'm not going to make any money on another cowman," and he let him have it for the exact price we had in it. While we were loading it on the car to go north, several people offered him $80 a ton for it in Helena, but Dad wouldn't sell it. At that time Minnesota slough grass cut on top of the ice and rolled up in bales sold for $70 a ton in Helena with quite a lot of ice in each bale.

I would feed our stock, go across the valley to Jim McMaster's ranch and help him feed his. One night we were coming into the corral with a four-horse load of alfalfa and four timber wolves came down the mountain with one of his heifers. They had hamstrung her on one side, and were tearing her flanks out. I had on chaps, I had my six-gun, but I had four horses and those horses were scared of the wolves too. So I had my hands full. But Jim fell off, ran in the house, and he got a .25 Remington pump gun he had and started shooting. He killed one wolf and wounded another. At that time there was $100 bounty on them.

Before we unloaded the hay, I got off and shot the heifer that the wolves had maimed, and after we had the hay unloaded, we got a lantern, took a saddle horse and snaked the heifer into a shed and proceeded to skin and dress that fat heifer out and hung her up. She froze hard as a rock by the next morning. We later had a lot of good steaks from her.

Jim's mother had a still in the basement. She was an old Scotch lady, a grand old lady. Whenever I packed the mail there or was over there to work, she'd call me aside, take me down to the cellar, and give me a good big drink of her home-grown whiskey. It was very good whiskey.

Jim and I were the best of friends. We worked together, helping each other out, hunted deer together, and altogether he was one of the best friends I ever had in that neck of the woods.

INFLUENZA . . .

It was the year of '21 or '22, and John Lawther and I were batching at the ranch. Towards spring I wanted to go to town, and he said he'd take care of things for a few days, so I rode into the Lamb ranch. George Middlemass, his neighbor, had his leg broken somehow. He was in a cast, propped up in front of the bay window in the house where he could watch the road and see people passing. The boys proposed we get a bucking horse and ride him for George to give him a little break from the monotony. So we saddled up the bronc and I rode him in front of the bay window. He was a good bucking horse and could do the whole job in about a 30 yard circle. He went crooked, swapped ends, and went high.

Middlemass got a great kick out of seeing me ride the bronc. I stayed with Middlemass that night. At three o'clock in the morning I started chilling. I just couldn't get warm. I went down to the kitchen, built a big fire in the cook stove, turned the oven door down and sat on that. It was about three o'clock when the chills hit me, and about four the man who delivered the milk in Helena came in and wanted to know if I wanted to go to town with him. I says, "Sure. I'm freezing to death here." I rode the milk wagon into Helena, where Dad and Mother had an apartment, I got to the door and knocked on it and when Father opened the door, I fell in on my face, out like a light. When I came to, they had me in the hospital in an alcove of a ward. The flu epidemic had hit Helena. There was a

Middle Fork of the Salmon River is rugged high mountain that is a fine habitat for sheep. This is typical of the terrain through which Elmer hunted and guided.

window on each side of my bed. For some reason that night the sister raised the windows up part way. I guess they thought I needed plenty of fresh air, but there was only a sheet and one blanket over me and it was about 20 below outside. By morning there was snow on my bed, my right lung was full of pneumonia fluid and the left lung half full. The doctor gave them all a good cursing when he came in. He certainly was mad.

Every day new patients would come in and be put to bed in the many cots on each side of the long ward. Usually of a morning they'd bring a basket along for some of them, lay it on the floor, load a corpse on it and pack it away. An old fellow across from me we called Jimmy would beg for water, and one young nurse came in and put up the desk screen around him. Instead of getting old Jimmy water, she made faces at the screen. This made all the boys in the ward so mad they cursed her out. Some of them even threw their bells at her until she left. My doctor said if we had some whiskey he might be able to save me.

Dad couldn't get any, and neither could Mother. There was no liquor to be had during prohibition. An old Catholic priest came in and sat by my bed and he says, "Doctor, I'll furnish the whiskey." He was true to his word. Every other day he'd bring in a pint bottle of Old Crow. It must have been some of the stocks they had on hand. At any rate, for several days I lived on egg nog, egg and milk, and whiskey.

But I wasn't getting much better. In the meantime, Mother and my brother Francis both came down with it, and they had them in another room in the hospital. Then my friend Bill O'Connell came in with the flu. He sent me notes and I'd send word back to him by my nurse, or try and scribble out a note to him, for several days.

My little brother, Francis, got worse and passed away. Mother almost went too. It was a sad time for the Keith family. As father was a Shriner, and my brother and I Masons, the Masonic Lodge took it up and held little Francis' funeral in the Masonic Lodge. Moth-

On top of the World! After a successful hunt, this pack string, loaded with game, is ready to return home. This photo shows the scrub growth in a burned-over area.

er got better and went out of the hospital to stay with some friends named Roberts. Finally they let me out, as I had improved some. I was badly swollen up on the right side and still in misery. Getting down to the Roberts's house, they fixed me up a bed by the window where I could look out and Father called in Doc Peak. I never had much use for Doc Peak. He was more of a horse doctor than a human doctor. At any rate he came in and examined me and he said, "The boy's gall bladder is enlarged and it's ready to burst. That's from riding all these bucking horses." He says, "If we can get him to the hospital within half an hour, and let me remove his gall bladder, he might make it." I didn't go for any gall bladder operation at all. I told Dad nothing doing. Peak says, "Don't pay any attention to the boy, Mr. Keith, I know what's best." Mother sided with me, but Dad was adamant that he was going to take me to the hospital. In desperation, I pulled the old .45 out of its holster where Mother had hung it on the bed by me, cocked it, and although I

was awful weak, I managed to train it on Doc Peak. I says, "Get out, Doc, before I blow you out." And he jumped. A good thing for him, or I would have let him have it.

Mother finally talked Dad into getting another doctor, a big fat fellow. I don't remember his name for certain, but he examined me and he told Dad and Mother "I believe the boy has empyema. I operated on over 200 cases at Camp Lewis." He says, "I think he is full of pus between the heart and the lung and that pneumonia fluid he couldn't cough up. I'll come back tomorrow with an assistant, and we'll tap him and find out." Mother told him about Doc Peak wanting to cut my gall bladder out and he was very perturbed. He said, "That would have killed the lad sure. It's a good thing, Elmer, you ran him off with your six-gun."

The next day they came back, turned me on my tummy and shoved a needle, so they called it, in my back. As soon as it went through my lung one gasp was all I could get out. It hurt like the devil. When they pumped the syringe attached to it, nothing came out but blood. The Doc says, "Well, I'll have to turn you over on your left side and puncture you from the side. 'Cuz I know you're full of pus somewhere there." I answered, "O.K., Doc. But first I want to take a look at that thing you call a needle." It was a big hollow tube tapered off to a sharp point that they called a trocar. So I says, "Go ahead, Doc." One more gasp and he shoved it through my lung. This time it came out full of pus. There was no doubt that his surmise was right, so they took me to the Protestant hospital which was only a little over a block away from Mrs. Roberts's house. They gave me enough ether to kill two or three men, and I was still talking to the doctor. Finally he started operating. He slit the skin over a rib after pulling my right arm up high. They cut the rib off near my back bone and then again around near my breast bone, leaving a big orifice to a lung. Then he cut through the lung, and put in two big rubber tubes to drain the pus.

My brother and Dad watched the operation. My brother got sick and left, but Dad stayed with me. Dad told me afterwards I talked to the doctor during the operation. The doctor asked me if it hurt. I says, "Hell, yes, it hurts. Go a little easy." I knew nothing of it myself, only what they told me afterwards. Dad got a special nurse to be with me during the nights, and they did everything possible to bring me out of it. I woke up the next day from the operation in a pool of blood. They had a rubber sheet underneath me and I remember one little nurse picked me up while another one gathered up that sheet with the blood in it and took it out. I couldn't hardly see across the room and could barely tell daylight from dark. I was just about bled out.

For ten days I lived on a little ice cream and root beer. The doctor said he couldn't understand what kept me alive, except the determination to live. One nurse was named Peterson. She got a cot and would shove it underneath my bed daytimes, then pull it out and sleep right beside me, one hand on me all night to check my breathing and take care of me. It was due to that good nurse that I survived. After a month in a solitary room, they moved me to a ward where there was a lot of other men. Some had broken legs, some had flu pneumonia, but anyway it was much better because I had company. Another nurse there, named Johnson, a short fat girl, a jolly little lady, she'd pat my pillows and shove bananas or candy bars under them when no one was looking. I had a ravenous appetite, as

This photo of a mountain goat was taken at a distance of 12 feet by Elmer. Although it was an easy shot, he passed it up and settled for the photograph as a trophy.

I was beginning to recover, and hospital fare was just a teaser.

One day George and Ed Lamb came up to see me and had a new saddle that George had bought. It was an R. T. Frazier bronc saddle, heavy skirting covered the fork, bars, cantle board and all, and was flesh side out to take the rough use of a bronc saddle. It had the best-shaped seat I'd ever seen in a saddle, and I kidded George about it. I said, "When you get throwed out of it I want to buy it."

"Well," he says, "I paid $67.50 for it. If I ever get throwed out of that, I'll sell it to you for just what it cost."

He was as good as his word. Before getting the flu and going to the hospital, George and I had taken a couple of broncs to break for Stadler and Kaufman. We named them Mabel and Bruce. He broke the mare named Mabel, and I broke the gelding named Bruce. Mine came out of it in good shape, but the mare was prone to buck. One day George came in and he says, "Do you still want that saddle?" I says, "Sure. Why?" He says, "Old Mabel unloaded me at Claysoil today. I was crossing a culvert with the water running underneath. She got halfway across, swapped ends, and went to pitching. I never did catch up with her." So I had Dad give him a check for $67.50 and I had the bronc saddle. We still have it today. My wife rides it sometimes instead of her regular saddle.

That flu epidemic was so bad there wasn't enough nurses to go around, enough doctors to go around, or enough cots in the hospital, and the dead were piled up in coffins waiting burial. They held funerals night and day for some time. Big strong men would come into the ward when I was there, and in two or three days they'd roll them in the old basket and haul them away. One of them was my friend Dan Floweree from across the river. I hated to see big Dan go. He was a prince of a fellow. Finally they let a bunch of us out on the sun porch of the hospital to get a little sun. I managed to get into some of my clothes before I went out there. One day I told some of the boys, "I'm going to quit this place. Don't give me away. I'm going to sneak out and go back to Mrs. Roberts's. She lives around the corner."

I was very weak, but I managed to get down the steps, across the street, and I was hanging on a parking tree when Mrs. Roberts's daughter, Olga, came along. She grabbed me and was going to rush me back to the hospital. I says, "No, Olga, I'm leaving that place. For God's sake, don't take me back. You go on to work and don't create any fuss here or they'll spot us. I'll make it all right." So she did. I worked from one parking tree to another, and finally got to the Roberts's house and knocked on the door. Mother was up by then and she and Mrs. Roberts took me in. From then on I was royally taken care of. Mother would cook me anything I wanted and all I could eat and I started to

rebuild. Olga would play the piano for me of the evenings after she came home from work. When I finally came out of it in the spring, and was able to get around, I went and bought a bouquet and big box of chocolates for each of my two good nurses.

They drove me back to the ranch. The doctor admonished me not to get on a horse because I still had a four or five-inch slit underneath my shoulder blade and a taped bandage over it. It had to be dressed daily, and you could see my lung when the patch was off. However, I had John Lawther run old Satan in and I saddled him up. He'd always pitched with me everytime I ever got on him, from the time I'd bought him from George Hammond at Ovando. This time was no exception. I tried to hack him with my spurs, but I was so weak that he could tell the difference. He made three crooked jumps, stopped, stuck his head around and smelled of one boot, then around on the other side, and trotted to Winston. Jumping fences was the only buck jumping he did. He never did buck with me after that, but would throw all and sundry other people that tried to ride him. Then they say a horse hasn't any sense. I believe they are much more intelligent than they are credited. Certainly this little horse was just as glad to see me as was John Lawther after the long stay on the ranch and me in the hospital.

After that winter Dad and Mother made a trip to Idaho to visit Cars Wilson and other old friends that had settled there. They decided to get out of Montana. They'd had enough too. A man named Malicoat had some 1200 acres of cheat grass range north of Payette on Willow Creek. Father traded him the ranch for it. It was a worthless piece of grassland except in the spring when it grew up in cheat, but then it would fatten a lot of cattle.

Chapter 4

COMPETITION AND MATRIMONY

BIG TIME AT CAMP PERRY...

I had been wanting to get into match shooting if I could, so I went to Bozeman and joined C Company of the Montana National Guard, an infantry company. When they held their camp at Fort Harrison for two weeks, I rode old Satan out there. Captain Finley wanted a good horse to ride, so I let him ride old Satan. By that time I had him gentle enough and he really enjoyed riding that good cow horse.

Each night sentries were posted completely around the camp and orders were that no one was to leave or enter after two o'clock in the morning. One night an Indian and I were walking the beat on the south side. He would walk his beat and meet me, and then I'd go back and meet another man at the corner. About 2:30 a car drove up in front of me with some officers and women in it, laughing and having a good time. I went over and told them to get off my beat and to get away from there because they weren't allowed in after two o'clock. They drove down in front of the Indian. The officers got out and started in. I heard the Indian yell for help. I snapped on my bayonet and went down there. They hadn't issued us any ammunition. Bless Moses, it was the captain and the first lieutenant of an artillery company. They told us who they

were, and that they was going on into camp. I says, "That's not my orders." The Indian stayed with me. I says, "You're going to the guard house." So to the guard house we took them and turned them over to the officer of the guard.

The next morning at reveille no captain, no first louie of that company showed up. The colonel was irate. He wanted to know what had happened. Finally Captain Finley asked me, he says, "Did they come in on your beat?" I said, "They come in on the Indian's, and we took them and threw them in the guard house. That was our orders." So they dug them out of the guard house. Later that day Captain Finley came to me, and promoted me to a corporal and then to a sergeant.

"Sergeant Keith," he says, "Colonel Williams wants to see you at his tent." So I went in, saluted, and Colonel Williams says, "Sergeant Keith did you arrest a couple of officers last night and put them in the guard house?"

"We did."

"Did you threaten those officers with a bayonet?"

"I did."

"Would you have used it?"

"I would."

"Very well, Sergeant Keith," he says,

"You're a good soldier. Dismissed."

I joined the outfit with the express purpose of shooting in the matches and going to Camp Perry, Ohio to the national matches on the Montana National Guard team. We held the state matches. The governor of Montana came out to call out the men to represent the team. He called Lieutenant Eben V. Phipps, an old Camp Perry veteran, Number 1. Number 2 was Sergeant Keith.

As I remember, we were several days going back to Camp Perry on the old rattler at that time. We stopped overnight in Chicago at a hotel right across the street from the LaSalle Street station. It was built kind of in the form of a square with a desk in one corner, and a stairs and hallway around in the next story above. You could look down on the desk in the big lobby. They quartered six of us in a corner room with three double beds.

Lieutenant Phipps said they'd stayed there the year before and they had several National Match rifles and spotting scopes and a lot of their belongings stolen. So he says, "Boys, one of us has got to stay here all the time, night and day." So we took it in shifts of three hours. In my afternoon shift there was six Negro women, one after another, that came in to polish and clean up the bathroom. I finally told them, I says, "Five of you have been ahead of this last one. I don't think it needs any more cleaning." That night the boys all came in. Lieutenant MacIntyre and Sergeant Jellison were among them, both old regular army men before they joined the Second Montana. They were both pugs as well. I didn't like the looks of things. Neither did Phipps. I slept with Lieutenant Phipps, so when I went to bed I laid my old .45 in the bed with me. About three o'clock in the morning, I heard somebody working on the door and heard a key turn. About that time Phipps put his hand over my mouth and whispered in my ear. I whispered back and I said, "Let me get out and over by the door and then turn on the light."

I got out of bed and when I went over to the door it was already open, so I stepped back a couple of paces. Just then the light came on. A big tall gent with very heavy black eyebrows was staring down at me. I tipped the old cocked .45 up in the middle of his chest and invited him on in. I had an idea if I could get him in there and lock the door, then we would let Jellison and MacIntyre work him over. He took one look at the old gun and his eyes got bigger and he turned and ran down the hall. I jumped out in the

hallway and pulled down on him to kill him and Phipps hollered, "Don't shoot, Keith. Don't shoot. That's an order." So I let the hammer down. He ran down the hall and got away. I came back and said, "Why did you do that, Lieutenant? I could have stopped that crook." He says, "I know you could, but that old gun of yours would have gone through him and the wall, and Colonel Williams is sleeping right down the line there."

The next morning the colonel took me down to the desk to find out about the deal. The man at the desk said he didn't know who the man was unless it was the house detective looking to see if we had any women or any booze. Colonel Williams told him, "The boys have got plenty of booze, but no women, and," he says, "Just as sure as hell if your man comes back tonight I've got a cowpuncher up there that's going to kill him." Colonel Williams says, "Elmer, if he comes back in the night, dump him." I told him I would. But he never came back.

Parts of Chicago was a tough town in those days. Parts of it still are, from what I can learn. At any rate, Lieutenant MacIntyre, Sergeant Jellison, Lieutenant Phipps and I went into a barber shop. It was a big shop, with six barbers in there. We had a shave and a haircut around and when it came to pay them they had an enormous price. As I remember it was about $3 apiece they wanted to charge us. MacIntyre, Jellison and Phipps didn't say anything. They just pulled off their blouses and piled them on me. They waded into those barbers. Very soon they had all six of them out cold and piled up on the floor. Lieutenant Phipps took his jacket, put it on, buttoned it up, went over to the mirror and got a comb, combed his hair. Jellison and MacIntyre did likewise and out we went and up the street. We never heard anything about it, but I'll bet there was six very sorry barbers we left behind that day.

The day before we left for Camp Perry from Chicago, Colonel Williams and another Lieutenant had friends there they wanted to visit. Lieutenant Phipps and I were walking up the street in what they called "The Loop" at the noon hour and the crowd was pressing us on all sides. I felt somebody a-diggin' in my hip pocket. I didn't have anything there only a handkerchief. I always carried my money in my breast shirt pocket. Anyway I swung with all I had and whirled and let him have it. The guy was taller than I thought and instead of hitting him in the face, I hit him right on the Adam's apple.

He just says "Quark" like a duck and down he went. Phipps says, "Come on. Let's get out of here." We went on up to where we could cross the street and came down the other side. People were still stepping over him there, so I guess I must have put him out. After all of this mess, I was glad to get out of Chicago, wishing I was back in the sagebrush of Montana. We went on to Camp Perry.

At that time the matches were held in October and we trained for a month, practicing every day before the official National Matches and Individuals came up. I had a good bull gun I'd had Larry Muesslein of the International team make up for me. In fact, it took most of my coyote money one winter to get it, but it was a good rifle. It had a 26-inch Winchester sniper barrel on a Springfield action, cut off striker, German double-set triggers, a Type C pistol grip stock, and International butt plate that you could adjust and hook under your right arm, and a good palm rest. It weighed about 16 pounds, as I remember. I came out high man for average through all the practice and through individual and team shoots that year at Perry.

Before leaving Montana I boxed all my guns up in some huge boxes, nailed them up tight, and left them with the ranch below us to be shipped. I'd also started three broncs and had them going good for my brother to ride to gather our cattle that fall to be shipped down to Weiser, Idaho. However Si didn't like the broncs, so he rode poor old Satan until he stiffened him all up gathering the cattle. I had traded all my other horses to Mr. Malicoat who swapped ranches with dad, sight unseen, for broncs that he had on Willow Creek north of Payette.

Camp Perry and the National Matches was a great show for me and I had a good time. I made the acquaintance of many fine people, some of them to last throughout their lives, such as James V. Howe, Colonel Townsend Whelen, Major, (later General) J. S. Hatcher, Lieutenant Sid Hines, later to become a general in World War II, and many others. The Hoffman Arms Company had an exhibit of their fine arms that they were then bringing out. Jim Howe had organized Griffin & Howe, then pulled out of that company and helped organize the Hoffman Arms Company. Morris Fisher, the Olympic champion, and I became good friends. Also Emil J. Blade of the Marine Corp and Sergeant Calvin Lloyd. The Marines at that time had a splendid team of expert riflemen, in fact some of the finest rifle shots the world has ever seen.

The weather turned quite cold in October in '24 at Camp Perry. It rained a lot. We piled all the blankets we could find on the cots. Lieutenant Phipps had warned us to take extra ones along, so we shipped a lot of blankets with us from Montana. In that way we managed to keep warm, but it was a wet soggy rain. We'd throw down a slicker to bed down on in our prone matches. The company streets were a muddy mess, and we were quartered in big army squad tents.

Lieutenant MacIntyre could imitate a donkey the best of anybody I ever heard, so he and Sergeant Jellison got some mule shoes, put them on sticks, made tracks around in the company streets and then Lieutenant MacIntyre would bray like a donkey. In a few minutes the military police would come looking for the mules. They'd trail his tracks all around the company streets but they never caught up with the donkey.

Range firing started at seven a.m. with a break at noon, and then we'd fire until about five in the afternoon. I learned early to skip breakfast, maybe drink a glass of milk or a pot of tea, and do the serious shooting, then eat bit in the evening. After a month's practice they held the individual matches, and then the national team matches. They were money matches in those days, and I managed to pick up more prize money than the rest of my team, a good part of it with my big bull gun in the individual matches. I shot in the free-rifle match and all the long-range individual matches with that rifle and did quite well.

At that time the Colt Company had J. H. Fitzgerald in constant attendance behind the firing line repairing pistols, adjusting trigger pulls, adjusting sights, and in general keeping all Colt guns in shape. I first met Fitzgerald at the Colt hut. One evening after dinner I changed clothes and strolled over to the Colt hut. There was quite an attendance there, including army officers and their wives, servicemen from all branches.

Fitzgerald was up in front of them all and had a man hold a gun on him and demonstrated how he could roll his big belly, grab the gun and turn it to break the man's finger before he could shoot him. I must have had a grin on my face because Fitzgerald spotted me in the back of the room. He says, "What are you grinning at, cowboy?" I told him I was just thinking what fools these mortals be. He says, "What do you mean by that?" "Well," I says, "You might get away with poking a gun in a man's belly back here, having him poke it in your belly, and whirling quick and grab-

It was Keith's prowess and experimentation with hand-guns that brought him the lion's share of his fame. Here he experiments with the Berns-Martin holster after it was first developed in the 1930's.

bing the barrel and breaking his finger, but you don't want to try it on Westerners that have used a gun all their lives and are thoroughly familiar with it."

"Why?"

"Well," I says, "They'd shoot you."

He says, "Do you mean to tell me that you can snap that gun in line with me before I can divert it and break your finger?"

"I think I can."

He says, "Come up here."

So I went up and he handed me a .45 automatic. I laid it down on the glass counter as there was a 7½-inch single-action .45 inside the counter, nickel plated. I told him to give me that instead. So I pulled the base pin, removed the cylinder and stood it on the counter. I jammed the gun in Fitz's big belly, and he was quicker than greased lightning, but as he whirled, I just tipped the gun upside down and snapped it. Had there been a load in it, it would have gone through the middle of him.

He says, "Try that again." The next time he was faster, but I was still able to get him almost center. The third time he was greased lightning, but I was tuned up too by then, and I would have still got a big steak off his belly if we had been serious.

"Well," he says, "You can't do it to my back." So he turned his back. I jammed my left thumb in his back hard, he whirled and grabbed the thumb while I snapped the gun three times. Later he put it in his book that he wrote, but he didn't say where he got the information or the source of it. We became great friends right until his death sometime after 19 and 40.

In 19 and 40, my wife and I and Fitz and his wife had dinner together at the end of the matches and that was the last time I ever saw Fitz because he died not too long after. He was a great man and a great gun man.

Chauncey Thomas was there representing *Outdoor Life* as he was then Shooting Editor for *Outdoor Life* Magazine. He proposed that Fitzgerald and I get on the Y.M.C.A. stage and demonstrate the quick draw for the whole assemblage. I couldn't get out of it, so finally agreed to go.

When the big Y.M.C.A. tent was filled to overflowing, and they put us on the stage separately, Thomas would act as an adversary and go for an imaginary gun while I drew and snapped the old single-action on him. Later Fitz performed the same deal. Fitz used a pair of 2-inch .45 Colt New Services and he wore them in cross-draw holsters. He shot from the side. He'd lift his left arm, grasp the gun, and shoot under his elbow with the right hand. He was very fast. He demonstrated the use of those 2-inch .45s with either hand, always turning the side of his body towards the target, wiping them out of the holster and snapping them.

Fitzgerald was busy every day under his big umbrella, adjusting trigger pulls, and sights on various Colts. He taught me how to file, polish, and fix a trigger pull on .45 automatics. I told him I had my old gun along that Johnny Linder had adjusted. He wanted to see it because it had a 3½-pound pull, but wouldn't "machine gun." I brought the gun over to his big umbrella and he had it apart in two seconds. He looked at the hammer. John Linder had taken a center punch and punched on the inside of the full-cock notch, throwing out a little burr on each side that limited the depth of the sear bite in the hammer. Therefore, it hadn't been stoned, it was still case-hardened, and it wouldn't wear. Fitz took that hammer out of my gun and put in another one. He says, "I've got to have that hammer." He tried to adjust the pull on the other one, but the old gun never did have as good a pull afterwards as the hammer that Fitz had to have that Johnny Linder of Helena had worked over.

Hoffman Arms Co. had an exhibit of fine rifles. Everything from .22 match rifles to the big .505 Gibbs on a Magnum Mauser action. Eric Johnson was one of the men there, since he bored the barrels for the Hoffman rifles. Jim Howe had done a lot of the sights and stocking as well, and Harry Snyder was president of the company. I had spent a lot of time with them looking over their fine rifles.

One day they wanted someone to shoot the .505 Gibbs. Apparently there were no takers, everybody being afraid of the big rifle. They had a running deer target, so I volunteered to shoot it. I managed to shoot twice, hit the running deer both times. I wasn't used to a rifle with that heavy recoil; so much more recoil than my old Sharps. Anyway the barrel raised halfway to the vertical and it turned me halfway around each time, but I also drilled a running deer each time.

Frank Kahrs was then public relations man for the Remington Arms Company, and we became good friends. When I left, he loaded half a trunk with ammunition he wanted me to test when I got back out West. I remember the first was 110-grain .30-06. He gave me a couple of hundred rounds of that stuff that I later used on coyotes and running jackrabbits.

Camp Perry at that time was a great show for a green cowpuncher out of the Montana sagebrush, and I enjoyed every minute of it. Little did I know then that many of the friendships I made there in 19 and 24 were to last throughout life.

Jim Howe introduced me to the famous barrel maker Harry Pope, and I spent one Sunday afternoon on the bench behind the 200-yard firing line where the Navy team was practicing, talking with Harry Pope. The old man had his pockets full of little boxes of bullets, padded in cotton, he'd put through the barrels of different Schuetzen rifles he'd made. He was a great source of information, and willing to dispense it to anyone who was really interested. That was one of the most interesting afternoons I ever put in. Later, after I acquired a Pope Ballard Schuetzen rifle, old Harry made me a mold and grease pump for it, and took about a year to write me a letter. He was a very interesting old man and one of the finest rifle makers in the world. In fact, Morris Fisher of the International team shot a 32-inch .30-06 barrel that Harry had fitted for him and won the Olympic Championship.

During the 19 and 24 matches we shot Model 1923 six-degree boattail ammunition loaded with high velocity powder in practice. Then they issued us some 1924 ammunition, also with high-vel powder. By the time we were through with our month's practice in the National Matches, our National Match rifles had their throats burned for three inches until they were almost black. In fact the finest accuracy was shot out of those rifles by the time we finished the matches. The International team would have the barrels cut off, rethreaded and rechambered, in order to get a new bullet seat that would give the finest accuracy after four or five hundred rounds practice. That high-vel powder was very erosive and simply burned the lands out for an inch ahead of the chamber and ruined the bullet seating area.

I had been an individual member of the National Rifle Association since 19 and 22, and at Perry got acquainted with C. B. Lester, who then headed the NRA and we became lifelong friends. He later wrote me up in *The Infantry Journal*. The Montana team didn't do too well in the National team matches, mainly for the reason we had one lieutenant who went to town, got on a good bender, and tried to shoot while he was enjoying a first-class hangover. The rain and damp cold weather didn't help any, and I remember one day the temperature changed about thirty degrees from the day before. That morning everybody was firing all along the line, all shots were down on the bottom of the target. Threes and fours instead of bullseyes were normal elevation due to that cold, damp, biting wind coming across Lake Erie. The temperature drop changed the elevation of our rifles all down the line.

During the practice month, Con Smith of the Minnesota team called on me to help him out. Several of his men had gone to town and hadn't come back from Saturday night, and they were scheduled for practice in the old infantry match, where two squads of five men each advance, one squad firing on the targets while the others ran forward, threw the butts of their guns out and went down prone, then they would start firing and the other squad would get up and advance and reload. Con and I tried to hold up the work of a five-man squad. We had one good five-man squad and he and I had to hold up the other end of the line. I ruined my National Match rifle that day as I put 120 rounds through it in that skirmish run. However, Con and I would beat down those five targets with the required number of hits per minute so that the other squad could advance. It had rained so much the water was standing in the blue grass of the range. We'd throw the butt of our rifle out, and hit the ground, only we hit the water instead. A man would splash on each side of him every time he hit the ground. My rifle got so hot that the wood was smoking when we finished the skirmish round. We did very well on it with just two men for one of the squads. I tried to get Colonel Williams to let me turn that rifle in. It wouldn't hold elevation after that, and I'm sure either the stock or the barrel had warped from the heat. However he wouldn't let me do it, so I shot a mediocre score in the National team match when I know I could have done much better if I could have drawn a new rifle. Medals and prize money were issued for the top echelon in all the individual matches, and I garnered some of both. When the matches were over, I re-routed my ticket to go to Missouri.

LIVING IN PAYETTE...

Mother and Father had already gone on to Idaho and my brother was gathering the cattle to ship them and my pet horse to Idaho, so I stopped off at Richmond, Missouri, and had a good visit with my cousins and my

Winter meat wasn't much of a problem in the game-rich area near the ranch at Winston, Montana. These deer helped the Keith family through the winter of 1920, and were taken by Silas Keith (left) and Elmer.

uncles. I remember my Uncle Irvin wanted me to go squirrel hunting with him. He had an old .22. I took it out, shot it at a knot on a fence post, and I couldn't even hit the post with it half the time. But I had a good .45 Colt single-action, and also my pet .45 auto that Bill Strong had given me. So I took the pistol instead of the rifle, and managed to dump every squirrel that we found, big fox squirrels, some of them swaying in the top of water oaks. I'd time their swing and manage to knock them out. My cousins and Uncle Joe and Uncle Irvin Keith couldn't understand how I could hit squirrels that far with a .45 single-action and that .45 automatic. They all used rifles for their squirrel hunting.

After a good visit with my relatives in Missouri, I entrained and finally landed at Payette, Idaho, where Father had rented a house on the banks of the Payette River just where it flowed into the Snake River. He'd also acquired a pet bear. I believe he traded a sewing machine for it. He called him Bobby. He was a brown bear. We had a crowbar driven in the ground, a good stout collar on Bobby, and a small light log chain from the crowbar to his collar ring. The little bear was a source of amusement to all the school kids. They'd come home from school and form a half-circle around little Bobby. He'd watch them for quite awhile, then he'd make a rush at them and "woof" and the kids would scream and run. The little bear got quite a kick out of that.

Dad also had a cocker spaniel, and he was quite the dog, he thought. He'd bluff out big dogs, sidle up to them and growl and rub against them, making them think he was going to eat them. Somehow he got away with it with most of the dogs. One day he tried this trick on little Bobby. He went up, rubbed his rump against Bobby, growled, then walked around to the other side, and did the same thing. The little bear regarded him out of the corner of his eyes, finally he lifted that left paw and Dad's cocker spaniel went clear over the top of a small apple tree. The dog went into the house howling, and never bothered the little bear again.

I found the mouth of the Payette was full of small black bass, and they took a fly quite readily. I had a lot of fun catching them. Also there was pretty good duck shooting upon the Snake River where they'd turn and come up the Payette. Dad's spaniels would get them for me. One day I shot an old loon. Thinking to have some fun with Mother, I took him in and told her I had a goose. Mom immediately got a sack for the feathers, a box to put them in and tried to pick the loon. She took hold of the feathers and pulled for all she was worth, but she couldn't get any feathers to come out of that bird's breast.

"Well," she says, "Elmer, I've picked a lot of geese, but I never saw one that looks like this thing. I don't believe it's a goose." Then I told her it was a loon, and took him out and gave him to the bear. Little Bobby rushed out of his barrel that he slept in, put a paw on the loon, got a good bite, pulled back, his teeth clicked and he had a feather or two. He put the other paw on the other end of the loon, got a good grip on the middle of him that time, again his teeth clicked and he didn't even break the skin. Back went that left paw. The loon sailed over the little apple tree to the right. Bobby stalked back in his barrel, disgusted, and wanting to let us know it. We had a lot of fun with that little bear.

Dad had a barrel of cider he'd shipped from Missouri and it had gone flat. It was awfully strong, and none of us could drink it. I filled a pop bottle with it and gave it to the bear. He took it in both paws, jammed the bottle down to the bulge in his throat and rolled over and drank it. When the bottle was empty he laid it on the ground, rolled it sideways with his paws, and stuck his little pink tongue in it. That little bear was a real clown.

One day a big swarm of bees came along after we had moved to the ranch on the Weiser flat. Mother had me beat on a dishpan. She had a big sheet spread out. She understood bees. She finally had the huge swarm on the sheet. We had set up a bee hive and were sitting there watching them go in. The queen bee went into the hive, then Mother knew the rest of them would follow. The little bear came up and sat down between us, watching the bees. Finally he put one paw out, raked it right through the middle of the bees, sheet and all. Mother was so disgusted she picked up a barrel stave and she whanged little Bobby on the rump. He took off and he hit the barrel he slept in so hard that he turned it up vertical. Then he raised up, put his paws on the rim and looked over at us.

AT HOME IN WEISER FLAT . . .

While my brother Silas was rounding up all the Keith cattle back in Montana, packing up personal belongings (including my boxes of guns) to ship to Idaho, Father rented a big farm on the Weiser flat from a banker we'll

Cyrus and Frankie Randall, Lorraine's parents, near the turn of the century in Idaho.

call B. I put in my time taking care of the 1200 acres of grass that Dad had traded for, as well as rounding up the horses I had traded for sight unseen from Mr. Malicoat. They proved a rough-looking bunch, and mostly greys. A Russian cavalry buyer came through and that appeared to be just what he wanted. We ran them into Clyde Kern's corral and he bought the lot at $40 a head. We four-footed them, dumped them, and sat on their heads while they put the iron on them for the Russian government. Evidently the Russian cavalry favored these iron grey mounts.

I also put out a coyote line that winter, and spent a lot of time experimenting with different rifles, different six-guns, and loads. Brother Si shipped all the cattle and my old horse Satan and our personal belongings down from Montana. We finally got everything installed in the ranch house on the Weiser Flat. Father had rented it crop rent. It was a big place, with two silos. We put up an awful lot of hay, and enjoyed first-class land with plenty of water. He was to get half of the crop, and half of the hay alone would easily take care of all of our stock. Father and Si fed the stock while I took care of the cheat grass up on Willow Creek and ran a coyote line and broke out a few broncs.

I also had some excellent duck shooting in the corn fields. They would come in there by the thousands and we were allowed 20 a day, or maybe 25. I remember shooting the limit one day and making several trips through the snow out to the road where a neighbor picked them up. I supplied everyone along the creek with ducks.

I had a little one-room cabin on this 1200 acres of grass in a basin. A spring was some 200 yards above it, and even at the best of times it still had a manure taste from the livestock. There was no way of keeping it clear. I'd put up a fence and they'd tear it down overnight. I also took an old horse that had to be destroyed and shot him 200 yards from the cabin. Then I cut a loophole in the cabin wall just over the table so it made a first class benchrest. I'd shove my bullgun through the loophole, rest my elbows on the table, and have some coyote shooting. I had a good deal of fun watching coyotes come in early in the morning, circle the old horse, set down and look it over, circle it again, and finally go in from the tail end. Just when they got interested in horse meat, I would put the crosshairs on their shoulder and set the set trigger, and tickle it. That way I garnered

several nice pelts.

I also joined the Idaho National Guard as I wanted to get on the next National Match Team to Camp Perry. This was a horse cavalry outfit at Weiser. The next summer when we held our two-weeks encampment, my job was mostly breaking broncs. That's about all I did the whole two weeks.

A SCHOOLMARM NAMED LORRAINE . . .

Batching on Willow Creek, breaking a few horses and running a coyote trap line was not conducive to fattening Little Willie up. So about every two weeks I'd ride down to Weiser and spend a couple of days with the folks, and fill up on Mother's good food.

Guns and broncs were my obsession. I worked with them all the time and that was all I was interested in.

Back in Montana before we moved, a neighbor lady, Mrs. Geiger, had wanted to marry me off. She'd hold parties, and have girls come from Townsend, Bozeman, and Helena and throw big parties and invite me over. As I was batching, I'd usually go over for the good feed anyway, and probably wind up in a back cabin. Their house was a series of log cabins joined together. Billy Geiger, her husband, would be back there and I'd talk over the old days when he was younger and hunting buffalo and game for the market. Mrs. Geiger and the girls would get rather provoked.

I remember one time her daughter came back and hit me over the head with a sheepherder's bible. She just about broke my neck. When I recovered from the shock, I went out and joined the party.

One day I went to the phone to call Jim Meyers to see if I had enough mail down there to bother riding the seven miles to Winston. When I took down the phone Mrs. Geiger was talking to another lady. She says, "I secretly would like to know just what kind of girl would interest that Elmer Keith." She says, "All he does is fool with guns and bucking horses and cattle. That's all he knows." She says, "He's a catch for some girl but I can't find any girl that he'll even look at." I got a earfull, hung up the phone, and decided not to call Jim until the next day.

People were the same in Idaho. One day when I came down from my cabin, my brother said he was going to a dance that night. Mother wanted me to go, as I was getting old enough that she thought I was getting to be an old bachelor. Then my brother says, "If he goes, he'll wear them old boots and that old Stetson hat and everybody will think I'm a hick too."

When he said that, I told Mother to hunt up my clothes as I was going and ride in the back of the buggy, that is, stand up in the little jockey box and hang onto the seat. Ray and Reva Wilson had a good buggy and a good team, and it was about all the team could do to pull a buggy through the mud that year. The dance was to be held at a little ranch house on the Flat. When we arrived at the dance, it was just one big room and part of another one connected. They had the music up in one corner. People were dancing back and forth. It was just a real good rancher's get-together and we were all having fun. I danced with Reva Wilson and then got in a corner out of the way. Finally she came back and wanted to know why I wasn't dancing, so I asked her for another dance, and later was back in my corner. She came around and brought a couple of young flapper girls, and introduced them to me. At that time when they wore their skirts above their knees we called them flappers. I wasn't interested in either of them, so didn't bother to ask them for a dance. After being back in my corner for a while, Mrs. Wilson came over again and she says, "Elmer, is there anybody you'd like to meet in the house here?"

"Well," I says, "I wouldn't mind meeting that little schoolmarm?"

She says, "How did you know she's a schoolmarm?"

"Oh", I says, "she's a school puncher all right. See her clap her hands and tap her toe to that music? She's been doing that for a lot of kids somewhere." Reva says, "Well, I'll bring her over. Her name's Lorraine Randall and I'll introduce you."

She did just that and I asked Lorraine for the next dance. I liked her from the start, so I asked her for the supper dance if she wasn't with someone.

"No," she answered, "I came with my two brothers."

I had several dances with her. The more I saw of the lady, the better I liked her. I asked her when the next dance was going to come off, and she said in two weeks at some other ranch. The next morning at breakfast Mother asked me, she says, "Elmer, did you see any girl you liked last night?"

I said, "I surely did."

Two weeks later, I saddled up an old bucking horse, rode down the day before on a

Friday, and decided to go again. This time when we got to the dance I saw Lorraine's two brothers, Chet and Edgar, but she was not there. I asked them where she was. She had the flu they told me.

Well, after that dance there was to be another one in two weeks at still a different ranch house. So again I rode down. This time I hired Ray Wilson. The roads had dried up a bit, and he had a car, so I hired him to take me in and ask Lorraine for the dance. I rode by her folks' big ranch north of Weiser, talked to her a few minutes, and asked her if she'd go to the dance with me. She agreed, so I hired Ray to take his car and take me along with him and his wife. After that I was put out to find transportation. I wanted to take her to more dances and get better acquainted, so I traded a cow for an old bug Ford. It had no fenders, it was a wreck of a car, and kicked like two wild mules when you cranked it. Every so often a wire would come loose somewhere and the thing would stall on me. I made it work, though, and managed to take the little lady to a number of dances that spring.

With the coming of spring, I moved all the cattle out on the Willow Creek grass. I had my hands full for quite a while there taking care of them, checking on water holes, and getting acquainted with some of the neighbors who also ran cattle there.

TO CAMP PERRY FROM IDAHO . . .

When it came time for our two weeks training with the National Guard, they gave us ten shots apiece at a 200-yard target, 8-inch bullseye them days, and that was all the shooting we got for the year. And on the basis of that, they were going to pick the Idaho National Guard competition team for Camp Perry. A friend of mine that I'd shot with some, his sights shot just right for me too, so we picked out a good rifle with a good throat in it, straight barrel, and he shot first. Then I took it over for my ten shots and I just assumed the old jacknife position, draping the rifle over my knees. My knees I drew up under my chin, and held my left hand over the stock and rested my cheek on it. I put all ten in the black, and was the only man in the regiment who did. I had no more than picked up my brass when a sergeant came up, tapped me on the shoulder, and says, "Major Lizear wants to see you back in the rear." So back I went with him. He asked me where I learned to shoot. I told him it sure wasn't in the darned army. He wanted more dope, so I told him I'd been shooting all my life and I'd also shot on the Montana National Guard team at Camp Perry the year before. He says, "Keith, you're on as a member right now, and you don't need to come to the regional tryouts at all later in the summer." And he says, "I'm promoting you to sergeant, so you be ready to go with us."

In the spring and summer of '25 I was quite busy for a good while, made a lot of friends, and when the two weeks National Guard training came up at Boise, my brother and another lad would take care of the cattle for me. The National Guard was quartered near the old Boise Barracks on the north side of Boise. We put in two-weeks training, and again my job was mostly breaking horses. Every time I'd get one broke so he'd stay in the column of fours or twos or whatever, they'd give me another one. With some of them I'd have to go down, cheek them, and spin them around like a top to keep them in formation. But anyway I got along pretty well with them. One day they put me on another one that was quite a bucking horse, they said. I found out they didn't underestimate him and all I had was a McClellan saddle with little taps on it and a pair of brass knobs for spurs. I wanted to bring in my old bronc spurs, but they wouldn't let me, knowing I had to ride a regulation saddle.

We'd been out on a three-day trip in the hills, camping out each night. Each of us had a half a pup tent and one blanket. So I teamed up with the biggest, fattest guy I could find in the company so that I could keep warm. We put our two pup tents together, one blanket under us and one over us, got our backs together, and managed to keep warm up in the mountains. Coming back to Boise, we were on the oiled road not too far from the barracks when this bronc, the new one they'd given me, went to pitching. He could jump plenty high. He turned over at the height of his jump and came down on the saddle. Fortunately I'd been fighting broncs for so many years I threw myself to one side as much as I could, but my head hit the pavement. He came down with my left leg between the fork and the cantle of the old army saddle. I didn't know a thing about it after the bat on the head. The horse tried to get up, and they said I reached over and cheeked him with one hand. Every time he'd raise his head to get up, I'd pull him back and we'd both hit the ground. Finally they

got a-hold of the horse and pulled me off him, then I passed out. I didn't know anything about it and I had to go on what they told me later.

They got an ambulance, got a cot and put me on that. Just as they was going to load me in the ambulance, I came to my senses again, took one look at the ambulance and said, "I'm not going to ride in that damn thing." I got up, went and caught the horse, climbed on him and rode on into the barracks. When I got there, I went to my place on the picket line, tied my horse up, but instead of removing rifle, saber, and pistol, saddle, blankets and grooming the horse, they said I just struck out for my tent in the company street, leaving the horse tied there with everything on him. About halfway to the tent I pitched over on my nose in the dust.

They took me to the hospital, x-rayed me and found I had a blood clot on the left side of my brain. They had me in the hospital nine hours and it finally cleared up. They put me in the charge of a medical sergeant in the hospital tent. I had a notion for some reason that I had a date with Lorraine Randall that night as she was going to summer school there and batching with another girl student. I had taken her to a show or two, and I was sure I had another date with her to go to a show. They told me I wasn't going anywhere, but they had my clothes all in a pile on a chair, so I bribed the sergeant to get some money out of my pocket and go get us some cold pop. He did and I grabbed my clothes and got into some of them, went down three company streets until I knew I had him lost, then went back, dressed and headed for town. I took the girls to the show all right, but Lorraine later told me I must have been out of my head, because she said when we came out of the show I wanted to go right back in another door. At any rate when we got to the girls' domicile, here was an army car and medical team sitting there waiting for me. They took me in tow again. I was all right by the next day.

Cliff Morehead, our stable sergeant, had a big bay horse. He'd weigh about 1200, maybe 1250, heavy-boned, and the last horse in the world you'd think could jump anything. But Cliff always maintained he was a jumping horse. He said he had won $200 at a logging camp by jumping a log seven feet high with him. I didn't believe it, but anyway he was a bit fractious so they wanted me to ride him in the big parade. We had the regimental parade at the fair grounds, with the governor, the adjutant general, and all the celebrities out there in the grandstand watching us.

My unit formed six abreast and we started parading. Lieutenant Townley was in front of the third horse to the right. There was one horse between me and the horse right behind him. How that bronc ever jumped that far I'll never know, but when the band started to play, that big bay went up in the air, straight toward Lieutenant Townley.

I yelled, "Look out, Lieutenant!" He turned his head up and the horse's front feet hit him on the head. He was knocked out cold. He fell off the horse, one of his feet catching in the little officer's stirrup, and his saber hanging on the other hand by a saber cord. His horse was a gentle horse at that, and sixteen hands high, and went trotting across the parade ground there dragging the lieutenant and his saber. My bronc started pitching and, man, could he go high. He headed for the grandstand right across the field, so I thought I might as well get with it. It looked like I'd killed a lieutenant and I had this crazy three-cornered saber, or what they called a saber in those days, in my right hand, so I started whipping him with that and trying to use those little brass knobs for spurs. I had a blanket tied in front of the saddle to use as buckroll on that McClellan saddle. He pitched straight for the grandstand, putting on a beautiful show, going high, wide and crooked, and turned just to the right of the grandstand where there was two lines of automobiles and room for people to walk between them. He sailed over the top of the first auto, hit the ground just like a bunch of springs, bounced over the second one, and took off for the barracks. That fence around the thing must have been at least six feet and maybe seven high, but he sailed over that, trotted up to his place on the picket line, nickered, stuck his nose around, and rubbed my feet.

I got off, tied him up and went over and sat on the corral fence. It wasn't very long until I had lots of company. Major Lizear gave orders that horse was never to be ridden again, so Cliff had me take him home with me when I went back to Weiser. I saw Lieutenant Townley five or six years after that and he said his head still hurt him at times where that horse had hit him. That horse could jump higher than anything that I believe I was ever on except one bronc that I broke at Winston. He came down springy with no jar to it. A sick baby could have ridden him, but

he was very spectacular. Cliff said they had bucked him at Pendleton and other places and everybody would yell for them to give the man the money. But he was so easy ridden they finally threw him out of all the bucking strings. After that experience I did not doubt Morehead's statement that he had jumped the seven-foot log in a logging camp and won $200 with that bronc. He was the last horse you would ever expect to be a jumper, but he could jump higher and over more things than any horse I ever rode.

In addition to riding and keeping our cattle pretty well under control, I'd go down to the ranch and help with the crops. We had two silos for corn. Then the haying started and we put up an enormous amount of hay. It was a beautiful stack. When we did break it, Si got on top of it and he could shake the whole stack and make it sway back and forth. He was a master at stacking hay.

Our 1200 acres of grass grew up in a solid mat of cheat grass. Wonderful feed when it's fresh and green, but later when it cures, it has heads on it with little barbs on them, and these were terrible things to contend with. Some of the cows would get a wad of them in their throat and we'd have to rope them and take a stick and claw it out. Others would get it in their eyes until you had to clean those beards out of their eyes. I didn't like the stuff. Finally in the summer part of it went to smut. It was up to the stirrups. You'd ride through it all day and you'd be as black as Coaly's bottom by the time the day was over. However the cows got fat on it and did right well. I used to ride with the man that took care of the cattle over the divide from our place, named Lee Hart. He'd help me and I'd help him. He could also make some pretty good prune wine, and we'd have a drink of that occasionally.

Whenever I went to a dance down on the Weiser Flat, I'd saddle up a bronc, as I was breaking them out for the neighboring ranchers, ride down to the big ranch at Weiser, get in my old bug Ford, and take Lorraine to another dance. We also took in some shows. That dilapidated creation of Henry's had the habit of stopping at every mud hole. A wire would come off or something would go wrong.

I taught Lorraine to shoot that summer. First with a little .22 Colt pump gun I gave her, then I graduated her to a .45 single-action with full loads, and finally to the 1903 Springfield service rifle. She did very well with all three.

October rolled around, and I had to go to Camp Perry with the National Guard team. This time we went right through Chicago with no problems. I took my old Springfield bull gun with me and did very well in the individual matches because I didn't burn up my Springfield with an infantry match. Our team did quite well also. From the start they found out I could judge wind, so they put me to coaching. Instead of letting me wait until the light was good in the morning and run up a high score, they made me take the weakest man on the team and shoot the first relay so I'd get the dope for the rest of them. The team captain said that worked out very well. Major Lizear would lie back behind with a pad and spot the shots, plot them on the bullseye, and pass them up to me while I was judging the wind, shooting myself as well as coaching my companion.

I entered all the long-range matches that were open to my bull gun and the old 5A Winchester scope, as well as entering the free-rifle matches, all three positions, and the unlimited re-entry match.

On a sergeant's pay, $3 a day, I couldn't afford many cards on the unlimited re-entry Free-Rifle match. But I did get four of them, and that constituted a score of 100. The target was the International target at 300 meters, and that center ring was 3.30 inches in diameter. Put that out at 300 meters (330 yards,) and it's a mighty small target. However, the whole black was about 26 inches in diameter. I had a Lyman aperture front, and Lyman 48 rear sights on the old bull gun. They allowed us five sighter shots in this prone Free-Rifle re-entry match. I fired my five shots and I was still not centered. My first shot for record was a 9, four inches from the center of the black. As the hold looked perfect to me, I made full correction. Then I ran a 99, and went straight from there. In the meantime everybody quit the other booths, and came over to watch me.

Later John Keith Boles says, "What are you trying to do, kid?"

"Why," I says, "I'm just going to show you International boys how to shoot. Give me my other two targets."

I knew I was good, and knew I could put the next ten in. But they refused. They said other people wanted to use the booth.

I said, "Why? There's three more booths open. Let 'em shoot on them."

"No, you better come back tomorrow."

I says, "I'm in team matches and it's hard to get away for these Individuals."

But they wouldn't let me fire my other ten shots.

The next day when I came back, I had the Camp Perry dysentery. I could only shoot about three shots, stand the bull gun in the corner and run for the ivy-covered. At that I got a couple of 49s as I remember. At any rate I came out with second place in the Free Rifle prone match.

Major Boles of the infantry, who'd been team captain on the International team, beat me by two points for first place. Sergeant Morris Fisher of the Marine Corps, who'd topped the International team at Switzerland, came in fifth. So I believe I was doing about as well as any. Had they let me fire my other two targets that evening, I'm certain in my own mind I would have won that match. There was a lot of horse trading going on at Perry in those days, and it was just as crooked as many horse races. It was a money match anyway, and you paid your entrance fee and you got so much back if you were good enough.

Next I entered the 600-yard any-rifle match. I took my old bull gun over to J. W. Fecker and asked him to check my 5A scope for parallax. He did and he said there was nothing vertical, but he said it was half the bullseye at 600 yards horizontal. The bullseye was 20 inches in diameter with a 10-inch V-ring in the center. Commander Si Osborn of the Navy, also a member of the 1925 International team that had gone to Switzerland, proposed to a bunch of us that the low man of the first ten shooters would take everybody to Port Clinton and have a big dinner, and the drinks, of course, from bootleg scotch that came across Lake Erie in boats and was planted out there with a string and cork on it. It was prohibition days and the camp was dry, except for the Marine Corps. I soon became acquainted with a lot of fine members of the Marine Corps. Everyone of them had a bottle at the head of his cot, a product of Scotland. Their International pistol shooter and I became friends. We'd take his two 10-inch Smith & Wesson pistols out on Sundays, illegally, I guess, and we garnered a lot of fat squirrels for a big feed. That was a welcome change from the regular chow line there at Perry.

When Commander Osborn proposed that the low man of the first ten take the other nine to town and buy them a big dinner and drinks, I started to back out of the crowd. Con Schmidt of the Minnesota team, who I'd shot with the year before in the infantry run and ruined my rifle, caught me by the shoulder. He called me "Montana". He says, "Stay in, Montana. You won't be the last, and if you are I'll foot the bill myself." So I did. I put my twenty shots all in the black with fifteen V's. Sergeant Odom and Sergeant Lloyd of the Marine Corps got 16 V's for first and second. Captain Joe Jackson of the Marine Corps and I had fifteen Vs, but he "out-Creedmoored" me. That is, he had one more V in the last ten shots than I had, so he got third and I got fourth in the 600 yard any-rifle match.

I next entered the Wimbledon Cup match, which had two sighters and 20 for the record at 1000 yards, with a 36-inch bullseye and a 20-inch V-ring. I got off well. My first shot was a good 5, well in. My second one was in the V-ring. I was the only man of all the assemblage at Camp Perry, between four and five thousand shooters, that ran it clean. I stayed in the black until the seventeenth shot. I had quite a gallery behind me. Chauncey Thomas of *Outdoor Life* was there. My friend Con Schmidt of the Minnesota team, and Captain Hyland Mitchell, head of the Oklahoma National Guard team. Suddenly, just as I was going to touch the set-trigger for my 17th shot, they pulled the target and flagged a miss. Luckily I hadn't fired. I rolled over in the sling, held my rifle up for the whole assemblage to see. I says, "Bear witness, everybody."

I picked out the loaded cartridge, and stood it in the other end of the box so it could cool off. The Marine Corps sergeant that was scoring phoned three targets on each side of mine. Nobody had lost a shot, no one had received an extra hit. Finally he says, "Sergeant Keith, commence firing." I put in two more shots, both in the V-ring, then he ordered me, "Sergeant Keith, cease firing. Your time is up."

I says, "Mister, you used up the time, not me. I always fire ahead of time, Slow-Fire or Rapid-Fire matches." Con Schmidt of the Minnesota team came up and had an argument with him, along with Captain Hyland Mitchell of the Oklahoma team, and Chauncey Thomas of *Outdoor Life*. But they made it stick. They wouldn't let me fire my 20th shot for record, so I came out with a 95 and $10.80 in prize money. They gave the cup to Ralph McGarity for a 99 and I helped him load his 200 Remington wind-buckers the day before on one of the benches.

Later I entered the Free-Rifle match, all three positions, 20 shots prone, 30 kneeling and 40 standing, as I remember. Eric Johnson and I tied for eighth place out of the whole

assemblage, including the International team.

That International match course is a tough, tiresome game. I was shooting very well, anyway. That winter I trained by snapping the set triggers and firing a few shots to verify my holding on them in hopes of trying out for the International team the next year. It was not to be. The high command at Washington decided that instead of holding regional tryouts, (the one I would attend would have been at Cheyenne, Wyoming) they would pick men of known ability and send them on the International team.

In 19 and 24 Morris Fisher ran a 10-shot possible on the International target at Camp Perry, but in 19 and 25 my 99 in the Unlimited re-entry match was the highest score put over the International target that year.

A CHANCE TO WRITE...

The year before Chauncey Thomas, who was then editor for *Outdoor Life,* had published a letter I wrote him in the *American Rifleman*. Then in 19 and 25, after I became acquainted with C. B. Lister, who was then heading the N.R.A., Lister asked me to write up the police matches at Perry, which I did for the *American Rifleman*. In fact this was my first article in the *American Rifleman*. I remember when I was typing it, hunting and pecking it in my slow manner, Sergeant Morris Fisher of the Marine Corps came over, and he said, "I'm a good typist. How about talking and let me type for you?" I thanked him, but I told him my thoughts weren't fast enough to keep up with his typing. He was the Olympic champion and in 19 and 24 had run a possible at Camp Perry on the International target. He was also a swell guy and a friend of mine for a considerable time. I met a lot of fine men at Camp Perry that year, and began friendships with some of them that lasted as long as they lived.

One evening a group of us were in the Colt hut. Chauncey Thomas said he'd give a leg, almost, to have a case of that good National Match brass to take back to Denver to reload for his .30-06 experiments. I told him to sit still a few minutes and I'd get him a case. The cases of fired shells back of each firing line were along the benches, and they were being patrolled by the Army regularly. So I sneaked out of the tents into a latrine, then when the guard passed I slid underneath one of the benches, and laid there while he came back. When he went back on his beat, I picked up a case of this fine brass, lifted it over to the latrine, from there to a tent, and very soon I set it down in front of Chauncey

Thomas in the Colt hut. He later went out to Fort Clinton and shipped it home.

He said, "Elmer, you took quite a risk."

I told him "No risk at all."

It was plumb easy to dodge those soldiers there. I'd been in the hills too long.

Frank Kahrs was then public relations man for the Remington Arms Company, and we became good friends, along with Harry Snyder, who was president of the Hoffman Arms Company. Eric Johnson, the barrel maker and I also became good friends.

I also met and had several long sessions with James V. Howe, who started Griffin & Howe. That Christmas of '25 Jim gave me my first real modern elk rifle, a .400 Whelen he had made up, and when they started the Hoffman Arms Company, Frank Hoffman stamped on the barrel "Hoffman Arms Company No. 1" and put it in the window of the showroom.

It was a grand custom rifle. I later killed twelve elk with it and my father killed another elk. It was a far cry from the .30-06 I'd used earlier on elk. It was the finest elk rifle for timber shooting I'd used. My load was 63 grains of 17½ powder with a 350-grain Western Tool & Copper Works bullet. It would stay on a silver dollar at 100 yards, prone with a sling. It only weighed about eight pounds.

It also kicked.

Ten shots would give me gun headache, as it had a Whelen-designed stock, having a 1¾-inch drop at the comb, and a 2¾-inch drop at the heel. The kicking of that rifle and the gun headaches I sustained from shooting it prone determined me to develop a stock that wouldn't kick my teeth out, and I did several years later.

NOT ENOUGH GUN . . .

My last use of the .30-06 on elk occurred in the fall of '24 after getting back from Camp Perry. All my heavy Sharps rifles were still in Montana, as my brother had not then shipped them. Dad had an invitation for he and I to join a party of seven for an elk hunt on the Little Salmon, and we took them up on it. They had pack horses and a big camp. All we had to do was drive up there and join them. We hunted hard for ten days. At that time, back from Perry, I only had two rifles that were at all suited for elk there at Payette, Idaho. One was a 19 and 22 Government Sporter Springfield, for which I had swapped three Sharps rifles and a batch of match am-

munition. The other was my old .30-06 service rifle. I could only find one box of .30-06 ammunition in Payette. Those were Remington bronze point 150-grain, far too light for elk shooting to my notion. I put one through each rifle to determine the sighting, then gave Dad the service rifle and ten rounds. I took the remaining eight rounds and I also had a batch of National Match 19 and 23 boattail. These, of course, were solids, but I gave him some and I took some.

One man named Riley had a little .25-35 carbine. Almost every day he would shoot and wound either a bear or a deer. He didn't see any elk, but he didn't bring in any meat. The other boys brought in three deer which the crew of us ate up. Finally, Riley wounded another bear one day, so I told him I was going to take him the next day for the rest of the hunt, and stay right behind his heels until we ran into something.

Sure enough, the next day we came up over a long rolling ridge covered with chaparral up to our waist. I heard game jump, heard logs rolling, and I knew it was elk from the sound. We hurried to the top, and across the canyon about 150 yards were three fine five-point bulls going up the hill. I picked the upper one as being best of the lot.

I told Riley, "You keep that damn carbine silent until I tell you and I'll get this one. We'll get some elk meat for all hands."

I held on the root of the tail of the upper bull and shot. It was good training from all the Camp Perry shooting. Down he went in the hindquarters, flounced around sideways, and I slipped him another one in the heart which killed him. The next bull I held on the root of his tail, down he went and rolled off the mountain. As the slope we were on curved, he soon rolled out of sight underneath us. The third bull went to the top of the ridge, ran down it, and stopped at 300 yards. With such good training it was easy to hold on him with that Government Sporter with a Lyman 48 sight, so I put the remaining five of those 150-grain Remington bronze points in him behind the right shoulder. Then my gun was empty. I could contain Bill Riley no longer, so Bill up and emptied his little carbine. We heard two of them go *plunk* and we later found they had hit the paunch. Then I stuffed in a clip of 1923 six-degree boattail Match ammunition. The bull turned around and faced me after Riley's second hit in the paunch. I hit him square in the neck, and for some unknown reason that boattail traveled the length of the spine and came out over the root of the tail, killing him instantly.

Then I told Riley, "We'd better go down the gulch and finish that other one with the broken back. Then we'll come back up the mountain and dress these."

When we got down to the foot of the slope, some three or four hundred yards, there was a little amphitheatre there about thirty feet across. Our wounded bull was there with a broken back. I had four rounds of six-degree National Match hardpoints, and Riley said he had three shells left for his .25-35.

I says, "Let's cut down a sapling and kill him with a club."

The only knife I had with me, was one of those candy-striped fish knives that Remington made with a four-and-a-half-inch very thin light blade. We finally managed to whittle down a little fir tree that was thick at the butt. We limbed it up and then we tried killing that elk. We took turns, hitting him between the horns right in the back of the skull just as hard as we could, but we couldn't even stun him. He'd hook at the club and throw it out of our hands with his horns.

I told Bill, "He's no bigger than a lot of cattle I've bulldogged and worked with. Let's bulldog him and cut his throat."

So I got the little knife out. We each grabbed a horn, but before I could even get the knife under his throat he heaved us both on over his head and into the brush. We tried it a couple of times more before we finally stayed with him. Then I cut his throat from one ear clear around to the other. I didn't leave anything except the spine and hide on the back of his neck, and with windpipe, trachea, and both jugulars cut, he still threw us into the brush. We crawled out of there. That time Riley had lost half of his shirt and I was peeled up a bit too. But that bull wouldn't bleed to death. A little blood would run down each shoulder. I guess the shot from that '06 in the rump stopped his heart beat from working normally.

He just wouldn't bleed to death, so I says, "Let's bulldog him, twist his head around, and break his neck."

At the first attempt he threw me one way and Riley the other, then he went for Riley, pawing with his front feet and got him jammed up against the brush. Riley said, "Shoot him quick!" His little carbine was handy and I grabbed it. Just as I shot he raised his head and I hit him too low for the brain. Still we hadn't killed him. That left Riley with one shell in his little carbine.

I says, "Let's tackle him again. As soon as we hit him, start twisting his head."

That time we did and broke his neck. That was the first and last elk I ever killed with a knife. After fifty head (in 1972 I killed my fiftieth one), I swore never to tackle another elk even though he had only his front legs, with a knife. Elk are "game" animals, and I've had several of them come for me when they could only pull themselves with their front feet, their backs broken—both bulls and cows. They will fight when wounded.

Dad's friends had five pack horses, including one huge 1600-pound work horse that had packed when it was a colt, so we went back to get the elk. We quartered two of the bulls and loaded them on four of the horses, and Dad wanted to take one of those five point bulls in, hide, hair, horns and all. We just took the feet off him, and with five men a-liftin' we finally got him on this big horse's back. I attached the swing ropes down through the cinch rings, then put on a diamond hitch, and I had all five of them pull on it at every turn, then lay on the tail rope until it was really cinched tight. I went back to the cinch rings, tied them up, and led this big horse on foot while the rest of them handled the other four.

We had some very steep mountains to go down, but that big black horse was a wonder. He would squat, sit right down on his bottom, slide for 20 yards sometimes down the steep places, but he was very careful and never let that pack get out of balance. He packed that elk about five miles to our camp whole. I don't know what it would weigh, but it was a good five-point bull that was fat and heavy. He must have weighed around 600 pounds. Dad and I and my cousin, Anson Merrifield, kept one elk, and let the other boys split up the other two so they each had a quarter of elk meat. Just before leaving we also got into some mule deer, so we all went home with meat. At that time in a hunting camp, you hunted until everybody was filled out. And as a rule somebody would be lucky and run into game and others would not. So that was the way we hunted then, even though it might be quite a bit contrary to the law.

The third bull showed (the one I had hit five times in the lungs) upon examination, all five of those Remington 150-grain bronze points went through the rib cage into the right lung. There they each blew out a little pocket about the size of a hen's egg, so that bull could have gone quite a ways with one good lung had I not drilled him in the neck after Riley shot him twice in the paunch. That was the second failure of .30 calibers for me on elk. The next year I had my old Sharps and then Jim Howe gave me his fine custom .400 Whelen with Hoffman Arms Company No. 1 on the barrel. The .400 Whelen had a ramp gold bead front, floating English leaf sights on the barrel, and a Howe-Whelen peep sight on the end of the bolt. This is still the finest receiver sight that I know. It's not on the receiver, it's behind the receiver, but it's the finest peep sight to my notion that has ever been designed and fitted to a bolt-action rifle. I still have a couple of them, one of them on a .375 Hoffman, and the other on my old .400 Whelen. The safety is on the right side of the sight itself, and can be rocked forwards or back as desired. The eye cup or aperture is just the right distance from the eye to give you maximum sight radius and yet still be far enough forward that it won't kick you in the face, or hit you, or damage an eye with the aperture ring.

TROUBLE WITH THE BANK . . .

Father and Si raised a good crop on the big farm on the Weiser Flat that he had rented for a half-share of the crop. Corn was cut and two silos were filled and the hay was all stacked. Father had wanted to plant some spuds but Banker B., the owner, wanted wheat. So Father agreed to give him an acre of wheat for every acre he put in spuds. That was fine with B. when the agreement was made. But when fall came and it was time to dig the spuds, spuds were up out of sight in price and wheat was only a nominal price, so B. insisted he get half of the spuds. Right there he and my father disagreed. Dad always kept his word to the letter and he wasn't about to let this banker run over him. B. at that time controlled the sheriff's office, controlled the local court, and he had his bank fail. Then his son-in-law took a big wad of money and went to Portland, so a good many people told me. My girl friend, Lorraine Randall, lost her savings from teaching school in the bank. It didn't pay back a cent. There were no laws to protect the depositors from bank failure in those days.

After getting back from Camp Perry, winter set in and we gathered all our cattle and moved them down to the big farm on Weiser Flat. I remember on one drive I had 113 head, and had to come down Sand Hollow and cut them through 3 big bunches of cattle inside of fences. I had quite a time. I had a good cow horse and a good cow dog. I also had a long stick of salami and a couple of loaves of rye bread. So I just stayed with them for three days to get them down there.

I remember getting into one batch of yearlings. One of them insisted he go with me. I cut him out until I got tired. So finally I got my old rawhide rope down, wild-wested him, and hog-tied him. I poured sand in one eye, turned his head and poured sand in the other eye. Then when I pulled my piggin' string off, he was only too glad to quit the bunch and go back where he belonged. I had the old Jersey steer that we had shipped from Montana that George Lamb and I had taught to buck. He was the best lead animal I ever had. All I had to do was start him down the road and then feed him the other cattle until I had the 113 head strung out over half a mile. That way they traveled good.

By the time I had the cattle down at the farm, the argument between Dad and B. had worsened. B. got out an order that they couldn't divide the crop at all. And there was our cattle, starting to snow and rain, and they needed feed. Father had a bunch of the local ranchers, Walt Tallboy, who was county commissioner, Cars Wilson, and another man, Arthur Cavaness, who later became sheriff for several terms and another man named Coates, come in and divide the crops. I happened to be down at the ranch at that time and was sitting in the kitchen with Mother when B. and his son-in-law, who hauled he bank loot to Portland, stopped the car in front of the place and came in.

I noticed instantly that this son-in-law had a gun in each overcoat pocket and had them poked out in front of him. When I saw that, I grabbed a pair of .45 single-action four and three-fourths, stuck them in my hip pockets, butts to the front, slipped into a jacket and went out in the mud after them. It had been raining, and the corrals and everything were muddy. Dad and the other ranchers were lined up by Jenkins Creek by a high board fence talking it over, and they had just divided all the crops. B. and his son-in-law headed straight for Dad. The other ranchers moved to one side when they saw him coming with his overcoat pockets sticking out. He didn't know it, but I was 20 feet behind him. Just as he came within ten yards of Dad, Dad put his hands up on the high board fence and he says, "I am unarmed." Dad knew I would take care of it, but I didn't know if he would shoot first or what would happen. Just then B. heard my boots squish in the mud, and told his son-in-law to look around. When he turned his head and saw me behind him, with both hands under my coattail, he sidestepped. I sidestepped with him. Then I told him, "Mister, keep them damn guns turned just the way they are, turn around real slow and head for the road, you and your crooked banker. If you vary a quarter of an inch, I'll riddle you."

They did just that, got in the car, and I watched them from the side of the road until they drove off. If he had made any break at all, I intended to kill both of them. In no time at all, it seemed to me, back came B., sans his son-in-law, but with the sheriff and a court order to evict the folks from the house on the ranch. He brought along his deputy, too. They moved all our belongings out into the road. As soon as they had completed the job, the banker and the sheriff headed back to town. Our stock was desperate for feed. They put a man in the house with orders to keep everybody out, and padlocked the big gate with a log chain.

My brother and I were determined to feed those bawling cattle. So we got Arthur Cavaness and Mr. Coates, our own four-horse team, and they each hitched up a four-horse team to plow through the mud with the big hay racks, and we drove over to the ranch. We covered the folk's furniture and stuff up with canvas. Si took a pair of clippers and cut the telephone wire. I knocked on the door until their guard came to it. I says, "Mister, if you'll keep your nose in the house tonight and the doors shut, you'll be all right. If you don't I'll bury you tomorrow."

We lifted the gate off the hinges, drove in, broke a stack of hay, loaded all three four-horse wagons with alfalfa, fed the stock good, and we put out enough feed for a week, loaded up again, and drove the three wagons over to Arthur Cavaness' ranch across the road. Our neighbors were all sympathetic and helped us every way they could because they knew what kind of a deal it was.

When we were moving things in the road, the little deputy told Mother, he says, "Elmer is getting awful mad and I've had all of this crooked deal I can stand." He pulled off his badge, threw it at the sheriff, and told him to take it and what he had coming as well. The next morning the sheriff and B. drove up and stopped at the folk's furniture. B. got out and started opening the dresser drawers, and went through Mother's things. I picked up my .400 Whelen, threw a shell in the chamber, pulled down on him and I says, "Mister, get out of that stuff right now, or I'll cut you in two."

The sheriff jumped out of the car.

I says, "I'll include you too, Mister. Both of you get back in the car real slow and easy and get the hell out of here."

They did just that and promised to come back with a warrant. I told the sheriff to be sure and get a good one because it would be the last one he ever served. I was young then, full of vinegar, afraid of nothing on two legs or four, and I figured I'd make the place a little bit better for someone else to live in. They didn't come back. They held a semblance of a trial, I don't remember just now how it came out, but at any rate my brother and I fed the stock and we fed out half of our crop in spite of them. I'd taken all I could and I used to cross the street if I saw the sheriff coming down the other side, and stop right in front of him and make him walk around me. He'd stick his hand under his coat where he carried his gun in a shoulder holster. I'd ask him if his damn gun wouldn't work or if he was getting old, but I couldn't get him to fight.

When spring came, I moved the cattle back on the Willow Creek grass. Father bought a nice bungalow home, dairy barn, silos and 20 acres of very rich farm land on the south edge of Nampa and moved there.

POPPING THE QUESTION . . .

One spring day I had Lorraine out at the rifle range coaching her with a .30-06 Springfield, and I proposed to her. I told her all I had were 13 bucking horses, a bunch of guns, an old team and wagon, some farm machinery, 20 head of Hereford heifers, and a bull. She said she had another $200 she'd saved since B. got away with what she had in the bank, so she says we can have something someday and she agreed to marry me. I got her a diamond engagement ring, went down to Nampa, rented an 80-acre farm, and put in spuds and alfalfa.

I moved my farm machinery with my old grey team a long drive across the desert down to Nampa. Mother helped me clean up the two-room shack on the farm as best we could. Lorraine agreed to get married anytime I got my crop in and everything in shape and we had a little time to get away. The place was full of pocket gophers, and I spent a good part of every day in my hip boots puddling those holes and shooting the little devils that I drowned out. I finally had a good crop of spuds and alfalfa growing and wanted to get away and get married. The neighbors took pity on me and agreed to irrigate for me for

Lorraine's parents, Cyrus and Frankie Randall of Weiser, Idaho, in later years.

ten days while I went to Weiser. I borrowed my brother's Ford coupe. He had gotten engaged a couple of weeks before, and on his way home cut off a telephone pole with the Ford, which didn't do it any good. He'd had it repaired though and straightened out until he thought it would work.

I piled a camp outfit in the old coupe and set out. First I tried to get a license at Nampa. No luck there. They were closed for some kind of holiday. Then to Caldwell with the same results. From Caldwell to New Plymouth—same results. On to Payette, and they were closed.

I got to Weiser and they were open so I asked the lady clerk if I could get a marriage license. She said, "Certainly. Who are you going to marry?" I told her Lorraine Randall. She said, "Not Si Randall's daughter?" I said, "The same." So I got my license, and drove out to the ranch.

Mr. Randall could not have helped but see the diamond Lorraine had worn for three months. He pretended he didn't know anything about it and thought we were both making a big mistake. I told him we couldn't agree with him. He said if he'd known about it he would have had a big wedding.

"Well," I says, "It's far too late now, Mr. Randall."

We went down to the little church that sits about in the middle of the street in Weiser and the old preacher married us. I gave him my last $5 gold piece in payment.

We drove way up the Weiser River for a salmon hunt taking food, bedding, and spears, to join some friends up there that were also going to spear salmon. We put in a very enjoyable ten days in spite of getting rained out the first night without a tent, and having to camp in the car in an old barn. Coming back down the Weiser River to Weiser, Lorraine gathered up her belongings, what we could haul, and we drove to our new home. It wasn't much of a place—two rooms, tin cans nailed over the woodpecker holes, and being on the very end of a ditch out of the Arrowrock Dam, the people upstream would juggle their headgates at night and steal most of my water. But I managed to get in a good crop of spuds, a crop of hay, then let it go to seed and harvested a good crop of alfalfa seed. However, I sold it on time and never did get a cent out of the whole crop.

OF CATS AND COW THIEVES ...

The place was just below the lake and the people in Nampa would sack up their extra house cats and bring them out and dump them. Soon we had a yard full of house cats. The things would scratch out the screens. We had no refrigeration in those days and Lorraine would set the milk pans in the cupboard for the cream to rise so she could skim it and we would churn our own butter. One day I shot a mess of bullfrogs in the ditch, cut their legs off and cleaned them nicely, put them in a pan and set them in the cupboard. I came in a little later and found the house full of cats and the frog legs all over the floor. That did it. I ran in the bedroom and picked up the .45 Colt and was going outside to clean up the cats.

Lorraine says, "Don't do it. It's seven years bad luck and we're just married."

So I let the hammer down on the old gun, laid it back on the dresser, and went out and sat down on the back door step. One big black cat sat there with his tail curled around on that dry old hardpan. I got an idea. I sneaked back and got the gun, came out, cocked it, and aimed the same as I'd take the head off a rattlesnake at close range right on the root of his tail, and let him have it. He went over the eight-foot netting fence in the strawberry patch in one jump, his tail a-hanging by one little leader. That looked pretty good to me. Mom came out and wanted to

know what I was doing, and I told her I was detailing them. So I did, I detailed every one there except the little white kitten she wanted to keep. The funny thing about it was ... none of them ever came back.

While Lorraine and I were on our salmon-fishing honeymoon, my brother agreed to take care of the cattle. But he went to California with Harry Berry for the ten days, and the end result was about 30 or 40 head of his and my father's cows were stolen along with four of my big brockle-faced steers. Si and I started riding the feed lots and we gathered up most of them, but we still lost about 12 head.

We heard that Slim Robinette was shipping three carloads of cattle down at Payette the next day, so I told my brother we would slip down there and be there at daylight. When we rode up, they already had a car spotted, and the gate open getting ready to drive a pen of steers in to fill that car. I rode up and took one look and there was my four brockle-faced steers. The wattles had been cut off their nose, and Sam Applegate's anchor iron was plastered over the top of my 7K on the right stifle. However, they couldn't cover up the breeching iron that I used on all cows that went around from the top end of the 7 clear across both hind legs under the tail.

I says, "Slim, you've got four of my steers there."

"No," he says, "Them's Sam Applegate's. I'll get a rope and show you."

I says, "Slim I can see all I want from here. I know those critters." I rode up to the fence, stepped off on the platform on top and slid down into the corral and hooked an arm around one of the 2x6s.

Slim says, "I'll get a rope and show you you're wrong."

I says, "I'll kill the first man that touches a rope, take it or leave it."

I knew that Slim and Humpy Nesbit had guns on them somewhere, but not in sight. The other two cowpunchers both carried guns. So I told Si to cut out the steers. Si opened the gate, rode in with his carbine in one hand, and he cut out the four steers. I backed to the gate, kicked it shut, and backed on off to my horse while I was watching them. Meanwhile Si got off his horse and laid the carbine over the saddle on them while I got on my horse and we took our steers. We never did find part of Si and Dad's cattle, however.

THE RANCH ON MANNING CREEK ...

Having no love for the little 80 acres that I had rented down at Nampa, I wanted to get a ranch in the hills, back in the hills and away from that flat land. I had liked the looks of the country over at Durkee, Oregon fairly well, and made one trip up the Weiser River with Walt Tallboy and I liked that country as well. I wound up renting a ranch on Manning Creek out of Durkee, Oregon. It was a creek ranch, scattered out for a mile, and part of it was pretty steep, but it had a good small house on it with four rooms. It looked pretty good to us.

In the fall of '26 I gathered up all the cattle and my brother Si and I moved the cattle. It was a three-day trip from Willow Creek down to the feed lot near Caldwell where Dad had bought hay for the winter. We moved them without incident and wintered them there, but somebody there stole my pet cow horse, Satan. Never did see that horse again and I did plenty of looking.

Spring came and I hired Si Widener Lorraine's cousin, to help me move my stock over to Durkee, Oregon from the feedlot at Caldwell. Lorraine asked me to stop at Weiser and pick up her little saddle horse and a steer she had there as well. Si Widener and I moved them without incident to Weiser, stayed all night at the Randall ranch there, and picked up her horse and steer. Her two brothers, Chet and Edgar, agreed to help us as far out as Rock Creek. We made that without incident, except that Edgar's horse threw him, so I put my saddle on him and took most of the buck out of him for him. From there we moved on down to the ferry on the Snake River. The water was high.

We put a good load of steers on the ferry boat and started across. When halfway across, all the rest of the cattle jumped in the Snake River and started swimming after us. I never expected to see any of them again. We also had a carload of Dad's steers that he wanted me to feed out. We got across and unloaded and started back. We could see white heads bobbing in the waves. Every one of them, though, came out on an island in the middle of the river. We counted them. There we were, wondering how we would ever get that bunch of cattle off. The river ran swift against the north bank, the Idaho side. On the other side of the river was Oregon.

Down where it made a bend, a quarter of a mile below the island, a couple of gulches ran down to the river and sand bars and gravel were thrown out there. Pretty soon one of them, an old white faced cow I had called Queen, took off and the rest of them fed in

behind her. Down the river they went, white heads bobbing once in awhile. She came out on that sandbar, and we sat there and counted the works of them as they came out one at a time. We rode around, brought them back up to the ferry boat and they were only too glad to get on and take a ride after the mile swim down the river.

We drove them on down to a canyon that headed up the back side of Lookout Mountain. People said we couldn't make it, that the snow was too deep up above. The bottom of the canyon had been placered out so we put the cattle above us and at the first grass we could find we camped below them.

The next day we got up into the snow and we took turns with our saddle horses breaking across the huge drifts. In some places in the timber it was four feet deep. I had Dad's old Jersey steer. We put him in the lead, and he'd follow any horse track I broke through the snow. We finally got over the top of the mountain and down Manning Creek to the little ranch and had supper with my wife. At last the little lady and I were in good country, had our cattle there, and proceeded to set up housekeeping and enjoy life.

It was good cow country, but there also was a considerable number of cow thieves there as well, like there were down north of Payette and Weiser. So I had to do a lot of riding, keeping my eyes open and my mouth shut. In the meantime, Dad bought and traded for the whole top of Lookout Mountain. That gave us a lot of good summer range. Si moved over and rented another farm from Bob Shook, and they moved all of their cattle over and put them on Lookout Mountain.

A neighbor that lived down below a couple of creeks was a one-armed man. He had a hook for a hand on the other arm. He had a long, tall, red-headed wife who was a real cowhand, and about a dozen Holstein cows. Every spring those Holstein cows had twin Hereford calves. I don't know what they done with the Holstein calves, but they broke out every spring with a pair of nice Hereford calves on each one of those cows. I was sure in my own mind they were collecting them off of Walter Dorset who had a big ranch on a side creek down by Wetherby.

One morning the sun was just starting to come up and I was up on top of Lookout Mountain looking things over, and I ran into this man and his wife.

Immediately he said, "What are you doing up here this morning, Elmer?"

*Elmer and Lorraine at home on their ranch in the winter
of 1929. It must have been a warm day!*

"Oh," I says, "I'm on our own land, and wanted to see how the stock were doing. I could ask you the same question."

He didn't answer. Then he said, "You wouldn't shoot a man for stealing cows would you?"

I says, "Just try it and find out."

While running cattle at Durkee, Oregon, a man named Lee Bland had a big Holstein bull that was badly diseased. I don't remember now what the vet called it, but every cow that he bred lost its calf and they had to be sold. I had four cows that went this trip, and Chris Lee in Baker had thirty he had to sell. It was against the law to run any dairy bull on the range, only Hereford, Angus, or Shorthorn, and good bulls, were allowed on the range. This man persisted in doing it anyway.

One day Bob Shook and I ran onto this big bull, and I had Mom's little "Snooks" horse. He'd weigh about 850 to 900 pounds, and was totally inadequate to handle a 2000-pound bull. Bob was riding his old horse, Duffy, a swell rope horse, weighing about 1450. He had a big roping saddle on it, with double cinches, and I asked him to put a string on the bull.

Old Bob was afraid of Lee Bland and he said that Lee would shoot him. I asked him if I could borrow old Duffy and I'd wild-west him and do it myself. Nope, he wouldn't let me have Duffy either.

A short time later Jay Keefer and my brother and I were gathering cattle about three miles west of where we'd seen the old bull this date. They were up the canyon above me about a half mile and I was going across a sagebrush flat when I jumped this big old Holstein bull out of an arroyo. I got my rope down. I had a 76-foot rawhide made by Injun Sam at Payette, an awful good heavy rope. My little horse didn't look half as big as the bull, but I put the rope on him and he took off. Little Snooks buck jumped trying to hold him but he couldn't hold him at all. He headed on over this sloping sagebrush flat, down towards a spring where there was scattered quaking aspen. He just drug us along anywhere he wanted to go.

We got down there and I managed to run around a quakey, flipped the rope up about four feet, and jumped the rope with Snooks. Then I had him on the spring of that aspen. I pulled a six-gun, shot three times quick, waited a few minutes and shot three more to let Si and Jay Keefer know I was in trouble. Pretty soon they came down the canyon. Jay heeled the bull, and got him stretched out pretty good. I got my rope from around the quakey, back on the saddle horn, and stretched him good.

Si decided to operate. I gave him my knife, but the bull kicked it out of his hands and we never could find it in the leaves. I did have a little tiny fancy pen knife about an inch-and-a-half long in the vest pocket of my old buckskin vest that Croft had given me. It had tweezers and everything on it. The blade, I believe, was three-quarters of an inch long. So my brother Si had to do the honors with that tiny little blade.

When I was going down to Bill Hall's store and post office at Durkee, several people told me that Lee Bland was going to kill me for working over his bull. This went on for some time and I didn't see the lad, but finally one day I went in to get my mail and Lee Bland came in, so I called him.

I says, "Well, Lee, you've been going to shoot me in the back for a long time. How about doing it to my face? We don't want to mess up Bill's store and post office, so you go out the side door and I'll go out the front and we'll just see about this little deal."

He wouldn't go out. He wouldn't move. He stayed there until after I got on my horse and went home. At any rate we got rid of a bull that was a detriment to all the good cattle in the country. He sold him for bologna later on, and I heard he weighed only 1400 pounds.

Chapter 5

MOVING ON TO SALMON

HUNTING IN CANADA ...

There was a lot of small game up there on Manning Creek; pheasants, California quail, cottontail, and sage hens, but no big game at that time. I didn't like that about it. There was plenty of blue grouse on Lookout Mountain, though, and we fared pretty well. I'd shoot a mess of birds with the six-shooter every day or so. I had good neighbors and if I would help them, they would help me. Then I received a wire from Harry Snyder asking if I was a good Dutch oven cook. He offered $5 a day plus all expenses to go to Edmonton and gather up enough food and liquor for a two-month trip down the Peace River with a hunting party. I wired him back I'd lived out of a Dutch oven for a good many years in the hills, and thought I could handle it.

About this time the *American Rifleman* advertised $100 for a prize story contest. I won it with an account of our elk hunt on Babcock Creek when my partner, Bill Strong was killed. Mom and I bought a cow, a two-year-old heifer, and a calf with the money; milk stock. One neighbor, Van Stull, said he would take care of the irrigating for me and ride for my cattle if I wanted to make the trip to Canada with the Snyder party. Five dollars a day was big money in 1927, so I took him up on it.

I went down to Pendleton, across the Snake River, and up to Kingsgate where we entered Canada. For some reason or other, there were three Mounties there and they were going through all the men folks for weapons. Had them line up, slapped them under the arms and on the hips for guns. I never did know why.

I had a 4¾-inch .44 Special, fully loaded, under my belt in front with the loading gate out, and my shirttail over it of course. When I saw them searching everybody, thank God I had my pants inside my boot tops. I wiped the loading gate shut, sucked in my tummy and let the gun go down in my boot. They didn't search my boots, and I got on the train all right to Edmonton. Coincidentally I got a pretty good scratch on my shin when I was climbing the steps on the train.

Arriving at Edmonton, I was directed to see Elmo Essery, who ran a big clothing store. He was a delightful chap who helped me in every way possible. I found out then that the party consisted of Prentice N. Gray, who later started the *Records of North American Big Game,* and who had been in charge of feeding the Belgians during the war; Carrol Paul, a retired Navy commander; and George Bates, son of a wealthy manufacturer in Quebec.

Several letters with instructions from Harry

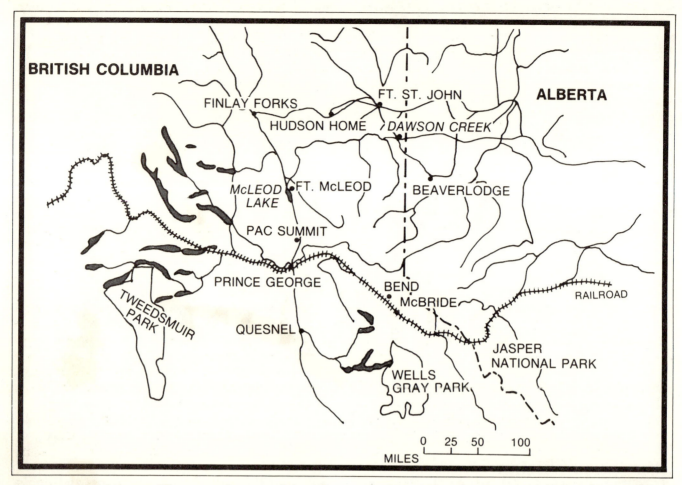

BRITISH COLUMBIA ALBERTA

FINLAY FORKS
FT. ST. JOHN
HUDSON HOME
DAWSON CREEK

FT. McLEOD
McLEOD LAKE
BEAVERLODGE

PAC SUMMIT

PRINCE GEORGE
BEND
McBRIDE
RAILROAD

TWEEDSMUIR PARK

QUESNEL

JASPER NATIONAL PARK

WELLS GRAY PARK

0 25 50 100
MILES

were waiting for me. He wanted me to buy all the good groceries in Edmonton where there was a better grade of groceries obtainable, and buy the coarse groceries and vegetables out at the little town twenty miles from Summit Lake where we were to take off in boats for the trip. We planned to go down the crooked Pac, Lake McLeod, Parsnip Rivers to Finlay Forks which forms the Peace River, and on down that to a few miles above Hudson Hope where it becomes impassable.

Harry also instructed me to get a couple of hundred dollars worth of liquor. He wanted a case of the best brandy he could get, and several cases of Grant's scotch, and a case of rum—the strongest I could get. Essery and I went in to the liquor store. I paid four bits, I believe it was, for the permit, and the clerk was writing down all the liquor I wanted.

Essery says, "This man is going on a hunting trip, taking this liquor for his party."

The clerk slammed the book shut, threw my half dollar back and says, "Very sorry, we're not allowed to sell to hunting parties at all."

We walked out of the liquor store and Essery said, "For once I should have kept my big mouth shut."

"Well," I says, "Harry is depending on me to get this liquor and get it I will if it is

possible. Who heads the Liquor Commission here in Alberta?" Essery says, "I know him well. I was taking my first degree in Masonry and he was in the lodge. He has an office up in the top of the Empson Building."

So we got a cab, took the elevator upstairs, and Elmo introduced me. I noticed he was a Mason right off and he also saw my pin. So I laid the cards on the table, and told him what I was up against.

"I can sell you all the liquor you want, but, I can't guarantee you taking it across the line as it's illegal to ship it from Alberta to British Columbia. When you cross the line you are liable."

He says, "If you want to take a chance on moving it some way I'll sell you all you want."

I told him I wanted some brandy.

"Well," he says, "I have twelve bottles here, Imperial Quarts, of the finest brandy on earth, I believe, 1852 is the date on it. I've had it at $7.50 a quart and it isn't selling, so I knocked it down to five."

I says, "I'll take it all."

He got all the liquor together, wrapped it up in burlap, and moved that down to the depot, along with all the fine groceries I'd bought. It was quite a job figuring out what

110

I'd need for two months and ten men. Essery saw us off along about ten at night as I remember it, with a man named Dewing that Prent Gray had sent in to help me. He was good help, a young lad, willing to work. We had no more than got out of Edmonton when the conductor came along, and I noticed he was a Mason, too, from his pin. He took one look at that corded liquor we had, burlapped and roped in front of the seat there and he says, "Boys, you're in trouble," and introduced himself. He told us what the score was.

"Now," he says, "I have a drawing room right through to Prince George, the little town where you should get off. You can have it for $3.75, right through, and I'd advise you to get that liquor in it."

I paid him. He got the Negro porter, and we moved into the drawing room right then. I told him, "This calls for a drink." I got a bottle of this fine old brandy and the porter brought some glasses.

The conductor says, "Give him a drink too."

I says, "Sure." So we each had a drink. It was amber-colored liquor, thick and syrupy. I don't think I've ever tasted any brandy as nice as that antique liquor.

The conductor says, "You're in trouble, boys, but I'll try and bail you out. Now, when we get to Jasper Park, we hold up there for about an hour. I'll go in and wire a friend of mine in code and see if I can't arrange things at the other end of the line at Prince George. You stay inside this drawing room. Don't go out of it."

Sure enough, he was gone for about an hour and, when the train finally pulled out for Prince George, he came back and said "Everything's arranged. Now the conductor and the fireman up there, they are Masons too. They're dumb, like the rest of us. In the morning when we get to Prince George, they're going to stop the locomotive in front of the station instead of pulling the passenger cars on up. When it stops, there will be an old Ford drive up right through the barbed-wire fence. This black man here will help you get your rifles, your bedrolls, and all this liquor in that old Ford. Say nothing. Do exactly as he tells you, follow his instructions, and you'll make it. You won't more than hit Prince George until the Mounties will spot you, and they'll try to find out your business. So don't go near wherever my friend puts you until you shake them."

The next day the engine stopped at the station while we were half a mile down the road it looked like to me. The old Ford drove up, the Negro helped us, and we piled everything into it. We took off on a dirt road off to one side of town, finally angled around in it, and came back. In the meantime we saw the Mounties running down the railroad track towards where we were loading the car, and we left them. We drove around in back of a hotel in the alley, got out, and he says, "Grab this liquor," and he took a load up some stairsteps to the second floor, unlocked a door, and says, "Put all this stuff, guns, everything, underneath the bed here, pull the counterpane down. Now you guys get out of here and stay out of here as long as those Mounties are following you. They'll be with you in short order. I'll leave it to you to get rid of them. Now, the hotel man here is a friend of ours. When you do get back, call him up for anything you need."

Sure enough we went and ordered a meal and had no more than sat down to it and here come the two Mounties. We asked them to have dinner with us, which they did. Then we started moving around to see the town. They were very curious, wanting to know what we were going to do.

"Oh," we told them, "we are looking the country over; might go on a hunting trip."

Finally we got into a saloon. We had some 12% beer, stout, a little of everything, so I ordered drinks all around, then Dewing would order drinks. Finally I knew we had to shake them some way or other. Neither of them seemed inclined to leave us alone at all. Finally I told them, "I've got to go to the little boy's room." Dewing says, "I have to go, too." I waved at the bartender for another round, he brought it, and we took off.

I says, "Dewing, let's find a hole out of the back end of this place somewhere." We found a hallway leading to a back door, and left the Mounties there with four drinks.

When we got back to the hotel, I called the manager. I told him I'd like to have a truck that would go out the twenty miles to Summit Lake at about four in the morning, and I says, "If it's at all possible I'd like to have $200 worth of rough groceries, spuds, onions, stuff of that sort."

"I think we can arrange it."

I says, "I'd like to have it here at four in the morning, and also a hole in the center of the stuff where I can cache some material we have here in the room."

He said, "It will all be arranged."

At three in the morning he came in with a pot of coffee, a bottle of scotch, and the grocer's bill, which I paid. At four o'clock the truck drove up. We threw the liquor in the center, rolled sacks of spuds on it, and took off for Summit Lake.

The man at Summit Lake, Slim Cowart, says, "Well, if they come out here looking for you, they'll have to go back to town and get a search warrant. We'll throw all this liquor in the cellar."

But nobody came after us. If they had, we would have sunk the liquor in the lake with a cork on a cord.

We got the boats ready, tried them out, and a couple of days later the party arrived. Prent Gray was to come in later and join us at Hudson Hope. Snyder, Carrol Paul, George Bates and I were to run the river. They gave me a 16-foot boat with a 3-horse Evinrude. Slim Cowart had a bigger boat, with an 8-horse Johnson on it.

From Summit Lake we took the Crooked River and it was really crooked. Sometimes I could hear Slim's motor within a quarter of a mile and yet I had to make a three or four-mile circle to get back to where he had been when I heard him. Beavers were in abundance. Every few hundred yards it seemed like at times we had to cut a hole through a beaver dam to drag the boat across. Slim would cut a hole and drag the big boat through, and by the time we got there the beavers would have it sealed up again.

We finally made it out of Crooked River into the Pac. We traveled down that until we got to Lake McLeod and old Fort McLeod. After crossing the lake, and stopping at the Hudson Bay post, we faced the Parsnip River from there on down to Finlay Forks, which forms the Peace River.

While crossing the lake, Slim Cowart says, "Elmer, you and I have got to stay sober." He broke out two cans of Carnation cream, opened them, and says, "Drink it. You've got to get your stomach coated so you can handle that Hudson Bay rum." Sure enough, when we got to the boat landing Zachary, the Hudson Bay factor, came down, invited us all up, and gave us an awful drink of Hudson Bay rum. We managed to get the party back on the boats and take off. George Bates and I in one, and the other three in the big boat.

We came to a division in the river. I didn't know which way to go, and one side looked like it carried more water than the other, so we took it.

It proved wrong.

A mile below, it made a sharp bend. A big tree had fallen over and was lying flush with the top of the water almost across the river. In spite of speeding up the little motor for all it was worth and steering for the bank, I still hit it. Just as I hit it, the bow was scooting up a sandbar. George Bates was a young athlete, 21 years old, and very strong and active. He had a-hold of the rope. I told him to hit it a-running, if he could. Just as the motor, the tail-end, and I went under, George landed on the bank and started pulling. I crawled out with him, hauled her out, bailed out the boat, and took off again. Finally we found Cowart and the rest of the party waiting for us where the river division came back together. They told us we'd certainly taken the wrong channel but had no way of knowing.

Arriving at Finlay Forks, we ran into two old prospectors that had started to Alaska in the gold rush. They had gotten that far and decided to stay there. They trapped for a living and mined a little. Neither of them had ever seen an airplane. This was about the time that Lindberg flew the Atlantic.

Just below Finlay Forks was Parle Paux Rapids. We floated down to the rapids, then put lines on each end of the boat, and long poles to hold them out just from the edge, and lined the rapids rather than try to run them. It was as well, as the swells were 15-feet high, and I think would have sunk us. From there we ran on down to some 12 miles above Hudson Hope, where Jim Ross met us with the wagons to transport the stuff on down to Hudson Hope. As the canyon narrowed down to the Hope, it was impassable for any boat that goes. At Hudson Hope, Prentice Gray joined us, along with the Calliou brothers—Jim, Pete, and Joe. The Callious were full-blood Cree Indians, and wonderful boys to be out with. We boated everything across the Peace River from the north to the south side, and started out with 32 head of horses, mostly packs except for a saddle horse for each of us.

We soon found we were overloaded, and Prent Gray and I gave up our saddle horses to pack with. We packed our rifles and hiked 20 miles a day, after which I cooked for the ten people in the crew.

We had hired another man, at Hudson Hope named McFarland. It took us ten days from the Hope, steady travel, to get back to the mountains. Prent Gray and I spent most of the time behind the whole pack string, pulling horses out of bog holes and repacking them. For a banker and man of his type, he was a revelation to me. He was a real man, and it didn't make no difference how tough the going got, he always had a grin.

On the tenth day we were going through some open timber when the pack string all stopped suddenly. Prent and I worked around to the side to see what was the matter, and there was two big bull moose standing exactly like a team of horses. George Bates and Carroll Paul fell off their horses, finally got their rifles, and started shooting.

They each emptied their guns into the chests of those bulls. Prent Gray told me, "Elmer, just to be sure," and he whipped his Springfield off his back and put 180-grains in the chest of each of them. I don't think that Paul or Bates ever knew that Gray shot, they were so busy pumping lead into the bulls. They'd take a shot and miss, and suddenly those two bulls whirled just like a team of horses and took off, with all that lead in their chest. We followed, and they only went about 50 yards, turned around a patch of timber, and there they lay side-by-side in death just as they had been in life.

I had to remove the capes and heads from both of them, so we camped there that night. McFarland took over the cooking while I worked at getting out all the meat we could handle, and taking care of the heads and salting the capes.

Next day's travel put us back in the mountains and some beautiful high meadows. We camped at one out in the open. I wanted to move into some timber but I was overruled. During the night the wind came up and flattened all our tents. Everybody was wishing we were in the timber.

There was considerable grizzly diggings all over the place, and the boys were out early the next morning looking for a grizzly. That was wild, primitive country south of the Peace River in 1927. We found one little group of settlers. They had some cattle, corrals, garden patches, and they had a grizzly skull on the top of every fence post. Jim Ross also took us to another farm where a trapper friend of his lived who had married a Cree Indian squaw. I don't remember just how many children they had, but there was quite a bunch of them. They were all neat and clean. They wore nice, neat, beaded moccasins, and were very polite. Although her husband was gone, she invited us all to have dinner with her. I never ate a nicer meal, or one better put up than that Cree lady had for us.

Aside from the moose, we saw no game south of the Peace River until we hit the mountains. Then grizzly sign was quite prevalent, also caribou and moose tracks. The first morning in the high country, as I was preparing breakfast, a caribou bull came right into camp. I woke Bates up. He managed to stick his .300 Magnum out of the tent while he was in his pajamas and shoot this bull. So we had plenty of fresh meat.

I had two No. 14 Dutch ovens and one shallow biscuit oven. Lorraine had taught me to make applesauce cakes, and also baking-powder biscuits. I could turn out a pretty pan of biscuits with that little Dutch oven. I'd simply mix up the dough, spoon it into the Dutch oven, first getting the lid hot, the Dutch oven hot until the grease would smoke, and put a bed of coals on top of the lid. About five minutes and they came out beautiful brown. We'd picked up some more wet groceries, as the spuds didn't amount to much up there in Canada. They were little knotty devils, but they grew some of the biggest parsnips, carrots, and rutabagas I ever saw. Some of the rutabagas wouldn't even go in a water bucket. I had to put them on a log and chop them with an axe. But the party seemed to want some stews, which we gave them in the big Dutch oven. However, when we got the caribou, even though he hadn't had time to age very much, I split his rump, put it in the Dutch ovens and just let it simmer all day until it fell off the bone, made brown gravy, boiled and mashed a batch of spuds, and poured a round of Grant's scotch at the table with the dinner. They seemed well pleased. We had also packed a lot of condiments, pickles, canned butter and preserves along, so between the roast caribou, mashed potatoes, brown gravy, and hot biscuits, they did all right.

Just before leaving on that trip at Durkee, Oregon I'd packed a big pail of slop to feed the hogs. I had to stand up on one board and reach over the top of it and pour it in the trough. It was muddy, my boot slipped and my left side came down on a brace that ran up about three inches across the top and broke two ribs on the left side. I guess Snyder must have noticed me a-wincing every now and then when I'd lift things on the trip, so finally he had to find out what was the matter. I told him I had a couple of broken ribs. He managed to get out his medical kit, and tape me up good and tight on that side. From then on I felt a lot better and worked better.

One day George Bates took off on his own and proceeded to get lost. Slim Cowart and I picked up his trail. We trailed him two nights and three days. We'd shoot and he'd answer. By the time we got to his old campfire he was gone again. Slim was mad enough to kill him, and I wasn't in a much better humor. Bates got into camp ahead of us, however, and informed all and sundry that we were lost instead of him. I understand today he is a great big-game hunter. He's hunted Africa considerable and got a 127-pound elephant and has

British Columbia was a paradise for game in 1927, and yielded Elmer's first caribou, shot with a .300 Hoffman Magnum rifle.

George Bates, Harry Snyder, and Carroll Paul at a remote British Columbia spike camp after a successful sheep hunt. Snyder's sheep was well up in the record book.

reformed, but at that time he was the hardest case I ever tried to guide. He knew it all, he wouldn't listen to anything you told him, and we had a terrible time with him.

Harry asked me to scout the head of the valley for moose and sheep. We got a skim of snow that night, so I took my rifle and legged it for about 12 miles back up the river and I didn't find any fresh sheep sign, but I saw one enormous moose. He came for me grunting until he was about 50 yards away, then I worked around to give him my wind. Then his hair all fell back down where it belonged and he took off. He was quite belligerent looking. I believe he would have gone 60 inches. He was a big moose.

During the day, to show how fast a grizzly is, I was trailing a grizzly through some shin-tangle along the base of a big mountain. The snow was melting. I knew I didn't have very much snow left. But what I came onto was a dead caribou with the rump, hams and loin pretty well eaten and a little caribou calf still hanging around. The tracks showed the grizzly had sneaked up in one of those little strips of scrub fir that came down on each side of snow slides in the mountains. From there the caribou cow and her calf had been bedded out about forty yards, I'd say, in the brush.

The grizzly's rush had carried him over there and he had shattered her rump bones in one blow, eaten his fill and taken off. Climbing to a higher knoll I saw his tracks two miles away in the snow where he was going over another hill. It's unbelievable the speed of a grizzly. Within the first 50 yards they'll catch the fastest horse that ever lived.

We made a semi-permanent camp for a few days while Jim Ross and Slim Cowart, and Slim's big old husky dog he also called Slim took off on a scouting trip for sheep. All they carried with them was a 9 mm Luger and a little rough grub. Jim Ross shot a caribou for meat. The dog packed about 30 pounds every day. They folded it up in canvas, put it across his shoulders, and they had a long strip of lamp wick that went around the front of his chest, crossed over the top of his back, down under his belly and back across again. That pack dog was a wonder. If he got hung up in some brush he'd howl until we came and got him out, but he'd carry that pack all day. They located sheep on Fish Creek, a branch of the Smokey, which in turn, I understand, runs into the Athabasca River. I don't believe those sheep had ever been hunted. They certainly showed no fear of man whatever, and would just stand and look at you.

From the time we got to the mountains, Snyder wanted me to start guiding them. He'd seen me work over the two moose capes and heads and he says, "From now on, you're through cooking." McFarland took over the job. While I could make good Dutch oven biscuits, I didn't have any luck with light bread. It would get so cold at night the stuff wouldn't raise even though I'd set it up. McFarland, however, was an old trapper, knew all the ropes and he'd take his batch of dough and put it in his sleeping bag with him nights, keeping it warm so it would raise. And he managed to make as nice a loaf of bread as you could wish for in the big Dutch ovens. So I turned the job of cooking over to him and was damn glad of it.

This was beautiful mountain country. High slide rock peaks, scrub fir growing up in little strips on them where the snow slides had cleaned them out. Immense spruce and fir thickets lower down on the slopes, interspersed with beautiful mountain meadows and little lakes, caribou sign everywhere, with some moose, wolf tracks and grizzly tracks. We were in a hunter's heaven.

LOST AGAIN . . .

While hunting one day we climbed a long, sloping tundra ridge overlooking a huge basin. It had rained during the night and heavy fog was hanging here and there in the different basins. I looked down in the basin and saw a huge grizzly waddling down on the other side of the draw at the bottom. Just then the fog closed in tight. The wind was right directly behind us, so I jumped and turned and went back over the ridge in a hard run to get down on the off side so that the wind wouldn't carry our scent to the big bear. Bates followed me on a run.

He said, "What are you doing this for?"

I says, "I saw a big grizzly just across the draw a-walking down that side, snooping around for feeding. We can get him. We've got to make a half-mile circle around here and come in from the other side and work down there. It's all open country and we'll have no trouble getting him."

Bates says, "I think you seen a porcupine."

I says, "Porcupine, hell! Man, I know a grizzly and I know porcupine."

"Well," he says, "I don't believe you. I'm going right down the draw."

I says, "O.K. You'll save me a big job of skinning."

So over the hill he went, and I followed him, much to my disgust. We got down just across the steep gulch from where I'd seen the bear, the fog so thick you could cut it with a knife. I caught hold of him and motioned him to set down. We did and about that time the wind blew around in behind us. Across the gulch I heard the big bear blow at us three

times. I heard that long, drawn "Whewsh-sh-sh-sh" and I knew instantly what it was. Then rocks started rolling and we could hear the old boy going up over the next ridge.

Bates says, "What was that, Elmer?"

I says, "That's your porcupine." We went across over there and looked at the big tracks, about 15 inches long, and five or six inches wide on the front paws. I was thoroughly disgusted with Mr. Bates. He wouldn't listen to me, but there was nothing I could do about it. I was delegated to guide him. I was working for Harry Snyder or I would have quit as far as Bates was concerned right then.

We worked on down the gulch and around through some scattered timber, probably three miles. I heard a caribou bark at us in some dense timber. A bull, I'm sure, but we never did get to see him. We worked on down the river, where this creek ran into a larger stream. Finally it was getting along in the afternoon, and I says, "George, we've got to cut back to our left and go to camp."

He says, "Where do you think camp is?"

I says, "Back here to the left. We made a big circle, and we've got to climb this timbered ridge here to our left and then we'll hit the open timber country and back up to camp."

Bates wouldn't believe me. He says, "Camp is on down this creek."

I says, "If you follow that down there, you'll finally get to the Athabasca River."

We argued. Finally I said, "Bates, I'm a poor man. You're a rich one. You've got a $200 magnum rifle and I have one, the Hoffman .300 Magnum. I'll bet you my rifle against yours I'm right." I says, "Put up or shut up."

He wouldn't bet.

I says, "Well, you can go on down Fish Creek here into the Smokey, and into the Athabasca if you want. As for me I'm going into camp. I've got a good eiderdown robe up there and something to eat."

I took off up the hill. I didn't look around, but when I turned to go around trees I could see him out of the corner of my eye, standing down there in the flat, undecided. I picked up speed, I was going just as fast as I could up the hill, to make him think I was going to run off and leave him. Just as I topped the hill, I saw him break into a run and follow me. We got through the timber, worked up the creek a couple of miles and finally we came in sight of camp.

Bates says, "I wonder who that is camped there. I thought this was virgin country."

115

"Oh," I says, "That must be some dudes pulled in while we were making the circle." We came on up to the camp. Harry Snyder was washing some socks in the creek. When we was 30 or 40 yards away, Bates says, "Why that looks like Harry Snyder."

Harry heard him. He says, "What's the matter, George? Are you lost again? You better learn to let Elmer do the figuring where camp is."

We had a great hunt on this trip. It was virgin country and I doubt if some of the game had ever seen a man. The sheep were quite tame. I remember the last three we got we took Bates and Snyder and Carrol Paul up to the top of the ridge. Prent Gray had had to get out and Slim Cowart had taken him and left. He'd already killed his sheep, including a couple on my license. We rode to one side of the ridge where Cowart had spotted the sheep the day before, crawled up on our hands and knees and peeked over. There were three fine rams bedded about 150 yards below us. I gave the skipper the first shot. He killed his, and as he jumped up, Harry Snyder, who was a very fine off-hand game shot, dropped his ram back in its bed. The third ram took off on a hard run. It went off 175 yards and whirled around. Bates sat down, made a good shot, and killed him with his .300 magnum.

Bates says, "How far is it, Elmer?"

I says, "About 175 to 200 maximum."

He says, "It's 600 yards."

I paced it, and it was just 175.

One day we took the saddle horses and explored another batch of country. I wanted to get a caribou and a goat on the trip. I'd already got a good 9½-inch billy goat, a big fellow that would weigh about 450. We were going to have lunch under a big spruce tree at the edge of Muskeg Flat. I built a little fire. Bates says, "Nobody's ever camped here. You can bet nobody was ever here before." When I scratched the fir needles away from under the big tree, there was a bunch of chopped sticks all charred. I says, "Somebody camped here. It might have been years ago, but they were here at one time."

Just as I was fixing up a lunch from the grub we had in the saddle bags, I looked out on the flat and there was an enormous caribou. I put the glasses on him. He had double shovels and great top formation. Bates had killed five caribou, and the rest of the guys had all killed theirs, so Harry Snyder, says, "Well, Elmer, that's your caribou." I says, "Fine." I laid down in the sling with my Hoffman .300 magnum, my hand loads of 61 grains of 15½ Dupont and some nine-degree

boattails. I'd filed off the point until the lead showed and then drove a 3/32nd-inch hole back in them. I held right at the top of his withers and was just squeezing the trigger when Bates says, "Don't shoot. I want to." So I turned the safety over. I was thoroughly disgusted with the lad. So was Harry Snyder. So Bates took Pete Calliou and made a circle to get a shot at the caribou, but the caribou was too wise for them and they never did get a shot. When they came back, Harry says, "Bates, you should have let Elmer have that caribou. He'd have killed him."

Finally we had about all the heads the party wanted. We had four grizzlies and we decided to head out towards the railroad. The first landmarks of consequence would be Mount Ida and the Three Sisters. We camped one night in sight of them. The next morning, after breakfast, I was munching on a sheep sandwich that I'd made from one of my baking powder biscuits and a slab of sheep loin. I happened to look across the valley. About two miles away I saw an old sow grizzly and a three-year old and a pair of yearlings cut across one of the snow slides and into the shin-tangle. So I hollered at Harry Snyder. I says, "Harry, there's four of Bate's porcupines over there." Harry took a look, grabbed his glasses, took another look. "My God," he says, "They're grizzlies."

Jim Ross and the Indians grabbed the horses, and everybody saddled up as quick as they could. Harry says, "Elmer, you guide Bates and, Pete," he says, "you guide the skipper and Jim Ross you guide me." The wind was blowing down the valley, so we rode a quarter of a mile down below them, where I'd seen the bear last, and then we worked up and tied the horses. We spread out up an open side where the snow had taken the timber off about 200 yards apart and started working up. Finally I poked my nose out of a batch of that scrub shin-tangle, that fir timber that grows stunted up there in the north, and here was the old sow a-digging. The three-year-old was up above her and the two yearlings were playing around. So I motioned for Bates to come on. I told him to set down. The wind was blowing awful hard and the bears were about 100 yards above us. I didn't like that part of it, but it was all we could do. So I says, "Set down, and get your elbows on your knees, take your time and hit her right through the shoulders."

Well she turned her rump to us about that time, a-quartering away. Bates insisted on kneeling. He was swaying back and forth in the wind. When he shot he hit the old sow in

116

the hip and out through the guts. Instantly the bears were all in motion.

Harry Snyder and Jim Ross had worked up to about 50 to 75 yards below us by this time and I saw Harry shoot the three-year-old right back of the shoulder (I could see the hair fly) with his .300 magnum and some 172-grain Western Tool and Copper bullets that I'd handloaded for him. The bear swung his head, bit at the entrance, and took off for the brush. I shot in front of them into the slide rock trying to turn them back, but I couldn't. They went right over the smoke from the rocks. In the meantime, the old sow got up on her hind legs a-bawling. Some of her entrails were out. She grabbed a piece six feet long, bit it off, shook it, and I says, "Bust her again, George." So he shot her again and she came rolling down the hill towards us. She got up again on three legs, her right hip seemed to be broken.

I says, "Bust her again, Bates."

He says, "I don't want any more holes in her hide."

I says, "Bust her again."

About that time Jim Ross hollered up the hill, he says, "Bates, shoot that bear or Harry and I are both going to shoot it."

So Bates shot again, and she went down that time. In the meantime the three-year-old and two cubs had almost run over Pete Calliou and the skipper. Carrol Paul always wore kid gloves on his hands and in the excitement of the bear coming at him, he fired his Springfield off in the air at first, then he threw in another shell and the three-year-old went up on his hind feet, but he missed him. He must have been excited. At any rate he didn't get any bear. Jim Ross and Harry Snyder came up the hill and Jim says, "You ought to shoot that bear again." Well he didn't want a hole in the hide.

Jim says, "I'll put one in it if you don't," so he shot the bear again, and finished her. We proceeded to skin the bear. I offered to trail up the three-year-old for Harry and get him, but Harry had a lot of faith in the Indians in those days, so he delegated Pete Calliou to do the job. I think Pete only trailed the bear out of our sight and sat down and let him go. I don't think Pete wanted any wounded grizzly.

At any rate, I told Harry I would still like to get a caribou before the trip was over, so he says, "You go ahead and hunt this afternoon, Elmer, and we'll stay in that same camp tonight."

I made a circle over into another valley and went through some heavy timber. I had just come to a big log. It must have been 3½ feet high, maybe four. I put my left hand on it to vault over it. I got up in the air and a bunch of hair unraveled itself over on the other side of the log. I know my hat must have been standing up on the end of my hair, but somehow or other I came back on my side of the log. Instead of a grizzly, which was all I could think of, out went a little cow caribou. She ran off 50 yards, reared up on her hind feet and whistled at me, went a little farther and reared up and whistled again. I worked from there on over into another wet meadow and found a little bunch of caribou with one nice bull. No record, nothing like the big fellow I'd seen on the flat before that Bates wanted, but a good head and one good shovel, so I decided to take him. I crawled far out in the wet meadow until I was soaking wet and was within 200 yards of the rutting caribou. When my bull came broadside I thumped him in the heart. He waltzed around, backed up a ways, finally reared up, and turned over. A young bull ran up and smelled of him, then he took off after the cows. I got up then and walked over, and the whole herd came up within 20 yards and formed a half-circle around me. They'd never seen a man, no doubt, and didn't know what I was. So I skinned out the head. The bull had been in a fight and his hide was punched full of holes, his entrails showed in places and he was a stinking mess, not fit for food. So I took the head and cape and packed it into camp that night.

The next day we packed up and went past Mount Ida and the Three Sisters. We came to a lake. There the Indians couldn't find tracks nowhere except Cowart and Prent Gray and their horses went into the lake. The Indians finally sat down like a bunch of whipped dogs. I went and cut a pole. I had a hunch they'd gone across the lake. Couldn't tell how deep it was, so I got this pole and started probing in front of me and I waded clear across only up to my waist. There I found the tracks where Slim and Prent Gray had come out. So we crossed with no trouble whatever, it was good hard bottom, went on past Mount Ida and the Three Sisters, and we came out at Bend on the C.N.R. and entrained for Edmonton. At Edmonton, Harry Snyder ordered a private dining room and a big dinner for the bunch of us. We took Jim Ross and the Indians with us there, and left the horses at the settlement in Bend to be picked up to go back to Hudson Hope. Harry gave us a fine dinner, gave me quite a send-off for my good hand-loaded ammunition and my cooking, and for taking care of all the trophies. Gave McFarland quite an ovation for his good light

Elmer Keith's first grizzly proved to be a hairy proposition in more ways than one, being first wounded at long range with a .300 Magnum, and then finished at 20 feet.

A hunt in the early 30s ended with this fine pronghorn for Keith. Julius Maelzer holds Elmer's rifle, a .280 Dubiel.

bread that he would make, and taking it to bed with him so that it would raise. I remember when they finally brought the finger bowls around after we'd had all the Grant's scotch and ginger ale we wanted, and a good feed, Jim Calliou, one of the Indians, he didn't know procedures so he picked up the bowl to drink it. Harry Snyder put his hand on his wrist, pressed it down, dabbled his fingers in the bowl and showed him how to wipe them on a napkin. The Indians had quite a time.

I remember one time on the trip Bates was still wanting a bigger moose. He and I were hunting a series of low ridges and little valleys with lakes in them. Just as we came up on one ridge I spotted the flash of the sun on the palms of a bull about a quarter-of-a-mile away over in the next valley, and we started up the moose trail that led over to it. About halfway up the moose trail I saw a nice yearling bull's horns a-coming not 50 yards away. I grabbed Bates by the sleeve and jumped over a big log and crawled back under it and motioned for him to do the same. The bull went right over us with one palm of his horns sticking out over us. He went on out to the lake as the wind was coming from the left and he evidently never caught our scent at all. He headed out into the lake. Bates wanted movies

of him, so I took his movie camera, and had him set it up. When the moose's head would go down into the water, I'd sneak up. I finally got within 30 yards of him, right at the edge of the lake, and I turned on the movie camera. Instantly his head came up and how the water did fly while he took off!

At the start of the trip, after we had lined past the Parle Paux Rapids, Harry decided to hunt for Stone sheep on the north side. The Stonies began north of the Peace River; none of them south, and no bighorn closer than about ten days south from the Peace River. The sheep on the north side of the Peace River are very dark, then they grade into Fannins, a grey sheep, then into spotted ones, and then the pure white Dall up around the Laird.

Harry decided that he, the skipper, and I would make a climb to the tops of the peaks on the north side of the river and determine if there were any Stone sheep there. They loaded me down with food for two days, plus cameras, and ammunition. The skipper had a half-gallon canteen full of cold water which he hung on my pack board. We made the climb all right, but halfway up the mountain I managed to get out of their sight, take a good drink out of the canteen, and poured it all out. I had load enough without packing water in a country that was full of little springs. Soon the skipper caught up with me, grabbed the canteen to take a drink, and shook it. He was very irate. I told him I wasn't going to pack water uphill for him. I says, "We only got to go over in the next draw, there's a nice little creek there and you can get all you want to drink."

We scouted the country thoroughly, but all the sheep tracks I could find were evidently made in the spring. They'd dried in the hard mud all summer, nothing fresh whatever, so we decided to go down. There was a steep slope behind the sliderock for half a mile, then a regular meadow on the steep slope with skunk cabbage. I told them I'd go down into the big basin of spruce and fir timber down below, make camp, and have supper ready by the time they got down. I picked out an old spike topped tree, told them I'd be close to that. So I lit out. They gave me their rifles. That and the pack together, I had a rifle in each hand and a load on the pack board. I made it down to the timber, found a good dry log with plenty of squaw wood, and I also ran into four little fool hens. So I took my six-gun and shot them where their neck joins the body, dressed them and washed them at a little creek. I spitted them on sticks, got a good fire going with a good bed of coals. I had the little grouse roasting to a turn by the time Carrol Paul and Harry Snyder caught up with me. So I broke out the rest of the food and we had lunch. Each of them wanted to know if I'd shot his rifle. I told them "No." I didn't tell them I had a six-gun under my shirt. I just let them guess at it. But anyway they enjoyed the grouse dinner. We slept under a spruce tree that night on coats and the next day made it back down to the river and the boat, which we ran on down in the canyon some 12 miles above Hudson Hope where the river becomes impassable, and from there on to the Hope we went around in wagons that Harry had Jim Ross bring up for the occasion.

We saw a wealth of Canadian game on that trip. It was one of the most memorable of my lifetime. It also proved to me that .30 caliber rifles were not the proper thing for grizzly or for big moose. I feel sure if Snyder had delegated me to trail up the grizzly he hit behind the shoulder, I would have got him. But I'm also quite sure the Indian, Pete Calliou, hadn't lost any wounded grizzly. I carried a .300 Hoffman Magnum Mauser on this trip, the last rifle made by the Hoffman Arms Company, and John Dubiel and Eric Johnson told me that all the crew had quit, but that they were going to stay on the job until my rifle was finished and shipped, which they did. It was for the old abrupt shoulder .300 magnum case that Holland & Holland called a Super .30. Later on, Western Cartridge Company revamped the case, and gave it a long sloping shoulder which became the .300 Holland & Holland. The old cartridge that I used in those days was called the Super 30, had an abrupt shoulder and was not so different in shape from the .30 Newton.

BACK HOME AGAIN . . .

After sleeping on the ground for two months in the wilds of British Columbia, it was good to get back to our little rented ranch on Manning Creek and my wife. She and Van Stull had done a good job. The crops were all in order, ready to put up. The rye crop on the mountain above the place had done well also. Van and I managed to bind the rye, and stack it just 440 yards from the kitchen door on the side of the mountain. The hay we put up in the bottom, and the second crop filled the hay loft in the barn.

For some reason our milk cow suddenly became dry. We'd see her in the day, and it looked like her udder was full of milk. But when we'd got to milk her at night, she didn't have a thing left. I finally discovered what was going on. We had some half-grown pigs and I caught the little devils. When the cow came in from the pasture, her tits all strutted with milk, those pigs would each get a tit and they would milk her dry. I had to corral the little devils.

By this time Lorraine and I were expecting a youngster. When she was asleep at night I could feel the baby's head up under her rib cage, and being an old cowpoke that had worked with a lot of stock, I knew something was wrong. The baby was turned wrong. So I took her down to her folks at Weiser between two and three weeks before we expected the baby. The doctor was named Waterhouse, an old friend of the family, so I hired him to take care of her. Finally, a neighbor rode up, told me that Mom was sick, and I got in the Ford Model T we had and bailed out for Weiser. I got down there ahead of the party all right. I'd told the doctor when I took Lorraine down that the baby was turned wrong and I wanted him to see what could be done about it.

"Oh," he says, "they turn every day."

"Well," I says "this one don't. I wish you'd take care of her."

However, he done nothing, as far as I could

Running a winter trapline occasionally got exciting for Keith. This Montana bobcat slapped the hat off his head just after this picture was taken in 1923.

It isn't all work on a ranch. There are always a few minutes for the youngsters, and here Lorraine Keith plays with Druzilla and Ted on the porch of the ranch.

learn from Mr. Randall. We had a breach birth with instruments that nearly killed the little lady, and the baby had the cord around its neck three times and just gasped a couple of times.

Lorraine said, "Elmer, is it all for nothing?"

That about took the heart out of me. She was a fine nine-pound girl, and it was one of the saddest blows of our life. Mother came up from Nampa, and we buried the little baby in the Weiser cemetery.

As fall came on I gathered the cattle and put them down in the pasture to clean up. I had a carload of Dad's steers, besides my own to feed-out that winter. I fed them on second-crop alfalfa out of the barn in the corral of a night. Then I moved them up on the mountain to the rye stack and threw a bunch of rye bundles over the fence and let them eat the heads off. Then I'd move the beef back down to the corrals, put the stockers up on the hill and let them clean up after the beef cattle.

In the morning I'd move the beef back up the hill for more rye heads and the stock cattle would clean up what was left of the second-crop alfalfa in the corrals. In this way I produced some fat steers. Several of Dad's steers were five-year-olds, and several of mine were fours, coming five. I finally sold them from my own corral at $10.80 a hundred weight. That was big money in those days. I put one cowpuncher in front, one behind, and

one on each side, and we never let them break a walk from Manning Creek down to the shipping pens at Durkee, Oregon.

One of Dad's steers was half Angus and half whiteface, a big black fellow. He was so fat his rear end just shook and wobbled as he walked. A bunch of the boys started betting on the size of this big black steer. They'd bid up thirteen-fourteen hundred, and finally agreed that whoever lost had to buy a case of "Sierra Tonic" from Bill Hall's store, because that was the only available liquor at that time, it being prohibition days. It was bitter stuff, but it was a fairly good wine underneath the bitters. When it came to my bid I bid 1700 on him. My brother, on the strength of it, went to 1550. When we put him on the scales he weighed 1710. I heard they shipped him to Portland, and from there to Alaska where they wanted big steaks.

I put out a long trap line for coyote, badger, bobcat, skunks, weasels, anything I could catch. It added up to a little more bacon and beans for the family. Lorraine and I both wanted a ranch of our own and the next spring we bought one from a Mr. Hyman, another creek over from Manning Creek. It was 160 acres and had very little water, mostly spring runoff, but it was good deep soil and I figured I could irrigate it from the runoff and a big spring that we had at the head of the field. In addition, there were 640 acres of dry land which I homesteaded and Van Stull helped me fence. That was a chore. We built many rock corners, and piled thousands of pounds of rock on the wire down in the bottom of gulches to hold it down, but we got the job done. Van and I drove up the wagon road, if it could be called a road, to the top of Lookout Mountain, cut down fir timbers, put them on the front axle, and dragged them back down to the ranch to build a big Mormon hay derrick. There was nothing there to hay with. I had a Jackson fork to fork it. I made boats, just rolled the hay on, skidded it into the stack yard, then with the Jackson fork put it up. I managed to get up a good hay crop and enough water to bring a good second crop up enough for a good pasture. I also had 40 acres of rye planted on the dry land. That did well.

Lorraine raised turkeys. She had a whole flock of them. She'd hatch the eggs under chicken hens, and then put the old turkey hen with them and let them run. The coyotes were pretty thick and they got onto it. There were several old three-legged coyotes that were awful tough. You couldn't trap them, and they were hard to get a shot at. Our house was on a slope with some big poplars for shade, and down the hill was the barn. The whole bottom half of the barn was stone and came up level with the hill at the top. The hay mow was just level with the ground there at the top of the barn and sloped down from the house.

We moved our bed out in the hay mow, cut a loophole through the barn facing the rye patch a quarter of a mile away, and laid the .300 magnum through this porthole. Every morning just before daylight I'd wake up, listening to the turkeys squawking and coming off the roost. They'd fly down in the meadow and then hike over to the 40 acres of rye and start feeding. It wouldn't be long until I'd hear them hollering over there, look through the scope and see a coyote would have one of them down. I'd center the coyote and kill him. I finally broke up the coyotes eating up our turkeys. We raised quite a crop of them, and went in debt for the little ranch.

I just signed a note for it. In those days they took a man at his word. If his word was no good, he was no good, and I had a clean record behind me. We turned the beef that I had raised into cash, along with the turkeys Lorraine raised, and we made our living from my trapline in the winter.

I also broke out a few saddle broncs for the neighbors to help out on the exchequer. Lorraine wanted to teach school to help out, but I was against it. She persisted, so I got her the

local school. However, she had to ride about three miles on a saddle horse, teach school all day, and come home. I was busy running a long coyote line, breaking horses, and feeding the stock, so I had little time around the house. Finally she got tired after one semester, said I wouldn't take care of the house and cook so she was going to quit school, which tickled me.

Rattlesnakes were very prevalent on this place and after we had sold out and left the country, we heard they found a den about a half mile from the house under a big cliff on the mountain, and took 130 snakes out of it. At any rate, Mom and I were killing them around the place every few days. I had a big saddle horse, an old bay, and he was bitten in the shoulder on Manning Creek. In spite of all I could do for him that winter, he died. Over on our new place I had a cow. She was half Angus and half Durham. I broke her for a milk cow, this nice young heifer, she was gentle. A rattler hit her on the left jaw and it swelled up until it was as big as a coal skuttle. I was coming down from the mountains where I'd been riding herd on the cattle and saw her standing by the homestead cabin. There was a spring about 100 yards from there and we also had a ditch down past the house where we got all our drinking water and water for the little garden. I got off my horse, went over to the cow, and felt of that great sack on the left side of her head. I had a good sharp jackknife, so I got one arm around her horns and I speared that thing and gave it a slash. Instantly a gallon or two of green stinking water hit me in the chest. I turned the cow loose, dropped the knife, and proceeded to take off my hat, unbuckle my gun belt, kick off my boots, spurs, and socks. I saved them. The rest of my clothes, underclothes, shirt and overalls I left in a pile. Over below the spring I went and washed off thoroughly. I came back, put on my hat, my boots and spurs, buckled on my gunbelt, and got on my horse. As I rode around in back of the house to the barn, Lorraine came out on the back porch to throw out a pan of dishwater. She stopped, took one look at me, and says, "What happened to all your clothes?" The cow healed up, but she dried up as well, and I sold her for beef the next year.

I had a little cow horse named Shorty. He was part cayuse, about as ugly a nag as anybody ever looked at. His head was so long I had to put an extension in any bridle, or let out a hackamore, to ride him. He cocked his tail off to the left and carried it that way. He'd been docked when he was a colt, so he

Elmer isn't the only hunter in the family, as Lorraine Keith proved many times. This mule buck was dropped by a 300-grain bullet from a .333 O.K.H. rifle.

had a short tail. But that little nag could walk five miles an hour all day long. He was a good swimmer. I remember a cow jumping into a big deep slough, when we rescued a bunch of Willow Creek cattle that had been stolen, and the little horse jumped in right after her, swam up and bit her on the tail until he finally chased her out of a little gulch that came into the slough down below.

Shorty liked to hunt. I'd hunt coyotes with him. At that time I was packing a big old 15-pound bull-gun, with scope sights, over my shoulder by the muzzle. When I'd see a coyote or an eagle, I'd just trail Shorty's reins, make my stalk, and get or miss them, but Shorty loved to hunt. Then I'd go up on Lookout Mountain, take my little 16-gauge Ithaca, and hunt grouse. The little horse learned it. He'd go along with his nose to the ground sniffin'. He would smell the fresh grouse tracks and I could tell it right then by his ears. When the chickens would jump, I'd trained him by hooking my left spur around his shoulder and reining him to the right to the right to turn his head to the right. I made a good many doubles off of that little horse with that 16-gauge. He'd whirl partly around, watch them go, and he'd hold his head down low. And if I

only shot once, then he'd shiver waiting for the second barrel. He was a grand old hunting horse. I could drop the reins anywhere, be gone a half-a-day or all day, and come back and Shorty would be standing there tossing the reins waiting for me.

When I got married I believe Mr. Randall thought I was just another saddle tramp going through the country. He was very opposed to our wedding. But after awhile he came over to see us, saw the hay all stacked, the fences up, and everything in good shape. I think he started to revise his ideas about things from then on.

On a trip down to the Randall ranch, we met Lorraine's uncle, O. J. Randall, from Salmon, Idaho. He had homesteaded on Lake Creek above Williams Lake. Had a homestead there, a bunch of cattle and some hogs. He was wanting to sell out. I had also found out there was considerable cattle stealing going on where we were out of Durkee. It was just a question of time until a fellow was going to have trouble with cow thieves somewhere. So I proposed we sell out, go over and take a look at the Salmon River country, and maybe buy O. J.'s place. Van Stull went with us for a prospecting trip over to Salmon. I bought the

The author's best antelope measured 17½ inches on both horns, with a 17½-inch spread, and fell to a 150-grain bullet in a .280 Dubiel. Keith shot the antelope at 362 yards in 1932.

first Model A Ford that came to Baker, Oregon and we set out in that. We made it down to Nampa, had dinner with the folks, went out past Mountain Home and camped on the sagebrush flat the first night. The next night we made it around up to Ketchum and over the Galena Summit and camped in the lodgepole at the head of the Salmon River. The third night we made it down to Twelve Mile Creek about twelve miles above Salmon, and stayed in an old house of Chauncey Stroud's. The road in those days was just the width of the Model A, and 25 miles-an-hour was really going places. We had to cross the river several times, and back up a lot when we'd meet some other traveler, but we made it.

The next day we drove around to the Mendenhall ranch, got horses and went up to see her uncle. He had a nice little place but it was awfully steep. He put up a lot of hay, and the ranch was up just below the lodgepole pines and pretty high. I was figuring on buying it, cattle and all. He had a bunch of hogs, about 30 as I remember it, but I didn't want them. Didn't see much way of getting them in and out.

At any rate I went back to Durkee, and started trucking everything to Salmon, Idaho.

Then I got pack horses and loaded six leather-bottom chairs and a rocker on one pack horse, a Simmons bedspring and mattress on another, and moved all our belongings up to O.J.'s ranch. Lorraine stayed down at Weiser with her folks.

I helped O. J. finish a two-room log cabin and put a roof on it, also get out a lot of lodgepole and rebuild the corrals. In the meantime I put out a trapline for coyote, lynx, etc., and ran it from Lake Mountain nearly out to Taylor Mountain along the divide. Caught a lot of coyote and lynx, and some marten. However, while I was scouting and putting out traps, I ran into a batch of larkspur, at least that's what I figured it was, in the first gulch above Williams Lake. I counted over a hundred old carcasses scattered up and down there, so I went to the forest service about it. They told me it was one of the worst poison patches in the country. That settled me from buying the place. I told O. J. I wouldn't take it on that account.

Lorraine came over and we spent the winter there until February with her uncle while I trapped. Then we decided to get out and look for another place, because I didn't want to be up there in that poison patch. Later, the forest service had big crews grubbing poison there from several springs.

Rather than pack all our belongings on packhorses for the trip around the narrow rocky trail and mahogany ledges, and back down to the Salmon River, I decided to make a sled. I got a couple of fir trees that grew out from the steep sidehill about three feet and then turned straight up, for sled runners. It was nothing but a trail clear out to the river, but either way, you took the high trail or you went around the lake and down the canyon. So I made this sled about 25-feet long and just a little narrower than the trail. I packed all our belongings on it, and hired Roy McCabe to come up from the river with a team to help me drag it down. I had all my guns in big boxes nailed up waterproof tight. I canvassed the whole thing, and roped it on good and solid. We hooked the horses up, one in front of the other, for the trip down to the lake from the ranch. Everything went well. I would stay on the tail end and steer it while he led the horses. Getting down to the lake we decided to hook them up as a team, which we did, and go across the lake. There was about a foot of wet snow on the lake in February. I was pretty green about the condition of ice in February on lakes and so was Roy. However, he had just sharpshod the team. They were big horses, about 14-1500 pounds and he'd shod them up good and sharp. We got out in the middle of the lake and I heard a funny noise and looked around and I could see the ice was sinking all around us. I yelled at Roy. He had a good 40-foot throw rope on his arm and he half hitched that onto the halter rope and he ran to the right and I ran to the left. Well, through she went, the team, the long sled, and Mom's old yeller tom cat in a gunny sack tied to the tail end. The team was dog paddling, with just their heads and feet out, and I ran around and laid on the rope to the right and we pulled for all we were worth and we drifted them around to where the ice was solid. The horse on the right side got one sharp shod foot up on solid ice, then another. Then he kicked and we pulled, and he got a hind foot up and we rolled him over. He jumped up snorting for all he was worth and the other one was pawing to get out. The braces held pretty good and I think that helped, and we finally got both horses out. Then the old Arkansas sled came up hit the solid ice, stood about 10-15 feet in the air and tipped over back onto solid ice and snow. The old tom cat says "Wow-r-r-r-r" and we saved it all. We made a beeline for the nearest promontory and got off that lake. It was a pretty narrow squeak from losing everything we possessed, and our lives as well.

THE RANCH ON THE SALMON...

Con Mendenhall graciously asked us to come down and stay with him and his brother Charley on their ranch while we looked around the Salmon River country to buy a place of our own. We'd sold out over at Durkee and had about $6000 to invest in another little ranch. Finally we located one on the North Fork and were going to buy it, but the man had about six to eight cords of creek wood, birch and willow, all bucked up. He wouldn't throw that in on the deal and I didn't want to start cutting wood when it was time to put in a crop, so the deal fell through. We looked a bit farther and found a much better place farther up the North Fork some four miles below Gibbonsville for less than half the money, which we bought. That was the spring of 1930. The place had plenty of good soil, right on the North Fork with all the water in the world if you wanted to repair the ditch. The ditches were grown up until only a trickle would go through. The house was a fine old log house at one time, but the roof had rotted, the shingles, even the sheeting and some of the rafters. And the cabins were in the same shape. I hired Dave Chard to help

me, and we put in a solid month re-roofing the house and cabin. Then we put in another month grubbing out the willows and rebuilding the ditch. In addition to that we had two hundred yards of flume to put around a slide-rock. By working night and day all spring we finally got the job done. We also put in a third of an acre of Mastodon Everbearing strawberries.

We were thirty miles from town, and most of it over a narrow road, that those days went around the Big Flat below Salmon. We put in twenty of the best years of our lives there. It was a wonderful place to live in the summer. In the winter, though, the snow would get three to four feet deep. The cows would break a trail from the barn and down to the stackyard and you could just see the tops of their backs sticking out of the snow. I kept my snowshoes there to go down and feed them. I also ran my trapline.

By this time I'd been writing quite a few gun articles in the *American Rifleman*. Major Askins bought my first one for *Outdoor Life* in 19 and 26. And I had done a lot of experimenting with six-guns at Durkee, Oregon. Harold Croft wrote me from Philadelphia and said the people back there in the gun club didn't believe any long-range shooting with six-guns, and would like to verify it. So I invited him to come out and stay a month with Mom and I at the little ranch we had there and see for himself.

He shipped out a case of ammunition: .44 Specials, .45 Colts, .44-40s, and I think there was one .38-40 in the bunch. Then he came out with a suitcase full of six-guns. I took him up to the ranch and he liked it there from the start. He wanted to see some long-range six-gun shooting, so we got some boards together, and nailed them up with braces in back to form a four-foot square. Then we put it in the old Model T, hauled it down across the meadow, across the road, upon the side of the mountain, and measured 700 yards. I asked him if that would do for a target.

"Sure", he says, "You couldn't hit that with a howitzer, let alone a six-shooter."

So I threw my saddle out there in the shade of one of the old poplars, laid down, used my saddle for a headrest, and held the gun between my knees. I hit the target before the gun was empty with everything except the two-inch .45 Colt slipgun he had. It required eleven shots from that gun, and I was aiming at a sagebrush on top of the mountain behind it and way off to the left when I finally lobbed one through the target. We could see the spurt of dust from every bullet, and I just

The ranch on the North Fork of the Salmon River was 30 miles from town over a narrow road, but it was a happy home for the Keith family, Elmer (left), Dru, and Lorraine in 1932.

A visit by Harold Croft to the Keith's in Oregon in 1927 led to a fast friendship and experimentation with hand-guns and ammunition that advanced the shooting sports.

walked them onto the target. With some of the four and five and 7½-inch guns I got three to four hits, and with one gun I got five hits out of six on it after I'd shot awhile.

That convinced Harold.

While there, he wanted better bullets. I had designed a .454-260 for Belding & Mull, and then I designed a 260 and 280-grain for Belding & Mull, all of them with a very blunt, round nose like the old .41 Long Colt. They shot good at close range, but were not very accurate at any distance. So I then (in 1927 I believe it was) designed the Ideal .429-421, a .44 Special. I found out by then that I could load a .44 Special much heavier and to give more power, more velocity and energy, than anything possible out of a thin-cylinder .45 Colt. Harold Croft experimented with me and we shot them at all ranges. We also shot jackrabbits, a couple of eagles, grouse, and other game with them. He became my lifelong friend.

When my forty acres of rye was ripe, the little turtle doves would come in by the thousands. I used to take the 16-gauge, go over and get about a dozen of them, dress them, and Lorraine would have dove and dumplings. One day we sent Harold over, I gave him a box of shells, he came back sans shells,

and also sans doves. He hadn't been able to hit them, he said.

While riding for cattle, I'd usually get a mess of grouse or the big sage hens nearly every day as soon as they were big enough to eat. One day my brother and another man were riding for cattle. Towards evening I told them I'd get ahead a little ways and see if I could pick up some grouse for dinner the next day. A big cock sage hen sat on top of a boulder as I came around a bend. I slid off my horse with a 19 and 17 Smith & Wesson with quarter-inch Patridge-type sights that Croft had given me. He'd had it made up in Philadelphia. I centered the old cock sage hen in the chest and he fell off the rock, caught himself and came flying right down the gulch over me. I shot him again in the belly, double-action, as he went over. He went on down and piled up in front of my brother's cow horse, which started to pitch and threw Si higher than a kite.

Mom and I liked our little ranch on the North Fork. North Fork's a beautiful, clear trout stream. With mining four miles above Gibbonsville, they used cyanide acids in treating the gold ore, and they'd killed all the salmon and steelhead run in the North Fork. So one day, John Kinney, the forest supervi-

The North Fork ranch was a good place for finding winter meat. This little two-point buck was shot at 400 yards by Keith, using a .334 O.K.H.

sor, asked me if I would like to have some salmon fry to plant. I told him I surely would. I proceeded to haul 40,000 chinook fry in two ten-gallon cans roped in the back of that little Model A Ford. I'd change the water at Boyle Creek, change it again at Fourth of July Creek, change it at the North Fork, then go up to the ranch and dump them in a slough.

Nobody would help me, nobody would loan me a dollar, and in 19 and 31 dollars were much bigger than my hat. At any rate I put 40,000 of them in the North Fork. Four years later there was a run of fish that averaged 16 pounds, and steelhead started coming with them. Everybody from town was down there with their spears to help catch salmon. Lorraine canned fifty-sixty quarts. We had no refrigeration in those days, but she'd can them in quart jars, put a couple of spoons of olive oil with them, and salt, so we had plenty of salmon put away. I'd also smoke a batch of them when I had time.

NO TROUBLE WITH MEAT...

About fifty head of deer wintered on the mountain in back of the house every winter, plenty of deer up Sheep Creek, and up Hughes Creek, so we had no trouble with meat. We'd go over to the Lochsa and get an elk or two each fall. We had plenty of good

meat and a wonderful garden, and raised practically everything we needed. It was a good thing too, because a good many of the residents of the North Fork lived on spuds and venison during the Depression. The strawberry crop I started selling at two-bits a quart petered down until I had to set up the boxes, pay for them, haul them to Salmon, and get seven cents a heaped-up quart for Mastodon strawberries. A five-gallon can of thick cream brought 90 cents at the creamery, so we just had to live off the land, barter and trade rather than buy things, because none of us had any money.

Again, Mom was expecting. I took her to Salmon and put her in a home with a good lady there to take care of her some three or four weeks before we expected the baby. In the meantime I hired the local doctor to take care of her, which he agreed to do. Elmer Hagel and I were placer mining above my bridge, cleaning off some of the rim, and getting out a little gold every day. One day the ranger, Al Wheeler, came up and told me my wife was sick and I'd better get to town. So I jumped in the old Model A and took off.

When I got to Salmon, the doctor wasn't there, so I started looking. I finally found him in a poker game in back of the saloon. I told him, "Doc, you promised to take care of my wife and she's been sick for a couple of hours. Come on."

He says, "As soon as I finish this hand."

I says, "Hand . . . Hell!" jerked the chair from under him, collared him, and headed him for the door. I says, "You're going with me now, Mister." I got out the door and there was Tommy Stroud, the sheriff, and Vaughn Clark, the deputy. The doctor says, "I've got to make a call on another lady. I promised her and then I'll come right on out."

I says, "Doc, you get in that Ford there right now or you ain't never going to make another call except to God Almighty."

Stroud came up. "That's pretty big talk, Mr. Keith," he says.

I says, "I'll include you too Tom. Get out of the way."

Vaughn Clark knew me well. He grabbed Stroud and says, "You better stay out of it, Tom. Elmer will do just what he says." So I threw the doctor in the car, and we went out. We got there just in time for him to put a little dope in the baby's eyes. The midwife had taken care of everything. We had a fine girl, naming her Druzilla. Druzilla was the name that Captain Clark wanted carried down in the family.

The first antelope season ever held in Idaho ended with Keith taking this 15-inch pronghorn with his .280 Dubiel in a Magnum Mauser rifle.

By this time I had acquired a pack string, a couple of good saddle horses, and eight or ten milk cows. I went into roan durhams, due to the fact that when I got a bull calf I could make him into a good steer, and they were good milkers—big cattle. The little ranch would put up enough hay for that much stock. Also room for a grain patch for the chickens and plenty of garden. So, although rather primitive (we had to pack the water from the ditch to the house in the summer, and from the river up to the house in the winter,) we still lived well.

The baby grew like a weed, and was a lot of fun. When she was a little tyke, she'd crawl to the rocking chair, crawl up in it, get her mother's big concert harp, and play any tune that came in on the radio. How she did it, I don't know. She couldn't walk or talk yet. Claude Coyle was the bandmaster in Salmon. He'd come out and visit us once in awhile. Claude says, "Elmer, you'll never raise her, she's a prodigy. I've never seen anybody that could play like that. A little chubby-handed baby and that big concert harp."

Though we didn't know it then, Claude's prophecy was right.

By this time I was selling occasional gun articles. At that time they usually brought $10 apiece if you had a few illustrations to go with them. I was always a good speller, and I remember when in Helena, in the eighth grade, we had a state spelling contest, taking representatives from every school and every county in the state. They brought them all to the Helena auditorium to have the final spelling match. A girl named Nora Boone, who was in my class, and I proceeded to spell down the whole state of Montana. Then they gave each of us every word in the book trying to spell one of us down. They couldn't do it, so they gave each of us a little silver medal.

Years later on Lake Creek, in the fall of '29, I put out a good trap line. A cousin of Lorraine's, Ruth Swearingen, and her husband, Morris, came out to visit her uncle, O. J. Randall. One day an Indian came down off the mountain. He says, "You gottum coyote trap on top of the ridge?" I says, "Yes." He says, "You gottum coyote up there." I told O.J., I says, "Well then, I'll have to go up and get him."

Ruth then said she would like to see a live coyote. "Well," I says, "I'll saddle another

Lorraine, Elmer, and Druzilla Keith "lived well" on the ranch tucked away on the North Fork of the Salmon River in Idaho.

horse and you can go along." O.J. remonstrated, saying it was a long, hard ride and would tire her out. So I says, "Well, I'll bring the coyote in alive."

O.J. had a little bay mare that had been swapped all over the valley between different ranches. She had a habit of tossing people off if she didn't like them. Every time O.J. Randall rode her, he'd get down to the Shoup Lane and she'd come all apart and unload him. Then she'd stop and let him get on and ride on into town. I'd promised him that I would take it out of her. He says, "Well, this is a good time to break that mare for me." And I says, "There never was a better. Run her in." So he ran the mare in. I put my old bronc saddle on her, buckled up my spurs, got on her, and tried to make her buck. She crow-hopped up on the woodpile, then up on the porch of the old soddy cabin. I knew she would have to do a lot better than that to throw anyone. I had a good cow dog, so I took the dog, and made the climb back up to the ridge between Lake Creek and Henry's Creek. Sure enough, I had a coyote there in the trap.

I tied the mare to a sagebrush, went over and teased the coyote with a stick until he grabbed it, and then I nailed him by the neck with the other hand, got the sagebrush back of his fangs, put a double half-hitch of buckskin around behind that so he couldn't open his mouth. Then I tied his legs together, took him out of the trap, and tied him to another sagebrush while I reset my trap.

I went over to the mare to put the coyote on her. She struck at me viciously with the left forefoot. I got a little blood on my hands from the coyote, as he was bleeding from the one foot that had been caught in the trap. So I pulled a red wool shirt off of my back that Mother had made me, got in close to her shoulder where she couldn't strike me, and pulled the shirt over her head so she couldn't see what was going on. Then I got the coyote and laid him across behind the cantle board. I ran a string around behind one shoulder and in front of the other and tied him, I thought, tight on that side. On the left side I had a loop in the cantle strings with the strap of my carbine boot going through it. I thought that would be close enough, so I tied his hind legs good with those strings beyond where I had the knot.

I got on, got my hackamore and bridle reins all sorted out, took a good grip on everything and pulled the shirt off her head. She went at it. She really could buck and this time she

A good load of prime venison from a mule deer taken by the author with a six-gun at over 90 yards. Venison provided a substantial part of the winter's meat in those days.

turned it on. Then the coyote came loose at the front end.

He'd whip under her belly and back up and hit me in the chest, all the time the mare was bucking as hard as she could down the ridge and making a crazy noise. It was almost a scream. I never heard a horse squall like that before. I was having my hands full riding her, and the blame coyote was trying to bite. He couldn't bite, but would strike like a snake because his jaws was tied together. But he'd go under her belly and between her hind legs and the next jump he'd come back and hit me in the chest.

She turned off into Henry's Creek where the slope was very steep. I knew she was going to fall and roll, so when she sunfished out down the hill, I jerked her head up and dallied it tight to the saddle horn and threw her. I kicked my left foot up, and we slid for thirty yards down into the bottom of Henry's Creek.

I just half-hitched her nose to the saddle horn so she couldn't get up, fished the coyote out from the side and got him back across the saddle, tied him good this time around the shoulders, and headed her back up the hill. I steered her with my hat and spurs. As soon as she got on top she went to pitching again and turned off down the other side which was just as steep. Soon she had me, saddle, coyote, and all up on her withers and I was about to lose them there. I finally got her stopped. By that time she was a bit winded and I managed to turn her back up the hill. She trotted to the top as fast as she could go, then started pitching again, but the fight was all out of her.

O.J. had said that he also wanted all the cattle brought out of the head of Lake Creek, so when we got over to the head, I told little Bobby, my cow dog, to go get them. He knew what was wanted. He made a circle and came back and I counted them and I says, "Bobby, there's a couple more."

The dog made another circle and back he came with them.

We headed down the canyon. Just when we reached the head of the hay meadow at the ranch, we met O.J. with another buyer looking the ranch over for a possible sale. He'd told Ruth that morning, "You will see, that mare will come in with the saddle under her belly and Elmer will come in a-walking about dark, and he won't have any horse or any coyote either." So I asked O.J. to count the cattle. He did and I said, "Well, I've got the coyote here behind." He seemed very much surprised. Just when I was talking to him, the mare decided to unload me again. So she came all apart and pitched for all she was worth. I kicked it out of her, and asked him where he wanted the cattle. He said, "Put them across the creek below the house." I drove them on down there, put them across the creek, untied the coyote and laid him on the porch of the old soddy, and unsaddled the mare. Morris Swearingen took a picture of me sitting on the porch of the old soddy with a live coyote across my knees. *American Rifleman* used it for a cover illustration on their magazine the next year, I think around 1930 or '31. That was as wild a ride as I ever had, and if I only had a good movie of it I think I would have had it made.

Chapter 6

BECOMING A WRITER

THE RIVER OF NO RETURN...

In the winter of 19 and 30, I went into partnership with Captain Harry Guleke, the old river rat who had long been running the Salmon River with freight to the mines at Shoup and on down the river. He also took out fall hunting parties.

We built huge scows, 8 feet wide, 32 feet long on the bottom, and with both ends sloping up at about a 45-degree angle. The front end was built up five feet to take the splash, and the rear end three feet. We double-boarded the bottoms and one board up on the sides and the ends. In the middle was a four-foot deck across the top of the gunwales that we stood on back to back. We had a king pin in each end and long sweeps that extended out, front and back, usually 2x6s. We used a pair of them for the sweep beam and then had a blade about 18 inches wide and about 14 feet long bolted to the 2x6s. We put a box in front of the handle of the sweep, weighted it with rocks until they were balanced perfectly so that we could raise or lower them instantly.

With these big scows we ran the Salmon River from Salmon down to Riggins through some of the roughest water ever run at that time. It was a one-way trip, as nothing had been able to come up the river. Later the Evinrude Company burned out four or five thirty-horse motors trying to push a boat up. It wasn't until they developed the jet boats that they were really able to master the Salmon both ways. In those days it was a one-way drift proposition, and we had to negotiate all the big rapids, dodge all the huge boulders, twists and turns, and it was a hard job. Today jet boats go skipping up and down the river like a bunch of ducks.

I had decided to make my living writing and guiding big game hunters and fishing parties. The first trip Captain Guleke and I ran in the spring of 1930 was a wild ride. The river was up fairly well and much of it was whitewater. We would no more than get out of one rapid and we were in another. I was always glad when we'd hit some quiet water and make a landing for a rest. Captain Guleke taught me the river and how to make every rapid. We ran the river together for ten years, up through 19 and 40.

Captain Guleke and I ran the river every year, sometimes several trips, spring fishing trips and summer and fall big-game hunts. On the fall big-game hunts I never made a trip down the river but somewhere on the trip, while I was guiding, an eagle would chase a blue grouse right to me. The grouse will fly and light right at your feet, ruffle up their

131

Captain Harry Guleke was an old river rat on the Salmon for many years, and, while he was sometimes wrong, he was always positive.

wings and fuss around, but they won't leave a man. They are not a bit afraid of a human so long as that old golden eagle is in sight. If an eagle lit, even though I was hunting sheep, I would always set down and kill him.

We had a favorite sheep camp below South Fork on the main Salmon. There was a big dead yellow pine up the hill that furnished an abundance of firewood for the cookfires. A couple of hundred yards downstream was a big yellow pine that hung out mostly over the river and one limb hung back over the bank, with a huge eagle nest in it some 4 feet across. One summer trip I asked Cap to fish the party while I climbed back up in the cliffs to see how the sheep were doing. I put in most of the day up there. There were 32 ewes in the band and there were more lambs than there was ewes. Some of them must have had twins. That fall when we hunted it, there was one lamb left.

When I came in one night from hunting rams (we got three big ones on that trip) an eagle lit on this old tree by the nest. The nest, of course, was long since deserted. I laid down and killed the eagle. When I went down to cut his tail feathers off to trade the Indians for a pair of buckskin gloves, Captain Guleke says, "I'll go with you." His feet was bother-

ing him and he had on house slippers. The skipper was getting pretty old. He hobbled down there, and while I was cutting the tail off the eagle for feathers for the Indians, he started picking up mountain sheep lamb legs under this eagle nest. I got interested, so together we canvassed the whole sidehill around that nest. We took all the legs down and spread them out on the sandbar and counted up nine mountain sheep lambs and three legs left over. Cap says, "Well, that's where our sheep crop went. Just one lamb left in those 32 head of ewes."

An eagle can't pack a big mountain sheep lamb, but it don't take long for him to cut him in two and cut him in pieces with that old hook bill. Then they can move parts of him anywhere they want.

On one trip down the river, we had just passed South Fork and our old sheep camp. Cap had a habit, when we got past South Fork of lying down in the boat and taking a nap because it was comparatively quiet water with only minor rapids and I'd run them with the rear sweep. This time when we turned a corner we were in a lake, and after traveling two or three miles every slowly in this lake, I knew something was wrong. It looked like a mountain must have fallen in the river down below somewhere. Finally Cap woke up. He looked out of the boat and saw everything so quiet and peaceful, and the boat barely drifting and he says, "Where are we?" I told him.

He says, "Oh, my God, something's happened to the river."

Pretty soon we could see waves a-kicking up ten feet high above the level of the river below us. Cap says, "Something awful's happened to the river." We finally drifted down there and tied up. A great cloudburst had come down a creek a quarter of a mile above Warren's Creek and it dammed the river up for four or five miles.

The falls looked like Niagara.

There we were with a big old scow that would weigh five tons, with all our bedding, grub, cookstove, and everything to move and no way of moving it around. A jumble of boulders and a deep gutter cut where this cloudburst had come out of the gulch. Down below the rapids you could see the roots of a huge yellow pine tree sticking straight up in the air above the water. Just how it had got stood on end and anchored there, we never knew. So the party asked us what we was going to do.

I says, "The only thing we can do is try and run it."

The early-day river boats on the Salmon were big scows, 32-feet long and 8-feet wide with long sweeps at each end. They were dismantled after every trip.

Immediately everybody in the party started packing everything off the boat, and carrying it around. That tickled Cap and I because it lightened up the boat. A couple decided to go with us. I threw some logs in to see where they would go and judged the current to see where we'd have a chance of making it. The river ran in an arc, and it threw awful hard against two big rock ledges that came out. I knew we had to get by them some way or it would smash the boat to splinters. We finally took off and put Florence Schultz, who we'd taken along to cook for us, up on a rock with a camera to get a picture of us. She said she saw only my hat after we went over the first big wave and never saw anything of us again until we came out far down below. At any rate we got over the first wave, about a ten foot drop, and up on the next one and headed for the cliff. Cap got knocked down by his sweep, and it was playing a tattoo on the deck beside him. I knew I should get in a good rake and straighten up the boat so it would miss the first ledge. Then we hit more heavy pitching waves 10 and 12 feet high. On the top of one wave I saw the next ledge coming up. I managed to dig my sweep deep in it and point the boat to the left of that ledge. We went by it all right, then my sweep knocked me flat, and would have knocked me overboard, but Cap grabbed me by the belt and hauled me back in. We came out in quiet water down below these awful rapids with the sweeps beating the deck right beside us. I jumped up and grabbed the rear sweep as we were tail-end-to, and made a landing.

Afterwards I talked to a party that came down ten days later and they measured the falls. They said the river took about a 60-foot drop there in just a couple of hundred yards. At any rate it was the roughest water I ever ran or ever want to run.

Next spring, high waters took all the dam out and the river was back to normal from then on. Captain Guleke and I had many rough experiences on the river. Many times we got hung up on rocks and we'd pry and crowbar until we'd get the scow loose and go on. We usually packed a 50-pound box of dynamite, and when we found a rock in the way we'd tie below it, get some long poles, make up a cartridge of several sticks of dynamite, grease it with cup grease, put two fuses and caps on it, run them up the poles and we'd work until we'd get those poles stuck underneath the rock. It was quite a job with a heavy current a-pulling, but if we'd get them placed right and then touch them off, why

Fall hunting trips down the river were often exciting, and in 1939, Doc DuComb (left) looks on as Gordon Koch shows the cinnamon bear he shot with a 30-06.

we'd move a rock and open up the channel so that we could get through better with the big scows. We improved the rapids quite a lot that way, but sometimes the next spring's high water would move more huge boulders half the size of a house around until we'd have to do it over again.

Captain Guleke was a grand old man. In the main we got along swell. When we'd get home we'd divide up the money we made on the trip, divide up the rope and materials we had left over. I'd go home and he'd give me a sack of vegetables from his big garden, and in the fall I'd come back with a ham of venison and a bunch of fresh meat for him. We had many close squeaks and went through some tough times together.

I remember one of the last trips I ran with Cap. He'd actually forgotten part of the river, but was in his eighties then, and not the man he was when we started eight or nine years before. Down at the Sam Meyers rapids we had to make a swing to the right and take the right hand channel before we took the long rapids.

For some reason, Cap had forgotten. He took straight across the big eddies. At the lower end, all the river throwed on a whole

bunch of boulders that stuck out in a circle. I didn't see any chance of us making it. Luckily before we got to this ring of boulders, we hit a big rock and the bow went up on it high. I immediately walked the tail end around so the boat wouldn't fill with water and there we sat. Cap said we always went that away, and I told him, I says, "You told me always before to go clear over again the other bank." But he had the front sweep and that's where he steered us. We sat there for about two hours wondering what to do for the rest of the party. I told him there was nothing we could do. If we went off we were going to hit that bunch of hard heads sticking up there and shatter the boat and we'd be lucky if any of us got out. We all had life jackets, but a life jacket isn't too much good in the Salmon River. If it sucks you in behind a boulder it may boil you around down there underneath for five or ten minutes before you come up, and that's too long for anybody to hold his breath.

Anyway finally along came a pack string. I yelled and asked him if he'd take a rope.

"Sure," he says. I always took 150 feet of half-inch rope and another 150 feet of quarter-inch rope, in case something like that did happen. So I tied a hammer on the

Something awful had happened to the river. It looked like Niagara ahead, and the only way through was to just grit the teeth and shoot the 12-foot rapids.

quarter-inch rope, asked him if he'd take a line and swing us off of that boulder and back into the channel before we cut loose. He agreed. So I threw and after several tries I finally got the hammer to him and quarter-inch rope, and we spliced on the half-inch. I told him he could have all the rope if he'd just take a good dally that would hold us with that half-inch. He finally found a boulder that he could go around two or three times, and snubbed our rope against it. I laid a 2x6 across the gunwale, and gave Ormy Beers, who was in the party, a hand axe. I told him to chop the rope in two when I told him, and all I had to do was give the boat one good hard flip with the sweep and off we came headed right for the bunch of boulders.

The man had taken up the slack good. I never did know who he was. We headed straight for that bunch of boulders and certain wrecking. Just when we were about 20 feet from them, the rope caught and swung us gradually around over into the channel. Cap wanted to take my rear sweep. I said, "No, you had your chance. Now it's my turn." So I ran the Sam Meyers rapids tail-end first, and took on quite a lot of water on account of only three-foot splash boards on that end. We made it all right.

Later on the same trip, we were down below French Creek and one of the officials there of the CCC boys wanted to ride down to Riggins with us. He was a big man. So we took him aboard. We had Doc DuComb along

that trip and two other sheep hunters that had finished their sheep hunting and were heading on out for Riggins. We managed to go over the falls there below Sheep Creek with no problem at all. But farther down the river, for some reason, the captain had forgotten the channel again and we were too far to the left. He hit another rock in the middle of the river, broke the front sweep beam, and bashed in the bow of the boat. I walked the tail end around as fast as I could so that the front end that was caved in was sticking up high enough not to take water, although we took quite a bit of water when we first hit. Bob Hagel was along too. Everybody was excited. Doc DuComb grabbed an air mattress and was going to jump overboard. Bob and I told him not to do it because he would be under the mattress and drown himself. The big man from the CCC camp was white as a sheet. I looked around and saw my can of tobacco bobbing around in the water in the tail end of the boat.

I says, "Bob, get my can of tobacco. I want to have a smoke." So I slowly filled a pipe and lit it, and set there to let them cool off a bit. Then Cap and I went to work with sacks, canvas, and boards. We patched the front end of the boat. We pulled in the sweep. We lifted it off the king pin, pulled it in, got another 2x6 out, spiked it on, spliced it, re-anchored the blade, and got it all back in position so it was all safe again. By hard pulling with both sweeps, we got back in the channel where we

There were peaceful times on the Salmon, too, and humor, as when a water ouzel landed on the sweep and rode with the hunting party all the way to Riggins.

should have been and we made it all right. The big man from the CCC camp suddenly remembered he had an awful lot of office work to do back in camp that he should have done, and he wanted to get off at the next sandbar, so we let him off. We ran the Lake Creek and Big Ruby rapids later on, heavy rapids down above Riggins, with no trouble whatever.

On one trip we made, there was a little water ouzel lit on Cap's front sweep beam when we stopped at Horse Creek. That little bird rode with us all day. When we camped he'd get off, dive under the water and go walking along the bottom picking up his evening meal. Next morning when we'd load the beds and everything back in the boat and get ready to go, the little ouzel would fly up and light on the front sweep. When we'd go through the rapids and the water would come over the sweep beam, the little bird would bounce up. He was a most cheerful little bird. The Cap called him our mascot. The little water ouzel rode with us clear to Riggins.

At that time there was a swinging foot bridge across the river at Riggins and we'd hang up a block and tackle on it and hoist all the heavy stuff out of the boat up to this foot bridge and carry it ashore to where we could back a truck up for the trip back to Salmon.

The boats were always left there in care of the postmaster to sell if he could. Most of them, however, were stolen, taken on down the river and broken up for backhouses or farm sheds. Half of the backhouses along the bank at Riggins were made from our old boats. You could see the nail holes and pitch seams where we'd calked them up.

When we unloaded the boat at Riggins that year, the water ouzel was sitting on the front sweep, going "tweet, tweet, tweet, tweet." He wanted to go on down the river with us. He seemed disappointed that that was as far as we'd go.

ON THE TRAIL WITH ZANE GREY . . .

In the fall of 19 and 31 I had booked a party led by novelist Zane Grey for a two months trip over in the Middle Fork country. We had also booked a boat trip.

Cap ran the boat trip, and took another man to run the rear sweep, but they sunk the boat at Salmon Falls, lost everything they had, and had a hard time getting out on foot. We never lost a boat when Cap and I were running together, and that was the last boat that Cap lost. Cap had a habit before we'd come to a big rapid, of tying up, getting out on foot and looking it over. He'd see if any logs had lodged between the boulders where we had to go, or if the heavy high water current had shifted some of the boulders and closed the channel. Then we'd come back, Cap would kneel down, and we'd offer up a little prayer.

He'd always say, "Elmer, isn't that right (or left) side of the boat a little heavy?" It was always where we had a gallon jug of moonshine tied with quarter-inch rope. I'd get the jug, we'd have a little nip, cut the ropes loose, and we'd run the rapid. This was regular procedure on all the major rapids, and we made them all. This was during prohibition, and we'd buy a gallon jug of moonshine from Old Man Moore at North Fork that he and his boy Johnny had made. Then when we got down below Campbell's ferry an old Tennesseean had a ranch where he grew rye and made it all into whiskey to supply the people riding up and down the river. He made very good whiskey, much better than the Moores. We'd always stop there and buy another gallon and that would see the party through to the conclusion of the trip at Riggins. All our early trips started at Salmon, and went from there on down. The road ended at Shoup. From there on was nothing but a pack trail around through the hills. Then as civilization began at Riggins Hot Springs, a few miles up above Riggins, the rest of the canyon was devoid mostly of trails and civilization, just people squatting along the river living on game and fish and taking out a little gold each year. We'd always stop at their camps and they'd give us their little retort buttons. Usually they'd retort all the gold they'd got in a potato, burn the quicksilver off, and we'd take the gold out to Pelton's Grocery. He'd weigh it up and fill their grocery orders. The next trip we'd take their groceries down to them.

I remember that prohibition officers finally caught Old Man Moore in his still. They took him to Boise and put him in the calaboose for six months. When he got out I talked to his son Johnny. Johnny said, "Elmer, the old man was so dry I had to pour whiskey in him for three days before his hoops would tighten up so he could hold it."

During the summer of '31 we had some bad fires on the North Fork. Al Wheeler hired me to take charge of a crew of some twenty-odd men, and we fought one fire on the Nez Perce for three weeks, another one on the North Fork, and another small one back of the North Fork store up the steep mountain. John Kinney, the supervisor, had promised me a fire permit anytime I wanted.

I'd booked Zane Grey and his three-ring circus for a trip. Grey told me he wanted to go into wild country, and that they were old mountain people and would come light. However, he brought in three cars and a big truck loaded with gear. I had my pack string and my partner's, and we hired (all told with our horses) 57 horses and seven men. Then we had to make three trips to relay that three-ring circus. I heard Kinney talk to the forest supervisor over the phone. He informed Kinney not to let Elmer Keith and Zane Grey go in the forest at all. It was terribly dry, and he was going to close the forest and call out the National Guard to stop all traffic on all roads entering the forest. John Kinney told him that I was a very reliable man, that I'd handled a fire crew and trenched more fire for him than any crew he had that summer. But it was to no avail. In the meantime I learned that Williams Lake, part of it was in private ownership and well within the forest, had excellent rainbow trout fishing, so we moved the entire Zane Grey crew and all their belongings up to Williams Lake, and ensconced them in a nice little park at the north end of the lake, the day before the supervisor clamped on the lid. I was within the forest then, and he couldn't stop me from going out and bringing in grub and mail, and he couldn't get me off because I was on private ground. We had to sit there two weeks until they finally lifted the ban on the forest roads. Then I took the party over to Meyers Cove, went the eighteen-mile pack down Camas Creek to the Middle Fork, forded the river, and set up a nice camp there. We fished there for awhile, then went on down below the old Mormon Ranch. He wanted me to take them to the mouth of Waterfall, and cross there and go up Big Creek, then across over into Cottonwood Meadows, back up to Cole Meadows, down Crooked Creek and up Monumental Creek to Thunder Mountain, an old mining camp, and write a novel on it, which he did later.

While waiting for the forest to be opened up, I managed to get a permit signed by President Herbert Hoover allowing Elmer Keith to take himself and party within any National Forest in the United States. That stopped the supervisor cold, and we were able to go on our proposed two month's trip. From the Mormon Ranch down the Middle Fork there was no trail, but I'd heard several old timers say they had hunted sheep down in there and they'd found horse droppings and tracks, and knew the Indians had worked through some way or other. I told them anywhere an Indian could go with a horse, I could, so I set out with the party down the south side of the river. We managed to make it, though we had to climb up around the cliffs and back and forth. It was an all-day trip from the Mormon Ranch down to the Waterfall. There was a nice campground there. The trail had come in over the other side as far down as this campground, punched through by the Forest Service at some time or other, or the Indians.

The next day we forded the Middle Fork, or rather swam it. One mule drifted down to the last sandbar. We almost lost her into the box canyon below, but she finally got out. We took the north side of Big Creek. The cliffs finally crowded us down, when one of the pack horses we had named Toots, slipped off a ledge. I saw her belly flash in the sun twice as she turned over down the mountain and she stuck on a ledge down there, pack and all. It took us two hours to build a trail down to her, pack her packs up, get her back on the trail and repack her, but she apparently wasn't hurt.

The cliffs finally crowded me down into the river, but I had a fine saddle horse named Brownie; 17½ hands high. He'd swim back and forth across the deep pools. We came out below old Cougar Dave Lewis's camp on Big Creek a short distance from where there was a blacksmith shop and a forge in under a huge cliff. From there we went up to Dave Lewis's, camped there, and the old man came over and had supper with us and came again for breakfast. I remember picking up a spearhead and twelve arrowheads there on the flat that evening that I gave to the Grey party.

Next we went up to Coyote Springs, hunted there, and killed several mule deer. From there we went down on the lower Cottonwood and hunted goats. They got their goats and some more deer. We packed up through Cole Meadows, down Crooked Creek, and up Monumental Creek to Thunder Mountain. This had been quite a gold camp. The old cemetery was in ruins. Trees had fallen across the headstones. A big mud slide had come down Mule Shoe Creek and dammed off Monumental Creek, and this in turn had formed a lake. Some of the buildings and the old saloon was floating around out in the lake. The beaver had built a nice nest in the attic of the old saloon, as it was floating around there.

This was a hard party to handle.

Romer Grey, Zane Grey's son, and his son-in-law Bob Carney, were the first to run the horses. I told them no more running of any of that stock because they had an awful long trip to make over the roughest country on God's green earth, and a walk was fast enough.

The country was crawling with game at that time, like this fat, well-antlered mule deer dropped by Keith with a flat-shooting .285 O.K.H.

They had a Japanese cook with them who was very agreeable and a fine person. I got along with him fine. They caught all the fish they could eat and then some, both up at Williams Lake in the two weeks there, and also on the Middle Fork.

From Thunder Mountain we went up Mule Shoe Creek, dropped over onto Marble Creek, went down it to where a trail cut to White's Gulch, and from there over into White's Gulch where we camped one night. I remember the next day I started counting mule deer when I gathered the horses.

From this camp on White's Gulch above the old White's Creek Ranger Station down to the mouth of the Camas, I counted 1000 mule deer that day, many of them within 30 or 40 yards. I could have loaded a truck with my six-gun alone, if I'd had said truck and somebody to dress the deer and handle them. The country was then crawling with game.

We made it from there down to our old camp across from the mouth of the Camas, then back up to the Ramshorn Ranch where the party had left their cars, ending this two month's trip. They took off for California.

I had cached six packloads of grub in the cellar at the Ramshorn Ranch, and when we got back somebody had stolen all of it. We were out of grub, so my partner Gerry and I had to come on home on my six-gun alone, eating pine squirrels, ruffed grouse, one snowshoe rabbit and one little porcupine. Zane Grey gave me some checks in the bank, and they bounced. I had the bank hold them and keep sending them back down to California until finally they caught some money in the bank and sent me the amount that was covered by these checks. This enabled me to pay off my seven men complete and clear all

In fording the Middle Fork of the Salmon River with the Zane Grey party in 1931, one mule drifted downstream and was almost lost.

Keith's method of carrying a rifle scabbard is shown on his horse, Brownie, the only profit he made on the two month Zane Grey trip in 1931.

debts, and left me with a good saddle horse for two month's work. I never did get the other $1500 he promised. The next spring he wrote me and wanted to go down the Salmon River. He wanted me to build two boats. I told him to send me the 1500 dollars he owed me, plus full payment for the two boats before I ever drove a nail in a board. I never heard any more from him.

This was a long, hard two month's trip on the horses, and Gerry Ravndahl and I had made a week's trip over there scouting before the trip, so it added up, all told, to about two months and a half of hard work, and for all of that I got a $100 saddle horse.

Later I had another California party on a sheep, deer, and elk hunt that paid off to a crooked partner I had, and I got nothing more from that than half the booking fees. Then I swore I would never take another Californian hunting without having full payment for the whole trip before I even ran in the horses or nailed on a shoe. After that the parties I got from California were all highclass people, and we had a very good time handling them.

I believe I showed Zane Grey the first long-range pistol shooting he'd ever witnessed. He and Bob Carney, his son-in-law, and Romer Grey, were shooting at a rock at 400 yards with a .30-06 Model 1895 Winchester with a Z.G. in gold on the left side of the receiver. They couldn't seem to hit it.

I laid down with my back to a log, took my old 7½-inch .44 Special single-action Colt and hit the rock repeatedly. Grey asked me why I packed a rifle. I told him I wanted the rifle for more power, the six-gun was just a handy weapon to use all time. We killed a rattlesnake just about every day at the camp on Williams Lake. There was quite a few in the

rocks there. Then we ran into more going down the Middle Fork. We had a beautiful camp across from the mouth of the Camas on the Middle Fork. One night we got a young cloudburst. It really soaked up the camp. There was a great puddle in front of Zane Grey's private tent, and snow was on the mountains down several hundred feet from the top. Grey took a look through his big spotting scope at that and ordered his secretary to bring out his long handled underwear. She hunted and couldn't find them. Then Grey told me that my packers had stolen his underwear. I told him that they hadn't stolen anything. Everything he had was there. His secretary was dressed in Gokey boots, slacks, buckskin shirt, buckskin jacket, and a black hat with silver conchos with a band around it and flat topped crown. She got mad at Grey and she took one of his war bags and crawled into it head first. Finally out she came with his long-handled underwear. She was so mad she went in front of him and threw them in the middle of this pool of muddy water. She pulled his hat off his head, threw that in on top and jumped up and down on the whole works until she'd tromped it well into the mud with her big Gokey boots. Zane Grey never said a word.

There were ten in the Zane Grey party, including Takahashi, the cook. Bob Carney had married Zane Grey's daughter, and Romer Grey had his wife, there was another man and his wife, and the two secretaries.

While we were camped at Williams Lake this one secretary had not yet come out from Chicago. Everybody told me what a beautiful woman she was and how I'd fall in love with her. I told them I was married and wasn't interested in any other girls. When she came out, the packers were all cowed down for her.

Down on the Middle Fork, we were packing up a mule string to send Romer and Bob Carney on a side hunt for bear. I'd given this secretary a little buckskin mare to ride. There were flat-topped rocks all over the place just like tables about two feet high. She came leading the little buckskin mare over and wanted me to help her on her horse. I told her to go ahead and step up on one of them rocks and climb on. The buckskin was gentle as a dog. She insisted that I help her on. I'd been heaving 150-pound packs on the sides of mules so I picked her up and tossed her up in the saddle. She didn't even grab at the horn. She just went over on the other side and plopped on her bottom.

She got up, and I've never heard an old mule skinner that could hold a candle to the cussing of that gal. I lost a lot of respect for her right then. I let her get up and get on her horse the best way she could.

Another time Grey ordered me to chaperone the girls down to the Mormon Ranch, as they had to go around a cliff that overhung the river a hundred feet or so and it was very narrow. If you met another pack string there, you were in trouble, because somebody would have to back all their nags up one way or another. This girl didn't want me to go. I told her, I says, "Zane Grey ordered me to go with you." She got in a huff. Romer Grey's wife, Betty, Bob Carney's wife, and the other secretary was very nice about it. They didn't mind having me along at all. The blond secretary got mad. She whipped the little buckskin into a hard run, and around all of that cliff she went, just as hard as that little horse could go. If she'd met a bear or met another pack string there'd been only one end. She'd have been in the river and smashed on the rocks below.

The girls said, "What are you going to do, Elmer?"

I says, "Nothing we can do. She's in God's hands instead of ours now. She'll either make it or she won't. There ain't a thing we can do." She made it to the ranch all right.

I came home about ten pounds underweight that fall, and my big saddle horse had lost 200 pounds. In fact, everything we had was pretty well wore out in the way of pack stock. Zane Grey wrote the novel *Thunder Mountain* from this trip. He sent me a copy of it, autographed, and it was loaned to somebody. Anyway, whoever it was never brought it back.

One day when fording the Middle Fork this blond secretary was right behind me on the little buckskin mare. There was a lot of big flat rocks in the river bottom. The little mare got astraddle of them and went down. I whirled my old saddle horse around, reached down and I got her by the shoulder of the buckskin jacket. I lifted her up in the air until her old horse got its feet under it again, and dropped her back in the saddle. In his book, Zane Grey had a big rescue scene on the Middle Fork and told how the river had washed the horses away, as he grabbed the lady and waded out with her. That was utterly impossible, because a horse can hold the bottom long after a man hasn't a chance. Anyway, he wrote *Thunder Mountain* from that trip.

HIGH COUNTRY FISH...

I had already replanted the North Fork of the Salmon River with 40,000 chinook fry. In the spring of '32, Al Wheeler, the ranger, came up wanting to know if I wanted to plant the Big Horn Crags with trout. It was along in June. I knew that high country would still be under snow, but they had an enormous amount of rainbow eggs, and wanted somebody to put them in those lakes. They had never been planted.

Kinney said all he could do was give me $4.80 a day and a man to help me at the same price. That was no pay at all, but I wanted the lakes planted, so I shod up ten head of horses and hired a Swede named Hansen to help me. He was a big husky man but weak in the head at times. At any rate we set out for the Crags.

At that time the road was building down the Salmon River below Shoup, and the CCC's had blasted it off as far down as Halfway Camp. They had blown out part of the trail, where the old road used to go around the cliff. When we got down there they had eight pack loads of eggs and our grub, such as it was. It was condemned forest service grub.

There we had a twelve-yard chasm across from one end of the trail to where it started again around the cliff, but they had lots of manpower and I had plenty of rope. We took each pack horse and cinched him up good and tight, tied the half-inch rope into the hoops of the Decker saddles, put 30 CCC boys up on top of the cliff to lift and hold the horse, and put another six or eight across on the other side to swing the horse over to where there was a trail. We swung all of them over there in spite of their screaming and neighing. We swung all the packs over, packed up, and headed on for the Crags. We got as far as Goat Lake. That was the end of the trail on account of snow drifts. There we belled and hobbled the horses and turned

Rain and fog fills the valley floor, but high above the Middle Fork of the Salmon River, Keith's pack string moves along in bright sunshine.

them loose. We took back packs and these fish eggs. What we had that we couldn't take on the first load we dug back into snow drifts and left them there and hoped that the bear wouldn't find them while we were gone.

We had to cut stairsteps in the snow cone to get out of the basin at the head of Goat Lake, and up onto a ridge. This ridge led back several miles past some little lakes and Clear Creek, and over a divide that dropped down into a basin with the big Ship Island Lake and a smaller lake they later called Airplane Lake above it. We made the trip okay and put 40,000 eggs in Ship Island Lake, and 10,000 in the little lake above. I remember it was about the 23rd or 24th of June. That night we got a howling snow storm and a blizzard as we were up over 9,000 feet. Mount Maguire on the north side was 10,067 feet, and we were down at the base of it, not too many feet below. We stayed under a big spruce tree that night, but got little sleep as the wind blew so hard we had an awful time keeping up the fire. The next morning we had a foot of wet snow to wade and we found Ed Withers old trap cabin about 300 yards from

us in a stand of heavy timber. If we'd known it was there we'd have spent the night in comfort. Anyway we planted nine lakes in the Big Horn Crags; Ship Island, Airplane Lake above it, three in Clear Creek, two in the left fork of Roaring Creek, and one lake in another creek that led down to the CCC camp on the Salmon River.

Coming back from Ship Island Lake, the stairsteps we'd cut in the snow cones to get up out of the Goat Lake basin had melted and the snow was pretty rotten. I started out on them and they all peeled away with me and away I went headed for a big cliff about a hundred yards below. I managed to start rolling over and over sideways, fast as I could, and I rolled past the cliff and slid down into a little meadow without incident. However, Hanson was afraid. I told him to get back and run and jump just as far as he could and land a-rolling and he'd make it. Finally I told him I couldn't help him. I wasn't going to try to come back, and he had to get up nerve enough to do it. Finally he did. He took a run and he came out in the meadow even past me because he really made a jump when he took off. We got back to camp and only two of my horses had crawled up under some cliffs and were there. The rest were gone. So we caught the two, saddled them up, and picked up the trail of the others. We had to trail them clear around on Clear Creek to Sagebrush Lookout before we found them. We got back at two in the morning.

We tried to get some sleep that night. We were out of grub, and we still had one lake to plant. That night the grizzlies scared the horses and they came into camp and stomped us out of our beds before daylight. So we built up a fire and as soon as it was light, we lit out. We went down the Garden Creek ridge. It turns an elbow. I told Hansen to go to the elbow and stop and wait for me and I'd fall off a 1500-foot drop down into Dome Lake and plant it and climb back out and meet him at the elbow. I planted the lake, and when I got out all I could find was horse droppings and broken halter ropes and tracks leading on down the Garden Creek trail. I scared up a pair of grouse, an old rooster and a hen. So I told the old hen she was going to have to get along without him and I shot the old rooster with a .45, drew him and carried him on with me.

I didn't catch Hansen until I got clear down to the carrot patch where some Mormons had started a homestead on Garden Creek. I was pretty mad. I don't know why he didn't do as I told him, but it made a long day for me.

The next day we ate the grouse. It was an old rooster and I think one Noah had on the Ark, because the Swede boiled him until two in the morning before he got tender enough to eat. The next morning we had nothing to eat for breakfast at all. We tightened up our belts and took off. We had a huge ham on the trip but it made us sick every time we ate it. It was condemned forest service grub anyway, so we finally threw it away and let the bears have it. We arrived back out to Halfway Camp and, bless Moses, they'd shot off the cliff again and there we were, stalled. It was Friday night and they'd quit for the end of the week. No grub, and very little horse feed, and what there was was up a steep mountain among the cliffs. So we turned the horses loose with bells on them and kicked them up the slope. That night we got a huge thunderstorm. Each of us had a bed underneath a big long boulder that hung out about six feet on the lower edge next to the river. Boulders came down off of that mountain the size of cookstoves and larger. The air was full of brim-

On a hunt on the Salmon with Doc DuComb in the 1930s, Keith shows the smallest of ten rams he has taken. It was dropped by a 180-grain bullet in .30-06.

stone from them hitting other rocks, and lightning struck all around. It was a wild night. Finally it let up Saturday morning. With nothing to eat, we tightened up our belts again for breakfast. That night we went to bed under the rocks again. The horses were above us getting some picking.

On Sunday morning when I woke up I had a sense that something was looking at me. I felt around in my bed and found my six-shooter. I turned my head a little to one side and then the other, then I looked over towards Hansen where he was under this other sloping boulder. He pointed behind me. I turned my head slowly and there was a big old mule buck with his nose not six inches from my face, in the velvet, and as soon as my eyes hit his, he snorted and jumped back a couple of paces and looked at me. Evidently he had never seen a man, but he was curious as to what I was. The Swede was motioning for me to shoot him. I started to and then I thought, "We can't eat him up in one day and if we build a fire and smoke him, why they'll know it and the game warden will be down and there'll just be hell to pay."

I let the hammer down on the six-gun, and the Swede started cussing. "Elmer," he says, "I could have ate the whole darn deer before they get here." Anyway I let the buck go.

Finally Monday morning here come about 50 men of the CCC crew, and they gave us two lunches apiece. We sat down and ate

142

them before we did anything. Then Hansen went up the mountain and gathered up the nags while I packed up and got things ready to move. That night we made it out to Shoup, camped there in the brush above the little mining town, and the next day we made it home. That ten days was one of the roughest I ever put in for $48.50 for myself and ten head of good horses, but we planted the Crags. Four years later I saw some ten and twelve-pound trout exhibited in a saloon here in Salmon that came out of Ship Island Lake, and from what I can learn, the fish "took" in all the lakes we planted, and did right well.

In 19 and 33 I booked Ben Comfort and Vic Asby from St. Louis for a month's sheep, goat and deer hunt in the Big Horn Crags. Gerald Ravndahl agreed to go with me and share the trip and what profits we made, which wasn't very much in those days. They were both good people to have out, but Ben weighed 255 pounds. I gave him my old brown horse, the strongest horse we had, but he was still really too much of a load in that steep country. After the month's trip Old Brownie had a sway back for about a month before he finally straightened out again. Ben could only sidehill around the mountain about half a mile in a day. That was as far as he could go. So it was pretty impossible to get sheep. Gerry and I had been in on a scout trip and had the sheep located. But our first night's camp at Goat Lake, here came some local people by with a big ram draped over the saddle and some canvas over him, before the season had ever opened. They'd been into our bunch of rams, shot them up and scattered them and killed one. Later we reported it to the game department, but nothing was ever done about it. We never knew why.

I finally located another bunch of rams on a steep mountain that sloped into Clear Creek. Gerry took Vic Asby and made the circle while I managed to get Ben across a canyon from the rams about 1000 yards away in hopes that if they came our way we might be able to head them off and get Ben a shot. Vic and Gerry got too close to them. They came down a gutter and the rams were only 30 yards from them and they jumped up and bounced around a corner before they could hardly get the safeties off their rifles. So we didn't get sheep, but we did get a good goat for Vic down Goat Creek. Also they both shot mule deer. While Vic and Gerry were off on a side hunt down Goat Creek, we got a three-day blizzard. Ben and I laid it out and he wanted to know what it would take to win the Wimbledon cup. I told him the best car-

tridge I knew would be the .300 Magnum. So he wanted me to design the rifle and figure out the load. So I drew out specifications for a .300 Magnum bull gun and he had Griffin & Howe build it. I told him to have Western hand load the ammunition, which he did.

The next year at Camp Perry he won the great Wimbledon cup, and sent me a picture of him drinking beer out of it. He was a big fat man and I surely enjoyed seeing that picture with him drinking beer out of the huge Wimbledon cup. Since then, only recently, has the cup been won with anything but the .300 Magnum, and that was the first winning with the rifle and 180-grain load I sketched for him to use.

On our trip out we had trouble again with the CCC outfit. We'd passed Shoup and were coming up the grade where an old ranch was across the river with only a cable car to cross over. Along came a CCC truck with a Sergeant and a Lieutenant on it. They started honking their horns. The horses were already nervous from bear after being over in the Crags for a month, and were very spooky.

I was riding a pinto called Dude. He was a firstclass bucking horse anyway and I had a $300 engraved Griffin & Howe Springfield with scope on it in one hand. I didn't want to carry it in a scabbard. Dude started pitching and this Lieutenant and his Sergeant beat on the horn to keep him going. The rest of the outfit stampeded. Gerry and Ben Comfort took off up the road to where the bulldozers had made a side cut. They managed to get all the pack string jammed in there. Dude was swapping ends and doing a first-class job of bucking me. Vic Asby was watching me, with this Lieutenant and his Sergeant laughing in the truck. Finally old Dude stopped and I kicked my feet clear of the stirrups and jumped. I just turned the safety over on the Springfield, set down in the road and took a bead on the driver.

I said, "One more honk out of that horn and I'll kill both of you, take it or leave it. You set right there. If you move that thing or hit the horn again, you're going to get it. Set there 'til we get this packstring up the road and get it out of the way."

They sat there all right. He said he'd go to town and get me arrested.

I said, "Go right ahead. That'll be fine. You make another squawk on that honker of yours and I'll silence it forever. So he let us move the horses down back to a decent place. Then I hung onto old Dude when he went by me, while Asby and Comfort and Gerry held the horses off the road. We had no more trouble that time.

Both Vic Asby and Ben Comfort were grand men to be out with. Ben was head of a petroleum company in St. Louis. Vic was a diesel engineer and traveled all over the world working on diesel engines. I saw the finest mule deer in my entire life on that trip. Ben Comfort and I had gone up a trail from camp, and across a canyon from us at 400 yards we saw a little bunch of deer. Then on the skyline behind them an enormous buck came out. His horns hung out it looked to me like 18 inches on each side of his body. There was so many points I couldn't count them, and he looked very heavy. He fed down towards where the other deer were, turned his rump to us and started feeding on the steep mountain. It was a good 400 yards across. Ben had a good .375 Hoffman with a Lyman 48 on it. He'd shot it on the range a lot and was a good shot. It was snowing, no wind to speak of, very damp, heavy air and quite a lot of snow falling. Knowing a rifle would shoot low in a deal like that, and knowing visibility was poor too, Ben says "How far is it?" I says, "Four hundred yards, but I'd set your sight for 500, and do as I tell you and you'll get the buck." He didn't set them for 500. He set them for 400, I found out later.

I says, "You set them for 500 and leave that white rump stick up right over the top of your gold bead, and, when I tell you, you shoot. You can take up the slack and wait."

I waited until the buck raised his head, then I knew he had the rump, the whole back, and the back of the neck for a target. I told him to shoot. Ben shot. He went between the hind legs and the forelegs, into the sod where the old buck had been feeding. He bounced into the air and around the hill while Ben missed him two more shots. Ben thought maybe he'd hit him so he was going to hike back to camp, that was about all he could travel with his weight, so I told him I'd go up above the canyon where I could get across, cross over, and make sure. I was certain he hadn't touched him. I got over there all right. I had on a pair of Bean rubbers and they'd worn slick in that decomposed granite from a month in the Crags. In fact the soles were about gone and we had about an inch of wet snow over there over everything. I found out he'd missed the deer clean, he hadn't even touched him. I started around above a cliff that dropped off about 20 feet. I stepped on a slab of rock and it was loose. My feet shot out from under me and down the hill I went, end over end and over the cliff. I curled up around my rifle.

Antelope hunting often calls for long shots, and the 12X Lyman target scope helped take this record-class pronghorn in 1935, mounted on Keith's .280 Dubiel.

I found out later I landed in about the only piece of soft dirt below the cliff. There was rocks on each side of where I hit. That was all that saved me, but I didn't come to for about four hours, and when I did the calf of my right leg was out in front of my shin and my left knee was swelled until it was about to burst my overalls. I took my knife and slit that. I tried to stand up and couldn't. My rifle was all right except for one little nick on the floorplate where it had hit a rock on one of the turnovers. I thought a lot of that engraved Springfield and didn't want to bust it.

I managed to find a limb with a crotch in it about the right length to use for a crutch, and tucked it under one arm. I put the rifle on my back with the sling and I tried to hobble that way but I couldn't, so I slid down the mountain on the seat of my pants to the bottom of the gulch. Then hand over hand, and with a little use of my right leg, I man-

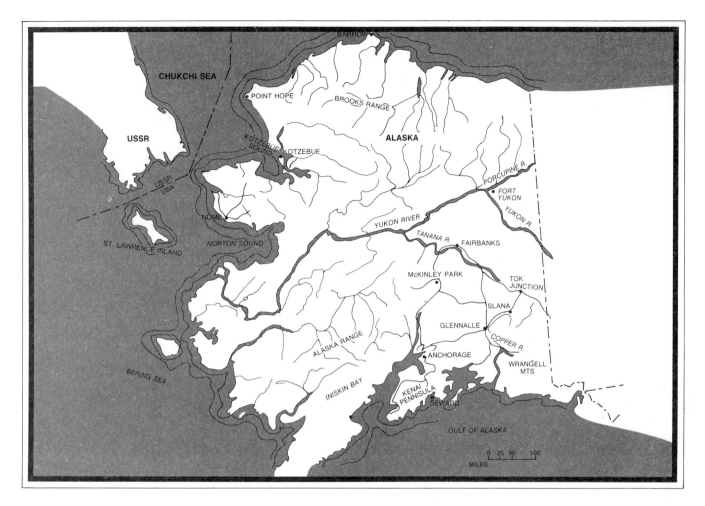

aged to climb back to the ridge. Then I slid down the next slope to the trail. There they found me at 2:00 A.M. when they was a-comin' out hunting for me. They boosted me on a horse, and got me back to camp, but I was worthless for the rest of the trip, and Gerry had to do the work and had to tail me up on my horse each day. That old buck would have gone way over a 40-inch spread, and with so many points I couldn't count them. I offered Ben $100 for his shot before he fired, but he wouldn't take it.

Another time I got Ben on a good buck and we were near the top of a ridge. I was lying down where I could clear the ridge. The buck was only a 100 yards away. Ben thought he was clear of the ridge and when he fired all he did was hit the top of the ridge in front of us and douse us with gravel and flying sand. The buck bounced away unharmed. A few days later I got him a shot at another buck about 80 yards from us in a swale and we were sitting up on a boulder. Ben had carried his .375 in a saddle scabbard. It had target knobs on the Lyman 48. Pulling it out and putting it back in the scabbard had rubbed the windage screw until the rifle was a good six inches off from zero. When he shot, instead

of hitting the buck behind the shoulder, he caught him back about the middle through the paunch. The deer jumped, kicked at his belly, and took off. I noticed the right ear was cocked low. He went around some brush out of sight. Ben said, "I missed him." I said, "No you didn't. You hit him all right. We'll just have to trail him up." The buck hadn't gone 50 yards. The 270-grain .375 had gone through the paunch, the right lung, and lodged under the skin on the right shoulder. So Ben finally had his buck.

Asby had a queer experience. He shot a big mountain goat broadside, square in the heart. The bullet split the heart, one whole side of it was open like you'd opened it with a knife. The bullet then turned around completely and came out three inches from where it entered. We heard it go by as it passed us going back. That blood in the heart must have caused it to turn. Anyway, it was a very queer experience and a queer performance for any bullet, but it happened exactly as related.

In '34 I booked Al Ellinger for a hunt in the Selway for elk and deer, as well as the president of radio station KNX in Hollywood and his brother-in-law. Ravndahl went with me on this trip to the Selway. It was a long

145

When not on hunting expeditions away from Idaho, Keith took parties hunting near home, as in this late elk hunt in 1946, with Lorraine Keith, Ted Keith, and two unidentified hunters.

pack trip dragging our horses down the river, up Spring Creek, out around Blue Nose, out past Square Top, Stripe Mountain, and clear out to Salmon Mountain. We went around the shoulder of it, and dropped off into a branch of the Little Clearwater where we made camp below an elk lick. I had W. L. Dickey along for cook. He killed a very fine six-point bull with a freak knob that ran out on the right-hand side about 18 inches with a huge ball on it. The old boy had been using it for a pillow when he slept until it was all polished and worn white on the end.

We had a good trip, though we didn't get Al the big head that he wanted. I had him within 30 yards of a huge bull. He was answering me and I told Al to run right at him hard and he'd get a shot. But he hesitated, and then the wind changed and I heard the bull go. I couldn't get Al to take off and run. If he'd run while I was holding the elk with the bugle, he'd had him.

One bad thing on the trip; we'd left the cars locked up at Paradise. When we came out we found out somebody had broken into Al's car and stole his fine .280 Dubiel Mag-

num Mauser. It carried a quarter-rim, folding sights, beautiful Circassian stock and a gold name plate underneath the grip cap, full-size of heavy sheet gold. We never saw that rifle again. However, he had his big .600 Jeffrey along, as he wanted to shoot it while he took movies, which I did, and they never bothered the big rifle in its case.

On the '34 trip, I again saw a 7x57 Mauser fail miserably on mule deer. The president of KNX's brother-in-law carried this rifle. I forgot his name. Anyway I got him a shot at an awful nice buck with a good head at about 250 yards across a gulch. He hit him in the neck and it took off a vertebra and over an inch of the spinal cord. The buck dropped and laid there, and while we were crossing the gulch he jumped up and took off again. He hit him again and piled him up, so we got the buck all right but that 139-grain 7mm had failed to do the job. It had cleared the spinal cord for over an inch and yet it hadn't put him down to stay. He was able to get up and run. Much like the experience Harry Snyder had when he put six slugs into a ram in British Columbia in '37.

LIFE AROUND HOME . . .

Ravndahl and I would spend a month each winter pulling down big dead yellow pine trees and sawing them into logs. We'd take a four-horse team and logging sled and haul them to each ranch, and then we'd put in eight hours a day on the end of a seven-foot crosscut, sawing up our winter's wood. Then we'd put in two weeks sawing ice on the pond, hauling sawdust, making bins, and putting down ice for the summer. There was no refrigeration then, no electricity. We had old coal oil lamps until we got gasoline laterns. We immediately quit the coal oil lamps for the gas lanterns, as they were so much better. Little Mom and Druzilla took care of the ranch, and ran things there while I was away on these many trips trying to eke out a living. Then in the winter, in what spare time we had, I'd write articles for the magazines.

In time I was writing for *Sports Afield* quite steady and also *Outdoor Life,* some for *Field & Stream,* some for *Hunting & Fishing,* and some for the old *Outdoors* magazine. I became acquainted with Captain Ned Crossman and we became very good friends. When he got a letter from some guy panning him about something he wrote, he'd send it to me and I'd take him apart in my column for the next month. When I got a letter from some freak giving me the devil, calling me a liar and one thing and another, I'd send it down to Ned and he'd take him apart in his column in *Hunting & Fishing.* That worked quite well. I never did get to see Ned. He was going to come up but he never did make it. He said it was too far to drive, especially during the hot summer months.

Lorraine raised turkeys on the ranch in addition to about ten head of cows. Between that and a good garden and what I would make writing, usually ten, fifteen, twenty dollars an article, we managed to live. Harry McGuire bought a lot of articles from me for *Outdoor Life* when they were in St. Paul, Minnesota. Later, that magazine sold to a New York outfit and has been there ever since. But I wrote extensively for *Sports Afield,* and found them a very fine magazine to do business with. They never changed any of my material in the least and always returned all my pictures. I enjoyed working for a magazine like that.

At the ranch we had about 50 head of mule deer wintering on the mountain in back of the barn. I was continually testing rifles, even the heavy Sharps, working up loads. As long as I didn't throw a slug up on the mountain,

Sheep hunting each fall was a big part of the Keith family income, and paid off in pride as well as money when the hunts were successful, like when this record ram was taken by Doc DuComb (left) in 1936.

they'd graze there above the flume, paying no attention to me whatever because they knew they were being protected. Every coyote that came out on the hill, or every golden eagle that lit there, I killed him if I could.

We had an old shepherd dog named Ring. She'd sit on the woodbox of a morning. If she saw a coyote or an eagle on the hill she'd just yip once, enough to let us know, and then she'd point her nose to where she'd seen him. She never lied. Lorraine would get the binoculars and I'd get the big rifle and go out to the bench with it and we'd watch. If it wasn't an eagle sitting on a stump or a log, why, sooner or later we'd see the coyote move. We got a lot of them that way. That dog had the best eyes I've ever seen on any dog in all my life. Seemed like she could see about as well as a mountain sheep.

After getting out of the elk camps in the fall of '35, our son Ted was born on the sixth of December. We had a good doctor, and everything went well. Now we had two youngsters to play with. Dru was old enough by that time to take quite an interest in the baby. The country was slowly coming out of the big Depression, and I did fairly well with my writing. Lorraine raised a big flock of turkeys each fall and all the garden we could use. I raised wheat for the turkeys and shot our meat for the winter's supply. We also speared and canned a lot of salmon each summer. After writing in the mornings, I'd take a fly-rod and pick up a nice bunch of trout for the evening meal.

The summers on the North Fork were very pleasant, although it would get terrifically hot at times as our ranch laid to the south, while the North Fork runs north and south. At our place it makes a sharp bend and the sun beat on that big mountain in back of it and made it much warmer than the rest of the North Fork. Hay grew clear up to the horses' hames. In fact, some years when harvesting I'd have to have a man go along with a pitchfork and throw it aside so I could make the next swath. It was so heavy the swathboard would have no effect on it.

In '36 I continued to run boat trips for fishing and fall hunts with Cap Guleke down the Salmon River to Riggins, so we were quite busy. Then when fall came, we had to lay in our meat. At that time on the North Fork the winters were quite cold and steady. I had a good screened meat house to hang our elk and deer in. They'd freeze hard as a rock. We'd go out and saw off what we wanted, and eat when it was needed. We had natural refrigeration. One winter, however, it started raining. The only way to keep the meat was to can it, so we put in nearly a week canning elk and deer meat to save it.

THE MEXICAN SHEEP HUNT . . .

I also hunted antelope in the Pahsimeroi Valley from the first season they opened for several years, killing five record heads. The largest went 17½ inches each horn and a 17½ inch spread. For a long time he was seventh place in the world's records. I also garnered some good sheep heads down the river for different parties, as well as a couple of fine ones for myself.

In the spring of 19 and 37 Doc DuComb of Carlyle, Illinois, asked me to go on a trip with him to Mexico for desert sheep. He said he would take care of my expenses, as he wanted me to guide him and help out. We booked with Charley Wren of Sonora, Mexico. I took a bus to California, had a good long visit with my friend, Frank Pachmayr and his father, Gus. Had dinner with them before taking the early morning bus out for Ajo, and Gila Bend.

Charlie O'Neil's antelope (left) and Elmer's were the result of this 1936 Idaho pronghorn hunt. The two men together designed a number of wildcat cartridges over the years that were very influential.

Doc DuComb met me at Ajo. He phoned a friend of his in California and had a long hour's talk. There was a game warden there, a big fellow over six feet, 200 pounds, red-faced, and carrying two guns. He had a United States badge, an Arizona badge and a Mexican badge. We knew nothing of it at the time, but he got the dope that we were going in hunting sheep via the telephone conversation.

Charley Wren came over in his car and took us over to his hacienda in Sonora. He had a huge adobe outfit there, but when it came to eating, they served the poorest meals I ever had. He had a can of sardines for each of us, and a huge bowl of yellow peppers. They were hotter than fire. He had a Mexican lady for a cook, I believe the ugliest buck-toothed woman I ever saw. She was sick, she said, so we told her Doc DuComb was a doctor. But when she informed him it was something with her heart, Doc said he didn't deal with heart problems at all.

Charley Wren had a big truck, and had extra casings over the tires to take the cactus and broken chaparral stumps we had to run over. We took off. Out in camp we seemed to

When they found the desert bighorn ram, the meat was worthless, but the rare trophy had splendid horns, and made Doc DuComb's Mexican hunt worthwhile.

have plenty of grub and we lived quite well. We hunted the Pinacates for several days, seeing only some ewes and lambs. Then we worked south and into the big lava flows between the Pinacates and White Mountains. Charley had a red-headed Mexican guide. One day I located two rams far out on that expanse of lava flows and we headed for them. One of them looked good. Before we got within half a mile of them however, Red started veering off to the left. He thought the sheep were over that way. I was sure I had them marked with some little hummocks of lava. So he went that way and I took Doc and headed on to where I knew the rams were. We came up behind a little hummock of lava and instantly the dust boiled out the other side of it. I knew we'd jumped the sheep at close range. Doc stood there undecided what to do. I just grabbed him and pushed him up on top of the lava flow. The rams ran out about 150 yards and swung around facing to the left. The big one was on the left side. I says, "Take the one to the left, Doc." It was a nice sheep, well-broomed, but a good heavy head. Doc shot. Both sheep jumped and ran

off. Where the big ram had been in the lead and bouncing high when I first saw them running, he now ran flat and low to the ground and the little ram took the lead.

Doc says, "I missed him."

I says, "No you didn't. You hit him."

I trailed the sheep for a good mile, I believe, by picking up traces of them here and there where there was a little dust or sand that blowed on patches on the lava flow. Finally I lost him. There never was any blood that we could see, but I was positive that he hit that ram center in the body, and I heard the flap of the bullet. The next day three miles, maybe four miles north, Charley Wren and I walked out on an escarpment and looked down into a basin below us. Instantly Charley, who was in the lead, motioned for me to get down and get my rifle ready. I walked out there and there was Doc's sheep lying down there. One look at him and I knew that broomed horn.

Charley says, "Shoot him."

I says, "He don't need shootin'." And I stood up.

The ram never moved. He was as dead as a mackerel. We called Doc up, went down, and drug the sheep out of the rocks. I found the bullet entrance at about the center of the left side. He'd been quartering towards us, so I felt around on his rump and right in the edge of the white patch I found a lump, took my sheath knife, and cut it out. Out fell Doc's 180-grain soft point, perfectly expanded. He wouldn't believe it was his bullet. I fitted it in the end of his Model 54 Winchester and then he believed me.

I told him, I says, "If you don't want him, I'll take him. He's a good head." He was blowed up to high heaven and the meat, of course, was soured and ruined. I pulled my sheath knife and peeled the cape off, taking it off behind the shoulders for a front leg to shoulder mount, turned the ears, and split the lips. Charley Wren had a three-pound sack of salt in the truck, so I rubbed it into every pore of the skin and managed to save the head for him. That sheep had gone at least three miles, and possible a little more, with that slug through his body. That again soured me on the .30-06. Of course, if he'd hit him six inches forward through the lungs, the sheep wouldn't have gone anywhere. It was a misplaced shot, but yet going through the paunch, through the whole body, through the right ham to the skin, you'd think it would have done better than that, and it would have, if it had been a heavier rifle with a bigger bullet.

A few days later we saw the other ram. Charley and I had shacked up in a cave in a cliff to get out of the terrible sun. We packed a gallon of water apiece, and even then we had to conserve it. We found the skeleton of one man that hadn't made it, his bones all bleached out by the sun. While we were lying in this sheep cave, along come this other ram, the same young ram that had been with the big fellow. He stopped at 200 yards and I put the scope of my .30 Newton on him. Charley begged me to shoot him. His horns were only, I figured, 32 inches, and came down to the bottom just a little past three-quarter but they were thin. I told Charley he would be a good ram in four, five, six years more, and I wasn't going to kill him. The old man didn't like it. He said I could drive the truck right to him and we needed the meat.

"Well," I says, "We'll have to eat some more of your sardines. I'm not going to kill him." I let him go. Had I taken him, I would have had the grand slam, but I still didn't want a little piddling ram if I couldn't get a good one.

Next we started hunting the Javelina. Charley had another Mexican guide. He had two saddle horses and a dog. He'd been packing water from the Crow tanks about 20 miles away every day and it was full of mosquito larvae. I started to strain it. Charley held up his hands in horror. We'd lose too much water from evaporation. So after that we'd just open our mouth, lay back our ears, and let it go, wigglers and all. It was wet anyway, and kept body and soul together.

One evening coming into camp I saw a big Gila monster. He was on a lava flow with white rocks in it, and he was colored black with white spots all over him. So I wanted to take him in and get his skin. I had a bunch of sash cord on my pack board, so I made a loop and roped him. The Mexican dragged him along. He was a big Gila monster. He'd keep him away from him so he couldn't bite. Finally I says, "How do you kill them?"

"Oh," he says, "We choke them to death."

"Well," I says, "Let's choke him to death and get on with it. We've got a long ways to camp, and lots of cholla and cactus to negotiate." He whipped him over between the forks of an ocotillo bush, put the rope around his hips, and set back on it with all his weight. After five, ten minutes I says, "Ain't he dead yet?"

"No," he says, "It takes quite awhile to kill them."

So he kept his weight on that monster for another five minutes.

Finally I says, "He must be dead. Slack up and we'll see." The monster slid down from the Ocotillo to the ground, opened his mouth and hissed at us. Red says, "You can't kill them quick."

"Well," I says, "Let's go on to camp with him and get a small pistol and shoot him." So he kept him away from him, swinging him, and took him on to camp. He tied him up to a sagebrush. We were bedded down around the truck. Doc DuComb says, "I'm not going to sleep on the ground with that thing." So he made Charley get out a cot and set it up. Raphael, our cook, said he'd kill him and skin him for me the next day.

The next morning Charley wanted to move early down towards the White Mountains. So I says, "Throw the monster in the back of the truck. Raphael can kill him and skin him today while we're hunting."

Doc DuComb says, "I'll have none of it." He grabbed his K-22. It was loaded with copper-coated Super X, I believe high speed, but I won't swear to it now 'cuz I don't remember, but I know it was a long rifle. He proceeded to shoot the monster. They'd just make a grey dent where they'd hit and glance off and richochet. Finally he shot him between the eye and the ear and that went in and killed him. However, Raphael didn't keep his word and I didn't get the monster hide.

Charley's Mexican guide had one saddle that was the queerest thing I've ever seen. The seat of it was about four inches above the bars on the horse's back. Doc DuComb rode it. Not being a rider, he was flapping around up there. It looked like he was floating on air. We took off on a hog hunt with his dogs. One old dog was a pretty good hog dog and he had his ears all cut to ribbons from previous fights with hogs. We got to trailing a bunch; the dogs barking, and the Mexican riding hell-bent-for-election through that cactus. I was equal to it, and stayed with him, but Doc got lost behind. Finally we came up on a point and Doc yelled and waved his arms.

He says, "I just saw two Javelinas go in a hole here." So we went back.

There was a little amphitheatre, probably twenty feet across, around the hole, and it was surrounded with cholla, all frosted white. The hole was fairly large where it entered. It went in about ten feet and then it choked down to a small hole and then there was another cavern behind that.

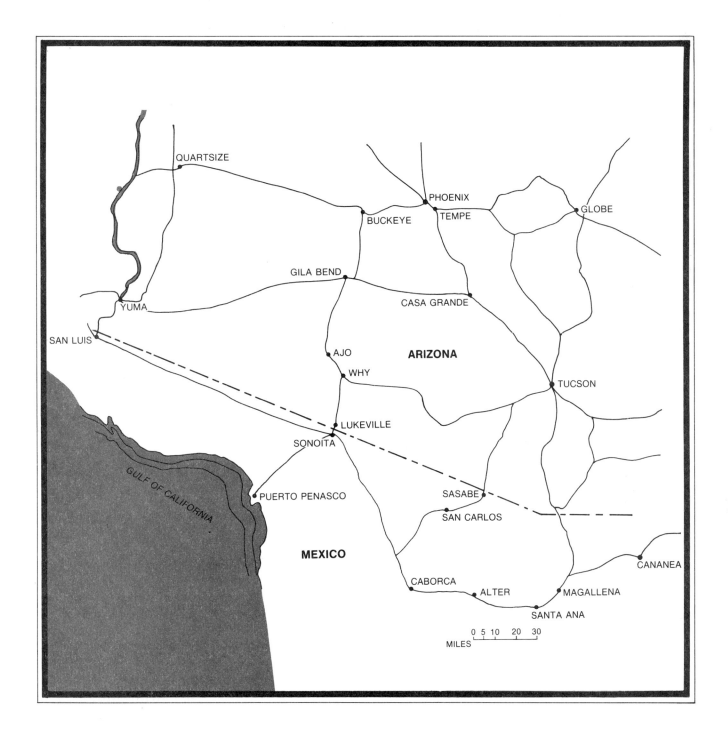

I took my .357 Magnum and crawled in, to see if I could get a shot. I got back to the orifice of the second cavern, and I could hear a pair of tusks clattering on one side and then another pair on the other. About that time the Mexican's reata hit my feet and spurs and he drug me out.

He says, "No bueno, no bueno," and he made slashing motions at his throat. He took a half-inch rope and tied it on the old dog. He called the dog "Pinto." He says, "Coche, Pinto, coche. Go get 'um."

Finally the old dog growled. Oh, he hated to go in, but finally in he went. As soon as the fight started, the Mexican pulled him back out. The rope had only one strand left. The old dog's shoulder was ripped open to the bone from the knuckle clear up to the top of the shoulder blade, and one ear was slashed wide again on the other side. He says, "Si, Senor, no bueno."

"Well," I says, "They've chopped the poor old dog up. We're going to get those hogs. Go get some wood, and we'll smoke them out."

Doc gathered up some of the old dead trees around there. I doubt if any water had hit them since before Christ, they were so dry. I whittled some shavings and set them afire and

151

it caught right now. I started throwing wood in. Fairly soon the hogs commenced coughing in there. I laid down in this amphitheatre in front of the hole with a six-shooter and waited. Pretty soon out come one of them for all he was worth, his little old tusks just a chopping. I shot him in the forehead double-action with a .357, and he went to jumping up and down about six feet in the air like a rabbit. The other hog came out of the hole and started going round and round in this circle. The dust was so thick I couldn't see anything. Doc DuComb was up on a cliff pointing the '06 down in there, and I was more afraid of him than I was the hogs. At any rate I backed into the cholla, good and square, and I was frosted, my whole backside. The other hog that wasn't wounded went back in the hole.

Well, we drug this one out that I'd killed, so I says, "Get some more wood and we'll set it afire," and I laid down again. My backside was burning. Finally we smoked the other hog out and I killed him. I says, "At least we've got a hog head apiece." Then they draped me over an old dry log, pulled my pants down, and Doc and the Mexican pulled Cholla spines, and they'd laugh and pull some more. I didn't set down comfortably for several days after that. That cholla is the most infernal creation of the devil that I've ever run into; worse than anything I saw in three safaris in Africa. It seems to me that the stuff will jump at you. And the wind will blow the burrs off and they'll collect in the low places and with tennis shoes they'll go right through them, sole, side or any other way. It's miserable stuff, barbed just like a porcupine quill.

We drove back to Sonora and Charley's hacienda and headed out for home. I had a date to meet Al Ellinger, Frank Mosteller and Mrs. Ellinger in Seattle for a bear hunt in Alaska. I just had time to get home and have one night with the family and make it. Charley sent us out to Ajo with his red-headed Mexican guide driving the truck. About half way out to Ajo a big black car with four men in it came by us. Pretty soon it circled around and went past us going to Ajo, came around another bend and went by us again and looked us over. I told Doc, "That's some officers looking for somebody." Then they passed us again headed for Ajo. We came around another bend and there the car was, laid square across a narrow place in the road. We stopped about a hundred yards from it. I didn't like the looks of things. One guy got out of the car and pulled out a .30-30 carbine, levered a shell into it and laid it down over the hood

on us. Then a big red-faced fellow with two guns on him, and two deputies with one gun apiece got out and came marching back to us. About that time a border patrol car came along from the U.S. side, swung past us in and behind us.

This big red-faced man says, "Are you Elmer Keith?"

I says, "That's the name I always went by."

"You Doctor DuComb?"

He says, "Yes."

He says, "Well I have a warrant for your arrest for killing sheep illegally in Mexico. I've got to take you back to Mexico to be there for trial."

I says, "The hell you say."

"Yup."

He pulled out the warrants and showed us his three badges.

He says, "I've got to search your car."

I says to go ahead. We left the sheep head and both hog heads with Charley Wren, and the Mexican had promised to jerk the pig meat and send that back to us, which he never did. He wrote afterwards that it was so good they ate it all. At any rate he started searching the car. He turned up my .357 Magnum and I just grabbed it, checked the loads and stuck it in my belt. Then he turned up Doc's 1917 Smith & Wesson. I grabbed that too, checked the loads and stuck it in my belt. While he was searching there I knew he would find nothing but dirty socks and empty shells, so I hiked back to the patrol car.

I asked the border patrol boys, "What in the hell is going on here?"

"Well," he says, "this guy has an Arizona badge and a U.S. Federal badge and a Mexican badge. He has the power to call us in. We know who you are, Keith. You're a friend of Charley Askins and George Parker on the patrol. You may have trouble with him. He's got several notches on his guns for Mexicans he's killed crossing the border. If trouble starts, you can turn your back on the border patrol car because there'll be no trouble coming from us." I thanked the boys, and I went back.

He says, "You fellows drive into Ajo and wait there. I'll go over into Mexico and get the evidence and we'll be back and then we'll take you to Mexico. Don't leave. You're both under arrest."

So we drove to Ajo. The whole town was incensed. The hotel men, the hardware men, everybody. They said, "They've been hauling these sheep out of here every year and hauling them over to Diego, and Sonora's been selling them licenses, $21 apiece, the same as you fellows paid for your licenses, and," he said, "Mexico D.F. don't honor Sonora's selling sheep licenses. There's where he's got you."

Well I told the people there, "Hell, I ain't a-goin to no Mexico with nobody. I gotta go home and got to go to Alaska on a bear hunt. Anyway I'm not interested in spending time in any Mexican jail."

At four o'clock the "galloping goose," we called it, (it was a motorized car) a kind of a trolley that came in on the tracks from Gila Bend over to Ajo was due. There was a big old adobe depot with an arch in front. Back of the arch on the right side there was quite a recess there, six or eight feet. The left side was square and ran back to the railroad track. There were a pair of swinging doors there where this trolley parked. Just as we were ready to go, or so I thought, this big black car pulled up across the street. One boy jumped out and levered a shell into a .30-30 and pulled down on us. I jumped back behind the arch on the right side so the rifleman couldn't get a shot at me.

I told Doc, "Load your Model 54 and pull down on that rifleman, and if anything starts at all, kill him and then help me with these three. 'Cuz if we ever get to Mexico, we'll never get back. Our only chance is to either kill them or bluff them. We've got to fight it out right here." I had two six-shooters in my belt, just stuck in the front. So in came the three of them, a deputy on my left, the big man in the center and the other deputy on my right. The big man had two guns and the others one apiece. He says, "Well, we've got to take you to Mexico City."

I says, "You've got to kill us first. And I just don't believe you're fast enough. Start in any time you feel lucky. I'm going to kill all three of you if it's the last thing I do."

I told Doc, "Kill the rifleman if it starts and then help me with these." Doc was as white as a sheet, but he did just what I told him. Well the big guy nudged the one on the left. I says, "Don't nudge him too fast or I'm going to throw both guns. I'll kill your deputies and they'll cross on you when I'm working fast double-action." I was in good training. When you draw a pair of six-guns and shoot at an object, for me at least, they always cross double-action. The right hand gun will start working to the left, and the left hand gun to the right. At any rate I knew I could kill them all and I intended to do it. But they wouldn't fight. Finally I said, "Well, gentlemen, if you don't want to fight, I'm going to go home." I backed to the door, pushed it

open with my foot, and caught hold of a brace that was hung on one side of the running board. I told Doc, "Switch your aim to these three." They didn't like the '06 pointed at the three of them all in line where he could kill them all with one shot. I hollered at the motorman to take it away. He did, and that's the way we left Ajo in the spring of '37.

When I got back to Los Angeles, I called my friend Ned Crossman, and told him what had happened. He says, "Elmer, the governor of Arizona happens to be a good friend of mine. We hunt quail together. I think I can take care of your game warden and his deputies. You go on to Alaska and have a good time. Just leave it to me."

I presume Crossman was as good as his word, because when I got back from Alaska, I had a letter from Charley Wren that said, "Elmer, I don't know what you did, but the big red-faced game warden and his deputies are all now sans badges, sans guns, and working on the section gang."

Anyway, it was a close squeak. Thank God Doc DuComb was a man that would do exactly what I told him.

TO ALASKA FOR BEAR . . .

So I pulled out, made it home, and had a day and a night with Lorraine, little Dru and Ted. Then I took off for Seattle, met the Ellingers and Frank Mosteller, and we headed north for Alaska on the Inside Passage on the old ship *Alaska*.

That boat trip was one of the finest I've ever had in my life. Fine food, music and the most beautiful scenery in the world up that Inside Passage. I didn't know then that two years later I'd be on the wheel four hours on and four hours off running another boat up through the same channel.

The *Alaska* was a good ship, well run, and we had a very fine trip up the Inside Passage to Seward, stopping at Valdez and several other ports along the way. Even went into Sitka, saw the Sitka Museum, and finally arrived at Seward. From Seward we took the old *Curesol*. It had been a yacht on the east coast, then it had been a Mexican gunboat, and then Alaskan, or some other line, had bought it and it run from Seward around to Kodiak and up the Cook Inlet to the towns there as far as Anchorage.

A very bad storm blew up when we left Seward. Everyone on the ship got seasick except Al Ellinger and I, the big Negro cook, and two of the stewards down in the galley. Frank Mosteller and I had a cabin on the left side of A deck. Al Ellinger and Mary had their cabin joined right up with ours except for the bulkhead on the other side of A deck. In other words there was a bulkhead between the cabins and they were crosswise of the deck. The seas got so heavy it knocked the transom out of the door in our cabin and water came in. They had a great old crockery pitcher and bowl that must have been relics of the Civil War, for people to wash with there. They came crashing down and shattered on the floor. I got our rifles and tied them to the stanchion of the upper berth with our belts. Frank was in the lower berth and I slept in the upper one if we could sleep in such seas. The boat was pitching like a bronc and rolling bad too. Each time it would roll to the left side, a mountain of water would come clean up over the door. Finally Al beat on the bulkhead between us and he says, "You hungry, Elmer?" I says, "I'm starving." Frank Mosteller groaned. He was sick. Mary was sick in the other bunk.

"Well," I says, "I'm hungry. If I can get to that galley I want something to eat."

Al says, "When she rolls my way you run like hell and get through the door into the room there above the galley that leads down to the dining room."

I did, and just got the door to the room closed when another mountain of ocean came up over it. I waited there. Finally here came Al down the other deck. I had the door ready to open for him, and he got in. We went down the stairs to the dining room. The Negro cook and the two stewards, they were very surprised.

"Why," they says, "the captain is down, everybody is down on the thing except the fellow on the wheel. Kermit Roosevelt is aboard, and he's sick too. You fellows want something to eat?"

I says, "We surely do, if you've got anything."

He says, "I've got a big cauldron of butterclam chowder."

I said, "There couldn't be anything better."

It was in a huge kettle that swung with the boat so that it wouldn't tip. It was swinging back and forth. So they sat us down at a table, and roped us to the table. They brought this butterclam chowder and bowls. On the next roll of the ship, away went the table, our chairs, us and the butterclam chowder clean over into the wall. The stewards cleaned us up the best they could. We went out in the galley with the Negro cook, hooked an arm around a stanchion, and held a bowl of chowder in one hand while we spooned it out with the other. We had a good feed.

Finally we got around to Kodiak Island, made the circle around it where they were dropping off freight and some passengers, and back up the passage to Seldovia where we debarked there, as that was where Ed Lovdahl had his little 47-foot boat, the *Vigilant,* that he was going to take us bear hunting in. Jim Simpson, the old Wyoming guide was the outfitter. He had Doc Reising, an old horse doctor from Boise, along as one guide; Ward Gay, who was formerly with Jonas Bros. in Denver, as a packer and to help guide Mosteller; and Ed Lovdahl to run the boat and do other guiding chores.

We set out for Iniskin Bay when the tide was right in the night, and we nearly ran over a beluga whale out there, and just managed to turn and dodge him. We anchored in the bay. A big old sea gull, mottle-colored, followed us all the way from Seldovia. When the boat was at anchor, it swung around on its anchor in the wind, and this old sea gull would perch on top of the masts. Jim Simpson and I had to sleep underneath a big old heavy 30-ounce tarp on the deck. That confounded seagull had the range, windage and everything. If we stuck a head out from under that tarp, it seemed like that's when he decided to unload, and we'd get part of it. I wanted to shoot him, but Tom O'Dale, the other guide, was very religious in upholding the law, and the law says you can't shoot seagulls. Poor old Jim and I had to dodge his excreta every time we stuck a head out from under that tarp for the whole trip. I swore then that if I ever had a chance I was going to kill seagulls.

We arrived at just about the right time, because the bears were just then digging out. One day Doc Reising and I watched one break the crust in the snow. I just happened to have the 20-power scope turned on a snow field and I saw the snow erupting. Out came a bear head. Finally out came a big bear. He had a ring of long hair around his neck and his head and the rest of him was rubbed as clean as an African lion. He made a circle, set around awhile, got rid of his rectal plug, came back and laid down across the hole. He was a big bear, but worthless. Frank Mosteller had a .375 Niedner. Al Ellinger had a .375 Rimmed double rifle and Mary had a .375 Hoffman, while I carried a .35 Whelen on a Springfield action with 275-grain Western Tool & Copper bullets and 57 grains of 4064 behind them.

On the entire trip I counted 88 bear that I figured were individuals, 78 of them brownies,

Mary Ellinger was one of the finest ladies Keith ever knew, and an avid bear hunter long before the Alaska trip. This is a fine black bear she bagged in Maine.

or grizzlies that would go for brownies, and the other ten were blacks. Doc Reising guided Mary and I, and he was a very poor guide. Ellinger said he had brought me along to take care of Mary, so I told him I'd keep her out of trouble all right as far as the bear was concerned. The big bear that I saw come out and make a circle when he first came out of the hole, Reising looked at him and said it was a woodchuck. I didn't know what was the matter with him, but I didn't think he wanted to make that climb over the deep snow. Anyway the bear was worthless.

On another day, Jim Simpson, Mary, and I were together and we located a big bear on a ledge in very heavy alders and about a quarter of a mile up the opposite slope from us. The snow was up to our hips. We managed to wallow down to the bottom and up the other side, each one pulling another out of a hole every now and then when it would break through deeper, up to our shoulders. We finally got up under the cliff the bear was bedded on. For some unknown reason, old Jim pulled off his hat, wiped his brow, and he says, "Whew, that was an awful pull." Mary and I held our hands up across our lips to silence him, but I knew good and well that the bear would hear that and go. Sure enough, we heard him above. I ran out to a ridge, saw him going across a swale there and up another ridge. I put the cross hairs of my little Noske 1½x scope on him, looked him over, but he

was rubbed to high heaven. There wasn't enough hair on him to make a good hat, so I didn't shoot him. Mary then wondered why Jim had said that and scared the bear. I don't know what got into him. He's supposed to be an old grizzly and sheep hunter, but he sure spooked that bear. However, it was just as well, as the bear wasn't worth killing.

One morning a big Japanese cruiser with its flag flying swept right past the entrance to Iniskin Bay right on up the coast. Tom O'Dale says they've got all this coast charted, while we haven't even a single chart of it that's accurate. There's all kinds of these green floats the Japanese use on their nets floating around the beaches, some big ones, some little ones, that broke off their nets.

One day Tom O'Dale, Ward Gay and I were crossing Iniskin Bay to the other side, when I saw a big brown bear on the beach about a mile away. Tom says, "Watch him now when we cross the wind." He was a good mile away but the wind was blowing quite strong. When our scent went to him, he stopped his prowling around and reared up on his hind feet. I turned the glasses on him and could see him twisting his nose, then he took off on a hard run for the hills. Shows how far they can scent a person.

Another day we located two three-year-olds, I figured they were. They weren't big bear but they were well-furred. They were playing, sliding down a snow slide. Then they'd go back up and slide down again. They'd cuff each other and roll. We worked out to the rim about 300 yards from them. A bear can't see very far, but they can sure hear and they've got one of the most wonderful noses of anything except possibly elk. At any rate the wind changed behind us. Instantly their frolicking stopped. One went one way down that side of the mountain, and the other followed on a hard run. That was the last we saw of those bears.

One day we elected to go up the Iniskin River. We ran the dory up it quite a ways not seeing anything of the big bear that we wanted. Finally we decided to come back down. Then we spotted a big black bear come running out towards the river. It was really a comical sight. He stopped at the edge, put one foot in, took it out and shook it, then put the other foot in and shook it, too. Then he backed up about 30 yards, took a hard run and jumped just as far into it as he could. When he got on the other side, the wind carried our scent to him. He lost no time making it to the alders. Another time on the Iniskin,

Even this small Alaskan brownie dwarfs the Hoffman .375 H&H Mary Ellinger used to drop him in 1937.

there was an old sow with two little cubs. They looked about the size of house cats. They were about 400 yards up the mountain on the left side from us in very deep snow. As soon as the old lady heard the motor she came charging down the ridge towards us about 50 yards, chopping her teeth and blowing. Then she'd go back up to the cubs. Finally she went up and stuck a paw under a cub and sent him up the hill as far as she could, then put a paw under the other one and sent him up there. She was a beautiful bear with beautiful fur, but we wouldn't bother a sow with cubs.

Next, a little farther up the river, we saw another sow with a cub across on the right side. Again she was a big, beautiful bear, well-furred, and she had either a very big cub or a small yearling, I couldn't tell which. Anyway we decided to pass her up. We didn't want to orphan any cubs.

Mary Ellinger was one of the grandest ladies I've ever guided. I'd rather guide a woman than a man any time. A woman will usually do what you tell her. A man, with his

natural ego, may think he knows more about the job than you do and then you get in trouble. Mrs. Ellinger was a wonderful companion to be with any time. One day across the bay we located a bunch of brownies playing on a snow slide. As I remember there were nine of them, all sows and cubs. They would go up to the top of this snow slide, some of them would go down on their bellies, some on the seat of their pants. They'd sail down the mountain in a cloud of snow, climb back up, and do it over again. Finally a huge old boar came out at the head of the snowslide, a big black bear. His nose seemed to say he was a brownie all right, but he was colored jet black as near as I could tell. He was a huge bear. Finally the wind changed and they got his scent. Every one of them took off in the alders on the hard run, with the big bear after them. The last we saw them they were topping the ridge and the big fellow was still chasing them. The rut was on.

On another occasion, Ed Lovdahl, Al and I were drifting down the river in a boat when we saw two three-year-olds. One of them was a dark-colored bear, deep brown, and the other was almost silver. That was one of the prettiest pelts I saw on the trip. I wanted Al to take it, but he wouldn't and I asked him to let me shoot him. No, he didn't want me to shoot him either, afraid we'd scare other bears, so we let him go. But that was the most beautiful bear I saw on the trip at nice easy rifle range.

We had some canned salmon bellies. Lovdahl would make up a mixture of potatoes and canned salmon bellies, a kind of stew. He also had some canned moose meat along. We wanted some fresh meat so Al shot a black bear. He wanted some black hides. We tried to eat him, but he'd evidently been on fish too long. The longer you'd chew that bear, the bigger he'd get, and he had such a strong fishy taste that we couldn't go him. I shot one black at about 200 yards. My rifle was sighted perfectly at 200 yards back on the Salmon River, but when I got up there it shot at least six inches low. At 200 yards I dropped underneath that bear's belly, then held higher and turned him over. Those 275-grain Western Tool & Copper slugs usually open well. We trailed him around the brush and finally killed him at close range. The bullet hadn't opened at all. I shot another one at about 50 yards with his head and shoulders up over a big boulder, got him square in the white place in his chest. It must have missed the spine. When he turned a back summerset and took off, we trailed him until he finally got into rocks and water where we could find no more trace of him. Evidently that bullet didn't open either.

Later on, Al, Doc Reising and Jim Simpson climbed the mountain on the right side where there was a bear they'd located, and Al killed him with a double rifle, hit him three times, I believe, with a double .375. They came down dragging that hide that night. The hides with the head and feet still left in them are a huge load for any man, and Lovdahl, Reising and Simpson would change off on it. Frank Mosteller and Ward Gay hunted over on the other side one day and they ran onto a nice bear that Frank killed at 200 yards with one shot with his .375 Niedner. The 270-grain bullet expanded perfectly, broke the spine, and lodged under the skin on the chest.

Once I was on deck cleaning the bear skulls and looking out for bear all around when I spotted an enormous bear on the ridge on the right side of the Iniskin River. There was a big spruce tree there so I could judge something of his size. He was at least a third bigger than anything I'd seen, maybe twice as big. He was enormous. Even when he lay on the ground it looked like his withers were about three feet off the ground and it looked like he was ten feet long, maybe more. He was a very dark-colored brownie. I showed him to Tom O'Dale. Tom had hunted bear all his life. He said, "Elmer, that's the biggest bear I've ever seen." So the next day Al decided to go up and get him. He took Lovdahl, and Simpson and I think Doc Reising went along too. He climbed halfway up the hill, Mary was still on the boat and watching through the glasses. I was cleaning bear skulls and watching the show. They got about two-thirds of the way up the hill and ran into another bear, shot at him and missed him. Instantly the big fellow on top of the ridge jumped up and the last I saw him, he was galloping up that ridge like a big work horse. We never saw the big fellow again. If they'd gone on up carefully and paid no attention to that smaller bear, they might have gotten the big bear. Years later, some Indians killed that bear. I'm sure it was the same one because there's not too many of them. They had an article in the *Alaskan Sportsman*, and somehow or other accidentally shot one of their group, but they spoke of this big bear on the right side of Iniskin Bay coming down the trail, and they gave him .30-30s in the heart at close range. Then one of them shot another and they had an awful time getting him out to help and a doctor. Some of them that skinned the bear said he went thirteen feet afterwards when they peeled the big fellow out. I'll bet any amount that it was the same bear I saw on that same ridge years before.

One day Mary and Al and Jim Simpson were hunting together and I was out with Ed Lovdahl and Doc Reising. Around a big arm of the bay, about three miles away, we located what looked like a good bear. We had to make many detours on account of the mud flats, the tide was out, and that old gooey mud from the silt from the glaciers was terrific stuff, holding lots of quicksand. We got around to where we knew we were close to them, came around a bunch of alders, and there was an old sow with two yearlings, and she was rubbed to high heaven, no more than thirty yards away. She then simply spanked both the yearlings and started them up the steep slope behind her, then she whirled around hissing at us. Doc Reising fanned out on the right with Ed Lovdahl to the left. The old bear singled me out. She came towards me in a rush and I yelled at her to hold it or I was going to kill her. She stopped and then she hissed. Finally she turned around to look

Two brown bear in one day is a rare dream for the most experienced of hunters, but Mary Ellinger did it.

and see where the cubs were. I started to back up. That was no good. She came again. I yelled at her, she stopped again. I was holding bead on the end of her nose. I knew I could shatter her skull if I had to, but I didn't want her because she was rubbed terrible, no fur on her. This seemed to me like it continued for an age. I finally just held my ground and talked to her. She'd look around to see where the cubs were. She started around to follow them, then she'd whirl around and come charging back hissing again and chopping her teeth. Finally she looked us all over and decided we weren't going to bother her. She stalked off looking back over her shoulder, and followed her cubs up the hill, which was just exactly the thing that we wanted her to do.

Doc Reising, Mary and I were out together one time when we located two brownies out on the flat. It looked like a three-year-old and an old boar, near as we could tell. We got within two hundred yards of them. Doc Reising carried a .405 Winchester. After he'd called one bear a woodchuck, I wasn't too satisfied with how he'd work out in an emergency. So I slipped the sling on my arm of the

.35 Whelen and laid down on the only piece of dry ground I could find there. He says, "My God, them are brownies. You're not going to lay down are you?"

I says, "I sure am. There ain't any two bear on earth can get to me if I'm in prone position and give them rapid fire with this heavy rifle." So Mary up and shot and she hit the big fellow. Into the alders he went a bawlin'. She shot again and she hit the little one about amidships. He took off up the hill in to the alders. Mary had iron sights. Doc Reising shot and he plowed up water and mud about three-fourths of the way to the bear. I could see the smaller one going up the hill, the big one had stopped somewhere, and I started in pecking at him. I'd hold in the middle of his shoulders and shoot and we could hear the bullets plunk. I emptied the gun and put in another bunch of cartridges. With my sixth shot, I didn't hear it plunk, but the bear turned a summerset backwards, down the hill.

Doc says, "You missed him."

"Well," I says, "I killed him anyway."

Mary couldn't see him through the alders. Then the big fellow went up and around an old tree. He turned around and looked at us, chopping his teeth and a blowin', and then here he came all out. I hit him in the shoulder as he came around the tree, and I hit him again in the chest pretty high up that went into the spine. He started rolling down the mountain, so we had Mary's two wounded bear stretched out. Neither of them had good hides, and I wouldn't have shot them, but Doc Reising was the guide, and the boss, and he told Mary to shoot, and she hit them all right. When they got in the alders, she couldn't see them with her iron sights and I could through the scope.

CAUGHT IN A WILLIWAW . . .

We decided to move from Iniskin up the inlet to another huge bay, Iliamna Bay it was called. So we up-anchored and moved up there. That night we got a williwaw, a hard Alaskan blow. At times it seemed like the wind would blow straight down. The boat would sink in the water clear up to the gunwales, then it would raise up high again. We had two anchors over, but we drifted anyway. Finally one of them got in the propeller and wound it up. We drifted ashore. So as the tide went out, we cut timbers and shored the boat up so it would stand. Then we got busy and cut that anchor line out of the propeller, got it all squared away and got the anchors all hooked up. Then we waited for the next tide to come in and float us. We got off and out to an anchorage again.

After the blow, Al Ellinger, Doc Reising and I started across the bay. A heavy wind squall blew up, but we were intending to go across anyway to hunt the other side. The waves soon were piling high. We were taking a lot of water over the front of the 16-foot sea dory. Ellinger said he had lots of experience in rough water with small boats, so we turned the motor over to him while Doc Reising and I bailed for all we was worth. We headed straight across. Al knew just how to ride it up at an angle on a wave, down in the next trough and up on the next, and shipping the least amount of water. We made it across and had to lay the blow out there before we came back to the sanctuary of the *Vigilant* and a hot meal and bed.

Lovdahl took Tom O'Dale, Ward Gay and Frank Mosteller across the Kenai Peninsula to hunt black bear, as Frank had his brown bear and only wanted one. So they went across Cook Inlet and Ed brought the *Vigilant* back. We then had much more room on it and a good bunk for everybody. Some friends of Ellingers from New Hampshire were camped with their guides and cook across an arm of the bay from us. We had a good visit with them. They were doing right well on bear also. Finally we up-anchored and pulled out from Iliamna and went on up to Snug Harbor to try that. Snug Harbor at low tide had a lot of quicksand flats. When we would try to go ashore, we would hang on the boat to see if the sand would support us. Several times we'd get out 30 yards from the boat and everything would start to sink and we'd back peddle to the safety of the boat as fast as we could. If the tide was high enough, we could run well up some of the little tidal arms, then we could usually find firm, sound footing. But we had to watch the tide on that account in order to get onto hard ground when we left the boat.

Mary had her two brown bear, but Al needed another one, and I hadn't shot one as yet. Ed Lovdahl, Al and I took the 16-foot dory and the outboard motor and went down the bay and then worked up the off side of Snug Harbor to see what we could find. They made quite a circle, several miles, while I ran the boat up and watched the tide to keep from being grounded. After several miles I located a good sized brownie out on the flat feeding. I signaled to Al and Ed where he was. I ran the boat up a little estuary as far as I could, but I had to stay with it and watch it because the tide was going out. But with my signaling they soon located the bear out on the flat. They stalked up within 150 yards of them. If you move while their head is down, or looking the other way, you can get quite close. Then they both started shooting, Al with his .375 and Ed Lovdahl with his 54 Model Winchester .30-06 with 220-grain bullets. Al was shooting 300-grain in the .375 Hoffman. Their first shots knocked the bear down. He was up and running directly away for the alders instantly. They proceeded to hit him twice more each. Before he reached the alders he stood up on his hind feet and looked all around. I believe then he saw them for the first time. He turned around and came for them for all he was worth. There were three or four inches of water on the flat and he surely threw up the spray, but you could see the flats of his hind feet as he came. Ed emptied his six shots from his 54 Winchester .30-06 into him, and Al's last shot, his fifth, finally turned the bear a summerset. I had to keep moving the boat out until the tide started to come in, then I could run it up close to the bear. We found a four-inch section of shoulder bone laying on the flat there where it had been driven out of him by the .375. He was not a very big bear, I would say around 600 pounds, but he surely took a beating. It shows what these animals can take, even from a heavy rifle.

Al now had his two brownies but they wanted me to get one. While I was cleaning skulls on the boat I located one high on the right side of Snug Harbor up in the alders. It was raining, and was snowing a little bit higher up. It was too late to go after him that day, so the next morning Ed Lovdahl and I ran the sea dory across the bay and as high as we could at high tide, flung the painter up another 60 feet up the bank, and took off up the mountain to where I'd seen the big bear in the alders. He was about halfway up the mountain when I saw him the day before. By the time we got up there, however, the storm increased and it started snowing. We were crawling around bear trails in the alders, the only way we could get through. It was tough going. Finally it got so tough that Ed said we'd just as well go back and give it up.

We started down the side of a wash. Alaska, in the spring thaws, leaves washes that will throw out a bank or rim on each side of it, and sometimes build up eight or ten feet. We were nearly down to the beginning of the slope to the tide flats, and were sitting on a cliff. I spotted a nice black bear go into some alders on the left side of this run or gulch we were following down. I told Ed I'd promised my girl, Druzilla, a good black bear hide, so I says let's go get him. We worked down on the right side of the draw, and were just climbing up on the rim to go down into it and over the other, where the black bear had gone into about two acres of thick alders. We figured on sitting on the other rim and watching until he came out and then I would bust him. However, just as Ed got on top of the rim, something made me look to the right, and here came an enormous bear's head over the wash about 20 yards away, followed by a huge brownie. I turned the safety and hung my sights on his nose instantly and I yelled at Ed, "Is his hide any good?" I hollered three times and finally I says, "Is his hide worth a damn? I gotta' bust him." He was coming at a crouching run, just like a cat will go across the yard after a sparrow. No high jumps, just that low crouching run. Ed whirled around, took one look, threw a shell from the magazine into the chamber of his old 54 Winchester and let go from the hip. By this time the big bear was on us. Ed's shot hit him in the outer edge of the right shoulder. He later determined that it penetrated 16 inches of shoulder meat and made a little nick in the flange on the shoulder blade. The entire wound

channel wasn't over 3/8 inch in diameter. As Ed turned around the big bear had crouched to jump on him. He evidently saw Ed's movement while I was standing still and holding a bead on his nose. At Ed's shot, he went up on his hind feet just 12 feet from me and only a trifle farther from Ed. I had to raise my rifle to quite an angle even though I was standing uphill above him, to shoot him under the foreleg. I gave him the 275-grain Western Tool & Copper there. It spun him away from me. I threw in another shell, not looking through the sights at all, just looking over the top of the 48 and the hood on the front sight, I gave him another one between the shoulders. Then he came around and back as he seemed to realize that I was doing him the damage. As he swung around Ed shot again. He thought then he'd broke his neck, but he hadn't. All he did was hit between the wrist bones of the right foreleg, penetrated between them an up the length of the foreleg and lodged under the hide on the chest. I'd thrown in another shell, and as he started to lunge towards me, I gave him another one through both shoulders and jumped back up the hill. His head came down among my empty shells. His hide wasn't worth a hoot. He was rubbed to high heaven. The whole neck and shoulders were full of deep fang wounds and full of pus. He was a stinking mess, an enormous old grizzly. We opened his belly so that he wouldn't gas up.

Ed says, "Let's go to camp, get our dory, and get back out to the *Vigilant.*"

When we arrived at the boat, of course Ellinger and Mary and Doc Reising wanted to know what happened. They'd heard the flurry of shots. I thought I'd let Ed tell the tale. He didn't answer at all. We'd been out of whiskey for some days and he went up to the pilot house and dug in under some bear skins in a bunk that was crossways of the back of the pilot house and came back with a quart of whiskey. He still didn't say anything. He got out a tincup for every person and proceeded to pour the whole quart into those cups for us to drink.

Then he says, "Al, I wouldn't be here if I hadn't had a damn good shot along with a big rifle. Will you take my 54 Winchester home and sell it and get me a .375?"

Though I have sustained other bear charges, that was the closest one that I have come to, and I don't care for more at that close range from such a huge bear.

The next day we went ashore and it required all of us to turn the brute over. They insisted on skinning him although I was sure

Some bears take a lot of killing, as did this one that charged four hunters and absorbed a lot of lead before going down. Al Ellinger, Ed Lovdahl, and Doc Reising examine Al's final trophy on the trip.

his hide was no good. I did want his skull, however, and those big front feet. They measured 10½ inches across the pad of the front feet before skinning. Doc Reising, who was an old veterinarian, and Jim Simpson, the old Wyoming guide, both estimated him at 1200 pounds and he was in poor condition as it was spring. The whole neck and shoulders were full of fang wounds, so he'd evidently had a big fight. We trailed him down to where we'd hung the painter from the boat. He'd come along the side of the tide flat until he found the boat, then he'd followed to where we hung up the painter. From there on he'd trailed us up, evidently an old sorehead that wanted trouble. We skinned him, left the head and feet in the hide, put it all on my packboard, and I got under the thing with two of them lifting, and it must have weighed 250 pounds. I carried it down to nearly the edge of the tide flat, and my legs and hips were killing me so I eased it down on a boulder. Ed Lovdahl, who wasn't nearly as large as I am, though one of the toughest little Finlanders I've ever seen, took it then and even in his big hip boots he sloshed through that knee deep

tidal mud and flat and out to the sea dory and dumped it in. I boiled and cleaned the skull and even six months later and dry, it still measured 17 inches long and 10 inches wide across his zygomatic arches. It would have been a very high record grizzly could it have been classified as grizzly. However, the Boone & Crockett Club said being as it was killed at the tidewater, it had to be a brownie and not a grizzly. But Frank DuFresne, head of the Alaskan Game Commission, and all the guides that examined the skull with its smooth even arch from the nostril back to the rear end of the skull, said it was grizzly and not brownie. Brownie skulls go from the front of the nostril back to the eye sockets, then they have a high arch there, and then on over the cranium.

Ed's first slug had done no damage. He told us that night while we were drinking whiskey that he broke his neck with the second shot. But we found that his bullet had only gone between the bones of the left forearm, under the skin up to the chest and stopped there. My first shot had gone through the top of the heart and exited on the other side as he was

Shooting a wounded brownie at 12 feet can ruin a man's afternoon, but it ended well as Elmer took this giant 10-foot bear in Snug Harbor in 1937.

broadside. My second one, when his back was turned, took off one side of his vertebrae and exposed the spinal cord for over two inches. My third one, as he came around, broke the near shoulder, went through part of the spine and lodged under the skin on the off side. That did the business. It was point-blank shooting, and from my empty cases to where his tracks showed he stood up on his hind feet was just 12 feet.

When Mosteller, O'Dale and Ward Gay left, Gay told me, "Now when you write this up, don't have any bear charges in it."

I says, "I won't without we sustain them."

A STORM IN THE INLET...

As our time was about up, we decided to up-anchor and head for Anchorage up the Cook Inlet. The morning we took off, however, a terrific blow came up, with waves up to 30 feet high. Ellinger, Doc Reising, and Ed Lovdahl got down below. We battened the hatch over them and they elected me to do the steering. Ed laid out all the charts, showed me where the beacons were, and told me to stay well out in the channel, because with waves this high there was a lot of shallow water where we might come down in a trough and knock the bottom out of the boat. We no more than got out, when Mary Ellinger, who was in the pilot house with me, laid down on the bunk, sick. She was really seasick. One wave would come in and bury the top of the boat until all I could see was the little binnacle light on the compass. Then we'd wallow out on top and I could look around and see the shore on each side. Then we'd dive into another wave. On about the third one we'd go clean under again. It was a pretty rough sea, but with the charts laid out there I managed to hold out to the middle of the channel all the way up Cook Inlet.

Ed could holler up through the hole where the steering gear went down and ask me how I was doing. I told him to just keep that motor running and we'd be all right. Mary was awful sick. I told her all she needed was a good old sourdough cocktail. She says, "What's that?"

"Well," I says, "We take a quart of seal oil and crack a dozen gull's eggs in it, and that will fix you right up."

Mary gritted her teeth and she says, "Elmer Keith, if I ever get you ashore, I'm going to shoot you with my .375."

Rough seas never made me seasick. In fact I never was seasick. When the water gets real rough, I usually get hungry.

We made it safely to Anchorage and hung up the boat by the side of the cannery dock. The tide there at Anchorage averages 34 feet, so we had to keep one man on the boat all the time letting out slack on the two ropes that we had it anchored to the dock with, as the tide went out until finally the boat was setting on the mud. The water was far out several hundred yards from the cannery dock. We were in hopes there would be no rocks under the boat to punch a hole through it, and luckily there weren't.

That was a great trip. The best bear hunt I ever had in my life. I had Guy Jonas from Seattle make a humidor out of the huge front paws of that bear, and I kept his skull, but the hide was worthless even after I got it home. So the only good skin I brought home was a black bear.

ONCE AGAIN TO CANADA...

Getting home to our little ranch on the North Fork, I just had time to put up our hay crop before I had another trip coming up in Canada. Dr. H.A.W. Brown, an Indian agent, invited me to come up on a two month's trip with him back into the Muskwa country where he wanted to interview some tribes of Indians there, and keep track of them. He hired me on as a horse wrangler. Before going, I had a gentle cow staked out in the orchard to eat some of the grass so it didn't get too high. I went out to untie her one day and the dogs scared her and she took off. I threw the chain around my hips, hedge-hopping behind her, and trying to stop her, when I stuck my foot in a hole, and broke my left ankle. Roland Westfall, a neighbor, made me a crutch out of a tree limb with a good fork in it and padded it up with sheepskin and I hobbled around on that. I was determined to go even though I wasn't much use as a horse wrangler. However, I did my share of packing, pulling nags out of mud holes, and cutting trees off of them, so that I earned my keep anyway.

The party consisted of Doc Brown, his son Dick, Al Robinson, the cook, a World War I veteran with crippled feet, Wesley Brown and Ed Dopp. We gathered all the horses, got all the tents, grub, everything together at Charley Creek out of Fort St. John. From there we started north over the old Hudson Bay tote road, so called. The trees had been cut off about two feet high. The trail wound around through these stumps, through bog holes and patches of timber. There were little low hills, and you could see the old buffalo trails where they'd been worn for centuries. The oldest Indian said they had a big snow one winter and all the buffalo died, how far back God alone

At the ranch in Salmon, Dru (left) and Ted were growing and learning to help with many of the chores.

knows. There was flat rolling country from Fort St. John north towards Muskwa. Owing to the muskeg nature of the country, the trees root very shallow. In fact, when the wind would blow some of them over, there would just be a big hotcake of roots and mud dried up. On the trail the weight of the horses sometimes would mash these roots down and turn a tree over on the horse, mashing him and his pack down in the mud. Then we'd have to chop the tree off, unpack the horse, pull him out of the mud, repack him and go on. A time or two, the tree came down on each side of the horse and mashed him down until just his head was out of the mud and water. How they ever built the Alcan Highway over that stretch of country is still beyond me, the muskeg seemed bottomless. You could stick a long pole down and it would keep on going if you wanted to shove it down full length.

We had a lean-to tent that we all slept in, and we built a fire along in front of it for evenings. Then we had a netting that we could drop down to keep the black flies, no-seeums and mosquitos out, which were very bad there in August.

We were 21 days going from Fort St. John until we reached the Sikanni Chief River and the old deserted Hudson Bay post there. A lot of Indians had been buried around there. Each had a little fence around the grave, and a little house built over the grave proper. Wild raspberries were all over the place. These were particularly rank and heavy with fruit around each of these graves. Evidently the old Indians had fertilized the ground as they deteriorated. Wes Brown and I took a couple of water buckets and filled them with wild rasberries from around these graves. Wes said it was customary to smoke a pipe at the grave of each Indian when we picked those rasberries, so this we did. Al Robinson proceeded to make us a lot of good rasberry cobblers and rasberry pies. We also had plenty of them with sugar and canned cream. So we really enjoyed the change to this fresh fruit.

Grizzly tracks were everywhere. There

seemed to be a lot of the big bear there. Where they'd rubbed on trees, the grizzly hair lots of times was eight feet up from the ground where they'd rubbed the back of their shoulders and head.

From the old Hudson Bay post on the Sikanni Chief we decided to cut a trail through to the Muskwa and into the sheep country. Before getting quite this far, however, we had interviewed the last pack of Indians. They had started a good many forest fires. Sometimes we had to detour several miles out of the way to go around these fires. Doc Brown asked the old chief why he started the fires.

"Oh," he says, "Burnum good. Make more feed for moose next year."

Both Ed Dopp, the other packer, and Wes Brown warned us not to let any of the Indians get on our beds as they were lousy, and for heavens sake not to camp near any of their old bed grounds. We saw many of their old camp grounds, nice spruce bough beds still in good shape. But both Ed and Wesley warned us that if we threw our bed on them, we'd be loused up in short order.

Around the camp fire one night, when we had the old chief and several of the tribe with him, there was one old lady, as near as I could make out her name was Carstair. Doc Brown couldn't hear too good, and when they tried to pronounce her name to him, he said horsetail. That made the old Indian very mad. She must have been around a hundred years old. She had two teeth, one above and one below in front. She was sitting there by the fire and she reached in under her skirt and pulled out the biggest old grayback I ever saw, and cracked him between those two opposing teeth. From then on I certainly wasn't going to get close to any of those Indians, or any of their beds. She was quite mad at Doc so he had his son, Dick, go and get a couple of plugs of what we called the heartburn tobacco. It was 20 cents, as I remember, for a plug that had a little tin heart on it. That tickled the old lady and she was happy then.

Cutting across the Sikanni Chief to the Muskwa we run into a lot of Arctic birch and willows, some of it so big and tangled we simply had to cut a way to get through. One day Wes Brown was in the lead, chopping off stuff. Ed Dopp was following him to finish cleaning it up, followed by Dick Brown, Doc Brown, and then myself. Both Wes Brown and Ed Dopp's saddle horses were in front of them with the reins strung up, simply following along behind as the boys cut a trail. Suddenly Wes says, "Look out for the bear," and he came running back as hard as he could run,

Stone and Fannin sheep were both to be found in the Muskwa River Valley in 1937, and Keith collected these two fine heads with his Winchester Model 70.

taking long leaps over those stumps he'd cut off. Out of the brush come a little old black bear, I don't believe he weighed over 250 pounds, but he had his ears laid back, his lips stuck out and he was hot after Wes. Wes was trying to get to his saddle horse and his .30-30 carbine. Ed Dopp, however, grabbed his right hand glove in his teeth and jerked it off, and pulled a .455 Smith & Wesson he always carried with heavy handloads in it. He shot the bear in the inside corner of the left eye and it came out the back of his head. The bear turned summersets right up to Wes Brown. His head rested on one of the stumps that Wes had cut off before. Wes had jumped to one side of the trail and raised the axe when he saw he couldn't make the horse, and he sunk that big old 4½-pound axe down between the bear's ears clear to the bit. That settled this bear. The wind was blowing from the whole packstring, 23 head of horses, and all of us, straight to the bear. There was no question about him having our scent. Evidently he'd never seen a human being or horses, didn't know what they were, and figured Wes was just a moose calf and he was going to catch him.

The boys cut on past the bear carcass and we led the horses past. First Ed Dopp and I picked him up, one at each end, and give him the old heave-ho out of the trail. The horses

Keith (left) and Wes Brown show the heads and capes of a Fannin sheep (left) and a Stone sheep. Note ax on horse at rear, which is handy for heavy butchering.

After the hunt comes the work of skinning, fleshing, and salting the sheep, but the results are smiles as Dick Brown, Doc Brown, and Elmer Keith admire the horns.

didn't even smell him until they got past him, so there was no question but that that bear had our full scent in his nostrils when he charged Wes. We didn't want his hide or want to pay the tithe on it to the game department. His teeth showed he was an old boar, a very scrawny, small-sized one.

Two trees had come down over a muskeg hole on Ed Dopp's saddle horse. He had a nice 8 mm Mauser, but when the trees knocked the horse down level with the top of the mudhole, they also broke the stock out of his rifle, so Ed had only his six-shooter, a .455 Smith & Wesson, for the rest of the trip.

Ed Dopp had trapped that country for years, said he had killed lots of sheep and had wintered on them for some years. Wes Brown had also trapped out to the north, but he preferred moose meat to the sheep, and said it would stay with him better.

Ed told me, "My rifle's broke and I've killed lots of sheep, so you shoot out my sheep license too. We need some meat, so the first good rams we run into I want you to bust one."

We put up a nice camp on the Muskwa River and scouted the first day. Coming back that evening, we saw five rams on the mountain to our left, about 475 yards from the trail, they later stepped it off. Edgar said, "Can you get one? We need some fresh meat pretty bad." I laid down in the sling. The .300 Magnum with 2½ or 3-power Hensoldt scope was sighted for 300 yards. As I knew the ram was a quarter of a mile or more, I held

up over his withers enough that I figured it would drop into him, and squeezed one off from a prone position. The ram stopped and stood still for some seconds, then he reared up on his hind feet and seemed to hold that position for a second or two, then pitched over backwards. They slapped me on the back and told me it was a good shot. We dressed the ram, and took the hindquarters and the forequarters. The boys bent over a tall spruce tree. Climbing up it, Wes Brown, who'd weigh over 200, would bend it over. So we tied the front quarters in the top of the tree and let it spring back up to keep it away from the bears. We took the hindquarters on to camp that night, with both Wes and Ed changing off carrying the weight.

The next morning when we came back up the trail we found a grizzly had also pulled that tree over and taken our front quarters of sheep meat. We went on and hunted some fairly open country. We climbed above most of the spruce until it was just shintangle and little strips of timber running down by the sides of the snowslides. Wes and I hunted together, and Doc Brown, his boy, and Edgar hunted together. We located a bunch of sheep across a canyon from us and it was very open country, but by getting down in the bottom of a gully and bending low, we managed to get up within about 600 yards of them. There we were stuck, with no chance of getting any closer so we decided to wait them out and see what they would do. All had white faces and necks and dark bodies. There was one, a Fannin, who had a light grey body and a white face and neck. He had beautiful wide-spreading horns, and I decided to kill him if I had any chance at all. Finally they started feeding around to the right to the head of the gulch above us. It was soon evident that they were going to cross too far above for a shot. But when they did cross the draw another big ram with broomed horns got up below them and within 400 yards of us. I looked him over. His head was very heavy. He was a much bigger sheep than any in the band. Even though his horns were broomed, I decided to take it, so I held over his withers and shot and down he went. The mountain was very steep and we saw him bounce out 20 feet from a cliff once before he rolled on below. The band we were watching then proceeded on around high above us a good 600 yards.

Just then another ram came out on the skyline, and one look at that right horn which bent way out and curved outward was enough for me. So I held over his withers and down he went. He rolled out of sight down in the crevices and cliffs below. The band we had been watching with the old white-necked ram worked on around above us, so we worked on down below the cliffs to see if we could find the sheep. We finally found the one with the broomed head, but we couldn't find the other one with the big wide head.

While we were searching for him, the other rams came out above us at what I figured was around 600 yards. I later wrote it up as 500, and was even called a liar on that. I found a boulder that I could lay down prone behind and get my rifle up at an angle and still shoot prone. I ran the sight up level with the top of his horns and a little over. He stood facing to the right and I squeezed one off. There was an interval before the bullet hit and down he went. He laid on the ledge with his feet sticking over. Then Wesley and I started searching for the other ram. We hunted high and low and finally I looked up a crevice and there he hung by his big horns. He'd fallen down part way and the crevice had gotten too narrow and his horns had caught. Wesley had a rope and he put it down from up above. I tied it on his horns and climbed up from below and I finally managed to dislodge him and Wesley eased him on down to me. We got him down on the flat. Then he went around to where the white-necked Fannin lay on the ledge far above us. He pronounced it six or seven hundred yards. However, on a horizontal line where gravity would pull on it, it probably was not over four hundred yards, but it was very steep.

At any rate, Wesley got up there and the rest of the band that he had been with just stood around and looked at him. They'd evidently never seen a person, and Wes wanted a sheep, so he pulled out a little Colt Woodsman and started plinking the best ram behind the shoulder. Just as the gun was about empty, he finally got one into its spine and that ram rolled off the mountain. He yelled down at me, "Find that one and take care of him, I'll get the big fellow down that you killed." We had filled mine and Ed Dopp's license, and Wesley also had a nice ram with his little .22 Woodsman, shot at about 15 to 20 yards. Evidently I'd killed the old leader and the younger rams didn't know what to do, so they just stood around.

Doc Brown, Ed Dopp, and Doc's son also came down the gulch to the right that they had hunted, and they had a couple of beautiful heads apiece. We managed to dress them all out and get the pack horses loaded, and we moved camp.

In the meantime, Al Robinson had taken a side of ribs and cracked them, a side of sheep ribs that I'd killed the day before, and he wrapped the ribs around the loin, put a pole through it, built a big fire, and had a nice bed of coals with a crotch pole at each end. These sheep ribs, after they were tied around the pole, hung about four feet above the bed of coals. He'd roasted that side of ribs and sheep loin all day. When we got there, he laid it on a lodgepole that he'd hewed flat on one side and cut it up in about four or five-pound chunks. He'd made a raisin bannock, opened a jar of sweet pickles, and a can of butter for the bannock, and we had a feast. I've never eaten finer sheep meat in my life, and mountain sheep is tops of all meat, to my notion. Al was a wonderful cook, and he proceeded to serve us sheep meat cooked the same way every day. He'd spend most of the day basting the meat and turning it. He'd leave some limbs on one end of the pole that he had through the meat so that he could turn it and tie it and leave it for a few minutes, then turn it again and baste another portion.

We spent the next few days in that camp, skinning out their heads, salting the capes, turning the ears, and splitting the lips. I jerked a couple of sheep, that is, all the meat except the ribs and loins which we turned over to Al for the next day's fare. The old heavy head I'd shot had a 15¼-inch base and a 34-inch length. It was so heavy it went into the records, while my best ram carried a 39½-inch right horn and a 38 left. He also went into the records. The first one I'd shot, being very small, Doc wanted for knife handles. The old Fannin had a beautiful head, but a small base, only about 13½ inches, and only about 36 and 37 on the curl, but it was a beautiful head nevertheless. While my best Stoney and the Fannin had very wide spreads, the heavy head was more of a close compact head. The heads that Doc and Dick Brown got were all close compact heads, but they had a couple of beauties.

We spent several days hunting that beautiful country. One day Ed Dopp and I counted 63 head of ewes and lambs in one bunch, all Stone sheep. The world-record head that has stood for a good many years, I understand, was killed on the same mountain that we killed our sheep on. We scouted other country for a week, and then moved to another location and scouted that several days. Doc wanted a goat but he didn't get one, and we turned down moose on account of the heavy heads and the long distance to be packed, and I didn't want a moose unless I could get a really big one. However, we ate up the sheep meat, except what we'd jerked to take home, and as we were out of meat Doc asked us to get a caribou if we could.

Wesley and I hunted one way while he hunted another. We ran onto a couple of caribou. One was a bull with a small head. It had several points but it was a small bunchy head, more like an enlarged cow caribou head. Anyway the bull was trotting to our left at 350 yards and I was carrying the .375 that day loaded with 300-grain bullets. So I held up on his head figuring that would give him enough lead by aiming at his nose that the bullet would drop into him. It did all right, right through the back bone just in front of the hips, and put him down. So we had enough meat to last us a good part of the way out.

Owing to the long range involved, the 300-grain bullet went right through the caribou and exited, just as my 180-grain open-point Western .300 Magnum had gone through the sheep that I'd shot. Of course, all of them were out at considerable range where the velocity had dropped off.

We decided to work back out on the old pack trail rather than down in the flats on the Hudson Bay tote road. We took a trail that crossed over into the Halfway River. I was following along behind the pack string with Al Robinson, the cook. Doc and Dick Brown were in the lead, in fact a quarter of a mile ahead of the string, watching for game, and Ed Dopp and Wes Brown were working the pack string along. I happened to look off to my left. A little over half a mile away I saw a

After tracking this fine grizzly all day, Keith finally dropped him, hitting him with three out of five shots at 500 yards with his .300 H&H Magnum.

grizzly standing on a sidehill feeding. I showed him to Al Robinson. I says, "If this had been in Alaska, I'd swear that is a grizzly over there." One look at him and Al sized him up for what he was. He whistled real loud and shrill and Wes Brown heard him and came back up the hill. I showed the bear to Wes, and said, "We'll go get him."

I took the .300 and we managed to get across the gulch from him, but there was still a good 500 yards.

Wes said, "Can you hit him?"

I said, "I'm sure I can hit him all right, but I don't know how this gun will do at that distance."

I held up over him as his rump turned to us digging and I hit him. We heard the plunk of the bullet and he rolled. Then he got up and went around the sidehill. I held over him again enough to drop the bullet in, but in my haste I forgot to lead. I shot right behind him. The next shot, however, I led him held over and I rolled him. He got up and started up over the hill. I hit him in the rump and down he went again, then he went over the shoulder of the mountain out of sight. Anyway I had three 180-grain open-point boattails in him. I asked Ed to let me have Wes Brown. They were going on down on the Halfway River to a big fishing hole, as they called it, to a celebrated camp ground.

We went over and looked at the tracks. Only a few tiny drops of blood. Dopp didn't think we would ever get him. Wes Brown, however, was confident. He said, "We'll get him all right. Drop off our beds and one pack horse and some grub and we'll go ahead after the bear, and tie up the saddle horses."

Ed left my saddle horse tied there with the pack horse and Wes Brown's old bay horse. We crossed over the gulch, picked up the trail, and trailed the bear. He'd gone over the hill

It takes a steady, experienced horse to put up with having a grizzly on its back, even a dead one that has been field dressed. Wes Brown's horse proved up to the task with Keith's bear in Canada in 1937.

and dug into the side of a log to cool his wounds, no doubt, in the cool earth underneath the log. From there he'd gone on over the hill. It was a maze of huckleberry bushes and buckbrush of some kind, with a few Arctic birch and spruce. It was the toughest trailing we ever did in our lives. One of us would get down on his hands and knees and look for a little drop of blood. As the frost had hit and discolored many of the leaves, we'd have to wet it with our tongue to see if it was frost-colored leaves or really blood. In this way, working all of a half day, we finally trailed the bear over the mountain and down on the other side about a quarter of a mile. The last drops of blood we found were only about the size of No. 6 shot.

Wes went back, got his old bay horse, and took the saddle off. I don't know why he did that, but he rode him down the hill towards where the tracks had headed, bareback. Pretty soon the old horse threw up his ears and snorted, so Wes came back.

Wes said, "He's down there all right. This

old pony don't fail. He can smell him farther than we can see him in this stuff."

The scrub fir and shintangle got thicker and we took turns, one of us on his hands and knees picking up a hair where it had sifted out of his belly where the bullet had cut it, or a drop of blood, while the other watched with ready rifle. I'd just taken over the .375 which I'd gotten from Dopp, and let him have my .300, when the bear raised up in front of Wes, I would say about 25 to 30 feet away. He stood up on his hind quarters and came out from under a spruce tree where he'd dug another damp, cool bed. As he came up on his hindquarters, I busted him through both shoulders with a 270-grain from the .375, and he simply grunted and sank back in his bed.

Wesley went back and got the old bay horse, who wasn't afraid of bear particularly, and came over. We gutted the bear to lighten the load all we could. At that time Wes Brown was considered the most powerful man in the Peace River, and I well believe it. We put a rope around the bear's neck and one shoulder and over the saddle. He would lift, and I had put a loop in my end of the rope and put all my weight on it and pull. We finally got his head up. It took about a half hour, I believe, until Wes finally got his back under that bear and got him across the saddle. We tied his feet together and to the cinch rings on both sides, and tied it back up to the fork of the saddle. We had him pretty well loaded. But the poor old horse had an awful load. We gave him his time, led him back over the hill and down to where we'd tied up the other horses. Then we rolled the bear off. Wes immediately got out the makings of bannock and a meal of the last of our caribou meat and he said, "I'll cook while you start skinning." I skinned out the four paws, got them all cleaned, made the splits on the belly and out to each leg by the time he yelled to come and get it. We ate a good tasty meal and then set to skinning. Wes wanted all the fat off the bear which he took for lard. He considered grizzly fat better than black bear fat. I cut the shoulders loose from the body and flopped them back, and took out the loins full length. I should have taken more meat, I believe, but Wes didn't think it would be very good eating. We loaded the bear skin wrapped in canvas onto the old pack horse, and lit out to travel as far as we could that night and camp. The next morning we took off again, and finally came to the big fish hole where Doc Brown and the rest of the boys were camped. They had been fishing but with small luck. Wes tied a rock on a line and put on some hooks. He'd stand there and swing that rock around his head, holler "Come, Fishie," and heave it across the pond and pull, and he'd get a fish nearly every time.

Al Robinson took my grizzly loins, hewed the top of a lodgepole that was laying crossways to the camp, spread them out on that, and took his old curved sheath knife and cut them into chops. The boys had dressed the fish, so we had plenty of fresh fish and grizzly chops. They were about as nice eating as any pork chops I have had in my life. Al Robinson said, "Elmer, why didn't you bring in the whole bear? We could eat him before we get back to Ft. St. John."

The three 180-grain bullets that I had hit the bear with had all blown up to some extent, but none of them had done a great deal of damage. One of them that hit him in the rump had gone up to the side of the ribs. Another one that had hit one shoulder, had angled across the chest, but it tore a very small hole. And the other one had hit a hind foot and went angling up a leg. But the .375 went into the skin on the other side and mushroomed out perfectly, breaking both shoulders. He proved a beautiful, well-furred silvertip, and I still have his rug on the wall in my den. We had a long, tedious, uneventful trip from there on out to Fort St. John. There I got a ride in a truck, one of the last ones going out through the mud to Pooskoopie, and went from there on to the railroad.

I had a flour sack full of nice jerked sheep meat, and Druzilla and Ted found that was about the nicest lunch meat they had ever had. In fact in little over a month those kids had eaten the whole sack of jerked sheep meat. They'd go around with a piece of it in their little chubby fists all the time.

THE FIRST BOOKS . . .

In 19 and 36, T. G. Samworth, who had been editor of the *American Rifleman,* and then operated what he called the Small Arms Technical Publishing Company, commissioned me to write three manuals, which I did. He offered me $250 down and another $250 if they sold. The first one was to be on six-gun cartridges and loads; the second one on big game rifles and cartridges; and the third on varmint rifles.

I wrote the three manuals which were to sell at a dollar apiece. He never did publish the last one. He paid me $250 down on it, and $250 on each of the others. The others sold all right, and plenty good. He later sold the *Big Game Rifles and Cartridges* to the Stackpole Company and it published a lot more of them. However, I never did get the final payment on either book that he published and, of course, not on the one that he didn't publish. Stackpole sold quite a lot of the *Big Game Rifles and Cartridges.* They are now out of print and I understand bring $8 to $10 a copy.

ON THE RIVER AGAIN . . .

After getting home from the August and September Canadian trip, Cap Guleke and I had another party booked for a big game hunt down the river. During the summer we had run a trip down and stopped at the Cottonwood. While they fished, I went up the Cottonwood to scout for goat as I had two men that wanted goats on this trip. I took the ridge on the right side of the creek. It was very cut up with cliffs and chasms and was awful hard, slow going, but I managed to get back on the ridge to where it was comparatively open timber and good traveling. I didn't go as far back as the head of the basin where I'd had the Zane Grey party in '31 and got goat there, but peeled off to the left at the lower end of the basin. I worked down a crevice and then it was too steep to go back up, and I didn't want to go down into the awful boulders that was in the bottom of the basin where Gerry Ravndahl, and I spent one night.

The scree slope starts out with very fine sliderock below the cliffs on that downriver side of the Cottonwood. But as it gets down, every pebble and rock gets bigger. Finally the boulders are almost the size of small houses and it's one devil of a job to climb in, around, and over them. I wanted to avoid that if I could, so I didn't drop off into the shale and go down around the cliff. I thought there should be some goats on that cliff as I'd seen them there in '31 when we hunted the head of the big basin. I went down another chimney that I couldn't possibly get back up and I could have worked around to the right and into the scree and small shale and worked down that, but there was a ledge that went around to the left, and I decided to take that around about halfway up the cliff. I came to a corner, and a cliff hung out over the trail. I had to stoop and bend about halfway over in order to stay on the ledge and get around; it was that narrow. Just as I came around the ledge, up jumped a big old yellow billy goat about ten to twelve feet from me. He stood there shaking his head at me. Instantly I had the old .45 six-gun on him. I didn't want to shoot him, it was in the summertime. He had hair about a half-inch long on him, no trophy, and out of season too. I didn't want to shoot him unless I absolutely had to, so I started talking to him. The old billy would shake his head, and I knew if he came I'd have to kill him or he'd knock me off that ledge, and not only that, but drive those little black rapiers into me as well. It seemed like a long time that we eyed each other and I kept talking to him. Finally the old goat sat down and he pulled his rump up against the wall as close as he could, put one forefoot over between his hind legs which projected out over the ledge. He kept watching me and I kept talking to him in a low steady voice. Then he put the other foot over, and looked at me again. He jumped and jerked his hind legs up so that he was turned the other way. He looked back over his shoulder at me and I said, "Go on, Bill. You can make it around there without any trouble, and I can't go back, can't even turn around on this place."

The old goat finally stomped majestically around out of sight. I worked around to where he'd been, to where there was one place wide enough so I could sit down, and I gave him plenty of time before I went on around. When I got around there, the ledge wound up in some nice small sliderock and I was able to take that down to the creek, cross it, and work down through an awful jumble of boulders and fallen logs on the other side to the river. In deference to that old goat, I didn't take any of the party there on the Cottonwood that fall. In fact, I never hunted the Cottonwood for goats again. A big mountain goat billy will weigh 450 to 475 pounds and they will fight when they are cornered that way.

I remember Harry Snyder told me about a friend of his finding a grizzly and a mountain goat below a similar trail around a ledge. They had evidently met and neither one would turn his back on the other. The grizzly had broken the goat's back but the goat had driven those long needles in to the bear's heart and they had died together.

That old goat was a gentleman. I had my loggers, the strings tied together and hung on my back with the string around my neck, and was hanging onto the side of that ledge with one hand and only had my right hand free, full of six-gun. If he had jumped me when I first showed, he no doubt would have gotten me, but he stood there shaking his head until I started talking to him. That fall when we ran our hunting party, I stopped at Horse Creek and got them their goats up on the left side of Horse Creek rather than hunting the Cottonwood.

Goats are notoriously tough. I've seen them take an unbelievable amount of heavy rifle slugs and keep on their feet as long as their spine or their brain wasn't hit. They require a lot of shooting at times. Properly placed, one shot will do it, but if it don't hit right, you can literally shoot them to pieces without putting them down.

GUIDING FOR BIG BEAR...

In the spring of 19 and 39 I went into partnership with Arthur Kinnan, a brother of Marjorie Kinnan Rawlings, who wrote *The Yearling*. He had a good 56-foot boat with a good sea hull, and an old make-and-break 20-horse motor. We proposed to run parties up to Alaska and guide big game hunters up there, especially for bear.

We put in ten days on Lake Union, near Seattle, repairing the boat, painting it, and getting everything in good shape before we went through the locks and out to sea. We decided to run the Inside Passage the same as I had in '37 with the Ellinger party.

Nelson Busick, who ran the Lord Baltimore Hotel in Baltimore, was the first to book with us for a brown bear hunt. Art's crew consisted of an ex-sailor named Jack, his wife, Martin the cook, myself and Kinnan to do part of the work and all of the navigating. Jack and I had the wheel, four hours on and four hours off. I remember it took us 93 hours from Seattle to Ketchikan. About a hundred miles up the coast, that old engine, which took up half of the bottom of the boat, quit on us. It had a make-and-break ignition system.

Jack and I put the dory over the side, let out a sea anchor, and rowed for all we were worth to keep the tide from piling us on some rocks. When we were still a quarter of a mile off the rocks, the wind and tide carrying us in, Art finally got the motor going and we headed on for Alaska. When the old motor was going good it sounded just like, "Let's quit and go fishing, let's quit and go fishing."

While crossing Queen Charlotte Sound, Jack and I put up a small sail he had on the aft deck and that spanked us along considerably faster. It upset Art's navigation, however, and where we should have turned to the left and gone through a passage in the islands, we went on north. Finally two small mountains showed up over the horizon. Art took one look at them and said, "Put her on 180, Elmer. You and Jack and that darn sail of yours have carried us past the entrance where we should have turned."

The only bad trouble we had, on the trip was while we were up in British Columbia territory on the Inside Passage. We had two 500-gallon gasoline tanks in the hold, and one of them sprung a leak. Art discovered it when he went down to check the motor while we were traveling. We pulled into the nearest Canadian port, I don't remember its name now, but as soon as he discovered this, everything was shut off. He said, "Nobody strike a match or light of any kind."

We opened all the portholes and doors to air the thing out. We got out the bilge pump and the whole bilge was full of gasoline. We pumped it all out into the sea. The trip did not cover going into a Canadian port, so we had to go to the customs officer and the old chap took us up to his office. He was a big man with a big red beard.

He said, "This is going to be painful and take a bit of time." So he got out a quart of scotch, gave us a drink, and Art finally satisfied him why we pulled into this port and what we were up against. He had quite a few papers to fill out and sign.

The next proposition was gasoline.

Art said he hadn't brought any cash along. He had a bank account up in Alaska, and we needed more gas to get to Alaska than what we carried. I happened to look across the bay and I saw a Standard Oil dock so I said, "Let's get the boat and go over there. I've had a Chevron card for years."

So we rode over. They agreed to sell us all the gas we needed. We bought another 500 gallons in fifty-gallon drums and put it on my credit card. As soon as we got over to the dock, it had aired out completely, and we'd pumped the empty tank full of water to be sure it didn't explode. We loaded the gas on the afterdeck, roped the barrels on, and headed on out for Alaska.

One night while I was on the wheel, I thought I saw a log ahead, and as the Inside Passage was full of floating logs from the big log booms that had been torn into, I turned the wheel hard over to the right to miss it. I stuck my head out of the pilot house and we just barely bumped it. Up came a flashlight out of that so-called log. Instead of a log, it was an Indian out there in the canoe asleep, fishing.

It was uncanny the way Art could navigate. I remember one evening he set a course, laid out the chart, had his watch hanging by the binnacle light, and he specified how many minutes, hours he would run on each course, exactly when to turn and take another course, and he went to sleep in the bunk. Jack and I were four hours on and four hours off all night. At daylight the next morning, we passed between two headlands, not much over 100 or 150 yards off either side of the boat and a bell buoy there which he told us we'd

pass between. How he ever figured that navigation so fine was more than I could understand. We were exactly on course, the bell buoy was on our left, just as he specified it would be after running all night and changing course several times.

On another night, about two in the morning, I ran into a heavy fog bank. It was so thick you could cut it with a knife, and couldn't see anything. I was on course exactly as he had written it out. Soon I heard people talking all around me, and then I heard some ship's bells. At that I kicked the bunk and woke Art up. He said, "Where are we?" I said, "I'm right on course, but stick your head out the window and listen." One second of that and he said, "Put her on 180, Elmer, quick." So I spun the wheel, put her on 180 degrees and around we came. We went out of the fog bank in just a few minutes, but just as we got out of the fog bank Art hollered, "Hard over to the right again, Elmer." As I looked back up, there was the bow of a big freighter hanging right out over us. The wash from it almost upset our 56-foot boat, but it missed us. Then from behind it came three more ships, one behind the other. How they ever got through without somebody getting run down in that fog bank I'll never know. I told Art, "I've had enough of this." So we pulled over into a little bay, got Jack up and he threw the lead until we got into a little cove where there was good anchorage, and we proceeded to put in six hours sleep.

We spent some time in Ketchikan, then went on up to Petersburg where Art had hired Jim Allen as a guide. We also took on Nelson Busick there for his bear hunt. He had flown up to Alaska. At high tide we took off and went over to Admiralty Island. We hunted for a time, and then Art wanted to go across to Baranof, but a huge storm kicked up. Allen, the guide, informed us that if the weather wasn't too rough for Art and Jack and I, that he'd like to go on across and start hunting over there. So we took off. The waves were plenty high and it was awfully rough. Jack and I both had to stay on the wheel and then it almost made a whip-cracker out of us. However the ones to get sick were Nick Busick and Jim Allen, the guide. The rest of us weathered it fine. We hunted all three islands; Admiralty, Baranof and Chichagof, as well as some smaller islands.

First on the ticket was to get some black bear. Art knew of an island that was simply loaded with black bear. I had never seen so many in one day in my life. We took the sea dory and went up a stream running in for a short distance, then got out and walked up the stream. There was quite a good trail that the bears had made along there while they were fishing for salmon. The river was loaded with humpies and dog salmon. In fact the salmon was so thick the river was roped up. I believe if they had held still, one could have walked across the pools on the backs of the salmon.

Nelson was shooting a .30-06 rifle with Peters 225-grain belted bullets. Originally Gus Peret and I had designed that bullet for Remington, but we wanted a soft point and instead of a soft point they made it full-jacket with a big hollow point and a belt of supporting metal just back of the point. We found it would not expand enough for black bear, and hardly enough even on grizzly before the trip was over. Nelson shot the first black through behind the shoulders at about 50 yards. He simply whirled his head around, snapped at the entrance hole and got in the brush. We never did find him. The next one he shot did the same thing, only this one was up a tree and Nelson knocked him out. He regained his feet and took off. In that almost tropical vegetation up there we couldn't trail them. There was bear tracks everywhere. So the third one, he hit him, knocked him over, the bear got up, and he knocked him over again. So I whipped the old .333 O.K.H. I had with me off my back, and just as the bear was hitting the brush across the river, I hit him in the tail end. We later found that the 300-grain bullet lodged in his left jaw. That finished him and we had one bear hide. After skinning him out and putting the hide and skull on the packboard, we worked farther up the creek and cut in again. We saw a bear fishing down below us about 150 yards. There were quite a lot of big rocks in the stream. Nelson shot at him, but he shot low and hit a rock right at the stern of the bear. I believe a fragment of the jacket hit the bear. Anyway he sat up from his fishing, and slapped himself on the rump as hard as he could several times. It was the most comical sight I ever saw, that bear a-pounding himself. I think he thought a bee had stung him. Anyway Busick clobbered him in the shoulders the next time, and he had his two black bear. Those 225-grain bullets just drilled, didn't seem to expand hardly at all.

As we were going back to where we'd left the dory, there was another black bear came out across the creek from us. The creek at this place wasn't over 40 feet wide, I don't think, and this black bear, oh, he was spoiling for a fight! He'd walk along, ruffle up his hair, look at us, then walk back, just acting like a dog

running along by another dog trying to pick a fight. I didn't want a black bear hide and had no way of getting across without we brought the dory clear up the creek, so we didn't bother him. But that was the most belligerant black bear I ever saw.

Martin was a good cook, and we had plenty of food aboard, so we lived quite well and had good bunks in the boat. It's really the only way to hunt bear in Alaska. Shore camps are just out. It rains all the time. Everything is wet and soggy and farther north on the Peninsula the ice is only about 4 to 6 inches underneath the top soil.

We next hunted, I believe, Baranof Island. We anchored out in the bay, took the sea dory, and went ashore and up a beautiful salmon stream. For some reason, there wasn't too many salmon running this particular stream. We finally came to the most beautiful setting I have ever seen for killing a grizzly. There was a great waterfall that fell 50 or 60 feet sheer into a pool, and the water was only about knee deep below it. The river was spread out over fine gravel and sand. On each side giant trees towered to the sky. There were ferns, devils club, and all kinds of underbrush, so you couldn't see six feet when you got off a bear trail along the river. A big old sow walked out in the middle of the river. She had a three-year-old with her. Our guide, Allen, told Nick to take her. We called Nelson "Nick." He shot her through back of the shoulders. She went down in a heap. The range was about 100 yards. We were standing by a big log so he could even have a rest. Instantly she was on her feet, bawling, and swung around and spotted us. The three-year-old took to the brush, but the old sow came at us all out. Nick shot again, hit her in the chest, and down she went. But up she got and came again. I could see the flats of her hind feet so she was really driving. Each time he shot, he put her down. His rifle carried six shells. He had one in the chamber and five in the magazine. Just when I decided it was time to take a hand, laid my camera down and picked up my .400 double rifle, he hit her high enough in the chest that he got into the spine and killed her. She proved a very dark grizzly and her fur, to my notion, was too thin on the middle of her back. I don't understand them having that early a bear season. This was the fall of 19 and 39.

The next bear we ran onto was on a little cove on a bay. He was a beautifully furred grizzly, typical grizzly, not brownie. He was frosted clear down the shoulders to the elbows. The first shot was at about 80 yards. The bear was just tipping over to the creek to go fishing. Nelson caught him forward of the right flank. The bullet came out low in front of his left shoulder. The bear swapped ends and came back by us. Nelson shot him again through the lungs right behind the shoulder. He swung his head and snapped at the bullet entrance and went into the devils club and brush.

A very steep mountain went up, and there was a bear trail about 30 yards to the right of where the bear entered the jungle. Jim Allen said, "I don't like to take Nick in there for that bear," so I told him I'd trail the bear if he'd work up the trail from the right and try to get Nick a shot if I located the bear. I had a .400 Westley Richards double rifle and I knew I could stop any bear with that if I had any chance for a shot. The bear was bleeding quite heavily, and I managed to trail him up the hill about three or four hundred yards. It was quite steep. I finally came to a big log. I could hear Nick and Allen, the guide, to my right as they climbed up a well-worn bear trail. When I came to this big log, it was chest high, I reached my hand up to climb up on it and just on the other side there sat the grizzly. He opened his mouth and hissed at me, so I swung the double rifle around, covered him and I whistled for Jim and Nick if they could hear me. They answered me.

I said, "Can you see the bear? He's just over this log from me."

Jim said, "I can see him all right."

I asked Nick, "Are you in the clear so that you can find a hole with no brush to deflect your bullet? If you can, shoot him through the head." Nick said, "We're all in the clear," so he shot. Down went the grizzly in a pile. Jim Allen came running over and vaulted the log. He straddled the bear, got him by the ears, and lifted his head up. He said, "My, ain't he a beauty."

Just then the grizzly came to life.

Jim Allen let out one wild yell, went over the log, over the top of my hat, and I think he went about 30 feet down the steep slope. The bear started hissing again, but I don't think he knew what he was doing. He was pretty badly hit from the other shot in the head, but Nick had missed the brain. So I told him, "Shoot again, and this time hit him at the base of the ear." Nelson shot again, and that did the trick. He was a beautifully furred grizzly. I don't like wounded grizzlies on the end of my gun barrel, but that was the case in this instance.

Nelson wanted a still bigger bear. Jack wanted a bear, and offered to take one of these on his license and decided to let Nelson

kill another one. We moved to another island. This time there was quite a salmon stream came in by a cannery. I don't remember the name of it. It was so full of salmon it didn't look like there was water enough to float another one. At the mouth there was an Indian and his squaw. They had a sea dory there and she had a rope about 30 feet long with several hooks tied on it about four feet from the bottom, with a boulder on the end of it. She'd heave the boulder into a pool there, wrap the rope around herself and head for shore. Each time she'd bring out from one to three flopping salmon. The Indian would knock them in the head with a club and throw them in the boat. When the boat was loaded to about six inches from the top, they'd get in and paddle over to an island. There they'd dress all the fish, and put sticks in them to hold them open flat. They'd split them and hang them up in the trees to dry. How they ever dried though was beyond me, because on that whole month's trip I saw the sun just once. The rest of the time it was either drizzly or pouring rain.

Allen, Nelson and I worked up this stream about two miles, finding fresh-killed salmon and some big bear tracks. One track crossed a gravel bar. It was sunk into the gravel a good two inches. I jumped up and down and I couldn't dent that gravel that that bear had sunk into two inches. This track looked very similar to the one we had seen on the island where we got the black bear, so we worked cautiously on up the stream. Nelson was following Allen, and I was bringing up the rear end of the procession, when I saw a big bear come out in the middle of the stream. This portion of the stream was swifter and much shallower than it had been down near the tidewater where the pools were deep. The big bear walked out in the middle. He was a jet black grizzly or brownie. At any rate there was not a white hair on him, but he was a big bear. I whistled low. The bear turned his head and looked at me. Nelson turned around and saw me, and I just pointed. His eyes were two question marks and I made the motion to shoot. He'd quit the .30-06 with the 225-grain Peters belted and had my .333 O.K.H. with 300-grain bullets, with 60 grains of 4350 powder behind them with Winchester 120 primers. I had my big .400 double and I watched. Nick shot the bear in the shoulders, square, broadside, the range probably 30 yards. It just looked like his front feet flew out each way and he came down on his big belly with his nose in the river. His ears wiggled, but that was all. Nelson shot again in his neck but it wasn't necessary. He was so big and heavy, he just laid there and the stream backed up and flowed around him on each side.

He was far too heavy for the strength of the three of us to move at all, so we waded out and skinned him right there in the river. It was quite a job. Then we got his big hide on my packboard, including the feet and skull. I didn't take time to skin out the paws. It made a terrific load.

When we'd gone down the trail a couple of miles, we met Art Kinnan. He'd been part way up when he heard the shots, so he came on up to see what was happening.

The first bullet Nick fired had evidently expanded when it hit the bear's wet hide. They were Kynoch 300-grain with thin jackets. Anyway it tore an inch entrance hole in that bear, and where he laid down in that river a rope of blood squirted out for four feet as big as my thumb for several seconds after he went down. The slug had taken off the top of the heart and lodged, fully expanded, in the far side of the right lung. It entered from the left side. The one he hit in the neck had broken the neck and laid there in the heavy muscles on the other side of the vertebrae. Jim and I were both tired from the heavy load, we'd been trading off, so Art Kinnan took on my packboard. After we'd gone down the trail a quarter of a mile though, he found a good big log and sat down on it. But he didn't figure the weight of the bear hide, and he got a little too far back. Over Art went with his long legs sticking up in the air on top of the bear hide and packboard. Jim and I pulled him back and we headed on back down to the sea dory, thence on out to the boat.

This bear hide, spread out on the deck of Art's boat, no one touching it, squared nine feet. It was a nice bear. One toe and claw of the front paw was missing. I don't know whether from a trap or whether another bear had bitten it off. He was jet black, not a white hair on him, a big hump on his shoulders, and I'd estimate his weight at around 800 pounds, possibly 900. It was all we could do to turn him over in the river while we skinned him.

We headed back to Petersburg where Busick could board a plane for his trip back home. On our way, we went pretty close to a huge glacier. It hung out from the cliffs and pieces were continually breaking off into the sea, and icebergs were sticking up all around us, which Jack dodged. I was on the deck cleaning bear skulls, and for once during the entire trip the sun came out and we had a beautiful day. We arrived at Petersburg in good shape and tied

up near the end of a floating dock. These docks were made to raise as the tide comes in and lower as the tide goes out. The harbor was full of shipping, and all around in the harbor, every now and then I could see the black fin of a killer whale cruising around. Seaplanes would come in and land. By this time it was raining again, and those seaplanes would break through the fog, it looked to me like, only 200 yards above the bay. They'd find an opening between the ships and splash down for a landing.

Art had a good radio on the ship and we'd hear all the calls coming in. There'd been an accident out on a fishing boat and a man had gotten killed. He'd leaned over to oil the main shaft from the engine back to the propeller. The collar on it had some nuts projecting out. He had a long silk scarf wrapped around his neck and it had been dangling, and one end of it had caught and wrapped around the propeller shaft and it had cut his head off. A man in an open cockpit plane with two seats agreed to go out and get him. He took off up through the fog out of sight. After a while he came back. When he came back he had the dead man in the front seat with his hands holding his head in his lap and he was in the rear seat flying the plane. It was gruesome.

One night Art and I were sitting in the cabin, waiting for the tide to raise so we could get out and go down the country towards the States. There was a bunch of halibut fishermen came in, three boats of them as I remember, and they were celebrating. They had a big catch of halibut and had made a lot of money. One of them, a Norsky, had been uptown. There the Norsky radio played all night all kinds of Norwegian dance music. This Norsky came back down to the end of the dock, had a portable radio in one hand, and it was playing the tunes. He had a quart of whiskey in the other hand. He got out on the end of the dock right near the tip of it and he would dance to this tune. The rain was pouring down, but he had on a slicker, rain hat, and hip boots. Finally he danced too far to the end, and off he went. I jumped up, opened the door and grabbed the boat hook to pull him out. Art grabbed me by the shoulder and set me back.

He said, "You can't drown them fellows. Sit down and watch the show."

So I did, sure that he'd sink. Up he came, however, with his thumb over the top of the whiskey bottle and carefully set it on the deck. Then he went down again and he came up and he laid the radio down, went under again and the next time, he heaved himself out on the dock, picked up the whiskey and had a drink, picked up the radio, and found it wasn't working. He shook it and threw it in the sea, finished the bottle, threw it in, and back up town he went. Within an hour he was back with a new radio and another bottle of whiskey.

The sea gulls were a pest in every port. They wanted to light on your masts, cover your deck with their excreta, and we had the job of cleaning it off and polishing the brass-work again. Martin, the cook, didn't like that. Once when we were at the end of the dock and the aft side of the boat was away from the town, Martin had an ingenious way of taking care of the seagulls. He had a short rod with a heavy reel and line on it. He'd bait it up and throw it out a porthole on the side away from the dock. The seagulls would come a-screaming down and grab it, he'd hook them, reel them in through the portholes, wring their necks and put them in a barrel. So we had a barrel of the darn seagulls to dump and bury when we next made a land-fall. Martin kept the brasswork clean with not so much scrubbing when he eliminated a few of the pests.

BACK AT THE DESK . . .

In 19 and 36 I'd taken a job as gun editor for the *Outdoors* magazine located at Columbus, Ohio. I held that position for twelve years until I resigned, after they had put on a new editor, a young chap. He accepted and published an article recommending an open-bored 20 gauge as the all-American shotgun; all-around for American use. He even wrote a paragraph recommending this article and signed my name and put it at the head of the article. I had no inkling of it, no knowledge whatever, until the magazine hit the news-stands. When I got my copy, I went to town and wired them that I was resigning, to take my name off the masthead and never to use it again in the magazine.

In late '39, when I got home from the Alaskan trip, I had a big bale of letters to answer, of course. About two months later I finally got the bill from Standard Oil Company for the 500 gallons of gasoline I bought for Art's boat.

In the winter of 1939-40, the magazine flew me back to Columbus for a ten-day conference. Not being used to a big city, I couldn't sleep nights at all. At the conclusion of the trip, they gave me some sleeping pills so that when I got on the plane I would do all right. I went on the plane and went to sleep after the stewardess had given me another couple of sleeping pills.

I woke up at Rochester, Minnesota.

At the time, I didn't know whether I was in this world or the next. The stewardess was bending over and asking me if I was all right. She had two sets of eyes, two mouths, two noses, and I thought I was seeing things. She asked me if I'd taken sleeping pills before I got on the plane and I told her "Yes." So she got me some black coffee and breakfast and that fixed me up. The pilot was Captain Davis, long since retired from the service. He had been reading my material in the magazines for years. As I was the only passenger from Rochester, Minnesota on this Northwest Airline flight, he sent the co-pilot back and asked me to come up and fly with him in the cockpit. I gladly consented, and let the co-pilot play cards with the stewardess while I went up and took his seat in the cockpit, and put on the headphones.

Cap Davis explained to me how I could raise or lower the plane, either with the wheel by pulling back or pushing ahead, and also with the large wheel between us down next to the floor. Also he explained the beam. It was dash-dot on one side of it, and when you got on the other side it dot-dash, and a steady hum when the plane was on course. So I flew the plane from Rochester until the calls came in from Miles City. I took it up to 10,000, and back down to 5,000.

I really enjoyed flying that two-motored DC-3. It was a good ship. When the calls came in from Miles City, Cap Davis said, "Go back and have the co-pilot come up and we'll take her in for a landing." We got stuck there in a three-day blizzard and couldn't move. The stewardess would take me down to the Metropole Restaurant and we'd have a big steak twice a day with all the trimmings.

Getting back in the air, we had passed Bozeman, and was crossing some mountains between there and Butte when we hit some very rough air. A lot of the baggage and stuff flew up against the ceiling and down, and one man commenced screaming that he had lost a lot of silver dollars he had in his pocket. He became quite irate and profane with the stewardess. Finally we went to Butte and then to Helena. When we got to Helena he finally got off the plane which was a good thing for all of us. Then when we made Missoula we made four passes at the field before we got down in a blizzard, but we finally got down.

About this time I hired out to a man to run a boat trip down the St. Lawrence, up around the east coast into Hudson Bay for a polar bear hunt. He had booked some people for the trip and some more were hanging fire when he wired me to come back to Michigan. I did so on a bus, taking along my own rifle and a .35 Newton for him, which he "bought" and never paid for. However, the trip blew up as some of the party backed out, and there wasn't enough to finance the trip or pay for the charter of the ship to go down the St. Lawrence and around and up into the Hudson Bay country.

BIRTH OF THE DUPLEX . . .

On my way back to Michigan, I ran into friends in Minneapolis, who gave me a fine dinner, and I became acquainted with Charley O'Neil there. Later on Charley and I started experimenting with various cartridge rifles. First we necked the .30 Newton down to a .22. Then we tried it in .25 caliber. A few shots from that thing, and the barrel would get so hot you couldn't hold your hand on it, especially ahead of the chamber. Finally we fired ten or fifteen shots through the thing one day and I actually put a cigarette on it and it started to smoke.

I told Charley, "We are firing the powder from the wrong end."

He said, "What do you mean?"

"Well," I said, "if we could ignite the front end of that charge, and start the bullet up the bore with a portion of it, then the pressure that drove the bullet forward would hold the powder back in the case until the fire came back and it was all consumed."

I could see no way of accomplishing this, but I gave Charley the idea. He had a good head. He went home and he went to work. He drilled out the flash hole in the primer pockets and then threaded them. He got some brass tube that was small enough to thread, and with a split collet wrench, screw them in from the front end of the case. We experimented with various lengths of tube, finding that a tube half the length of the powder chamber was about right and gave the best results. This carried the flash of the primer to the forward end of the powder charge. We worked with it quite awhile, finding that we had something, so we applied for a patent. We got one on it. At that time the war in Europe was going on, and it looked like we would be into it. I didn't want to give it any publicity, other than tell the results, which I did in the *American Rifleman* and others. The then head of the "dope bag" in *The American Rifleman* wrote a piece and said we were mixing powders, which we were not doing at all, but I didn't want the dope to get out for the German technicians to get ahold of, because I was sure it would greatly boost velocities with

a lot of the artillery, especially with their 88's.

O'Neil and I had already developed the .250 O'Neil Magnum which we made by making down a Holland & Holland belted magnum case. That proved to be quite a rifle, but still was not the answer for anything but pests. I wrote up the .250 O'Neil Magnum in the April, 1937 issue of *The American Rifleman,* and in the September issue, 1938, of *The American Rifleman,* I wrote the results of our duplex loads. Then again in 1939 in *The American Rifleman,* I wrote up the .285 duplex on game. I killed five elk with the .285 O.K.H. duplex before I had a failure and found out that the caliber was too small, and the heaviest possible bullet was still not my idea of an elk gun.

After the story in *The American Rifleman* that we were mixing powders, a lot of people started mixing powders to gain higher velocities. They blew up several rifles in their efforts. I still would not let the dope out until after the war was over and finished.

Nelson Busick had used my .333 O.K.H. with duplex loads on his big bear, and I did also in finishing off a black for him that he had wounded. O'Neil tried various calibers, necking the .30-06 down to the seven millimeter, really .285 inches. That made quite a rifle, and was as fine a shooting long range rifle I had used at that time, even beating the .280 Dubiel that I used for several years.

I conducted some trajectory tests, sighting the Winchester Model 70 in .300 H & H Magnum with 180-grain Western boattailed ammunition and also the .285 O.K.H. with the 180-grain bullet I designed for Western Tool and Copper Works and 55 grains of 4350 in the duplex case. With both rifles sighted to print dead center at 400 yards with a benchrest, I then turned them on another target at 200 measured yards. The .300 H & H Magnum with 180-grain boattail printed 7½ inches above the center of the bull where I held, while the .285 O.K.H. printed just five inches high, showing a third less trajectory height over a 400-yard range. Next I turned them on some ⅝-inch armor plate that Don Hopkins had sent me at 20 yards, shooting out of the cabin and with a feather bed and feather pillow padded around so that there was just a hole for the rifle and the scope, because a lot of fragments come back from steel shooting. The .300 H & H Magnum 180-grain went about three fourths of the way through, and left a big dent on the other side of the plate. The .285 O.K.H. 180-grain blowed a clean hole through the whole plate.

I next set the plate out at 50 yards. The .300 Magnum went about a third to a quarter of the way through with a dent on the back, and a big splash on the face of it. And again the .285 O.K.H. cut a clean hole right through the steel. So I knew we had something. I killed five elk with that rifle and load before it failed me on one over on the Yellowstone Park line.

Next we brought out the .333 O.K.H., as Don Hopkins had joined us by then. He put up money for O'Neil to experiment with, and barrels of powder. We did a whale of a lot of experimenting. The .333 O.K.H., with 60 grains of 4350 and Winchester '06 cases, with everything in 250 to 300-grain bullets performed beautifully. I killed a good many elk and deer with it. That was the first rifle I used on elk after using the .400 Whelen Jim Howe had given me in 19 and 25. With a duplex load, instead of a sharp crack it was more of a "Ker-whoom" sound, and the recoil was different too. It was not as sharp. And the powder that started the bullet up the bore also built up pressure and held the rest of the powder in the case until it burned back. Later I was to work out duplex loads for caliber .50 Browning machine guns back at Frankford Arsenal for ordnance.

Each fall three or four of us would drive over to the Lochsa and put up camp and hunt elk until each of us had an elk for our winter's meat. We could get deer at home but elk were scarce there then. The .333 O.K.H. on the .30-06 case proved a wonderful killing load. But even then I wanted the same caliber, using the British .333 Jeffery bullet in a big magnum case, either by expanding the neck of the .300 Holland & Holland, or necking down the .375, which O'Neil finally did, and we called it the .334 O.K.H..

That proved the best long-range big-game cartridge for everything from deer to elk or big bear that I had used. Now, with a very slightly changed form, it is the .340 Weatherby; the main differences being that the caliber is increased from .330 to .338 inch.

We next brought out from the .375 case what O'Neil named the .424 O.K.H., using .404 caliber .423 inch bullets. We finally introduced the .475 O.K.H., using the 500-grain .470 bullet from the .375 Magnum case straightened out.

They all proved to be excellent loads, and some are still in use. We also experimented some with a little 6.5 Mannlicher case with a 7mm necked to 6.5 with a duplex tubing. It worked well, and was wonderfully accurate, but was still too small for anything much over deer. We never tried duplex loads with a .250 Magnum, but I believe they would have

worked well with a 120-grain bullet, as it was a .275 Holland & Holland case necked down to .25 caliber.

Between spring bear hunts and fall hunting parties, I worked getting in a supply of wood for winter, getting the ranch in shape for next summer, did some trapping, and my writing. I was kept very busy. In fact, I have never been out of a job all my life, never expect to be, and I don't intend to retire. I would rather die with my boots on any time than in some hospital cot.

Gibbonsville, above my ranch, had been a rich placer mine, with some rich quartz mines in the early days from the nineties through 1900. I prospected along the rim above the bridge and found some very coarse gold, but it didn't go back very far towards the highway. I managed to clean off quite a little along the rim, enough to buy a second-hand Buick car. Elmer Hagel, Bob Hagel's father, and I rebuilt an old ditch out of Sheep Creek, carried the water through a big pipe that went under the highway, and washed out a pit above my bridge. It was good on the edge, but as we got back farther it quit, the main part of the channel being down in the bottom across the creek. At that time we hired Bob Hagel to clean the tail place for us. He wasn't very energetic, but he did manage to get it done. I ordered his first rifle for him, a Krag 30-inch for $1.50 through the B.C.M. He later hunted a lot with that rifle, and killed a lot of elk and deer with it. At that time, he was just a stringy kid, then he started wanting to write. I went over some of his first articles, and I bought some of them from him and published them in *The Outdoorsman,* and got him started in the writing game. Today he writes for several magazines. Bob and I also have hunted elk and deer together on several occasions.

I had worked some with John Dubiel who had been with the Hoffman Arms Company during their span of existence. I had worked with him on the .276 Dubiel, and later on the .280 Dubiel. He rebarreled my old .300 Hoffman Magnum to .280 Dubiel. At that time, that was the finest long-range cartridge I had ever used. We killed a lot of game with it and used it several winters on coyotes at long range with a 12-power Lyman Targetspot on it. We only had No. 15½ DuPont to work with, as that was before 4350 came out. I soon found that our duplex load in the '06 case with a .285 O.K.H. outranged the .280 Dubiel with the same 180-grain weight bullets. The .280 Dubiel, however, had a .2889 groove diameter. John was building me a fine .280

Dubiel sporter-weight rifle at the time of his death. His boy later told me the rifle was all finished except checkering. I had sent him a Howe-Whelen peep sight for the Magnum Mauser Monroe Good had given me, to be put on. However, someone stole the rifle on John's death, the boy told me, and I never got a chance to see it.

With my heavy-barrel .280 Dubiel I took a good many coyote out to a full 500 yards. Also worked on golden eagles. At that time, the State of Idaho paid a dollar bounty on these killers and it should be on today to my notion, as I have seen them kill full-grown mule deer and antelope, an old mountain sheep ewe, and God knows how many times I've seen them working on mountain sheep lambs and mountain goat kids. I wish some of these ecologists and biologists could watch the depredations of the golden eagle that I have seen in a lifetime of hunting. They would most certainly have a far different impression of that old bird.

O'Neil and Hopkins wanted a belted magnum case on our .333 O.K.H. that would still function in standard length Mauser actions. We developed the .333 O.K.H. belted, a shortened version of the .375 case necked down to .333 O.K.H. Today, with some slight variations, it is a .338 Winchester Magnum with a .338 bore instead of a .330 groove diameter. It then proved a wonderful cartridge, and both Don and Marge Hopkins used it in Africa on all the plains game. Today the .338 Winchester Magnum is one of our finest all-around cartridges for American shooting, and it is also very good on the plains game of Africa.

In the early 19 and 30s, Bill Weaver sent me his first little scope with a grasshopper mount, which I tested and wrote up in some magazine. I worked with Bill on a number of scopes, and on improvements in his mounts. I also asked him to bring out the double crosswire with 6-inch spacing between the two wires, so that the top wire could be set for 200 yards, and the bottom one would come on at about 500 to 600 for most long range rifles, which he did. This is still an excellent reticule.

More recently, in fact quite recently, Bob Thomson of Glenwood Springs, Colorado, brought out his Double-Dot Colorado reticule which uses the same principle, 6-inch spacing between the large center dot and the smaller lower dot, which gives approximately 300 to 500 yards range with the two dots in his reticule. However, Bob went a long step beyond our fondest dreams when he applied it to the 3x9 Redfield scope with the big dot in the center for 300 yards, then the lower dot can be used for spacing in between and turning the power back from nine to seven or six, you can put it dead on at any range from 300 out to 600 yards. His application of the power changes in this 3x9 Redfield scope, which is equally applicable to the 3x9 or 4x12 Weaver scopes, or other scopes with double crosshairs or double dots with 6-inch spacing. It has worked for everyone who has tried it at all ranges. Once you shoot over the range, write down the power change for the longer ranges using the lower dot, and you're sighted dead center at any range you wish merely by turning your eyepiece.

"THE RIFLEMAN'S RIFLE" . . .

In 19 and 35, Don Martin, Cinque Thompson, Col. Jay Williams and Oscar Waterood and I had worked for about a year and half and designed the Winchester Model 70. They finally sent all the papers and specifications in to Ed Pugsley, who was then head of Winchester. Ed Cave was then their advertising manager. In spite of current claims in some books, we five designed the Model 70 Winchester. Martin and the others were all Alaskan sourdoughs, while I was living on the ranch on the North Fork. We corresponded a lot in that year-and-a-half before we sent in the final papers. Frank Dufresne, who had headed the Alaskan Game Commission, and was later head of U.S. Fish & Wildlife, was back at Winchester at the time visiting them. Ed Pugsley showed him the pilot Model 70.

Ed told Frank, "We have over $200,000 in this pilot model Winchester. If it don't sell, there's four Alaskan sourdoughs and one Idaho cowpoke that had better hunt their holes."

We never had to turn gopher.

They gave each of the boys one apiece. Don Martin took an '06. Jay Williams took a .375. I don't know what the other boys asked for. I took a .375 and a .300 Magnum as they gave me two rifles, and I carried them both on many trips.

When Winchester brought out the .375 and .300 in the Model 70, they first produced a 300-grain softnose bullet load. This proved the most accurate .375 Magnum load I ever fired at that time and for many years later. I put sixteen consecutive shots at 200 measured yards in 1 9/16 inches, center-to-center, for the widest bullet holes. That with a 330 Weaver scope and a Stith mount on the heavy straight tapered 24-inch barrel Model 70 they gave me for helping design the rifle. Later when they brought out the Silvertip, Bob Hagel and I tested it from a benchrest, and we could only get 3½ to 4-inch groups at 200 yards. While my 16-shot group was fired prone with sling with a tarp throwed on the snow and elbow holes pounded, I would fire two shots, stand the rifle up against the fence, snowshoe over to the target, have a look at it, come back, load two more and fire them. The reason I did this was I had sent the rifle to Stith, down in Texas, for mounting a 330 Weaver scope with a flat-top post reticule. When it came back, I took it out to sight it in and at a 200-yard "A" target, the first two shots landed almost in the bottom of the target, but they were right together. I became interested, so I came back, kicked off my webs, crawled into the sling and laid down on the tarp again, fired two more, snowshoed over to the target and they bracketed the other two. I kept that up for eight trips to the 200-yard target until I'd fired 16. Of course the rifle had a chance to cool with the bolt open standing against the fence while I made the 400-yard round trip on snowshoes. This again upsets the idea that you can't get into the sling and move and get back again and hold the same group because the entire group was just 1 9/16 inches center-to-center.

Jim Wade of Peters took a composite of it and carried it in his wallet for a long time. I published it in several magazines. Winchester, however, later improved the Silvertip until it is wonderfully accurate. Back at New Jersey with Bob Thomson and a group of his friends, I put three .378 Weatherby Magnums with 300-grain Silvertip bullets in one hole at 100 measured yards. A dime covered the three holes completely. You couldn't see any trace of the hole if you laid a dime down over the three shots. So Winchester made a vast change in the Silvertip bullet from the first ones that Bob Hagel and I tested down at the ranch to the present production.

On my Michigan trip with the proposed Hudson Bay polar bear hunt I became acquainted with Charley Kohler of Saginaw, Michigan. He and his brother had the Kohler Iron and Steel Works. Later after I was home, Charley said a bunch of people in his club there didn't believe Ed McGivern put six shots *double-action* through a can while it was falling 18 or 20 feet. I wrote and told him I was quite sure that Ed McGivern had done every stunt he ever wrote up many times before he ever went to print on it, or told anybody about it. However, Charley asked me if I would practice that winter and see if I could find out if it was possible for me to do it. He sent me a new 5-inch Smith & Wesson heavy duty .38-44 with 500 rounds of ammunition. I practiced a little bit every day I had time. I'd

fire the six shots, take a gallon can in my left hand, hold the gun in my right hand, throw the can up 20 feet and start on it double-action. Several times I caught myself following the can with the gun when I wasn't looking over the sights at all, and still hitting it. I remember in Ed's book there is a picture of five clay targets in the air, all being broke or busted already, and the dust cloud from them. He had a gun in each hand. Ed always said he used the sights. But this picture proved he didn't always because the line of fire from the guns to the broken clay targets in the air is way below the line of his eyes to the targets. I know he just focused his eyes on the target and shot by the feel of the gun the same as any other good hip shot does. At any rate, I would fire six shots and then I would snap on the empties and save my firing pin from breaking. Then I'd load another six rounds and fire it again. By spring I got pretty good. I had the neighbors come in for witnesses, threw my can up and hit it six shots straight before it hit the ground, five times in a row, then I quit except for some exhibition shooting down at the CCC camp with the officers and CCC boys, and some two-gun hip shooting at tin cans while firing both guns double-action at the same time. McGivern wanted some pictures for his book, so I had a photographer come out from Salmon and take the pictures of me tearing a little stump to pieces with two guns, a triple-lock .44 Special and a .357 Magnum that Major Wesson had given me for helping him design that cartridge and bring it into being. I sent the pictures to McGivern. However, he didn't use them, as he had pictures of a boy from Philadelphia that had trained to do much the same stunts and used them in his book. With practice I got so I could throw the two guns at once and keep them on a very small target at ten yards.

I worked with John Berns when he was a Navy man stationed at a radio station in Alaska. He wanted to design a holster to carry a long 7½-inch single-action up high out of the snow. It was quite deep up there. We developed an open-front holster with a spring to hold the gun. Later he and Jack Martin made quite a number of them. They made me one for two guns and two rolls of ammunition, a belt with two quick-draw holsters. Jack Martin made them for years. A lot of the F.B.I. used them and I remember seeing Walter Walsh demonstrating quick draw at the N.R.A. convention at San Francisco in 1950, using one of the Berns-Martin open-front holsters. They are still being made by one of our large holster companies, but I doubt if they know the history of their development.

In the early '30s, Herbert Bradley brought Don Martin down to the ranch on a Sunday. We had an impromptu bit of pistol practice that day, busting cans, shooting rocks, and one thing and another. We got well acquainted. He has been my lifelong friend since then. Don was one of the finest men I have ever known. He was in the army down on the Mexican border with "Blackjack" Pershing while they were chasing Villa. Later he was in the six-inch field artillery in France during World War I as a dispatch runner and forward observer. Still later he was Sheriff of Lemhi County for two terms. When I met him, and for seven years more, he was a Deputy U.S. Marshal in Alaska until politics changed his job, then he came back to his ranch here on a branch of the Salmon River. We have hunted elk and deer together, and gone on many tough trips. He is a dead shot with either rifles or six-guns. He had done quite a bit of arms writing over the years for various publications. He is well grounded about all phases of rifle or pistol work or reloading. He has been the first reader of several of the eight books I have had published, and has written the foreword for some of them and I think will now write the foreword for this book. He was brought up in the tough old Western school the same as I was, and we share like thoughts on a great many subjects. I could never ask for a better friend.

BACK TO CAMP PERRY...

In 19 and 40 I decided again to go back to Camp Perry, and with that in view started training rapid fire and also long-range plains shooting with a Springfield .30-06. Don loaned me his old 1903 Springfield for rapid-fire work and I'm afraid I about wore it out. Col. George Busby, a friend of mine, came out and spent a week with us at the ranch. He had been captain of the cavalry team on several of the National Match shoots at Camp Perry. He was the best rifle coach I ever had. Col. Busby later ran an armored outfit under Patton through France and Germany. Later he was Provost Marshall of the American sector of Berlin for three years. He was later military advisor to Paraguay for seven years, and is now retired and living in California. While at the ranch on his visit, I drove him up to Don Martin's ranch on Boyle Creek. We had an impromptu pistol shoot. We set up a bunch of bottles around 20 yards away, and the three of us lined up. Don winked at me. I understood him thoroughly. Every time the Colonel would level on a bottle, we would bust it

before he could shoot. Between Don and I we cleaned up all the bottles and the Colonel didn't fire. He was exasperated to say the least. Col. Busby was a West Pointer and as fine a military school man as I've ever met.

I trained for two months in the summer of 1940, and went down to Nampa to the state matches and managed to win first place there, with a gold medal which put me on the Idaho Civilian team for Camp Perry. We had an old '34 Buick, which we drove back to Camp Perry, taking us five days. We drove as far as the suburbs of Chicago when the fuel pump went out. We found a garage that had a kit and could repair it. In the meantime, we took a cab into Chicago in that awful traffic and went to the Field Museum and enjoyed a very good day there looking at Carl Akeley's work and other museum specimens. We could have spent a month there but we only had one day and had to get on the road again for Camp Perry. We made the camp on the fifth day, and were quartered in a tent along with other Idaho civilians with the team.

Our Idaho Civilian Team consisted of ten shooting members, two alternates, a coach and a team captain. On the whole we had a very good team. Several of the members took their wives, so we had quite a group of ladies along with the team. There was a course of instruction and qualification for the ladies at Camp Perry, and most of them took it, my wife included. The course included several days of training, position, and sight picture until the final shooting. When they passed the course, each was issued a certificate of proficiency.

For proficiency with .30 caliber rifle fire this Idaho team was the best team I had served on. After the team matches started, the captain soon found that his coach would chase the spotter rather than judge the wind and make corrections before they shot, so they put me on the job again of getting the dope and doing the coaching. Likewise they squadded me with the weakest man on the team to take the first relay and get the dope for the rest of the team.

With many of our wives along, we had a very enjoyable time in 19 and 40 at Camp Perry. It was easy to see that our nation was then preparing for war. Practically all the army officers knew it was coming. They just didn't know when. All of our training was with that concept in mind.

We were issued a good 1903 National Match Springfield rifle, one of the most accurate military rifles this world has ever produced. After several weeks of practice to get the zero on our rifles at the various ranges, we were ready for the National Matches. We did quite well in many of them but still did not get on top. With all the service teams, all the National Guard teams, and also all the Civilian teams from each state, there must have been 5000 shooters in the camp.

I had a good single-shot bull gun with 26-inch very heavy barrel made by John Buhmiller on a remodeled Enfield action with no magazine or floorplate. It was a wonderfully accurate rifle. It would stay on the 10-inch spotter at 1000 yards if you could hold it. I borrowed another Model 70 .300 H & H bull gun, the same caliber as mine, from the Winchester people to use in the Herrick Team match. My rifle did quite well, but for some reason every shooter that fired the Winchester didn't do quite as well. I believe that particular rifle was not up to the usual standard for accuracy.

The rules of the 19 and 40 matches were a great deal different from those of 1924 and 25. Gone were the sighting shots. The rifle had to be on, as you were not allowed any sighters. That went for the whole team as well as the individuals. We shot through all the individuals first, then the team matches, all leading and building up to the great National Team Matches. We had two southpaws on the team and they were two of the best men we had even though they had to reach over the stock with that left hand to work the bolt. One man, Walterman, had but one eye, a blacksmith by trade of Blackfoot, Idaho, as I remember it. Every day either he or I would get a possible in the rapid-fire practice matches, either 200 sitting from standing, or 300 yards prone from standing. At 200 yards we had one minute to go down in a sitting position, and put in your ten shots after the target started up. At 300 yards you had a minute and ten seconds to go down to prone position, fire your first clip, reload and put in the other one. When you make a possible at those ranges on a ten-inch bull, you're working the Springfield. You must be in good training to get your ten shots off all perfectly aimed. Each day, however, Walterman or I would get a possible, and sometimes both of us. One day I got it at both ranges, which is unusual for most people. One man on our team, Johnny Grey, had also been on the Idaho National Guard team with me back in 19 and 25. It was good to have my old shooting buddy back again.

Next our team entered the Infantry Match, a skirmish run. Starting at 600 yards were seven riflemen and one BAR automatic rifleman. The team captain told me to do the coaching, as I'd had more experience than any of them and could judge the wind. Our run was scheduled for seven in the morning in pretty dim light. I noticed that the smoke from the old furnace house that heated all the camp had drifted clear across the range from right to left. There was apparently no wind. All the flags were hanging straight down. But from my shooting in 1924 and 1925 on that range, I knew there was a drift there somewhere. I made every man put the mike on his Springfield rear sight and check it. I had their elevations written down for all ranges. 600, 500, 300, and two, on a piece of tape and taped it to my gun stock. I had every man put the mike on and check his sight until he knew it was exact. Then I told them to put on a half-point right windage.

A lot of them thought I was crazy. The Infantry captain detailed to razz us was doing a fine job yelling at us to hurry up; anything to distract us. That was the way of the matches, sorta simulate warfare, I presume. At any rate, when the targets came up at 600 yards, we hit the grass, we took one to two shots, a few of us fired two shots, but most only one. All the targets went down. We had to have the prescribed hits on each target.

Then we moved up to 500.

I had every man again check his mike for elevation, then I told them to cut the windage to one-third point right. They all did. Again we put all the targets down with a shot each. We moved up to 300. I asked the team to cut the windage to one-fourth point right and to again check all sights with their micrometer. This Infantry captain was razzing us for all he was worth. Johnny Grey, who was later killed in London when a buzz-bomb landed on him, carried the automatic rifle. He was a big man, a prince of a fellow, and could almost drown out an old bull for volume. He'd yell, "Pay no attention to this brass hat, gang. Take your orders from Keith." He about drowned out the captain that was sent to distract our attention. At 300 yards we downed all the targets again and I let Grey open up with his automatic rifle, which was a mistake, I believe, because he climbed right out over the targets. Then we advanced to 200. I then had all sights checked and the windage cut to one eighth point; there we had to put in all our remaining ammunition. I fired all of mine. Walterman, two places over, fired all of his. We had one man named Burnham. He'd been making hay with a long magazine follower that would jam in the individual rapid-fire matches. He'd fire five to seven shots, call an alibi if one of them stuck in the magazine, and he'd pick up a spotting scope to check his group to see if it was right. Then he'd correct sights and get in another. He also bedded the toe of his stock in the ground, which was illegal in the prone position. At any rate I told him to take that magazine follower to the armory and grind off the front of it or he'd cause us trouble in one of the big matches, which he surely did.

Johnny Grey fired some more at the 200-yard range with the automatic rifle, the prescribed number of shots. Walterman was asking if anybody had any ammunition, and so was I. Burnham was in between us, fighting four cartridges stuck in the magazine with that long follower tipped down. We didn't know it until time was up. When it was over we got eighth place out of the United States and all the Service teams, and we had never had one practice run. The two Marine Corps teams had laid there all summer practicing that Infantry Match and we didn't have one single practice run.

The next day I changed clothes and was over at the bulletin board looking them over. A Marine Corps colonel and Col. Waller and a captain came up and were looking over the board. Idaho civilians—eighth place. The first Marine Corps team was down below us, and the second Marine Corps team was way down. Col. Waller asked the Captain who had been razzing us the day before who was standing there. He didn't recognize me when I'd changed clothes. He asked, "Where the hell did that Idaho outfit crop up?"

The captain saluted and he says, "Sir, I was the officer detailed to razz that bunch. I think they're a bunch of old Idaho coyote hunters. They got a cow-puncher that did all the coaching that surely knows how to judge wind. There wasn't one single bullet from the seven rifles that missed the black. The BAR climbed out, but I never saw such rifle fire. None of the seven men missed the black at any range from 600 to 200 yards. If they had not turned in four rounds unfired from a jammed magazine, they would have won the match."

For each unfired round we were penalized five points, or twenty points for the four rounds that Burnham had to turn in. If it hadn't been for his utter stupidity, playing with that long magazine, we could very well have won the infantry match over all the service teams and all the civilian teams as well.

We had Sundays off, and one Sunday the whole team with their ladies chartered a small boat for a run out to Perry's Island where we spent a most enjoyable day looking over this historical old place. Jorgensen, the oldest man on our team, could smell a pub even on Sunday. He came up with a pillow case full of whiskey bottles. Where he got it, none of us knew, but he could find it if anyone could. We had a great day going out, touring the whole island, had lunch, then went back. The boatman sipped a bit more of Pete's whiskey than he needed, so coming back my wife, Lorraine, ran the ship all the way from Perry's Island back to the dock at Camp Perry.

Remembering the deal I had in the Wimbledon Match in 19 and 25, I wanted another try at it. I had my old bull gun well tuned up, but just before I was scheduled for the Wimbledon Match, I went over to the Marine Corps and asked for the names of all my old friends that I'd shot with there before. The colonel of the Marines told me, "I knew them, Elmer, but they are all gone now. Either dead or retired out of the service."

At seven that morning, with all the flags hanging down like a wet rooster's tail, a Marine had gone out and run 27 Vs. That won the match. The wind picked up soon after that and when I was there at two in the afternoon, the wind was blowing a hurricane and puffing from about eight o'clock. It was blowing so hard that men firing the service rifle had to use from 2¾ to 3¼ points left windage to stay on the 1000 yard target. Not only being puffy, it would lull occasionally, just enough to throw everybody out when they corrected with that much wind. You had to hold hard and firm with plenty of sling tension or it would rock the rifle as you lay on the grass. The Marine Corps dope that I cranked on my 12-power Lyman scope was correct, as my first shot landed well in the black. I corrected and ran several Vs in a string. But three times while I was aiming, the wind lulled, and I had no chance to detect it as I was concentrating on the final trigger squeeze, and I got three fours.

I wound up with a 97 in the Wimbledon Cup match. I would liked to have fired that match at seven in the morning along with the Marine that won it. However, such is luck in a rifle match. You have to take the relay you draw and conditions may be impossible for a good score, while others may have perfect conditions as in this case.

Fitzgerald of Colt's was again at the matches, under his big umbrella, adjusting trigger pulls on all the Colt guns for pistol matches. We renewed acquaintance. He and his wife, and Lorraine and I, went out to dinner one evening, and had a most enjoyable meal. Fitz was not feeling too well then and died not long after that. He was a grand old man. It had been 15 years from 19 and 25 until 19 and 40. Personnel had changed greatly. However, some of my old friends from the industry were still there and we renewed acquaintance. I missed the old boys, however. It was not quite the same as back in 19 and 25. Too many of them had passed away. However, in the practice in the Individual Matches I again came out high man.

Burnham had been on several Idaho Civilian teams and been top man each time, and claimed he was going to be top man on this team as well. However, the 1000 yard match proved him wrong and I came out top for the team. I do not now remember just where we placed in the National Team matches, but I do know it was not good enough to get in the medals, though I did garner several medals in the Individual matches as did some of the rest of our team. We were given a considerable number of lectures.

We also were shown the M1 rifle, and watched it fired until the barrels would bend and the groups would start going below the target. The M1 may be a good combat rifle, especially for close-in fighting with its seven shots in the magazine, but it certainly is not a match rifle. Each team was issued ten of them so we could try them out and become acquainted with them. One day Burnham made a possible at 600 yards in practice. My rifle wouldn't shoot that good, so I sneaked up behind him, grabbed the rifle with one hand and got ahold of his neck with the other. I said, "Just wiggle out of that sling, Burnham. I want to try your rifle."

I laid down and held my ten shots perfect, got a nice juicy 43 with two way out. I noticed Burnham had the toe of the stock dug in the ground when he fired his ten shots. How he got that possible I will never know, because the rifle simply would not do it.

The team captain then said, "Keith, it must be you. Burnham just shot a ten-shot possible."

I said, "Bring my old Springfield up and let me see how I do with that."

I put in 20 with the Springfield straight without a miss, so I said, "Now, Captain, do you think it's me or do you think it's this damn rifle?"

After the matches I wrote up the M1 rifle. General Hatcher told me he'd like to see the article for possible use in *The Rifleman*. However I was not very complimentary about the M1 rifle for long-range accuracy, and the article was returned to me. I published it in *The Outdoorsman* magazine and I also wrote a piece

on it for, I believe, *Sports Afield,* and they published it. I believe that those two articles stopped me from getting a commission in the war. There must have been considerable politics attached to that M1 Garand rifle. At odd times I tested the ten that we were issued. I went over and asked the Montana team to let me test theirs, which I did. I didn't find any of them that would stay in the black for ten shots at 600 yards with perfect holding. There are no guard screws in the rifle. The stock is simply clamped on with the trigger guard. The barrel is heavy at the base but has a very rapid taper. On top of that, the whole front hand-guard, stacking swivel, bayonet catch and sight assembly are hung on that light barrel. When The Army fired them at our instruction, we watched them. They fired them until they got so hot the wood was smoking, and every one of them would lose elevation until finally the bullets at 600 yards were going into the target butts instead of in the paper, because as the barrels heated they bent downward.

At the end of the matches we each headed home, back to the West, and God's country. But all of us well-knowing we were in for a war, and that it would be very soon from the preparation that was well demonstrated to us at Perry by all the Army personnel.

While at Perry, I questioned several members of the Marine Corps team. They told me they had three or four rifles issued to each of them. They claimed that with the Garand they might fire 500 to 700 rounds before they really got it shooting, then after that it might quit them any time in the middle of a match. The consensus among all the old match riflemen on the team, was thumbs down on the Garand for accuracy, although it was a good combat rapid-fire weapon at reasonably close ranges. The Garand had the best sights I've seen on any military rifle; positioned right. However, that rear sight wouldn't always stay put. The screws would work loose with the chatter of the gun in rapid fire.

My idea of a new military rifle was to combine the best points of the Model 70, the Springfield, the Enfield, and the Garand. The trigger mechanism of the Model 70 is the best of all. The Mauser receiver, with its internal flange, is the strongest of all. I wanted the good long Mauser extractor as well. Then for sights, a combination of the Enfield and the Garand. Wings on the front sight protect the 3/32-inch blade. The rear sight is also protected with wings and adjustable from zero for both windage and elevation, with graduations in units of 100 yards each, from 200 yards to

1000 yards. The stock should be longer than the Enfield and similar to the Garand, but at least 13 to 13¼ inches long with a comb high enough so that it could be cheeked well. The hand-guard should cover the barrel completely from the receiver forward on top, the complete rifle to weigh around eight pounds if possible, but with fairly straight taper and stiff barrel for finest accuracy. The cartridge would be a .30-06 necked down to 7mm and would employ a 160-grain boattail bullet at around 3000 feet velocity. This would have made a real military rifle. I never did believe in an average infantryman using a machine gun. The rifleman should be an individual to pick out individual targets and kill them when he finds them. Spraying the landscape with bullets had best be left to the artillery and the machine gun companies. Its no place for any real rifleman. My published criticism of the M1 Garand and my advocacy of this new proposed military rifle and cartridge did not enhance my chances of getting a commission.

"THEN THEY HAD THIS WAR"...

I was on the train on my way home from a hunting trip when the news of Pearl Harbor came through. As a patriotic American I wanted to get in the war and do my part. I wrote to General Uhlio in Washington offering my services for consideration in all branches. I received a nice letter back saying, "Very sorry, Mr. Keith, no place for which you are qualified."

Next the Marine Corps advertised on the radio wanting rifle instructors. I wrote the head of the Marine Corps at Washington telling him I had three certificates from the Camp Perry firing school as a rifle instructor, giving him my background of a lifetime of experiments with all manner of small arms, and offering my services either as a non-com or as a commissioned officer. I had a nice letter back from him stating he appreciated my patriotic offer, but was very sorry he could not use me because I was not a former Marine. I wrote back and told him that while I was not a former member of the Marine Corps, to look up the 19 and 40 National Match records and he would find that I was a coach and shooting member of the Idaho Civilian Team that beat hell out of both of his Marine Corps teams at Camp Perry in the Infantry Match. I never heard any more from the Marine Corps.

Next, my friend, General Hatcher, who headed Ordnance during World War II, asked me to come to Washington and he'd get me a commission in a few months. However, I didn't have money to take care of my family at home and stay around Washington at the high cost of living there until such had come through, so I turned that down. Next my friend, Captain George W. Busby, later to become Colonel, asked me to come to Fort Riley and enlist as a buck private. He said he'd talked me over with all the officers, would put me in Officer Candidate School, and make me a captain in ten months. He wanted me for a combat unit. However, I again couldn't see what the family would live on at home and me at Fort Riley on a buck private's pay this time, so I turned that down. Next my friend, Major Wesson, then Colonel, head of the 9th Corps Area at Salt Lake, asked me to come down there and go into Civil Service and Ordnance, which I did.

They shipped me to Rock Island Arsenal, with residence at Davenport, Iowa, to go through the ack-ack school along with Bliss Titus from Heber, Utah. We roomed together. We studied the .50 Browning machine gun, the 37mm automatic Browning cannon, the 40mm Swedish Bofors cannon, and the big 90mm ack-ack rifles.

They vaccinated all of us for smallpox. One man died from the vaccination, and I came very close. About nine days after I'd taken the scratching on the left arm, I became very sick at the school. The teacher advised me to go home and go to bed. I managed to get out to the bus stop, and was hanging on a park tree getting so sick I could hardly see across the street. A red-headed lady came running across the street and wanted to know what was the matter with me. I told her I didn't know unless it was the smallpox vaccination. She asked me where I lived. By that time I was getting too sick to know very much about what was going on. I told her I had a room in a hotel in Davenport and she said, "Have you got your key with you?" I gave it to her. How she got me on the bus, and got me to the hotel, I'll never know. But anyway the old Negro porter told me he helped her get me up to the room, undress me and put me to bed, and was supposed to call the doctor, but doctors were scarcer than hen's teeth in Davenport, Iowa, at that time. I was out of my head part of the time. Bliss Titus would call on the officers at the arsenal every day and try to get them to send a doctor. None ever came. Between him and the old Negro porter they managed to keep me alive somehow or other on soup and ice cream and jello. The fever finally broke and I started to come out of it. My left arm swelled up to the size of a ham. A hole rotted out underneath the vaccination

Keith had participated in a number of rifle matches at Camp Perry before the outbreak of war. This was taken as he posed with his Hoffman Magnum Mauser there.

Never content to accept the status quo, Keith kept experimenting with newer and more efficient firearms during his term of service at the Ogden Arsenal.

until you could see the bone of my arm. Finally the fever let up and the swelling started to go down, and I was able to get out and back to the school.

In my absence they had been studying the 37mm Browning automatic cannon. The instructor said, "Being as you haven't been here, Keith, you don't need to take this exam." I said, "I'll take it anyway." I did take it and got the highest grade in the class because it was so similar to the Browning .50 caliber machine gun.

After finishing the school I was shipped back to Salt Lake first, then Major Kerr and other officers at the Ogden Arsenal requisitioned me for service at Ogden Arsenal. I was slated to go to Fort Richardson out of Anchorage and be the civilian head of an ack-ack crew there. Major Kerr and the other officers there decided they needed me worse at the Ogden Arsenal as a small arms expert, so I took the position as inspector and head of small-arms testing at Ogden Arsenal. This was the base arsenal for the whole Pacific Theatre, and in addition we had 330,000 .50 caliber barrels there to spot-inspect for both Theatres.

I had a crew of from 10 or 12 to 25 people

at various times. I had more women than men on my crew and I taught them to do stock inspection and clean the rifles and pass them to me. I did the real inspection, checking the barrels, checking the actions, and I did all the proof firing. At one time we processed 500 rifles a day. I had another building added to grease and repack the rifles for shipment. Enfields, Springfields, M1 rifles, .30 carbines, .45 auto pistols; all went through the shop. The .50 caliber guns I'd proof fire of the evening after the arsenal was closed so the noise didn't bother the rest of the people.

They had us firing into a bank of sand in the same building, and put up boards to shoot through, but even then the lead dust from those bullets grinding up would soon have a cloud hanging over all of the firing room. All of us were coughing, spitting up black lead dust, until Major Kerr made them build a new proof house.

They also sent in carloads of bazookas. Word got out that some bazooka crews had been killed because they had blown up on firing. All the lathes in the machine shop were worked over until they would wrap wire around the body of the bazooka tube, and then it was soldered to hold it in place. They thought this would stop them from blowing up, but I had other ideas. I asked for gauges to gauge those bazookas. They gave us some dummy rockets, but that wasn't enough. At that time, however, the 30 men employed in the machine shop were building ornaments out of shell cases for the Officers' Club. I wrote General Hatcher about this and he corrected things. He relieved the colonel in command at that time and sent in Colonel Capron. He told me to take anything I saw off-color in the arsenal to Colonel Capron and he would handle it. He certainly did, from start to finish. His father had been at the Battle of Wounded Knee in charge of the cannon there. Like his father, he was an old West Pointer. He'd also been at Pearl Harbor during the Japanese strike. He was a very fine officer.

The whole small-arms crew was working on these bazookas for a couple of months. I finally got a gauge made slightly larger than the rocket and so that it would still slip through a normal bazooka tube. We started gauging them. One lad had come back wounded from Anzio, and was out-of-service. I decided he needed a soft job. I remember his first name was Charley, and, I believe, the last was Brown, so I gave Charley Brown this job. He would drop the gauge in. Every now and then we would find a bazooka tube where the gauge would stick right where the front sight was welded on. The welding of that front sight had thrown up a burr or a hump on the inside and the rockets would stick there, then blow up. That, to my notion, was the cause of the trouble with them in blowing up some bazooka crews.

I had a mandrel made, long and heavy, and just barely under the size of the normal inside diameter of a bazooka tube, but larger than the rocket itself. Charley would drop the gauge down. If it went through easy, that bazooka tube was passed. If it hung up, it was piled out to one side. Then he would drop the mandrel in, and using a ballpeen hammer, peen it around that front sight and that would relieve the thing until the gauge and the big mandrel would drop through easily. From then on they quit the expensive job of wrapping wire around the whole tube that had been going on for months.

I put in three and a half years at Ogden Arsenal in charge of proof-firing and final inspection. Much of it was very hectic as I had to fight some officers who knew nothing of guns but wanted to dictate what I did with them. I told the officers when I took the job I would not put OG.E.K. in the little rectangular box, my proof mark, on any gun I was not willing to go into combat with myself. They backed me on it, as did General Hatcher, who headed Ordnance at that time. However, the officer in charge of small arms had to have the head inspector sent out from Washington, D. C., and he backed me up on all of my decisions. I had a warehouse full of guns I had condemned. Finally they had 83 BARs. The lieutenant called me from down at the shop and wanted to know if he should blue the actions. I told him, "No." I said, "Polish the breech blocks and scrub out the inside of those receivers after they are blued or they won't work." The 83 guns came up to me for proof firing and final inspection with the breech blocks all blued. The girls laid them out on long tables, and I had a high bank of sand to shoot into, turn them sideways, let them kick off ten rounds flat movement and come back on the other ten rounds. Those 83 guns would fire one to three shots and balk. I condemned the whole lot. I also had another carload of Winchesters, M1s that came in with cracked hand guards, and everything wrong with them. I condemned the lot of them. Finally the officer in charge, who had been a second looey when I went there, had been promoted to a major and he decided that I didn't know what I was doing. I'd thrown out a lot of rifles with crooked barrels. So he had a rod turned up .300 diameter and showed the colonel who pushed that rod through the barrel, that they was straight. He didn't know that a rod would bend. Anyway he said I couldn't judge rifle barrels whether they were straight or crooked. Colonel Capron backed me up, so they took down the numbers of two cases of rifles and wrote down what I'd written on the tags of the ones that I'd condemned or asked to be rebarreled. They took all my tags off, brought them up, and I had the girls clean them. The colonel sat behind my desk and watched the procedure. I passed on the whole bunch of them, they'd mixed some good rifles with them. I threw them out without a bobble from start to finish, the good ones and the bad ones. Colonel Capron said, "I guess, Major, you'll have to admit he knows what he's doing." We had an awful lot of trouble there. I finally went to General Hatcher with it and Colonel Capron and the General cleaned up the thing. The Major was relieved of all duties within the arsenal and the Lieutenants were shipped off to war.

They then asked me to take charge of the Salt Lake plant for Remington, who'd been making .50 caliber ammunition for the war.

In the meantime, however, I told General Hatcher of my duplex loading. I wanted to work on it for a 90mm ack-ack rifle and the British anti-tank rifle. The upshot of it was they shipped me back to Frankford Arsenal, but they put me on caliber .50 instead of the big artillery pieces I wanted to work on at Aberdeen. I put in a month at Frankford Arsenal duplex loading caliber .50. I gave them 202 feet more velocity for normal pressure, and the head man stationed there said it was the most uniform pressures that ever went through his guns.

A Dr. Smith, Ph.D., seemed to be in charge. Major Greenhall was the officer in charge who'd taken over after Colonel Whelen had been given another assignment. Dr. Smith informed me that my idea of a duplex load wouldn't work. He said he'd tried it all. I told him I knew he hadn't. However, he kept me sitting at a desk for nine long days. I went into Major Greenhall's office, picked up a phone in the side room, and called General Hatcher in Washington. I told him what they'd been doing, that I couldn't get tubing for duplex .50 caliber cases and they kept me there at a desk, and that Dr. Smith had said he'd tried it and it wouldn't work. About that time the conversation was cut off. I could hear Major Greenhall, "Yes, General. Yes, General. We'll have the tubing tomorrow. A range will be available for Mr. Keith's firing."

From then on I progressed with the job and got it done. I got the final report from ordnance that I'd justified all claims for duplex loading; absence of muzzle flash, longer barrel time curve, and reduced pressures, the most uniform pressures of all at 202 feet higher velocity for caliber .50 at normal pressures. I was burning 258 grains of powder as compared to 240 of a normal load, and where the normal load went around 2800 feet, I was getting a little over 3000 feet-per-second velocity from normal pressures. But the report stated that due to the exigencies of war, they couldn't change over at that time to manufacture .50 caliber stuff with duplex loads.

I wanted to work with artillery shells which already had a tube going half way up the case, a plug in the end of it screwed in, perforated, and the tube filled full of black powder to fire the cannon powder. All I would have had to have done in those artillery cases was eliminate the holes along the sides of the tubes, eliminate the screw front and fill the tube with black powder as they did, and put a wax wad over the front of it to hold the black powder in place. Then I know I could have given them higher velocity with the 90,

the 40, and the 37, and the 51mm British anti-tank rifle; all of that artillery would work well with our duplex system. However, I didn't get a chance to try it.

Getting back to the Arsenal, Colonel Capron wanted me to go over to Salt Lake and be a civilian head of the old Remington plant that had then been turned over to Ordnance with around 380 people working there. He sent me over in a staff car and I looked it over and I told him I'd try it, take it on long enough that they could find somebody capable of handling it. I met a major there, a red-headed man from Carolina, a very fine officer. He said, "Keith, if you want to come and handle the civilian end of the deal, I'll keep all the red tape off your neck. I know what you were up against at Ogden."

At the arsenal, Major Kerr who was head of safety, had condemned our proof house. As an end result, Colonel Capron asked me as the head of small arms to draw up plans for a new proof house. My plan was to have an outside firing court and a concrete pit for sand some 50 yards from the building to catch the bullets. Then the sand could be cleaned out and fresh sand put in when it became too full of projectiles and started richocheting and coming back, the same as they did at Rock Island Arsenal.

The major in charge wanted to have a pit and a big tank of water and fire into that against steel plates. He didn't know that water wasn't compressable. Ordnance adopted my plans completely and turned down the major's. They built the proof house exactly to my specifications. I was going to go to Salt Lake and take charge of that for a couple of weeks until they could find somebody else to handle the job, as I was tired of working at $9.60 a day putting in 12, and often 16 hours a day in some cases.

At one time, the government bought up 5,000 shotguns to use in Army military police units. I put in two solid months, Sundays and all, test firing those shotguns. I fired from a case and a half to 2½ cases of 12-gauge buckshot from the shoulder every day. At that time I'd gotten out of the bedbug-infected dormitories and took a room with Major Kerr down in Ogden in a clean private home. My hands would swell until I could hardly get my clothes on or shave. Major Kerr would help me, as he roomed next door.

My service at Ogden Arsenal had been anything but pleasant. The lieutenant, who became major as the result of our work, wanted me out of there so he could put in a friend of his, and so that he could ship guns that were in no condition to be used at all. They did everything they could think of to get me out of the arsenal, but I was too bullheaded to give in.

They plugged shotgun barrels with rags for six inches, and hammered them tight from both ends thinking I would be fool enough to fire one of their guns without looking through it. They did the same thing with rifles. They filed the sears on .45 automatic pistols until they would machinegun. They also fixed up automatic twelve gauge shotguns until they'd rip off the whole six rounds fully automatic.

The first time this happened Alta Brockway was standing in the truck where we had the racks of shotguns for testing. I'd drive the big truck out, we'd test each shotgun, and if they'd fire all right with a full magazine, then they were passed. However, a great many of them would have to go back to the shop to be worked over again. On the first one of them that went fully automatic, Alta was standing in the truck and I was just behind it. The gun climbed until the last shot almost hit the canvas hoop over the top of the truck. I told Alta to put the safety on and load it again, hop down, and put her back against the truck and put her hands on my shoulders and when I grunted to start pushing. She did this and after several trials with the six rounds in this Browning automatic, I was able to hold it well on the target at 50 yards through the whole sequence, but the recoil was pretty steady. With her pushing hard on my shoulders I could keep it on target. I kept this shotgun, put it behind my desk in the proof house, and didn't send it back, or condemn it. When we started getting more of them fixed the same way, I knew what the score was. They were trying to blow me off the job some way or other.

Colonel Capron got wind of it, however, and he asked a bunch of the officers to come out and he asked Alta and I to demonstrate. So we did, with the satisfaction that we could handle the thing fully automatic. They finally dropped that phase of the thing.

Later, an Enfield was doctored up, I believe the firing pin was extended. At any rate as I threw the bolt forward to drive the cartridge out of the magazine into the barrel, it went off. The blast cut that Enfield in two pieces. One hunk of the receiver went by my head, and dug a hole in the concrete. Another piece clipped the top of my thumb, but it ricocheted over the little lady's head who was passing rifles out to me. It made me pretty mad. I went down to the proof house with the intention of killing the man in charge there as I figured he'd been putting a lot of the armorers up to these various stunts.

The big civilian head there grabbed this half of an Enfield as I swung it at the head of the man I considered responsible. I was so mad I picked up the 250-pound civilian and tossed him over on top of the man I was after.

He held on, and my whole left side from my ear to my hip was numb from firing that rifle with my hand on the bolt. At any rate the head of the small arms shop was fired and Jiggs Burgess was put in charge; a good man.

During this time I had a little run-in with Major Boehmer, Lt. Brophy, and his second lieutenant. They had blued the breech blocks on 87 Browning Automatic Rifles, and I condemned the lot. They would only fire one or two shots . . . then jam.

Major Boehmer shipped the shop foreman, Jiggs Burgess, and I to the Rock Island Arsenal for an inspection trip. It was unnecessary, but it worked to get rid of us while he shipped those condemned BARs to Benicia Arsenal.

A train wreck stopped Jiggs and I in Denver, and we waited a day and a half before the track cleared. About midnight we went down Larimer Street to see if we could get a train out, and three crooks came out of a saloon and demanded two bits "or else."

Jiggs pulled and cocked a .41 double Remington derringer, pointed it at the biggest man's belly, and told him, "Here's your 'or else.' Where do you want it?" They turned and ran up the alley.

When we finally got back to Ogden, the acting foreman told me Major Boehmer had shipped those 87 BARs as soon as we got on the plane. Years later I had a soldier tell me he was issued one, and it wouldn't work during a fire fight, so he threw it in the mud and left it.

I called Boehmer on the phone and demanded to know where the BARs were, and he ordered me down to the office at seven the next morning. He added that Colonel Capron had a copy of all telephone calls. I said I hoped the colonel was on the phone listening.

Next morning I loaded two .45 autos, fully cocked them, and stuffed them in my belt and pulled my shirt over them. When I knocked, the Major let me in, locked the door, and put the key in his pocket. Not liking the looks of things, I picked up a chair and went to the far corner of the office and sat in it, backwards. The major gave me a ten-cent lecture, and when he was through I called him for the crook he was.

Lt. Brophy jumped up, shucking his jacket,

and said to let him take care of me. I told Brophy to sit down or he was a dead man, then I called Boehmer in terms he could understand. I cussed him out good, as he cared nothing for the boys overseas in the mud, but merely wanted more brass on his shoulders. I asked them to go ahead of me to the colonel, but Boehmer said he couldn't stand another reprimand from him. I made all three get behind the major's desk, and told Boehmer to unlock the door, or I would shoot the lock off it. He unlocked it, and I went straight to the colonel.

He relieved Major Boehmer of all duties in the arsenal, sent Lt. Brophy to the paratroops in Germany, and the little second lieutenant went to the South Pacific.

That is only a sample of the hell and grief I went through in those three years and a half at Ogden Arsenal. They even had the civilian head of inspection flown out from Washington, D. C. to go over my work, and he backed me up in all instances. That settled the deal as far as their trying to get rid of me. Had it not been for my daughter getting worse, I would probably have served out the rest of the war there.

While at Ogden Arsenal, I was amazed at the lack of knowledge of the potential of the .45 Government automatic pistol in combat. I remember the head of the small-arms shop as well as several armorers there who said you couldn't hit anything with them beyond 20 or 30 yards. I told them they were very foolish, that I could kill a man with no trouble at all up to 250 yards if I could see where my bullets struck and walk them on the target. The argument got all over the arsenal until finally Colonel Capron ordered us out to the range on a Sunday. The head of small arms insisted that he could stand up at 60 or 80 yards and I could shoot at him all day, and barring an accident, couldn't hit him.

We repaired to the rifle range, which was a 200-yard range. A slight slope raised up behind the range and 50 yards beyond the 200-yard target butts was a snowdrift around three feet long, eighteen inches high in the center tapering to each end. I had asked Colonel Capron if I could bring my own .45 automatic into the Arsenal and he granted me permission. Then I asked him if that target would do. We had quite an assemblage of officers and people from the small-arms shop. I laid down on my left side in a reclining position, bracing my head with my left hand, and cradling my .45 auto in the hollow of my uplifted right knee. My first shot landed low, just over the target butts. I was holding all of the

front sight up, lining it up with the notch in the rear sight, and perching the snowdrift on top of it. The next shot I held up too much of the slide between the sights and went over the snowdrift. I corrected my point of aim, and the next five shots in the clip went into the snowdrift. I put in a new clip and put them all in the snowdrift. Then I asked the head of the small arms shop if he'd like to go up and lay down where the snowdrift was, and let me shoot another clip.

Colonel Capron said, "Amen, gentlemen."

At one time at the Ogden Arsenal the whole small-arms crew was ordered out to the range to load clips while all the officers from Hill Field and Ogden Arsenal were given a complete course in the firing of the various small arms; M1 carbines, the Browning Automatic Rifle, Springfields, Enfields, M1s, and .45 automatic pistols. They gave them the old FBI crouch position for firing the pistols. We, of the small-arms crew at Ogden Arsenal, were busy loading clips behind the firing line. I noticed a line of officers shooting at the targets which were placed 15 yards from the firing point and were the old Army target of a man's head and shoulders. Those firing the .45 autos from the hip were digging into the ground about halfway to the target. There was more dust raised than there were hits on the targets. Finally out of a clear sky the head of the guards at Ogden Arsenal picked up a megaphone and he said, "Elmer Keith and Buck Lee will now demonstrate hip shooting for the assemblage."

I called him on that. I said, "Captain, you are an ex-Texas ranger. There is not a quick-draw rig in this whole arsenal and you know it as well as I do."

Buck Lee had made up a rig for a .38 Smith & Wesson and had been coaching the Ogden police. I knew very little of what he was doing. However the captain said, "Well, I have a Colt single-action and a 1917 Smith & Wesson."

I said, "Either gun will do to demonstrate hip shooting, but I have no holster or rig here."

"Well," he said, "You can hold the gun down at your side while I count three, and you and Buck can fire in place of the count four."

I agreed. He had the 1917 Smith & Wesson .45 there and the single-action was back at his office. So Buck and I stood up on the 15-yard firing line, he counted three, and instead of four I raised the old gun, poked it at the target and turned it loose. I saw my first bullet cut halfway into the silhouette target and into the 1x4 on which it was nailed. I lifted the gun slightly, and put the other five in a space I could cover with my hand in the chest. I pressed the latch, opened the cylinder, handed the gun to him and walked back between the benches on which all the officers from the arsenal and Hill Field were seated. I went on back and loaded clips. I noticed as I went between two benches of officers that Buck Lee was still firing and dust was raising between him and his target. The captain then picked up the megaphone and he said, "The colonel wants to see you do that again." That was before Colonel Capron was put on the job and the former colonel was relieved of duties. This colonel had very thick lenses on his glasses. In fact his eyes looked like crawdads when he looked at you. So I came back and reloaded the 1917 Smith with a couple of clips. That time when he counted three I put the gun up and put the six in my target in a space I could cover with my hand. I opened the cylinder, spun the gun on my finger, handed it to the Captain, and went back again. As I went between two benches there was a colonel on one side and a major on the other. The major said, "Colonel, we've seen something." I went on back and went to loading clips, but never again was I called on to go out and load clips or to demonstrate when they had another course of training for the officers in firing the various guns. Many memories of my service years come back to me now. I often wonder how we ever won the war if what I saw was an overall sample of the combined effort.

At Frankford Arsenal, half of the cafeteria was roped off for officers only, and there were a great many officers there from lieutenants to majors. I asked the head ballistician what they were doing there as I didn't see any of them doing anything around the testing branch of the arsenal. He said, "Elmer, they are politicians' sons given good commissions and put here in Ordnance so that they will be safe from any action in the war."

There seemed to be more uniformed officers in their half of the cafeteria than there were workers in ours. They apparently had no duties within the arsenal as near as I could learn, merely spending their time at the Officers Club and various amusements around the arsenal.

At Ogden Arsenal, I saw a great many pickup trucks, vintage of '38 and '39, all put through the machine shop, completely reconditioned, filled up with Prestone, then all of them parked in a vacant lot and bids called in from outsiders and they were sold by the

ton at very low prices. I could not conceive of how this could help the war effort in any way.

My mother passed away in 1940, just before we got into the war. My father passed away while I was in service at Ogden Arsenal in 1943. Mother was 65 and father was 69.

DRUZILLA . . .

During this time, Lorraine and my daughter, Druzilla, had been down to see a doctor at Hazelton who was treating Lorraine. There was a prisoner-of-war camp there and one day when she was going from her place of residence in town out to see this doctor, the P.O.W. truck barged halfway across the highway, ran a stop sign, and stalled there. My wife's lane was open, she was on the right side, so she drove on, but a car coming the other way at very high speed swerved over to miss the truck and hit her head-on. Druzilla went through the windshield and was badly cut. We didn't know it at the time, but she had also crushed a vertebra in her neck. Mrs. Keith was not seriously hurt.

I had been on the ranch on the North Fork. I went to Salmon, got a plane, and went down to see them in the hospital. I couldn't do a thing against the man that had pulled over on her side and hit her head-on. No lawyers would take it and there was nothing to be done. The car was a total wreck.

During my service at Ogden Arsenal, my daughter Druzilla had steadily gotten worse. She was growing, and as she grew the vertebrae in her neck did not grow and was choking the spinal cord. Sometimes she would drop on the floor. We had to take her out of school. She was a natural musician and spent most of her odd time playing the piano.

When I went home to Salmon for a short vacation before taking over an assignment down in Salt Lake, Dru got much worse. I wired the colonel and told him I had to give it up. I told him I had to have either a major's commission or a decent salary for all the work I had been putting in and the people I'd been handling. I have a letter from Colonel Capron saying that I had done my share ten times over and when I came back from the Frankford Arsenal, the Colonel had me get in his staff car and go around to the various buildings at the arsenal.

He said, "I want you to tour it and see what you find." I was amazed to see the young people that I had trained and coached in charge of various branches of small arms. Alta Brockway was in charge of .45 automatics, and so it went down the line. The colonel then told me when I decided to quit for good,

Keith and his family at his corner of the study-trophy room just prior to World War II.

192

"You've done your job in this war, Keith. I hate to lose you, but under the circumstances I don't blame you a bit." The draft board had me on A-1 right along, and when they went to Colonel Capron, he said "You'll take Keith over my dead body. He's doing a job here that's needed." I was 45 years old, but I was still top priority for the draft.

General Hatcher had visited the arsenal while we were busy on bazookas. He looked over in the corner, spotted me and left his other officers and came over and he said, "What are you doing here, Keith?"

I said, "This is the best I've been able to get in this war."

He said, "They're certainly not making use of your ability." He was quite perturbed about it. This ended my war service.

I went home to the ranch and gathered up some more horses. Mrs. Keith had been forced to sell my pack string except for the saddle horse during the very hard winter while I was at Ogden Arsenal.

I, like everyone else, lost money in the war and my little salary left only about 100 to 150 dollars each month to send home to my wife after I'd paid for very poor lodging at the Arsenal. Down at Ogden where I finally got into a private home, I at least had a good clean room without the bedbugs of the dormitories at the arsenal.

As nearly everyone that was footloose went to war work in the arsenals at one place or another, the big game built up tremendously on the North Fork; in fact, all along the Salmon River. It was like the old days, game everywhere. I counted over 50 elk wallows in Twin Creeks alone, so I started back in my guiding business, having some very good parties and having very good luck with them.

Druzilla had been badly injured in that car wreck. Doctors told me later they knew we would lose her, but they wouldn't tell us at the time. One day Mrs. Keith, Dru, Ted and I were in town shopping. I wanted to go to the restaurant and Lorraine said, "Let's go have our dinner here and I won't have to cook when I get back to the ranch." However, Dru appeared pale and wanted to go home, so we went home. She took down with the flu and the next morning it hit me.

I was carrying in a pail after milking the cows when it hit me. I set the pail of milk down and asked Lorraine to take it. I managed to get in the house, get off my clothes and get in bed. I went into pleural pneumonia.

Druzilla got worse, and at two in the morning we lost her. Lorraine had phoned Doctor Mulder from Salmon at the Ranger Station.

Lorraine and Druzilla Keith with a fine 15-inch antelope on a 1933 hunt, taken with a .280 Dubiel.

He came out and was treating me. He thought I was going into empyema again, and said he would operate while I sat up in bed, with a local anesthetic. Having had one empyema operation with a rib gone on the right side, I wanted no more of that. I told him I'd rather die in one piece unless he could cure me otherwise.

When we lost Dru, the Masons helped Lorraine take care of all the arrangements. I was so sick they thought I was going to die the day they buried my daughter. I couldn't even get out of bed or move, the pneumonia had one lung full of fluid, and the other one nearly so. It was a sad state of affairs at the Keith ranch. I couldn't even go to my own daughter's funeral, being so bad that day. Our son, Ted, however was a lot of help to his mother.

After the war, it seemed like everyone wanted to go hunting. Elk and deer had both built up tremendously. I can remember on the North Fork, after the boys all got home from the war and started hunting, from daylight to dark there wouldn't be five minutes that you couldn't hear the crack of a rifle somewhere up and down the North Fork of the Salmon. It was the same all over Lemhi County, lots of game and a barrage of hunters after them. Many of them would come in ill prepared to hunt elk. They'd go back and kill an elk as

After the war, Keith spent many months developing new loads with C.M. O'Neil, shown here with a fine 16½-inch antelope in Idaho's Pahsimeroi Valley.

far as they could hike from their car, and then with no way to get it out, they'd leave it to sour. They did the same with deer. They'd kill them so far back they couldn't pack them out. They weren't men enough to quarter them up and take them out in pieces. We found a lot of game dressed out and left to spoil.

In 19 and 46 Herman P. Dean who headed the Standard Publishing Company solicited a book on big-game rifles. I wrote it. It was titled *Rifles for Large Game*. He printed 2,000 copies and promised to push it for 20 years. He sold out to the Stackpole Company, and it was never reprinted. It was a ten-dollar book for regular copies and, I believe, $15 for a limited leatherbound edition.

Then in 19 and 48, Little, Brown & Company of Boston solicited a book on big-game hunting. I wrote it, covering all species and the hunting of American game to the best of my knowledge from all my experience of guiding in Mexico to Alaska. It sold through three editions and I understand now *Rifles for Large*

Game is priced at $150 a copy, if anyone can find a copy, and *Big Game Hunting* by Little, Brown is at $50 a copy.

I went into a partnership with George Turner of Eagle Nest, New Mexico, on a new scope mount. It was a good mount as long as George made it, and it made us a little money. We even made one up at the start of the war for testing by the Marine Corps as a sniping rifle, but it was not adopted. I believe it would have been much better than what they used. After the war, Turner let the patent out to others. Finally the King Pike mount came out, a copy of it. Later Stith of Texas adopted it. It was a good mount when George Turner made it. Variations of the later companies that took it over have, to my notion, never been as good as the old original.

George was an old timer of New Mexico. His father had freighted in to the Army posts there in the early Indian days.

I was a busy boy after the war. I put in a lot of time helping develop new loads, make

The combination of the .280 Dubiel rifle with 150-grain bullet, and the 12X Lyman target scope helped Keith bag many fine antelope in the Pahsimeroi Valley.

improvements on rifles and scopes, and worked with Weaver on my double horizontal cross wires, and with O'Neil on our OKH cartridges. Between testing guns, ammunition, writing articles, and handling my assignment as gun editor of *The Outdoorsman* Magazine plus big game guiding, I was a busy boy.

I had a close call out of Ashton on an elk hunt. I'd had Don Hopkins over there on an elk hunt. We were hunting in about two to three feet of snow on snowshoes in a heavily jackpine-timbered country. On my own and looking for my own winter's meat, I crossed the tracks of five or six elk. I turned back on the trail where they'd spread out to see what was in the band as I wanted a big dry cow if possible. Just then I heard somebody say, "Don't shoot. I see red."

In looking to the side, the lad had a .30-30 carbine trained on me through a crack in the trees and his partner had seen my red shirt. Those two boys had been trailing the elk for several hours, so I told them to go ahead. I was no hand to cut in on anybody's track.

However, after having my partner, Bill Strong, killed in 1919 in front of me, I was glad I was wearing red that day.

After resigning as gun editor of *The Outdoorsman* after 12 years service, I accepted a position on the technical staff of *The American Rifleman* under General Hatcher, and was kept quite busy answering up to 500 gun inquiries a month in addition to getting out articles occasionally for *The American Rifleman*. In 19 and 50, the NRA convention was held at San Francisco, and General Hatcher ordered me there along with others of the technical staff. During the program I was scheduled to speak at the Marine Memorial Theatre. I did so.

The podium was set up on a semi-circular stage facing the audience, with floodlights reflecting back into my face. Evidently it had been built for dancing girls and the usual theatre. General Hatcher introduced me. I was to talk on various hunting trips, which I did for an hour. The silence was really confusing to me. I could hear a pin drop and after an hour's talk I thought everybody had left except possibly my wife and General Hatcher. Then the general got up, turned up the lights and broke it up. I was to speak for an hour, and then questions and answers for a half hour. He asked the crowd, which by this time had filled all the seats, the aisles, and some were sitting on others laps, if they wanted more talk or if they wanted questions and answers. There was a roar, they wanted me to speak some more. So I did, telling of other trips and other hunts for another half hour, and then excused myself and tried to get out of the assemblage. However, I had to autograph a lot of my books, sign drawings various artists had made of me; and it was quite late before Lorraine and I and Harold McFarland and his wife got out of the theatre.

I was ordered to, and took in, all the NRA conventions for the next eight years. One of them was held at Jacksonville, Florida where Roy Weatherby and I had to speak for the assemblage again. While at Washington on one trip, General Hatcher had to go to Florida for the pistol matches and asked me to run his office for a day, which I did. During the day I talked into a dictaphone and answered 40 gun inquiries that had come in, answered numerous phone calls, received several people that came in to see the general on various questions and, all told, had quite a day.

In 19 and 50, General Stackpole who then headed the Stackpole Publishing Co. at Harrisburg, Pennsylvania, solicited a book on shotguns, which I wrote for him. Later in 19 and 55 he again solicited a book, this one to be on six-guns. He had been selling the old Samworth manual for some time and wanted a big book on the subject. I agreed to write it if he would again publish *Rifles for Large Game*, which he had bought from Standard Publishing Co. and Herman P. Dean. He agreed that if *Sixguns* would sell, he'd be only to glad to republish *Rifles for Large Game. Sixguns* went into three editions for Stackpole and recently they sold it to Bonanza Books where it is now in its tenth printing. They also sold *Shotguns* that had sold out three editions. Bonanza Books edition of *Shotguns* is now sold out.

A CHANGE AT CAMP PERRY...

In 19 and 53 General Edson, head of the NRA, had wired me to come back to Camp Perry. He said so many people wanted to see me and talk with me there. So I grabbed some airplanes and got back to Cleveland, I believe it was, and there I was stuck getting to Camp Perry. However, I ran on to an airplane captain I knew and had flown with. He took me to another office and introduced me

to his girl friend who promised to get me transportation to Camp Perry. She soon found a flyer with a little Navion plane and we took off for Camp Perry. At Fort Clinton there was the start of an air field. There was a tiny hanger and one plane sitting in one corner of the field. There was two big ditches and a slough across the middle of it that hadn't been filled. We buzzed it a couple of times. I pulled off my hat and he ran the canopy back so I could stick my head out, and I told him I could tell him when to lift the plane to jump the ditches and the slough. This we did and taxied up to the hanger and this one little plane stiting there.

When our little Navion stopped, there sat Al Freeland in a car. He said, "Where are you going, Keith?" I said, "I'm trying to get to Camp Perry." He said, "Grab your bags and hop in. There's where I'm headed." Al was then one of our top small-bore shooters, and was engaged in the matches.

One day he was gathering up his equipment at Perry to move up when his relay come up. I picked up his scope, and one of the shooting cases, while he got his rifle and mat. We went forward to place it. The soldier who was to score Freeland's target said, "Who's that with you?" Freeland told him it was Elmer Keith. He said, "If that's Elmer Keith, who the hell are you?"

I put in two weeks of the most terrible hot weather there at Camp Perry that I have ever experienced. The temperature was running around 100 and so was the humidity. The nights seemed just as hot as the days. The only way we could get any sleep was to go to the bath house, soak up a couple of sheets, go back to the cot, lay one down, and spread another wet sheet over us. While evaporation was in progress, we'd doze off and get a couple of hours sleep. It was miserable weather. There was apparently no ice in the camp. We had plenty of whiskey and mix, but no ice. I remember one night a friend and I were sitting out on the sea wall about one o'clock in the morning. The heat was so oppressive we couldn't sleep. We saw some distant lightning and heard a little thunder far across Lake Erie, but none of it ever came our way.

I renewed acquaintance with a great many old friends, and also became acquainted with Tom Frye, a trick shot for Remington. He invited me out to his home—a welcome break. His wife served us all the ice-cold lemonade we could drink, and he asked me if I'd like to see him do the shooting he usually showed around over the country. I told him I'd be delighted, so he took me out to a farm and we proceeded to do considerable shooting. He had me throw up five clay targets at once, taught me finally how to throw them so it would make an even spread, one below the other, and he'd break them all. He said, "Elmer, I can teach you to do that in half an hour."

I told him he was certainly crazy. He handed me a little 20-gauge Remington automatic and threw up one target. He said, "Hold at the bottom of them," then two, then three. After a half-hour's practice, he threw up five and I got them all—three times straight. He said, "See, there's nothing to it—it only takes practice."

One day I decided to get into some of the individual matches, so I signed up for and took a National Match M1 rifle. I was anxious to see it. They said they'd improved it a great deal, but the Marines I talked to said they each had three and if one went sour they'd pick up another one.

Finally a colonel of the Marines there said, "Keith I have already targeted my rifle here and you can use my target." So I put in my ten shots there, offhand, calling my shots within an inch of where we hit. "Keith," he said, "You must have shot matches before."

I told him I'd been on the 19 and 24 Montana National Guard team, 19 and 25 Idaho National Guard team, and 19 and 40 Idaho Civilian team. "Well," he says, "tomorrow come back and at 600 yards I have my data down pretty well and you can use my target." So I came back the next day, laid down prone, fired my ten shots and called them for a possible. Up come the target. I had one bullseye, then a four, then a three and then I was off the target. I couldn't understand it. The colonel came up and I showed him my rifle. He said, "Grab that screw, Keith, before it falls out of the rear sight." I was so disgusted with the thing, the sight had come loose in that tenth shot. I took the rifle back, cleaned it up, and turned it into Ordnance, and swore off the M1 rifle for life.

THE .44 MAGNUM BEGINS . . .

Having wanted a .44 heavy load at the time I worked for Major Wesson back in the 30s on the .357, I casted bullets for him to take down to Winchester, which was the start of the .357 Magnum. After I put 1000 rounds of 10 grains of No. 80 behind my 173-grain bullet through a heavy duty 5-inch Smith & Wesson, I still wanted a heavier .44 Special load. I had been handloading 18½ grains of 2400 behind my 250-grain bullet for my .44 Special with excellent results, both on game, long range, target, anything I wanted to turn the

gun on. I met a Mr. Peterson, who was then head ballistician at Remington. I put in all the available time with him that I could during the two weeks I was at Camp Perry, asking that he bring out my heavy load on the .44 Special. He and other Remington officials wanted me to come up to the Remington plant and spend a week with them after my assignment at Camp Perry. Also my friend, Carl Hellstrom, president of Smith & Wesson, wanted me to come up and spend a week at the Smith & Wesson plant with him. I asked General Edson's permission after my two weeks assignment at Perry and he agreed for me to go on and tour the Remington and Smith & Wesson plants.

I wanted two things from Remington. I wanted them to factory load my heavy .44 Special load, and I also wanted an ounce-and-a-quarter magnum 16-bore load that I'd been loading successfully for years. There was no problem whatever on the 16-bore load. Peterson had called the boys all together, and they agreed on it right away.

But they were afraid of the old triple-lock Smith & Wesson with my heavy loads. I told them I'd been shooting it for 10 to 15 years in the old gun I'd got from McGivern with no problems whatever, fine accuracy, no undue pressure. But they were skeptical of the old gun holding it. So I told them why not make the case 1/10-inch longer and call it a .44 Magnum? They agreed that would be a good idea but on the other hand, they said, where are you going to get the guns? I told them I believed I could get Smith & Wesson to make the gun if they would make the ammunition. After a week of going through all the production of rifles, shotguns, and ammunition at the Remington plants, I flew up to Springfield as a guest of Carl Hellstrom. I put in a week there going through their wonderful plant.

He had taken over Smith & Wesson when it was $13,000,000 in the red, and the government wanted to put in the men there to oversee it. Carl Hellstrom said, "I will have nothing to do with it if there is a single government man here. If you'll turn me loose, I'll have Smith & Wesson out of the red in a few years." He showed me where he'd bulldozed a small hill into a swamp, leveled it up, and built the Smith & Wesson plant, one of the finest arms plants in the world today for its size. He could go underground if necessary, as complete facilities were both underground and above ground.

There I watched the building of Smith & Wesson handguns for a week, from the forgings through the shapers, trimmers, then rifling machines and finally the lapping of the barrels, then the Magnaflux checking of all parts before they finally went on to assembly, down through assembly, proof-firing and final inspection. It was a most enjoyable week for a man who had spent most of his life experimenting with arms of all types.

I also became acquainted with the heads of Smith & Wesson. The last day I was there Carl Hellstrom called me in his office and we put in the whole morning together. Several delegations came in from South America and Canada wanting to see him, and he would have his secretary tell them he was in conference with Keith and he would see them in the afternoon. I asked him to bring out a .44 Magnum and have Remington bring out the loads. He finally promised, "I'll wrap a gun around any legitimate load that Remington will bring out."

I suggested he invite the heads of the Remington plant, the technical boys, up and have them work with Bill Gunn, his foreman, and see if we couldn't produce a .44 Magnum and ammunition. This he agreed to do. He took me out to the old Smith & Wesson residence which had been turned into a club. There we had dinner, and a few drinks. Afterwards, he sent his car and his chauffer to take me down to the Colt plant and see that I got in touch with the Colt people. That was September 19 and 53.

After a lapse of several months the advertising manager, whose name I cannot now recall, phoned me. He said, "Elmer, your dream has come true. The .44 Magnum is now a fact. Carl had the Remington boys up here and they are making the ammunition. The first .44 Magnum ever produced, the tool-room job, is on its way to you now by air parcel post. Remington will send you a supply of ammunition within a few weeks." Which they did.

That was the start of the .44 Magnum. As I remember it arrived in February. Emmett Steeples and I took it down to Wagonhammer Springs, and pulled off the road there to sight it in. About 60 yards from the parked car there was a little black stump of mahogany about four inches in diameter projecting out of the snow. And just six or seven yards to the left of it was a big old buck mule deer, bedded down. When he saw us he pulled his head down into the snow. His horns were long gone, but his old white face and the way his ears flopped out to the side, proved him to be an old buck. I believe I fired 16 shots at that little stump, adjusting the sights with a screw driver, and resting both arms out the car window, until I hit the stump three times

The introduction of the .44 Magnum cartridge revolutionized handgun hunting, making it possible to bag some of the biggest animals on earth.

straight—or what was left of it. Emmett says, "That old buck thinks we don't see him." We pulled out and left him lying there in his bed with his head pulled down tight in the snow thinking we hadn't seen him. He well knew if he jumped up that we would see him. Out of season, we had no intention of bothering him whatever, but it was interesting to watch how he pulled his head down and thought he was hid. We left so he could stay hidden.

Next Pete White from the slaughter house phoned me. He said, "Elmer, I have ten big bulls out here I wish you would come out and shoot. You have some heavy six guns and we don't have anything out here but a .22 and it is inadequate."

I drove out at seven in the morning, but I got there a bit early as the crew hadn't arrived. While I was standing there by a fence, a big goshawk flew into the top of a cottonwood across a slough around 100 yards away. I rested both arms on the top of a fence post, pulled down on the old goshawk and I killed him. That was the first shot at game of any kind with a .44 Magnum to my knowledge.

The bulls were run into a chute by the side of the killing floor. There I put up a ladder so I could shoot them in the forehead and had no trouble killing the bulls with the big gun. They'd drop, and while the gun was still in recoil their noses would hit the concrete. One they had me shoot from behind, the back of the head. Both of his eyes popped out of their sockets when the big gun cracked. Many people tried to claim credit for the .44 Magnum, but those were the facts as I experienced them. I had been loading 18½ grains of 2400 behind my 250-grain bullet a good many years in the .44 Special, and testing it on game, target and long range.

Remington ammunition came in plain boxes. I still have a little of it. With a part jacket around over the base band and under the breach in the grease groove. The lead was quite soft, it expanded well, and was very accurate. The velocity was around 1400 feet per second. Pressures ran around 34-35,000 psi. I shot the big gun a good bit that spring and summer and worked out a load of 22 grains of 2400 behind my bullet as my favorite load. This developed 34,000 psi with less than three thousand pounds variation. It was also wonderfully accurate. Velocity ran around 1400 feet per second. That fall I went down to Kriley's ranch on Clear Creek, intending to shoot a buck with a six-gun.

One day Judge Don Martin and I were shooting the big gun over at the city dump. When we started back, I spotted a rock down the canyon below the dump at what looked like 500 yards from the road. We estimated the distance at that and I told Don to park the car and turn off the motor and let me see what I could do with it. The rock was about three feet long by about 18 inches high in the middle tapered a little bit at each end. Resting my arms out the window, my right arm on the back of the car seat as well, I tried it. The first shot was low. Holding up more front sight and perching the rock on top of it, I managed to put the next five on the rock. Don said, "Damn it, I seen it, but I still don't believe it. Let's go down there."

We paced the distance down to the rock, both ways, and as near as we could figure it was five hundred yards. There was five splashes of lead on the rock and one bullet that dug into the dirt short. This shooting, just before hunting season, had given me a pretty good idea of just how much front sight to hold up at long range.

Paul Kriley and I hunted up Clear Creek on the right side where it is partly open bunch grass meadows and partly patches of timber. We hunted all day, and although we saw several does at 80-90 yards, one at 60, that I could have killed. We passed them up,

as I wanted a buck. Toward evening we topped out on a ridge. There was a swale between us and another small ridge on the side of the mountain slope about 300-400 yards away. Beyond that, out on the open sidehill, no doubt on account of the cougar, were about 20 mule deer, feeding. Two big bucks were in the band, and some lesser ones, the rest were does and long fawns. As it was getting late and the last day of the season, I wanted one of those bucks for meat. Being a half-mile away I told Paul, "Take the .300 Magnum and duck back out of sight here, go around through this swale to that next ridge and that should put you within about 500 yards of them. I'll stay here (the deer had seen us), let them watch me for a decoy." Paul said, "You take the rifle."

I said, "How is it sighted?"

He said, "One inch high at a hundred yards." I told him to go ahead because I wouldn't know where to hold it. I always sighted a .300 Magnum 3 inches high at a hundred and I wouldn't know where to hold it at 500.

I said, "You go ahead and kill the biggest buck in the bunch for me." Paul took off, went across the swale and climbed the ridge, laid down and crawled up to the top. He shot. The lower of the two bucks, which he later said was the biggest one, dropped and rolled down the mountain. I then took off across the swale to join him. Just before I climbed up the ridge to where he was lying, he started shooting again.

When I came up on top, the band of deer was pretty well long gone. They'd gone out to the next ridge top, turned up it slightly and went over. But the old buck was up following their trail, one front leg a-swinging. Paul had hit it. I asked Paul, "Is there any harm in me getting into this show?" He said, "No, go ahead."

I had to lay down prone, because if I crawled over the hill to assume my old backside position, then the blast of his gun would be right in my ear. Shooting prone with a .44 Magnum is something I don't like at all. The concussion is terrific. It will just about bust your ear drums every time. At any rate Paul shot and missed. I held all of the front sight up, or practically all of it, and perched the running deer on top of the front sight and squeezed one off. Paul said, "I saw it through my scope. It hit in the mud and snow right below him." There was possibly six inches of wet snow, with muddy ground underneath. I told him, "I won't be low the next shot." Paul shot again and missed with his .300 Magnum.

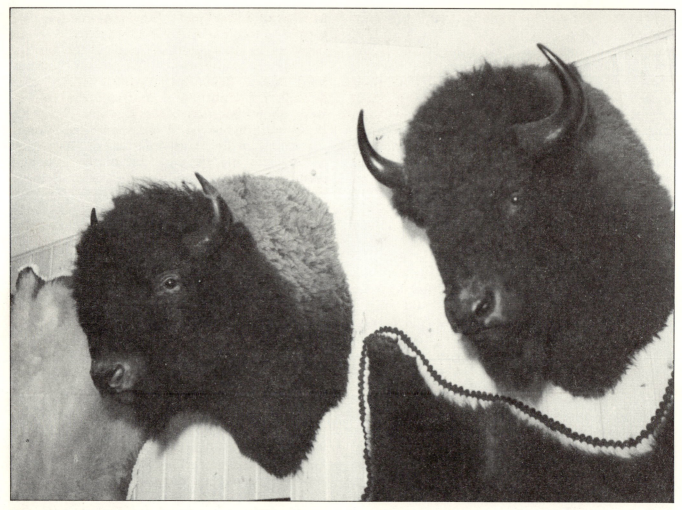

These two record bison heads decorate the wall of Elmer's study. One was taken with a .45-120-550 Sharps. The other fell to a .476 Westley Richards double rifle.

The next time I held all of the front sight up and a bit of the ramp, just perched the deer on top. After the shot the gun came down out of recoil and the bullet had evidently landed. The buck made a high buck-jump, swapped ends, and came back toward us, shaking his head. I told Paul I must have hit a horn. I asked him to let the buck come back until he was right on us if he would, let him come as close as he would and I'd jump up and kill him. When he came back to where Paul had first rolled him, out about 500 yards, Paul said, "I could hit him now, I think."

"Well," I said, "I don't like to see a deer run on three legs. Go ahead." He shot again and missed. The buck swapped ends and turned around and went back right over the same trail. Paul said, "I'm out of ammunition. Empty." I told him to reload, duck back out of sight, go on around the hill and head the old buck off, and I'd chase him on around. Paul took off on a run to go around this bunch-grass hill and get up above the buck

and on top. He was young, husky, and could run like a deer himself. I got on the old buck again with all of the front sight and a trifle of the ramp up. Just as I was going to squeeze it off when he got to the ridge, he turned up it just as the band of deer had done. So I moved the sight picture in front of him and shot. After an interval he went down and out of sight. I didn't think anything of it, thought he had just tipped over the ridge. It took me about half an hour to get across.

When I got over there to the ridge, I saw where he'd rolled down the hill about fifty yards, bleeding badly, and then he'd gotten up and walked from the tracks to the ridge in front of us. There were a few pine trees down below, so I cut across to intercept his tracks. I could see he was bleeding out both sides.

Just before I got to the top of the ridge I heard a shot up above me and then another shot, and I yelled and asked if it was Paul. He answered. I asked, "Did you get him?" He said, "Yes, he's down there by that big pine

The second deer ever taken by a .44 Magnum round hangs on a bridge in Idaho. Keith took the buck at 40 yards using a 6-inch Smith and Wesson Model 29.

tree below you. Climb a little higher and you can see him." Paul came down and we went down to the buck. Paul said the buck was walking along all humped up very slowly. He held back of the shoulders as he was quartering away. The first shot went between his forelegs and threw up snow. Then he said the buck turned a little more away from him and he held higher and dropped him. Finally we parted the hair in the right flank and found where the 180-grain needle-pointed Remington spitzer had gone in. Later I determined it blew up and lodged in the left shoulder. At any rate I looked his horns over trying to see where I'd hit a horn. No sign of it. Finally I found a bullet hole back of the right jaw and it came out the top of his nose. That was the shot I'd hit him with out at 600 yards. Then Paul said, "Who shot him through the lungs broadside? I didn't, never had that kind of shot at all."

There was an entrance hole fairly high on the right side of the rib cage just under the spine and an exit just about three or four inches lower on the other side. The deer had been approximately the same elevation as I

was when I fired that last shot at him. We dressed him, drug him down the trail on Clear Creek, hung him up, and went on down to the ranch. The next day a man named Posy and I came back with a pack horse, loaded him and took him in. I took a few pictures of him hanging in the woodshed along with the Smith & Wesson .44 Mag.

I took him home and hung him up in the garage. About ten days later my son Ted came home from college and I told him, "Ted, go out and skin that big buck and get us some chops. They should be well-ripened and about right for dinner tonight." After awhile Ted came in and he laid the part jacket of a Remington bullet on the table beside me and he said, "Dad I found this right beside the exit hole on the left side of that buck's ribs." Then I knew that I had hit him at that long range two out of four times. I believe I missed the first shot, we didn't see it at all, and it was on the second that Paul said he saw snow and mud fly up at his heels. I wrote it up and I've been called a liar ever since, but Paul Kriley is still alive and able to vouch for the facts.

This first Smith & Wesson .44 Magnum has a 6½-inch barrel.

By the time Ted was eleven, he'd accompanied me on several hunts. Often times I'd let him take the saddle horse and the pack string on the trail while I hunted off to one side. He soon became very proficient with horses, and also a good shot for a kid. He killed his first bear and deer when he was eleven and twelve years old with a .45-70 Model 86 lightweight Winchester, one shot for each animal.

After termination of my services of eight years with *The American Rifleman,* I also took on the job as gun editor of the little *Western Sportsman* in Denver for the four years that it lasted before it folded up. They, like the *Outdoorsman* magazine, left me holding the sack for my last two month's wages.

Having guided for and killed most game in North America, I had long dreamed of hunting Africa. At 50 years of age, I decided to quit guiding. I'd served my time. I'd killed eight good rams myself, and guided for 25 more—to say nothing of many elk, deer, and bear hunts. I decided to put in my time writing, so I rented out the ranch and bought a good home in Salmon a few months after Druzilla's death. We moved to Salmon during some of the worst weather we have ever had here—the winter of 19 and 48. U.S. Highway 93 was being built and was simply a mud puddle all the way. I rented a truck and finally succeeded in moving everything to town and we had a good home there. During the winter of '48, we had two months of hard weather, but nothing to compare with what I'd seen in Montana in the winter of 19 and 19, and 19 and 20. We did have two months of 20 to 43 below. Lorraine, Ted and I enjoyed a good modern home in comparison to the ranch down on the North Fork.

General Hatcher is one of the finest men I've ever known. He and his wife visited us for a couple of days here in Salmon on one of his trips to the West. My associations with the NRA were very good until a new editor took over in the latter part of the eight years I spent on that assignment. This man rewrote and changed some of my articles; changed a bull elk into a caribou from one paragraph to another; changed a 450-pound goat that I wrote up on that episode on the Cottonwood to a 150-pounder. I had to buy a lot of whiskey for old timers here in Salmon who'd come along, put their arm around me and say, "Elmer, why didn't you kick that little kid off the ledge?"

At that time I was drawing $400 from *The American Rifleman* monthly. Bev Mann, who had been a former editor of *The Rifleman*, asked me if I wouldn't do a column for him each month and take on the arms assignment for *Guns* Magazine in Chicago. I had signed a contract with the NRA in July. It allowed me to write for any and all magazines I desired, so long as I answered the 300 to 500 letters *The Rifleman* sent me each month and furnished what articles they wanted for the magazine. This agreement I had kept to the letter. However they didn't keep the contract with me. My name was taken off the staff, off the masthead, and I was changed to a contributing editor in fine print at the very bottom of the page. Many people jumped me at various conventions wanting to know why I was writing the way I had. I told them that it was not

my doings. The editor had changed my text. Then they went after him. He in turn jumped on me and I told him he would have to accept the blame for any changes he made in my material. Things went from bad to worse between us, and after eight years on the technical staff of *The Rifleman*, as contributing editor, I had accepted an assignment to write a column on guns each month for *Guns* magazine in Chicago for $150 a month. I received a call one morning from the editor wanting to know if I was quitting *The Rifleman* and going to write for *Guns*. I told him I had no intention of quitting *The Rifleman* and I told General Hatcher I wanted to make it my life work. However he said he and Mr. Lucas would take a very dim view of me writing for two magazines at once. I told him he'd better read the contract which allowed me to write for any and all magazines as long as I filled my assignment with *The Rifleman*. He said, "You write me a letter to that effect that I can show to Mr. Lucas."

I said, "You have ears. I'm not going to write any letter."

Some two weeks later he again phoned at seven in the morning and wanted to know if I'd sent that letter. I told him, "What letter?" He said, "The one telling me you are going to write for *Guns*."

I said, "I told you at that time that I wasn't going to write you a letter, and I haven't." "Well," he said, "Mr. Lucas and I would take a very dim view of you writing for two magazines at once."

I said, "Mister, and you can tell Mr. Lucas, you can take any damn view you desire." In 15 minutes I was terminated from my assignment with *The American Rifleman* magazine. Lorraine asked me, "What are you going to do now, Dad, on $150 a month from *Guns* magazine?"

I said, "I'm going to Africa."

Chapter 7

HUNTING BIG GAME

GETTING THE "WORKS" IN AFRICA ...

Two years before, a friend had phoned me from New York City telling me that John Lawrence of White Hunters Limited wanted me to come over to Africa. He said Lawrence would give me a free trip if I would pay my round-trip fare and my hotel expenses, all licenses, and shipping charges on the shipping of trophies, etc. At that time I wrote John that I would accept, but he would have to give me another year, so that I could save up enough money for the trip.

John Lawrence wrote back and he said, "Elmer, you have done enough for us over here recommending adequate rifles to Americans coming over, that we feel we owe you a trip and we are going to give you one. So, you pack up and be here in Nairobi on the first of November next year, and I'll take you on a safari myself."

I was determined to keep my date with John Lawrence, so just before the first of November, 19 and 57, I flew to New York City, then took a Belgian Airline plane that took me to Shannon, Ireland. We arrived there very early in the morning. There was a tea house there by the side of the airport. We had to wait a considerable time for the next plane to take us on to Brussels, Belgium. Good

scotch whiskey was $1.75 a fifth—and about all brands, but, my pockets were full. I had no place to put any so I ordered a double shot of Irish Whiskey and some tea, had that, and we took off for Brussels. At Brussels you could still see plenty of evidence of the war. Cigars were around six bits to $1.50 apiece, and a bottle of warm beer was 75 cents, so I didn't drink much of it. From Brussels we flew to Prague, Czechoslovakia.

The pilot told us we would have to have our passports and we would have to get off there at the tea house while they cleaned the plane and put on more food to go on to Athens, Greece. As we came down the gangplank, two Russians stood there with their red shoulder boards, hollered "passports" at us, and snatched them out of our hands. We went into the tea house and were there for a couple of hours. I was beginning to wonder when the hell we were going to get out of there. The pilot called the plane two or three times, but I could go nowhere without my passport. Finally an old German came over and asked if he could sit down at my table. I told him certainly. I ordered coffee for him and a warm beer for myself. He told me he'd been in the Kaiser's Army during World War I. I asked him how we were going to get our passports

203

Keith and Truman Fowler look over some of the tusks taken on an elephant-only hunt in Africa in 1967.

back. At that time there was a half dozen Russians sitting across the room from us with their backs to us. They had our passports as far as I knew. There was three American couples there also and they asked me what I was going to do. I told them I wasn't going to leave without my passport because I couldn't go anywhere. The old German told me. "Mr. Keith, I know a lady. I'll see what I can do. Don't mention my name or say anything to anybody about it." With that he went out the back door.

The captain of the plane came in again and asked me if I was going with him. I said, "Not without my passport. My big double rifle is laying under my seat in a case. Will you please lay it on the dock if you have to leave without me?" He agreed. Just then a huge woman came along and she said "Keek" and she went on out into the courtyard. I got to thinking maybe she meant "Keith." She said "Jah" and handed me my passport. The other three couples got their passports so we boarded the plane. However they held us there for another hour, motors running a good part of the time, for no reason under the sun only to show their authority, the captain said. A cou-

ple of squads of Greek soldiers had also boarded the plane. They were going back home.

We flew over Budapest, illegally, as my passport plainly stated not to travel in Hungary. From there on to Athens. As we came down the gangplank at Athens there was a dark-complexioned Greek and a red-headed lady asking all passengers if their name was Keith. When they came to me I told them I was. They said, "We've been ordered to take good care of you and will you come with us." I went into an office with them and the gentleman said he understood I was missing one piece of baggage. I told him I was. So I gave him all the dope to send it to White Hunters Limited of Nairobi and he agreed to do so when it showed up. The lady then took me in tow and went to a Greek restaurant. We had a very good dinner of curried chicken and rice. It was a long table, family style, and people sat facing each other across it, not too wide but with ample room. In front of each plate was a huge bottle of wine and a bowl with a couple of delicious apples in it.

At Athens a great many South African Dutch people were to board the plane on for South Africa. They were fine, big-boned, tall people, clean, neat, and very high-class people. A lady sat across from me. I noticed she was eyeing the apples. She ate the two she had and was eyeing mine. She said, "Mr. Keith, aren't you going to eat your apple?"

"No," I said. "They are falling off the tree at home. Take mine." She had only drank about a half of a bottle of her wine and I told her I could use the wine if she didn't want that, so we made a trade.

We landed at Khartoum, one of the hottest, dirtiest, stinkingest airports I believe I was ever in. Beer, warm, was 90¢ a bottle. On the trip I flew with a South African soldier, a very nice chap. We didn't bother with any of their warm beer, but had a cup of tea and finally took off for Nairobi. There was a thunderstorm on at the time and we flew around for some time before we landed on the runway. Mud was ankle deep on each side of it.

Colonel Caulfield met me and took me in tow and up to the New Stanley hotel where I had a room. Rooms there then were $4 per day. This also included a breakfast. There was a table covered with all kinds of breakfast food and various kinds of fruit for you to make a selection. Then you went to the table and ordered your toast and bacon or toast and eggs. I didn't see any hotcakes listed on the menu.

Caulfield told me that John Lawrence would be in off a hunt sometime the next day. Sure enough, he came in and I liked him from the start. He had enlisted in the King's African Rifles as a private and at the end of World War II had come out as captain of his company. They fought the Italians and later fought against the native uprising against some other settlers, and was headed by the man who is now head of the Kenya government. I met and got acquainted with several of the firm's white hunters—all fine chaps. I took along two rifles: a best-quality detachable lock single-trigger ejector .476 Westley Richards, and a .333 OKH Mauser made up by Iver Henrikson with an Ashurst barrel. I had both solid factory Kynoch loads for the big double, and also my own handloads, and some 200 of the .333 OKH.

White Hunters Limited were having a meeting at this time, and John went with them while I stayed around the office and prowled around the town. It was quite a city, even then. They asked John what he was going to do and he told them he was going to take his jeep and a trailer and four boys and give me a rough, tough trip but a good one and try and get me the big five. They informed John, "You're not going to do any such thing.

Keith's favorite African rifles included his .333 O.K.H. Mauser with 26-inch barrel, mounted by a K-4 Weaver scope, and the .476 best-quality Westley Richards with detachable locks and single trigger.

You're going to take the big truck, ten boys, and give Elmer 'the works' because he has done enough for us in recommending adequate rifles for Americans coming out here for many years now. It's time we gave him the full treatment." This they did.

I wanted elephant, buffalo, and I had my heart set on a sable. I didn't think much about getting lion or leopard. I thought they would be very hard to get, as well as the greater Kudu, but John said, "We're going to get them all, Elmer," and we did.

John drove his jeep while one of his boys, his "boss boy" he called him, drove the big truck with ten boys and all our safari equipment, and we headed for Arusha where we had to go through all the formalities of obtaining the licenses, registering my guns and ammunition, and finally made it out into the bush. John's two gun bearers, which he called trackers, were Galu-Galu and Goyo. Goyo had fought with John during the uprising. Galu-Galu would weigh about 80 pounds soaking wet, and his wife had just died in childbirth. I guess she was a very young girl from what John said. So John said the best thing for the little guy was to take him out on a hunt.

WAITING FOR "OLD SPOTS"...

Arusha lay not far from one snow-capped peak, whose name I forget, and Kilimanjaro was also plainly visible on clear days. We drove south and camped on the east side of Lake Manyarra. John said the first thing to do was get some baits up for leopard and lion. I shot a wildebeest and we hung him half in one place and half in another. The next morning we had leopard on both of them, and they'd pulled it down and ate one half of it, but no lion. I killed another wildebeest and we put him out for lion. We got no lion on the baits whatever, but a large leopard was working on the bait to the west of camp. We sneaked out there early in the morning to a little hideout we'd made higher on the slope and about 100 yards from the bait tree. No leopard was in evidence. The bait was in plain sight. We waited until the sun had come up and was getting quite hot, and John said, "Well, there's no leopard here today, though he was here yesterday, so we'll go up and see what he did to the bait." We only got about halfway when the leopard jumped out of a swale right at our feet. He ran by a long stretch of high grass of some kind about four feet high. I sat down and swung the crosshairs in front of him and was going to shoot, and John said, "Don't shoot, Elmer, unless he stops. You've got to kill these things dead." So I refrained from shooting, watching him run along the side of that grass for 200 yards, and finally turn into it.

John said, "Well, he fooled us. But we'll get him yet today. They can't count, so we'll go back to camp and have breakfast, and about three o'clock we'll take everybody but the cook, go down there and raise a good hubbub. While we're doing that we'll figure out another good hideout to one side of where the last one was because he'll come around and investigate that before he goes into the bait.

He came in all right, about a hundred yards away just at dark. It was too dark to shoot. I saw his head come around a tree three times, but he'd pull it back every time, so I motioned back. John didn't hesitate. We took off, went back to the jeep and on back to camp. I didn't want to take any chance on wounding the spotted devil.

The next day we went down, covered the bait with some toilet paper to keep the buzzards off, and waited until about three o'clock. The boys made a great hubbub, and we bedded down just on the south side of the bait but only 40 yards away in a thick clump of thorns. The boys cut out a hole through

which I could view the bait and shoot. We lay there in the hot sun, with the tsetses biting us all afternoon. We dared not move or make any noise. If we did, the leopard would see us and John said he's probably watching out there. But after we bedded down awhile, the rest of the boys were prowling all around and they got in the truck and drove off. John whispered in my ear, "The leopard can't count, and he won't know we're here." Soon along came an old yellow legged Francolin. I had my rifle poked out through the hole in the thorn. He wasn't a yard from the muzzle of the rifle. He looked at me and said "Arp, arp-arp, arp," and I looked him in the eye and never moved or batted an eyelid. If I had, the jig would have been up. Finally he walked on up the hill going "arp, arp-arp, arp," and John just squeezed my arm. Later after we went back to camp, he said, "That was a good job you did, Elmer. If you'd moved, he would have taken fright, squawked differently, and the leopard would have known we were there."

Just as dark was closing in, I finally saw the bait swing. By looking real close I could see his shoulders on the left side. His head was down in the hole he had eaten in the wildebeest's hindquarters. It was getting awful dusk and poor light, but I held back of that shoulder for a heart shot as close as I could and squeezed it off. Instantly the big bloom of flame blinded me. I said, "Take him on. I'm blind." The leopard came out of the tree with one of the nastiest growls I ever heard. Each time he hit the ground, he let out another squawl. In the tall grass he told us off there for several minutes. I got up, trying to accustom my vision after the flash of the big rifle. I told John, "I have now committed the cardinal sin. It's after dark and I've wounded a leopard."

He said, "Don't feel too bad, Elmer. That sounded like the last back-talk he'll give us. The boys will be up with the jeep in a few minutes."

When they came up there, we loaded both shotguns. I had Colonel Caulfield's double, and John had a Remington pump gun. We loaded them, pushed off the safeties, and as the steering wheel and gear shift is on the right side of cars over there, John drove with his left hand and held his shotgun poked out in front with the right. I held mine out the other side. John says, "If he comes, Elmer, don't try to raise your gun at all. Poke it like a spear and pull both triggers. You'll have time for nothing else and he'll hit you."

Elmer Keith's seven-foot leopard had to be photographed by using the headlights on the hunting car.

Three of the boys stayed in the back of the jeep behind us with a pangas. John said, "If he lands on us, they'll chop him off." We eased into the tall grass where we heard the last growl from the leopard. I had never heard such vicious growling in all my life. It sounded like shoving a buzz saw into an old mahogany knot. John would ease it along in four-wheel drive and in low gear, a few feet at a time and we'd watch. Finally I spotted the leopard stretched out broadside across in front of us. I told John, "I see him." I jumped out and hung the shotgun on him. John stopped the jeep and jumped out the other side. Then he asked little Galu-Galu to go up and pull his tail. There was no movement. My slug had gone in behind the left shoulder and out right where the knife cut went down over the right front leg to the center cut. The heart was blown clean out of him, and how that beast managed to go 50 yards and growl at us for that length of time without any heart, I'll never know. He was a beauty, seven feet long with a peg at his nose and one at his tail, not stretched or pulled in any way. He had a very white background with small spots, a beautiful leopard. John took some pictures of him with the lights of the car, using gas lanterns, and a time exposure.

The next day we hunted to the south seeing myriads of game, great bands of zebra, and wildebeest. I shot one oryx from the top of an ant hill at 400 yards, square in the lungs. He lit out on a hard run, wringing his tail. I made no attempt to shoot him again, thinking he would roll the same as an elk would, put my empty case in my pocket, sat there watching him go when I could have hit him two or three more times. Suddenly he turned into the bush and he was gone. We trailed that oryx for seven long miles. No blood, but the slug had hit him square in the right ribs. He finally joined up with another bunch of oryx. Then we saw eland and a myriad of game. They'd run by on one side or the other and raise the dust high in the air. Once I saw a great yellow head come up out of the grass about 400 yards away and told John about it, and he watched for some time. The game on each side where this head came up out of the grass broke and ran away from there, so I know I saw a lion there.

Taking fast game like the oryx requires a good shot. Keith took this one running at 200 yards with a 300-grain bullet in his .333 O.K.H..

One day we followed quite a herd of oryx, trying to get in range. They were off five or six hundred yards. Finally we got to within 400 to 450 yards of them and they stopped. One bull that looked good to John was standing with his rump to me and his head up, but between us was a smaller oryx. Beyond the oryx was a big anthill. I had an anthill to shoot over for a rest. Using the lower crosswire I figured on dropping into the back of his neck. However, just as I shot he swung his head to the right and the bullet plowed into the anthill beyond him. We followed him around for quite awhile. The great herd of wildebeest and zebra complicated matters. They would get between us and the oryx. We also saw a good bunch of eland. Finally, however, we had them separated and John and I jumped out of the car and moved to a bunch of trees. One of them had a nice crotch in it. The oryx started to barge across our front at 200 yards. John said to take the third one in the procession. They were running as fast as they could. I swung way ahead of them and held high enough for the vertebrae and shot. That hit the oryx just behind the shoulder but in line with the spinal column and she went

down in a cloud of dust, turning summersets. It proved to be a cow with 30½-inch horns, a nice head.

By this time we found out that my 300-grain steel jacket Kynoch soft-nose bullets from the .333 OKH were blowing up badly and not penetrating. I shot a little 40-pound "Tommy" quartering away at 80 yards in the left flank. The bullet never went through him, just blew to pieces. I actually had missed but the one shot when the oryx swung his head out of my sights just as I shot. John said the boys came to him and told him, "We have a good bwana this time. We're going to have a good trip. He can shoot."

The next morning when we went out to our little canvas-covered johnny there was a big lion track in the mud where he'd crossed within a foot of the little tent that covered it. Lion, however, were protected in this district.

John told me, "I'm going to break a precedent. We usually take a client out and let him shoot all the lesser game first before we go for elephant. However the boys and I are satisfied with your shooting. We're going to pull out in the morning and head for the Kisego River down in southern Tanganyika."

Africa is still a game-rich area, where kob can be seen frolicking with big tuskers along the upper Nile.

While walking up a reed buck we saw go into heavy grass, I fell down a deep ant bear hole. In the back of the hole there was a root stuck out and this caught me between the shoulders. It evidently displaced some of my vertebrae. The boys pulled me out of the hole, but my right shoulder and arm hurt like fury, and my right hand would go numb. John wanted to go back to Arusha and get a doctor, but I insisted that we go on because it would ball up the schedule of the trip and probably cut it short. We drove through Babeti and on to Singeta. There we went to a doctor who carried a big, full red beard. He looked like a grizzly bear. He was a very fine gentleman. He told me, "Keith, I'm not a chiropractor. You have a vertebra out, misplaced a bit between your shoulders. That's causing you the trouble. I can't do anything for you, and there's no chiropractor or osteopath around here. Every day, when it gets to hurting too much, lay down across the seat of the jeep and have a couple of the boys pull your feet, and have John pull your head and work it back and forth, turn your neck. Your neck will stand a whole lot and your head won't pull off, but it will relieve you."

This we did for the rest of the long trip. About every two hours I would have to be stretched again, to relieve the pain and get some life back in my right hand and arm. It was miserable, working on dangerous game part of the time, with a numbed right hand. I'd have to put my trigger finger in front of the guard, get on the game, then put my finger back in the trigger guard, get my aim again and squeeze my whole hand and fire the rifle. That went on for the rest of the trip.

We stayed all night in Singeta. The next morning our two little trackers were not in evidence. John said, "I know where we'll find them. We'll go to the police station." Sure enough, the police had them in the pokey. John bailed them out and we headed on for Mayoni. From Mayoni we went down on the Kisego River, if it could be called a river. It was just a deep riverbed of dry sand. We made camp in a beautiful little bend of this sand river, and below us was some open water with monkeys and guinea fowl in profusion. Above the open waterhole the elephants had dug great pits, ten to fifteen feet across, and four or five feet deep. Then with their trunks they had bored a hole down to clean water.

209

They weren't about to drink after guineas and monkeys. Their great droppings were all over the place. That night an elephant came in and laid down close to our tents. We didn't even hear him. The next morning there was his tracks and the print of his old hide where he'd laid there and slept for a time within 50 yards of our tents.

BIG TUSKERS . . .

The first day out at our elephant camp we walked down an elephant road, and found tracks of cows and calves in profusion. Finally we crossed the tracks of two great bulls heading off to the right. We trailed them for several hours, and finally found them kegged up in a noonday siesta underneath a big acacia. The wind was shifting. We started to work in from one side and it shifted again, so we beat a slow, careful retreat and came in from the other side.

Just then along came a giraffe, "twiga" the boys called him, with his long neck stuck out and his head up above the acacias. Everybody had to freeze still. We didn't dare move a muscle or hardly breathe. The old giraffe went over to the tree under which the two elephants were taking their siesta, plucked a few leaves off the top branches, and finally strolled on, unconcerned. Then we worked on into the wind to the left so that we could approach the elephant. They were turned head to tail. One bull, facing us, had both tusks broken about halfway off. They were big and heavy but were badly damaged. The other one had one great tusk resting against the bole of the tree. It looked very good, looked like it was five or five-and-a-half feet out of the lip and heavy. In order to get into position we had to cross in plain sight of them within 40 yards. Little Goyo went across first, taking several seconds for each step, moving just as slow as possible and still move. John followed and I emulated their tactics and the three of us got across the open space and behind a little bunch of thorn. We were 40 yards away. There was another bush about halfway to the elephants. I whispered to John that I could make that all right and take this old boy with the big tusk resting against the bole of the tree. John whispered, "We haven't seen the other tusk. Wait."

I remember we sat there for over half an hour. I remember the sweat was dripping off my elbow and making a little puddle in the sand. Finally the elephants decided to shift position. The big bull facing the tree backed up a bit so he could get his tusk around the tree and the other one came around and took

up this elephant's position. As the bull came around that had the great tusk on him, I was all set and ready to take him as he came around. But he only had one tusk. The trunk hung down limply on the left side and that great right tusk out front. John shook his head. We waited for 15 minutes until both of them went to sleep again. Their eyes were open, apparently, but they were dozing. We repeated our slow tactics of a step at a time back across the open space and into the bush and took off. After we got out of hearing I told John I thought I ought to shoot that old boy for his one tusk. I asked him what it would go. John said 90 to 100 pounds and he said, "Elmer, we want one with two tusks."

The boys headed for camp. How they knew which direction, I'll never know with the sun beating straight down and being hotter than the hinges of Hell. Finally we made camp, had a couple of gin tonics and then as evening approached we moved into the tent, dropped the mosquito netting in front of it and set down for a wonderful dinner our old cook had prepared. I had never seen such camp cooking in my life before. They served everything in a three-course dinner with all the trimmings, separate plates for each course, and silverware laid out like you were in a very fine hotel.

The next day we drove back up the truck trace for several miles and then started scouting. We cut the tracks of a big bull that went into the elephant road. But after we found his droppings and all the limbs and stuff he had digested and chewed up fine, John shook his head. He said, "He's a young bull." We cut back towards the truck trace where we'd left the jeep and in doing so cut the tracks of four elephant. One of them was a very big, heavy track. We followed them for six miles down into the jungle away from the truck trace. Finally they merged with a herd of cows and calves and we could hear them trumpeting all around. John said, "Elmer, you and Goyo stay here by this baobab. Galu and I and the native boy we picked up at the village will make a circle."

This day we had made a 20 mile circle and stopped at a village where John had picked up this native guide. Then we had hiked as hard as we could for two hours in the dim light just as daylight was coming until we hit the Kisego River. There we found where these four elephant had watered and climbed a steep bank. They took off across open country for four or five miles.

In all, we covered about 14 miles when they

finally crossed the truck trace. It was very hard tracking. The boys would lose it and I would find it. I would lose it and John would find a trace. We finally crossed the truck trace. There John sent Ungani, one of the boys, back to camp to bring the big truck back there where we left the jeep and bring water. We'd followed this herd of four for a good six miles when they merged with the cows. Goyo and I tried to find some shade under that baobab. The sun was beating straight down, there was very little shade, and a lot of tsetse flies to keep us occupied. Finally the native that John had picked up at the village came back. He asked me, "Piga tembo, bwana?" I knew then they had found elephant. He led the way and Goyo and I followed. In about half-a-mile we came to John and Galu-Galu sitting under the shade of a bush, and four great elephant were off to their left about 60 yards. I asked John what he would go, and he said he looked 70 or 80 pounds and he said Galu-Galu had gone in and he had two tusks this time.

We moved up to about 40 yards and John motioned for me to take a rest, but I knew I didn't need it. The big bull was quartering away facing into the wind. There were two other bulls his size, but with very small ivory, with their heads turned toward the back track watching. There was a small bull in between the two and the big bull. The left front leg, off side, lined up with about where the heart had to be, so I took him offhand. I raised the sights up until I touched his chest, and then raised them two feet higher where I knew the heart ought to be, and squeezed the trigger.

At the blast of the .476, all hell broke loose. Trees came down, and a big log sailed up in the air. The other three elephants swapped ends, and the old boy took off following his trunk in the direction he was headed. I pulled the gun down out of recoil, swung with him a little farther back and gave him the other one in the heart also. John shot in the air and all the boys yelled to keep them moving. I had asked John if I should brain him at the start, and John said, "No, if you do, we'll have the other three on our necks and have to shoot them." So I'd given him the heart shots as directed. John and two of the boys, Galu-Galu and the native guide, took off at a run after the elephant, yelling. I ejected my empties, and shoved in two more loads. I closed the breech and started to run, but Goyo caught me by the shoulder and motioned for me to just walk.

Soon we heard a great crash ahead of us.

The bull had gone about 150 yards and was piled up in very thick thorns, still alive, still breathing. John and the boys were trying to cut in towards the back of his head. I circled and finally I came around by his back. John had motioned to me before that to come in where he was. I did, and he said, "Give him a couple between the shoulders, Elmer I've never seen one get up after he's hit there." I did as directed.

Then I made the circle around him to come in and finally I was in front of his chest. John and boys were back to one side and John said, "Give him two more there for the heart," which I did. Still he was alive. When I started to circle, he raised his head, saw me and threw his great trunk out at me. John yelled at me to stay out of reach and come on around from the other side. I did. The boys continued to chop with their pangas until they cut through to the back of his head. John took the .416 then and shot. No reaction. Finally he shoved the gun at the back of the elephant's head and he says, "Halfway between the eye and the ear, and halfway down." That time the left hind leg stiffened and came up in the air and we knew we had him finished.

Eighteen inches of his left tusk had been broken off years ago. John was sick when he saw it. He said, "Elmer, we'll sell this ivory and I'll get you another elephant."

There were only a few hairs on his tail and John said he thought the tusks would have only six inches to a foot of nerve and they'd go about 60 and 80 pounds. We finally made the trip back out to the truck. On the way, however, we were passing through a little open spot with some old rhino wallows that had long dried up. Buffalo tracks in them also dried hard as concrete. Suddenly an elephant trumpeted to our left and came towards us, with trees coming down. The boys all came back by me, John included. I was so tired, both feet were blistered from the long trek, but I snicked the safety on my rifle, put two more shells between the fingers of my left hand and I was standing there, going to wait for the charge when he came out. I was too tired to run or do anything. I had about 20 yards of open space that he would have to break through.

Just then John came back, grabbed me by the shoulder and pulled me his way. We'd only run about ten yards and he pinched my arm to stop. We did. The bull stopped, and everything was perfectly quiet. Finally after about ten minutes there was a little rodent of

Keith's first elephant had 18 inches of his left tusk broken off, but the close shooting with the .476 Westley Richards made him an elephant worth remembering.

some kind, I had a glimpse or two of him, he wasn't over a foot long. He went in over the dry leaves where the elephant was. We could hear him going pitter-patter all over the place, and he came back out and across the trail. Still no sound whatever from the elephant. Then John told Galu-Galu to go in. All he had on was tennis shoes and a pair of pink slacks, more of a lavender color really than pink, that somebody had given him. He shucked all of them and he went in naked. After about ten minutes, he came back out and motioned us to come on. He told John that "somebody's wounded an elephant."

How that great beast could go across all those dry leaves and thorn without making a sound, or without making a single tree top shake is beyond me, yet we could hear the little rodent all through the place.

The local native then told John a white man had killed a hundred-pounder and wounded another one about a week before. So this must have been his wounded elephant. By the time we got back to the truck trace, I was all in. The boys on the truck saw me and they come a-running, put a shoulder under each arm, practically carried me to the truck and

handed me the big long water sack. I believe I absorbed half a gallon before I turned it back to them. That morning John had said we were going around to the Kisego River, and I had worn tennis shoes thinking we would be doing a lot of wading. It was a grave mistake in that terrific heat. I had blistered the balls of both feet and three toes on the right foot. So John said, "The boys and I will go back in the morning and cut out the ivory and get the front feet for you. You stay in camp and rest." I told him I was going along with them if I had to crawl. He opened all the big blisters on my feet. We had a good feed, a couple of gin tonics and a good night's sleep.

The next morning we went back and cut out the ivory. It was quite a sight. Then John sent the big truck around to get the jeep and bring it back. The night before the truck had made the trip to the native camp. It came back festooned with natives, all it would hold and all that could hang on. The jeep was also festooned with villagers. They were all hungry for elephant meat. The next day the rest of the band of natives had trekked across the flat, the whole 20 miles, and followed us down to the elephant.

After the ivory was out, John told them they could have the elephant. All we took were the ivory and the front feet. The feet were filled with triangular shaped bones from the first joint up from the foot down. It was a terrific job to dig each one of them out all set in cartilage. At the bottom was a great cushion of a fibrous material, gristle in character, some two inches thick. That's the pad on the bottom of the feet. Finally we had it all out, however, and headed back to the truck trace. The nerves proved very long and John shook his head and he said, "This elephant won't weigh very heavy." We had covered about half of the six miles and stopped to rest. Some of the Negro women came along with loads of elephant meat on their heads and they were in bad shape for lack of water. John had sent two boys back to the truck and they came with the big canvas water sacks on a pole between them. The native women cupped their hands and John poured a handful of water for each of them. After that they picked up their loads and started down the trail.

We finally made it out to camp with the tusks and front feet and enjoyed another good dinner. The longest tusk was seven feet on the curve and the shorter one had about 18 inches of the same length broken off, lost years before. Between the number that the boys hauled on the truck and the jeep, which were both loaded coming back from the village, and the rest of them that trekked across country 20 miles to the elephant, I believe most of that band of natives were at the elephant. When John turned the elephant over to them, he stuck a spear in his side because he had been killed the day before and was gassed up. There was a geyser of water and gas for a time. When that subsided, they started cutting him. Each native had a curious knife. The blade was only four or five inches long, maybe less in some cases, and it was attached to a stick of hardwood of some kind, a long, slim stick not much bigger than my thumb. It would hook right in the skin and cut down from the top of the back to the bottom, move over 18 inches, and do it again. Then one would grasp this section of hide while another would cut behind it. That way they peeled the hide off the elephant in strips. Soon they were cutting out chunks of him and throwing it over to the other natives, who carried it to the women who kept out of sight and back in the brush. They built fires all around the elephant, and as soon as the trunk was off they started cutting it up and putting strips of elephant trunk in the fire to fry and cook. As

soon as it was halfway cooked, they started eating it. They put strips in their mouths and held on while they cut it in front of their noses with these curious knives. Before starting the cutting up operation one native had a small pipe. He was a small boy. I believe it was some kind of ritual. It was a gourd and the stem went around in a circle. Just where the tobacco was I never learned, but he would smoke that. Then they all started to work. One native started to cut into the elephant before the ivory was out. John had warned him not to. John made a run and jump, landed on the carcass and kicked him clear over in the thorn bush. That seemed to satisfy his urge to get to cutting up the meat before the other work was done. Galu-Galu supervised the cutting out of the ivory and he was an artist at it. After the tusks were out, of course, they had to chip the bone shell away from the ivory which is a tedious business, especially with the curious axes they had.

When the body cavity was opened, the intestines rolled out. Two or three of them crawled inside after fat around the elephant's kidneys. It was a bloody orgy from the start to finish. As much as three days later we still saw some of the Negro women packing my old elephant in baskets on their head. They'd carry about 40 pounds to the load. John said they would clean up every morsel of that meat and that that would keep this village of natives in meat for the next six months, as they flayed it, put it on the thorn bushes to dry, then they'd pack it home. They simply camped there for three days and nights until they'd cleaned up the entire carcass.

SABLE COUNTRY...

From our camp on the Kisego I saw a sable track one day. It was a different track than I'd ever seen and I asked Goyo what it was and he told me in Swahili—gave me the name that they called kudu. We moved from there deeper in the bush. In fact we went as far as anyone had ever been in some of that bush as far as motor transportation was concerned. There'd been some woodcutters in there and we found traces of them. It was very thick bush in this place and with a lot of game. There was one waterhole there and sure enough a poacher's hideout was under the roots of a huge tree right at the edge of the water. The pool was probably 60-70 yards across, it looked just like thick cement. There was buffalo, elephant, rhino and practically all species of game watering there, and they'd stirred it up into a thick soup. How the boys

This old, well-broomed sable fell to a single neck shot from Keith's .333 O.K.H. at 195 yards.

ever produced drinking water out of it is beyond me, but we had a big still for it. They would strain this soup until they'd get moisture, then they'd put that in the still and distill it until finally we had water for cooking and drinking.

This was John's sable cover. The first day out I saw buzzards circling off to our left. I pointed them out to John, so we moved over there. From the tracks, two great lion had killed a small rhino and eaten a good part of him. We cut out the hide with the horns on it to turn into the game department. That afternoon we made a hide in some thorn bush within nice range of what was left of the rhino carcass and waited until dark. Tsetse flies were terrible. They were so thick that when we were traveling, the boys wore their rubber rain coats. There would be a patch of them the size of my hand between their shoulders where they couldn't get at them with the switches they were flopping around continually to try to keep them off.

Little Goyo had a winning way with them. He'd take a long thorn, catch them, stick it through them and then shove the thorn into a tree until he caught another one. This way he

had several strings of them on thorns.

The lion never did come back.

The next day we looked all over the place hunting a suitable hide to hang a wart hog carcass that I'd killed after we left the elephant camp, for lion bait. Again the tsetse flies were terrible. Their bite feels like a red-hot needle shoved into you. While searching for a good tree with a suitable hideout within 100 yards for the lion bait, I happened to look up on a ridge to our left and there stood a big sable. I motioned to John and pointed. He took one look through the glasses. He said, "Put him down quick, Elmer. He's a bloody good sable."

Resting my left shoulder against a tree, I took it offhand and when the crosshairs settled on his neck, I let him have it. Down he went in a pile. Instantly the gun bearers and John were on the run. They rushed up to the sable, one grabbed his horns and pulled them around one small tree. Another one grabbed his hind feet and bent them around another, while a third boy shoved a knife in his chest to the heart. I had my sable. He was a very old sable with only a 38½-inch length of horn, but at least six inches had been broomed away. He had rubbed them on rocks and in sand banks to keep them sharp. There was only 2½-inches of straight horn beyond the annual rings. He was so old he was turning grey.

We dressed him out loaded him in the jeep after the boys drove it over as close as they could and hauled him to camp where we hung him to a tree and took some pictures. Then the skinner set to work taking off my head and cape. The boys cut up all the meat, fileted it, and put it on bushes to dry. I asked John if we were going to have some of it to eat. He took me over and he showed me the meat. There was some great white worms, nearly as big as a lead pencil through the meat and you could see where the boys had cut them in two in several places. Just how long the worms were I have no idea, but I saw plenty of sections. John shook his head and he said, "We don't eat any of that."

The next morning at daylight we again run the lion bait, but no lion was on it. However, just beyond I saw another bull sable. He turned and watched us and I tried to get pictures of him, but it was too far for a camera without a telephoto lens. The sable turned to run, then he made a buck jump and flashed to one side as hard as he could go. I caught a glimpse of a long yellow object close to the ground sneaking off to the left. I figured it must be the lion. We went over and sure enough there were their tracks. We trailed them for several miles over a hill and into a donga until a herd of buffalo came along and obliterated their tracks. There we lost track of the two rhino killers and had to return to the jeep and to our camp.

One day I spotted an elephant standing broadside, a small cow. She had been shot in the left side of the head and evidently in the left hip, because she was very lame we found out later. I got in fairly close and got a good picture of her, then she sensed me when she heard the click of the camera and she whirled and screamed and came for us. I beat it back to the jeep. Goyo got out, and she chased him around as he teased her in the heavy bush. The little man could get away from her as she was so gimpy in that left hind leg she couldn't go fast. The next day, however, we saw the same cow five miles from there. This time I got my camera ready and she screamed and came for us. John revved up the motor, put the clutch in, and waited. I got on the running board, and got a good picture of her charging while one of the boys held onto my belt. Then he jerked me into the car, we took off, and she came plowing along where the

jeep had been, but I got my picture. Poachers had evidently shot her in the left side of the head, as pus streamed down that side of her cheek, and also evidently in the left hind leg or hip because she was very lame. Why they would want to kill such a little cow elephant I don't know, as she couldn't have carried more than ten pounds of ivory to a side.

John said those lion were a pair of old buffalo killers and probably wouldn't come to the bait at all, and they didn't. The next day we packed up camp to pull out. That morning when I got out I saw where a rhino had gone right through camp leaving his big tracks between the tents. As we were leaving the hills and past where the woodcutters had made camp, we saw another sable with a herd of cows that the old boy had. He was a beauty. John estimated him at 42 inches. However, I'd shot out my sable license so I had to wish him luck. He stayed at about 60 yards.

From there we went back through Mayoni to a place where John knew there were some greater kudu and put up our kudu camp about a quarter of a mile from a native village. On the way a rhino crossed the road ahead of us a considerable distance. John and I trailed him up and came up with him and he turned facing us at about 40 yards. One look at him though and John shook his head and we slipped away and left him. Farther on we caught a glimpse of a good wart hog crossing the trail. We left the jeep and walked up through the open bush to try and intercept him. He ran across to the right and one of our natives spotted him, and pointed him out to me between two trees. I took it offhand at 150 yards, killing him instantly with a .333 OKH. He proved a very nice wart hog with excellent tusks. I had them remove the head, clean it and cook it, strip it of all meat, and kept the skull with the ivory in it as a trophy. It was so ugly I didn't want to mount that head. The carcass of the wart hog we roped on the back of the big truck for lion bait at our next camp.

The kudu camp was in heavily bushed rolling hills with some little grassy valleys in between, and at one time the Germans had had farms all over the place, but they were now growing back to the bush. There was a big native village only a quarter of a mile from our camp. At that time they had on a big dance and beer bust, and for three days and three nights they never stopped singing and dancing, as near as we could determine. Our first day's kudu hunt we saw a small bull and some cows in an old meadow, but nothing

This fine wart hog sports tusks 11 inches long with a 14-inch spread, and was shot for lion bait.

worth hunting for. The next day we went back over a heavily bushed hill for some distance. We came to the edge of another old shamba, as these old farms were called. It was pretty well grown up. John and Galu-Galu had the glasses and were on a perch to my right looking out over this old shamba where it had been farmed. I was carrying the .476 and little Goyo had the .333 OKH. Goyo moved in front of me and looked down the steep hill in front of us. Instantly he whirled around, his eyes shining. He came back, grabbed the .476 and passed me the .333 OKH and motioned me forward. I moved out to where I could look down the hill, and there 90 yards away stood a great kudu bull facing quartering towards us, his head slightly to the right, and he was eating leaves out of the trees. I aimed at the junction of his neck and shoulder. Just then John Lawrence had turned around, put the glasses on him and he said, "Hurry, he's going to leave." As I squeezed off the shot, I says, "He's too late." Sure enough down he went in a heap.

I threw in another shell to give him another if necessary as I didn't trust those blow-up 300-grain bullets. However, when I looked over the rifle all I could see was the seat of

John's well washed shorts bounding over the bushes down the hill towards the kudu, accompanied by all our trackers. Just as he arrived at the kudu, the big bull jumped up. John just shot him in the rear end and out the chest with a .416. Down he went again. Then John went around to one side and put another one through his shoulders. It was getting late and soon would be dark and he wanted to leave no chance of that great kudu getting away. I reloaded the .333 OKH, put the safety on, and started down the hill. John turned around and I asked him, "What kind of head has he got?" He held both hands above his head, his fists gripped together and he yelled, "He's a bloody beauty, Elmer."

We skinned out the head and cape up to the head, and unjointed the skull. John took this load and the boys took all the rest of the meat that they could possibly wiggle with and we started for home. We had to go over this big timbered hill covered with thorn and acacia and rhino tracks criss-crossing it here and there. John said, "Elmer, you've got to be the insurance on the way back."

One of the boys hung my .333 OKH around his neck in addition to his load of meat, and I took the .476 as well as John's

A single shot at 92 yards finished this 54-inch greater kudu, with Keith using the .333 O.K.H. offhand.

.416. One of the boys took it in addition to a load then, and left me in the lead with the .476 in case a rhino jumped us. However, we made it across and to the jeep by dark, and were soon in camp. There the old skinner took the cape off and salted it that night, so there was no chance of it spoiling. The next morning John measured it and claimed it was 54 inches on each side. Both horns were perfectly symetrical. Nothing out of the ordinary at all. It was a beauty. John decided to break camp the next day, go through Mayoni, back to Singeta and on over to Makalama Mission. We packed up everything and he told the boss boy explicitly to stop the big truck in Mayoni, as we had to check out my kudu and wart hog and my big elephant there and have the elephant ivory stamped, while we went on to a friend of his who had taken over an old German pig ranch.

We visited him and saw some wonderful paintings of lion that his son was turning out in oil, ate lunch with him, and then drove on to Mayoni. After leaving the old pig farm we saw half-a-dozen great kudu bulls out in an open meadow. One of them had only one horn. Several of them were as good as the one I killed, or better. They were simply beauties.

John said, "I'll know where to bring my next party for kudu."

Arriving at Mayoni, there was no trace of the big truck or all of our boys. We only had the two little trackers with us. John was stumped. We toured the town and finally found out they had gone on through. So we jumped in the jeep and John drove like a mad man, he's a race driver anyway. He could surely put that jeep over the road and somehow or other keep it on two wheels on the curves and stay in. We chased them for over a hundred miles and finally caught up with them. There he gave them a thorough dressing down, called them "bloody bawboons" and that's about the worst thing you can call a native in Swahili. So back we went to Mayoni, there to have my ivory checked and report the kudu before we could turn around and head back for Singeta.

We stayed all night at Singeta at a little hotel and pub there. The next morning as usual Galu-Galu and Goyo were missing. The rest of the boys we assembled all right. John said, "I know where we'll find them, Elmer. Let's go to the police station." Sure enough, they were in hock again.

John bailed them out and we took off for

217

Makalama Mission. On the way we passed an old German fort built out on a sort of peninsula, you might call it, in a gulch. It was surrounded by high walls all around and really a fort. It was just this narrow neck of land leading out to the higher land in the middle of the gulch upon which the fort was built. John told me that during the German occupation, the Germans had had trouble with the natives there. So they called in the chiefs of all the different tribes around there, got them inside the gate, shut the gates and machine-gunned them all. That was the German's way of avoiding further trouble with the natives.

THE MAKALAMA LION...

At Makalama Mission the next evening, we learned that the old priest who had been there had been bitten by a bad tsetse, contracted sleeping sickness and had been taken out. They saved his life, however, and two young priests had taken over the mission for him. They were nice friendly chaps, invited us in, gave us a drink of good brandy, and wished us well.

At Makalama Mission the first day, we went out and killed zebra, cut them up and hung them for lion bait. The next morning we were at the hideout at daylight but found nothing. We finally found that something had pulled our bait down and taken it. We saw lion tracks, but whether the lion had gotten it or some of the natives had stolen it, we didn't know for sure.

Next we drove over towards the Great Lake. I wanted to get a hippo if I could, but the natives there told us that the hippos were over on the other side of the lake, probably 20 miles around and we didn't figure we had time to go around there and get boats and try and get a hippo. We saw a good eland bull there, but he was quite wild. While we were trying to intercept him a little native jumped out of some brush and went screaming as loud as he could yell and headed for home, I guess. At any rate he certainly was afraid of us, and his carrying on spooked the eland bull and he took off. The natives informed us there was a pride of lion there, as well as a big red-maned lion that a white man had been trying to get for two years. We cut his tracks after a rain, so we left the jeep and followed them on foot. Finally we came to where we knew we were getting close from the tracks. We jumped him all right. John was off to the left, I to the right, and the boys trailing in between us so we could protect them. I just saw the brush move and heard him give a low, heavy growl,

but John saw him, said he was a full-maned lion with a red mane. So it must have been the one the other hunter had been after for a couple of years. John said we'd get him all right so we took off and hunted up a kongoni, which I shot. We loaded it in the jeep and hauled it back within a reasonable distance of where the lion had been. We tied it onto the jeep with a rope and made a circle. We found where the lion had gone into about three acres of very dense, thick thornbush, inpenetrable for a human. We made a circle around it and dropped the lion bait. Then as the boys went on with the jeep we dropped out behind some heavy bush about a hundred yards from the bait. John said, "Now as soon as the vultures come, the lion will come out to chase the vultures away and you'll have your lion."

It didn't work out that way.

There had been so much poaching in the country by the Arabs and natives, they'd no doubt poisoned all the vultures, because never a vulture showed up in the sky that afternoon. We sat there until dark when the boys came back with the jeep and picked us up. We took the kongoni carcass in several miles and tied it up in a tree at a good suitable place for a lion in a little gulley. We could work up within a hundred yards and it would give me a good shot if the lion was on it. The next morning we ran the other bait where we'd lost part of our bait, and the wart hog was gone. We put up another piece of zebra. We came back, and ran this bait only to find a leopard had been on it. He'd eaten quite a lot of the neck where we'd taken off the head and cape. So we pulled the bait down and carried it about a half a mile in the jeep and hung it up in a tree in the middle of a long opening down through heavy bush that extended for a quarter of a mile and was about 30 yards wide. The Germans had some day cut a road through there and it had grown back up.

This bait was about 12 miles from Makalama Mission. In the afternoon we went around to the native village. They had been losing cattle to a pride of lion right along. John suggested that they give us some of their old black robes that they used for capes and clothing and we'd drape in them and he and I would guard their cattle, herd them one day in hopes the lion would kill another cow so we could take him. The old chief wouldn't allow us to do it. I remember he got out a huge gourd full of milk, passed it around. John signaled to me not to touch it, which I didn't.

The next morning at daylight, we left the car about a mile from our lion bait and went

It was a long shot, a full 400 yards, but the .333 O.K.H. proved effective in dropping this Kongoni for lion bait.

in only to find that the natives had stolen our bait. Then we headed back towards the lake in the jeep and I shot a good roan. I was using solids on him as I didn't have much faith in those soft-points. It took several to put him down. Finally I hit him in the rump with one and it came out his lower jaw. That finished him. We hung the roan up for bait.

The next morning we were back again, left the car a mile from there and worked in. Lion had been on it all right, the bait was pretty well eaten up, and there were tracks all around. So John suggested we go get another zebra, and put up some more bait. We drove back to the mission and off on the other side I killed a big mare zebra. We hauled her back and hung her up. Then the boys opened her up. She was in foal. That little zebra was one of the prettiest hides I ever saw and I wanted to get the skin. But John said, "No, that's the best lion bait of all. Leave it."

We drove over across some open flat plains simply covered with little Tommies towards the east scarp of the Serengeti Plains to the native village there of Daturo. They were fine clean-looking natives, the best I saw on the whole trip. They reported that a lion had

been in their corral the night before and they'd killed him with spears. His hide was draped over the thorn bushes and there wasn't six inches that didn't have a spear hole in it. Also the Masai had raided their camp for cattle and women a few days before and they had killed one of the Masai, and the Masai had killed one of their men with an arrow. It was still Africa.

CHARGED BY A RHINO . . .

We trailed up one rhino only to find that it was a cow with a little toto and we let her go. Another time we went down a long arroyo, or donga, trailing a rhino and finally we ran onto her at about 20 yards. It was a cow with tremendous horn, looked to me like 25 or 30 inches. John motioned for me to shoot. However, just as I raised the rifle, the rhino wasn't over 10 yards away, something caught my eye to the left. Looking that way there was a little toto about two feet high. I motioned and pointed to John. As soon as he saw the little toto he shook his head and motioned back. We sneaked back and left her undisturbed with her baby. We finally cut the track of a fairly good-sized bull, so we took it. After trailing it for five miles around some low scrub-covered mountains, I caught a glimpse of his hind legs running across in front of us and motioned to John. We fanned out, John following after him and I cutting off to the right to intercept him. I got into some very heavy bush with some waitabit thorn. Just as I got tangled up in some waitabit thorn until I could hardly move, there was a rhino 20 yards away facing me. I raised the rifle to shoot him in the chest. His horn didn't look very long but it was too close to take chances. However, when I raised the rifle and aimed at his chest to look him over, he dumped his head and charged. My slug caught him in the end of the nose just below the horn. It stood him on his nose and he crow-hopped towards me with his nose rooting the ground, finally stopping. I waited for him to come up, and thought I'd break one shoulder and turn him as the horn was in the way for the brain. He came up all right. I aimed for the left shoulder, but just as I shot he fell on his nose again from the effects of the first 520-grain slug in his nose. That put him down again.

My gun was empty and I yelled for John to take him on as I opened the gun to reload it, hampered by the waitabit thorns hooked around my arms. John shot from the side, hit him at the back of the right shoulder and later found that his .416 solid went clear

Solids weighing 520 grains from Keith's .476 Westley Richards ended the career of this rhino.

through to the skin on the left hip. The rhino jumped about six feet in the air but, thank God, he swapped ends and headed back out of the brush towards the open. By that time I got reloaded and I tore my way through to the right. As he came barging across the front John shot again nicking the top of his withers, and I swung under his chin with the .476, and broke his shoulder and his spine. He rolled end over end. As we went up John said, "Pour the other one down between his ears, Elmer." He'd fallen with his back towards me.

He proved a young bull with only a fairly short horn. However, I had to take him as it was him or me. As the skin is quite valuable, they split it down the back and took it off in two slabs. John would later trade it off for something back at Nairobi. We took the skin off the nose with both horns on it, and both hams and the shoulders. The boys wanted all the meat they could get. The jeep was pretty heavily loaded as we headed back for Makalama Mission.

An old Darky, a hermit, lived alone beside a dry wash. He had a little garden and some little figure four traps, little cages he'd made up out of small limbs to trap small birds, with corn underneath. He eked out his living trap-

ping small game birds like guinea and yellow legs, and also from his garden. John yelled across the wash to him and he came over. We told him to help himself to some meat. He took a whole shoulder of rhino, balanced it on his head and he was all smiles as he left. John said that would hold the old guy a couple of months. He'll dry all the meat and mix it with his beans, squash, corn and he'll live high. His lean-to was open on two sides and thatched on two sides and he had a bed in one back corner and a little fire out in front. Why the lions didn't eat him I'll never know. Guess they didn't want him.

We hung up the rhino hams for more lion bait. The next morning we were out again before daylight, and left the car a mile from our hideout.

The tree was about 100 yards from where we'd fixed our hide at the end of the road which was heavily timbered, some of it quite big timber. We found the lions had pulled down the rhino hams, and had taken them off in the brush. We could hear them there, about forty yards away.

We sneaked out, and came back the next morning. This time the situation had improved. They had eaten on the zebra and the place was full of lion. Right in front of the hideout was a young maned lion laying on his back, all four feet in the air, snoring. Past him on the left was a sow lion and three little spotted cubs. Another female lay there beside her. Up at the tree another big female that was either full of rhino meat or the baby zebra, was making a half-hearted effort to pull the zebra down. The tree was 90 yards from our hideout. Ten yards beyond it lay a great lion on his side with his belly toward us. It was still too dark to shoot. I looked over the .476 and couldn't make out the sights. Daylight was fast approaching. Soon flocks of little green parrots went fluttering by and then daylight broke.

As soon as I could see the bead down in the bottom of the V of my sights on my .476 I lined them up on the grass right over this young lion sleeping right in front of me, as I figured the big fellow past the tree was what we were looking for. It had just got light enough that I could see the center line in the back sight and lined up my sights perfect when he rolled over towards us and raised his great head up. I aimed just back of the knuckle on his shoulder and squeezed the trigger. With the bloom of cordite flame, he jumped up, gave a couple of burping low growls, and turned to the left and into the thorn bush.

The sow with three cubs went to the right into the thorn. The other two sows went into the thorn to the left. The young punk laying there on his back sleeping, kept right on snoring, even though John took a snap shot at the big lion as he went into the brush. However, he was handicapped. When he started to shoot the sow got in the way as he raised his rifle, then he took a snap shot just as he disappeared, but missed. We moved out from the tree we were hiding behind and went forward about ten yards. I was watching the right and John the left. Then I saw the old sow lying there under the bush. I didn't see the cubs, but the lioness was lying there watching with her tail a-popping. I asked John to hold it while I hung the .476 on her. He said, "What do you see?" I said, "This lioness is laying here flat on the ground with her tail a-popping back and forth." He said, "Give her both barrels, Elmer, if she comes."

Just then she disappeared. I don't know yet how that lioness got out of sight. Of course it was very dark underneath the bushes, and I saw her plainly over my sights, and then she wasn't there. I told John then, I said, "We'd better hold it right where we are until the

boys come up. They'll have heard the shots." Soon they came up with the jeep.

John said, "Get on the left side of the jeep away from where that sow and cubs are as she could be dangerous."

The boys drove slowly and we managed to go down to the bait tree. I walked on past it to where the big lion had laid. There was no splash of the bullet in the sand and grass in front of where he laid and none behind. So I knew he'd took it. John said, "You hit him good, Elmer. I not only heard it but I saw him shake from the impact."

We started looking to the left, fanning out along this very dense thorn. Finally John said, "I'll go up to where he went in." Just then I worked around below the boys and I spotted the lion, so I told him to hold it, that I could see him. I hung the .476 on him again and John came down and looked and says, "It's lion all right, but we don't know which one. I'll go up where he went in." He did, parting the bushes and thorn with his .416 until finally he came to where he could see him. He says, "You can relax, Elmer. It's your old tomcat, and he's deader than hell."

The boys got a big thick rope from the jeep, and tied it on him but they were unable to move him. He was a very big lion. Finally they tied the rope to the jeep, put it in low gear, and we dragged him out of the thorn. We worked for over half an hour, the six of us, getting that lion aboard the back of the jeep. He seemed to be the heaviest, hardest animal we'd tried to load. We'd loaded 600-pound zebra without too much difficulty, but that stinking old lion was certainly a job. We got a rope around one shoulder and his neck, with two boys up in the jeep a-pulling, while the rest of us lifted. We finally got him loaded and headed back for the mission. However, the natives drum telegraph preceded us. When we arrived at the mission there were over 100 natives assembled to see the lion.

My 520-grain soft nose had hit nothing but ribs just back of the right shoulder. It took the whole heart off and left it loose in his chest and pooched out the skin on the left side behind the left shoulder—perfectly expanded. John said if the lion hadn't hit thorns so thick he couldn't get through, he would have gone 200 yards even with his heart loose in his chest. He said if he'd known where we were and headed our way, he would have been able to make it to us and do damage, unless we put him down with another shot. Such is the tenacity for life of these great cats. I asked John what he would weigh. He said about

Goyo (left) and Galu-Galu admire Keith's fine lion, killed with a single heart shot at 100 yards.

The leopard swung his head, gave me that coughing growl and went into the thorn just about where the old lion went in a few days later after I'd plugged him. John said he happened to look up as he passed the tree and he said the big cat was all set to jump on me, but just as he launched himself he saw John come out from behind the tree, too, and he arched his back and sailed over my hat. I was mighty glad he did. John said if either of us had been alone, that leopard would have killed us. It was much too close for comfort, and I'm mighty glad John Lawrence was so close to me and the leopard spotted him even as he leaped.

In addition to the killing of big game, we also had some good bird shooting, sand grouse, Francolin and guinea fowl. They were excellent eating. Also some lesser bustards. When we were at the elephant camp I told John to tell the boys that when I got an elephant and got the ivory to camp, we'd take a day off and hunt birds for them to eat. They were very happy about this, so after we had the elephant in camp we drove quite a ways that day just hunting birds. We must have killed about 30, all told. As soon as we were back in camp the boys started picking chickens and cooking them. John said they would be no good tomorrow and they surely weren't. They sat up all night cooking and eating birds. Our cook prepared some of the lesser bustard, the sand grouse, yellow legs, and guineas for us. We had some wonderful feeds for a couple of days. But the boys ate themselves so full all they wanted to do the next day was sleep. John would have to keep waking them up and making one of them stand up and stick his head out through the hole in the roof and look for game.

Another day we went to a small lake. Again there was a poachers hideout up in the top of a big tree. There was quite a flock of Egyptian geese there, and they started circling. I killed six that day with the Colonel's shotgun and the German ammunition I bought at Nairobi. One goose I hit hard with one barrel after the other and we could see it going for nearly a quarter of a mile. Two of the boys took after it, however, and in about half an hour back they came with the goose. They were better than bird dogs.

One comical incident happened. I had downed a guinea with a broken wing at long range. I'd killed one with the first barrel and winged the second one. Little Goyo took after it. He ran that guinea all over a half acre. He finally came to a deep small donga, or wash,

550 to 600, he thought. He said I could kill another hundred lions and never get a bigger one. His mane was only about two or three inches long, badly rubbed off. Not a heavily maned lion at all, but an enormous old brute. His head, back, and neck was covered with scars from fights he'd had. He was quite an old animal. This was the 16th morning we had run lion bait before I finally got a shot.

I had a very close call at this same place on one of the earlier morning hunts for this lion. We came to the hideout tree, saw no sign of any lion, nor did we hear any, and we moved up to the bait tree, 90 yards from where we'd hidden. I walked just past the bole of the tree looking at the ground for tracks. John followed close behind me. A big leopard, probably the same one that had eaten on the kongoni the first night, was up in the tree hidden by the leaves. I didn't know he was there, had no inkling of it. The first thing I knew he jumped out over me and his tail hit my right shoulder. He landed about 15 feet from me. He was a good foot longer than the fine leopard I'd killed. I swung the .476 on him to shoot. John yelled, "Don't shoot, for Christ's sake don't shoot." So I put the safety on.

A large crowd was waiting in camp to see Keith's large black-maned old lion, taken with a single shot.

and the guinea flew across. While Goyo was looking for a place to cross, the guinea started jumping up and down in his death throes. Little Goyo laid down on his back, kicked his heels in the air, and laughed for all he was worth at the antics.

The amount of bird life in Africa is a constant source of amazement to me. The crows there have big white splotches around their necks. They are bigger than our crow, but they seem to be the same kind of a bird except for this big white collar. The old secretary birds stalk along with the tufts of feathers sticking up for all the world like an old secretary with a bunch of pencils behind his ear. They live on snakes, lizards and stuff of that sort. The maribou storks, one of the homeliest birds of all, and the buzzards clean up anything that's left from a kill. They are the undertakers of Africa.

One day we spotted a great spur-wing goose standing on a sand bar near the river. We were about 200 yards from him, or little more, so I laid down with the .333 OKH and put a solid in, shot him through the shoulders. It didn't kill the great goose but the boys took after him, ran him down, finally caught him

and got a wing stretched out each way while a third cut his throat. He was a huge goose. I believe he weighed 30 pounds. We had some fine goose dinners from the little Egyptian goose that was just about the size of our lesser snow geese, speckle bellies and blue geese in this country. The boys ate the old spur wing. Right at the elbow of each wing was a horny spur about an inch long and quite sharp, and I am quite sure he would have used it to an advantage if I hadn't shot him through the shoulders with a solid from the .333 OKH.

I killed 32 head, or 33, on the whole trip. Much of it, of course, was meat for the natives and baits for lion and leopard. I wanted to shoot the old lion with the .333 OKH and scope because I could see so much better, but John would have none of it. He said, "Use the big gun on him," and after seeing how far he went with his heart completely severed from the aorta, I was happy that I took his advice.

One day I saw an African weasel. He looked exactly like our weasels, a brownish-red color with a black tip on his tail. He was about the size of a small mink, or about twice the size of our ermine here. John thought he was a golden mongoose. However, he ran like

223

It took two heart shots from the .476 to anchor this bull, and although the range was just 40 yards, the angle of the elephant prevented Keith from noticing the broken tusk.

a weasel, traveled like them, and I was sure he was a weasel. When we were camped at Makalama Mission one morning, a golden mongoose came along and stood up on his hind feet right in front of my tent about fifteen feet away and he had a sheen of gold in his hair. His tail tapered, heavy at the butt and tapered to a point like an otter. So I knew I'd seen a golden mongoose then. After that we saw several more of those weasels. John said if I got a chance at another one to shoot him with a shotgun and I could get a hide for a specimen, but we never got another chance.

We saw a great many mongoose at the different camps. They'd travel in groups of four to a dozen spread out several feet to yards apart and they seemed to drift along at a fast run and shift back and forth. They were hunting snakes and lizards. There were several different kinds of them. One was a little brown mongoose that John said made a wonderful pet. He'd had one for several years. He'd put him in a cage or in a lantern when he moved camp, and then turn him loose. The little fellow would clean up any snakes or vermin around the camp and sleep in his bed with him. He said the natives caught them and

tamed them. They made wonderful pets and kept the snakes away from camp.

The boys killed a big old adder in front of my tent after we'd gone hunting one morning, and another one we found had crawled under the tarp that covered my trophies, and we killed him. I saw very few snakes on the trip. One day after we'd trailed a big rhino all day from one water hole to another, I saw about six feet of a great dark-colored snake go into a bush. I was in the tail end of the procession, all in as we had covered about 20 miles, and I yelled at John about it. John says, "Ah, come on. It's nothing but a darned cobra." He didn't even stop, so I went on. Another day we were driving up the road and two long slim pale green snakes were wrapped around each other. John stopped the jeep, got a club and proceeded to hit them as hard as he could. One of them he killed, and the other one slithered away into the grass. I asked him what they were and he didn't answer. However, on a later trip in '69 I saw some of them in a zoo. They were mambas.

At one camp where we hunted rhino, the natives at the village said a huge bull rhino had killed one of their men about a week before. He was coming home from a beer bust at a neighboring village when the rhino closed from behind and hit him in the buttocks with a horn and it went clear up through his heart. From this we knew that was a good bull rhino. We cut his trail one morning and we trailed him for several miles, finally getting into very dense thorn where we had to bend over and crawl. The wind was constantly changing and we'd move one way or another to keep the wind from the tracks in our face. Finally we got within 30 or 40 yards of him, possibly closer. We could hear his great jaws chomping as he ground up the thorn bush.

John and Goyo crawled under some more intervening brush and thorn and motioned me to do likewise. I got as low as I could but my jacket scraped on some of the thorn. Instantly we heard the rhino snort and he took off. Thank God he went the other way. Had he come our way he certainly would have run over us because he was right on top of us. I doubt if even our heavy rifles would have stopped him. We found where another big rhino was wallowing and when we'd get there at daylight there'd be a smoke from a fire and poachers there waiting for him. Poachers were in evidence wherever we went. They had taken all the fencing wire at one old German ranch and cut it up to make snares out of it to snare game.

I saw numerous leopard tracks on the trip. After I'd killed my leopard, we were driving through some open timber and I saw a beautiful leopard come down a tree, head first just like a squirrel. I believe it was a female, because it wasn't as large as the one I'd killed. She ran out about 60 yards and stopped. I dropped out of the jeep and had the pleasure of putting the crosswires on her shoulder and squeezing the trigger, though I didn't take the safety off as I'd killed my leopard and shot out my license. We also encountered a poacher with his poison arrows wrapped in corn husks, and John talked with him in Swahili for some time. Each night about two in the morning, heavy trucks would go by. John said they were Arabs loaded with ivory, horns and biltong from poached game and were taking it to the coast. There were not enough game wardens to even slow down the poaching, he said. I noticed that all the game at this camp was very wild, showing evidence of poaching. At no time did we see any buzzards or maribou storks, while up north around Manyarra and other camps, we'd no more than leave an animal until a cloud of buzzards and maribou storks would form a great flopping mass ten feet high over the carcass. The Arabs and the poachers had poisoned all the undertakers in that section of Africa so that they wouldn't eat up the meat of an animal killed by a poisoned arrow until they could find it and turn it into biltong, which is jerky over here in this country. They simply filet the meat and hang it on a thorn brush and let it dry.

This was one of the finest hunts I've ever had in my life. John Lawrence was not only a fine companion but one of the ablest hunters I have ever been out with. He knew the game, knew how to track, and knew how to outwit them. He was also a first-class mechanic. We had some breakdowns with the big truck, but he'd soon get it in operation some way or other. I shot two little "Tommies" for meat, also a Grant's. They were very fine eating. One day while hunting rhino, we spotted a little dik-dik. He had the longest horns I've ever heard of on a dik-dik. John got a glimpse of him. He said, "Elmer, if you see that dik-dik again, blow his hips off with that .476 because he's a world record dik-dik."

The horns stuck up twice as far as the ordinary dik-dik's did. I killed one with a shotgun and rolled another one over twice with a shotgun and he still got up and ran away while I was reloading. The one I killed, however, proved very good eating. He tasted like buck meat, although he wasn't any larger than an Idaho jackrabbit. I now had an oryx, sable, roan, greater kudu, elephant, lion and leopard. John was anxious to get back up north before the small rains, which had just started, got any worse. He said that gumbo would be impassable in another week. So we headed out, first to Singeta, then to Babeti. At Babeti we broke down again with the big truck and we had to spend some time getting repairs on it. From Babeti we headed on north, back towards Lake Manyarra.

A great many natives had bicycles. In fact I never saw so many bicycles in my life except in later years in Rome. But this time John would drive along and he'd honk a horn at them. Instead of getting off their bikes and standing beside the road, most of them would just turn into the brush and roll head-over-heels in the thorn. One day an old Masai was coming down the road with his sword belt and short sword, and his big spear over his shoulder. He was right in the middle of the road. John honked the horn at him, and back went the old spear and we took the ditch. He stalked on by us proud as a peacock. John said the old devil would have chucked it through the windshield too, if we hadn't taken

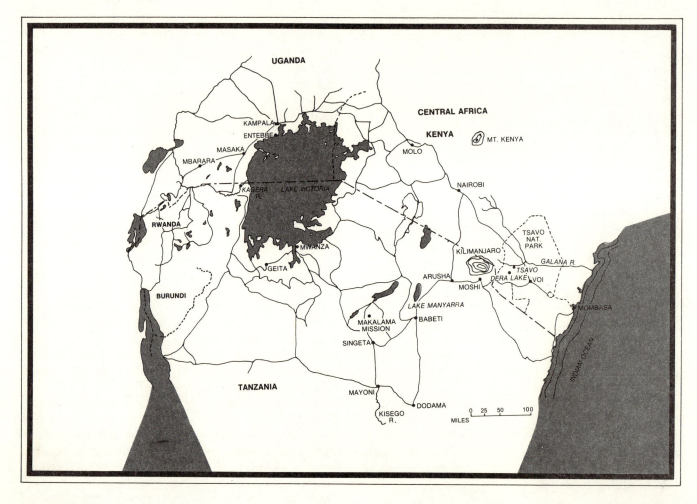

UGANDA

CENTRAL AFRICA

KENYA

MT. KENYA

KAMPALA
ENTEBBE
MASAKA
MBARARA
KAGERA R.
LAKE VICTORIA
MWANZA
GEITA
RWANDA

MOLO

NAIROBI

TSAVO NAT. PARK
KILIMANJARO
GALANA R.
ARUSHA
TSAVO
MOSHI
DERA LAKE
VOI
MOMBASA

BURUNDI

LAKE MANYARRA
MAKALAMA MISSION
BABETI
SINGETA

INDIAN OCEAN

TANZANIA

MAYONI
DODAMA
KISEGO R.

0 25 50 100
MILES

the ditch. Personally, I ducked my head down below the cowling. Those Masai spears would weigh about eight pounds and the Masai are very adept with them up to about 20 yards at anything standing or running. They keep them filed sharp as razors, so they are really quite a weapon.

BUFFALO BUSINESS . . .

I still wanted a good buffalo. At one time we'd trailed up a small group of buffalo and they went into some very heavy bush right to the side of a donga. The boys passed us our rifles and we crawled up until I know we weren't over 30 feet from them. We could hear them breathing, belching up their cuds and chewing them but we couldn't see a thing. Finally the wind shifted. Instantly they were all in motion. We got glimpses of black hides through the brush and they pitched into a deep donga and out the other side. We worked down into the donga and crossed. When we came up on the other side, there they stood about 60 yards away. One great old bull, he was a monster, his horns were both broomed and he was looking back over his shoulder. But for a trophy he was hopeless, so we let him go.

At Lake Manyarra we'd crossed a wide plain where the natives grazed their cattle and their sheep. There wasn't a sprig of grass on it. It was as bare as a tennis floor. The lower end of the lake was grown up in reeds anywhere from six to twelve feet high and the water was from ankle deep to waist deep. There was a great herd of buffalo, the natives told us, about a hundred head that had been out on the flat there at daylight and then had turned and gone back into the reeds. We went in after them. We could follow their trails around and we could see from six to ten feet at times, and sometimes from ten to thirteen yards. Buffalo manure was everywhere, and between wallowing through the mud, and smears of buffalo manure on us, we were soon a sight. The farther we got in, the worse the going was, the water deeper and the reeds thicker. The sun was beating down on top of us and the mosquitoes and tsetses were working on us. Finally I told John, I said, "This is hopeless. If we do find the buffalo, he's going to be right on the end of our gun barrel. It may be something we don't want at all, and still have to kill him. So let's get out."

We had a little native with us armed with nothing but a spear. I believe he was about 14

226

years old. The little fellow was certainly game. He wanted buffalo meat and he wanted it bad. John told him to head out, in Swahili. He started, but I could soon tell that he was taking us in a circle. John called him then and told him to head out, that he wasn't going to make any more circles. The little fellow was trying to lead us back into the dense reeds again hoping we would run into a buffalo. When we were about 200 yards from the edge of the reeds and the open plain, up jumped a bull right in front of us. He was about seven yards from John and eight or ten from me. I had the safety off the gun and hung it on his nose instantly and John hung his .416 on him, while John started talking to him very softly.

The buffalo would shake his head. A bunch of reeds hung over one horn and one eye. The little native stood in front of John with his spear poised. What he hoped to do with that ton of buffalo and that little spear I have no idea, but he certainly was a game little man. Finally the buffalo grunted, swapped ends, and was gone just as quick as he had jumped up out of the muck. We headed on out. I managed to get into a deep place up to my armpits and boys pulled me out. I was glad to get out of that stinking mess because it certainly wasn't my idea of a place to get a good buffalo head.

From Babeti we drove back to our old camp past the diamond mine on a little hill east of Lake Manyarra. The next day we hunted to the south, where it had been almost bare ground, the grass and reeds had grown up while we were farther south on the small range. When we started out on our hunt, there were several lakes there, just dry beds a hundred to 200 yards across with the mud covered with deep cracks going down a foot to eighteen inches in the mud. When we came back, the lakes were full and there were great big fish three feet long jumping in them. I asked John why. He said they were a type of mud cat. He said when the lakes get low, they bury way deep in the mud and they survive there through the drought of the dry season until the next rains. When it is soaked up, they burrow out and again become live fish.

We crossed several huge tracks of very big bulls in that dense grass that had grown up three feet high. We could see out of the jeep fairly well, but we didn't see a sign of a buffalo that day. Just tracks, and some of them very fresh, but just where they were, we never did learn.

Later on, we headed north, up the side of Lake Manyarra. We crossed a great field of grass there that was full of ant bear holes. We had to put the boys out in front to pick a trail through there in order to get the jeep through. These holes were about eighteen inches to 2 feet in diameter and some of them go down 6 feet like the one I fell in at the start of the trip. My right arm was still paining me and bothering me until I could only sleep 3 or 4 hours a night. It had been miserable the whole trip, but I still managed to do pretty well with my shooting.

This day we first spotted a little baby eland. Don't know where his mother was. He couldn't have been more than a few days old. Finally we came to some reeds and dry pans where there'd been water in the rainy season. We saw a pride of lion, a young male, and old sow, and three more half to two-thirds-grown lion. They stalked across one of these pans and went into the reeds. I had my old tomcat, however, so we were not interested in lion. The boys would take off from the truck every now and then and search the hills for buffalo sign while we drove along the edge of these pans where it was pretty fair going for the jeep. The hills, however, were covered with volcanic boulders and we couldn't put a jeep through there at all. So we'd drive along these pans and the boys would get out and cut sign if they could find any. Finally we crossed another big pan, the boys went out and looked and back they came running, their eyes shining. We knew they'd found buffalo.

They said there was a big herd of hundred or so shaded up in a batch of thorn bush and acacia trees. So we got out, loaded the big rifles, climbed the slope up on to this bench and started working forward. Off to the left I spotted a half-dozen bulls feeding towards an old baobab tree. I wanted to work that way and look them over. Galu-Galu wanted to go too, but John spotted another bull to our left front, feeding all alone, and he motioned me over there. I moved over to where John was. He looked him over for some time and I asked him what he'd go. He said, "I believe 40 inches. It's a pretty head. I saw it turned once." Well, I decided this was the last day of the hunt anyway, I'd better make the best of things and get him. We moved up to 60 yards of him and I sat down. He was pointed to our left feeding. When his head was down, we'd slip forward. I sat down and rested my elbows on my knees and held the bead of the .476 just over the knuckle of the left shoulder where I knew the heart had to be. I should have held higher for the spine, but that was

Elmer Keith's first buffalo was taken at Lake Manyarra, Tanganyika. The young, 36-inch bull was shot through the heart and spine with the .476 Westley Richards.

my first African buffalo, and I didn't know any better. Anyway I shot him through the heart. Up went his head and tail and he took off on a hard run in the direction he was headed. John shot and nicked the top of his withers. I saw him flinch from it but he didn't break his stride I pulled the big Westley down out of recoil, swung under his chin and ahead for a lead and gave him the other barrel.

It hit square on the shoulder and from there on into the spine where it ground it to bits, and killed him instantly. His head hit the ground and his front feet folded back. His hindquarters stood high in the air and he skidded for a good ten yards before he hit a pile of volcanic rocks and stopped. His hindquarters dropped to the ground and he never even kicked. My first slug had gone through the heart and over to the hide on the other side. The second one broke the shoulder, broke the spine and ground it to bits there. It proved a pretty head but only a 36-inch spread. He had a fairly deep curve, though, and perfect horns, so I was happy to get a good buffalo as we had to pull out. We took one more day at this camp to clean up and salt the buffalo cape, then we had to head for

Arusha and back to Nairobi.

Two of the boys took the head and cape, one of them holding a horn in each hand, and dragged it across the hill and down to the jeep, while the others loaded up all the buffalo meat they could carry, while I packed the two rifles. We hadn't even got out of sight of the buffalo until a great rope of buzzards came from the direction of our camp. It looked like a rope of buzzards about ten feet through and extending as far as the eye could reach. In no time at all it was a flopping mass ten feet high over where the buffalo had been. Then maribou storks came as well, standing around the edges, looking at the flopping mass. I'm sure that buffalo didn't last very long. It was getting dark and John took pictures of him just before we left, before we skinned out the head. It turned out very well in spite of the dim light. John was also an excellent photographer. We had 20 miles to negotiate, a lot of that through bear holes, and John was anxious to get started back to camp. We finally made it to the truck trace before it got too dark to see. We made it to camp all right where the old skinner by the light of a lantern started work on the buffalo. The next day he finished caping out the head, salting the cape, turning the ears, splitting the lips, and we were ready to pack up and head for Arusha where we had to check out all of our trophies, and then, after a day there, head for Nairobi.

By this time little Galu-Galu wanted another wife. He came to John and asked John to put up money for him to buy him a wife when he got to Arusha. I remember John telling him, he talked to him in Swahili and he'd translate to me. He says, "Now Galu, I'll put up the money all right, but you've got to work it out on the next trip. And you go buy a wife your age. Don't get any 13 or 15-year-old kid that'll die in childbirth. This time get you a woman your age."

While we were going through all the formalities, checking out trophies and one thing and another at Arusha, Galu-Galu got his wife, because the next day when we headed for Nairobi there sat his wife with him on top of the big truck loaded with our camp equipment and our trophies.

We had seen a lot of baboons on the trip. In one bunch I believe there was a hundred, including lots of old dogs. John said they were very dangerous if you got them stirred up. I remember one time near some sandhills and huge boulders close to the German fort, we encountered quite a bunch sitting on top of the rocks about 100-150 yards away. I shot several of them with the .333 OKH. Evidently the bullet blowing up quick worked wonders on those big old baboons. They are nasty-looking . The old dogs have very long fangs, and the natives claim that they destroy a great deal of their crops. That was one reason John told me to shoot them there, because there was a native village not too far away, and they could wreck a whole corn crop in one night. The leopards work on them quite a bit when they can catch a small one out alone. But they don't dare monkey with a big herd because the old dogs if they ever get a leopard cornered, will tear him to pieces.

On the way from Arusha to Nairobi while we were crossing flat, level plains, we saw considerable game such as wildebeest, kongoni and zebra. While we were doing 70 miles an hour, a little red Volkswagen went by us like we were standing still. At Nairobi I turned all my trophies over to Rowland Ward of London. They were to dip and ship my trophies later on. Then we went up to Molo to John's home where I spent Christmas. We had a nice dinner and a very nice time. Molo was about 8800 feet and I had to wear a jacket all the time although it was right under the equator.

The cooking was done on the outside in a fireplace by the native helpers. The living room had a big fireplace that was the only means of warming it. It looked very much to me like the hills of Ohio with neat little farms scattered all around over the hills.

George DeBono came by one evening with a client. They had been up in the rain forests after bongo. He had a very nice bongo head to show us. We went back into Nairobi, where John belonged to an automobile club. They were to have a good dinner there for all the members and their wives, however, the cook got sick. They were wondering what they'd do when we came in for a gin tonic. John says, "We'll take care of that. Elmer and I will go over to town and get my old cook." So we went over and got the old boy with all his rags and brought him back. They proceeded to dress him up in white. They told John, "Your old cook can't cook for an assemblage like this." John said, "Just try him." So in desperation they did try him. He cooked as fine a dinner of chicken curry and rice with all the trimmings as you can imagine. Then they wanted to hire the cook. John said, "Nope, you're not going to steal my old cook. Come on, Elmer, let's take him back over across town and hide him," which we did.

Thanks to John Lawrence's expert guidance and his knowledge of the game and the country, I now had the big five of Africa. I have never been out with a finer hunter or a finer gentleman, and when you hunt, sleep, and eat for a month and a half to two months with a man, then you begin to really know him.

John Lawrence had arranged with Bob Foster to take me on another elephant hunt right after Christmas, sell the ivory I had and try and get a hundred pounder. Bob Foster was the dean of elephant hunters among all at White Hunters Limited. He was a grand old gentleman. I spent some time in the museum, going over it, then we went to the game department to see if there was any control work to be done, as he wanted to get me some elephant shooting. However, from the third day on the trip that right arm continued to pain and hurt until I could sleep only 2 or 3 hours at a stretch, and usually then after a couple of highballs in the evening. It was getting worse. We went to all the doctors in Nairobi but the only osteopath or chiropractor had gone to London for a two-month vacation. The M.D.'s could do nothing for me. Finally I decided there was no use in trying to go on another hunt, especially on elephant. My arm hurt continuously night and day, and half the time my right hand was so numb I couldn't even feel the trigger. So I packed it up, changed my tickets from Sabena, (I didn't want to go back through Russia again,) and left Nairobi on BOAC for London.

I hated to pass up the two-week elephant hunt with Bob Foster. This was the greatest disappointment of the entire trip, but I was simply physically unable to enjoy it. I thought I would get home and get my vertebrae straightened out.

A BOUT WITH RED TAPE...

The plane landed at Entebbe for a time, then another town in Africa on the coast of the Mediterranean, thence to Rome where we had to spend several hours. I went up and had a haircut and a shave and got acquainted with the Italian family that ran the barbershop. He didn't want African money or American money, so we had to go to the bank and change some into Italian lira to pay for my haircut and shave. From Rome we flew over part of the Alps in Switzerland, France was all under fog, and landed at London. Twenty-three hours from Nairobi with no sleep, as my shoulder was still giving me fits.

As I came off the plane at London, some official grabbed my rifle out of my hand. The .476 was in its little trunk case, and my .333 OKH was checked as baggage. He also grabbed that and put them in the Queen's Warehouse, so he called it, and informed me that I couldn't possibly carry guns on a plane. I told him I'd carried them from America to Africa, checked them in, checked them out, and I wanted to take them home with me on the plane. "No," he said. "You cawn't possibly do that. You have to put them in the Queen's Warehouse, then inform your gunmaker to get them and pack them up and ship them over later on by sea freight."

I told him, "Yes, and have them rusted and ruined. Besides if they were shipped that way, then they'd have to go through brokerage in New York City, which would cost another hundred dollars." I told him I wanted to take them with me. I had a ten hour wait between planes thereafter, no sleep for 23 hours from the other trip. I knew if I went up to London or anywhere and got a room and went to bed, I never would wake up, so I decided to stick it out. When plane time approached I asked them for my rifles. They said they had to be shipped. "Well," I said, "we'll see about it. I went and wrote out a cable to the U.S. Embassy in Washington. I asked for the phone book to get me the number of the U.S.

Embassy in London, and sent a cable on to the State Department in Washington. They said, "You cawn't do that, don't you know."

I said, "The hell I cawn't."

So I threw down the money for the wire to the State Department in Washington, and a telephone conversation to get the consulate in London. When they saw I was going through with it, they produced my rifles. Just as we were getting on the plane, however, one man grabbed them, took them on the plane and up to the captain's quarters which was all right with me. I just wanted my rifles on the plane. After we went through the "Mae West Drill" and were well out over the ocean, the captain of the plane came back and said, "You Elmer Keith?" I said, "Yes." He said, "Do you want your rifle back there with you or leave them up there in the cabin with me?"

I said, "Just leave them there if they aren't in your way, and be sure I don't get off the plane without them, because I'm dead for lack of sleep."

We landed at Gander, Newfoundland again, thence on down to New York. Before reaching New York we had to fill out a bunch of papers, and I went to the bathroom to shave. I left my camera in the pocket in front of my seat, with the strap hanging out. When I came back and landed at New York, the camera was gone. Some passenger had noted it and managed to pick it up. I never heard of it again.

After arriving home, I received a letter from John Lawrence saying that I had been elected an honorary associate member of the East African Professional Hunters Association, and he sent me the bronze emblem to be put on a car, some four-inches across. I decided rather than put it on a car for someone to steal, I would put it on a walnut plaque, which I did and hung it with my trophies.

A LITTLE HOUSE IN TOWN...

After the loss of our daughter on the ranch, the little ranch never seemed the same to Mom and I. It brought back too many memories, so it was good to get into our home in Salmon. This old home was built in 19 and 11. It had old wiring, so when we put in a new electric range, we also had an electrician put in a new stove cable. However, unbeknown to him or us there was a flaw in the cable. Somebody had possibly kinked it in its manufacture. One night Johnny Austin and Ted were sleeping in one bedroom, Lorraine and I in another, when at three o'clock in the morning the barking of our old Stub dog

When old Stub wasn't clowning around in clothes, he was a serious member of the Keith family, saving them from a disastrous fire in the 1950s.

woke me up. I could smell smoke. I jumped up out of bed. The fumes were so heavy at about that level that it floored me. Down on my hands and knees on the floor, I yelled at Mom that the house was on fire. I also yelled at Ted and Johnny Austin. It seemed that the level of the gas that had knocked me down was about head high. Lorraine bailed out of bed like a covey of quail and ran into the boys' room to get them up. They were already up, however. Ted got out in the hallway and got the phone off the hook, but it choked him down and he had to crawl back into the bedroom. I went to the window and when I stood up to raise it, it floored me again. It just seemed like it would turn your knees to butter when you got a whiff of that gas. So from then on I crawled to the door, opened it, crawled into the hall which was a furnace, reached up and undid the night latch on the door, and managed to get my head and shoulders out before I passed out again from the fumes. I yelled at Ted to keep Mom in there, not let her come back, and take her out the window. He and Johnny did so. Ted had the phone off the hook and the operator heard my voice and recognized it, yelling at them that

the house was on fire. Ted ran to a neighbor lady's, turned in the alarm, and came back.

I managed to get my pants and shirt on and headed for my nearest neighbor. I woke him up and told him the house was on fire, then I ran back. Ted came around and I told him to get the hose, put the nozzle on it, and bring it to me. The kitchen and the dining room were just a mass of flame. I soon had the kitchen hosed down and the fire out there. Then I turned it onto The French doors into the dining room and hosed it down until I had the fire out there. It was still burning in the hallway. Just then the fire department came and they kicked in some windows and drug the big hose in and put out the fire in the hallway that I hadn't reached from the window. However, the fire was still burning. They asked me if they should turn the hose on. I supposed it was water, I didn't know it was an acid hose. So they turned it on and completely eliminated the fire. However, the fumes from that acid hose rusted everything we had in the house including my guns.

Judge Martin and I worked three days with solvent cleaning them to save them. The ground floor of the house was a shambles. I lost twelve heads in the fire, big-game heads that hung on the wall, and some more were badly damaged. Capes were burned off sheep and the antelope, three of them record heads. The caribou horns melted and ran on the floor looking like so much pitch and tar. We had to tear out the knotty pine panelling. The house had originally been plastered and I covered the rooms with heavy fibre board, except for the living room and the hall which I covered with knotty pine. It all had to come out and we had to reline the whole ground floor.

For a month we took our meals downtown and set up a bed in the garage. It was another sorry day for the Keith family. My hats burned up, most of our clothes, and I had one little dress hat that I saved. No one knew me in town for about a month. We lost $16,000 in personal belongings in the house and the insurance man had not done what I told him when I asked him to put half of the insurance, the $12,500 I had, equally on the house and on the contents. However, he did allow us $4,000 for the damage to the house which relined the ground floor and we had to buy all new furnishings for the house.

Two of Mother's fine oil paintings burned up, one of an African lion, and one of a pair of English setters on point. Also two fine oil paintings that I had made, one of Stone sheep and one of a pair of big antelope up the Pahsimeroi. Such things could not be replaced. I also found out that insurance people are very nice and friendly when you are insuring with them, but when it comes to making a settlement, it's the devil's own job to get anything from them.

While we had much more room in our new home in town, I missed my rifle range down on the ranch. Now I had to drive out of town to the National Guard range to test guns and ammunition, which I was doing constantly. I was also experimenting with new types of scopes, rifles, and bullets. The year after the African trip, I wrote and sold $8,700 worth of articles. That, and my assignment with *Guns* magazine, and *Western Sportsman*, kept us in pretty fair shape.

I worked with an engineer of the Lyman Gunsight Company to develop a double-crosshair reticule, the upper wire to be adjusted with the regular adjustments in the scope, the lower wire to be adjusted separately with a little tiny screw in the front of the capstan, and the cap on both the windage and elevation so it could be adjusted separately for elevation. It worked out very well. They made me two scopes with this special reticule in it.

Elmer Keith and Judge Don Martin, conferring on the Keith front porch in the 1950s.

The top wire set for 300 yards on the .334 OKH brought the bottom wire on at about 550 yards. I could adjust it so I finally adjusted the bottom wire to 500, the top to 300. It worked out beautifully.

I put one on the .375 Model 70, and I put the other one on the .334 OKH with jack-frosted stock and beautiful wood, and O'Neil had fitted the barrel from Johnson Bros. in California. It made the finest long-range rifle I had ever used at that time. Later, with a slight shoulder change and an increase in bullet diameter to .338, it became the .340 Weatherby.

During the four years I was with *Guns* magazine, they upped my salary from $150 dollars to $500. *Western Sportsman*, however, folded up still owing me two month's wages. After four years with *Guns* magazine, Tom Siatos phoned me from Petersen Publishing Company in Los Angeles and asked if he and Mr. Petersen could come up and have a visit with me

They spent three days here. One day looking over my guns and trophies, another day at Williams Lake, fishing, and the third day we went up the Pahsimeroi. Judge Martin went with us. We put in the day shooting jackrab-

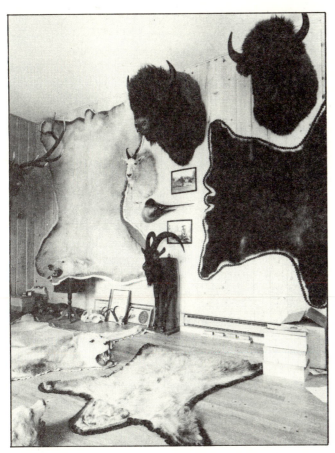

The new house in town gave Elmer the room he needed to display the many trophies collected on two continents.

bits. Don and I would drive along to the mouth of the coulee where the sagebrush was heavy and Tom and Pete would get out, one on each side, hunt up it, cross over to another coulee full of sagebrush and come down. They had a lot of jackrabbit shooting as they were quite thick then, with the heavy benchrest rifles they were packing. I took along only the 6½-inch .44 Mag. Smith & Wesson.

This one jackrabbit jumped and ran across the road behind the car around two hundred yards away. I decided to try him for luck anyway. In spite of a good lead, my first bullet landed just behind him. I had the elevation all right, but not enough lead. Of course the jack went into high gear. I gave him considerable more lead and again landed behind him. The third shot I swung way out in front of him, the same amount of front sight held up for range, and that time I rolled him. He turned several summersets before he came to a stop. A lucky hit, of course.

It was a very hot day, and Judge Martin and I preferred to do the driving and sip some cold Scotch we had on ice in the back of the jeep. We finally came to the Hooper Lane. The right side of it had a considerable sage-

brush flat that always carried a good number of jackrabbits. So we let Petersen and Siatos out there, and they started hunting it while Don and I waited in the car. They jumped a big old jackrabbit. She came out of the sagebrush and across the bare flats studded with prickly pear. I told Don I was going to try her. So I jumped out, and with both hands got on the jackrabbit. The range looked to me around 100 yards, but the rabbit was running all out. I got on the rabbit, started my trigger squeeze, swung the sights well ahead, and just as the rabbit crossed the white line in the road the gun went off and I saw hair fly. The rabbit was going so fast she went across the barrow pit and hit George Santee's netting fence and bounced back in the barrow pit. Judge Martin said again, "I seen it and I don't believe it. I'm going to pace it off." The Judge paces a meter rather than a yard. So he got out and paced it off. I believe it was 96 paces, so it was a trifle over a hundred yards. I went over to the old bunny and picked her up by the ears. My Remington lead gascheck slug had caught her through the middle of the back just blowing away that section. When I picked the old rabbit up by the ears four young rabbits fell out of her. She was about to give birth to that litter, so I wrote it up as killing five jackrabbits, running all out at around a hundred yards with one shot from that 6½-inch Smith & Wesson .44 Magnum. I've been called a liar ever since, but I had Bob Petersen, Tom Siatos, and Judge Don Martin as witnesses. Honest facts are always stranger than fiction.

Back home that evening Petersen offered me a $250 raise over what *Guns* magazine was paying me. I told him and Siatos I hated to quit *Guns,* as they had been very fair with me, and their editor, Bev Mann, had also been my editor when he was editor of the *American Rifleman,* and that I would at least give them a chance to see what they would do before I would accept. They took off for California, and I phoned Bev Mann at *Guns* magazine in Chicago. When I told him of the offer they had given me, he gasped. Then he said, "We'll hold a meeting and we'll call you back tomorrow on what our decision is." I waited through the next three days, staying home by the phone, but no call came.

On the afternoon of the third day Pete White at the slaughter house phoned me and said, "Elmer, we have eight big heavy bulls to kill this afternoon and I have only a little .22. Will you come out and kill them with your heavy six-gun?"

The Smith & Wesson in .44 Magnum Keith used to "kill five running jackrabbits with one shot at 100 yards."

So I went out and shot the big bulls for them at the slaughterhouse. When I got back that evening Lorraine said there was a long distance phone call came in. I asked her who and she said she didn't know. So that evening I called up Tom Siatos at Los Angeles and told him that I would accept the offer as I had heard nothing from *Guns* magazine. The next morning I had a call from Bev Mann. "How would you like to work for us, Elmer?"

I said, "I think I have been working for you the last four years."

"Well," he said, "we have agreed to meet Petersen's offer if you'll stay with us."

I said, "That's fine, Bev, except for the fact that I phoned last night and accepted their offer."

He said, "You haven't signed any contract?"

"No," I says, "My word is as final as death and taxes. I have never yet broken it and I'm too damned old now to start in."

Bev cussed me out for some time over the phone, but I told him that was final. So I went with Petersen Publishing Company, and it has been one of the best assignments I have had in my whole life of writing. Later, after

Bev Mann had had time to consider everything and look at my side of the picture, he agreed that I had done right and we are still good friends. I have been with *Guns and Ammo* magazine as Shooting Editor and Executive Editor ever since. I have also written for their annuals, with articles for the column each month. I answer a great many longdistance phone calls from shooters all over this country, and have a pretty heavy mail load of gun inquiries each month.

Lorraine and I made two month-long hunts to Alaska hunting the Slana, a branch of the Copper, and the Copper River itself for caribou, moose, sheep and grizzly. We obtained two good moose, one with a 54-inch spread, the other going 65¼. We also took a nice grizzly on Gillette Pass. This was the headwater branch of the Slana, and the pass went over to the Big Tok in Alaska. We found a big grizzly feeding on the offal from our first moose, and I decided to save him for Lorraine. However, we got a three day blizzard, and when the guide and I came back, we saw his tracks going over a mountain two miles away. He had finished the moose offal and took off. It would have been an ideal setup, as I had a shot picked out for Lorraine to shoot from above the alder patch and about a hundred yards up the hill. I wanted her to kill the big bear.

These two trips were by horseback, followed by hunting on foot. We had a good time both times. I obtained a nice caribou on the first trip and on the second Lorraine and I located a band of caribou some four or five miles away. The next day when we went after them, one of the guides had quit so Al Pabst of Texas went with us. We finally located the band again. There was one grand caribou in there. Al asked me to take him as we'd found them first, but I gave him the caribou. He proved a very fine 40-point head with double shovels, and Al killed him at 275 yards.

On the second trip, the Indian guide and I observed two airplanes driving a bunch of caribou towards the Copper River. When they had them well out on the flat near the river, one plane landed on a sand bar and the two men took off for the edge of the river and started shooting while the other airplane continued to herd the caribou up to the guns. There was two old white-necked bulls in the bunch, and they put them down. They also killed three cows that got in the way of the bulls. My Indian guide and I rode over and admonished them for their crazy shooting. Both caribou bulls were still floundering. They

An experimental Model 70 Winchester in .338 Magnum caliber was used with a 300-grain bullet to take this record-class caribou on the Slana River in 1966.

would get up and fall over while this man from Chicago and his guide took movies. I asked why they didn't finish the poor things off. They said, "Oh, they can't get away."

I jerked my old six-gun and killed the one that was nearest. The other one was 200 yards away, getting up, falling down again. Finally they went over to him. I guess they finished him off. I was so disgusted, we rode on. Our outfitter reported this infringement of the law to the game department, but kept himself out of the picture. However, I testified to what I had seen. Later, after getting back to Idaho, the game department subpoenaed me and I had to fly back to Alaska for the trial. The trial was cut and dried, eleven men and a woman on the jury. They were ready to hang the guy that was flying this hunter with two planes, herding the caribou up to the guns.

However, the judge wouldn't play back my testimony for the little prosecutor at all. He was a youngster out of college, a good boy trying to do his job, but the trial was bought and paid for, I'm quite sure. The judge dismissed the jury, and took it under advisement and threw the case out. He never let it come to the jury trial it was supposed to be. Such

was the conditions up there in the late sixties in Alaska. I doubt if they have changed very much today.

POLAR BEAR . . .

Ken Oldham of Anchorage, one of the best guides in Alaska, wanted me to come up and have a polar bear hunt with him. I also wrote my friend, Charley Shedd, and Charley booked up and went with us. We flew up to Anchorage, and from there to Kotzebue. Oldham and his wife, Mary, were already there. Mary had gone out and killed a good bear the day before. Ken Westenberger, who flew cover for Oldham, also came in the next day in a blizzard. Several flyers had set out from Anchorage, but most of them had stopped at Nome, but Ken came on through that swirling blizzard. How he ever found the place is beyond me. He had a peculiar way of circling, turning the plane upside down, and then straightening it out and making a landing. When we saw him make that crazy turn, we knew it was Westenberger. Charley and I had cleaned the bolts of our rifles with gasoline to be sure they wouldn't freeze up. When we stood them out in the snow one of them still

Alaska's Slana River produced this massive 65 1/2-inch moose for Elmer and Lorraine on a late fall hunt.

didn't want to operate. We sprayed it with graphite, then they both worked. We had sighted them in carefully here in Idaho three inches high at 100 yards and then tried them at 25 yards where they printed one inch high at 25 yards. So up there in the swirl and blizzard to prove our rifles we put up a box with a small target on it and laid down at 25 yards and each fired a shot, finding it went exactly one inch over the point of aim, so we knew our rifles were okay.

Charley carried a Model 70 .375 H & H with a Weaver four-power scope. I had my old .338 Winchester made by Iver Henriksen on an old Halger Magnum Mauser action with a single set-trigger.

We finally got a break in the weather. We took off early in the morning for the Chukchi Sea over on the Siberian coast. It was a long flight, but the planes were equipped with an extra gas tank and a great deal of radio equipment. We flew over a great many open leads, some of them from 50 yards to a quarter-of-a-mile wide, and extending as far as the eye could see on either side of the plane. We knew if we ever came down out there we were well marooned. We saw several bear.

The first ones were sows and two-year-olds, as near as I could make out. They were beautiful bear. We finally found one in a jumble of pressure ridges. Ken flew low over him until we got a good look at him, but he was only about an eight or nine-foot bear, Ken said, so we passed him up. Finally some ten miles from the Russian coast we spotted a big bear. Looked to me like he was two feet to three feet between his hind legs when he was going away from us. So Westenberger and Charley Shedd flew on ahead of his course, set the plane down, and climbed up on a pressure ridge and waited for the big bear to come along. Oldham and I stayed in the air and watched them. He was a beautiful bear, but on the right side of his head he was all a mass of blood. Didn't know what the matter was, but Ken said the rut was on and he'd probably been in a fight. Finally he approached the pressure ridge where Westenberger and Shedd were waiting. Charley let him have it, and I saw him bite back of his shoulder, then his left hip gave way and he started spinning around. I told Ken, "Let's go and set the plane down." Knowing Charley Shedd, I knew that the bear would be ready to skin by

Lorraine Keith and her saddle horse are dwarfed by Mount Sanford in Alaska's Wrangell Mountains.

the time we got there. We sat down and taxied up to their plane, climbed over a couple of pressure ridges and the bear was dead. Charley had shot him twice more.

It was around 30 below with about a 30-40 mile breeze blowing, so it was really colder than hell. I never did a faster job of skinning in my life. Shedd and Westenberger held up the feet while Ken Oldham and I proceeded to rip the hide off. I worked out the paws and the claws, got them done, made the splits from one foreleg to the other, and from under the chin back to the rectum. We soon had the big pelt off, but it was a load. Then we took off his skull and I proceeded to knock all the meat off it I could in a few minutes there. I had a pair of buckskin gloves I was wearing for the skinning. Of course, they were soaked with grease in a few seconds of work. I noted that the tongue and the inside of the mouth of the polar bear was not pink like a lot of taxidermists do them up. It was dark blue shading to black at the lips. We loaded Charley's hide and skull in our plane. I supposed we would head back for Kotzebue, but Ken Oldham said, "Elmer, how would you like to go bear hunting?"

I said, "I thought we just did."

"Oh," he says, "The day's young yet. We'll get one for you next."

So we took off again. We jumped some more bear, but they proved small, around eight feet, so we passed them up. Finally, nearing the coast of Siberia (I don't believe we were more than three-to-four miles off the shore,) I spotted a sow and a two-year-old running to the right of the plane. My window frosted up so badly, I had to crane forward and look out of Ken's side window. Both planes were Super Cubs, with a flyer in front and a hunter behind. I had my rifle in a Boyt scabbard that I'd designed for Boyt years before. Ken said I'd better get it out. I told him I couldn't get it out in the plane.

I said, "You set the plane down ahead of any good bear. I'll take care of the bear. You just take care of this plane because we are a damn long ways from home."

I punched Ken on the shoulder and pointed to this sow and two-year-old. He says, "I've got news for you, Elmer. Look what's following them."

He swung the plane around and there was a big boar chasing the sow and the two-year-old. Charley Shedd's bear had the whole right cheek split wide open from the jaw nearly to the top of the head. While we were skinning him, I told Ken, "I'd sure like to get the bear that chewed this fellow up. He must be a good one."

I asked Ken what this bear would go and he said, "Ten feet."

I said, "That's plenty good enough. Let's get ahead of him and set her down."

So Ken flew on ahead of both the old boar and the sow and two-year-old until we found a place that looked favorable for landing. There were quite a few drifts of snow on top of the ice that made a rather bumpy landing. We got her set down some 300 yards from a pressure ridge. Ken got out and put a shroud over the engine to keep it warm. I piled out and dug out my rifle, threw a shell in the chamber, and went over and set down with one of the wing struts for an elbow rest and waited. Soon the sow and two-year-old went by along the pressure ridge. I kept on waiting. Next came the old boar.

He came over on our side of the pressure ridge, and even at 300 yards and with one eye, we found out later, he spotted the plane and stopped. I laid the crosshair well up on his neck at the junction of the shoulder figuring to try and hit the spine or just under it. As my rifle raised in recoil I heard the thump of the 275-grain Speer and the big bear went down in a heap. He was up instantly. As I threw another shell in the chamber, he was over the pressure ridge. Then he would come up and show two or three inches of fur over the top of the pressure ridge and go down again. Ken was admonishing me to shoot again or I was going to lose him. I told him I didn't think so. There was no use pounding ice.

I said, "If I get a target, I'll shoot. If I don't, I'll wait." In the meantime Ken Westenberger and my friend Shedd were circling. They'd dive on the bear, circle, come back and dive again. They did this three times. After the third circle I hadn't seen any more fur over the top of the pressure ridge 300 yards away. They set the plane down and taxied up beside ours.

When we went over there the big bear had milled around in a circle about 30 feet in diameter and he was deader than a mackerel. We later found that the slug hit just behind the right shoulder as he turned slightly to jump over the ridge just as the bullet found him. Instead of hitting him in front of the shoulder I hit him just behind, but we cut it out from under the skin on the left buttock, a

full four feet of penetration. It was nicely mushroomed but held together and retained most of its weight. I had my big bear. His left eye was clean out of the socket and on the outside of his head and turned backwards. No doubt he was the one that had chewed up Charley's bear.

As we were in Russian territory we lost no time with the skinning. Charley Shedd and Ken Westenberger held up the feet, while I made the cuts, unjointed the paws, and skinned them out to the last joint, leaving the paws on the skin. We made a record time of skinning him out clear to the end of the nose. Then I cut off the skull and removed all the weight I could from the cheeks and the tongue. We dragged the hide and the skull and put them in Westenberger's plane as we had Charley's in our plane. About that time along came a big Russian jet flying over. They had gotten us on their radar screen and were looking for us. We laid down on the bear hides and with the tops of the planes being light-colored, they didn't spot us. We lost no time in loading and taking off. When we were a half hour out from the Siberian coast crossing the Chukchi Sea, the Russians came back much lower down looking for us. Oldham radioed Westenberger to hit the deck and we took both planes down just skimming over the tops of the pressure ridges as low as possible. We slipped by underneath the big plane and they didn't detect us. We headed for Kotzebue and home.

After another half hour out, and still an hour and a half from home, Westenberger's plane threw a jug. It would smoke and come down nearly to the ice, while Ken and I prayed and he got on the radio to Nome and Point Hope and Kotzebue, telling them all to keep a triangulation on us as we were afraid we were going to have to set down. Ken was on the radio for a half hour. Westenberger would come down until we'd think he'd hit the ice and black smoke would boil out of the exhaust pipe, then he'd raise it again. Finally Oldham says, "Keith, I believe he's going to make it. That old devil can fly if there's any power left at all. So I guess you know that I've been busy. If he does have to set down, all we can do is dump the bear hides, rifles, coats, everything that we don't possibly have to have, take the seats out. Then I'll lay the three of you in my plane like cordwood, sit on you, and fly you into Kotzebue. It's death to stay out on this ice overnight."

When we got to Kotzebue, darned if Westenberger didn't make that crazy old upside-

238

Keith's ten-foot polar bear was taken almost within sight of Siberia on the Chukchi Sea with a single heart shot from a .338 Winchester Magnum at 275 yards.

down turn and taxi in. Oldham says, "The old devil will stunt on only three cylinders."

Charley's bear went 11′ 4″-spread out on the snow, and mine 10′ 4″. We paid some Eskimo ladies $20 apiece to flesh them. They worked all night on them and were very adept at it with their round curved knives, which were very similar to a knife used by a leather worker because he can rock back and forth across a sheet of leather. By morning they had them fleshed right down to the skin and then the old Eskimo and his wife took them out over the bay and chopped a hole in the ice, tied a rope on each, took a pole and punched them down under the ice in the salt water. They'd bring them out then and spread them and kick snow on them and dance on them awhile, and then they'd poke them back down the hole for more salt water. In this way they cleaned them as clean as a whistle, leaving not a trace of blood on either pelt, and these bear, unlike a lot of polar bear hides, were snow white. They still are. Neither of them had the yellowish tinge of bear killed late in the season.

THE .41 MAGNUM IS CREATED...

The year before the polar bear hunt while we were attending the NRA convention in Washington, D. C., Bill Jordan, the old border patrolman, came to me and says, "Elmer, you've got the .44 Magnum. How about getting a .41 Magnum for the police and sheriffs' departments over the country that don't care for the recoil of the big .44?"

I told him, "Bill, there never was a better time. All the arms company heads are here as well as ammunition company heads. So if you'll side me, we'll get them all together and get the job done right now."

I contacted Doug Hellstrom and Bill Gunn of Smith & Wesson; Bill Ruger of Sturm, Ruger; Ted McCawley and Earl Larsen of Remington; several of the Winchester boys, some Colt representatives, and Nils Kvale of Norma Precision. We held an impromptu meeting that night.

I asked them for a .41 Magnum, case length to be the same as the .44 Magnum, bullet diameter to be .410 so that no old .38-40s or .41 long Colts could ever be revamped to handle the larger bullet as they go around .403. I wanted a 220-grain bullet. Doug Hellstrom also insisted on the .410 diameter to preclude the possibility of a cartridge ever being used in the old .41 guns which would not take its pressures. Earl Larsen of Remington said he could make the ammunition if the other boys would make the guns. Doug Hellstrom and Bill Gunn of Smith & Wesson agreed to bring out the gun as did Bill Ruger. I couldn't get any commitments from the Colt representatives or from Winchester and Norma on the ammunition.

Some six months later, just as Charley Shedd and I were leaving for the Arctic and our polar bear hunt, a pair of 4-inch Smith & Wesson Magnums, with target sights, and triggers trimmed to ⅜ inch, the hammers cut back about ¼ inch arrived. They had rosewood grips and my name on the side plates of the pair, consecutively numbered, No. 1 and No. 2. Also most of a box of Remington ammunition arrived in a plain box. Clyde Stone of Salmon took a picture of us with the guns about an hour before we took off for Alaska. We drove Charley's car to Seattle, stopping at Wagonhammer Springs some 15 miles out of town where I sighted both guns on a little mahogany stump at about 60 yards. We carried them with us to the Arctic.

After our polar bear skins were cleaned and ready for shipment, Ken Oldham says, "Now I'll take you caribou hunting and you can try out those six shooters."

We flew across Kotzebue Bay and up a river, counting 17 Eskimo dog teams on the ice going up the river to hunt caribou. Finally we located a little band of caribou and Ken managed to set the plane down on a rocky ridge. How he ever did it I'll never know. At any rate the caribou ran and then came around and poked their heads up a little over 100 yards away. I lay down, as the wind was blowing a good 30 miles an hour, used both hands, and I held up a little front sight right between the base of the horns of the bull. I shot. It went over him, showing me that the .41 Magnum is a bit flatter in its trajectory than the .44 Magnum I was used to.

The caribou ducked down out of sight and across a small canyon and came out again 400 yards away across the canyon where they all stopped broadside, pawing. I finished emptying the gun, holding into the wind and holding as much front sight up as I thought it would take to carry. I emptied the gun and reloaded it. Then on my fourth shot of the second gun full, I saw snow fly right over the bull's shoulders I was shooting at. So I cut down the sight picture and my eleventh shot dropped him cold in his tracks. Other caribou joined the band until there was quite a herd. They went out over the top of the mountain and out on a ridge. We circled and Ken set

the plane down again on this ridge. It was quite rocky but he managed to keep the skis out of the rocks someway. He left the engine running and the caribou were traveling at a very fast trot across our front about 150 to 200 yards away.

I shot out the side window with the plane vibration playing the sights up and down on the bull, but I nailed him. When he went in the air about ten feet, the band took off. Ken says, "We don't dare run them, so let's leave them go for now because if you run them in this cold they'll freeze their lungs and all die in the spring."

We circled back and, going through a pass, we hit a willawaw, what they call some of those crazy Alaskan winds. The plane was upside down and in every position you could think of. I was hanging on for dear life, and it just whirled us around like a leaf until we got through that pass. Then Ken says, "How you doing, Elmer?"

I says, "I'm still hanging on."

He said, "I'll level it up as soon as we get out of this windy pass," which he did.

We circled back over the tracks of the caribou and saw a black spot in the snow where the bull I had shot had ended. I said, "Shall we land?"

He said, "No, we'll wigwag the Eskimos. They know they'll get them all and they need the meat." From there we flew on out over the Sound.

Ken said, "I'd like to land. There's an old Eskimo family lives on a point over here in a log cabin." The Eskimos, there was one woman and three men there as I remember, they asked us in and wanted us to stay for dinner. They gave us some coffee but it was such vile stuff I could hardly get it down. Then for dinner they had an old copper wash boiler on the stove and there was the head and part of the neck of a caribou, hide, hair, eyes, ears, and all boiling. That was to be dinner. I told Ken I wasn't hungry. We excused ourselves, went back to the plane and took off again.

Part way out on Kotzebue Sound, we saw an old Eskimo with a mound of ice blocks around one side of him to break the wind, and a hole in the ice. Ken said, "I know that old guy. He's a friend of mine. He's shee fishing. Shee fish are gigantic Arctic whitefish, very fat and very fine eating." We flew on past him, then we spotted three little caribou on the ice. They must have been yearlings. Their horns were about six inches high. I don't believe they'd weigh over 80-90 pounds apiece. Anyway Ken set the plane down, taxied up in range and he said, "Give me one of those guns," which I did. He proceeded to empty it fast and didn't hit a caribou at all. The engine was still running and the plane vibrating. I told him, I said, "Ken, shut that engine off and I'll kill them caribou." So he shut it off and I plugged one through the lungs. It went down, got up and I hit him again and he went down to stay. The next one I shot through the lungs and then through the shoulder, and it went down to stay. The third one turned end to me to depart. I hit him in the seat of the pants, the bullet came out his chest and whipped up snow beyond.

Then I found out my gun was empty, and the one Ken had shot was the last ammunition we had for the two six shooters. So I told Ken he would have to kill him with his rifle. He had got out and got the .300 Weatherby. The little caribou was out about 125 yards by then, and he turned broadside. Ken shot him through the lungs twice with that .300 Weatherby Magnum. It didn't even knock him off his feet, and then Ken, I think, got a bit rattled that the caribou didn't move, and thought his gun was off. Anyway he missed him with the last shell he had. So he put the rifle up. That was all he had with him was the three shells in the magazine. So I said, "Maybe we can crank up the plane and knock him over with a ski." Then I thought of an automatic shotgun he had in the plane full of buckshot for wolves. So I grabbed it and I ran right at the caribou as hard as I could run until I got within 30 yards of him before he took off and I rolled him with the buckshot.

Ken said, "If you don't want these caribou, Elmer, what do you say we give them to that old Eskimo that was shee fishing?"

I said, "Capital idea. I wanted to try out my guns and the Eskimos need the meat."

We took the rear seat out of the plane and we piled in all three caribou. I asked him if he didn't want to dress them. "Hell no," he said. "They eat the guts too and the moss in their stomachs they make a salad out of that." So we just loaded them in, feet, horns and all. Ken finally got into the plane and into position and gave me the engine shroud to help me keep warm while he flew. He took off. I heard him land again and pick up the old Eskimo and heard them take off again. They headed for the mainland where the old Eskimo had his family and his camp. After about an hour of my dancing around on the ice to keep warm and watching and listening for the plane, I heard it coming. Believe me I waved that engine shroud around because there was snow blowing and I had my doubts about his finding me. But Ken said he would find me all right, and he surely did.

When he landed, he had two shee fish, I would imagine they ran around 17-18 pounds apiece that the old Eskimo family had given him. And he said the Eskimo family was very happy to have the three caribou. They hadn't had any fresh meat all winter. So we did them a good turn. Flying back to Kotzebue, Ken put one of the fish on his arm and we took it into a butcher shop and had them saw it up into slices, scales, guts and all. Then we took it home and Mary proceeded to peel the skin off, clean it out and that night she served us a wonderful dinner of fried shee fish.

Charley Shedd and I had a great time in Alaska, thoroughly enjoyed it and all the good people up there. One man at Kotzebue had been killing whales for the Eskimos in the summer months and he showed us his huge brass whaling gun with the big dart and an explosive head on it that he used to shoot whales. He said they'd got one at 70 or 80 feet the year before. We had an uneventful flight from Kotzebue back to Nome, thence on across the many bends of the great Yukon and all the forest wilderness there on the west side of Mt. McKinley, and finally landed at Anchorage. We proceeded to get another plane out for Seattle, and got out of the place only a short time before the great earthquake leveled a lot of Anchorage. We arrived in Seattle at three in the morning. I wrangled the baggage and the guns while Charley went and got the car. In spite of being lost in Seattle for an hour before we found the route out of it, we arrived back at Salmon, Idaho, that evening in time for supper with my wife.

THE BULLS OF UGANDA . . .

In 19 and 68 Truman Fowler invited Lorraine and I down to Las Vegas to the Southern California Safari Club meeting, which we took in and had a good time. At that time he asked me to come as his guest on a month's elephant hunt in Africa. Both Fowler and I consider elephant the greatest game on earth, so I told him to give me another year to finish recuperating from a bad coronary, so we could hunt in '69. After we had the plans about all formalized and Fowler had booked with the Galana Game & Ranching, and Mike Hissey for our guide, then Bob Petersen and Tom Siatos of *Guns & Ammo* invited me to go with them on a 30-day hunt in Northern Tanganyika starting from Kampala, Uganda.

They were to leave the middle of August.

I told them I had already promised Fowler to put in a month with him on the Galana on straight elephant hunting, so they said, "Come ahead and go with us and get in ten days on the Kagera, as it is good hippo and buffalo country."

I wanted a bigger buffalo than I'd gotten in '57. I also wanted one set of hippo ivory. I flew to Los Angeles and there I met Petersen, Siatos, Dave Shane, who was also to go, and Bob D'Olivo their official photographer for the magazine. We flew to New York, thence to Athens, Greece, where we spent the night, and then to Kampala, Uganda. At Kampala we met John Northcote and Nicky Blunt, the two white hunters that both Petersen and Siatos had hunted with the year before.

We drove a Toyota, a Land Rover, and several big trucks 238 miles south to Kagera Crossing where we crossed the Kagera on a boat rigged up on cables. The natives pulled on the rope and towed us across. It was quite a large, deep stream, muddy and of considerable depth. Nicky Blunt's boys had already set up a camp in an elbow of land surrounded by the river. It came in on the left and made a big lagoon, then made a bend to the right around the other side of camp. It was a beautiful campsite in a beautiful setting. Hippos were in the river in profusion. I would walk out from the tent and count 20 of them in the evening in a very few minutes. Some nights they would grunt, roar, bellow, and make all kinds of noises all night long.

I only had ten days before I would have to leave and go to Nairobi and meet Fowler for our elephant hunt, so we decided to make the best of it. As I was interested only in buffalo, hippo and elephant, I took but one rifle with me, a 24-inch barrel Charles Boswell .500 ejector, formerly owned by George Neary. Neary had killed six elephant and a good many buffalo with the rifle. It was superbly accurate, putting both barrels under a dollar at 50 yards and just right for elevation. Dave Shane had a .338 Winchester Magnum. Petersen had a .416 and a .375, as well as some lesser rifles for the small stuff. Siatos had a .404 Jeffery for his heavy rifle and a .375 for a lighter one. I went with Bob Petersen, John Northcote and Bob D'Olivo the first day.

We looked over the remains of an old ranch with its old buildings dilapidated, formerly owned by a man who had been killed by a buffalo. He had found a buffalo, his boy reported, so he went out and shot the buffalo one morning. Then he went back to have tea

The buffalo was a young 32-inch bull Keith took with a .500 Boswell, but the odd thing was the dead tick bird Kim displays, who was grazed by the exiting bullet and killed. Professional hunter John Northcote looks on.

and breakfast. After breakfast he walked down to have a look at his buffalo without taking his rifle with him. The buffalo had shammed death, jumped up, and killed him.

While we were looking over this ruin, Northcote and the boys spotted a pride of lion to the south of us. We drove over within reasonable distance. The pride of lion got up and moved across a donga. It was beautiful open country, scattered acacias, grass, and patches of brush. The donga was two to three hundred yards wide in places and simply a choked mass of jungle, fronds, vines, and creepers until at times you couldn't see over six feet. Northcote got Petersen within about a hundred yards of the pride, and a lion jumped up and started to go for the brush. Pete shot him with a .416, but I am quite sure the lion moved just as Pete shot, and instead of hitting him back of the shoulder, he caught him through the guts in front of the hips. He had a whole pride with him, and they scattered in all directions. The old tomcat went into the brush. We drove over there.

Northcote told me to get on top of the Land Rover with a big double and watch in case of trouble from any of those lionesses. He and his boy went in. Pete wanted to go with him, but he told him, "No." He refused to let him go into the jungle.

John trailed the big cat around for a couple of hours. He could hear him but he could never get a sight of him and the lion refused to fight. Petersen felt very badly about wounding him. I looked at the trail and told them it was gut blood. Northcote thought he had hit him too low in the chest or shoulder. But the brown blood and dripping near the center of the tracks told me it was a gut shot.

All three wanted leopard, so we proceeded to let them shoot lesser game and hang up leopard baits. Then we drove several miles up a donga and finally located a small herd of buffalo, 25 or 30 I would say. John wanted me to kill one for lion bait to hold Pete's wounded lion in the country until he could get another shot and finish the job. He was a fine-maned lion and we had to get him. We couldn't leave a wounded lion at any time. The buffalo were milling lazily around in a small amphitheatre, sort of a depression on the far side of a big donga. We had to get down on hands and knees at times and crawl through buffalo trails across that jungle-choked donga for some two hundred yards. Then the bank raised up steeply with a few scattered big acacias. We climbed up there and there was one bull in the bunch, and the rest were all cows that we saw. The party had ten buffalo licenses. Bob Petersen asked me to kill one to hold his lion so that I would get some shooting. The range was 140 yards. I sat down beside an acacia, and John Northcote says, "Can you do it, Elmer?" I said, "I believe so." He said, "Wait until the bull turns broadside." Finally he turned broadside as he hooked at a passing cow. I held high for the spine behind the shoulder and squeezed off the old .500.

The buffalo went down in a heap. We heard the heavy 570-grain slug strike. The cows milled around him and were into the donga in short order as they only had about 30 yards to go. My slug had broken the bull's back. Although he could shake his front feet around, and raise his head and growl, he was down and out. As we walked up I put another one down through his shoulders through the spine to finish him. Later, in California, Tom Siatos showed me the movies.

I saw no flash from my big rifle when I fired it, but there was a brilliant flash from the cordite flame in front of the muzzle when it went off in the color movies. Likewise, while we were walking up, another bull buffalo had been bedded behind a bush. He jumped up and took off and none of us knew anything about him or even saw him. You can be looking at one buffalo and get clobbered by another one if he has been wounded. I paced the distance back to where I'd shot from at 140 yards. At the shot John Northcote pulled off his old camouflaged hat and yelled, "Christ, what a shot." I wanted to take the head and cape for a taxidermist friend even though it was only a small 32-inch head.

The October 1972 *Guns & Ammo* magazine, pictured this bull and had a caption about a great trophy bull. I don't know who put the caption on it but it was a young 32-inch spread bull that I shot for bait to hold Pete's lion that he had wounded with a .416 the first day out. Northcote's boy did cut off the head so we could keep the horns for my taxidermist friend.

We left the bull just as he fell, hoping that Pete's lion would get on him.

He did, the next night.

He ate considerable around the neck and the testes, but was unable to tear open the belly on account of his own wound. A queer thing happened at that shot. There was a little tickbird perched on the other side of the buffalo's back behind the shoulders. My big slug went through, broke the spine and took all the tail feathers off the tickbird; didn't even break the skin but it killed him. When we were examining the bull, John's boy picked up the little tickbird that the slug had just kissed as it went through.

Northcote said we had to get that wounded lion before we left that part of the country, so we figured this buffalo bait would hold him. He had quite a pride of lionesses and also another young-maned lion in the pride. This Kagera River country of Tanzania is great game country. We saw rhinos quite often out in the open. With the heavy acacia bush clumps all along the river, the rhinos had dug beds beneath them so that you never knew when one was going to come out from under one of these bushes. We saw several bulls, but they were protected there.

Northcote, Bob Petersen, Bob D'Olivo and I were driving along over a flat one day when two cow rhino jumped up from under one of these bushes about 30 yards away. One old gal came at us a-huffin and a-puffin. D'Olivo got his movie camera out and got some fine pictures. Northcote kep the motor going, held the clutch down, and when she got too close he figured on slipping the clutch and taking off. However she was bluffing as she didn't come on in to the finish.

The Kagera River country was full of plains game like this fine roan bull, taken for lion bait by Keith.

Out in the open, a rhino charge offers little problems to any good rifleman with a heavy rifle. However, in dense thorn where you can't see more than ten feet, they are as dangerous as anything in Africa. Their utter stupidity is one thing that makes them so dangerous. They cannot see too well, but they can hear the slightest sound and they have a nose second to none. They are nearly always accompanied by little tickbirds and when you get close to them, the tickbirds will fly up into the air and start their chattering and warn the rhino. These little tickbirds are the rhino and buffalo watchdogs.

The country was simply crawling with impala. All three of the boys killed some beautiful heads. Likewise there were a lot of topi in the country. They were protected. I saw no zebra, though there were eland, and I killed a nice roan bull with Pete's rifle. After killing the buffalo for lion bait, we drove on up the valley along the west side of the Kagera and ran into quite a herd of buffalo. There were 30 to 40, right in the truck trace. Northcote looked them over for some time as they crowded and jostled each other around, watching us. We were in plain sight.

We circled down toward the river through scattered bush. It was beautiful open bush, beautiful hunting country. We ran into a bunch of cows and calves kegged up under a clump of acacias, but there was no bull among them. John Northcote was in the lead, I was next, and Petersen was behind me with one of the boys. D'Olivo brought up the rear with the cameras.

Northcote spotted a big leopard sitting with his back to us about 50 yards away. Nicky Blunt, Tom Siatos, Dave Shane, and their boys were hanging up a bait for leopard about a quarter of a mile away. The big cat was sitting there listening and watching for them. Northcote signaled for Pete to come up. He had solids in his rifle for buffalo and when he got up, after shifting and putting in a soft nose, the big cat ran. Pete got one running shot at him but he zigged to one side and Pete shot where he had been. It was too bad Petersen had not been where I was. Although I didn't see the cat at all, I would only have had to have taken three steps and had him dead to rights, at fifty yards, with his back turned towards him.

Another day we spotted a big herd of buffalo on the plain next to the donga that led back up-country toward the hills where I'd killed the bait for the lion. We drove fairly close, then got out of the car and tried to stalk them. They were feeding up toward a low pass in the hills, and even though we hiked along as good as we could, I was a handicap to the rest of the crew. They could have caught up with them. But my chest would hurt from the old coronary attack if I moved too fast or tried to hurry it. Northcote took my big rifle in a sling and hung it over his shoulder, took the lead, and then I managed to keep up with him. We moved from one ant hill to another, trailing the herd while he watched in his binoculars to see if there was a good bull among them.

My .500 double weighs 12¼ pounds and John said, "My, that gun is heavy," as we stopped behind another ant hill. So he signaled for the boys to bring up the Land Rover which they did. We got in and attempted to head the buffalo from the pass to have a good look at them. John drove like mad in second gear up that slope over rough terrain, with all of us hanging on and bouncing.

The buffalo herd took off for the pass too.

We did get close enough so that Nicky could study heads as we were going along and John said there wasn't a trophy head among them, but there was about 100 buffalo in the band. They beat us to the pass, went over the hill and down the valley on the other side, and we could see a trail of dust a quarter of a mile in the air for miles.

BIG BUFF . . .

The next day we drove back up this donga from the Kagera River, and hung up some leopard baits as the boys were all anxious to get leopards. We found where the big lion had worked on the dead buffalo, then we crossed back to the Land Rover and started down the other side. Soon Northcote spotted five great buffalo bulls across the donga and a half mile below us. He looked them over for some time and he said, "Elmer, there's a forty-inch head in the bunch. Do you want him?"

I said, "Sure."

I only had a few days left to hunt before I had to leave for Nairobi and my date with Ted Fowler. We drove down the donga a ways, left the Land Rover, and proceeded to cross this donga some 300 yards wide choked with fronds, vines, and every conceivable amount of bush. The only way we could get through was to bend over low and crawl through the buffalo trails. When we got out

the other side of the donga, it raised up steeply about 75 to 100 feet then broke away into beautiful open plains and lush grass, with just a few scattered acacias and anthills. Northcote took the lead, and I followed him. Behind me was Bob Petersen and D'Olivo and the boy, John's gun bearer.

John picked out an anthill with scattered trees growing out of the top of it. It was an old one. We got that between us and the buffalo, and then single-file we all managed to make the cover of this anthill. Northcote looked them over and he said distinctly, "The second one from the right, Elmer." I started to climb up the anthill, as I wanted to lay my big rifle over the top over my hand. But just as I climbed the anthill my boot scraped on that dry hard sand, the buffalo heard it, and they whirled around like a cavalry troop facing us and their noses stuck out straight at us. I heard Northcote say, "The second one from the right, Elmer," and I nodded. Then I laid the sights right under his chin. However D'Olivo and Petersen focused the big movie camera with the telephoto lens on the second bull from the left.

In this country we go from left to right in describing anything. In England and Africa they go from right to left. They even have the steering wheels and gear shift on the right side of their cars.

Just as I squeezed the trigger on my .500 Boswell, and the big gun raised in recoil off the anthill, I saw the buffalo's head tip down and to the right. Whether he was hooking at the bull next to him or whirling to run, I'll never know. At any rate we heard the heavy slug strike and he went down in a pile. Pete and D'Olivo had focussed on the wrong bull, and the small field of the telephoto lens only got the other bulls and their frantic disappearance. Again Northcote yelled, "Christ, what a shot," and pulled off his hat. We walked up and I could see the bull's eyes were still blinking. I remember telling John to stay clear of him, but John seemed to have a lot of faith in that big rifle and my shooting by then. He circled around. So did I until I was square with his back, then I put another one down through the spine between his shoulders just to make certain.

It was unnecessary.

The first bullet had gone through the right ear as his head tipped down, and it hit in the bulge of the neck, breaking the neck and killing him instantly. He was a beautiful bull, a fine head, and very deep. We measured it, or tried to at the time, and after the skinner

Keith's third buffalo was his all-time best, sporting a horn spread of 44 inches, and 41-inch horns. One shot from the .500 Boswell broke his neck.

removed the cape, I got 42 inches. After I got it home, and got it at right angles, it measured a full 44 with the left horn going 41¾ and the right 41. A beautiful buffalo head and just what I wanted.

John's boy was an expert butcher. He soon had the shoulders off, which they drug to a tree and hung for additional bait for Pete's wounded lion. The rest of the animal, practically all of the meat, the head, and the cape, we loaded in the back of John's Land Rover and he and I took off for camp, while D'Olivo and Petersen stayed around in case the wounded lion came out on any of the baits or the buffalo we killed before. The load was so heavy in crossing ditches the front wheels would come up off the ground. We had quite a time getting back to camp. We had one bad mudhole in another donga we crossed.

The meat was a welcome sight for all the natives around the Kagera Crossing by our camp, and there soon was a long line of them there begging for meat. This was a delightful camp on a little peninsula as the river made quite a bend. John said that during the last few years, the game department had slaughtered some 6,000 hippos trying to keep them

down so that they wouldn't eat up all the range adjacent to the river. They make two trails, one with the feet on the left and one with the feet on the right, leaving a little ridge of grass in between, in a way like the huge brown bear does in the snow or grass of Alaska. They feed back as much as two or three miles from the river at times, with a mouth so wide and their big lips, they crop the grass short. It takes a lot of grass to feed a big hippo, which may weigh well in excess of two tons.

Bob Petersen kept the camp supplied with some of the lesser antelope, which were fine eating. One evening his old cook had taken an oribi and baked him over the coals, spitted him on a stick, and basted him with some kind of gray dressing. I don't know what it was, but when the little oribi was finished, Northcote cut him up and I've never eaten anything more delicious in the meat line.

Dave Shane shot an eland bull in the heart with a .338 Winchester using 250-grain Silvertip ammunition. The bullet actually lodged in the heart wall, but the eland bull took off and they had to trail him some three miles before they got another shot and finished him. Impala were everywhere, some were in small groups and some were in bands of up to 50. They are beautiful animals with their high jumping, jumping over each other's backs when they take off. We enjoyed watching them and the boys all got good ones. Personally I was only interested in buffalo and hippo at this camp, but did take a good roan bull.

Another time, I went with Tom Siatos, Nicky Blunt, Dave Shane, and Nicky's gun bearer. He was named Kim, and he was a Masai prince, though he'd been with Nicky seven years. He said he had to quit that fall and go take charge of his tribe because his father was getting old.

As we were climbing a long slope to go over into the upper part of the valley, Nicky spotted a lion pride down on a flat in scattered acacias and tall grass—nearly a mile away. He had wonderful game eyes. The old tomcat and his whole pride was down there. We tried to contact Northcote and Petersen. We ran up aerials, got out the radio, and Nicky just heard Northcote signing off from a talk with the office at Kampala and we couldn't reach him. We drove on over the hill and came back on the upper river side of where we'd spotted the lion pride. Finally I told Siatos I thought the best thing we could do, as it was nearly four o'clock, was to move in and kill that wounded lion while we had a chance. Just then, however, Kim spotted the other Land Rover going over the hill from where we had come. So we whirled around, took off and chased them over the big donga and caught up. Petersen had killed a fine 44-inch buffalo that day and had his head in the back of the car. So Petersen and Northcote drove down along the donga, came around below the lion pride, and we went back over the hill and came in from the upper side. So we had him between the two cars, the hill and the river, so somebody should get a chance to finish the wounded lion.

As we moved in, we saw several lionesses head for the brush along the Kagera River with one young maned lion. Nicky was easing his Toyota along while we watched. Then we heard a shot on ahead of us followed by another shot. That sounded very welcome to our ears. When we drove up, Pete had his wounded lion. They'd gotten a shot at around 100 yards, quartering away. Pete had hit him in the flank with the .375. When the lion whirled around to fight, he hit him again in the chest and that was it. He was a beautiful-maned lion, over nine feet long. Northcote and Blunt of course were very happy to know they had the wounded lion in the bag.

AFTER OLD BIGMOUTH . . .

One day we had a terrific wind and rainstorm, turning to hail, and actually piling hail on the ground. It blew down some of the tents and almost wrecked the camp. Other tents had water standing in them. It was a typical tropical storm, yet it hailed considerable. While I was out with Petersen, D'Olivo and Northcote, Tom Siatos got a big hippo. He said he shot him in that pink patch back of the ear. He went down in a heap, but got up bellowing bloody murder and he had to go in and shoot him again in the back of the head with a .458.

I wanted one good set of hippo ivory to complete the big six of Africa. I went with Nicky Blunt, Dave Shane and D'Olivo on a hippo hunt up the river. We drove a considerable distance and finally climbed up on a bluff where a recent fire had burned off most the grass. We saw hippo signs all along the river and one little toto not over 30-inches high next to the riverbank. The little fellow turned, ran into the dense jungle and into the river. Finally we spotted the rear end of a giant hippo in some dense bush just below us. We slipped out of the truck, and sneaked down there, but we couldn't get at him from that direction, so Nicky took the lead and we worked around to the left. When we came around there, however, the old hippo's back was in plain sight. He was behind a huge log, feeding. We were only twenty feet away from him and he raised his head slightly once and I saw his ear and massive neck. Although vines covered all the lower part of it, I figured I could center it and break his neck. So I aimed into the vines low enough to center the spine and the neck and squeezed off the left barrel of the .500. Down he went in a pile.

He didn't have far to fall as his legs don't appear to be over a foot long. What massive beasts they are!

I stepped around to the right then until I could see his head and slipped him another one under the ear through the brain. It wasn't necessary, but I like to be certain on that kind of game. D'Olivo took movies of him and we measured the brute, going 14 feet from his buttocks to the end of his nose and very wide and heavy. Nicky said, "He is as big as they get." Kim got the axe and proceeded to chop for about an hour, cutting through his skull back of all the ivory. They have two great incisors below and shorter ones above out on each corner of the mouth. Then in the bottom there are the four straight tusks and in the top of the head or palate there's four more straight tusks. The hippo has a whole mouth

Bob Petersen's lion was finally stopped by a Winchester Model 70 in .375 H & H Magnum caliber.

full of hard ivory. We loaded the nose in the Toyota and hauled it to camp where the skinners cut away most of the meat, boiled it and pulled the ivory. The longer tusks went 24-inches and Nicky said that was as good as they went for a typical tusk. Some have been found where the upper tusk has been damaged or lost and the lower one then grew in a great curve in a circle the same as I have seen with a few rabbits, woodchucks, and one beaver.

After ten days we broke this camp and I had to get back to Kampala and on to Entebbe and enplane for Nairobi. Nicky Blunt drove me back. Along the route I was amazed at the dress of the natives. The Negro women had long flowing skirts, looking like bustles, and very wide padded hips. They also had puffed sleeves with a great puff of cloth at the shoulder and tight necks. They reminded me of the dress of the women when I was a little kid in Missouri and early Montana. Banana groves were all along the road from the Kagera Crossing back to Kampala. We also went through several villages.

Northcote took the rest of the party, Petersen, Siatos, Dave Shane, and the boys, and moved to a new camp deeper in Tanzania. It

was with reluctance that I bade them all goodbye. They wanted me to go on with them the rest of the 20 days they were going to hunt, but I had already promised Ted Fowler I would meet him in Nairobi on September 30, which I did. At that time Kampala was quiet and I had no trouble getting the big rifle through customs. However when I carried it on the plane one little official came along and he wanted to take it away from me. I wouldn't let him. I handed it to the purser, and told him to take it up to the captain. It was cased in one of my Boyt scabbards. This little Negro official went aboard the plane and got my gun. I was worried a bit, but when we got to Nairobi, the purser brought it back to me. He passed it up through a window to the captain, I presume. At any rate I arrived in Nairobi and met Fowler. I have never been out with more enjoyable companions or had a more pleasant ten day hunt in my life than with Bob Petersen, Tom Siatos, Dave Shane, and Bob D'Olivo and the good white hunters, Northcote and Nicky Blunt.

My big buffalo head and cape, the skull of the small buffalo, my roan head and cape and the hippo ivory were left with the Jonas Bros. office at Kampala to be shipped to me in the

One neck shot with a .500 Boswell turned this giant hippo into trophy tusks for Keith.

States later on. However when they did arrive, I found they had almost ruined the heads of all three on account of cooking them to death. The extreme edges of the horns were charred until you could rub your hands on them and the particles would come off like soft black coal. The capes of the buffalo and the roan, however, were well-salted and cured when they arrived.

I found Nairobi was a very changed city from what it had been in 19 and 57 when I was over with John Lawrence. I had a room in 19 and 57 for $4 a day, including an elaborate breakfast. You could pick up all the fruits and cereals you wanted, then move to a table and order your toast and bacon and eggs or whatever, all for $4 a day. In '69 Fowler and I shared a room and it was $14 each for this one room with no breakfast and very poor accommodations in the New Stanley Hotel as far as meals were concerned. However, we went out to another restaurant not over two blocks away where the food and the service were excellent.

My old friend, Bob Foster, had passed away before I arrived at Nairobi, but his good lady and their ranch foreman came in and we had lunch together. Bob was one of the most fa-

mous elephant hunters around Nairobi at the time and had accounted for a lot of 100-pound tuskers. He and Lawrence had also shot on control for the game department a great deal. He was considered one of the finest elephant hunters in Africa as well as one of the finest gentlemen.

Truman Fowler had booked a thirty-day hunt on the Galana for us with Mike Hissey, a brother-in-law of Northcote, as our white hunter. We were to put in a solid month on elephant on a concession from the Kenya government to Galana Game & Ranching, Ltd. This section south of the Tsavo Park no doubt carries more elephant than any portion of Africa. It is simply alive with the great beasts. They have already killed most of the timber in the Tsavo Park until it is largely grassland now, and when they have a drought they suffer. In 1971 such a drought occurred. They lost thousands of elephant. Even the ranch managed to pick up a good many tons of ivory from the dead beasts that had died of starvation, and some from the poacher's arrows where the poison had not taken effect quickly enough. Mike Hissey is a grand old elephant hunter and has had a great deal of experience over 20 years of hunting them. He

249

also had a great crew, composed of Old Macaou who had also worked for my friend, Don Hopkins, for years, and Genghi, and a little ex-poacher named Boro Dbassa.

After the first day I told Mike I wanted little Boro for my gunbearer. He couldn't understand English, nor I Swahili, but we got along perfectly by signs and both being old hunters, we hit it off together first rate. The little man had been on the Ten Most Wanted list of poachers in Africa for many years. When they finally captured him they gave him his choice of turning gunbearer for hunters or go in the pokey for ten years. Boro, being a hunter, of course decided to be a gunbearer and he is one of the most expert little hunters I have ever been out with. A book entitled *"The Elephant People"* by Dennis Holman and currently available in Nairobi describes little Boro along with the other poachers that the game department fought for years before they finally captured them.

On the banks of the Galana River we had a beautiful permanent camp. Rock and cement walls ran up about six feet and then a thatched roof went over that so that the wind could blow through underneath the roof. It was quite comfortable; good beds and mosquito nets to pull down and tuck in around you each night. Lizards ran around among the poles of the thatched roof, but they were welcome because they captured a lot of bugs, flies and insects that otherwise could cause you trouble.

The Galana concession from the Kenya government comprises 1,500,000 acres. They run over 20,000 head of cattle on the entire place scattered out in little bands with a little group of native spearmen herding each band. Lion were taking their toll of these cattle every few nights. The lion down on the Galana carry no manes at all, the leopard down there are smaller. There is a world of giraffe and other small species. There is also a lot of buffalo, but they are the smaller coastal variety. They've got heads up to 42 inches. Waterbuck, eland, lesser kudu were in profusion and quite a lot of other game. Some wart hogs, zebra and myriads of lesser game were all over the place.

Elephant, however was the principal game. I have never even dreamed of seeing so many elephant. From the Lahli Hills some two or three miles from camp, we could sit up there and sight a thousand elephant at one time on several occasions. On almost any day herds of 300 to 600 could be spotted out on the flat in the scattered bush. It was in the main fairly

open bush and easy hunting. The dongas carried some very dense growth and taller trees where the elephant would keg up at noon for their siesta.

Both Ted Fowler and I consider elephant the greatest trophy in Africa, with the buffalo second choice, rather than the antelope. We had agreed to hunt elephant exclusively for 30 days, which we did. Truman Fowler is one of the finest hunters I've been out with. Cool, level-headed, never excitable, a deadly shot, and he carried a big 15-pound Lancaster Ejector, caliber .577, probably one of the finest elephant rifles obtainable today.

From Nairobi we drove to Tsavo, stayed all night, and the next day made it down to the camp on the Galana. The Galana at that time was fairly low. We saw one crocodile lying on a sand bar as we were going down. However the Galana Game & Ranching charge an enormous fee for everything killed on the ranch. You have to pay after you kill it. Both Truman and I were interested only in big elephant, though we did decide to take a couple of the lesser kudu which were in profusion along the Galana. Each day we would see a good buck somewhere on our drive. They are one of the most wary animals I have ever hunted, and are very hard to get a shot at. We decided that sooner or later we would run into some along the road and get a shot, which later happened.

Going through the park we spotted a great many elephant feeding along the roads, apparently unconcerned and unafraid of man. They were used to the protection of the park. But we didn't see any bulls with over 50-pound ivory on a side. In the next 30 days, Mike Hissey, Fowler, Macaou, Genghi and little Boro took off before daylight, driving out on the great flat expanse or else to the Lahli Hills where we would climb up to several hundred feet elevation and look out over the plain and spot elephant. We saw elephant every day. We stalked bulls every day, for the 30 days we were there. Most of the time, however, we would get up to them within good shooting range and find they were only 40 to 50 pound elephant, and we would turn them down and move on, sneaking out as carefully as we'd sneaked in on them.

After crossing the Galana River, they have a guard outpost prohibiting anybody from crossing the river on account of bad elephant. Three years before they killed about 600 on control in that section and many of those elephants still remembered it. So the average tourist, anyone except those going to the

Boro (right) supervises the cutting of the ivory on Keith's third elephant, whose tusks ran 55 and 58 pounds.

ranch to hunt or for other purposes, were stopped at the Galana Crossing. Across the river we saw one great old bull about a quarter of a mile away. Mike said he would go over 100 pounds. That was probably the best elephant we saw on the entire trip. However he was still 50 miles inside the park and people that had seen him said he never left. He was a wise old bull.

THE WRINKLED MONARCH...

From the first day on we saw huge herds of elephant. We'd drive out to the Lahli Hills, climb them, look them over, and go on over the hills toward John Lawrence's Waterhole, named after the old white hunter of my '57 safari. It is great country and we never failed to spot big herds of elephant every day wherever we went. On the third of September we were again perched on the Lahli Hills and spotted a herd of some 500 out in the flat, maybe more. We didn't see anything extra long, so we went on some 20 miles to where Mike had gotten a 96-pounder. At Lawrence's Waterhole we picked up the tracks of an old slick-heeled bull. It was apparently quite old and Mike decided to trail him. He had his

askari with him. We trailed him back through the scattered bush, much of it quite tall and we couldn't see very far. We had to dodge around some groups of cows and calves and pick up the trail again. Finally we came onto him again and his askari in fairly open bush. I asked Mike what he would go. He said 80 to 90 pounds and very long.

The bull was 30 yards away from us and quartering away. Mike moved around to the left and motioned for me to come around to the side for a brain shot. However I'd sat down under a thorn bush and the elephant knew Mike was there. He'd swung his head once and I knew he would again. When his head came around the next time and the ear came back I figured six inches behind the ear hole and four inches lower would center that great bonnet on a car and hit the little football of a brain inside, so I squeezed off the left barrel. Down came his hind quarters, the trunk and head he threw high in the air, then down came the front quarters and over he came. I'd drilled his brain center. He was a very old, decrepit, wrinkled elephant. Mike said he thought I'd done him a kindness by killing him because he probably wouldn't have lasted too much longer. However the ivory was a great disappointment, seven feet long on the curve, but they had great forty-inch nerves and ran 55 and 58 pounds. Mike offered to take them off my hands and pay the tithe to the ranch on them but I said, "I've killed him. I'm going to keep him." They are now on my wall here in the living room. Boro cut out a lot of meat on the side of the head opposite to where I'd shot and carried it in as the boys were very fond of elephant meat. He found my 570-grain slug in that meat and gave it to me. It went through the brain and almost to the skin on the right side of the head.

Each day one or two of the boys would climb the hills to look for elephant and usually leave Ted or I or both of us to guard the truck, as nearly every day elephant would come up to the tall bush beside the truck trace and we could see their trunks turning and twisting above it and you never know when one of them is going to decide to wreck our transportation. Each day we would see and stalk bulls only to find them around the 50-pound class and turn them down. We worked out as far as the Dakhadema Hill and also to Dera Lake where some 3000 or 4000 elephants were watering.

On the fourth of September we had stopped and looked over seven big bulls about 10:30 in the morning. None were over 60 pounds. One was an enormous old beast. In addition to elephant each day we saw myriads of game. Everything from ostriches to lesser kudu. One morning on the Lahli Hills we watched a herd of some 30 or 40 buffalo just below us, and out on the flat was a herd of elephant that must have numbered a thousand, as they were scattered all over the place.

Truman Fowler, who we called Ted, was to take the next elephant. Mike Hissey told us of several unusual experiences. He had a very old friend in Nairobi, a Colonel Kirkwood. He was over 85 and nearly blind, but was still driving. One day he was driving down the street in Nairobi and he heard something rattling under his car. He got out and looked under it and he said, "Would you believe it? I had a rather extraordinary experience. I looked under the car and there was a bloody native on a bicycle."

Mike also told us of the big ground hornbills, the largest of these birds. They build their nest in a hollow stump or the top of an anthill. The old lady bird lays her eggs, and the old male and last year's offspring carry mud and build a solid mud hut over her, sealing her in except for a hole to feed her.

Then after the eggs are hatched in three weeks, the old male and last year's kids would go up, peck on the mud hut and listen and when they hear the young chicks they break the mud hut and let her and the brood out. They all take turns packing food to her, poking it through a hole until the chicks are hatched then they break her out of seclusion so they can raise the young.

For Africa the temperature was not too bad. Each day about 10 in the morning a monsoon wind would come up from the Red Sea, blow steady and quite hard, sometimes 20-30 miles an hour. Other days it would get muggy, with a few drops of rain, and no wind. The truck traces from various bands of cattle scattered over the concession were usually covered with elephant tracks and the sansaviera which the elephant pull up and chew. It is a sizable green plant with a sharp spear on the end of each leaf. It must be the elephants' chewing gum as they chew up tons of it and finally spit out a ball of white fiber after all the juice and greenery is absorbed from it.

Some evenings by moonlight we could see elephant coming down and watering across the river from us. One night one old bull came right in camp and woke Mike up flapping his ears 30 yards from his tent. It was great country. We'd see quite a lot of lesser kudu, Grant's, impala, topi, kongoni, and little dik-diks like jackrabbits in Idaho. Oryx were quite common, as well as zebra, some gerenuk and giraffe.

But we were only looking for the very big elephant.

One day we saw a cow elephant in a band of about a dozen with a very young toto or calf. The little fellow didn't look much bigger than a shepherd dog. This particular cow had tusks shaped like a mastodon. They went out, curled up and curled back, thin but very long—a beautiful set. Every so often a huge herd of elephants would come out of the Tsavo Park, across the truck trace which was the line, and feed out on the flat, then go down to the Galana River and water. They might stay a day or two and then work back into the park. This procession occurred a great many times while we were putting in our 30 days. Many times we watched small herds of elephant in groups cross our truck trail and the smaller tracks of the car. Some of them would scream, the old cows, and some of them would bunch up and stand completely silent for half an hour listening and watching. They all knew what the smell of those tires on the road meant.

One Sunday morning we were watching a

Keith's record-class lesser kudu was downed by a shot from a Model 70 Winchester rifle in .375 H & H borrowed from Mike Hissey.

herd of a good thousand elephant out on the vast expanse of bush between us and the Galana River. Some looked like good bulls in the center but there were too many elephant all around them to ever work in and get a shot in that open bush. A pair of lesser kudu bulls were out in the middle. About ten o'clock that Sunday morning, for some unknown reason, all those elephants started moving together until the whole herd of them was bunched in about a quartermile circle. The kudu bull tried to hide under a bush but an old elephant went over and shook the bush and chased him out. They were jumping back and forth frantically, surrounded by elephants in every direction. Mike said he'd never seen anything like it and couldn't understand it. I told him the solution was simple. It was Sunday morning, ten o'clock, and they're holding prayer meeting.

Several times we saw some good bulls out in the middle of great herds from the Lahli Hills, but there was no way to get at them without working through several hundred elephant to do so, which would be too dangerous in case of a stampede. If we could have

caught one of the great tuskers out on the edge so that we could slip down and kill him, then go back to the safety of the hills, we would have done so. But such opportunity never came. So we started driving farther down the Galana River to contact herds of elephant that stay there the year around. Probably 3,000 to 4,000 elephants stay on the ranch at all times, in addition to the great herds coming out of the Tsavo Park.

On September 8, we had driven down the Galana River several miles and cut the tracks of a very large herd going into the bush to the north. We found another truck trace that would take us around and downwind from them as the wind was blowing in from the Indian Ocean every day about ten o'clock. Mike parked the Toyota and sent Macaou, Genghi and Boro in to see if they could locate the herd.

They did, in heavy tall bush.

We moved in and worked the edge of the herd for two hours, finding a great many groups of cows and calves, also a lot of bulls, some of them quite heavy with ivory. This was Ted's chance, and we wanted to get him the best bull possible. Ted and I spotted a great red bull much taller than his companions. The ivory looked heavy and it went right down into the grass. We motioned and showed him to Mike. By this time we were in heavy bush and elephants were all around us. We passed several groups of cows and calves. There was five bulls kegged up head-to-tail in front of us, another group to the right, and another group even farther to the left. For a time we could do nothing. Thank God the wind hadn't come up that morning, so we just stood around there with elephant all around us, waiting for them to move so that we could get a chance.

We showed Mike this big red bull but he whispered that he'd seen a bigger one. Finally he handed me his glasses and pointed out in the open to our right front. There was the elephant Ted had been looking for, over six feet of ivory projecting out from each side of his big head. He was a monster elephant and a beauty. However we were surrounded by elephant, and we knew that the first sound, the first time they knew we were there, there would be a melee to get out.

I took one look through the glasses and I said, "Let's go get him if we have to fight the whole herd. Mike, you and I can keep them from coming over us while Ted kills the big bull." Ted and Mike got within 50 yards and Ted raised his big rifle for a brain shot and the bull whirled and ran at the same time.

Truman Fowler (right) nearly had to fight an entire herd of elephants to get a shot at this giant tusker, who had nearly 100 pounds of ivory on each side.

Out at about 90 yards I told Ted to take him and try for the spine. He put one shot in the rump and another one right beside the back bone. The old bull swerved and turned to the right. As Ted reloaded and put in two more, he stumbled and I thought he was going down. Ted reloaded and put in two more and the bull swung around to the right. Then on his last shot, Ted hit the neck. Down the great tusker went. He was a beauty, over six feet of ivory out of the lip and a 20-inch circumference at the lip, a perfectly matched pair. Ted had what he'd come for.

He thought he would go well over 100 pounds a side and he would have except that after we got the tusks out and got them home, when we pulled the nerves we found they were 37½-inches long. The tusks both went 8' 4" in length but with the long nerves they weighed 92 and 98 pounds.

The next elephant was to be mine. We were up, had breakfast before daylight and were in the truck for the drive out to cut the tracks of herds every day. We worked them hard, looking for another big bull, and then went back after dark. We had ample opportunity to observe elephants under any and all conditions

conceivable, and we learned a lot about them. I'm quite sure in the 30 days there Truman Fowler, Mike Hissey and I were up against more big bull elephant than eight or ten American hunters ever see in several safaris. When Ted shot the big bull, all the elephants in every direction started moving. After his second shot, there was pandemonium, dust raising in the air, elephants going by on both sides screaming their heads off. It was a melee.

Mike and I had to watch behind us, but thank the Lord all of them seemed to split and go around us each way. It was fairly open where Ted had downed the great tusker and I believe we could have stopped any two or three elephant that came for us there. However none showed any fight. They were all wanting to get away. Any time you work out into the middle of a big herd of elephants, you are asking for it. Anything can happen.

Both Fowler and I broke out with hives. We never knew whether it was some of the fuzz on the grass that got in our skin, or whether it was something we had eaten or drank. We were a sight, and we would scratch until we'd rub the hide off. Truman was worse than I, one hand swelled badly and hives all over the back of it. It never bothered Mike or the natives so they were evidently immune to whatever caused us our discomfort.

On the 10th of September, we picked up a slick-heel track at Lawrence's Waterhole. It was a big elephant, and the last six inches of the heel was all worn slick, so he was old enough and big enough that he should carry heavy ivory. We trailed him back into the bush until the wind came in from the Red Sea and dried all the dew off the grass. It was easy tracking as long as there was dew there, but after the sun reached the zenith and the hot wind started blowing in at 20 miles an hour, then all the brush dried up, and the ground was as hard as a cement floor.

We finally lost this big bull.

While we were spread out searching for him, little Boro was ahead of me with my .500 over his shoulder which he grasped by the muzzle. I had taught him to carry the rifle that way with the buttstock sticking back toward me. I was a couple of steps behind, so I could grab the rifle in case of an emergency. Suddenly, Boro froze. He slowly pushed the big rifle back at me. I grasped it and slipped the safety catch off.

Ahead of us, I could, just see the tips of a rhino's horns sticking up above a bush. Boro faded back behind me while I watched. He signalled to all the others, and we slowly backtracked. Thank God the wind was in our favor. I didn't want a rhino on the Galana Ranch as they ran about $1500 each.

On another day, we located a group of bulls from the Lahli Hills and we worked down in the bush to try and contact them. Every so often Boro and Genghi would climb a tree and look around and listen. We ran into a herd of buffalo, however, and spooked the bulls. All we could see of them was their legs under the brush.

Then we spotted a rhino.

We dodged around him, but the wind changed and he got our scent. There were a lot of giraffe, "twega" they were called, and they'd spot us with their great long necks and heads up over many of the trees and they'd stampede. At any rate the buffalo stampeded and the twegas started wringing their tails and going away at a gallop, and they spooked the elephants. We circled around this rhino but he got our wind and started trailing us. A quarter of a mile farther on, here he came. I whirled around, not wanting any rhino, but not wanting his horn rammed into me either. At 50 yards I snicked the safety and decided if he came around another bush I was going to

bust him. I was waiting to see what Mike was going to do as he was the boss. Mike pulled off his old campaign hat, heaved it at the rhino and yelled at him and the rhino turned. If he came around the next bush I intended to bust him, but he took off and we were free of another rhino. They were quite thick at times and you had to dodge them, circle around them, and keep the wind right because you never know what those animated tanks are going to do. One day we ran into a big elephant herd out at Lawrence's Waterhole. A great many bulls were among them. There was some anthills and bush so we managed to stalk them and get up on top of a big anthill and look them over. To save us we couldn't see anything over 50 or 60 pounds, so we kept the wind right and sneaked back on our back track and left them to their grazing and their noonday snooze. They feed early in the morning and about noon they like to keg up in some bush and they'd rest and sleep for a few hours. Then they'd feed out again in the afternoon towards the Galana River where they no doubt watered during the night.

Each day produced more elephant experiences—all different. Bulls came along through open bush while we were eating lunch, then when they'd get our wind they'd flap their ears, wring their tail and take off. Some in great herds of 300 to 600 and some even of 1000. Contrary to the popular opinion that big tuskers and a few askaris go off alone, these herds prove entirely different. The big bulls usually were well out in the center of the herd with cows and calves scattered all around. Those old boys were wise and knew the cows and calves would give the alarm. They were in the center of the herd usually for protection. We saw a great many skulls from the elephant control shooting of three years before. Yet all, or practically all of the other bones would be gone. The hyenas had gathered them in. How they can crack up huge bones like elephant, I don't know, but they manage to get away with them until only the old bleached skull remains where the elephant was killed. We saw three mambas crossing the road at different times in high gear, and we ran over two great vipers. The boys got out and finally located them and killed them. They are very tough snakes. One of them we ran over lying endways in the trail with both tires with the four boys and the three of us in the car, and he took off as soon as we crossed over him. Mike said the only way to kill those big snakes was to drive on them and just as you hit them, set the brakes and skid them along under the tires and that would kill them.

On the 11th we stalked some eight or ten bulls at the edge of a herd. Mike thought they'd go 70 pounds and he wanted me to shoot one, but I turned him down. I was still hoping for another great tusker like Ted's.

Gary Roberts, a ranch hunter, reported the lions were killing cows every few nights. He sat up on a kill one night and shot a lion through the heart with a .300 Winchester Magnum. The boys didn't find the lion until nearly daylight because he went about 200 yards after the heart shot. He had no mane at all. I saw quite a few gerenuk in the bush, little fellows standing on their hind legs and reaching their long necks up to flick leaves off the bush. I had no desire to kill them. Neither did Ted, and anyway we didn't want to make any sound at all to frighten the elephant.

It was hot and dry every day but in one way this was a blessing because the snakes were in countless thousands on the Galana and most of them holed up in the anthills. Mike said that in March and late February, when the rain starts, the road is literally full of poisonous snakes. Coming to camp one night Mike jammed on the brakes and said, "Christ, look at the cobra." He extended clear across the road and his head was three feet up in the air. The throat looked white. Mike said he was an Egyptian cobra. We made no attempt to molest him, and sat there in the car until he went on into the bush.

THE BACHELOR'S CLUB...

On the 12th we drove back down the Galana and on out to where we'd seen that group of bulls. We called it the Bachelor's Club. When we tried to work into the herd, however, we ran into several groups of cows and calves. The wind not being right, all we could do was work around the edge and try to dodge them. We ran into one young bull that was on the prod. We could hear him screaming and raising hell for quite a while before he got our scent. We had to back track in a hurry and run for it several times trying to get away from that youngster, and yet when we'd move from one side or the other, we'd run into more elephant kegged up. So we had a hectic time there for a couple of hours. The bush was quite tall and there was other smaller bush. We could move around in it quite well but each direction we went we'd run into more elephants. We were too far out in the herd for comfort. This day, for some reason, it

was muggy. The wind hadn't come up and we worked through quite thick brush with elephant all around us. Mike would look them over, shake his head and we'd move on. Finally we came past a herd of cows and calves on our left and five bulls kegged up under some tall trees on our right, and we came to a little open place. There in front of us was a whole troop of bulls, the ones we'd been looking for, walking slowly across our front. One of them looked very good and Mike told me to take him. When they stopped we were 55 yards from them. An intervening bush prevented my sitting down and resting my elbows on my knees as I had on my first elephant of the trip, so I had to take it offhand. Mike thought I was going to shoot him in the heart. Remembering my friend, Charley Shedd had broken the shoulder bone on one with a .470, I figured the .500 would do it as well. So I went up the left foreleg as the bull was almost broadside, traversed my sights up that shoulder until I figured it would hit the shoulder and then into the spine, and I squeezed off the left barrel. Mike shouted, "Christ," he said, "you've broken his left shoulder." It looked like the whole left side caved in and over he came. I whipped in the other barrel for the heart as he came over and he was down. He proved a beautiful bull with tusks about the same configuration as Truman's great bull, but instead of being 8' 4", mine was 7' 4". They carried their weight well, and were a beautiful pair. After we got them out and the nerves pulled we found they had 34" nerves. Back at camp that evening we weighed them at 76 and 78 pounds, my best pair.

Cutting out the ivory is a big chore, and also little Boro liked to cut into the abdomen and go in and get fat from the kidneys. When he came out he was a bloody mess. He was a small native, the top of his head coming to about the top of my shoulder, but a very powerful little man. He took one of those tusks on his shoulder, along with about 20 pounds of elephant meat in one hand and walked out. With my shots, the whole herd stampeded everywhere. You could hear elephants running and trees coming down, snapping off from the impact of great bodies as they went by. But nothing came our way and we had no trouble. Boro packed that great tusk and 20 pounds of meat in the other hand clear out to the Toyota. I wanted to go with him, but Mike signalled me to stay with them. I didn't like the idea of that little man going through that bush infested with rhino all alone, as one day when we'd sent the boys

It took two shots from Keith's .500 Boswell to down his largest elephant. The tusks ran over seven feet long.

in to look for a herd, a cow rhino had treed them for a couple of hours before she went on.

We cut out of the open bush, Mike got the Toyota, and we loaded up and headed for camp. My first slug had broken the shoulder bone and gone on into the spine which accounted for the whole left side of that bull apparently collapsing. An elephant is helpless on three legs. They can't go anywhere and you have ample time if you do need to put in other shots if you ever break a leg. When we went up to this bull he was still breathing so I put another slug into the brain through the back of the skull. This bull had a great thatch of hair on his tail on one side from which the boys at camp made me some fine bracelets. The first one I killed didn't have any hair on his tail, and Ted's elephant also had some good tail hair for making bracelets.

As Ted wanted a leopard, we killed a zebra, cut it up and hung up baits in various places and put one out at John Lawrence's Waterhole. A day later as we drove by, the boys spotted a leopard high in the top of a tree off to one side of the bait. He had been eating on it and was up this tree watching it. Of course

he disappeared into the bush. Ted took his .338-378 KT and loaded it up, Mike likewise his old .470, and they crawled into a blind the boys rigged about 60 yards from the bait tree where we'd hung part of the zebra. I took the Toyota and the boys drove on down the road a half mile and parked. It was then about three o'clock. I remember motioning to the boys and pointing to my watch that about 5:30 I told them "boom." Sure enough about 5:30 we heard Ted shoot. So we started up the Toyota and drove back up there only to see Ted and Mike coming out from the blind. My heart fell then. I thought he must have missed. Mike didn't say anything but got in the car, dug out his Browning over-under shotgun, loaded it with buck, and went back. He hadn't investigated after Ted had shot. Ted said the leopard cartwheeled out of the tree at his shot. He was up with his hind feet up above his head and reaching down to work on the bait with his head. Ted said he shot for the shoulder. They went in only to find the leopard dead as a mackerel. That 275-grain Speer, backed by 95 grains of 4831 powder, went through shoulder and spine, edging

Mike Hissey (right) admires the 76 and 78-pound tusks of Keith's elephant after some close shooting in thick brush.

it on the right side and through the right hind foot. So Ted had his leopard, a 6½-foot tom.

Ted wanted a rhino to complete the big five if he could find a good one. After killing his great bull, we'd celebrated that evening until quite late. The next day Ted had a hangover and a headache. He wanted to sleep. I was in the middle, Ted on the left and Mike driving on the right when we were coming back from Lawrence's Waterhole. We spotted a great bull rhino right in the road eating off a bush on one side. Ted was asleep. Mike stopped the car, I shook Ted awake, pointed at the rhino, and told him to load his .577 and go kill him. Mike dug out his old .470, loaded it up and they stalked up the road after the rhino. He crossed the road and went over to the left and went to feeding again. I didn't even get out of the car. I knew Ted Fowler would take care of him very easily in that open country with his big .577. They approached to about 50 yards and there was a little thorn tree with a crotch in it. Ted laid the big rifle in his left hand and the crotch of the tree and took the old rhino. He hit him just forward of the shoulder above the spine. Down the bull went in a pile. Then he started

screaming. I believe you could have heard him clear to the coast. Ted reloaded the left barrel, then he gave him both through the shoulders. One of those heavy slugs passed through the rhino and richocheted and we could hear it howling for a fraction of a second heading for the sea coast. Ted had his rhino. He was a nice one. The boys took head and cape, and all four feet for ash trays.

Several times when we were a long way from camp and out of the elephant district, we would collect a bunch of the big guinea fowl. They are beautiful birds, much bigger than the other normal guineas we found in Tanganyika on my '57 trip. I killed several of them as did Ted. The boys would bake them or boil them of an evening and we'd take them with us for lunch the next day.

I had contacted dysentery and had a hard time staying in the car for over an hour at a time before having to hit the brush. One day when we were driving along past Lawrence's Waterhole, I had reached for the toilet paper and was just going to tell Mike to stop and let me go for the brush, when Genghi pounded on the roof. Mike stopped and whispered in Swahili to him. Genghi had seen a kudu, a

258

Truman Fowler framed in camp by tusks of elephants he and Elmer shot during a 30-day safari.

good bull, back under a tall tree. Nearly every day we had seen a good bull kudu, but by the time we stopped the car and got out, they were always in the bush. We made circles trying to get a shot and they were very elusive, keeping a tree between you at all times. So I laid the toilet paper down and took Mike's .375 and we walked back up the road. Finally I spotted the kudu at what looked like 100 yards away under a big acacia. An intervening thorn bush came up high enough that I could only see his head and horns. By that time the wind was blowing in from the Red Sea at a good 20-mile clip and was puffy. I had to take it offhand. I had shot Mike's rifle once and it was dead on at a hundred yards so I figured that it would do the trick. It was fitted with an old Texan scope that Charley Askins had given him. It was an old Model 70 Winchester action. The rifle had been shot out and the English had rebarreled it. It was a good rifle. It had a post reticule. I timed the swing of the rifle and the wind and as the post started under the kudu's chin I finished the trigger squeeze. The gun went off, it backfired, filling both my eyes with dust. Then I backfired—filling my pants.

I said, "Here, Mike, take your damned rifle. It backfired." Mike grabbed it. I rubbed my eyes and when I could see I made it to the Toyota, got a water jug and a roll of toilet paper and headed for the bush for a much-needed cleanup. When I came back they had dragged the kudu out and they'd paced the distance at 105 yards. The 300-grain Winchester Silvertip .375 H&H had hit him right under the chin and gone out the back of the neck. He never knew what hit him. Mike was very excited about the head. He put his tape on it. The right horn was 30½ and the left horn 29½. He says, "Elmer, you've got yourself a record kudu."

They are a beautiful beast. In fact I believe the lesser kudu is probably one of the most beautiful antelope in all Africa. Although I like the great sable and his long symmetrical horns, nevertheless, for coloration, the lesser kudu is a beauty. He is blue in color, with white slashes across his throat, white spots on the sides of the head, white stripes down his sides, and a tail much like a white-tailed deer; tan and white underneath, and the legs from the knees down are a tan color.

The same day we were going out on the

It took only one shot offhand at 105 yards to finish this lesser kudu, who later went in the record book. Keith used a .375 H & H Magnum for the chore.

plain we ran into a bunch of Grant's gazelle and the most unexpected thing that happened on the trip, in a way. There was a lesser kudu bull a good 25 inches right among the gazelle. The wind was blowing hard and Ted took it with his .338-378. I held on to the door of the car, held it open for Ted to keep from the wind as much as he could where he sat down in the road. He took the kudu through the neck and he then had his trophy.

We drove out to the Lahli Hills on the 18th of September. We looked over a huge herd that had come out of the park and joined up with other local elephants. At the rear end of the herd was 15 or 20 bulls and some of them looked very good, though they were about three quarters of a mile away. Mike said we had better go in and investigate them. So we went back to the Toyota and drove around opposite where the herd had crossed parked the car, loaded our rifles, and were just going in when I happened to look up and there 60 yards in front of us was a mass of elephant. I couldn't see through them at all, crossing the road back into the park at a walk. I poked Mike and pointed and he jumped up on top of the Toyota with his glasses looking for big

ivory even though they were safe when they crossed that truck trace into the park. I happened to turn around and look behind us and the same thing was going on 150 yards to our rear. So I picked up a pebble and tossed it up and hit Mike and pointed. As soon as he saw that other herd going across the road behind us, he jumped down and said, "Everybody in the truck, quick." Just then ten or twelve trunks came up over the bush right in front of us twisting this way and that to get our scent. Mike put the Toyota in reverse and back down the road we went toward the herd that was crossing in our rear. This bunch of bulls came across the road then, ten or twelve of them. One old bull put his trunk down and sniffed the ground right where we had been standing, screamed and took off for the bush. About that time we heard a blast, a heavy one, and the elephants started moving in a fast walk or almost a run. Then we heard another heavy blast and the stampede was on. I saw an old cow reach down and pick up her little toto and hold him under her tusk as she crossed the road. Dust raised high in the air for a quarter of a mile. On both sides of us was this solid mass of elephant. We couldn't

Keith and Boro (right) admire Fowler's great tusks, weighing 92 and 98 pounds, after the big bull was killed by a .577 Lancaster double rifle.

see through them and don't know just how wide the herd was, but for five minutes they crossed in front of us there while we stood on the off side of the Toyota with rifles, safeties off, ready to abate all comers.

Back at camp we learned that Tony Dyer and Barry Roberts had been blasting preparatory to building a bridge across the Galana. They had put off three small shots they said that we didn't hear at all but then they fired the two heavy ones. Mike was very mad. So was Ted because had we gone on out after that little bunch of bulls at the tail end of the herd and got back out there, we wouldn't have had a prayer unless we could pile up enough elephants in front of us to turn the herd. What split the herd and turned them so that part went by on each side of the truck, we will never know. But thank God they did split. Otherwise we would have had a very tough time of it, and probably gone under. Another 15 minutes and we would have been on the edge of the herd when they turned around and headed back for the park from those blasts. Mike gave Roberts and Dyer the devil that evening about it. He was very incensed. Why they didn't tell us what they were

going to do we will never know.

Many times we would spot elephant crossing in front of us, get out and load our rifles and try to head them off. Their normal stride when they are slouching along, stepping about seven feet to the step, makes you almost run to keep up with them. My chest would hurt from the old coronary and I would sit down and signal to Boro and he'd sit down with me until my chest would stop hurting, then I would take off after the bunch again. We fought the crooked road, turns, bumps, and everything out to Little Dera Lake where for 300 yards all around the lake the bush was all tramped up with elephant. It looked like there must be 2000 or 3000 elephants watering there as well as some buffalo. But the bush was so thick and tall you couldn't see ten yards in any direction when you got out in it. Tony Dyer said he had seen a 100-pounder out there from an airplane, but we couldn't see much chance of ever getting a shot,

One day the boys spotted a young bull elephant in a waterhole. The ranch had bulldozed out great pans to catch the rain water to water the various herds of cattle. The soil was gumbo, and when we drove out this little

Wildebeest were occasionally shot for camp meat and lion bait. Keith dropped this one in 1957, with the help of Galu-Galu, a superb native tracker.

elephant was in it, just his head out, stuck in the mud. So for the rest of that day we gave up hunting, sent the boys back to the ranch to get tractors, cables and everything. We finally pulled the little bull out of the mud. He made no effort to fight. The boys cut bush to feed him but he was too far gone to feed. Probably been in there a week. He was very emaciated. Barry Roberts sat up with him that night to keep the lions off him, but the next morning he couldn't raise his head or his trunk so Barry had to shoot him to put him out of his misery.

On the 21st we drove down the Galana again to the Bachelor's Club where Ted had gotten his big elephant and I had gotten my 78-pounder. We saw one small herd that day crossing fairly open country. When they came to our truck tracks they all stopped, smelled of them and kegged up for some time. Then an old cow took the lead and went across. One bull, Mike said, would go 80 pounds but I was still hoping for a big one so I turned him down. That mythical hundred-pounder you don't get many of in a whole year in Kenya.

John Baker and his wife ran the great ranch project and were very fine congenial people.

We had them up for dinner one evening at our camp and they also had us down to their home on the Galana as well. We saw a good many rhino, but nothing like the big bull that Ted killed with 22-inch circumference of front horn and 22-inch length and a good heavy secondary horn. I didn't want a rhino, anyway, but they kept us dodging at times to keep the wind right and not disturb the beasts, especially when we were trying to find a big elephant.

Each day we would look over as many as 20 to 30 bulls, but nothing over five feet out of the lip with ivory that Mike guessed would go about 70 pounds.

On the 27th it rained and that gumbo mud was a sight. We spotted four bulls crossing the road ahead and took after them. But soon our feet were as big as snowshoes, caked with gumbo and grass until it was very hard to move. We did catch up with them and found out there was nothing over 50 pounds to the side among them so we let them go on their way. We crossed the tracks of another herd on the 27th and sent the boys in to try and locate them in the bush. A good part of the ranch was quite heavily bushed with tall trees.

They ran into an old bull buffalo and he put them up the trees. He was belligerent and wouldn't give ground. They had to stay there until he left. We wondered why they were gone so long, but it was probably a good thing we weren't there. Otherwise we would have had to shoot the buffalo because neither Ted nor Mike or I are very adept at climbing thorn trees. These elephant herds had a great many small calves, many of them not over two feet high. They couldn't have been very old and yet the old bulls were with them, all mixed up, but usually the cows and calves were on the outside perimeter of the herd and the old bulls stayed in the middle.

A SPECIAL BULL . . .

On the 28th of September we still had found no good bulls like Ted's. We drove on down the Galana to the Bachelor's Club where we'd seen more heavy ivory than any other place. While we were crossing the great plain covered with grass and a very few scattered trees, we heard a herd off to our right about a mile away. Mike and the boys went over to look them over. They sent little Boro back, his eyes shining by signs that they'd seen a big one. So Ted and I got out and took off. I couldn't keep up with Boro and I had to stop several times, my chest would hurt and whenever it did I would stop and sit down. Finally we caught up with Mike and by that time the herd had moved into a great donga. It wasn't very deep and carried heavy and tall trees with very thick bush surrounding them. We could only see a few feet. We worked up to the doubtful shade of a thorn tree some 200 yards from the edge. As far as we could see to the right and left were elephants kegged up, cows with little calves and big bulls scattered around through them. Mike had seen a big one, but by the time we got there he had moved into the dense heavy bush and we couldn't locate him. The wind was blowing in steadily so we had to keep that in our faces. We waited for a couple of hours while the elephants had their noonday siesta, then they started moving out. So we worked to the right up the donga, keeping the wind right and finally cut through above the herd. We got into the edge of the herd where we could watch them at about 100-150 yards. The whole plain was covered with elephants all feeding slowly toward the Galana. I saw one bull that had a tusk that looked like seven feet out of the lip and very slim, and the matching tusk only went half as far out, so he was out for a trophy. Then we located one

great bull and his askari standing by a thorn tree. His right tusk was very great, curved around in front of him. He'd lay his trunk on it and rest it. The left tusk was evidently shorter, they looked heavy to me. Soon along came about 15 or 20 calves. One little toto went around right underneath the old bull between his legs and the old bull paid no attention to him. We waited there until three o'clock. Never could Mike locate the big bull he'd seen that he thought might go 90 pounds with long heavy tusks. As this was the 28th and I knew it would take a day to come in and cut out the ivory, and we had to leave on the 30th, I decided I'd better take this bull. Mike estimated him at 65 and 67. Ted said 65 and 70. I thought from the looks of that ivory, he carried his weight well, that he would go quite a bit heavier. At 3:30 we hadn't seen anything better. Mike said, "So you still want to kill that bull?" I said, "I think I'd better, because we might have a remote chance of finding that big one you saw tomorrow and we might not. If I kill this one it will take them a day to get the ivory out, and leave the next day."

So we worked into the bush after all the other elephants had apparently gone except this old bull and his young askari. We worked downwind from him and got around to a little opening in the bush 65 yards from the elephant. Mike said, "Sit down." I had already done so, and I snicked the safety on my .500 Boswell. I think Mike thought I was going to shoot him in the heart. He was quartering away like my first elephant. From my earlier experience that's the shot I prefer on an elephant. The back of that great skull is square and if you aim on a line with the spine, and center that little football of a brain in that great mass of bone that comprises their head, the bullet has every chance of going through. On the side shot you have the zygomatic arch. If you're up too close, that's in the way and may turn a bullet. It happened to one friend of mine. If you're in front you have a target three inches wide and five inches high between the tusks to reach the brain as the tusks come up above the eyes. Mike thought I was going to shoot for the heart, but instead I motioned Boro and pointed to the ear. The little poacher nodded and grinned. I waited until the ear came around and it looked like to me again about six inches behind the ear hole and four inches low would center the head so I squeezed off the left barrel. Down came his rump, down came the forequarters, the trunk and tusks

Elmer with skulls of Wildebeest, Grant's gazelle, and Oryx. Salted Leopard skin is rolled up in foreground.

thrown high in the air, and he came over against the tree he'd been standing beside. He bent the tree over and I thought it would break, but the tree sprung back and threw him over on the right side. They nearly always fall on the side the bullet enters, but in this case just the opposite happened. Instantly the young bull came charging around towards us, demonstrating, wringing his trunk and tail, flapping his ears, and screaming his head off. Then between 30 and 50 more elephants came out of the bush that we didn't know were still there. They formed a quarter circle around us, all of them screaming and demonstrating, especially some old cows. Mike said shoot over their backs. He and Ted did shoot over their backs but I kept my big double loaded. I figured if this askari came in, or any of the rest of them, I was going to dump two of them. Finally an old cow picked up her little toto under her tusks and went into the bush. The others started following. But the young askari would run back out to the old bull, sniffing at his trunk and come charging back at us while we cussed him out and told him to go on. Finally he gave it up and took off after the herd.

As it was getting late, we cut the tail off the bull after looking him over and drove back to camp. The next day it took us half a day to work the truck in to him. The boys were going ahead picking up branches from thorn trees which would pierce the truck tires. When we cut out the ivory and pulled the nerves, they proved only 24-inches long, and one of them had a whole spoonful of little ivory beads in the nerve that they call elephant pearls. Mike dug them all out for me. Back at camp we weighed the tusks. I'd figured 70 and 80 and I was very close to right. The short tusk went 73 and the long crooked right tusk went an even 80 pounds, a very good elephant. That ended our elephant hunt.

The next day Barry Roberts was to drive us out. Mike Hissey had to go on back to pick up another party and go on another hunt that he had booked. So Barry Roberts loaded our four sets of ivory, the rhino head, horns, our kudu, and everything in the Land Rover and he and I, Fowler and three of the boys set out for Nairobi. We drove about thirty-forty miles inside the park, but had not yet gone over the hill and down to the Galana crossing at the guard camp. We had been passing little groups of elephants, ten, twelve, fifteen head, a few old bulls, but mostly cows and calves. The wind was blowing in from the left at about eight o'clock. Finally we passed a group of twelve to fifteen elephants on our right side, all cows and calves.

One old cow threw up her trunk, folded her ears back, screamed, and here she came.

They are wise. She didn't head right at the truck. She headed up the road to intercept us. I don't know why to this day Barry didn't shift gears and pour on the coal. We were lugging uphill with all that load of ivory and six of us in the Land Rover, and the old cow was headed for us wide open. Barry Roberts looked around when she was about 50 yards behind and he said, "Bug off you old bitch," but he still didn't shift gears. When I looked around she was 30 yards behind us and gaining. Our guns were all cased, packed up, our ammunition was all packed up. We didn't have a thing to fight with and didn't have a prayer if she caught us. Then Barry started pulling away from her slightly. But she chased us another 300 yards up the road, screaming her head off, wringing that trunk and reaching for us. Finally she gave it up, turned, and headed back for the little group of cows and calves. We went on over the hill toward the Galana River and had a flat tire. What would

Buffalo can take a lot of killing at times. This last buffalo Keith shot in 1957 took a shoulder shot and a heart shot from a .476 Westley Richards double before piling up.

have happened if we had had that flat tire going up that grade with that old devil after us can best be left to imagination.

In 1971, Fowler went back. He asked me to go, but Mrs. Keith was not feeling too well so I turned down the trip. He went back to the Galana again to try for a hundred pounder. Again he had Macaou, Boro and Genghi along and Mike Hissey, the white hunter. Conditions have changed greatly, he told me, since we were there. Now the place was full of poachers and Mike had found several poached elephant that the boys had not been able to contact and get the ivory. The poison was probably too weak and they'd gone too far. They reported it to the game department but they hadn't done anything at that time. Poaching got so bad that all the old bulls were out in the middle of the herds and cows were on the rampage around the edges at the slightest sound or smell of a human being. Ted said that even then if a group of elephant came to a truck trace, or if they smelled the track of a native as well as a white, they'd turn and stampede back on their track. He finally picked out one bull for insurance how-ever that went 65 and 66 in a bunch of 15 or

20. He clobbered him in the neck as his head was covered with bush, and the heart and shoulder shot too, but he could see through to the neck so he slipped him the .577 in the neck, killing him instantly. By the time he had reloaded the rifle, the other bulls in the herd came right back past them. They got behind a tree and Ted said they went by close enough that he could have touched them with his gun barrel, stampeding in their back track on account of all the poaching going on. Ted said they saw some they thought would go 80 or 90 pounds, but always out in the middle of a herd and there was so many belligerent cows out around the perimeter that they could never work in. One old gal chased them until he and Mike were all in and they had to run many times to dodge these old cows. This was caused by the poachers working on them constantly due to the high price of ivory, as good ivory had gone to $10 a pound on the ivory market in Mombasa. So Ted came out with this one 65 and 66 pounder and swore he'd never go back to the Galana again. Since then Mike Hissey wrote that the elephants had killed three poachers, the buffalo had killed another one, and the game department had

Tom Siatos, publisher of Guns & Ammo magazine took this 49½-inch buffalo with a custom Mauser in .460 G&A.

over Africa. The elephants, however, seem to be on the increase wherever they have been protected. In fact they've increased until they've destroyed the range and the only answer is control shooting.

Each year thousands of acres of bush is cleared and the game killed to make room for more natives to plant crops and raise their villages. This in turn forces the elephants into ever smaller areas until the various parks where they are protected are, in the main, overloaded with elephant. We heard of four girls in a Land Rover touring the park down in Rhodesia. They came on to a herd of elephant and very foolishly drove right up in the midst of the herd, in the edge of it. One old bull got curious and came over and smelled of the car, put his trunk on the radiator and got it burned from the hot radiator. Instantly he turned the Land Rover upside down and smashed it and the four girls to a pulp. They said the whole oufit was no higher than the frame when he got through stomping it.

THE PROBLEM OF TAXIDERMY...

Back at Nairobi I turned the lesser kudu and my elephant tusks all over to Major Rowe of Rowland Ward, who had taken care of dipping and shipping my trophies in '57 and did a very fine job of it. They arrived home safely and at less cost than the shipment from Kampala that Jonas Bros. shipped on a couple of buffalo heads, a roan head, and some hippo ivory. Ted, however, took his trophies to a local taxidermist in Nairobi and he did about the worst job of mounting his great rhino of any I have ever seen, not a wrinkle in the skin, that front horn separated and anchored with screws when it arrived home. His 6½-foot leopard was turned into a rug, but eight-feet long and you can imagine how wide. The ivory however, they did a nice job on it, setting it up on pedestals. I would advise all Americans hunting East Africa to take their trophies to Major Rowe of Rowland Ward and have him ship them direct to the States and have a local taxidermist here do the work.

Arriving back in Nairobi, I found I had a three-day wait before I could get out on a plane that would take me direct from Africa to New York, and I certainly didn't want to go back through Greece and have trouble there as we did coming over from the states. A Baptist minister friend asked me to come on and get out of the hotel, go home with him and go fishing, which I accepted. I took a lot of pictures of the massive bird life at Lake

rounded up most of the rest of them and put them in the pokey for five years and he said things were getting back to normal on the Galana again.

In spite of the hives, dysentery and all the hard work, this was the greatest hunt I was ever on. I know in that time, the 30 days, we must have looked over 3000 to 4000 different elephants and God knows how many bulls we saw of 30 to 60 pounds that we turned down. Last year's drought killed elephants by the thousands. The ranch alone picked up seven tons of ivory from dead elephants. What the future is of those great herds I do not know, but they have already destroyed most of the bush, and most of the timber in the Tsavo Park is now grassland. In last year's drought the grass didn't grow, so the elephant didn't have much to feed on and that was what caused the enormous loss. Several thousand elephants died of starvation and malnutrition. Much of Africa formerly teeming with game is now a thing of the past. Native villages have sprung up where John Lawrence and I had our camps in '57. The same is going on all

Here Elmer demonstrates correct shooting form with his .500 Boswell. Notice that the left hand grasps the side-by-side barrels ahead of the wooden forend.

Naivasha and another lake between there and Nairobi.

We hired a boat and went out bass fishing. It had an outboard motor, but it was connected up with controls in the front seat. We drove it up the lake about 12 miles, caught some bass, and then the wind came up. We moved into the shelter of a bunch of islands covered with papyrus. Many of them were just floating islands of papyrus. My minister friend hung his bass plug on a root of that so he said, "Take my rod and reel in while I start the motor and run the boat out." I got up on the bow, standing on the deck and was reeling in when he started the motor, but bless Moses, the boat was set for high gear. Instantly, when the motor caught, the boat shot out from under me, throwing me high in the air. I came down on the gunwale just in front of the motor on my right side breaking two ribs off close to my spine. He grabbed me and pulled me into the boat and got the motor stopped.

Then, with about ten miles of lake to traverse, the wind came up and the waves were three feet high, so we had to pound that all the way back to the boat dock. However he was a great guy. He went into the tavern, got me a double shot of scotch and some aspirin to relieve the pain. Then we drove back to his home at the mission. I couldn't eat except a little ice cream that night. The next day I was still sick but I had to get back to Nairobi for that plane. He got me there, got a wheel chair, got my big rifle through customs, and wheeled me out to the plane. I paid another $316 to change my ticket to first class so that I could sit up in the front of the plane and not have to move too much. I was in misery. I couldn't eat and I couldn't sleep, those two broken ribs were gnawing all the way.

They got me back to New York and I got another wheel chair to wheel me around through customs. I'd had my big rifle turned over to the captain of the plane and the steward brought it to me when we got off. They had a wheel chair for me, so I went through customs with my .500 Boswell in its case lying across my knees. At Salt Lake they phoned my son, Ted, in Boise to meet the plane there. Got another wheel chair and took me off the plane and wheeled me around and Ted met me, took me home and I spent three days with them recuperating. Finally, I was able to eat a little food and keep it down. I finally got home from my last safari in Africa. I was too sick all the way home to eat the fine dinners prepared on the plane, and about all I could do was sip a little scotch whisky. Back home it was still several months before those broken ribs healed and quit hurting me.

After Truman Fowler's 1971 elephant hunt on the Galana, he wrote me that the old cow that had given us such a fright in the Tsavo Park had moved down on the Galana. She had chased the ranch manager and his wife for some distance up the road. They had finally outrun her and got away from her. Mike and Ted had gone out to the Lahli Hills one morning and, bless Moses, this old cow took after them. She chased them down the road, but because it was fairly straight there they outran her. Then they got out, loaded up the guns, went back and Ted gave her a 750-grain solid through the brain which settled her. There was no mistake about it being the same old cow elephant because her tusks crossed and one of them was longer than the other and they had worn together. The last look I had at the old gal was out of a Land Rover at 30 yards and she was screaming bloody murder and coming for us in the park in '69 Ted had a bracelet made from her tail feathers and sent it to me as a memento of the old elephant. Several months after getting home my ivory trophies came in and now I have them mounted and on the walls.

Chapter 8

RANDOM THOUGHTS

Most of my adult life I have been experimenting with all manner of arms and ammunition. In the .41 Magnum I wanted a 220-grain bullet, but Remington came out with a 210-grain softnose. I also asked them for a softer, lighter load for police use at close quarters in the cities. Earl Larsen brought out a lead bullet load at around a thousand foot-seconds for this. On a full load it develops 1400 fps or a bit over with the 210-grain.

I later designed a bullet for Hensley & Gibbs of Murphy, Oregon, makers of some of the finest bullet molds in America. One was a 220-grain for the .41 Magnum, an exact copy of my .38 Special and .357, .44 Magnum, and .45 Colt bullets. They came out with a beauty of 220 grains. I worked up a load of 20 grains of 2400 for my guns. In some of the guns we tested, it showed pressures a trifle high. Maybe they were chambered different or had a little tighter bore, but the 20 grains of 2400 made the 220 Hensley & Gibbs bullet shoot perfectly in my pair of guns. It also works perfectly in the 4⅝-inch Ruger that Bill Ruger sent me. In spite of some arms critics saying that the cartridge never got off the ground, or it died a-borning, Earl Larsen of Remington, and the Smith & Wesson officials, as well as Ruger, tell me they have been back ordered in both guns and ammunition, since it was first brought out. A great many police outfits, sheriffs' departments, and highway patrols, adopted the .41 Magnum as a standard police gun.

Smith & Wesson brought it out both in a fixed-sighted standard police model as well as a target sighted model. Ruger brought it out in a Blackhawk target model. Personally I have no use for any six-gun without adjustable target sights.

Back in the 30's I worked for D.D. King of the King Gunsight Company at San Francisco in the development of a long range pistol sight. It was a square flat-topped blade, but with three gold inserts down the face facing the shooter. One at the top, one at the middle, one lower on the front sight blade, to give the shooter a definite aiming point for long range. You could hold up the second bar for longer than point-blank range, and for extreme range the third gold bar was held level with the top of the rear sight blade, giving you an exact elevation.

Enough shooting at various ranges soon enables the shooter to learn which bar to hold up level with the top of the rear sight. It is

Lorraine and Elmer Keith with dog Stub and two sheep trophies in 1960.

very effective and for a time Smith & Wesson fitted some of these sights to their guns.

COYOTE KILLS . . .

While the little lady and I were paying for our ranch on time with beef and turkeys that she raised, I made a good part of our living hunting and trapping coyotes and other fur. At that time I used the heavy bull gun for my coyote shooting. Wanting a definite aiming point for various ranges, I had Bill Weaver fit the double crosshairs in his scope with a six-inch spacing at 100 yards. The top wire for a lot of rifles would be sighted dead on at 200 yards when the bottom wire would come on at 400. With higher velocity rifles up in the 3000-foot bracket with long heavy bullets, we could sight the top wire for 300 yards and the bottom would come on at 500. This worked out very well, holding for rifles around 2700 feet, sighting in for 200, and using the top wire for 300 yards, and the bottom for 500- and holding halfway between for 400 yards.

Keith firing a custom 25-pound rifle shooting .50 caliber B.M.G. cartridges. The rifle, made by Al Weber of Lodi, California, was tested in 1967.

270

I made some very long coyote kills as well as big game using this arrangement. Weaver called this reticule his range finder, as the six-inch spacing between crosswires could be used on an animal like a deer of around 18-inches from the chest to the top of the back. If you filled the spacing in there, then you knew he was 300 yards away. It worked out quite well. However, full use of the double crosswires did not come into being until much later when R.W. Thomson, an old guide from Glenwood Springs, Colorado, and an old Navy combat flier as well, inaugurated his two dot system, a big dot on the crosswire for point-blank range, and a small dot, the center of which was 6-inches from the center of the upper dot. Then in conjunction with Redfield variable-power scopes, he worked out the finest sighting system for long range of any yet to date on sporting rifles. It works equally well on Weaver scopes with my double crosshair reticule. The top wire can be sighted on heavy rifles from around 2800 to 3000-foot-second velocity at three-inches high at a hundred and they are practically on at 300 yards. Then you can hold between the upper crosswire and the lower one for 400-yard shooting. At 500 yards, use the lower crosswire, and turn the scope back to 7X for 600 yard range.

If you want to go to 600 yards, instead of holding over with the bottom dot you can turn the scope power ring back from 9 to 7 power and be on at 600.

With rifles of less velocity the change is different, but it can be worked out on any modern rifle, so you can have a definite aiming point, both for point blank and for long range shooting.

R.W. Thomson, Keith, and Dale Williams examine the first Keith grade Champlin and Haskins rifle in .458 Winchester. Keith designed the rifle for Jerry Haskins.

Thomson checked it out with several men who had never fired at long range before and had them hitting the black at 200 to 600 yards within a few day's practice. The system works equally well with Weaver scopes of 2 x 7, 3 x 9, 4 x 12 power, just as it does with Redfield scopes of similar power, and will work out with others so long as they have the two dots or the double crosswire for six-inch spacing. We proved that beyond a shadow of a doubt both on target and on long-range elk and deer shooting.

Redfield also put a range finder in the top of their variable power scopes, especially a 3 x 9, and 4 x 12. You can put an animal between those upper crosswires and then at the bottom of the scope on the right hand side, read off the range. If you know the spacing, that is the distance from the bottom of the chest to the top of the back, and on most game animals it proves very accurate. This is in connection with Thomson's system, changing the power, and cutting it back for longer range. As the power is cut back, so the spacing is wider.

I've done a good deal of long-range antelope shooting both here and the plains of Africa. Of course, every real hunter likes to get as close to his game as is humanly possible, and should always do so whenever terrain permits closer stalking. There are times however, when it's a long-range shot across canyons, and there's not a Chinaman's chance of ever getting close to anything. When such an opportunity presents itself, with a good long-range rifle and scope, and enough work on the range to verify your holdings, you can still lay down or get a rest and make a clean kill where it would be impossible with poor sighting equipment.

Bullet construction has always interested me. Back in the black-powder days, when we used a bullet of 1 to 16 tin and lead temper and of moderate velocities, there was no problem. It would expand so much. Also in the days of 2200-2300 fps velocities with the old .30-40 Krag 220-grain, the .30-30 with 170-grain bullet, .35 Winchester 250-grain, the .405 300-grain, no problems existed because those bullets would expand out to about the limit of their effectiveness and dig a uniform wound channel through anything they hit. They were very reliable. But with the coming of high velocity and trick bullets, trouble started. Many of them would blow up at short range, or they would fail miserably to expand at long range. And that problem still presents itself today though our bullet makers have come a long way towards solving the problem with many of our new bullets. I designed bullets for Western Tool & Copper Works and others in various calibers. Gilding metal jackets are rather brittle. At extreme high velocity the point tends to fragment. I've long felt that a pure copper jacket was much better, like those made by Fred Barnes that will furl back in strips, as they split on the land cuts, rather than fragment and blow into little pieces. They just furl back with the lead adhering to them, making them much more reliable for game shooting.

Over the years I have carried a good six-gun. First it was a .32-20 caliber, later came a .38-40, .45 Colt, .44 Special and still later .44 and .41 Magnums. The six-gun is a firearm of opportunity. If you have it with you all the time, you will find many opportunities to use it on game. I've killed over 40 head of big game with a six-gun; elk, caribou, deer, mountain goat, bear, and an endless variety of the smaller game. I've also killed flying birds with them. If you shoot enough, and know your gun well enough, you have a lot more "accidents" like that of downing a bird flying at a hundred yards or more. Most people say and feel that it's impossible to hit something of that sort with a 4-inch barrel six-gun. However, they probably haven't used one as much as some of us old timers and don't know its possibilities.

In 19 and 49 when I was 50 years old I decided to quit the guiding business and stop booking parties. I decided to do some hunting on my own, and take it easier the rest of my life. I'd had enough backpacking in heads and quarters of meat, and decided it was time I got in some hunting on my own instead of guiding dudes over the hills and following up their crips. After moving to town in '48 and getting a good home in Salmon, I had a lot more opportunities to work with, experiment, and test various guns, ammunition, and to help develop even more. Also I had more time for steelhead and salmon fishing, something I like very much. I miss my old 800-yard benchrest range down at the ranch, but we do have another benchrest some six-seven miles out of town, and a good range there where I usually do my test work.

SEMINAR HOPPING...

A number of years ago, Winchester started holding annual seminars and bringing the gun editors of America together to show them their new developments in arms and ammunition and give them a chance to test it on game, either at Nilo, where they have their big game farm, or else take them other places. One time they took us over to Italy where we shot on the King's estate and later my group went to Portugal for shooting red-legged partridge, which is a European chukar. This was a great trip. On another trip we were taken down to Cabo San Lucas on the very lower end of Baja California. Part of the group was to fish one day while the others flew over to the mainland and shot doves. My group went fishing. I managed to get a 155-pound blue marlin that day and had one hell of a fight with him. It took an hour. The sea was fairly rough, with 8 to 10-foot swells, and when we came up on top, at times I could see my fish. Lots of times he was out 200 yards from the boat and we counted 15 times that he went straight up in the air and shook himself and fell back. Then he sounded twice and I thought I'd never get him up. The reel seat

This 155-lb. blue marlin gave Elmer an hour's fight before it was landed off the coast of Cabo San Lucas, Mexico, during a Winchester seminar.

was not very substantial. The reel got around on the lower end of the rod. Likewise there was a chair for me to sit in in the back of the boat, but there was no belt, and there was no straps to go around my shoulder to the eyes on the reel. Whenever the fish would go over to the side, he'd jerk me into the scuppers.

When he was directly behind the boat I could set down and rest while I cranked on the reel and worked on him, but it was a tough fight. Jim Rikhoff of Winchester got a 160-pounder that day, and Larry Kohler caught both a sail and a blue marlin that day. We had a grand fishing day. The next day the weather socked in and we couldn't go over to the mainland for our dove shoot, so we went fishing again. My boat had no luck that day, though Slim Pickens had a strike and thought he had hooked him, but the fish threw the bait, hook and all. Others did better and it was quite an eventful trip.

When we had landed in Mexico and gone through customs there was half a dozen boys came out in full Mexican regalia with their guitars. Another half dozen boys had trays of margaritas. We'd had no breakfast and we had half of a chicken sandwich apiece and a bottle of whiskey in each plane to nibble on. Those margaritas tasted very much like lemonade. My good friend, the late Pete Kuhlhoff was in the plane with me. He had several and I had three, I believe, at this airport. In all I drank eight drinks practically on an empty stomach. Pete Kuhlhoff told me he drank thirteen. Then Jim Rikhoff of Winchester told us to go to our rooms and dress because there was going to be a formal dinner and they'd present their new arms, which they did.

I finally got to my room and just kinda sat down on the floor. Big Pete Kuhlhoff, being wiser than I, backed up to his bed until he could get ahold of it with both of his huge hands and sat down. I says, "Pete how are you doing?"

He said, "Elmer, I'm drunker than a skunk."

I said, "So am I. But we must make this dinner. That's what they brought us down here for."

I managed to get down a flight of stairs into the bathroom, had a cold shower, then a hot one, then a cold one until it sobered me up. I went back to the room and Pete said, "I can't make it."

I pulled him off the bed, took him in the shower, gave him the hot and cold treatment, and he came out of it too. After that, however, we decided to stay on scotch and soda if

273

The most famous names in gun writing a few years ago gathered for a picture at a Winchester seminar, including (standing, from left) Bill Edwards, John Amber, Pete Kuhlhoff, Warren Page, Jack O'Connor, and Elmer Keith. Front row, from left, are Ray Ovington, Larry Kohler, Tom Siatos, Pete Brown, and Jack Seville.

we wanted a drink and leave those margaritas alone. I remember Jim Rikhoff had warned us, "Margaritas are not senoritas."

On the European trip we found much of interest in Portugal, the old castles on every hill, the quaint two-wheeled carts which they all went around in, the women working in the fields wearing flat-crowned, flat-brimmed black hats. The industry there seemed to be mostly cork trees, and olives for oil. There was huge olive and cork tree groves. The aristocracy had fine homes. Usually back of each one was a pigeon range.

They do a lot of shooting in Portugal as well as in Italy. In fact, we were informed when Winchester showed us their new shot shell plant in Italy that Italy actually used more shotgun shells every year than did the whole of the United States.

Shotgun hunting is popular in Portugal, as Keith discovered when he hunted there during a Winchester seminar.

On the 13th seminar, Winchester took us down to Altair, Texas for a goose shoot. It was all small geese, blues, specks, lesser Canadas and snow geese. We had a grand time and a very good goose shoot.

We put out an acre of white pillow slips, plastic sheets, and one thing and another to simulate snow geese in the field. However, the two days we shot there I didn't see any geese decoy to those white sheets. For some reason it was all pass shooting. Our five managed to collect 19 the first day, and we filled out the second day as well.

It was a grand goose shoot. These little geese would run around four pounds, or possibly five for some of the specks, but they were very fine table birds, and fat as seals, as they were feeding in the rice fields. We had a wonderful time down there.

Each year at these seminars we were given a chance to test all their latest developments in ammunition and arms. The point was to give us an advance look at everything before it was put on the market, to get our criticisms and our opinions. I believe these seminars have proved not only beneficial to all arms editors of the country, but to the company itself, as many of the boys come up with new ideas at each session.

Remington started seminars a little later on. For many years they took us to the game farm in Maryland out of Great Oaks. There we had fabulous goose shoots every year. The honkers land by the thousands on a little lake in a preserve on the Remington game farm. They have bought up a bunch of the old colonial homes and farms there and turned them all into a huge game farm, different but similar in its ultimate ideas to Nilo that Winchester has out of Alton, Illinois. The quaint old colonial buildings, many of them built in the 16th century, are still in good condition with very steep stair cases, and tiny little doors. Evidently the people of that age were smaller than the present line. The little churches and old graveyards have many graves dating back to the 16th century on their headstones. One year Remington took the group of us up to Maine for a waterfowl shoot. However, we arrived there in bad weather and the ducks and geese, with the exception of some fish ducks and mergansers, had already turned and gone south. So that was kind of a dry run as far as shooting was concerned.

Another time, however, Remington took us down to the YO ranch in Texas, allowing each man a little Texas whitetail buck and a turkey gobbler. That was a great time.

Grits Gresham and I hunted together. They gave us a 6mm Remington rifle, which I don't consider a big-game gun at all. One hundred grain ammunition, scope sighted, and they said it was targeted in. Grits took his buck, four points on the side, which they called an eight-pointer down there, and we here in the Northwest call a four-pointer. At any rate he was 80 yards broadside. Grits shot him right over the heart. He jumped, kicked at his belly, ran about 50 yards and piled up. On opening him we found the 100-grain bullet had exploded in the chest cavity, made a mess of heart and lungs, but hadn't even touched the opposite rib cage.

Later that morning we jumped a doe and a five pointer, (five points on each side). I whistled and he stopped at about 80 yards, so I took the little rifle and laid it right over the knuckle on his left foreleg for a heart shot and squeezed one off. Like Grits' buck, he jumped, kicked at his belly and took off. But he only ran about 40-50 yards as the guide screamed at me to shoot him again, and I told him it wasn't necessary. If the gun was any good he was a dead deer. About that time he started running in a circle and piled up. We found the same identical performance. The little 100-grain bullet exploded inside but didn't even get to the other ribs. To my notion the .30-30 would be a better all-around gun for these little deer because sooner or later you are going to have to take a raking shot and anything that will blow up in the lung cavity without touching the other rib cage certainly wouldn't reach the vitals from a raking shot.

In the afternoon we hunted turkeys. We were lucky to see a big bunch of gobblers run into some oak brush. The guide had us in a Scout with the top removed. He took us over logs, rocks and everything in second gear around this bunch of oaks, as the turkeys were coming out on the other side and taking off. We each got a nice 17-pound gobbler with one shot each, so we didn't use much Remington ammunition down there.

Our little deer, the first time I'd had an opportunity to shoot a Texas whitetail, went 98 pounds for Grits' 4-pointer, and 103 pounds for my five-pointer, with the entire intestinal tract, lungs, heart removed, but the feet still left on. So they are tiny little deer.

At one Winchester seminar at Nilo, we shot International trap and normal trap, as well as shooting quail, chukars, and pheasant that had been turned out, and flighted mallards.

I understood my old friend, Townsend Whelen lived in St. Louis nearby. So one sem-

The YO Ranch in Texas provides hunting for deer and other more exotic animals, including this ibex Keith bagged while hunting with guide Button Forehand.

inar I proposed to the Winchester boys that they go get the Colonel and bring him out for dinner and let him meet all the new crop of arms editors. This they did. Colonel Whelen had a great time with us. He put on my hat and paraded around the building there, enjoyed the pheasant dinner with us, and had a great time. He was one of the grand old men of the gunwriting profession.

These seminars are usually largely shotgun shooting. They also show us all rifle developments too, though seldom do we have a chance to try them out except down in Texas when we got a chance to shoot deer. The late Major Charles Askins, father of Colonel Charles Askins of today, taught me more about shotgun ballistics than any other man.

We corresponded at great length for many years. I also have his Magnum 10-bore, the first Magnum 10-bore ever built by Ithaca. Also his special 16 bore that was built with all the extras that Ithaca could put on it. Both guns were full choke, both fine shooting guns, and the guns I use today by preference to my Westley Richards, Purdy, and everything else I have. The Major was a big man, and why his guns fit me I don't know. They were stocked with a 14¼ inch length of pull, which fits me exactly, although I am a much smaller man. I have done some of my best shooting with these guns.

TED FINDS A WIFE . . .

Son Ted was around twelve years old when

we moved to town from the ranch. After he finished high school he wanted to marry his girl friend, and take a job as a grease monkey at a local garage. I was against it. Iver Henriksen, a gunsmith from Missoula and a lifelong friend, happened to be with me. Mrs. Keith was down to Weiser with her folks. I told Ted, nothing doing. I said, "You are too young to get married and if you get married now all you'll have is a grease monkey's job the rest of your life, possibly working up to be a good mechanic. You've got to go to college, get an education, get a job so you can support a woman and a family, and it would be much to your advantage to do so."

Ted says, "Well, I haven't the money for college."

I told him, "You get out and work, save all the money you can each summer, and I'll put up the rest. I haven't much money either, but between us we'll manage." Iver Henriksen gave him the same advice. So in the morning he said, "Dad, do you still mean what you told me?" I said, "I do," and we shook hands on it.

He put in three years in the Forest Service at lookouts, the first two on a lookout on Sage Creek, then one on Bear Trap, and he put in a summer as assistant to the ranger down at Indianola. Then he went into the smokejumpers, put in two years out of McCall, Idaho.

When he was seventeen he wanted to enlist in the National Guard. Lorraine was against it, but I was all for it, having served two hitches in the National Guard, and I figured they did me no harm and I learned a lot. So I insisted he go ahead and join, which he did. All told, he put in nine years in military service. The last years, when he was going to camp down in California, one of the officers informed him, he said, "Ted Keith, you're already out of it. You turn around and go home. You have your papers, you've put in your time."

While down at Fort Bragg, in the Green Beret outfit, jumping, he had a lot of experience. Another time he came back from some fort in Carolina, I believe it was, and he was alive with chigger bites. There wasn't two inches square on his whole body that didn't have chiggers under the skin. I went to the drugstore and the druggist fixed me up a concoction, made him take a hot bath, and rubbed that on three days straight to kill all the chiggers.

I told Ted to study for a doctor and he'd get rich quick.

"Nope," he says, "I'm not going to be looking down both ends of people and doing that."

"Well," I says, "be a dentist."

"Nope," he says, "I'm not going to be looking down their necks either."

So I told him, "You go ahead and pick out any profession you want, but get your sheepskin."

Ted Keith leaves his lookout tower for a walk through the woods, followed by Stub and his two canteens of water.

When Ted was 12, he helped his Dad lead a pack string out of Sheep Creek after a successful elk hunt.

He put in two years, then came down with bad tonsils which had to be extracted and he lost a whole semester. But he went back and finished up.

While I was at a Winchester seminar at East Alton, Illinois, I received a wire from him. He said, "Betty and I are getting married the 13th." I just had time to come home and drive the wife down to Nampa to take in his big wedding.

Ted was jumpmaster for his squad while he was in the smokejumpers. Also while in one of his camps down in Carolina, he was to take his squad out and lose himself while the other squads hunted for him, and live off the land. Ted told me he found a good hideout on a mountain, and found a little hill farmer there who made good moonshine and would supply them with some chicken and eggs, so they did quite well. When the week was up, they hadn't been caught or contacted by the squads that were hunting for him, and he led his squad in, tied up the guards, and went in and reported, much to the discomfort of the other squads that were sent out to catch him.

He took accounting and business management at college, got his sheepskin, and now is the internal auditor for the big Boise College, and is also a C.P.A. Needless to say we are proud of the lad.

When he first brought his girl over from Moscow, he phoned me and he said, "Dad, can I bring my girl home?" I didn't even know he had another girl.

I usually get up from two to four o'clock in the morning due to my many years of punching cows, and 30 years guiding. I got up and went downtown for a pot of tea. A light skim of snow had come. Ted and his girl came in late that night, in fact early morning. We told him over the phone which room to put his girl in, and he could sleep in another room. When I went out that morning, I found the long slim tracks of a woman beside Ted's tracks where they got out of the car and came in the house. I heard them come in and I got up soon afterward. The next morning I told Ted I'd saved the duck shooting until he came home so we could hunt together. His girl, Betty Swain, asked if she could go along. So we hunted her up some of my outdoor pants, heavy underwear, a parka and some oversize boots with a lot of socks. We all went duck hunting.

Mom and I got on a good pass while Ted and Betty hunted the creek down the Lemhi. We got a nice bunch of ducks that day. When we came home, I took all the ducks to the basement, and got out tubs to save the feathers, as I always saved duck and goose feathers. Lorraine makes pillows from them. Ted got a knife and axe and chopped the wings and legs off. Then Betty come around and she says, "I want a sharp knife, Elmer." So I gave what she asked for.

The next thing I knew she was in the sink cleaning ducks. There is not much worse a job a woman can get into, but she went at it with vim. The next morning as I came out for breakfast, Ted says, "Dad, can I keep her?"

I says, "Anytime, Ted."

He gave me an answer while I was at the Winchester seminar. Later on they had three girls: Heather, Heidi, and Holly; beautiful little girls.

BETTY WINS THE IVORY...

I had one set of elephant tusks hanging on the wall that I killed in '57, with one tusk broken off about eighteen inches. After my last trip to Africa, Betty said, "Why won't you let Ted and I have one of these sets of ivory? Let us have the one on the wall." So I told them I'd loan them to them. Lorraine and I hauled them down there in the back of our Cad. Ted and Betty cleaned off a wall and hung the ivory up. They were very proud of those tusks.

I told Betty, she was cooking breakfast, I said, "Now if you'd come up with a grandson, I'd give you that ivory." I thought she was going to throw the skillet at me. She says, "Three kids is enough."

However, the next October Ted told me one day, he says, "Dad, we've got an eight pound boy." I said, "Tell Betty she won the ivory." They named the little lad Gregor William Keith. He is doing fine this date.

THE CORONARY...

In '67 I had a bad coronary.

I had two small attacks first, didn't know what it was or what was the matter with me. Finally, one day while talking and answering questions with a couple of gun cranks that had come over from Missoula, Montana, I had a good one. It felt just like an old Masai had throwed a spear through the center of my chest. I laid down on the floor too sick to even move. Lorraine called Doc Blackadar. He arrived in his car within a few minutes, gave me a shot and some pills, and says, "Shuck your boots and your six-gun. You're going to the hospital."

I was there 22 days.

For several days they didn't think I'd make

Heidi, (left), Betty, Ted, Gregor, Heather, and Holly Keith at home in Idaho, sit beneath "Betty's ivory" for a picture.

it. They had me under an oxygen tent. I put in quite a tough session. After 22 days they wheeled me back on a cart again and packed me in the house, and gave me a wheel chair to set up in. I tried to get around corners and doors with that thing. Finally one day I hung up on the corner of the door again and I caught hold of the wall and pulled myself up until I was standing. I gave the wheelchair a kick and it folded up. I told little Mom, I said, "Take it back to the hospital. I'm going on my own from here on, win or lose."

I did. I could only travel eight or ten yards at a time and would have to stop, as my chest would hurt. I persisted, and kept going. Jack Nancolas took me out deer hunting. We'd driven way up a ridge into the edge of the timber with his Scout, looking for deer. Jack walked down below me a short space, probably 50 yards from me, and waved for me to come down quick. He had a big buck spotted at nice range. I took off but I could only go about a third of the way and I had to stop and rest even though it was downhill, then set

off again. By the time I got to Jack, the buck had disappeared.

Farther down the ridge that day we ran onto another buck. He ran off 200 yards and stopped. I got out my .338. Jack said, "Head or nothing." "Well," I said, "Will you continue to haul me around until I get another shot if I miss?"

He said, "I will. Head or nothing."

So I put the crosshair right under the chin. The 275-grain Speer landed on the inside of the right eye and out the back of his head. I had my buck for that fall.

Then Jerry Haskins of Champlin & Haskins phoned me from Enid, Oklahoma. He said, "Elmer, I've designed a rifle action that I believe is superior to anything on the market. Will you come down, at our expense, and design a rifle to go around it? We want the best that you can possibly design."

I told him I would as soon as I got through with the Remington and Winchester seminars and gained a little strength. We were hauled out in cars at the Remington seminar to our

Their 50th wedding anniversary in 1976 found Elmer and Lorraine Keith "all duded up" for a special party at their home in Salmon, Idaho.

goose blinds and had a good goose shoot. Out at Winchester it was raining. The first day they insisted I stay and shoot trap. I know nothing of trap, never shot enough of it to even learn the positions. However I did manage to get 22 at International Trap. Those birds would really get out and go and you could swing with them and hit them. With the regular 16-yard trap they go like hell for a few feet, fall off, and I think I was overshooting the straightaways. When they went to the side, I could get them easy enough, but the straightaways I knew I was losing for elevation. Whether I was shooting over or under I never knew. However, the next day the dog handler at Nilo says, "Elmer, you get in the truck with the dogs and I. You can walk along these paved roads here while we work these strips of corn, millet, and one thing and another, because a lot of birds come across the road." Quite a lot of them did, and I had a good time downing every bird that came across the road.

Another time at Nilo we arrived there after

an awful sleet storm. All the limbs broke off the trees, and little twigs were as big as your finger all coated with ice. There was also six inches of snow on the ground. It was impossible to turn birds out in that and hunt them with dogs. We had a good flight of mallards where they'd kick them out of the tower, they'd sail over the blinds and down into a little lake. That worked out fine. But for the pheasant shoot they decided to put everybody down in a deep draw heavily timbered while the truck backed up to the edge, some 50 to 75 feet above and level with the top of the draw, and they'd fold the pheasants wings up and throw them to start them flying out over the timber.

The Winchester people asked the dog handlers who they wanted for backup gun to get up on the other bar in timber in back of this timber-choked draw or gulch. They said, "We'll take that cowpuncher with the big hat," meaning me. I waded through the snow with Cotton, the dog handler, and old Lucian Carey, and we parked about 50-60 yards back

Lorraine and Elmer Keith ford the Middle Fork of the Salmon River in 1958, where Keith crossed with the Zane Grey hunting party 27 years before.

of the draw. From where they were throwing the birds it was too easy, and there was Bill Talley, Jim Rikhoff, and Johnny Falk of Winchester, plus all the gun editors down in the bottom of that draw, all good shots. They killed every bird that was thrown that came over them, and I'd raise my gun, see them coming, down the birds would go, and I would take my gun down. Finally they decided that was too easy, so they moved the truck and the pheasants to a higher point and farther to the left with more timber. Then they started throwing them. I let two birds go by. I'd gotten tired of raising my gun and taking it down again. Cotton says, "Keith, I want you to kill those birds, don't let them get loose, because they will freeze to death this winter anyway. They're pen-raised."

I said, "Where can I start taking them?" He said, "If they come by that big dead snag in front, you take them." I downed the next 15 birds that came over, and the only ones that got by the firing squad. I had to use the

second barrel several times as I wasted the first one on limbs and tree boughs, the birds passing over the heavy timber.

Lucian Carey was standing to my right and he shot a couple of times. He says, "Elmer, did I get them?" I said, "You sure did." When he wasn't looking I ejected my empty shells towards old Cotton who looked at me and grinned. Lucian was a grand old boy, not too good for health, and he had a fine over-under Westley Richards 20 gauge. But I knew he wasn't hitting there, and I wanted to be sure he had some fun out of it.

Another time at a Remington seminar, Lucian was out in a blind, well in front of us. The rest of us had all killed our geese and Lucian had shot, but he hadn't got a goose yet. So the boys proposed that I sneak down a draw there, crawl up in the corn field and out in front of Lucian and kill him a goose. I got in position, over came a lone honker. I waited and waited and waited and hoped I'd hear his

General J.S. Hatcher and Keith visit with ailing Colonel Townsend Whelen during an N.R.A. convention in Washington, D.C., in 1956.

gun and didn't, and I thought "He'll surely shoot now," so I shot. I got the goose all right. It must have fallen pretty close to Lucian's blind. Anyway when they called us all in for lunch. Lucian came out dragging the goose with a smile on his face, so we were all happy.

Bill Talley had loaned me his 12-guage Model 21 fancy-engraved shotgun. It was a good gun, fitted me perfectly and I did good work with it.

A CLOSE CALL IN WASHINGTON . . .

We were packing up to go home at Great Oaks Lodge in Maryland from a Remington shoot on the day President Kennedy was shot. Tom Siatos had a car he had rented at Dulles Airport and had to take back to Washington, and we had to lay over in Washington about three days before going down to Atlanta and Albany, Georgia, to a quail shoot and seminar that Winchester was putting on for us that fall. He asked several of us to ride with him back to Washington, which we were glad to do instead of waiting for the chartered bus.

Pete Brown of *Sports Afield,* Jack Lewis of *Gun World,* Tom Siatos, publisher of *Guns & Ammo* and I formed the party. We got into Washington D.C., and for some reason the

boys got lost even though Pete had a sister living there and Tom had been in the place a good many times. I had never prowled around the town or knew anything about it, so we proceeded to get lost in the Negro section of Washington, D.C.. Tom was driving, and while we were going up a wide avenue, all the radios were blaring in the street about President Kennedy being shot.

There was a big black car across the street that pulled out, revved up its motor, and headed for the side of us to ram us. I yelled at Tom and he poured on the gas. The big car barely missed us, going behind us. Then it turned sharply back across the street to our right and swung around for another go at us.

Tom asked, "Have you got your gun, Elmer?"

I answered, "I've always got my gun."

With that I rolled down the window just as the big car swung at us again. When the driver saw my gun, he made a very sharp right turn away from us. Tom poured on the gas some more, and we left. From the crash we heard, I think he hit a lamp post or some other car across the street. At any rate, we got away unscathed and were glad to get out of the mess. We made it to a big motel in Washington, D.C. and spent the next two days there as radios were blaring all over town advising everyone to stay off the streets. Sentiment was very strong. By that time the news had come that Kennedy had died. It was quite an upset bunch of Negroes all over Washington. I think the fact that the four of us wore light-colored Stetson hats, they must have thought we were Texans and for that reason decided to ram us. At any rate I am glad it wound up as it did.

Between assignments there was winter meat to get in, such as this buck shot by Lorraine Keith in 1961 at 300 yards with a Weatherby rifle in .300 H&H caliber.

282

From Washington we flew down to Albany, Georgia, and were driven out to a hunting camp, an old plantation that had been turned into a quail-hunting camp. Part of the delegation, however, never made it. They got their wires crossed some way. Winchester then showed us the first of their new Model 70s with the forend free floating from the barrel. I took a look at it and I told them that it would never go, that they would surely lose money on it.

We had a great quail shoot. We were shooting pairs with a dog handler with two dogs. It was scattered timber—grass with quite a few rattlesnakes—plenty of quail. Jim Rikhoff of Winchester proposed we throw ten dollars each in the pot and the winning team would take the pot. Charlie Askins and I teamed up together. The Colonel is a very good wing shot and had a nice over-under Browning 20-bore skeet gun, ideal for the purpose. As the Winchester guns had not arrived at the game farm, I had to shoot an old Dakin 30-inch full-choke 20 bore with about a ten-pound trigger pull. For some reason the second barrel wouldn't go off half the time, and if it did the trigger pull increased to about 20 pounds. In spite of that, I had the best quail shoot of my entire life.

We quit an hour early at noon and after lunch we again quit at four while the others were still shooting for about an hour. We turned in 87 quail to win the pot, and each of us gave the dog handler $10 apiece to make him happy and give him a very good day's salary. Charlie would take the first rise of the quail and I would pick out a long shot for the full-choke barrel. Charlie carried most of the load, but I dumped a good many long-range shots that day.

Each fall I look forward to these seminars. It's a gathering of the gun editors of America, some of the finest people you could possibly be out with. I believe we also help the companies because I notice that many of them have adopted our suggestions and put them to work. First Remington adopted my stock design, and I see now that Winchester has come to it and adopted it as well.

For several years after '64, Winchester products were not up to our ideas of a Winchester gun. We knocked them both at the seminars and later in print. Finally Winchester got on the ball and accepted a lot of our recommendations. Today they are back in business with guns that truly represent the name "Winchester." High-priced labor and high-priced materials are what led to their cheapening their guns with the stampings, plastics, aluminum, and what have you. I believe they lost money in those years, but now should regain their old standard of excellence. I notice that at the various stores now the present product is being acclaimed again as the old Winchester standard and people like it.

TO DESIGN A RIFLE . . .

Late in '67 I flew to Denver on a little DC3 headed for Enid, Oklahoma. We didn't get out very far until one motor went dead on us and we had to land at a town in Colorado. There they held us five or six hours, then flew us back to Denver. We embarked on another plane then that was to take us to Oklahoma City. In the meantime they phoned Champlin-Haskins to get me there. It didn't get off the ground either. Something went wrong with the windshield wipers, and there was a good storm on, so they had to cancel that flight. Later they put me on another flight to go to Wichita, Kansas, and see if there was a flight coming out of Chicago to go from there to Oklahoma City, so I boarded that flight and landed at Wichita. A boy going to school at Enid, Oklahoma was with me. The plane out of Chicago threw a motor and had to go back and land at Chicago. There wasn't to be another one until well along the next morning. However this lad called some of his school cronies and they had enough money for gasoline to get them to Wichita. So I told him to tell them to come and get us. I'd take care of things, which I did. We all had breakfast together, filled them up with gas and we all made it to Enid, Oklahoma.

There I put in a couple of days with Doug Champlin and Jerry Haskins, and designed the Keith-grade Champlin & Haskins rifle, their top-grade rifle. They were able to machine-taper octagon barrels and I wanted them with quarter-rib, a front ramp, and a lug underneath the barrel to be all integral, which they did. Next I wanted the best French walnut or Circassian they could get, and my stock design, which they approved. I also wanted the rear tang extended back over the nose of the comb for added strength, the lower tang to go back to the edge of the pistol grip, the trap grip cap to hold an extra front sight. Then I wanted English type wide angle sights with platinum or gold center line, and folding sights on the quarter-rib. I wanted the front sight to fold down in the ramp when not in use. To this they agreed.

I also wanted a square back for the trigger guard so the trigger guard wouldn't pound your second finger when using rifles with heavy recoil like the .458, .378 and similar heavy rifles. This they all agreed to. They brought out the No. 1. They asked me to pick out a barrel. I looked through their barrel stock. Some were good, some not so good, but I found one made by a man in Kalispell in .458 bore with an 18 or 20-inch twist. It looked very good, so they decided to make the first Keith-grade rifle a .458. I still have it. It's a beauty. It will cut clover leaves at 110 yards with benchrest and double sandbags anytime you want to try it. We used Redfield mounts, and I had the front mount base built integral with the rib and forward of the receiver ring so as not to weaken the receiver in any way. This worked out very well for low-power scopes that have plenty of tube at the front end for such installation.

Later they made me a .338-378 K.T. that Bob Thomson and I designed. On that rifle we wanted the 3x9 Redfield and Thomson's two-dot reticule range finder with all the trimmings. So we had to use the mount then on top of the receiver ring, and regular Redfield mounts, which we did.

They made another rifle for R.W. Thomson of Glenwood Springs, one for Bill Jordan, and one for George Gelman of Bakersfield, California, which they took to Africa and killed over 30 head of game each, including buffalo. We didn't design the .338-378 K.T. for buffalo, but Jordan and Gelman claimed it worked very well on them with shoulder shots. With a shotgun safety on top of the tang, extended straps, a tapered, octagon barrel, and a Keith-designed stock, it all added up to what I consider to be the finest sporting rifle ever produced in this country in bolt-action persuasion.

The company had made up a rifle for Doug Champlin's father, and it had been engraved by Frank Hendricks of Texas. Frank had done a very elaborate job on it. So I asked Doug if he would make me up a rifle like that but instead of the barrel being all engraved I'd rather have some bas-relief and gold animals, with most of the work on the receiver in case I ever wanted to shoot out that barrel and change to another one. It was agreed, so I traded him a fine best-quality self-opener ejector single-trigger cased Lancaster .303 I had

Lorraine Keith glasses the ridges on a recent hunt with R.W. Thomson of Glenwood Springs, Colorado.

284

and a batch of ammunition for a hand load I'd worked out that fitted it perfectly. Hendricks put in three months on the engraving. About six weeks of it paid for by Champlin, and the other he wanted to donate to me.

It is the most beautiful bolt-action rifle I've ever seen or expect to see. Clayton Nelson stocked it in a gorgeous piece of French walnut which sets off the general line and beauty of the rifle. It is in .375 H&H caliber and it stays under an inch at 100 yards with factory loads and even better with careful hand loads. Barrels are 25 inches to take advantage of the slow-burning 4831 powder and heavy bullets to gain maximum velocity.

THE .338/.378 IS BORN...

While at an NSGA show in Chicago, R.W. Thomson proposed that we neck down the .378 Weatherby to .338. I told him the case is too big. It's way over bore capacity for any powder we have unless it could possibly be H570. However, 4831 is a good powder and I believe if we cut off a quarter inch of the case, shove the shoulder back a quarter of an inch, and neck it to .338 it will work. We contacted RCBS, and they agreed to make up a dummy case that I could send to a reamer maker, Keith Francis, in Oregon. He made up a set of reamers and we turned them over to Champlin & Haskins. They made me a beautiful rifle and made one for Thomson. Then Bruce Hodgdon, the powder man of Shawnee Mission, Kansas, got a barrel from Champlin, made up a test rifle and chronographed it. We got 3008 fps with 103 grains of 4831 with a 250-grain Nosler, over 2800 fps with a 275-Speer, and over 2700 fps with the 300-grain Winchester bullets.

We knew we had a cartridge.

Test firing proved it would shoot into less than a minute-of-angle at 100 yards. In fact, I put five in one hole that a nickel covered completely at 110 yards from my rifle. Bill Jordan killed everything in Africa with it including a couple of buffalo, and even followed wounded buffalo into the brush for others and finished them off, saying that the 250-grain Noslers he used went clear through the shoulder and put them down in great style. Gelman also killed his buffalo with it. However, I do not recommend any small caliber for African buffalo.

Bob Thomson fitted 3 x 9 Redfield scopes, selecting ones with no parallax and the 3 x 9 settings with the range finder and his Colorado two-dot reticule on both my rifle and his. All screws we put in were Loc-tited as well

as the clamp rings on the scopes. These two rifles have shown exceptional long-range accuracy. We had not had the opportunity to shoot them at long range like Mr. Gelman and Bill Jordan and several others who have taken this rifle to Africa with our cartridge since then. However, Bob has killed three elk and two mule deer at long range. I have killed two elk and three mule deer, all at long range. I killed my first mule deer at 400 yards with one shot, the second at 300 yards with one shot, and the third at 500 yards. I didn't take the time to estimate the range thoroughly and went over him with the first shot, but killed him with the second shot. My first elk, was a big old six-point bull at 300 yards, the second elk I took at 350 yards, a spike bull, both with one shot each.

I used a 275-grain Speer bullet with 95 grains of 7831 for my shooting. This long heavy bullet does not expand so much as some others, but does open out at 500 yards. It produces clean kills with a minimum of meat destruction, and great penetration. For all shooting under 250 or 300 yards, I believe the 300-grain Winchester Power Point would be the most lethal bullet of them all. Certainly it carries the most weight and expands well at even at fairly long ranges, and at close range it holds together well.

Looking back over 30 years of guiding, and Thomson also put in that much or more outfitting and guiding parties, we realize what a time we could have had with such rifles when we started that business. We believe it is the finest long-range big game cartridge in the world today. It will take everything up to and including the African plains game and all fauna of North America. Previously our old .334 OKH, which was later turned into the .340 Weatherby, was the greatest long-range rifle that I had ever used on our game.

WINTER MEAT...

For several years Lorraine and I flew to the Selway and hunted our elk there. We also drove over into the Selway where I ran our own camp, often with parties, during the elk season and usually collected our meat there. Mule deer were in profusion and also lots of elk were in that country at that time.

Around home on the North Fork, poachers usually started hunting about two months before the season opened. When we waited until the season opened and took off, we could find the tracks, empty shells, and gut piles, where they had dressed game before the season opened.

Lorraine Keith with Elmer's fine caribou bull, taken on the Slana River in Alaska in 1960.

After the war one fall, Oscar Bohannon and I hunted ten days from our ranch for elk without success. Then we decided to pack up and go out to the head of Sheep Creek and hunt out the meadows. Lorraine packed up the food supply for us to manty up with a pack horse. She says, "I'm going to make you boys hunt this time." She meant it because she didn't put in any lard whatever and no meat except a little bacon to go along with the beans and for breakfast. Just as we crossed Sheep Creek, below Carnes cabin, a big buck came out at about 300 yards. I slid off my old brown horse, and thumped the deer in the lungs with a .285 OKH I was carrying. He jumped, kicked at his belly, and ran into the timber. Our little Stub dog took after him, so I told Oscar we'd go on to the cabin, unsaddle, unpack, hobble and bell the horses, and then come back and see what happened.

A short distance in the timber we found my little dog sitting beside the big buck guarding him until we came. We had to use deer tallow for grease for cooking on that trip. Lorraine

meant what she said. She was going to make us hunt. However, we did all right getting our elk and deer to bring home for our winter's meat supply.

Elk became scarce in this country due to the game department lowering non-resident license fees to less than our surrounding states. Californians, Texans and hunters from other states flocked in here by the thousands, and soon depleted our elk herds. Likewise we had some poachers here locally who worked on them the year round, some with jack lights.

Bob and Jean Thomson invited us to hunt elk with them in Colorado, so for several years we have made an annual trek to Glenwood Springs and hunted with Thomsons, with the exception of '67 when I had my coronary and couldn't go anywhere. Bob Thomson put up and ran the finest tent camp I have ever seen in the hills, well organized, with good guides, good packers, good horses, and some of the most beautiful country on God's green earth. We hunted Avalanche Canyon several years and for two years we went out of Fort Defi-

286

The second deer ever killed by a .44 Magnum pistol is packed out by Ed Pozzi in 1956.

ance on the Flattops. God willing, we'll be with them again.

MY IDEA OF A SCABBARD . . .

Back when I was on the technical staff of *American Rifleman*, Harry Lynn, who then headed *American Rifleman* and the NRA, came out with his wife and paid us a visit. Jim Boyt of the Boyt Leather Works in Iowa had asked him to have me design a saddle scabbard that would really work.

I have seen so many rifles lost over the years in the usual saddle scabbards, especially when carried with the butt to the rear. When the horses were fording creeks, jumping logs, or going up a steep hill, the guns would slide out of the scabbard, and I later trailed up and recovered several rifles for parties I was out with. I have always used the old northwest position for carrying a rifle on the near side of the horse, butt forward and with the gun lying almost parallel with the horse's barrel, the scabbard strapped around the fork of the saddle at the front end as high as I can get it

and the rear end through either the cantle strings or the rear cinch, and carried low enough so that the rifle stays in the scabbard without any trouble.

I wanted a scabbard that would protect a fine rifle, and not scar it all up. So I had Jim Boyt make this scabbard out of heavy saddle skirting, the inside to be lined with an imitation fleece, thick and heavy and treated with a rust repellent. The full length of the scabbard was sewed solid except the front end and a heavy zipper went clear around the front end so that the rifle was completely enclosed against dust, rain or snow. When you wanted it, you could fall off the horse on the near side, and the rifle was on your side of the horse, all you had to do was unzip the scabbard and pull out a perfectly clean rifle.

In the early days of Montana I used an old Army saddle scabbard carried with the sight up and if I was riding broncs I ran the scabbard between the stirrup leathers. Then my weight on the stirrups, especially the narrow bronc stirrups I always used, would hold the

Lorraine Keith's horse sports a Boyt scabbard in Elmer's favorite northwest position, on an elk hunt in Avalanche Canyon, Colorado.

rifle scabbard between the stirrup leathers and blanket. I've rode many a bucking horse and had my rifle intact at the end of it. Try this with one of the old southeast Texas positions with the rifle stuck under your right leg and the butt up about the height of the cantle board and you will soon see the difference. A bronc will practically always buck it out of the scabbard. I trailed up many such, including one for Carroll Paul on our trip to Canada in 19 and 27. I found his fine G&H Springfield in a creek where he had jumped a log some six miles back from where we'd camped.

As a youngster I tried all positions of carrying a rifle, even went to the southeastern Texas position with the rifle under my right leg and the muzzle down fairly close to the stirrup and the butt up high by the cantle board

behind. I was riding a big bay horse one time, and he stuck his foot in a badger hole while we were going along at a nice swinging lope. He turned a summerset. The butt of the 95 Winchester that I had in the scabbard hit me in the back of the head. I didn't come to for two hours, and when I did the old horse was grazing nearby. I had a knot on my head that wouldn't allow my hat to go down for several days. That cured me permanently of any rifle position on a horse except the old northwest position.

You can soon have a bronc trained to where you can get up to the near side of him. To get on the off side, or the Indian side, (the Indians always mounted from the right side), then you have trouble. Furthermore, if you jumped off your horse on the left side the darn rifle is over the horse on the other side. I wanted a scabbard that would allow one to reach down, pull the rifle out, either mounted or on foot, and on the near side of the horse. This Boyt scabbard turned out to be one of the finest in existence. I carried my two rifles in it to Africa in '57 and for six trips to Alaska.

The Boyt Company finally changed hands and they quit making this fine scabbard. It used to sell for around fifty dollars.

Recently Milt Sparks of Route I, Star, Idaho, has taken up the manufacturing of these fine scabbards, but now on account of the increase in cost of materials he has had to go from $80 to $115 for them, but they are worth it. They are ideal for carrying a rifle in the trunk of a car without scratching it up or on a horse. And you can bet you have always got your rifle and it's clean and dry.

Bob Thomson had the most beautiful elk camp I believe I've ever seen. It was ideal from every standpoint. There was a spotting scope in front of the cook tent where you could sit and watch elk on the mountain up to 12 to 13,000 feet above a great flat. It had plenty of bunch grass and buffalo grass for the horses, heavy spruce timber between the camp proper and the creek, and a big meat pole back there in the shade where the elk and deer could hang and age.

On the first trip out of this camp one year, a doctor client had a rifle in one of these Texas scabbards on the right side, butt to the rear with the muzzle of the rifle fairly well up, his leg pretty flat on the horse. I told him that morning, "You'd better tie that rifle in or you will lose it." As he was going up a steep trail, sure enough he lost the rifle. Though the boys looked high and low for it, it was never found, a fine scope-sighted, bolt-action rifle. I am glad that Milt Sparks is again making this fine scabbard as it is always in demand by anyone that has used it or seen it used.

THE BERNS-MARTIN HOLSTER . . .

I worked with John Emmett Berns when he was stationed in Alaska. He wanted a six-gun holster that he could get a long 7½-inch single-action out of quickly and yet be able to wade snow and keep the gun clean. Between us we designed his open-front holster with a spring clip around the cylinder and a slight pocket at the bottom of the holster for the muzzle to ride in. You push the gun forward and then jerk it upward. It is fast, but not as fast as a plain box holster at the right angle because you have to rock the gun forward and then lift it. It was used extensively by the FBI,

and is still made now under other names since Berns' patent has long since run out.

I next designed the No. 120 holster for single-action Colts, and another for Rugers later on, for the George Lawrence Co. of Portland, Oregon. I also designed the No. 34 for double-action guns. I used the Chick Gaylord plain-clothes holster quite a bit, but if you tipped over on your face or kneeled you would very likely lose your gun. If you carried the butt well forward for quick draw, it would not hold the gun tight enough. Hank Sloan of the FBI, who was instructor for them for some 20 years before his retirement, designed an even better plain-clothes holster that rides close against the body. There is stitching around the bottom and up the sides within two inches of the trigger guard. Then the filler is left loose and a heavy screw goes through the top of it. You can press this leather in until it rides hard on the gun frame just in front of the trigger guard. Turn the screw up tight, and it requires a jerk to free the gun. You can turn summersets with the gun in that holster and it won't fall out.

I showed it to Milt Sparks and we decided to improve on it. Hank Sloans' version stood a little too straight up and down to suit me. I like the butt of the gun tipped farther forward for quick draw. So we designed the same holster but left it open at the bottom which shortened it a half inch so it won't push your belt up when sitting in a car with a four-inch gun. This has worked out to be the best plain-clothes quickdraw holster I've seen.

When it comes to fancy gun rigs, my old friend Ed Bohlin of Hollywood, California, stands alone. He has made, and makes, the finest silver-mounted hand-carved quick-draw belt and holster outfits in existence. He has made a great many of the silver-mounted saddles that are used in the Rose Parade, as well as the gun equipment also carried there.

HOW HUNTING CHANGED . . .

During my 30 years of guiding, I became quite proficient in calling bull elk during the rut. The rut in Montana, and here in Idaho usually starts around the 20th of August and runs to the 15th of September. The bulls are pretty well run down after that, and the rut fairly well over. Each bull will gather his harem of cows and attempt to fight off all comers. This is nature's way of having the cows served by the finest bulls in that part of the country. Big bulls will whip off the little fellows and they will sire the herd.

A buck law or a bull law is a sad mistake.

Wherever it has been they no longer get any good heads. The bulls don't live long enough because most people, especially hunters from cities, are after heads. For that reason they want to kill more heads than they do cows and does. The old hunters, the old hillbillies, and ranchers, of course, will pick a cow in preference to an old bull elk unless he could catch that bull elk when he is fat about the end of August or by the 20th.

you and you have to walk around into the wind and give them your scent before their hair will go down and they'll leave. Some that would come on in had to be killed. They don't always quit.

Today this section of Idaho, Lemhi County, is completely shot out. Over 500 hunters checked through the game department station at Carmen after the first three weeks of the season. Some took boat trips down the Salm-

Hunting in the United States has changed a lot since Keith took many of these heads.

I have made a good many bugles out of two sections of bamboo. I leave the end closed, drill out the center note, and put a whistle plug in the other end and tape the whole thing so it won't crack and split. This makes the most natural call of any I have used and over the years I have called a lot of them. One old bugle I have now has called over 50 bulls up to close range. Many times they will come within ten or fifteen yards of

on, or fly-in trips to remote ranches back in the interior and pack trips, as well as car hunting all over the county and into some surrounding counties. The hunters in the first three weeks had checked out 12 elk and 24 deer which shows what a sad state of affairs Lemhi County, Idaho, has come to as far as big game is concerned.

Yet the game department protects all predators with the exception of the coyote, and I look for them to put them on the list next. They protect the cougar, yet their average kill is two deer a week.

The last one that Don put up last spring, when he back-trailed the old cat he found where he had killed a six-point bull elk the day he treed him, and one day farther back he found where he had killed a cow elk, which shows the rate they work. I can remember when the Middle Fork was simply alive with deer. I counted 1000 from the time I started wrangling horses on White's Creek at daylight until I got down to Loon Creek. One thousand mule deer, and they were quite tame. I could have loaded a truck with my six-shooter alone. Today there are very few deer in that section. Here in Lemhi County at the close of the war we had plenty of game. When I came here in '29 I know there was at least a thousand deer for every one there is today. Also, 13 bands of sheep ranged down the river and ate up a good part of the summer's range and much of the game's winter range, yet they managed to survive. Today the Forest Service says there isn't enough feed for them, and any way you want to go from Salmon, Idaho, you'll find feed up to the knees, buffalo and bunch grass and lots of it, but no game to eat it. With the restrictions on the ranchers, they pretty nearly have to have their own summer range in order to run cattle or sheep profitably.

Now since poison and cyanide guns have been taken off, Jack Nancolas, our government hunter here, is hard put to keep the coyotes, bear and cougar down. The coyotes have been so bad that several of the sheep men here are thinking of selling out.

The golden eagles get a lot of the lambs, and the coyotes do too. This theory that the

Keith admiring one of his fine double rifles in the trophy room of his home in Salmon, Idaho.

biologists pass along that the coyotes and cougars will eat only the old crips is false. I have trailed cougar right by three-legged does wounded in the winter and they paid no attention to them, but went on and killed the biggest, fattest buck they could find in the band. Also cougar prefer mountain sheep lambs and mountain goat kids. Yet he is protected. I don't believe in exterminating anything, but we could do with a hell of a lot less eagles in this part of the Salmon River country. I remember when the Idaho Game Department paid a dollar bounty on eagles and I used to ship their heads down there for the bounty.

Alaska at that time also paid a dollar bounty on eagles up there. They were mostly bald eagles. The bald eagles kill sheep, too, just as the golden eagle does. I had one bald eagle tackle me when I was out with John D. Hart. He was a young bald eagle as his head and tail was still black. They don't turn white until they are about five years old. Game mismanagement by biologists with four years of college training, against the lifetime experiences of old timers here has now relegated our big game almost to a thing of the past. I don't believe the deer will ever come back. If we could get the 2800 head of elk surplus they have in the Yellowstone Park and plant them here in Lemhi County we could at least have elk shooting and a nucleus of breeding stock all over the county. But the Forest Service bucks it, saying that they will eat up all the range. What they want the range for now is beyond me. The ranchers have a hard time getting their quota of cattle on the range, and sheep the same way. Yet the range is in better shape now than I have ever seen it since I came here in 19 and 29.

This used to be a great game country but that is now a thing of the past. Both big game and small game at present are scarce. I see no chance of further improvement unless we can get a two or three-year closed season, which is unlikely with the game department so hungry for dollars from the licenses each fall. Man is the greatest predator of all, and many years ago upset the balance of nature until it can never come back. Today with so many hunters in the field, we need no predators.

I remember when Winchester took us to Italy to shoot on the King's estate at Lamandria, they gave us orders to shoot every hawk, every owl, every housecat or fox we saw. When my contingent of the group was shipped on to Portugal to shoot red-legged partridge, (really a chukar) we were given the same orders, to kill every hawk, owl, housecat or fox we saw. Those people have been raising game birds for hundreds of years, even before America was discovered, and they have found out that with man as a predator they don't need others.

Here in this country our biologists labor under the delusion that the predators kill off the old, crippled and sick game which could never be farther from the truth. Take a band of sheep. If an old ewe leaves the band and lays down to die, which she will, will the coyotes eat her? No. They never touch her. They want to kill the finest fat lamb in the flock.

All my life I have worked with guns, ammunition, sights and improvement on everything and also studied all phases of big game and small game alike. It has been a lifetime work in the main, and I can now see the writing on the wall. Except for some big ranches over in the Southwest, down in Texas, and other natural game preserves, we are soon going to be out of the big-game class entirely. Alaska is going the same way and fast. Only Canada seems to have better conservation efforts on the part of the game department and enforcing laws to a greater extent and still have considerable amount of big game as well as waterfowl and small game. These ecologists have never seen a mule deer out in crusted deep snow up to its belly as it floundered along, and a pack of coyotes or wolves crowding along beside eating the poor animal alive. First the guts hurtle out and they eat them up and pull them out. Finally the poor thing goes down and they literally eat him alive with no attempt to kill him clean first.

I'll say this for the cougar. He usually kills his game before he eats it. Not so with an eagle and a deer with a broken back. He just starts eating on the hams, and a coyote or a wolf simply eats them alive. Coyotes, skunks, foxes, all often kill far more than they have any use for. I've seen as many as 23 lambs killed by one coyote, and he had eaten very little from only one of them in one night's foray. The old cougar often kills more than he will eat and he won't go back to a cold dead animal if he can find a fresh warm one to eat.

These things are not given consideration by the ecologist. He hasn't had the experience, he hasn't been there and watched the game hard winter after hard winter to see how it lives or how it dies. Weasels, mink, skunk, foxes, coyotes, horned owls and hawks get an awful percentage of our female duck population while they are on the nest. The same goes for the pheasant population. The owl hunts of a

292

night. Wherever we have chukars in this country, whenever you get up to where the chukar tracks are thick and start jumping them, invariably you will see an old golden eagle circling along about two yards over the sagebrush ready to drop on one. In the winter time, both up the Lemhi, over on Birch Creek, or up the Pahsimeroi, whenever a bunch of sagehen gets up and flies, then you will see a pair of eagles (or as many as eight or ten) circling where those birds went down. They have no protection except their coloring, and sooner or later the old eagle with his eight-power-binocular eyes will spot them. Down he goes and eats that chicken. Then he'll go up and circle until he finds another one. They have about cleaned out our sagehens in this country.

Last spring we had a good crop of antelope, but by now you see very few fawns among them, plenty of does, a few bucks, but very few fawns. Eagles and the coyotes got them.

In some sections of Missouri, whitetail deer have been brought back in suitable quantities. When I was a small boy, I doubt if there was a deer left in Missouri, or a wild turkey either. With proper management, game can be brought back. But it requires proper management by men who have lived with the game and understand it and not by some biologist with a four-year degree from college alone.

At one time the Middle Fork of the Salmon was lousy with deer. A hard winter killed off most of them, but after that the cougars pretty well cleaned them out of that part of the country. Then they moved over on to the Salmon River where we used to have an awful lot of mountain goats, and they cleaned them out. From there they moved on over into the Selway country and Sid Hinckle's hired man on the ranch at Selway Lodge accounted for 16 one winter a mile and a half from the cabin. Sid flew in two good dogs for him to use and he really cleaned up. Before he cleaned out that bunch of cougar that winter, we could find an old cow elk or an old bull elk, but rarely a young elk. The cougar accounted for practically all of them. Now he is protected in Idaho. Non-residents have to buy a big-game license and a ten dollar tag to kill one of them.

PRIMITIVE WEAPONRY . . .

Another thing that is common in many states out here in the west and also in the east is a law permitting the archers to hunt for a couple of weeks before gun hunters are allowed in the field. They not only spook the game and scare the hell out of it, but they also wound a lot of game with arrows. I have found enough dead and soured animals with an arrow sticking in them to know what goes on. Many of these archers are not trackers, and if they think they missed but don't find their arrow, they don't trail the game far enough to know what did happen. By the same token the laws won't allow expert pistol shots to use a heavy six-gun on the game, which is far more deadly than any bow and arrow. Any good six-gun shot can kill game clean, from deer to elk, with a .44 Mag or a .41 Mag, a heavy loaded .44 Special, or .45 Colt, at three times the range of any archer.

In some states they are now permitting the use of muzzle-loading rifles rather than all shotguns on deer. This is great stuff in the right direction, because a good shot with a flintlock or percussion caplock rifle of .50 caliber, or at the smallest .45, can place his shots on game, and he will not shoot until he gets a shot because he knows that he has but the one load. It takes time to reload. This is far more humane and better for the game than simply blasting after an animal with buckshot that is probably out of range.

I believe every state permitting archers to hunt big game should also permit a muzzle-loading cap or flintlock rifle as well as heavy caliber six-guns at the same time. Rifle hunting could be scheduled later. But I believe in the main they should open the season for a specified period and let anybody hunt with whatever he wishes to use from a bow to a muzzleloader or a modern rifle. I cannot see it being fair to let one set of hunters use one item to the exclusion of all the others until the game is well scared or spooked. It don't make sense to me.

FEELINGS ON IRON SHOT . . .

Getting back to this ecology business. Biologists have found that over the Midwest, especially the muddy marsh sections of the country, a considerable number of ducks are killed by lead poisoning.

Fine shot that stays on top of hard surfaces, or near the top of mud flats, is shoveled up by the ducks and in time they die of lead poisoning. Now there is a hue and cry to use iron shot. They've tried about everything. Copper shot would be preferable to iron, both for the protection of the gun bore and also as to the range it will actually kill. However, Remington, Federal, and Winchester have been working with iron shot. At the last Winchester seminar I was privileged to watch a test that is being carried on at Winchester-Western. They are going at it in a scientific manner, but it is very hard on the ducks. They have a short railway rigged up. They clamp a duck on it in flying position and send him past the gun at 20 miles an hour. The stations for the guns range from 20 yards to 80 yards. I witnessed about an hour of the 80-yard firing using a Winchester shotgun with a telescope sight tuned to center the pattern on the duck when he passes the range at 20 miles an hour.

Now wild birds fly 45, maybe 60 if there is a tailwind. So they are really catching a lot more shot owing to the stream of the pattern at a 20-mile speed than if the fowl was flying at 45 to 60 miles per hour. Nevertheless while I watched, every duck was hit. Most of them were crippled. I saw one that was hit in the head and actually killed.

It's hard on the ducks and the poor things suffer, but this is in the aid of science. The same as they allowed so many biologists here to kill so many deer just to see what they were eating. Another biologist over at Coeur d'Alene was given a permit to kill 30 pregnant whitetail does, just to see how the fetus was doing. It seems to me this ecology business is getting more out of hand all the time. These Winchester experiments are very thorough. They count the number of pellets that hit the bird, and keep him for ten days to see whether he lives or dies. In my humble opinion, if they adopt iron shot all over the country, the killing range, even with No. 4s, is limited to 40 yards. And even at 40 yards there will be cripples. It takes a No. 4 iron shot to equal the pellet energy of a No. 6 lead shot.

I am convinced that the use of iron shot will cause three to four times the cripples which will eventually die over the total amount that die now from lead poisoning from the ingestion of lead shot in the mud. Lead shot does not hurt gun barrels. Iron shot will score them badly and in time ruin them. Quite a number of ring bulges have occurred just back of the choke after using iron shot. So

A 1976 antelope hunt in Wyoming ended with Lorraine taking this representative pronghorn with a shot at 400 yards with a .338/378 K.T. rifle and a 275-gr. bullet.

I would never fire a load of such shot through any good gun of my own, and I know a great many hunters who will do the same.

blind. These tests by Winchester-Western and Federal are further proving how hopeless iron shot is beyond 40 yards. No one is going to be

Keith leads a pack string across the Flying B Ranch bridge on the Middle Fork of the Salmon in 1958.

It's true that the license fee and duck stamps help further the promotion of ducks and geese all over our waterways. That was what the money was originally designed for. Yet for several years not one cent of it went for production of ducks or geese. It went to the usual pork barrel. Now, however, it's being used. If hunters are forced to use iron shot, many will quit altogether. They don't intend to ruin their fine guns with any such shot. That will cut down the license fees and also the number of duck stamps sold.

It's far better, it seems to me, to use No. 4 shot or even No. 3. No. 3 is the best wildfowl shot anyway for ducks and geese at long range, and if they use the standardized No. 3 shot, and nothing smaller on waterfowl, it would sink deeper in the mud and would also tend to move to the bottom of any gravel bottomed stream or wherever there were waves. The companies are not going into it

able to stop the average shooter with his little knowledge of range, lead estimation, or his own capabilities. He is going to shoot at ducks at long range just the same as he always has. If he uses iron shot it's going to cripple three or four birds where he would otherwise kill with lead shot.

After many years of experimenting, hundreds of rounds on the pattern board, plus considerable duck and goose shooting with 12, Magnum 12, Super 10, and Magnum 10 bore guns, I have found that for me at least No. 3 shot is the best and most reliable killer of waterfowl of any size tried. In No. 2, the pattern gets a bit thin at long range. With No. 4 the pellet energy is about done at 70 yards. No. 4 lead shot, however, kills pretty reliably at 60 to 65 yards with heavy charges, while No. 4 iron shot, all the companies claim, is done at 40 yards. Anyone who has ever panned gold or washed gold by placer meth-

Keith hefts Al Weber's 25-pound rifle made to shoot the .50 Browning Machine Gun cartridge at a gun show, while Col. George Busby and Al Weber look on.

ods of any kind well knows how lead shot bullets as well as the gold sinks to the bedrock at every possible opportunity if there is any movement of the sand and gravel caused by the waves, riffles, stream flow or whatever.

As I see the problem it is only contingent on marshy muddy ground, shallow water where there is no wave movement to wash it and this is true of some places along the California inland lakes and along the midwest Mississippi flyway. However, these sections should not condemn the whole country to the use of iron shot because of a few thousand birds lost that way. I believe it is a sad mistake and will result in a far greater loss of birds through wounding.

A NATION IN TROUBLE...

The communistic anti-gun crowd would like to disarm America and leave an open gate for Russia whenever she wanted to attack. Likewise, they believe in killing off all the game, as near as I can figure, from the way they are managing it at the present, so that people couldn't live in the hills even though they had the chance or were forced to do so.

A disarmed country is a whipped country. Look at little Switzerland, for example, where every man of military age has his rifle, pack, and ammunition in his own home ready to go at a moment's notice, where shooting is a national sport, and men, women and children shoot every Sunday—even fully automatic weapons. They are well versed in the use of all arms. Switzerland has survived two world wars. The Kaiser would like to have taken her, likewise Hitler would have taken her, but his generals informed him that if they did take little Switzerland, they wouldn't have an army left to fight the rest of the world.

Taxes based on real estate alone are making it tough for the older people. I've witnessed many changes in this country from the start of the airplane age and the automobile down through the years. I remember when horses were the only means of propulsion except for the railroad. Today it is far different, and times are changing ever faster. What the next ten years will bring, God alone knows.

FISH FROM THE RIVER . . .

After moving to Salmon in 19 and 48 we had three very dry years. The Lemhi River practically dried up. Our little power plant and its dam about a half mile up in the main part of town took practically all the water.

The salmon run backed up down at the mouth of the creek wanting to get up the river. I asked the game department man here then, and who is now head of all the game wardens in Idaho, what he would do about it, if he could help to get that salmon run up.

"No," he said, "we wipe our hands of the salmon. To hell with them. Let them go. We're not going to spend a dime or do anything about it."

I then went to the head of the power company, a Mr. Peterson.

He said, "Elmer, I'll give you all the help you need. What do you need?"

I told him I needed a carpenter for a day's work and we'd rebuild the ladder over the dam, take out some of the boxes, and make the others big enough so a big salmon could turn around and jump. Then we'd need a bulldozer for three days because we'd have to build a big holding pond below the dam where they could rest and jump until they got over. Then we had to throw all those little trickles into one big ditch clear down to the river, a distance of a mile or so.

He agreed.

He got me a carpenter and we rebuilt the ladders. He said, "Can you work nights?"

I said, "Sure."

He said, "I can get you a good man and a bulldozer of a night," which he did. My boy, Ted, then about eleven or twelve years old, helped me steer that cat at night with a flashlight and a gas lantern. After we had dug out a good holding pond, we then threw all the little trickles into one big ditch down to the bridge that goes over to the dump. There the

Elmer Keith and his son, Ted, in Salmon, Idaho in 1977.

297

boy and I shoveled out while the cat crawled around and got down fences and got in below and worked the ditch out to the mouth of the Lemhi where it opens into the Salmon River. For a couple of hours after we made the final cut, the spray was three feet in the air as that run of salmon was going up. We had to do this same procedure for three years straight, except we didn't have to dig the holding pond or rebuild the ladder.

One night while I was sitting in the front room writing for the magazines, two game wardens came in, one of them the same man that had washed his hands of the salmon. They had my boy. They said, "Well, Elmer, we're going to take your boy to St. Anthony."

St. Anthony is a home for all boys gone wrong.

I said, "What did he do?"

Ted told me afterwards, "I was standing at the dam watching the fish jump and they asked me what I did with my tackle." Ted was an innocent little lad and the same as all other boys in Salmon, he had a big treble hook with a big sinker wired to the bottom of it and a sash cord tied to the eye of it to throw over a fish and jerk him out.

"Well," he said, "we caught your boy with this illegal tackle. We're going to take him to St. Anthony."

I said, "Mister, you are the man that washed your hands of all the salmon. You've done nothing for them, and neither has the Idaho game department. Now you say you are going to take my boy to St. Anthony's. Mister, you get yourself and your partner out of this house before I kill you in it. And don't you ever darken the door again or I'll shoot you. If you ever touch that boy for any offense, I don't care what it is, I'll hunt you down the same as any other coyote, which you are."

He left and he hasn't been back since. That is one sample of what we have for a game department here in Idaho.

There is many a good officer in the department, but some of the heads of it I couldn't care less for.

A BIRD PROBLEM . . .

All hawks and owls are protected in Idaho. Likewise the blue crane, the fish duck and even the little kingfisher. Why they are trying to raise trout and steelhead and salmon is beyond me. Wherever they make a plant of trout or steelhead fry you can see a dozen to fifteen cranes at work on it every day.

One of their fish biologists, Don Corley, stopped me a few years back and he said, "Elmer, you wouldn't believe what I found today."

I said, "What was that?" He said, "I shot a fish duck."

I said, "Don't you know it's illegal?" He said, "Oh we can shoot them whenever we want to study them. I found a ten-inch trout in that fish duck."

I said, "Don, what do you think an old blue crane could do? How big a fish do you think he could handle?"

I've seen them fork out a two-pound trout, cut him up with that long beak of theirs, put part of him down their bill, and pack the rest off for the nest. The department now claims we have a surplus of green-head mallards and not enough hens to go around. They don't realize the protection of the predators gets the hens while they are nesting in the spring, so that there is a shortage of hens and also a shortage of young ducks. Coons, skunks, bobcats, coyotes, the great horned owl, and all other owls are protected.

Coming from steelhead fishing down the river two years ago, I saw a turtle dove get up in front of my car. It hadn't got ten feet in the air when a little sparrow hawk hit it in the back and killed it deader than a nit. I got out and examined the dove and how that little tiny sparrow hawk, the tiniest of all the falcons, could kill a bird as big as a turtle dove, I don't know, but I watched him do it. Down the river when Guleke and I were running below the pack bridge at Horse Creek, we heard a flock of honkers coming up the river. They got almost opposite us and seeing the boat they swung up over the sliderock on the left. We were in heavy whitewater. Two eagles dived on the flock of honkers, and broke it all up. Each eagle hit a honker in the back and killed him dead in the air. They fell way up in the sliderock. Then the eagles went down to eat one of them and I presume they ate the other one the next day. But that is what is going on. Ecology and biology are all right in their place, but they should be mixed with a little common horse sense and a helluva lot more experience than most of these biologists now have.

The primitive area starts a half mile from my back door and extends almost to Lewiston, Idaho down the Salmon and Snake Rivers, yet the big game is scarce all over, due to the hard winters killing a lot of it.

I remember the hard winter of '48 here. I begged the game department to get feed in

298

Each fall in recent years, Keith has traveled to Colorado to hunt elk with his friend, Bob Thomson.

here and feed the ducks and pheasants. At that time we had lots of Chinese pheasants and myriads of mallards, along with a few green-wing teal. My answer from the same man that ignored the salmon run was that they didn't want to make pensioners out of them. As a result, ducks and pheasants died by the thousands.

They would get out in the feed lot and eat the manure from horses and cattle trying to find some substance that the livestock didn't take out of the feed when they ate it. They died by the thousands and they have never came back. I doubt now if they ever will. A few thousand dollars worth of grain could have saved the bulk of that crop of pheasants and ducks that winter. And with all the intake and money from the licenses, the constant raise in price, I wonder where all the money goes. There are plenty of cars, plenty of game wardens cruising up and down the highways, but damn little of the money ever goes to propagate the game, at least in this section.

Erv Malnarick formerly ran the Selway Lodge, and for the past good many years has conducted a packer and guide school over at Hamilton, Montana. He takes each class, teaches them all phases of guiding and packing from shoeing horses to packing, including the dressing of big game, and skinning out capes and curing them. In fact, he goes through the whole gamut of what a guide should know. After the school and a long course of study, he takes them on a two-week pack trip back into the roughest country in Idaho, usually in the spring of the year when the rivers are high and they have one hard time fording, swimming horses, making rafts, and getting their equipment across streams. He really gives them the works. Each time he also brings them over here or has Lorraine and I come over to Hamilton and we give them instruction with both rifle and six-gun.

A LOVE OF FLYING ...

For a good many years now I have occasionally flown down the Salmon River with Fred Pearson, an old sourdough and bush pilot friend of mine from Alaska. We would go down either to Mackay Bar or Crooked Creek or a little ranch in between with a short landing field to fish for steelhead. It's been great fun, but we have also run into some terrible weather at different times. One time the runway at Crooked Creek had been cut in two by a cloudburst. We stopped with the front end of the plane looking right down into the cavern that the torrent of water had cut through the runway. After we caught our steelhead, I had to hang onto the plane while he revved the motor up. I never did get the seat belt fastened as we took off on that humpety ride. We'd go up one hump, down a swale, up another hump and the last swale you'd better

make it because there is nothing but the river in front. However, we made it.

Another time we came down the river and decided to land at this little ranch. The wind sock was an old dishtowel hung on a pole. The wind had wrapped in around so tight we couldn't tell which way the wind was blowing. The water was ruffled and we couldn't decide which way. Finally we decided the wind was blowing up the river. So we came in for the landing.

We had to go up the river a considerable distance to find a place in the canyon wide enough to turn the Cessna 185 around. Coming down, we landed right by the house, at the head of the runway. Then we skipped nearly three-fourths of the runway before we hit again. Just then we headed for the river. I unsnapped my belt and was ready to try to get the door open when Fred ground looped the plane and spun it around, and we were going back up to the ranch at about 45 miles an hour. How he did it, I don't know. I asked him where he learned to turn a plane around that way. He said, "I've run out of runway in Alaska a good many times." We got through that one okay, too.

On another trip at Mackay Bar, we ran into solid overcast snow blizzards clear across the canyon going down, and had to pull around and circle until it cleared. We finally got down all right and caught our fish and were going on down to Crooked Creek. When we took off, we ran into solid cloud formations, which were snowstorms by the time we got to Mackay Bar.

Up above us on the South Fork was a hole through to clear sky. Not knowing how high it was we decided to go up and see. Fred said the plane was good for twelve-thirteen thousand. I thought that would get over it. He thought otherwise. Anyway we squirreled up through this opening until we were on top and headed for Salmon. We didn't know whether it would be overcast at Salmon and we would have to go on to Leadore as long as gas lasted, or if we could find the highway.

When we tipped out over the range west of town, all was clear in the valley and we ran into no trouble. I am a fatalist, believing firmly that nobody is going to die until his time comes. When that time comes, however, you will fall down and break your neck or something will happen.

The worst scare I had in an airplane, however, was when I attempted to fly to Seattle, and finally did get there after three days, with a couple of flat-country fliers in a small single-engine plane. We fought our way at high elevations through a hard snowstorm and iced up and finally came out with a hundred-foot ceiling right over the center of the Clearwater River above Lewiston. That really spooked me as it did the two fliers.

Had we been two hundred yards to either side we would have crashed. There was no visibility in the last hour of that flight.

ON PLACING THAT FIRST SHOT . . .

I believe it is time more people in this country hunted with single shot rifles, took their time and placed that one shot. If they don't get a good shot, they should not shoot. I am dead against the use of automatic rifles and spraying the brush in hopes of making a hit while shooting at too long a range.

Recently articles have appeared in *Guns & Ammo* Annual, and also in other gun magazines, of 1000-yard whitetail deer shooting across canyons in Pennsylvania. I am dead set against any such shooting.

One thousand yard target work is great sport in developing rifles for thousand-yard sniping, which is useful in any war over open country. However shooting at fine game animals at such ranges is beyond my ken. I can't understand it because I have seen so many game animals kick at their bellies, jump and run off, (and many never were recovered) by people I was guiding, in spite of my best efforts. I am an expert tracker and have been for many years, but I will not condone any thousand-yard shooting at big game. If one was to do it, it should be open country and then with a big 25-pound scope-sighted rifle with a Browning .50 caliber machine-gun cartridge. Nothing smaller is capable of administering a killing hit except on the brain or spine at a thousand yards.

You can go behind the thousand-yard targets at Camp Perry, Ohio, and pick up a hatful of the old 173-grain boattails or presently the 150-grain flat-base variety, showing how near spent they are when they kick through the target at a thousand yards, hit

Keith doesn't believe in extremely long shots at big game. This 54-inch moose was shot in the shoulder at 50 yards with a 300-grain Kynoch bullet from a .338 Winchester Magnum in Alaska.

the grass, bounce a few times and lie there.

To think of shooting at a big game animal at such range is simply beyond my comprehension. Furthermore if they are set up at a benchrest with a big spotting scope and Army range finder at a thousand yards, who is going to get across the canyon to where the deer was hit and find him in brush over there (where he probably can't see 50 yards) while across the canyon they show up plain?

It is inevitable that they must lose several deer for every one they kill.

I would prefer to shoot big game at ranges close enough so I could see their eyes. Whenever possible I stalk close enough to do just exactly that.

I have had to do long range shooting a few times in my life or forego the game that I wanted badly. I can remember killing one mule deer at 600 yards before about 30 people at Gibbonsville, on a bet. I didn't want to shoot at that distance, but they kidded me until I showed them it could be done. I also remember killing two mountain sheep at 600 yards, one at possibly 650. I also remember killing two coyotes, one at a measured 600, and the other one my father stepped at between six and seven hundred.

I do not believe that the average person has any business shooting over 300 yards at big game unless he is a trained expert rifleman with a background such as I have had of a lifetime of shooting, and then only from a rest or a prone position.

Otherwise more cripples are represented than clean kills.

I checked with different guides around this section of the country for several years. The consensus of opinion on elk is that the hunters coming in here and using rifles of .30 caliber, even the big magnums, lost at least two and possibly three elk for every one they bagged. Such shooting at long range, especially antelope, mule deer, sheep and goats, and the use of too small a rifle, is conducive to further elimination of all our big game.

The hunter training programs initiated by the National Rifle Association all over this country have done a great deal to help tyro hunters and others to realize the possibility of the arms and their own capabilities, and they should then limit the ranges at which they shoot to those capabilities.

When it comes to big game rifles I like to do all my hunting before I shoot. Many years ago I decided that for elk, moose, and our big bear, nothing smaller than .33 caliber or a minimum bullet weight of 250 grains at

around 2200 feet or better, was adequate for these species.

This allows us a little .358 Winchester with 250-grain bullet, a Remington .350 Magnum with 250-grain bullet, a .338 Winchester Magnum, the .340 Weatherby, the .378 Weatherby, our line of OKH cartridges, the .333 OKH, the .334 OKH, and our great .338 .378 that Thomson and I designed. Also my .338-74 Keith from the 9.3 x 74 German cartridge, as well as other .35 caliber and .375 magnum cartridges.

These are all adequate, and I consider them a bare necessity in an all-around rifle. Usually small deer can be shot with these big rifles with a heavy bullet at moderate velocity with far less meat destruction and cleaner kills than are accomplished by high velocity .30 caliber and smaller bullets that simply blow up on impact or inside the animal. Furthermore, you get a blood trail with heavy bullets of large caliber, while small high-velocity bullets go inside and blow up. The hide shifts on the outside when the animal moves, and you have no blood trail whatever.

POLICE PROTECTION . . .

Police armanent in this country has also been a sad mistake, to my notice, for many years. Many departments are depending entirely on standard .38 Special, round-nosed, 158-grain bullet loads. They have proved inadequate in so many gun fights that it is simply pitiful. So many good officers have been killed after hitting an opponent from one to several times, and the .38 Special still never killed the crooks. For many years I have recommended nothing smaller than the .38-40, .44-40, .44 Special or .45 Colt. All four are heavy loads as well as the .44 Special especially with my heavy bullet, and the .41 and .44 Magnum.

I spent 30 years working to get the .44 Magnum produced, and finally accomplished it with the aid of Carl Hellstrom and the Remington people. But it only took six months to get the .41 Magnum in action, and I consider it today one of the finest police cartridges extant. Some police outfits and sheriff's forces have adopted the .45 Colt automatic. It's a good gun. It's totally dependent on perfect ammunition and perfect functioning, however it does throw a 230-grain hardball that will usually take the fight out of any man with one shot if it is placed at all. On the other hand, some police departments are out with 9 millimeter guns which are no bet-

302

ter than the .38 Special, if as good. A .38 Special lead bullet may upset some, especially if it hits a bone. The full-jacketed 9 millimeters are too light and too small.

When Colt brought out the .38 Super in the thirties with a 130-grain bullet at 1200 fps, everybody hailed it as the ideal gun for both police use and game shooting. I bought three of them, tried them out extensively on everything from jackrabbits to woodchucks to deer. They failed miserably in most instances. Only if I hit the skeletal structure and broke the animal down, would it work.

Even on woodchuck. You can shoot a chuck with a .45 auto and he will go down. His tail will come up and wiggle a little bit and go down and that was all she wrote. With the 9 millimeters, the Luger that I tried then, or the Super .38, you could knock a chuck down and

he'd lie there a few seconds, then he'd jump up and run in his hole. They required from two to three shots for the same killing effect, as near as I could tell, as one 230-grain .45.

Today Smith & Wesson is out with a new 9 millimeter automatic. Like their older version it carries a double-action feature with the first shot and is really a very accurate and fine weapon. However the new model has a staggered magazine and holds 14 rounds. I guess they intend to accomplish with two or three shots what could be accomplished with one shot from a heavy six-gun or the old .45 ACP. I cannot see it for police use. It's simply too small. I haven't seen this new version, nor have I tested it, but I have done enough shooting with Lugers and the older model Smith & Wesson 9 millimeter to know what can be expected.

The technical staff of the American Rifleman gathers for a photo in Washington, D.C. From left, back row, are Bob Wallack, Rudy Etchen, and Harold McFarland. Front row are Phil Sharpe, General Julian S. Hatcher, author Elmer Keith, and Bud Waite.

COURTS ARE LACKING...

Today the courts and many of the judges favor the criminal and not the police officer who risks his life every day and night in the performance of his duty. Of all the 50 states and their laws, the judges seem to turn the criminal loose, rather than helping the common citizen who pays all the taxes.

The only exception is Nebraska with their Legal Jeopardy Act that the legislators were wise enough to pass over their governor's veto. This law protects the citizen, not the criminal. In fact, it makes open season on the criminal which should be standard procedure in every state in the union.

I have been in law enforcement long enough to know that the cop sees all the sordid end of life. He is up as a target. He is not supposed to shoot until he is shot at. Often by then it is too late as far as he is concerned, and seldom is his family very well taken care of if he is killed. In my opinion we are better off with fewer criminals and harsher laws.

Likewise I do not believe in removing the death penalty for serious cases. Anyone who has been in law enforcement for any length of time will check the records after fingerprinting a criminal, and look at a long line of felonies that each of them has committed.

Most of them are repeaters. They spend their sentence in jail figuring out their next crime when they get out. There are some instances to the contrary, but they are not prevalent. Most are hardened criminals, never reformed.

The best remedy for them is the Legal Jeopardy Act of Nebraska and a heavy chunk of lead where it will do the right action and save the court expenses and Mr. John Q. Citizen from further jeopardy. Personally I would like to see every state in the union adopt the Legal Jeopardy Act and start either killing or prosecuting properly all criminals convicted, rather than turning them loose in two or three years after they are convicted for the most vicious crimes. If this act were adopted by all 50 states, and the police were armed with the minimum of the .41 Magnum, it would go a long ways toward ending the crime wave in this country. My sympathy is all with the police officer and the sheriff's outfits rather than with the criminal.

In the old days in the west, the criminal was given very short shrift—usually six feet of rope and a limb ended his depredations in short order—even for horse stealing. It was a very polite and much better society then than it is today in many cases.

This country now boasts an army of competent and clever lawyers waiting to take on the case of most any hardened criminal so long as they can see either publicity or a bit of profit in the transaction. It's about time the honest citizen was considered rather than the hardened criminal.

AFRICAN RIFLES...

Each year I receive a lot of letters pertaining to African hunting—the proper arms and cartridges to use, as well as where to go. Africa, like the States, is fast being shot out in many sections. Also the political situation in east Africa is getting steadily worse. Where we hunted in Uganda they are now at war with Tanganyika, (now Tanzania) which used to be German East Africa. I believe the African colonies were never so well off as when under colonial rule. Today it is reverting back to cannibalism in some sections and tribal warfare in others, and it will get worse.

When it comes to rifles for the great game of Africa, I favor nothing smaller than the .338 Winchester Magnum, the .340 Weatherby with a minimum of 250-grain Nosler or the new Sierra boattail for use on plains game.

When it comes to the heavy game there are dangerous reasons. However, while these rifles will take the leopard very nicely, with lion, buffalo, elephant, rhino or a hippo in the reeds at close range, I favor the use of nothing smaller than a 480-grain bullet and .45 caliber. From there on up the larger the gun you can handle, the better off you are. It's a mistake to get a gun too heavy or with too much recoil for you to handle. Usually, however, the bigger and heavier a man is, the more recoil seems to bother him. Small, wiry people shoot the great .577 and .600 without trouble.

This choice of mine takes in the .458 Winchester, the .460 Weatherby, (both fine cartridges for Africa) through all the run of the big British double-rifle cartridges; the .450 Nitro Express, .465, .470, .475, .476, .500 and the best stopper of them all, the big .577. Anyone going out to Africa now should take a shotgun along for birds, one of these medium rifles for the plains game, and a heavy double or a bolt action in .458, .460 Weatherby on up, will be well prepared for anything he will encounter in Africa.

I suggested a .500 to John Buhmiller, who has had a lot of African experience, especially in control work on elephant in Tanzania.

This cartridge was made up with John test-

Hunters should never go to Africa undergunned. These tusks were taken by Keith and Fowler using heavy caliber British double rifles with solid bullets.

ing it, and in .450 caliber before Weatherby ever saw or heard of it. That later became the .460 Weatherby. The same case, namely the .416 revamped by Weatherby into a belted case and the neck expanded to .500 caliber to take the .570-grain bullet, and the .500 Nitro Express, make probably the finest of all heavy bolt action cartridges.

On any game, even with the heaviest of rifles, the bullets must be placed for best results for certain one-shot shot kills. However I believe in using all the power you can handle and killing the game cleanly and with one shot rather than risking your own neck and that of the natives you are hunting with by using too small a rifle.

Times change and the game of the whole world is becoming ever scarcer. India is becoming shot out. Now we have laws prohibiting the bringing of spotted hides into this country. In the main they may have been aimed at stopping the poacher. However, all it accomplishes today, as I see it, is to prohibit

the honest sportsman from killing a leopard or tiger or many of the other spotted cats and bringing their hides back to this country as a trophy. The total of all trophy hunters combined is not one single drop in a bucket compared to the number of poachers. It's the poacher who gets away with the leopards, tigers, and other spotted cats, and ships their hides. All our government has to do instead of stopping shipment of hides brought in here as trophies only, is to stop the sale of hides commercially to fur dealers.

I have had several letters recently from men who have been over in Africa and killed nice leopards and they are tied up in customs and cannot bring them in. It's not the trophy hunter that affects the game, but the poacher. That and the demand for leopard and other spotted cat coats has brought about this crazy law. It should apply only to the poacher and he should be given the full extent of the law. Honest sportsmen going out to Africa should be allowed a trophy. In many sections of

Africa, leopard are on the increase and they take an awful toll of the smaller animals. Again this ecology business has gone too far. They don't stop to consider all facets of the situation before passing some crazy law.

I MISS OLD BRONCS...

Over the years I have witnessed many changes from the horse and buggy days when draft stock was used for practically all farming, and when transportation was saddle horse, buckboard, spring wagon, or surrey. Today's rodeos are another example. Only the Brahma bulls seem to be the equal of the old ones we had back in the twenties. Bucking horses are now a thing of the past. What goes for bucking horses today would not even have been considered a bucking horse in the old days.

A bucking horse drags his hindquarters. He don't kick up in the air fighting a flank rope. Only Charley Russell could paint a bucking horse as he truly was, and having rode enough of them myself, I know the difference. Today they have a lot of horses that will run, and some few will swap ends, but very seldom. You never hear them bawl when they hit the ground like the old broncs used to, and they kick up at the flank rope, fighting it. Sure they may be hard to keep in the saddle with that rear end kicking high in the air all the time, but still they are not a bucking horse at all. A good bucking horse may do his whole stunt in a 30 yard circle. Then he'd swap ends until one stirrup hits the ground and then the other as he sunfishes. The old Roman-nosed broncs with a strip of long hair down their nose, pig eyes, that would bawl every time they hit the ground, are now long gone and we will never see their like again.

...AND FAREWELL...

All my life I have tried to dodge trouble as much as possible, yet for some reason it seems to follow me. Life is a fleeting thing, and one realizes how short it is only after he begins to reach old age. Over the years I have known many fine men and women who helped make

Elmer Keith and his wife Lorraine in Colorado. Still hunting every year for more than 50 years together.

Elmer and Lorraine Keith at the 1973 presentation of the
Outstanding American Handgunner Award to Elmer.

this country what it is today.

I was a junior in the old school of arms writers and gun editors of this country; Captain Paul Curtis, Captain Ned Crossman, Colonel Townsend Whelen, General Julian Hatcher, Monroe Good, Al Barnes, F. C. Ness, Major Charles Askins, Chauncey Thomas, James V. Howe, as well as many others that I could name.

Though I will be 80 in March of 1979, I have no intention of retiring. You retire, you become a vegetable and usually last six months to three years. I don't care for that kind of an end. I'd rather keep working and die with my boots on if necessary.

Though I can no longer climb at high altitudes on foot or do heavy lifting, I can still sit a good horse all day, anytime, anywhere he can set his feet. I still like to get out each fall and ride a good horse, as I did with the late Bob Thomson, and hunt some of that beautiful Colorado Canyon rim country as we did the past several years.

After publication of my African book *Safari*, I swore I would never write another book, but so many friends have asked me to do one on my entire lifetime that I finally agreed to do this one last book, which will be my ninth. I only agreed to do it after I was told I could tape it and have it typed and avoid pounding it out on a typewriter myself. It is an accurate account of many of the highlights of my life. A great many of my old friends who helped me no end on many occasions have now passed over the Great Divide. A man's work is seldom recognized until after he is passed away, and it is too late now to thank the many fine friends, both men and women, who helped me over the years. I cannot help but recall a little poem written by my old friend, the late E. A. Brinninstool, a great many years ago. Brinninstool was a very close student of the Custer Battle and wrote a great deal on it. Both from the side of the Indians and the few participants he interviewed as well. I think with his little poem I will end this book.

"If with pleasure you are viewing any work a man is doing,

If you like it or you love him, tell him now. Don't withhold your approbations until the parson makes orations,

As he lies with snowy lilies o'er his brow. For no matter how you shout it, he won't really care about it,

He won't know how many teardrops you have shed. If you think some praise is due him, now's the time to pass it to him,

For he cannot read his tombstone when he's dead."